Lecture Notes in Computer Science 9671

Commenced Publication in 1973
Founding and Former Series Editors:
Gerhard Goos, Juris Hartmanis, and Jan van Leeuwen

More information about this series at http://www.springer.com/series/7409

Alessandro Bozzon · Philippe Cudré-Mauroux
Cesare Pautasso (Eds.)

Web Engineering

16th International Conference, ICWE 2016
Lugano, Switzerland, June 6–9, 2016
Proceedings

 Springer

Editors
Alessandro Bozzon
Department of Software and Computer
  Technology
Delft University of Technology
Delft, Zuid-Holland
The Netherlands

Philippe Cudré-Mauroux
Department of Informatics
University of Fribourg
Fribourg
Switzerland

Cesare Pautasso
Faculty of Informatics
Università della Svizzera italiana (USI)
Lugano
Switzerland

ISSN 0302-9743 ISSN 1611-3349 (electronic)
Lecture Notes in Computer Science
ISBN 978-3-319-38790-1 ISBN 978-3-319-38791-8 (eBook)
DOI 10.1007/978-3-319-38791-8

Library of Congress Control Number: 2016939066

LNCS Sublibrary: SL3 – Information Systems and Applications, incl. Internet/Web, and HCI

This Springer imprint is published by Springer Nature
The registered company is Springer International Publishing AG Switzerland

Preface

ICWE aims to promote research and scientific exchange related to Web engineering, and to bring together researchers and practitioners from various disciplines in academia and industry in order to tackle emerging challenges in the engineering of Web applications and associated technologies, as well as to assess the impact of these technologies on society, media, and culture.

This volume collects the full research papers, short research papers, vision papers, tool demonstrations, posters, tutorials, and extended abstracts for the keynotes presented at the 16th International Conference on Web Engineering (ICWE 2016), held in Lugano, Switzerland, during June 6–9, 2016.

ICWE is the flagship conference for the Web engineering community. Previous editions of ICWE took place in Rotterdam, The Netherlands (2015); Toulouse, France (2014); Aalborg, Denmark (2013); Berlin, Germany (2012); Paphos, Cyprus (2011); Vienna, Austria (2010); San Sebastián, Spain (2009); Yorktown Heights, NY, USA (2008); Como, Italy (2007); Palo Alto, CA, USA (2006); Sydney, Australia (2005); Munich, Germany (2004); Oviedo, Spain (2003); Santa Fe, Argentina (2002); and Cáceres, Spain (2001).

The 16th edition of ICWE accepted contributions related to different research areas revolving around Web engineering, including: Web application modelling and engineering; human computation and crowdsourcing; Web applications composition and mashups; social Web applications; Semantic Web; and – for the first time – also the Web of Things.

As opposed to the previous two editions of the conference, and with the full support of the Steering Committee, we switched the conference program organization from a multi-track system based on topics to a multi-track system based on types of publications (full research papers, short research papers, vision papers, demo and poster papers, as well as PhD symposium papers). This enabled us to offer the community the opportunity to submit their work at different stages of maturity and target multiple, staggered paper submission deadlines. Additionally, we are proud of the vision paper track, providing the Web engineering community with a new venue and format in which to reflect upon its future. The Program Committee was also reorganized from having multiple track chairs and sub-committees dedicated to each topic, something that often made it difficult to balance the reviewing workload and was hard for experts to choose which areas to sign up for. Instead, we introduced a tiered Program Committee, with a senior Program Committee composed of well-known experts from the field. This made it easier to run the virtual Program Committee meeting of the full research papers track and the discussion about each paper, which resulted in a meta-review. We also had a positive experience by introducing a shepherding process for borderline papers.

This year's Call for Papers attracted 125 submissions from around the world, out of which the Program Committee selected 19 full research papers (21 % acceptance rate),

16 short papers (45 % acceptance rate), and three vision papers. Additionally, the Program Committee accepted 11 demonstrations, five posters, and seven contributions to the PhD symposium, where PhD students received personalized advice and guidance on their work from senior researchers in the Web engineering field.

ICWE 2016 accepted five tutorials on cutting-edge topics in the field of Web engineering, entitled: "Design Science Research in Information Systems and Software Systems Engineering"; "Using Docker Containers to Improve Reproducibility in Software and Web Engineering Research"; "Recommender Systems Meet Linked Open Data"; "Distributed Web Applications with IPFS"; and "A Declarative Approach to Information Extraction Using Web Service API." Moreover, seven workshops were selected to be co-located at ICWE 2016.

The excellent program would not have been possible without the support of all the people who contributed to the organization of this event. We would like to thank the conference chairs for their hard work. Our thanks also go to Xin Luna Dong (Google Research), James Lewis (ThoughtWorks), and Panos Ipeirotis (New York University), who accepted to be our keynote speakers.

Special thanks are extended to Florian Daniel and Martin Gaedke for their wisdom, advice, and encouragement in setting up ICWE 2016 in Lugano. We are grateful to our local organizers Elisa Larghi and Mauro Prevostini for their logistical support, and to Springer for publishing this volume and together with EnterpriseWeb for offering travel grants to support student authors. In addition, we thank the reviewers for their meticulous work in selecting the best papers to be presented at ICWE 2016. Last, but not least, we would like to thank the authors who submitted their work to this conference and all the participants who contributed to the success of this event.

April 2016

Alessandro Bozzon
Philippe Cudré-Maroux
Cesare Pautasso

Organization

Technical Committee

General Chair

Cesare Pautasso   USI Lugano, Switzerland

Program Chairs

Alessandro Bozzon   Delft University of Technology, The Netherlands
Philippe Cudré-Maroux   University of Fribourg, Switzerland

Short/Vision Papers Chairs

Oscar Diaz   University of the Basque Country, Spain
Tommi Mikkonen   Tampere University of Technology, Finland

Workshop Chairs

Sven Casteleyn   Universitat Jaume I, Castellón, Spain
Peter Dolog   Aalborg University, Denmark

Demonstration Chairs

Saeed Aghaee   University of Cambridge, UK
Marco Brambilla   Politecnico di Milano, Italy

Poster Chairs

Giovanni Toffetti Carughi   Zurich University of Applied Sciences (ZHAW),
                                     Switzerland
Manuel Wimmer   Vienna University of Technology, Austria

PhD Symposium Chairs

Flavius Frasincar   Erasmus University of Rotterdam, The Netherlands
Gustavo Rossi   Universidad Nacional de La Plata, Argentina
Marco Winckler   Paul Sabatier University, France

Tutorials Chairs

Cinzia Cappiello   Politecnico di Milano, Italy
Philipp Leitner   University of Zurich, Switzerland

Publicity Chairs

Domenico Bianculli	University of Luxembourg, Luxembourg
Michael Weiss	Carleton University, Canada
Liming Zhu	Data61, Australia

Proceedings Chair

Mourad Khayati	University of Fribourg, Switzerland

Local Organization Chairs

Elisa Larghi	USI Lugano, Switzerland
Mauro Prevostini	USI Lugano, Switzerland

Steering Committee Liaisons

Florian Daniel	Politecnico di Milano, Italy
Martin Gaedke	Chemnitz University of Technology, Germany

Program Committee

Senior Program Committee

Boualem Benatallah	University of New South Wales, Australia
Jordi Cabot	Internet Interdisciplinary Institute (IN3) - UOC, Spain
Philipp Cimiano	Bielefeld University, Germany
Gianluca Demartini	University of Sheffield, UK
Schahram Dustdar	Politecnico di Milano, Italy
Jacques Pasquier	University of Fribourg, Switzerland
Oscar Pastor Lopez	Universitat Politécnica de Valencia, Spain
Jian Pei	Simon Fraser University, Canada
Daniel Schwabe	Pontifical Catholic University of Rio de Janiero, Brazil
Steffen Staab	University of Koblenz-Landau, Germany and University of Southampton, UK
Stefan Tai	Technische Universität Berlin, Germany

Program Committee

Silvia Abrahao	Universitat Politecnica de Valencia
Lora Aroyo	VU University of Amsterdam, The Netherlands
Sören Auer	University of Bonn, Germany
Alberto Bacchelli	Delft University of Technology, The Netherlands
Marcos Baez	University of Trento, Italy
Wolf-Tilo Balke	TU Braunschweig, Germany
Hubert Baumeister	Technical University of Denmark, Denmark
Devis Bianchini	University of Brescia, Italy
Domenico Bianculli	University of Luxembourg, Luxembourg
Maria Bielikova	Slovak University of Technology in Bratislava, Slovakia

Michael Blackstock	University of British Columbia, Canada
Cinzia Cappiello	Politecnico di Milano, Italy
Fabio Casati	University of Trento, Italy
Sven Casteleyn	Universität Jaume I, Spain
Michele Catasta	EPFL, Switzerland
Ciro Cattuto	ISI Foundation, Italy
Pieter Colpaert	Ghent University, Belgium
Oscar Corcho	Universidad Politécnica de Madrid, Spain
Alexandra Cristea	University of Warwick, UK
Florian Daniel	Politecnico di Milano, Italy
Olga De Troyer	Vrije Universiteit Brussel, Belgium
Emanuele Della Valle	Politecnico di Milano, Italy
Tommaso Di Noia	Politecnico di Bari, Italy
Oscar Diaz	University of the Basque Country, Spain
Djellel Eddine Difallah	University of Fribourg, Switzerland
Vania Dimitrova	University of Leeds, UK
Peter Dolog	Aalborg University, Denmark
Filomena Ferrucci	Università di Salerno, Italy
Flavius Frasincar	Erasmus University of Rotterdam, The Netherlands
Martin Gaedke	Chemnitz University of Technology, Germany
Irene Garrigos	University of Alicante, Spain
Jose Manuel Gomez-Perez	Expert System Iberia, Spain
Peter Haase	Metaphacts, Germany
Stephan Haller	Bern University of Applied Sciences, Switzerland
Christian Hammer	Saarland University, Germany
Sebastian Hellmann	Universität Leipzig, Germany
Tobias Hossfeld	University of Duisburg-Essen, Germany
Geert-Jan Houben	Delft University of Technology, The Netherlands
Artem Katasonov	VTT Technical Research Centre of Finland, Finland
Tomi Kauppinen	Aalto University, Finland
Roman Klinger	University of Stuttgart, Germany
In-Young Ko	Korea Advanced Institute of Science and Technology, Korea
Agnes Koschmider	Karlsruhe Institute of Technology, Germany
Matthias Kovatsch	ETH Zurich, Switzerland
Markus Krause	University of California Berkeley, USA
Angel Lagares	Carlos III University, Spain
Philipp Leitner	University of Zurich, Switzerland
Olivier Liechti	University of Applied Sciences of Western Switzerland, Switzerland
Zakaria Maamar	Zayed University, United Arab Emirates
Maristella Matera	Politecnico di Milano, Italy
Simon Mayer	Siemens Corporate Technology, USA
Nikolay Mehandjiev	University of Manchester, UK
Santiago Melia	Universidad de Alicante, Spain
Hamid Motahari	IBM Research, USA

Moira Norrie	ETH Zurich, Switzerland
Luis Olsina	National University of La Pampa, Argentina
Hye-Young Paik	University of New South Wales, Australia
Jeff Z. Pan	University of Aberdeen, UK
Jose Ignacio Panach Navarrete	Universitat de València, Spain
Jan Paralic	Technical University Kosice, Slovakia
Heiko Paulheim	University of Mannheim, Germany
Vicente Pelechano	Universitat Politècnica de València, Spain
Alfonso Pierantonio	University of L'Aquila, Italy
Venkatesha Prasad	Delft University of Technology, The Netherlands
Judith Redi	Delft University of Technology, The Netherlands
David Resseguie	Oak Ridge National Laboratory, USA
Werner Retschitzegger	Johannes Kepler University Linz, Austria
Till Riedel	Karlsruhe Institute of Technology, Germany
Gustavo Rossi	Universidad Nacional de La Plata, Argentina
Harald Sack	University of Potsdam, Germany
Fernando Sánchez	Universidad de Extremadura, Spain
Ansgar Scherp	Universität Kiel, Germany
Quan Z. Sheng	The University of Adelaide, Australia
Beat Signer	Vrije Universiteit Brussel, Belgium
Elena Simperl	University of Southampton, UK
Philipp Singer	GESIS Leibniz Institute for the Social Sciences, Germany
Andrea Tagarelli	University of Calabria, Italy
Farouk Toumani	Blaise Pascal University, France
Christoph Trattner	Know-Center, Austria
William Van Woensel	University of Dalhousie, Canada
Maria Esther Vidal	Universidad Simon Bolivar, Venezuela
Evelyne Viegas	Microsoft Research, USA
Maja Vukovic	IBM Research, USA
Manuel Wimmer	Vienna University of Technology, Austria
Marco Winckler	Paul Sabatier University, France
Erik Wittern	IBM Research, USA
Eric Wohlstadter	University of British Columbia, Canada
Guandong Xu	University of Technology Sydney, Australia
Nicola Zannone	Eindhoven University of Technology, The Netherlands
Gefei Zhang	Hochschule für Technik und Wirtschaft Berlin, Germany
Jürgen Ziegler	University of Duisburg-Essen, Germany

Short/Vision Papers

Cristóbal Arellano	University of the Basque Country, Spain
Sven Casteleyn	Universitat Jaume I, Spain
Oscar Corcho	Universidad Politécnica de Madrid, Spain

Srgio Firmenich	Universidad Nacional de La Plata, Argentina
Flavius Frasincar	Erasmus University of Rotterdam, The Netherlands
Martin Gaedke	Chemnitz University of Technology, Germany
Geert-Jan Houben	Delft University of Technology, The Netherlands
Gerti Kappel	Vienna University of Technology, Austria
Ora Lassila	Pegasystems, Sweden
Maristella Matera	Politecnico di Milano, Italy
Santiago Melia	Universidad de Alicante, Spain
Juan Manuel Murillo Rodríguez	University of Extremadura, Spain
Moira Norrie	ETH Zurich, Switzerland
Luis Olsina	National University of La Pampa, Argentina
Daniel Schwabe	Pontifical Catholic University of Rio de Janiero, Brazil
Antero Taivalsaari	Nokia Research Center, Finland
Markel Vigo	University of Manchester, UK
Bahtijar Vogel	Malmä University, Sweden
Marco Winckler	Paul Sabatier University, France

Posters

Marco Brambilla	Politecnico di Milano, Italy
Jordi Cabot	Internet Interdisciplinary Institute (IN3) - UOC, Spain
Cinzia Cappiello	Politecnico di Milano, Italy
Sven Casteleyn	Universitat Jaume I, Spain
Florian Daniel	Politecnico di Milano, Italy
Roberto De Virgilio	Università degli Studi Roma Tre, Italy
Davide Di Ruscio	Università degli Studi dell'Aquila, Italy
Sergio Firmenich	Universidad Nacional de La Plata, Argentina
Irene Garrigós Fernández	Universidad de Alicante, Spain
Michael Grossniklaus	University of Konstanz, Germany
Tanja Mayerhofer	Vienna University of Technology, Austria
Nathalie Moreno	Universidad de Málaga, Spain
Moira Norrie	ETH Zurich, Switzerland
Werner Retschitzegger	Johannes Kepler University Linz, Austria
Gustavo Rossi	Universidad Nacional de La Plata, Argentina
Giovanni Toffetti Carughi	Zurich University of Applied Sciences (ZHAW), Switzerland
Antonio Vallecillo	Universidad de Málaga, Spain
Manuel Wimmer	Vienna University of Technology, Austria

Demos

Charith Perera	The Open University, UK
Maristella Matera	Politecnico di Milano, Italy
Daniele Bonetta	Oracle Labs, Austria
Jordi Cabot	ICREA and OUC, Spain
Andrea Mauri	Politecnico di Milano, Italy

Carmen Santoro   ISTI-CNR, Italy
Jean-Sebastien Sottet   Luxembourg Institute of Science and Technology,
                                  Luxembourg
Hugo Brunelière   Ecole des Mines de Nantes, France
Ivano Malavolta   Gran Sasso Science Institute, Italy

PhD Symposium

Devis Bianchini   University of Brescia, Italy
Maria Bielikova   Slovak University of Technology in Bratislava,
                                  Slovakia
Marco Brambilla   Politecnico di Milano, Italy
Cinzia Cappiello   Politecnico di Milano, Italy
Alexandra Cristea   University of Warwick, UK
Damiano Distante   Unitelma Sapienza University, Italy
Tommaso Di Noia   Politecnico di Bari, Italy
Peter Dolog   Aalborg University, Denmark
Martin Gaedke   Chemnitz University of Technology, Germany
Ivan Jelínek   Czech Technical University in Prague, Czech Republic
Ralf Klamma   Aachen University, Germany
In-Young Ko   Korea Advanced Institute of Science and Technology,
                                  Korea
Manuel Wimmer   Vienna University of Technology, Austria

Web Engineering in Practice

Mike Amundsen   API Academy
Obie Fernandez   2U, USA
Ronnie Mitra   API Academy
Mark Nottingham   Akamai
Jonathan Robie   EMC
Silvia Schreier   InnoQ
Eberhard Wolff   InnoQ

Additional Reviewers

Alberto Tonon	Francisco Ibarra	Markus Ast
Alessia Amelio	Jean-Paul Calbimonte	Michael Luggen
Alexandra Mazak	Joerg Waitelonis	Mingdong Ou
Alfonso Murolo	Jon Iturrioz	Pablo Becker
Anna Lisa Gentile	Juan Carlos Preciado	Riccardo Tommasini
Babak Naderi	Julia Neidhardt	Robert Bill
Belen Rivera	Khoi-Nguyen Tran	Roberto Interdonato
Bettina Klimek	Kristína Machová	Runze Wu
Carlos Rodriguez	Laura Rettig	Simon Steyskal
Chifumi Nishioka	Luca Berardinelli	Yongrui Qin
Ciro Baron Neto	Madalina Drugan	
Daniele Dell'Aglio	Magnus Knuth	

Sponsors

Abstract of Keynotes

How Far Are We from Collecting the Knowledge in the World

Xin Luna Dong

Google, Mountain View, USA
lunadong@google.com

Abstract. In this talk we ask the question: How far are we from collecting the knowledge in the world? We analyze the knowledge that has been extracted to Freebase in three categories: head knowledge in head verticals (e.g., music), long-tail knowledge in head verticals, and head knowledge in long-tail verticals, showing the limitations and challenges in current knowledge-collection techniques.

We then present two key efforts at Google on collecting tail knowledge. The first, called Knowledge Vault, targeted on tail knowledge in head verticals. It used 16 extractors to periodically extract knowledge from 1B+ Webpages, obtaining 3B+ distinct (subject, predicate, object) knowledge triples. The second, called Lightweight Verticals, targets on head knowledge in tail verticals. It uses a crowd-sourcing approach to collect knowledge by annotating websites, and currently has millions of active Google Search users every day. We present some key technologies under both projects, namely, knowledge fusion for guaranteeing knowledge correctness, and knowledge-based trust for finding authoritative sources for knowledge curation.

1 Bio

Xin Luna Dong is a Senior Research Scientist at Google Inc. She is one of the major contributors to the Knowledge Vault project, and has led the Knowledge-based Trust project, which is called the "Google Truth Machine" by Washington's Post. She has co-authored book "Big Data Integration", published 65+ papers in top conferences and journals, given 20+ keynotes/invited-talks/tutorials, and got the Best Demo award in Sigmod 2005. She is the PC co-chair for WAIM 2015 and serves as an area chair for Sigmod 2017, Sigmod 2015, ICDE 2013, and CIKM 2011.

Microservices - The Hunting of the Snark

James Lewis

ThoughtWorks, Chicago, USA
jalewis@thoughtworks.com

Abstract. The microservice architectural style is now one of the most talked about topics in software architecture. Large organisations are using them to deliver value into production faster than ever before. But what actually are they? What do they look like? Why should you use them?

"They sought it with thimbles, they sought it with care; They pursued it with forks and hope".

In this keynote, James will take you on a journey to hunt down the snark - what he finds may surprise you.

1 Bio

James Lewis studied Astrophysics in the 90's but got sick of programming in Fortran. As a member of the ThoughtWorks Technical Advisory Board, the group that creates the Technology Radar, he contributes to industry adoption of open source and other tools, techniques, platforms and languages. For the last few years he has been working as a coding architect on projects built using microservices; exploring new patterns and ways of working as he goes. James has spoken at many international conferences. His previous topics range from domain driven design, SOA and the future of the web to agile adoption patterns and lean thinking. He's also heavily involved in the fledgling microservice community. He rather likes the fact that he got to describe his take on things jointly with Martin Fowler in a paper[1] that is influencing how people see the future of software architecture.

---

[1] http://martinfowler.com/articles/microservices.html

Adventures in Crowdsourcing

Panos Ipeirotis

Department of Information, Operations, and Management Sciences,
Leonard N. Stern School of Business New York University, New York, USA
panos@stern.nyu.edu

Abstract. Crowdsourcing is becoming increasingly popular in many fields. In this talk, I will describe a set of systems that we built over the last few years, which combine human and machine intelligence, to create systems that are better than using humans or computers alone. I will cover a diverse set of topics surrounding the creation of such systems, including worker quality control, fair payment schemes, vulnerability detection for machine learning systems, and how to use online advertising systems for targeting knowledgeable users. Time permitting, I will conclude with an illustration of how Mechanical Turk workers and mice are not that different after all.

1 Bio

Panos Ipeirotis is a Professor and George A. Kellner Faculty Fellow at the Department of Information, Operations, and Management Sciences at Leonard N. Stern School of Business of New York University. He received his Ph.D. degree in Computer Science from Columbia University in 2004. He has received nine "Best Paper" awards and nominations, a CAREER award from the National Science Foundation, and is the recipient of the 2015 Lagrange Prize in Complex Systems, for his contributions in the field of social media and crowdsourcing.

Contents

Short Research Papers

Vision Papers

Poster Papers

Tutorials

Full Research Papers

Medley: An Event-Driven Lightweight Platform for Service Composition

Elyas Ben Hadj Yahia[1,3](✉), Laurent Réveillère[1], Yérom-David Bromberg[2], Raphaël Chevalier[3], and Alain Cadot[3]

[1] LaBRI, Université de Bordeaux, 33400 Talence, France
{elyas.bhy,reveillere}@labri.fr
[2] IRISA, Université de Rennes, 35000 Rennes, France
david.bromberg@irisa.fr
[3] CProDirect, 33700 Mérignac, France
{raphael.chevalier,a.cadot}@cprodirect.fr

Abstract. Distributed applications are evolving at a frantic pace, critically relying on each other to offer a host of new functionalities. The emergence of the service-oriented paradigm has made it possible to build complex applications as a set of self-contained and loosely coupled services that work altogether in concert. However, the traditional vision of Service-Oriented Architectures (SOA) based on web service specifications does not meet the trend of many major service providers. Instead, they promote microservices, a refinement of SOA focusing on lightweight communication mechanisms such as HTTP. Therefore, existing approaches for orchestrating the composition of various services become unusable in practice.

In this paper, we introduce MEDLEY, an event-driven lightweight platform for service composition. MEDLEY is based on a domain-specific language for describing orchestration and a compiler that produces efficient code. We have used MEDLEY to develop various compositions, involving a large number of existing services. Our evaluation shows that it scales both on a mainstream server and an embedded device while consuming a reasonable amount of resources.

Keywords: Web composition · Domain-specific languages · Services orchestration · Event-driven programming · Microservices

1 Introduction

Since the early days of distributed computing there was a primitive notion of services that took its origins from RPC mechanisms [1]. The concept of services was significantly refined across the last decades to have a strong impact on the distributed computing landscape, in particular, due to the emergence of the Service Oriented Architecture (SOA) paradigm notably via the use of the Web Service stack as defined by the WS-* specifications.

© Springer International Publishing Switzerland 2016
A. Bozzon et al. (Eds.): ICWE 2016, LNCS 9671, pp. 3–20, 2016.
DOI: 10.1007/978-3-319-38791-8_1

From a higher perspective, SOA has promoted at least two major trends that have a long term impact. First, it has promoted a standardized way to build an application (that can itself be seen as a service) as a set of well specified, independent, self-contained and loosely coupled services that work altogether in concert. Second, it has proven that services act as a valuable paradigm to design complex applications.

As a result, we live in a service-oriented world. Applications ranging from the simplest smartphone application to the Web's most complex one, strive, in one way or another, to interact with value-added services, potentially made themselves from other services. In other terms, applications are increasingly built using the SOA paradigm and integrate a plethora of composable services. Moreover, as services are autonomous and deployed, undeployed or upgraded independently from each other, SOA enables application developers to have a fine-grained control on how to smoothly update their applications and how to make them scalable in production.

Hence, nowadays, the development of SOA-based applications comes together with continuous service development and continuous service integration practice[1]. This new trend coupled with the steady proliferation of services is not without challenges, and potentially obsoletes the traditional vision of SOA [19], along with their classical implementations based on the WS-* specifications (such as SOAP, WSDL, BPEL). For instance, the use of BPEL, the *de facto* standard, as a workflow to compose a plethora of services may be inadequate according to the developers' expectations. In fact, BPEL is a low-level and verbose language that describes *how* services need to be composed instead of defining *what* should be realized. Consequently, the quantity of code developers have to write in BPEL is proportional to the number of services they want to compose. Therefore, the complexity of the code increases making most often the use of BPEL not really suitable in practice. Furthermore, existing workflow languages typically require strongly-typed and well-defined interfaces from composed services. However, defining such interfaces is not the trend anymore due to the fast proliferation of services that most often expose their Web APIs without any contracts (such as with REST for instance) [15]. Thus, there is a need to write some glue code to compose services in an ad hoc and fast manner.

From another perspective, with the emergence of continuous service integration and development (often referred to as *DevOps*), workflow languages need to support not only static composition of well-specified services, but also on-the-fly integration of services that have not been previously planned at design time [23,25]. Finally, workflow languages are usually bundled with an execution engine such as an Enterprise Service Bus (ESB). However, ESBs are well known to be heavyweight containers. It does not meet the trend of lightweight containers, as popularized by Docker, which enables developers to deploy their service compositions wherever they want, such as personal clouds, according to privacy requirements [10].

---

[1] J. Lewis and M. Fowler, Microservices
http://martinfowler.com/articles/microservices.html.

Hence, the SOA paradigm has to evolve. Well known service providers such as Netflix, SoundCloud, Amazon, Spotify, have already widely adopted a refinement of the SOA paradigm named microservices. Microservices is no more than a SOA instance constrained to the basics of HTTP, i.e. with a RESTful style, without the WS-* specifications, and coupled with a variety of tools to promote fast deployment and undeployment of services. However the challenge to compose services stays open to microservices practitioners that are free to use the programming language they want.

In this paper, we introduce MEDLEY, an event-driven lightweight platform for service composition. MEDLEY's architecture is specifically designed to tackle the aforementioned four problematic issues encountered when orchestrating a composition of various services. Additionally, MEDLEY meets the current trends in terms of continuous service integration and development as expected to promote a continuously evolving SOA. Our approach is based on a domain-specific language (DSL) for describing orchestrations using high-level constructs and domain-specific semantics. Once defined, a MEDLEY specification is compiled into low-level code run on top of an event-driven process-based and lightweight platform. By providing an abstraction layer between the low-level implementation and the high-level business logic, the language allows users to express compositions with fine-grain tuning of both control flow and data flow.

The rest of this paper is organized as follows. Section 2 presents the range of issues that arise when orchestrating a composition of several services. Section 3 describes the MEDLEY architecture and introduces a DSL for describing orchestrations. Section 4 describes the main challenges in code generation, and then presents an event-driven lightweight platform to support execution of service compositions. Section 5 demonstrates the efficiency of MEDLEY and its scalability both on servers and embedded devices, and presents a comparative study of supported features. Section 6 discusses related work. Finally, Sect. 7 concludes and presents future work.

2   Issues in Service Composition

The composition of heterogeneous services is a daunting task for many developers. Several languages, including BPEL, have been proposed to ease the orchestration of service compositions. However, they all fail in the context of microservices. We illustrate issues developers have to face in the remainder of this section.

Complexity of Orchestrations. An orchestration may require monitoring a service for new events or state changes. This monitoring can be performed either synchronously by repeatedly polling the endpoint (pull mode) or by registering a callback for an asynchronous notification (push mode). When services only support polling, clients have to initiate a request to the server to retrieve the current state of the service. Then, the client compares this state with the previous one to detect any changes. Despite the advantages of push mode, developing applications based on the asynchronous paradigm is known to be challenging for many developers. When data needs to be propagated between subsequent asynchronous actions, the corresponding information has to be stored by the runtime system at the point of the asynchronous call. The runtime system then passes it back to the stored continuation function when the corresponding response is received. Integrating services based on active polling may also be challenging for the developer. She needs to set up a reasonable frequency for polling to avoid resources waste while preserving good responsiveness. When the same service is used several times, its invocations could be factorized among several clients. However, identifying such global optimization opportunities is difficult when the orchestration code is hard-written and each composition is developed independently from each other.

Heterogeneity of Unspecified Interfaces. Existing orchestration languages such as BPEL require strongly-typed and well-defined interfaces from composed services. They rely on description languages like WSDL that have been extensively and successfully used for many years. The microservices architecture, however, promotes the use of RESTful services for which such description languages do not necessarily exist. Therefore, off-the-shelf tools are unpractical in that context. In addition, services that provide similar content are often heterogeneous either in the communication paradigm they rely on (synchronous *vs.* asynchronous) and in the format of data they provide. As an example, consider a custom daily news digest where a user receives an email containing information formatted to her liking about her favorite news. The developer has to specify how to interact with these news providers, what information to retrieve and how to aggregate data to produce a digest. As the number of services increase, this task becomes laborious.

Dynamicity of Service Composition. Compositions of services are usually statically specified and make explicit the connections between the interacting composed services. This design-time coupling prevents an orchestration to dynamically adapt its behavior to new services being deployed, undeployed or upgraded. Microservices architecture, however, promotes dynamicity although not providing insights on how to achieve it in practice. Supporting adaptation at runtime is known to complexify the task of the developer as she needs not only to focus on the orchestration of several services but also on how to smoothly react to service changes. As an example, consider the custom daily news digest orchestration scenario. To prevent failure in case the mail service become unavailable for some time, the user would like to specify a pool of mail services that can be used indifferently. However, defining such mail service selection policy in languages such as BPEL requires explicit handling of errors by the user.

Privacy Preservation of Execution Platforms. Orchestration languages including BPEL rely on execution environments such as ESB. Although powerful, they are well known to be heavyweight containers. Therefore, their deployment requires a significant amount of resources and renders their usage in small or personal entities more difficult. Sharing an execution platform, however, implies that personal sensitive data goes outside the boundaries of the personal network of the user.

To preserve privacy, one would want to deploy its own execution platform in her house or company. The emergence of low cost embedded devices such as the Raspberry Pi makes it possible. Execution platforms targeting these constrained devices need to be both lightweight and scale well with the increasing number of services users want to compose.

3   Medley Platform

To abstract away the low-level details when composing heterogeneous services from the users, we introduce MEDLEY, a lightweight platform coupled with a DSL that enables users to express service compositions from a more abstract level as opposed to several other languages, such as BPEL. Overall, MEDLEY enables users to reason and to focus on business logic rather than be disrupted by technical implementation details and issues. In the remainder of the section, we introduce our approach to create composite services with the MEDLEY platform and we present its associated DSL.

3.1   Approach

Based on a particular set of services to compose (See Fig. 1 ❶), a user specifies, via the use of the MEDLEY DSL, two kinds of information: (i) how to assemble together the services, (ii) the composition logic (See Fig. 1 ❷). In particular, with MEDLEY, services are mapped to processes, and the process workflow is expressed in terms of patterns of events. Accordingly, the user is expressing in a simpler manner which processes to invoke according to events that may occur. The written specification is then given as input to the MEDLEY compiler (See Fig. 1 ❸). The compiler in turn generates the adequate low-level code enabling communications among the assembled processes. In fact, service orchestration is instantiated as an event-based inter-process communication, conceptually similar to what we can encounter in traditional POSIX systems (See Fig. 1 ❹). Each service orchestration mapped to a set of processes (e.g. C_1 to C_n) is isolated

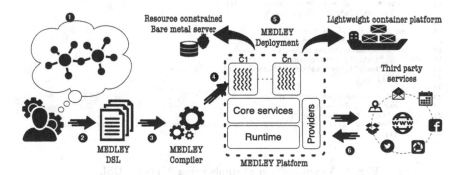

Fig. 1. Steps involved in the scenario described above

from each other, and run in a sandbox. Hence, for instance, several users can deploy different services orchestration without interferences among each other.

The MEDLEY platform is lightweight, and hence can itself be run and deployed on either resource-constrained bare metal servers like Raspberry Pi, or on lightweight container platforms such as Docker (See Fig. 1 ❺). Finally, the MEDLEY platform takes charge transparently, on the behalf of the users, of the interaction with third-party services (Fig. 1 ❻) as expected by the users according to the MEDLEY specifications they have written.

3.2 The Medley DSL

The MEDLEY DSL allows users to declare and configure processes to use and to compose. In particular, the MEDLEY DSL enables users to express how to compose processes altogether according to the events that can occur on their respective output streams. Figure 2 gives an overview of a composition of a set of processes and enables us to introduce the DSL, with the help of Fig. 3 that gives a subset of the grammar.

Figure 2 describes a composition that periodically (line 2, 13) checks for new high-priority issues created on a specific GitHub[2] repository. If a new issue is detected, it notifies the user by sending her an email containing the issue's URL. The email service is selected from a pool of interchangeable services, enabling fault-tolerance on service unavailability. It also notifies the user if an error is encountered with the GitHub service when polling for new issues. Furthermore, this example enables us to highlight some key language operators of the MEDLEY DSL, and concepts of the MEDLEY platform.

```
1   composition {
2     process tick = require("Medley/Tick");
3     process getNewIssues = require("Github/GetNewIssues");
4     getNewIssues.init({"credentials": "<label>"});
5     process gmail = require("Gmail/SendEmail");
6     process outlook = require("Outlook/SendEmail");
7     // ...
8     pool process sendEmail = require("Medley/Pool");
9     sendEmail.add(gmail, outlook);
10    sendEmail.init({"strategy": "round-robin"});
11    on (tick:out) do {
12      stream issues = getNewIssues.invoke({
13        "repository": "medley/repo"
14      });
15      on (issues:out as issue) do {
16        if ({{$.issue.priority}} == "high") {
17          sendEmail.invoke({
18            "to": "john@doe.com",
19            "body": "New issue: {{$.issue.url}}"
20          });
21      } }
22      on (issues:err as error) do {
23        sendEmail.invoke({
24          "to": "john@doe.com",
25          "body": "Error encountered while fetching new issues: {{$.error.message}}"
26        });
27  } } }
```

Fig. 2. A composition example using MEDLEY DSL

---

[2] A Git repository hosting service.

Language Operators. The init method (Fig. 2, line 4, 11) allows the user to configure the process with initialization parameters. These parameters persist throughout the lifecycle of the process instance. The invoke method (line 14, 19, 26) allows the user to invoke a process with a set of arguments. When a process is invoked, it returns a reference to its output stream (line 14). The events of an output stream are tagged according to their types: out for successful executions (line 13, 17), err for erroneous executions (line 25), and close to signal the end of stream. Thus, users can listen to these event types using the on construct (line 13, 17, 25), then react according to the event type. Process invocations separated by semi-colons are executed in an asynchronous manner. As such, p1.invoke(); p2.invoke(); represents a parallel execution of both p1 and p2 processes. If a sequential ordering is required, on blocks can be nested (line 13, 17). Due to the intrinsic nature of the web, some requests may never receive a response. In that case, we make sure to set a timeout on aggregation operations, and flush the memory if the aggregated services take too much time to respond.

Additionally, users may need to aggregate data from different sources before performing an action. For this purpose, we introduce the and operator. It allows users to express synchronization points when dealing with asynchronous processes. The and operator is implemented as a built-in process that generates an output event only when it receives an event from both its two input streams. Incoming events are buffered in a circular FIFO memory enabling the runtime to provide load shedding by discarding events that occur more frequently from one source than the other. For each discarded event, an error event is generated on the output stream allowing the composition to react to it.

The language also provides basic control flow constructs, with the if/else keywords. These constructs provide filtering capabilities on data from output events and can be used to conditionally execute a branch of the program. For example, Fig. 2 (line 18) shows how to express the invocation of the sendEmail process only when the value of the priority field is high.

Core Services. In addition to the set of operators provided by the language grammar, we provide a wide range of core services to facilitate the use of the language and enrich the expressiveness of compositions. For instance, a require function (Fig. 2, lines 2–9) is available globally and serves as an import mechanism for instanciating processes. require returns a new instance of the specified process. Processes are looked up by name and loaded from MEDLEY's internal repository which includes a set of predefined services. For instance, to periodically check the existence of a new issue, a predefined process Medley/Tick is used, which emits tick events at a predefined frequency.

Providers. In MEDLEY, integration of third-party services is achieved through process providers. A process provider is in charge of developing the interaction logic with the desired service, by implementing a MEDLEY process, and then deploying it in MEDLEY's process repository, in a plugin-like fashion. Once deployed, the process is indexed and becomes available for use on the platform (Fig. 2, lines 2–9).

$$
\begin{array}{rcl}
\textit{comp} & ::= & \texttt{composition} \ \{ \ \textit{decl}^{+} \ \textit{rule}^{+} \ \} \\
\textit{decl} & ::= & \texttt{pool}^{?} \ \texttt{process} \ \textit{ident} \ = \ \texttt{require} \ (\ \textit{string} \ ); \\
& | & \textit{ident}.\texttt{init} \ (\ \textit{json}^{?} \ ); \\
& | & \textit{ident}.\texttt{add} \ (\ \textit{ident}^{*} \ (, \ \textit{ident})^{*} \ ); \\
\textit{rule} & ::= & \texttt{on} \ \textit{event} \ \texttt{do} \ \{ \ \textit{action}^{+} \ \} \\
\textit{event} & ::= & \textit{evt} \ | \ \textit{event} \ \texttt{and} \ \textit{evt} \ | \ (\ \textit{event} \ ) \\
\textit{evt} & ::= & \textit{evt\_kind} \ (\texttt{as} \ \textit{ident})^{?} \\
\textit{evt\_kind} & ::= & \textit{ident} \ : \ \texttt{out} \ | \ \textit{ident} \ : \ \texttt{err} \ | \ \textit{ident} \ : \ \texttt{close} \\
\textit{action} & ::= & \texttt{stream} \ \textit{ident} \ = \ \textit{ident}.\texttt{invoke} \ (\ \textit{json}^{?} \ ) \ ; \\
& | & \textit{ident}.\texttt{invoke} \ (\ \textit{json}^{?} \ ) \ ; \\
& | & \texttt{if} \ (\ \textit{expr} \ ) \ \textit{action} \ (\texttt{else} \ \textit{action})^{?} \\
& | & \textit{rule} \\
\textit{expr} & ::= & ! \ \textit{expr} \ | \ \textit{expr} \ \textit{binop} \ \textit{expr} \ | \ (\ \textit{expr} \ ) \\
& | & \textit{ident} \ | \ \textit{string} \ | \ \textit{integer} \ | \ \textit{float} \ | \ \textit{jsonpath} \\
& | & \textit{method} \ (\ \textit{expr}^{*} \ (, \ \textit{expr})^{*} \ ) \\
\textit{jsonpath} & ::= & \{\{ \ \textit{string} \ \}\} \\
\textit{method} & ::= & \textit{ident} \ | \ \textit{jsonpath} \ . \ \textit{ident} \\
\textit{binop} & ::= & < \ | \ > \ | \ <= \ | \ >= \ | \ == \ | \ != \ | \ \&\& \ | \ || \\
\end{array}
$$

Fig. 3. Subset of the DSL grammar

Process Pools. We also define a construct to specify pools of interchangeable processes, using the `pool` keyword. More specifically, it consists in a set of processes that share a common interface, and are semantically equivalent (i.e. they can fulfill the same functional need, such as sending an email. See Fig. 2 for an example). A process pool is typically used to allow a composition to dynamically adapt to service outages, all while being transparent to the developer.

3.3   Data Processing

A crucial aspect in composing multiple web services is being able to reuse and pass data from a service to another. In our DSL, we provide the necessary mechanisms to have fine-grain control over the data, such as on-the-fly substitution and evaluation expressions, as well as document traversal and templating.

Substitution. To extract data from inbound events, we use JSONPath [12] expressions. JSONPath is the XPath [30] equivalent for JSON. It provides a set of operators to traverse JSON documents from their root (noted as $), and selectors to match queries on document attributes. In the snippet presented in Fig. 2 (line 21, 28), we use the double curly braces notation {{...}} as delimiters for JSONPath expressions. The document root $ represents the payload of the incoming event. At runtime, these expressions are evaluated: placeholders are replaced with the corresponding values. To enrich the expressiveness of event processing, we provide an additional set of primitive methods on JSONPath expressions, to perform arithmetic operations and text processing, such as `contains`, `startsWith`, `endsWith`, etc.

Evaluation. In addition to data substitution, we also provide an environment for evaluating expressions on JSON primitive types. The evaluation environment is accessed through `<@ expr @>` delimiters, where `expr` is the expression to evaluate. As such, users can easily manipulate and transform data through evaluated expressions. At runtime, a pre-processing phase takes place, where JSONPath expressions are first substituted with the appropriate values, and then eval environments are evaluated.

4   Implementation

Our implementation of MEDLEY comprises a compiler for the MEDLEY domain-specific language and a runtime system. The runtime system relies on Node.js, a JavaScript runtime built on Chrome's V8 JavaScript engine. From the MEDLEY specification of an orchestration, the compiler generates JavaScript code that can then be linked with the runtime system. The generated code runs on devices ranging from desktop computers to resource-constrained devices such as home appliances. The runtime system defines various utility functions and amounts to about 1,200 lines of JavaScript code. The MEDLEY compiler is around 600 lines of code. We first describe the main challenges in code generation, and then present the runtime system.

4.1   Code Generation

The main challenges in generating code from a MEDLEY specification are the propagation of data through subsequent process invocations, and the routing of events through publishers and subscribers.

Data Propagation. An orchestration usually defines a hierarchy of handlers, the actions inside an on clause. Code inside a handler can access not only the data associated to its input event but also its inner events. Figure 4 shows an example of orchestration in which a handler manipulates data (line 4) associated to one of its inner events (line 1). Because each process invocation is asynchronous, data associated to events must be maintained across multiple invocations, resulting into a hierarchy of data. Maintaining data hierarchy can, however, have serious performance penalty. Furthermore, propagating the whole payload of an event might not be necessary when only a subset of the data is required at a later stage.

The MEDLEY compiler implements a backward dataflow analysis to identify data fragments that must be maintained across multiple process invocations.

```
1    on (foo:out as f) do {
2      stream bar = getBar.invoke();
3      on (bar:out) do {
4        p.invoke({"id": "{{$.f.id}}"});
5    } }
```

Fig. 4. Hierarchy of handlers

$$\frac{e = \langle l, d, \delta \rangle \qquad \vDash \textbf{on } (e) \textbf{ do } \{stmt_1; \ldots; stmt_n\}}{e \vDash action_1 \quad \ldots \quad e \vDash action_n} \tag{1}$$

$$\frac{e_1 = \langle l_1, d_1, \delta_1 \rangle \qquad e_2 = \langle l_2, d_2, \delta_2 \rangle \qquad \vDash \textbf{on } (e_1 \textbf{ and } e_2) \textbf{ do } \{stmt_1; \ldots; stmt_n\}}{e_1 \Rightarrow \langle and_{in}, \{(l_1, d_1)\}, \delta_1 \rangle \qquad e_2 \Rightarrow \langle and_{in}, \{(l_2, d_2)\}, \delta_2 \rangle \atop and_{out} \vDash stmt_1 \quad \ldots \quad and_{out} \vDash stmt_n} \tag{2}$$

$$\frac{e = \langle l, d, \delta \rangle \qquad e \vDash p.\texttt{invoke}(j)}{e \Rightarrow \langle p_{in}, j, \delta \cup \{(l, d)\} \rangle} \tag{3}$$

$$\frac{e = \langle l, d, \delta \rangle \qquad e \vDash \texttt{stream } s = p.\texttt{invoke}(j)}{e \Rightarrow \langle p_{in}, j, \delta \cup \{(l, d)\} \rangle \qquad p_{out} = \langle l', d', \delta' \rangle \qquad p_{out} \Rightarrow \langle s, d', \delta' \rangle} \tag{4}$$

Fig. 5. Rewrite rules for event routing

These data fragments are implemented as an environment structure that is added to the event payload. Processes forward this environment from their input channel to their output channel, adding information only when it may be required at later stage. To reduce memory footprint, the environment structure contains only references to data stored inside a global environment maintained by the runtime system. The MEDLEY developer does not need to be aware of these details.

Event Routing. Each process in MEDLEY has its own input channel for listening to events and output channel for publishing events. Events associated to a process are isolated in the namespace of the process, preventing them from interfering with other processes. To implement the logic described in the MEDLEY specification, the compiler generates a set of rewrite rules. Rewrite rules are used to intercept events, rename them, and publish them under a new event name. Rewrite rules are described as inference rules with a sequence of premises above a horizontal bar and a judgment below the bar (see Fig. 5). An event is described as $\langle l, d, \delta \rangle$, where l is the label name of the event, d the data associated to it, and δ the environment structure of the call hierarchy. A rewrite rule of the form $e_1 \Rightarrow e_2$ means that once the event e_1 occurs, the runtime system raises the event e_2. A judgment of the form $e \vDash stmt$ means that the runtime systems interprets the statement $stmt$ when the event e occurs. In other words, $stmt$ is the callback associated to e. The second rule shows how MEDLEY implements the and operator by rewriting each event into the input event of the and process. This process is provided as a builtin process. When it receives both the events $\langle and_{in}, \{(l_1, d_1)\}, \delta_1 \rangle$ and $\langle and_{in}, \{(l_2, d_2)\}, \delta_2 \rangle$ on its input channel, it generates the event $\langle and_{out} \{(l_1, d_1), (l_2, d_2)\}, \delta_1 \cap \delta_2 \rangle$ on its output channel. The third and fourth rules are for invoking a process p. In that case, we rewrite the event e that trigger the invocation of p as the input event of p.

4.2 Runtime System

The runtime system relies on Node.js as the backing messaging system. It encapsulate each composition in a scoped environment by assigning it a unique namespace. Therefore, events generated within a composition are restricted to their composition scope, and cannot leak over to other compositions. The run-time system is also responsible of managing the lifecycle of a process. It provides basic operations to initialize, start, stop and destroy a process instance. The init operation is usually used to pass user credentials to the process instance so as to interact with third-party services.

Our current implementation supports most of client authentication methods ranging from HTTP Basic Auth [9], API keys, to OAuth protocols. To handle these authentication mechanisms, MEDLEY provides a dedicated user interface through which users can authorize third-party services by providing their cre-dentials. The runtime system also supports OAuth 2.0 refresh tokens (used in Google APIs, for example). Refresh tokens are short-lived access tokens that expire after a predefined amount of time. A process can not be started unless all its credentials have been correctly set.

During its lifecycle, a composition may have to handle several kind of errors. A process may throw an error on its output channel (events of type err) based on its internal implementation. An error may indicate that a request to a third-party service has failed, that authentication has failed or any other service specific errors. These errors are reported as events and thus are accessible at the language level. Therefore, users can describe in their orchestration their own error handling policies. In addition, the runtime system catches errors such as network failures. In that case, it rolls back the failed process and tries it again later, increasing the time interval between each successive retry. When too many errors are raised by a composition, the system may decide to kill the running instance and release corresponding resources.

5 Evaluation

To assess our approach, we first present a performance evaluation of our imple-mentation and then describe a comparative study of the supported features.

5.1 Performance

The MEDLEY specification used for our experiments is depicted in Fig. 6. It con-sists in periodically polling a stock exchange service for a quote, and notifying the user by SMS if the value of the stock quote is above 100 USD. The period corre-sponds to the time elapsed between two successive executions of a composition. To measure the intrinsic scalability of our implementation, the processes used in our experiments do not actually communicate with third-party services. Instead, we simulate real-world latency by defining a randomized delay for response times between 50 and 100 ms. Similarly, we mock the behavior of the stock exchange service. The value it returns is randomized and varies between 80 and 120 USD.

We run our experiments on two different kinds of hardware platforms, from embedded devices to mainstream servers. The server we use is powered by 2 quadcore AMD Opteron 4386 CPUs at 3 GHz and 16 GB of RAM. We configure our runtime system to use a pool of 7 working threads, and one thread for

```
1   composition {
2     process tick = require("Mock/Tick");
3     process getQuote = require("Mock/GetQuote");
4     process sendSms = require("Mock/SendSms");
5     //...
6     on (tick:out) do {
7       stream quote = getQuote.invoke({ "symbol": "MSFT" });
8       on (quote:out as q) do {
9         if ({{"$.q.value"}} > 100) {
10          sendSms.invoke({
11            "text": "Current price: {{$.q.value}}",
12            "number": "+33601234567"
13          });
14  } } } }
```

Fig. 6. MEDLEY specification of the stock exchange composition

the main process. Therefore, we allocate one thread on each physical core of the server. We increase the memory limit of our underlying execution engine to 4 GB which is its current maximum on 64-bit systems. As an embedded system candidate, we use the Raspberry Pi 2 model B with 1 GB RAM and 1 quadcore BCM2836 CPU. We configure our runtime system to use a total of 4 threads, mapping each of them on a physical core. We raise the memory limit to 1 GB, which is the maximum of memory available on this device.

Our benchmarks measure the memory footprint of the MEDLEY runtime when gradually increasing the number of simultaneous compositions. We perform a staged rollout by instanciating and starting a new composition every 10 ms, and collect a snapshot of memory usage every second. The period used in our experiments vary from 30 s to 5 min. A small period increases responsiveness but requires much more resources as the composition needs to be executed more often.

Performance results on the server are shown in Fig. 7 while those for the embedded device are shown in Fig. 8. On the server, the total number of simultaneous compositions varies from at least 22,000 with a period of 30 s to up to 125,000 with a period of 5 min. Similarly, the Raspberry Pi 2 enables at least 4,000 simultaneous compositions with a period of 30 s to up to 27,000 with

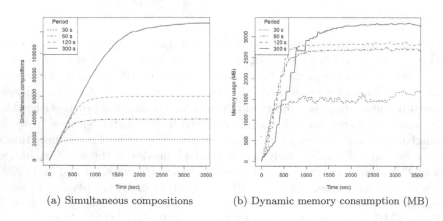

(a) Simultaneous compositions   (b) Dynamic memory consumption (MB)

Fig. 7. Benchmark results on a server

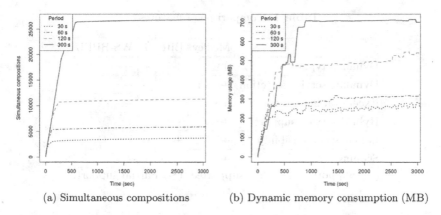

(a) Simultaneous compositions   (b) Dynamic memory consumption (MB)

Fig. 8. Benchmark results on an embedded device

a period of 5 min. When the period is too small or the number of simultaneous compositions is too high, the event queue of the runtime becomes full and no composition can be instantiated anymore. We are currently investigating the scheduling of the various compositions out of the main thread to significantly increase the scalability of the runtime. As illustrated in Figs. 7b and 8b, the memory consumption of the runtime follows the same growth as the number of simultaneous compositions. In the worst case, the runtime consumes up to the total of memory allocated to it. Our current implementation relies on Node.js which limits the memory of a single process to 4 GB. However, as compositions are independent from each others, it would be possible to increase the number of simultaneous compositions by distributing them over a cluster of several instances of Node.js processes.

5.2 Features

We present a comparative study of the features supported by MEDLEY compared to Bite [27], S [3] and the WS-BPEL standard [20]. We select these solutions because they address the problem of composing web services and provide a language to describe such compositions. We rely on the work of Sheng et al. [28] to identify the following features:

- *Dynamic typing*: the ability to manipulate arbitrarily-typed data structures.
- *Dynamic service selection*: the ability to select and bind services at runtime.
- *Exception handling*: the ability to handle and respond to runtime errors.
- *Hybrid service support*: the ability to compose services of different types (REST, SOAP, etc.).
- *Language extensibility*: the ability to extend the language and provide new features.
- *Scoping*: the ability to define and use nested blocks and localized variables.

Table 1. Comparison of features

	Medley	Bite	S	WS-BPEL
Dynamic typing	+	+	+	−
Dynamic service selection	+	−	−	−
Exception handling	+	~	~	+
Hybrid service support	+	−	−	~
Language extensibility	+	+	−	−
Scoping	+	−	+	+

(+) Supported, (−) Not supported, (~) Partial support.

Table 1 summarizes the results of our comparative study. All approaches support dynamic data typing except for BPEL, where data types are defined by their corresponding WSDL interface. Furthermore, even though all solutions enable static binding of services, MEDLEY also provides a construct to handle pools of services, enabling dynamic binding based on user-defined strategies. All four solutions also support handling runtime exceptions, although at different levels. For instance, Bite enables defining exception handlers at the activity and composition levels, while S just relies on standard error handlers provided by the JavaScript language. On the other hand, MEDLEY enables reacting to error events from the output streams of the invoked processes. As for the supported types of web services, they all enable composing RESTful services except BPEL, even though recent works aim to address this aspect by proposing extensions to BPEL. Moreover, since services are wrapped and exposed as processes in MEDLEY, we can easily integrate other types of web services such as SOAP. Since the adaptation is handled at the process level (by the process provider), it is transparent at the language level, enabling the composition of hybrid services. Regarding language extensibility, MEDLEY can be easily extended by implementing new processes, whereas the same can be achieved in Bite by implementing new activity types, allowing further customization of these languages. This aspect is not covered in S and BPEL. Table 1 also shows that scoping is supported by all solutions except Bite, since it relies on a lightweight composition model.

6   Related Work

Ever since service-oriented architectures (SOA) emerged, the aspect of composing web services became prevalent and necessary. To this end, several languages and tools have been developed [28]. Among them, the most popular is WS-BPEL (Business Process Execution Language) [20]. It provides a model for describing the behavior of a composition based on its interactions with the composed services. BPEL is standardized by the OASIS organization since 2004 and relies heavily on WSDL [4] interfaces to define links with partner services. However, not all web services are exposed through a WSDL interface.

Nowadays legacy web services are rapidly decaying, in favor of the more flexible REST architecture style [7]. Although REST became the building block for major service providers, it lacks an official standard for describing interfaces. Some initiatives including Swagger [29], WADL [11] and RAML [26] have been proposed for describing REST interfaces but they are all far from wide adoption by the majority of service providers. A consortium of several major API vendors came together to found the OpenAPI Initiative [21] (founded in November 2015), as an effort to standardize how REST APIs are described. Therefore, there is a fundamental mismatch between the REST architectural style and SOA orchestration solutions, since these solutions are not directly applicable [32].

Several efforts have been made to support composition of RESTful services. Some approaches such as Bite [5,27] and S [3] define a domain-specific language to express compositions. Bite follows a workflow model while S is an extension of JavaScript. Both of them require services to be statically binded and provide limited support for error handling. As opposed, MEDLEY has the notion of pool of services that enables dynamic binding based on user-defined strategies. This mechanism also improves robustness by providing fault-tolerance to service unavailability. Other approaches propose to extend BPEL by addition new activities to manipulate REST resources as first-class entities [22,24]. However, in practice, popular BPEL orchestration engines have limited support for composing REST services.

Among existing solutions, some tackle service composition using a goal-driven semantic approach [13,16,31]. They rely on ontologies and on reasoning engines to dynamically select services that fulfill the user-provided requirements. However, very few REST services have a well-defined semantic description thus limiting the applicability of these techniques in practice.

In the commercial world, several SaaS (Software-as-a-Service) solutions and integration platforms have been built around the concept of composing these emerging services, providing user-friendly web applications in which users can describe simple orchestration scenarios. For instance, Zapier[3] and IFTTT[4] allow end-users to express compositions as pairs of *(trigger, action)*, such as *"on trigger do action"*. However, *action* is limited to one per *trigger*, which hinders the expression of more complex scenarios. Workato[5], Azuqua[6], Node-RED[7] and NoFlo[8] on the other hand do not have this restriction, and enable users to express more complex compositions. However, these platforms do not provide error handling mechanisms to the users; they merely log the errors encountered. Node-RED provides a generic *"catch all errors"* node, that serves as a single access point for all errors. On the other hand, MEDLEY provides error output streams on a per-process basis, which allows for localized error handling.

---

[3] https://zapier.com/.
[4] https://ifttt.com/.
[5] https://www.workato.com/.
[6] http://azuqua.com/.
[7] http://nodered.org/.
[8] http://noflojs.org/.

Additional processes can be attached to these error streams to execute error handling logic, such as invoking other services.

Nonetheless, most of these solutions may not be suitable for large businesses or organizations which handle sensitive and business-critical data. Instead, the emergence of private personal clouds [18] enables these actors to deploy a secure environment, where sensitive data is not exposed over external services. Further works investigate how to enforce access-control levels on data at a fine grain [2]. MEDLEY being lightweight and embeddable enables these actors to deploy private orchestration platforms, granting them control over the confidentiality of data and business processes.

As for the existing aforementioned orchestration languages, MEDLEY draws its inspiration from several existing concepts, such as flow-based programming, and process algebras. MEDLEY applies both of these concepts to the particular context of microservice composition. The notion of Flow-Based Programming (FBP) was first introduced by John Paul Morrison in the early 1970s [17]. FBP introduces the concepts of processes, bounded buffers, information packets, named ports, and separate definition of connections. FBP views an application as a network of asynchronous processes communicating by means of streams of structured data chunks known as *information packets*. Information packets are passed between the inputs and outputs of processes. Each process may have multiple inputs and outputs, and multiple processes may be connected to a specific inport or outport. FBP encourages loose coupling of components, relying on linking black boxes in order to build microservice architectures. This approach is applied in MEDLEY, complemented by an event-driven communication layer.

Process algebras are abstract languages used to specify the execution of concurrent processes. Languages like FSP, CSP, LOTOS provide the necessary semantics to express interactions (emission, reception) between two or more processes [6,8,14]. These formalisms are founded on algebraic laws, enabling one to reason formally on a system and perform various model-checking techniques to verify properties, variants and invariants of said system. MEDLEY reuses process algebra principles in a more concrete manner to express dataflow between third-party services. MEDLEY defines the required mapping between the user-provided input and the system input, and enables reasoning on data types and type compatibility, which is otherwise not possible.

7   Conclusion and Future Work

In this paper, we have presented MEDLEY, an event-driven lightweight platform for service composition. MEDLEY is based on a domain-specific language for describing orchestration and a compiler that produces efficient code. We have used MEDLEY to develop various compositions, involving a large number of existing services. Generated compositions consume a reasonably low amount of resources and the platform scales well both on a mainstream server and an embedded device such as a Raspberry Pi. Compared to traditional approaches based on BPEL or ESB, MEDLEY enables smooth adaptation at run-time of compositions of services based on their availability. In addition, we show through several examples that MEDLEY raises the level of abstractions enough to hide to the programmer intricacies of underlying communication paradigms. The MEDLEY platform is currently under beta test and will be shortly distributed as a product of CProDirect. We are working on a visual editor on top of the MEDLEY language for defining orchestrations.

There are a number of interesting avenues of future work. The first is to extend the language to specify when a change of a remote resource has to be reported as a new event in the case of polling. In this regard, we are currently defining new algorithms to efficiently compute diffs of XML or JSON documents. Complementary to this, we are investigating dataflow analyses of orchestrations to detect compositions that may expose sensitive data to unauthorized users.

Acknowledgment. This work was partially supported by CProDirect and the French funding agency ANRT under contract CIFRE-2013/0891.

References

1. Alonso, G., Casati, F., Kuno, H., Machiraju, V.: Web Services: Concepts, Architectures and Applications. Data-Centric Systems and Applications. Springer, Heidelberg (2004)
2. Biswas, P., Patwa, F., Sandhu, R.: Content level access control for openstack swift storage. In: Proceedings of the 5th ACM Conference on Data and Application Security and Privacy, pp. 123–126. ACM (2015)
3. Bonetta, D., Peternier, A., Pautasso, C., Binder, W.: S: a scripting language for high-performance RESTful web services. ACM SIGPLAN Not. **47**(8), 97–106 (2012)
4. Christensen, E., Curbera, F., Meredith, G., Weerawarana, S., et al.: Web services description language (WSDL) 1.1 (2001)
5. Curbera, F., Duftler, M., Khalaf, R., Lovell, D.: Bite: workflow composition for the web. In: Krämer, B.J., Lin, K.-J., Narasimhan, P. (eds.) ICSOC 2007. LNCS, vol. 4749, pp. 94–106. Springer, Heidelberg (2007)
6. Ferrara, A.: Web services: a process algebra approach. In: Proceedings of the 2nd International Conference on Service Oriented Computing, pp. 242–251. ACM (2004)
7. Fielding, R.T.: Architectural styles and the design of network-based software architectures. Ph.D. thesis, University of California, Irvine (2000)
8. Foster, H., Uchitel, S., Magee, J., Kramer, J.: Tool support for model-based engineering of web service compositions. In: Proceedings of the 2005 IEEE International Conference on Web Services, ICWS 2005, pp. 95–102. IEEE (2005)
9. Franks, J., Hallam-Baker, P., Hostetler, J., Lawrence, S., Leach, P., Luotonen, A., Stewart, L.: Rfc 2617: Http authentication: Basic and digest access authentication (1999). https://tools.ietf.org/html/rfc2617
10. Fuchs, A., Gürgens, S.: Preserving confidentiality in component compositions. In: Binder, W., Bodden, E., Löwe, W. (eds.) SC 2013. LNCS, vol. 8088, pp. 33–48. Springer, Heidelberg (2013)
11. Hadley, M.J.: Web application description language (wadl) (2006)

12. JSONPath. http://goessner.net/articles/JsonPath/. Accessed 05 September 2015
13. Klusch, M., Gerber, A.: Fast composition planning of owl-s services and application. In: 4th European Conference on Web Services, ECOWS 2006, pp. 181–190. IEEE (2006)
14. Magee, J., Kramer, J., Giannakopoulou, D.: Behaviour analysis of software architectures. In: Donohoe, P. (ed.) Software Architecture. IFIP, vol. 12, pp. 35–49. Springer, New York (1999)
15. Maximilien, E.M., Wilkinson, H., Desai, N., Tai, S.: A domain-specific language for web APIs and services mashups. In: Krämer, B.J., Lin, K.-J., Narasimhan, P. (eds.) ICSOC 2007. LNCS, vol. 4749, pp. 13–26. Springer, Heidelberg (2007)
16. Mayer, S., Inhelder, N., Verborgh, R., Van de Walle, R., Mattern, F.: Configuration of smart environments made simple: combining visual modeling with semantic metadata and reasoning. In: 2014 International Conference on the Internet of Things (IOT), pp. 61–66. IEEE (2014)
17. Morrison, J.P.: Flow-Based Programming: A new approach to application development. CreateSpace (2010)
18. Na, S.H., Park, J.Y., Huh, E.N.: Personal cloud computing security framework. In: 2010 IEEE Asia-Pacific Services Computing Conference (APSCC), pp. 671–675. IEEE (2010)
19. Newman, S.: Building Microservices: Designing Fine-Grained Systems, 1st edn. O'Reilly Media, Sebastopol (2015)
20. OASIS: Web services business execution language version 2.0 (2007)
21. OpenAPI. https://openapis.org/. Accessed 14 January 2016
22. Pautasso, C.: BPEL for REST. In: Dumas, M., Reichert, M., Shan, M.-C. (eds.) BPM 2008. LNCS, vol. 5240, pp. 278–293. Springer, Heidelberg (2008)
23. Pautasso, C.: On composing RESTful services. Software Service Engineering (09021) (2009)
24. Pautasso, C.: RESTful web service composition with BPEL for REST. Data Knowl. Eng. 68(9), 851–866 (2009)
25. Pautasso, C., Alonso, G.: Flexible binding for reusable composition of web services. In: Gschwind, T., Aßmann, U., Wang, J. (eds.) SC 2005. LNCS, vol. 3628, pp. 151–166. Springer, Heidelberg (2005)
26. RAML. http://raml.org/. Accessed 05 September 2015
27. Rosenberg, F., Curbera, F., Duftler, M.J., Khalaf, R.: Composing restful services and collaborative workflows: a lightweight approach. IEEE Internet Comput. 12(5), 24–31 (2008)
28. Sheng, Q.Z., Qiao, X., Vasilakos, A.V., Szabo, C., Bourne, S., Xu, X.: Web services composition: a decade's overview. Inf. Sci. 280, 218–238 (2014)
29. Swagger. http://swagger.io/. Accessed 05 September 2015
30. Urpalainen, J.: An Extensible Markup Language (XML) Patch Operations Framework Utilizing XML Path Language (XPath) Selectors (2008)
31. Zhao, H., Doshi, P.: Towards automated restful web service composition. In: IEEE International Conference on Web Services, ICWS 2009, pp. 189–196. IEEE (2009)
32. Zur Muehlen, M., Nickerson, J.V., Swenson, K.D.: Developing web services choreography standards—the case of rest vs. soap. Decis. Support Syst. 40(1), 9–29 (2005)

REST APIs: A Large-Scale Analysis
of Compliance with Principles
and Best Practices

Carlos Rodríguez[1(✉)], Marcos Baez[1], Florian Daniel[2], Fabio Casati[1],
Juan Carlos Trabucco[3], Luigi Canali[3], and Gianraffaele Percannella[3]

[1] University of Trento, Povo, TN, Italy
{crodriguez,baez,casati}@disi.unitn.it
[2] Politecnico di Milano, Milan, Italy
florian.daniel@polimi.it
[3] Telecom Italia, Trento, Italy
{juancarlos.trabucco,luigi.canali,
gianraffaele.percannella}@telecomitalia.it

Abstract. Quickly and dominantly, REST APIs have spread over the
Web and percolated into modern software development practice, especially in the Mobile Internet where they conveniently enable offloading
data and computations onto cloud services. We analyze more than 78 GB
of HTTP traffic collected by Italy's biggest Mobile Internet provider over
one full day and study how big the trend is in practice, how it changed
the traffic that is generated by applications, and how REST APIs are
implemented in practice. The analysis provides insight into the compliance
of state-of-the-art APIs with theoretical Web engineering principles and
guidelines, knowledge that affects how applications should be developed
to be scalable and robust. The perspective is that of the Mobile Internet.

Keywords: REST · APIs · REST principles · Mobile internet

1 Introduction

By now, Web applications leveraging on remote APIs or services, service-oriented
applications or service compositions [21], mashups [5], mobile applications built
on top of cloud services and similar web technologies are state of the art. They
all have in common the heavy use of functionality, application logic and/or
data sourced from the own backend or third parties via Web services or APIs
that provide added value and are accessible worldwide with only little development effort. The continuous and sustained growth of ProgrammableWeb's API
directory (http://www.programmableweb.com/apis/directory) is only the most
immediate evidence of the success that Web services and APIs have had and
are having among developers. On the one hand, today it is hard to imagine a
Web application or a mobile app that does not leverage on some kind of remote
resource, be it a Google Map or some application-specific, proprietary functionality. On the other hand, to some companies today service/API calls represent
the equivalent of page visits in terms of business value.

© Springer International Publishing Switzerland 2016
A. Bozzon et al. (Eds.): ICWE 2016, LNCS 9671, pp. 21–39, 2016.
DOI: 10.1007/978-3-319-38791-8_2

Two core types of remote programming resources have emerged over the years: SOAP/WSDL Web services [21] and REST APIs [6]. While the former can rely on a very rich set of standards and reference specifications, and developers know well how to use WSDL [4] to describe a service and SOAP [3] to exchange messages with clients, REST APIs do not have experienced this kind of standardization (we specifically refer to JSON/XML APIs for software agents and exclude web apps for human actors). Indeed, REST is an architectural style and a guideline of how to use HTTP [7] for the development of highly scalable and robust APIs. While the freedom left by this choice is one of the reasons for the fast uptake of REST, it is also a reasons why everybody interprets REST in an own way and follows guidelines and best practices only partially, if at all.

It goes without saying that even small differences in the interpretation of the principles and guidelines underlying REST APIs can turn into a tedious and intricate puzzle to the developer that has to integrate multiple APIs that each work differently, although expected to behave similarly. For instance, while one provider may accompany an own API with a suitable WADL [10] description, another provider may instead not provide any description at all and require interested clients to navigate through and explore autonomously the resources managed by the API. Of course, if instead all APIs consistently followed the same principles and guidelines, this would result in design features (e.g., decoupling, reusability, tolerance to evolution) that would directly translate into savings in development and maintainance costs and time [18, 23].

With this paper, we provide up-to-date insight into how well or bad the principles and guidelines of the REST architectural style are followed by looking at the problem from the mobile perspective. We thus take an original point of view: we analyze more than 78 GB of plain HTTP traffic collected by Italy's biggest Mobile Internet (MI) provider, Telecom Italia, identify which of the individual HTTP calls are targeted at REST APIs, and characterize the usage patterns that emerge from the logged data so as to compare them with guidelines and principles. We further use the maturity model by Richardson [8], which offers an interesting way to look at REST in increasing levels of architectural gains, to distinguish different levels of compliance with the principles. The dataset we can rely on allows us, at the same time, to look at how conventional Web applications leverage on REST APIs as well as to bring in some insights regarding the use of APIs in the Mobile Internet. Concretely, the contributions of this paper are as follows:

- We descriptively characterize a *dataset* of more than 78 GB of HTTP requests corresponding to one full day of Mobile Internet traffic generated by almost 1 million subscribers.
- From the core principles and guidelines of REST and the structure of the dataset, we derive a set of *heuristics* and *metrics* that allow us to quantitatively describe the API ecosystem that emerges from the data.
- We *analyze* the results, study how well the data backs the principles and guidelines of REST, and discuss how the respective findings may impact API maintainability and development.

The paper is structured in line with these contributions. We first recap the theoretical principles and guidelines that we want to study in this paper (Sect. 2). Next, we introduce the dataset we analyzed and how we collected it (Sect. 3) and discuss its key features (Sect. 4). Then, we specifically focus on the REST APIs (Sect. 5) and conclude the paper with an overview of related works and our final considerations on the findings (Sects. 6 and 7).

2   REST APIs

The Representational State Transfer (REST) architectural style [6] defines a set of rules for the design of distributed hypermedia systems that have guided the design and development of the Web as we know it. Web services following the REST architectural style are referred to as *RESTful Web services*, and the programmatic interfaces of these services as *REST APIs*. The principles governing the design of REST APIs are in big part the result of architectural choices of the Web aimed at fostering scalability and robustness of networked, resource-oriented systems based on HTTP [7]. The core principles are [6,23]:

- *Resource addressability.* APIs manage and expose resources representing domain concepts; each resource is uniquely identified and addressable by a suitable Uniform Resource Identifier (URI).
- *Resource representations.* Clients do not directly know the internal format and state of resources; they work with resource representations (e.g., JSON or XML) that represent the current or intended state of a resource. The declaration of content-types in the headers of HTTP messages enables clients and servers to properly process representations.
- *Uniform interface.* Resources are accessed and manipulated using the standard methods defined by the HTTP protocol (Get, Post, Put, etc.). Each method has its own expected, standard behavior and standard status codes.
- *Statelessness.* Interactions between a client and an API are stateless, meaning that each request contains all the necessary information to be processed by the API; no interaction state is kept on the server.
- *Hypermedia as the engine of state.* Resources as domain concepts can be related to other resources. Links between resources (included in their representations) allow clients to discover and navigate relationships and to maintain interaction state.

Together, these principles explain the name "representational state transfer": interaction state is not stored on the server side; it is carried (transferred) by each request from the client to the server and encoded inside the representation of the resource the request refers to.

2.1   Best Practices for Development

Along with the general principles introduced above, a set of implementation best practices have emerged to guide the design of quality APIs [16,19,22,23].

These best practices address the main design aspects in REST APIs: (i) the modeling of resources, (ii) the identification of resources and the design of resource identifiers (URIs), (iii) the representation of resources, (iv) the definition of (HTTP) operations on resources, and (v) the interlinking of resources. We overview these best practices in the following; a summary with examples is shown in Table 1.

Resource modeling. REST APIs can manage different types of resources: *documents* for single instances of resources, *collections* for groups of resources, and *controllers* for actions that cannot logically be mapped to the standard HTTP methods [16]. While modeling resources for REST APIs is not fundamentally different from modeling classes in OO programming or entities in data modeling, there are a couple of recommended naming practices that are typical of REST APIs: singular nouns for documents, plural nouns for collections, and verbs only for controllers [16], no CRUD names in URLs [16,22], no transparency of server-side implementation technologies (e.g., PHP, JSP) (http://www.ibm. com/developerworks/library/ws-restful/).

Resource identification. Resource identifiers should conform with the URI format, consisting of a scheme, authority, path, query, and fragment [2]. In the case of Web-accessible REST APIs, the URIs are typically URLs (Uniform Resource Locators) that tell clients how to locate the APIs. In order to improve the readability of URLs, it is recommended to use hyphens instead of underscores, lowercase letters in paths, "api" as part of the domain, and avoid the trailing forward slash [16]. In addition, in its purest form, REST services should avoid declaring API versions in the URL [16].

Resource representation. Resources can support alternative representations (e.g., XML, JSON) and serve different clients with different formats. Which representation to serve should be negotiated at runtime, with the client expressing its desired representation using the HTTP `Accept` header instruction. This fosters reusability, interoperability and loose-coupling [22]. APIs should therefore use content negotiation instead of file extensions to specify formats (e.g., `.json` or `.xml`). In addition, it is recommended that APIs support (valid) JSON among their representation alternatives [16,22].

Operations. To manage resources, REST APIs should rely on the uniform set of operations (`Post`, `Get`, `Put`, `Delete`, `Options`, `Head`) defined by the HTTP standard [7] and comply with their standardized semantics:

- `Post` should be used to create new resources within a collection.
- `Get` should be used to retrieve a representation of a resource.
- `Put` should be used to update or create resources.
- `Delete` should be used to remove a resource from its parent.
- `Options` should be used to retrieve the available interactions of a resource.
- `Head` should be used to retrieve metadata of the current state of a resource.

REST APIs should thus never tunnel requests through `Get` or `Post`, e.g., by specifying the actual operation as a parameter or as part of the resource name.

Table 1. REST API design best practices with compliance (✔) and violations (✖)

Resource modeling

Singular noun for documents, plural noun for collections, verb for controllers, avoid
   CRUD names in URIs, and hide technology:

✔ http://api.test.org/universities

✖ http://api.test.org/university/deleteCenter?id=1

Resource identification

Use hyphens instead of underscores, lowercase letters in paths, and avoid the
   trailing forward slash:

✔ http://api.test.org/universities/12/faculty-centers?page=1

✖ http://api.test.org/universities/12/Faculty_centers/

Resource representation

Content negotiation instead of file extensions to specify desired formats, support
   (valid) JSON format among the representation alternatives:

✔ GET http://api.test.org/universities

   Accept: application/json

✖ GET http://api.test.org/universities.json

Operations

Avoid tunneling requests through `Get` and `Post` and instead make standard use of
   the methods:

✔ DELETE http://api.test.org/universities/1

   Status 204

✖ GET http://api.test.org/api?action=delete\&target=university\&id=1

Hyperlinks

Links should not be constructed by clients but obtained from the resource
   representation, they should follow a consistent structure and be sensitive to the
   current state of the resource:

✔ GET http://api.test.org/universities/1

   Accept: application/json

< {"name" : "UniTN",

<   "links" : { "faculty-centers" : "/universities/1/faculty-centers" }

   }

✖ GET http://api.test.org/universities/1

   Accept: application/json

< { "name" : "UniTN" }

2.2 Assessing REST Compliance

Next to the lower-level development best practices, concrete APIs may follow
the very principles underlying REST to different extents. The maturity model

by Richardson [8] offers a way to explain the respective degree of compliance by means of different levels of maturity:

- *Level 0*: At this level, APIs work by *tunneling* requests through a single endpoint (URL) using one HTTP method. Examples of services working at this level are XML-RPC and those SOAP/WSDL services that transmit all communications as HTTP `Post` requests and use HTTP purely as transport protocol. Yet, also some REST APIs adopt this technique.
- *Level 1*: At this level, instead of using a single endpoint, functionality exposed by the API is split over *multiple resources*, which increases the addressability of the API and facilitates consumption. However, services at Level 1 still make use of payload data or the URL to identify operations.
- *Level 2*: APIs at this level make proper use of the *HTTP methods* and *status codes* for each resource and correctly follow the uniform interface principle.
- *Level 3*: APIs at this level embrace the notion of *hypermedia*. Thus, not only resources can be accessed through a uniform interface but their relationships can be discovered and explored via suitable links.

Each level of compliance comes with greater benefits in terms of quality and ease of use by the developer familiar with REST. We will come back to these levels when analyzing the adherence of APIs to the principles and best practices.

3   Mobile Telco Infrastructure and Dataset

In order to study how well the state-of-the-art landscape of REST APIs complies with the introduced principles and guidelines, in this paper we rely on a dataset of 78 GB of plain HTTP traffic collected by Italys biggest Mobile Internet (MI) provider, Telecom Italia. To understand the nature and provenance of the dataset, Fig. 1 provides a functional overview of the underlying cellular network architecture (upper part) and of how data was collected (lower part).

The cellular network uses 2G (GSM/GPRS), 3G (UMTS) and 4G (LTE) base stations (Node B) for the connection of mobile devices. The Radio Network Controllers (RNCs) control the base stations and connect to the Serving GPRS Support Nodes (SGSNs) that provide packet-switched access to the core network of the operator within their service areas. Via the core network, the SGSNs are connected with the Gateway GPRS Support Nodes (GGSNs) that mediate between the core network of the operator and external packet-switched networks, in our case the Internet. The GGSNs also assign the IP addresses to the devices connected to the Internet through the operator's own network.

If a mobile device issues an HTTP request to a server accessible over the Internet, the request traverses all the described components from left to right. Special hardware probes tap into the connection between the SGSN and the GGSN to intercept raw traffic. The probes forward the traffic to multiple, parallel data collectors that filter the intercepted data by purpose (we specifically focus on network usage and HTTP traffic) and produce purpose-specific log files as output; each file contains approximately 15 min of traffic. For our analysis,

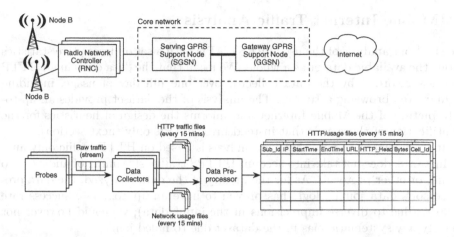

Fig. 1. Cellular network architecture with probes for the collection of Mobile Internet usage data and an excerpt of the structure of the data studied in this article.

a pre-processing of the files is needed to join the HTTP traffic records with the network usage records, so as to be able to correlate traffic with network usage properties like cell IDs or data sizes.

The result is a set of joint, enriched HTTP traffic files of which Fig. 1 shows an excerpt of the data structure: Sub_Id and IP are the subscriber identifier and IP address (both fully anonymized), StartTime and EndTime delimit the HTTP transaction as registered by the cellular network, URL contains the complete URL requested by the mobile device, HTTP_Head contains the full header of the HTTP request, Bytes contains the size of the data uploaded/downloaded, and Cell_Id uniquely identifies the base station the device was connected to.

The available dataset was collected throughout the full day of 14 October (Wednesday) by one data collector located in the metropolitan area of Milan, Italy. The average amount of HTTP traffic recorded per day is about 150 GB (about 340 mln individual HTTP requests), the usage data is in the order of 200 GB/day; the enriched HTTP traffic files amount to approximately 180 GB/day. The pre-processor joining the HTTP traffic and network usage files is implemented by the TILab software group in Trento using RabbitMQ (https://www.rabbitmq.com) for the parallel processing of chunks of input data and Redis (http://redis.io) for in-memory data caching of joined tuples to be added to the enriched HTTP traffic files in output.

Please note that, in line with similar Internet usage studies [1], personal identifiers were anonymized prior to the study, and only aggregated values are reported. Data are stored on in-house servers and password protected. Before publication, the work was checked by Telecom for compliance with Italian Law D.Lgs 196/2003 (which implements the EU Directive on Privacy and Electronic Communications of 2002), Telecom's own policies, and the NDA signed between Telecom and University of Trento.

4   Mobile Internet Traffic Analysis

We start our analysis of the use of REST APIs with a set of descriptive statistics about the available dataset as a whole. We recall that the data contain all HTTP requests recorded by the data collector over one full day of usage, including regular Web browsing activities. The analysis of the dataset provides an up-to-date picture of the Mobile Internet and informs the design of heuristics for the identification of those calls that instead involve APIs only (next section).

It is important to note that our analysis is based on HTTP traffic only and, for instance, does not take into account HTTPS traffic, streaming of audio/video media, or other protocols. As for the quality of the data analyzed, the data pre-processor's data joining logic has proven to have an approximate success rate of 90 % (due to diverse imprecisions in the input data); we could however not identify any systematic bias in the dataset due to failed joins.

4.1   HTTP Requests and Responses

Figure 2 summarizes the key characteristics of the dataset we leverage on in this paper. Figure 2(a) reports on the different *HTTP methods* (also called "verbs") used by the recorded HTTP requests, along with the respective count. We can see that the two most commonly used methods (Get and Post) dominate the traffic in today's Mobile Internet, followed by other methods such as Connect, Head, Put, Options and Delete. The less common methods Propfind and Proppatch are used by Web Distributed Authoring and Versioning (WebDAV), an extension of HTTP for web content authoring operations (see RFC 2518 [9]). Source (used by the Icecast multimedia streaming protocol), Dvrget and Dvrpost (used for multimedia/multipart content and streaming over HTTP), and List are other non-standard HTTP methods.

The identified usage of HTTP methods provide a first indication of the potential compliance of the RESTful APIs with the REST architectural style guidelines [6], which, as we have seen earlier, advocate the use not only of Get and Post, but also of Put, Delete, Options, Head, etc. for the implementation of what is called the "uniform interface" of REST APIs. Our dataset shows that by now these request methods are not only being used by some APIs, but have turned into state of the art.

In this respect, it is good to keep in mind that the mobile app market is largely characterized by applications that heavily leverage on Web APIs to provide their users with mobile access to large content repositories and highly scalable computing power, two resources that are typically limited on mobile devices. Since our dataset captures Mobile Internet usage, there may be a bias toward a more rich use of HTTP methods. On the other hand, it is important to note that the Connect methods are used to establish HTTPS connections, that is to switch from plain HTTP to its encrypted counterpart HTTPS. Once a communication switches from HTTP to HTTPS (e.g., when a user logs in to Facebook) we are no longer able to intercept tunneled HTTP requests and, hence, to follow the conversation. The estimation of the telco operator is that, of all the mobile internet traffic, around 25–30% corresponds to HTTPS traffic. We acknowledge the lack of such type of traffic as a limitation of our dataset.

Figure 2(b) illustrates the counts of the *HTTP response codes* corresponding to the requests in Fig. 2(a). According to the figure, the recorded requests feature a rich and varied usage of HTTP response codes. Responses are dominated by successful and redirection operations (2xx and 3xx codes), and errors (4xx and 5xx) are mainly due to clients requesting resources not found on the server (404) or forbidden to the client (403). In 2005, Bhole and Popescu [24] did a similar analysis of HTTP response codes and identified only 5 different codes in their dataset, with status code 200 representing 88 % of the analyzed traffic – despite the HTTP protocol specification (version 1.1) dating back to 1999 [7]. In other words, after approximately one decade HTTP responses are characterized today by a much richer use of response codes and APIs that effectively work with the standard semantics of both request methods and response codes.

Figure 2(c) looks more detailedly into the different HTTP request methods and shows how much data is transmitted/received per method. Overall, the median of transmitted data is 1463 bytes, while the median of received data is 1643 bytes. The same numbers approximately hold for all methods, except for the Source method, which presents significantly higher values; we recall that the method is used by Icecast to stream multimedia content.

In 1995, Mah [13] showed that the median HTTP response length was about 2 KB. Pang et al. [20] registered a similar response length in 2005, and Maier et al. [15] approximately confirm analogous numbers in 2010. In the end of 2015, our dataset too confirms a similar median response length. This almost stable picture is somehow surprising, as over the last years we all have witnessed a Web that has grown more complex, in terms of both content and functionality. On the other hand, Mah also showed that in 1995 the median HTTP request length was about 240 bytes [13], while our dataset presents a median request length of about 1.5 KB. This change of the length of the requests must be explained by a different use of the Internet in upload between the two dates. In fact, from 1995 to today, the Web has evolved from Web 1.0 to Web 2.0, that is, from mono-directional content consumption to fully bidirectional content co-creation. The increase of request lengths provides evidences of this paradigm shift. A confirmation of this, however, would require an own, purposely designed study.

4.2   Media Type Usage

"Media types" are the generic Web synonym of "representations" in REST. Studying the media types returned by the HTTP requests allows one therefore to obtain a first indication of which representations state-of-the-art APIs use. Figure 2(d) shows the ten most used media types in our dataset. Keeping in mind that the dataset contains generic Web traffic (not only API traffic), it is of no surprise to find text/html on the first place, followed by image/jpeg and image/gif. More surprising is that the data format application/json is already on the forth position, while text/xml is only on the ninth position. As can further be seen in the figure, both text/javascript

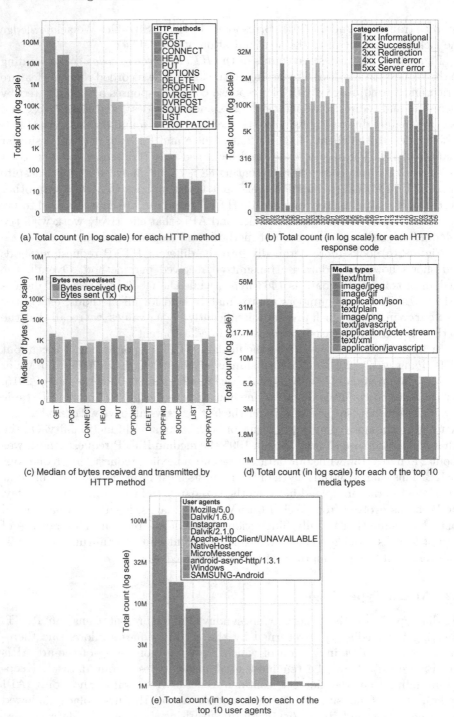

(a) Total count (in log scale) for each HTTP method

(b) Total count (in log scale) for each HTTP response code

(c) Median of bytes received and transmitted by HTTP method

(d) Total count (in log scale) for each of the top 10 media types

(e) Total count (in log scale) for each of the top 10 user agents

Fig. 2. Descriptive statistics of the available dataset characterizing state-of-the-art Mobile Internet traffic as of October 2015.

and `application/javascript` refer to the same media type and, hence, the naming of the media types is not consistent throughout the different applications and/or APIs. In fact, it is good to note that the figure only shows the ten most used media type declarations; overall, the dataset contains 1134 different media type declarations.

The two media types that are of particular interest in this paper are of course JSON and XML, as these are meant for machine consumption and therefore refer to the invocation of an API or service. We exploit this property later on to identify calls to APIs among the huge amount of calls in the dataset. SOAP web services [21] too transfer XML-encoded data, yet the respective XML-encoded SOAP envelope is always associated with the media type `application/soap+xml` and transmitted via HTTP `Post` requests. It is therefore easy to distinguish calls to SOAP web services from potential calls to REST APIs.

4.3   User Agents

Finally, with Fig. 2(e) we would like to shed some light on the user agents used to issue the requests logged in our dataset. The figure again shows the ten most used user agents from a total of 57571 different user agent declarations. On the first position, we find Mozilla/5.0 with an extraordinary predominance. To understand this result, it is important to notice that the user agent string in the header of HTTP requests can be assigned arbitrarily by the user agents themselves. And this is what happens in practice, as nicely explained by Aaron Andersen in his blog http://webaim.org/blog/user-agent-string-history/: in order to prevent user agent sniffing and being discriminated, most modern Web browsers declare to be compatible with Mozilla/5.0 (even Internet Explorer, Edge, Safari and similar). More interesting to our own analysis are the user agents Dalvik (Android virtual machine), Android and Windows that testify the presence of mobile devices, while the user agents Instagram and MicroMessenger represent native mobile apps able to issue HTTP requests. Indeed, a closer inspection of our dataset revealed that 40.8 % of the traffic corresponds to native apps, while the rest 59.2 % is traffic generated from mobile, web browsers. As a follow up, future work we would like explore these two worlds with an own, dedicated study to understand whether and how they differ from each other.

5   REST API Analysis

Given our dataset, which can be seen as a generic dump of HTTP requests that interleaves requests directed toward APIs for machine consumption with requests directed toward Web applications for human consumption, the first problem to solve is identifying which *requests* actually refer to the former. This is necessary to be able to effectively focus the analysis on APIs for software agents (from now on simply APIs) and not to be distracted by regular Web navigation activities. Given the limited amount of information available about the recorded HTTP requests, the problem is not trivial and requires the application of API-specific heuristics.

Recalling Fig. 2(d), we remember that among the top-10 media types used in our dataset we have JSON and XML, which are typical data formats for the exchange of data between software agents. It is thus reasonable to assume that requests returning any of these two media types are directed toward APIs. In order to identify such requests, we considered only those requests that contain the strings 'json' and 'xml' in their media type declaration. Examples of these include the common media types `application/xml` and `application/json`, but also less common media types such as `application/vnd.nokia.ent.events+json` and `application/vnd.wap.xhtml+xml`. The total number of such requests in our dataset is 18.2 million, 9.3 million for JSON and 8.9 million for XML.

In order to assure that these requests really return JSON and XML and to characterize the typical responses, we sampled all JSON and XML requests independently and representatively for the whole dataset using a 95 % confidence level and a confidence interval of 3. This corresponds to 1067 requests to the corresponding, presumed APIs randomly picked for both media types to obtain their payloads. Figure 3(a) shows the cumulative density function of the payload sizes. The medians are 1545 and 2606 bytes, respectively, for JSON and XML.

We also checked the formal validity of the payloads. Checks were performed using Python's internal libraries, which reported that 75 % and 76 % of the requests contained valid JSON and XML, respectively. The main reasons for invalid payloads were either empty payloads or, in the case of declared JSON payloads, the presence of JSONP callbacks (JSON wrapped in Javascript code) instead. As for the empty payloads, an inspection of the respective HTTP status

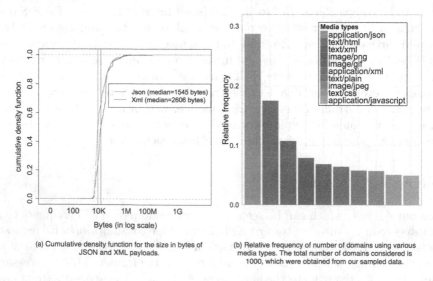

(a) Cumulative density function for the size in bytes of JSON and XML payloads.

(b) Relative frequency of number of domains using various media types. The total number of domains considered is 1000, which were obtained from our sampled data.

Fig. 3. Size in bytes for JSON and XML payloads, and media type distribution by host

codes reveals that most of them are explained by 4xx and 5xx error codes, that is, by resources that no longer exist or are not addressable on the server or because of session expiration. Overall, the counts of the status codes (in parenthesis) in the sample are: for JSON 1xx (0), 2xx (1204), 3xx (1), 4xx (243) and 5xx (53), and for XML 1xx (0), 2xx (1280), 3xx (0), 4xx (233) and 5xx (2).

The next step toward the identification of APIs would be deciding which concrete URLs serve as APIs *end/entry points* (e.g., api.server.org/universities), starting from where clients can start exploring the APIs. Doing so is however not feasible without inspecting each API individually. We thus limit our analysis in this section to individual HTTP requests, without trying to infer API endpoints.

Given an HTTP request, the options for end points may range from the plain host name (e.g., api.server.org) to the full URL at hand (e.g., api.server.org/universities/45/people/3). We discard this last option as too fine-grained, while, ideally, APIs should be accessible through a dedicated host name not used for other purposes. This would make the host name an identifier.

We tested this assumption: Using the same sample of 1067 requests as above, we identified the respective individual host names (incidentally precisely 1000) and went back to the full dataset recorded by the data collector to retrieve all media types that are accessible through these host names. If the host names were used only to provide API access, the media types would all be media types oriented toward software agents. In order to keep the computation manageable, we used a 15 min time slot of the full dataset collected during a high traffic hour. The slot contains a total of 3.2 million requests that, when joined with the 1000 different host names, corresponds to 3.2 billion comparisons. Figure 3(b) shows the relative frequency for the top-10 media types identified. The media type `aplication/json` has the highest frequency, followed by `text/html`, `text/xml` and others. The presence of `text/html`, `text/css` and `text/javascript` indicates that through the same host names also content oriented toward human agents (Web sites) is delivered, not only content oriented toward software agents. Hence, we conclude that host names are not good API identifiers in general.

5.1 Compliance with Design Best Practices

Next, we specifically focus on the set of 18.2 million API requests identified previously and study how well the designers of the respective APIs followed the design principles and best practices introduced in Sect. 2. We define a set of heuristics based on the request metadata available in the dataset as well as on the payloads we obtained from our representative sample of API invocations, in order to derive empirical evidence of compliance (or not).

Since some of the best practices as well as the maturity levels discussed in the next section do not apply to individual HTTP requests (which would be too fine-grained), we group requests by host names. This means that rather than studying the compliance of APIs or HTTP requests we study that of API providers, in that we look at the full traffic toward the APIs accessible under one and a same host name. Differently from the data underlying Fig. 3(b), here we only focus on requests targeted toward JSON and XML resources and, hence, we are sure we study API-related traffic only.

The heuristics are summarized in Table 2, implemented in JavaScript for node.js and Python, and the respective code is available on https://github.com/mbaezpy/api-analysis. For instance, rUnderscore uses a regular expression to tell whether an invoked URL contains underscores; we recall that the guideline is instead to use hyphens. rLowercase checks whether URLs comply with the guideline to use only lowercase letter, while rSlash checks that URLs don't end with a final slash character. We refer the interested reader to the online resource for the concrete implementation of all heuristics.

Table 2. Description of heuristics to identify compliance with design best practices.

Heuristics	Description
rUndescore	Number of URLs avoiding the use of underscores in URLs
rLowercase	Number of URLs using lowercase in paths
rSlash	Number of URLs avoiding the trailing forward slash
rVersionInPath	Number of URLs avoiding version number in the path
rVersionInQuery	Number of URLs avoiding version number in the query params
rApiInDomain	Number of URLs with API as part of the subdomain
rApiInPath	Number of URLs with API as part of the path
rCrudResource	Number of URLs avoiding CRUD operations as resource name
rHideExtension	Number of URLs hiding the implementation technology
rFormatExtension	Number of URLs avoiding media type as resource extension
rQueryExtension	Number of URLs avoiding media type as query param
rCrudInParam	Number of URLs avoiding CRUD actions in query params
rActionInQuery	Number of URLs using action params (to tunnel operations)
rIdInQuery	Number of URLs avoiding resource IDs as part of the query
rResNameApi	Number of URLs avoiding use of API as resource name
rMatchMedia	Number of URLs not violating the use of content type
rCacheQuery	Number of URLs avoiding the use of CACHE in query params
rHypermedia	Number of URLs containing hypermedia links for control

Figure 4(a) illustrates the mean, median and standard deviation of the compliance of the identified host names with each of the heuristics. For example, if we take heuristic rUnderscore, we can see that, on average, 75 % of the resources accessible through a host comply with this heuristic, with a median of 100 % and a standard deviation of 41 %, approximately. The figure shows that all except one heuristic (rApiInDomain) have a median of 100 %, and that they reached means higher than 95 %, the exceptions being rUnderscore, rLowercase, rSlash and rApiInDomain as well as rHideExtension and rFormatExtension.

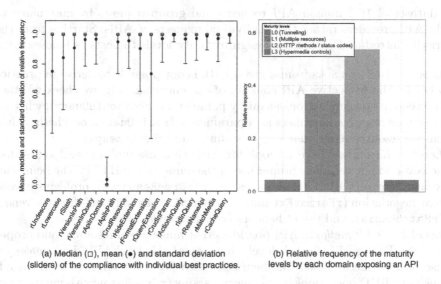

(a) Median (□), mean (●) and standard deviation (sliders) of the compliance with individual best practices.

(b) Relative frequency of the maturity levels by each domain exposing an API

Fig. 4. Compliance of APIs with best practices and maturity levels of API providers.

Overall, these results are better than we expected. The lower compliance with the former four heuristics is not major issue that affects the quality of the actual service provided through an API; they refer to naming conventions, which may or may not be shared by all developers. However, the still rather high compliance with the first three heuristics tells that most of the developers actually do follow the best practice, while they don't seem to like the use of "api" in the URL (consistently with the finding above that host names typically intermix content for human and software agents). The low compliance with the heuristics rHideExtension and rFormatExtension, instead, may have a negative effect on the maintainability and future evolvability of APIs. In fact, making implementation technologies explicit in the URL (e.g., the file suffix .php) hinders the switch from one server-side implementation technology to another (e.g., node.js). By the same token, showing resource extensions (e.g., .json) prevents content negotiation between client and server to agree on which representation format to exchange (e.g., XML instead of JSON). Of course, both cases can still be implemented (e.g., by using javascript inside an endpoint with suffix .php and by delivering XML through a resource with extension .json), but conventions have their meaning, and developers would be confused and software agents (e.g., Web servers) may not properly handle these mismatches.

5.2 API Maturity Levels

In order to estimate the compliance of the identified APIs with the maturity levels by Richardson, we leverage on some of the above heuristics to implement composite logics representing each of the four levels of maturity. Again, we study the dataset of 18.2 million API requests and group requests by host name to study API providers rather than individual requests or APIs. Starting from the heuristics introduced earlier, we assign maturity levels to hosts as follows:

- *Level 0, Tunneling.* As from a given URL is not possible to derive in practice whether the respective API consists of one endpoint only, we check whether the requests declare actions as query parameters (rActionInQuery), whether they pass resource identifiers as a parameters (rIdInQuery), or whether they have a resource name that suggests tunneling (rResNameApi).
- *Level 1, Resources.* Here we look for APIs that use multiple endpoints that however do not yet make proper use of the semantics of HTTP. The heuristics we use here are CRUD names as resources (rCrudResource), problems in content negotiation (rFormatExtension, rQueryExtension), self-descriptiveness (rMatchMedia), and use of headers (rCacheQuery).
- *Level 2, HTTP methods.* API providers that make use of resources and proper use of HTTP qualify for this level. However, at this level APIs don't make yet use of hypermedia links. The heuristics used for this level include the avoidance of CRUD operations in the query params (rCrudResource), media types as resource extension (rFormatExtension), media types as query parameters (rQueryExtension), "cache" in query params (rCacheQuery), as well as the matching of media types with actual content (rMatchMedia).
- *Level 3, Hypermedia.* Hypermedia means links inside resource representations to enable the client to navigate among resources. The rHypermedia heuristic helps us identify resources in this level by looking for hypermedia links inside the payload of HTTP responses.

The following pseudocode implements the logic for the identification of levels (dNumResources is the number of individual URLs accessed through a given host, dNumMethods is the number of different HTTP methods used by the requests):

```
function calculateLevel012(){
  if (dNumResources == 1 && dNumMethods == 1 && (rActionInQuery < dNumResources ||
    rIdInQuery < dNumResources || rResNameApi < dNumResources)) {
      level ="L0";
  } else if (rActionInQuery < dNumResources || rIdInQuery < dNumResources ||
    rCrudResource < dNumResources || rFormatExtension < dNumResources ||
    rQueryExtension < dNumResources || rMatchMedia < dNumResources ||
    rCacheQuery < dNumResources)) {
      level = "L1";
  } else {
      level = "L2";
  }
  return level;
}

function calculateLevel3(){
  resources = resourcesInL2.sample().getPayloads();
  numResources = count(resources);
  rHypermedia = 0;
  for resource in resources{
    if (resource contains hypermedia links){
      rHypermedia = rHypermedia + 1;
    }
  }
  estimatedLevel = rHypermedia / numResources;
  return estimatedLevel;
}
```

Compliance with Levels 0–2 is computed on the full dataset containing the 18.2 million requests, including both XML and JSON. Since the computation of Level 3 needs access to the actual payload of the requests, Level 3 is computed over a representative sample of the hosts complying with Level 2 (which is a prerequisite for Level 3) for which we were able to access the respective payloads. The sample consists of 1048 different requests with a confidence level of 95 % and a confidence interval of 3, along with the corresponding payloads.

The result of this analysis is illustrated in Fig. 4(b), which reports the fractions of the studied dataset that comply with the four maturity levels. Few hosts reach Level 0; note that we explicitly focus on requests toward REST APIs and therefore excluded invocations of SOAP or XML-RPC calls by discriminating the respective media types. A significant part of the dataset complies with Level 1, yet the respective APIs do not make proper use of HTTP. The biggest part of the dataset, however, does make good use of HTTP and complies with Level 2, while only few hosts qualify for Level 3. These data indicate that the current use of REST APIs is mostly targeted at providing CRUD access to individual resources (Level 1 and 2), while full-fledged APIs that properly interlink resources and use hypermedia as the engine of state are still rare (Level 3).

Despite big steps towards resource-oriented services, there is still a large percentage of services not taking full advantage of the HTTP protocol to provide true standard interfaces. Developers should be more aware of the benefits of standard interfaces, e.g., to be compliant with the increasing number of libraries and frameworks (e.g., backbone.js, ember.js) based on RESTful principles. The limited support of hypermedia, comes as no surprise as there is no agreement on (de facto) standards or formats, at least not in JSON, to make the required investment by both service providers and clients worthwhile.

6 Related Work

Large scale analyses of HTTP requests have been presented in several works, but focusing mainly on quality of service [11], user profiling [14] or the general understanding of Internet traffic [15]. Analyses of RESTful design patters and anti-patterns have been the subject of recent studies [18,19]. Palma et al. [18] presented a heuristic-based approach for automatically detecting anti-patterns in REST APIs, namely SODA-R, that relies on service interface definitions and service invocation. The authors analyzed 12 popular REST APIs, finding anti-patterns in all of them, with more anti-patterns than patterns in services like Dropbox and Twitter. As an extension, the same authors [19] also looked at linguistic properties in 15 widely-used APIs with similar results. These studies provide insight into design patterns and tell us that even popular REST APIs have their issues. However, these works focus more on the validation of the proposed frameworks rather than on a large scale analysis of API design practices.

In contrast, in this paper we perform a large-scale analysis of REST API design best practices and of the underlying principles by studying up-to-date Mobile Internet traffic traces. Although limited by the metadata available, the large scale of the analysis presented in this paper gives us insights into the current practice that was not present in the aforementioned studies.

7   Conclusion

The work described in this paper advances the state of the art in Web engineering with three core contributions: First, to the best of our knowledge this is the first work that empirically studies how well the developers of REST APIs follow the theoretical principles and guidelines that characterize the REST architectural style. Second, the work defines a set of heuristics and metrics that allow one to measure implementation anti-patterns and API maturity levels. Third, the respective findings clearly show that, while REST APIs have irreversibly percolated into modern Web engineering practice, the gap between theory and practice is still surprisingly wide, and only very few of the analyzed APIs reach the highest level of maturity.

These findings all point into one direction: The implementation and usage of REST APIs – as well as that of Web services more in general – is still far from being a stable and consolidated discipline. On the one hand, this asks for better, principled Resource-Oriented and, in general, Service-Oriented Computing (SOC) methodologies, tools and skills [12]; pure technologies are mature enough. On the other hand, keeping in mind the ever growing strategic importance of APIs to business, this asks for better and more targeted service/API quality and usage monitoring instruments, such as proper KPIs for APIs [17].

Acknowledgement. This research has received funding from the Provincia Autonoma di Trento under the project e2Call (Enhanced Emergency Call), grant agreement number 82/13. The authors thank all partners within e2Call for their contribution.

References

1. An, X., Kunzmann, G.: Understanding mobile internet usage behavior. In: Networking Conference, IFIP 2014, pp. 1–9. IEEE (2014)
2. Berners-Lee, T., Fielding, R., Masinter, L.: Uniform Resource Identifier (URI): Generic syntax. Technical report (2004)
3. Box, D., Ehnebuske, D., Kakivaya, G., Layman, A., Mendelsohn, N., Nielsen, H.F., Thatte, S., Winer, D.: SOAP Version 1.2. W3c recommendation, W3C. http://www.w3.org/TR/soap/
4. Christensen, E., Curbera, F., Meredith, G., Weerawarana, S.: Web Services Description Language (WSDL) 1.1. W3c note, W3C, March 2001
5. Daniel, F., Matera, M.: Mashups: Concepts, Models and Architectures. Data-Centric Systems and Applications. Springer, Heidelberg (2014)
6. Fielding, R.: Architectural styles and the design of network-based software architectures. Ph.D. dissertation, University of California, Irvine (2007)
7. Fielding, R., Gettys, J., Mogul, J., Frystyk, H., Masinter, L., Leach, P., Berners-Lee, T.: Hypertext Transfer Protocol - HTTP/1.1. Technical Report RFC 2616, The Internet Society, (1999). http://www.ietf.org/rfc/rfc2616.txt

8. Fowler, M.: Richardson maturity model: steps toward the glory of rest (2010). http://martinfowler.com/articles/richardsonMaturityModel.html
9. Goland, Y., Whitehead, E., Faizi, A., Carter, S., Jensen, D.: HTTP Extensions for Distributed Authoring - WEBDAV. Rfc 2518, The Internet Society (1999). https://tools.ietf.org/html/rfc2518
10. Hadley, M.: Web Application Description Language. W3C member submission, Sun Microsystems (2009). http://www.w3.org/Submission/wadl/
11. Khirman, S., Henriksen, P.: Relationship between quality-of-service and quality-of-experience for public internet service. In: Proceedings of the 3rd Workshop on Passive and Active Measurement (2002)
12. Lagares Lemos, A., Daniel, F., Benatallah, B.: Web service composition: a survey of techniques and tools. ACM Comput. Surv. **48**(33), 1–41 (2015)
13. Mah, B., et al.: An empirical model of http network traffic. In: INFOCOM 1997, vol. 2, pp. 592–600 (1997)
14. Mai, T., Ajwani, D., Sala, A.: Profiling user activities with minimal traffic traces. In: Cimiano, P., Frasincar, F., Houben, G.-J., Schwabe, D. (eds.) ICWE 2015. LNCS, vol. 9114, pp. 116–133. Springer, Heidelberg (2015)
15. Maier, G., Schneider, F., Feldmann, A.: A first look at mobile hand-held device traffic. In: Krishnamurthy, A., Plattner, B. (eds.) PAM 2010. LNCS, vol. 6032, pp. 161–170. Springer, Heidelberg (2010)
16. Masse, M.: REST API design rulebook. O'Reilly Media Inc, Sebastopol (2011)
17. Musser, J.: KPIs for APIs. The Business of APIs Conference (2014). http://www.slideshare.net/jmusser/kpis-for-apis
18. Palma, F., Dubois, J., Moha, N., Guéhéneuc, Y.-G.: Detection of REST patterns and antipatterns: a heuristics-based approach. In: Franch, X., Ghose, A.K., Lewis, G.A., Bhiri, S. (eds.) ICSOC 2014. LNCS, vol. 8831, pp. 230–244. Springer, Heidelberg (2014)
19. Palma, F., Gonzalez-Huerta, J., Moha, N., Guéhéneuc, Y.-G., Tremblay, G.: Are RESTful APIs well-designed? detection of their linguistic (Anti)Patterns. In: Barros, A., et al. (eds.) ICSOC 2015. LNCS, vol. 9435, pp. 171–187. Springer, Heidelberg (2015). doi:10.1007/978-3-662-48616-0_11
20. Pang, R., Allman, M., Bennett, M., Lee, J., Paxson, V., Tierney, B.: A first look at modern enterprise traffic. In: Proceedings of the 5th ACM SIGCOMM Conference on Internet Measurement, pp. 2–2. USENIX Association (2005)
21. Papazoglou, M.P.: Web Services - Principles and Technology. Prentice Hall, Upper Saddle River (2008)
22. Pautasso, C.: Some rest design patterns (and anti-patterns) (2009)
23. Pautasso, C.: Restful web services: principles, patterns, emerging technologies. In: Bouguettaya, A., Sheng, Q.Z., Daniel, F. (eds.) Web Services Foundations, pp. 31–51. Springer, New York (2014)
24. Bhole, Y., Popescu, A.: Measurement and analysis of HTTP traffic. J. Netw. Syst. Manage. **13**(4), 357–371 (2005)

MIRA: A Model-Driven Framework
for Semantic Interfaces for Web Applications

Ezequiel Bertti and Daniel Schwabe[✉]

Department of Informatics, PUC-Rio, Rua Marques de Sao Vicente, 225,
Rio de Janeiro, RJ 22453-900, Brazil
{ebertti,dschwabe}@inf.puc-rio.br

Abstract. A currently recognized barrier for the wider adoption and dissemination of Semantic Web technologies is the absence of suitable interfaces and
tools to allow suitable access by end-users. In a wider context, it has also been
recognized that modern day interfaces must deal with a large number of
heterogeneity factors, such as varying user profiles and runtime hardware and
software platforms. This paper presents MIRA, a framework for defining and
implementing Semantic Interfaces for Web applications, including those on the
Semantic Web. A Semantic Interface is defined as being one capable of understanding and adapting to the data it presents and captures, and its schema, if
present. Moreover, the interface must also be able to adapt to its context of use –
the device being used, any available information about its user, network conditions, and so on. Using a model-driven approach, MIRA allows developers to
define such interfaces, and generates code that can run on clients, servers or both.
We have carried out a qualitative evaluation that shows that MIRA does indeed
provide a better process for developers, without imposing any significant performance overhead.

Keywords: HCI · Interface · Adaptation · Semantic Web · Data-driven
design · Model-driven interface design

1 Introduction

In his ESWC 2013 keynote talk[1], David Karger defines a Semantic Web application as
"one whose schema is expected to change". Analogously, we define a "Semantic
Interface" one that is able to cope in an effective manner with this variability. Along a
different dimension, a Semantic Interface should also exploit the semantics of interactions themselves, allowing the interface to exhibit similar characteristics to the way
humans interact among themselves – namely, a degree of context awareness of the
interaction process itself.

It has long been observed that the design and implementation of the interface
components of Web applications (and other as well) consumes over 50 % of the
development effort, as reported by Myers and Rosson already in the nineties [12]. Since
then, in spite of the lack of published similar measures, it is safe to assume their figures

---

[1] See this blog post for a summary and slides - http://goo.gl/vqXglr. Video available at http://
videolectures.net/eswc2013_karger_semantic/.

© Springer International Publishing Switzerland 2016
A. Bozzon et al. (Eds.): ICWE 2016, LNCS 9671, pp. 40–58, 2016.
DOI: 10.1007/978-3-319-38791-8_3

must have surely increased, due to the evolution of the computing platforms, the advent of the Internet and the Web, and the now popular gestural and vocal interface modalities. Sources of heterogeneity affecting application development include:

- Different computing platforms, affording a variety of interaction modalities and diverse input/output capabilities;
- Multiple, often dynamically varying contexts of use, be it at a desktop with a wired network or on the go using a smartphone, head-mounted display or a watch, wirelessly connected in a variety of underlying network infrastructures. Such environments may have high degree of noise, and sometimes restricted bandwidth;
- Multiple, ever evolving set of tasks that must be supported, derived from an increasing number of different workflows that users adopt and must be supported by the application. The example of Homebrew Databases cited by Karger [1] well illustrates this point;
- Highly diverse types and profiles of end users, ranging from very novice to experts, being from many different cultures and speaking a multitude of languages;
- The increasing need to integrate data with no schema, or whose schema changes frequently. This data typically comes from different sources, often not under the control or responsibility of the application designer. A prime example is the use of data in the Linked Data Cloud.

To further aggravate the situation, the context of use, i.e., each component of the triad <user, platform, environment> often changes dynamically while the application is being used, which calls for so-called Plastic UIs [5], capable of adapting while preserving the "user experience" while the user is engaged with the application.

A common approach to deal with such complexity is to use formal models to represent various aspects of the artifact being designed, breaking up the problem into smaller, more manageable tasks. Regarding interfaces, the Model-Based User Interface (MBUI) development approach has been used to address these challenges and maintain or decrease the level of effort necessary to design and implement application interfaces, through the introduction of suitable abstractions.

The Cameleon Reference Model is a current reference framework for User Interfaces gaining adoption [4], the item of several years of research of a major European research project, which proposes four abstraction levels for modeling UIs: Task and Domain, Abstract Interface, Concrete Interface, Final User Interface.

The Domain model describes the domains of the application, and the Task model describes the sequence of steps needed to perform the tasks (with respect to interactions with the User Interface).

The Abstract Interface model describes the composition of interface units in an implementation and modality independent way.

The Concrete Interface model describes the interface in terms of platform-dependent widgets, but still modality- and implementation language independent.

The Final User Interface is the actual running code that the end user accesses when interacting with the application.

When considering the Semantic Web, and particularly applications leveraging Linked Data (so-called Linked Data Applications, LDA's), there exist several proposals of development environments or frameworks for supporting their development, such as

CubicWeb[2], the LOD2 Stack[3], and the Open Semantic Framework[4]. In addition, semantic wiki-based environment such as Ontowiki[5], Kiwi[6], and Semantic Media Wiki[7] have also been used as platforms for application development over Linked Data. There are also proposals of frameworks for building visualizations such as Exhibit [9], or Fresnel[8], among others.

While useful, they do not present a set of integrated models that allow the specification of an LDA, and the synthesis of its running code from these models. Therefore, much of the application semantics, in its various aspects, remains represented only in the running implementation code.

We have been working in the past years on the Semantic Hypermedia Design Method (SHDM) [7] and its implementation environment Synth [3], which aim to support Model-Based development of Web Applications, including Linked Data based ones.

Our experience with SHDM and Synth [13] has led us to observe that the abstractions used for designing the interface are also applicable in a more general context, beyond LDAs, and independently of the other models in SHDM.

In this paper we present MIRA[9], a framework incorporating an updated version of the User Interface models used in SHDM, its implementation architecture, which can be leveraged by any application that provides a REST interface to its "business logic". This includes, for example, RDF-based applications.

We present our approach in this paper as follows. After describing the example we are going to use through the paper in Sect. 2, we present our approach for interface modeling in Sect. 3. We discuss the implementation in Sect. 4. Section 5 discusses the evaluation of MIRA, and Sect. 6 presents the related work, discusses future work and draws some conclusions.

2 A Running Example

To help make the concepts discussed in the paper more concrete, we first briefly show an example interface[10] built with MIRA over the Europeana RDF database[11]. Suppose the user starts with a query string "da Vinci"; Fig. 1 shows an interface with the resulting items.

---

[2] http://www.cubicweb.org.

[3] http://lod2.eu/WikiArticle/TechnologyStack.html.

[4] http://openstructs.org/open-semantic-framework.

[5] http://ontowiki.net/Projects/OntoWiki.

[6] http://www.kiwi-project.eu.

[7] http://www.semantic-mediawiki.org/wiki/Semantic_MediaWiki.

[8] http://www.w3.org/2005/04/fresnel-info/.

[9] http://mira.tecweb.inf.puc-rio.br.

[10] Examples and source code available at http://mira.tecweb.inf.puc-rio.br/.

[11] http://data.europeana.eu/.

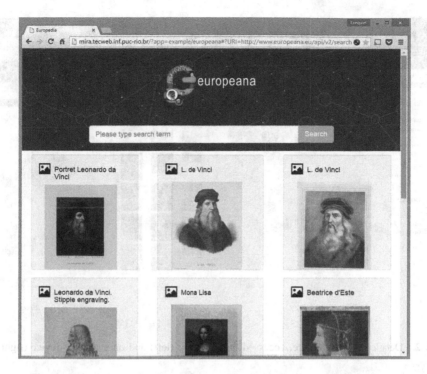

Fig. 1. Search items for the query "Da Vinci" in the Europeana collection

Clicking on the second entry leads to the interface shown in Fig. 2 Items in this collection have a variety of properties, including some with links to DBPedia. When present, this link is shown next to the other properties using DBPedia's api, but *only* in the desktop version. In addition, datatype properties can have different formats, and an appropriate interface widget is used to display each format. Figure 3 shows an item with an audio datatype property, and its audio player widget.

3 A Semantic Interface Model

The MBUI approach leverages abstractions to deal with complexity by following the principles of "separation of concerns" - the challenge here is the proper identification of the relevant concerns. Web (and interactive) applications exhibit many different behaviors, catering to different concerns. Some behaviors address the actual goal of the application, i.e., the so-called "business logic", such as adding a product to a shopping cart, or proceeding to checkout. Other behaviors address the interaction between the user and the application, e.g., choosing one item from a large list of options - e.g., picking a book from a large list of known titles. The latter must be supported by the interface. This separation is consistent with the SOUI/SOFEA architectural style, where the interface flow (logic) is separated from the business logic (see for example [17]).

Fig. 2. Detailed item interface, accessed on a desktop (left) and on a mobile device (right).

Fig. 3. An item with an audio datatype property

Based on this separation of concerns, the Interface Model in SHDM [16] distinguishes the "essence" of the interface, determined by the needs of the business logic, from its look-and-feel, which determines how the interface supports the business logic. This is achieved by decomposing the interface specification into an Abstract Interface Model, and a Concrete Interface Model.

Briefly, the Abstract Interface focuses on the roles played by each interface widget in the information exchange between the application and the outside world, including the user. It is abstract in the sense that it does not capture the look and feel, or any information dependent on the runtime environment. The Concrete Interface model is responsible for the latter.

In its essence, the interface must be able to display information to the user, upon request from the application; capture information provided by the user; or signal to the application the occurrence of some event caused by the user or by the environment.

Accordingly, the Abstract Interface meta-model (see An Element Exhibitor is used to provide the Abstract Interface with some domain model information needed to be either shown to the user (e.g., the author's name), or used by the interface to help in the interaction, e.g., a label for an input form field; help information regarding a value to be informed by the user; or some business-logic related info needed to ensure that the user inputs correct values, such as a minimum stay period for hotel or air travel reservations.

Given an Abstract Interface, a mapping specification made by the designer determines how each abstract widget will be mapped onto one or more Concrete Interface elements, based on several possible factors, discussed later.

Figure 4 defines an abstract interface as a composition of abstract interface elements (widgets). These in turn can be an Element Exhibitor, which is able to show values; and Indefinite Variable, which is able to capture an arbitrary input string; a Defined Variable, which is able to capture input values (one or several) from a known set of alternatives; and a Simple Activator, which is able to react to an external event and signal it to the application.

An Element Exhibitor is used to provide the Abstract Interface with some domain model information needed to be either shown to the user (e.g., the author's name), or used by the interface to help in the interaction, e.g., a label for an input form field; help information regarding a value to be informed by the user; or some business-logic related info needed to ensure that the user inputs correct values, such as a minimum stay period for hotel or air travel reservations.

Given an Abstract Interface, a mapping specification made by the designer determines how each abstract widget will be mapped onto one or more Concrete Interface elements, based on several possible factors, discussed later.

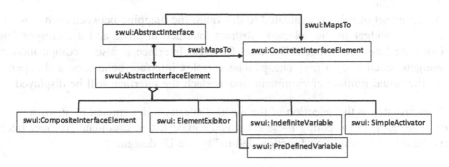

Fig. 4. The Abstract Interface metamodel in SHDM

SHDM follows the basic abstraction levels of the Cameleon Reference Model. The Concrete Interface in SHDM conflates the Concrete and Final Interfaces proposed in Cameleon, as we found that, in practice, there is little advantage in making such distinction, especially due to the adaptability of SHDM Concrete Interfaces.

The Domain Model, in SHDM is simply a set of RDF triples, which form a graph, and may include RDFS or OWL definitions. It is often the case that there does not exist any schema definitions in the Domain Model, only instances of resources representing information items. In MIRA, the domain model is simply a JSON structure of <attribute:value> pairs; a particular case is Linked Data, rendered as JSON-LD.

A mapping specification made by the designer determines how each abstract widget will be mapped, on one side, onto one or more Concrete Interface elements, and, on the other side, onto which Domain Model elements, including the operations defining the application behavior to achieve the desired tasks.

3.1 Information Flow in the Interface

In the traditional MVC (Model-View-Controller) architecture, each request to the model is accompanied by the view that will be used to display the items. In MIRA, the request does not include the view to be used. Instead, the following steps, summarized in Fig. 5, determine the actual interface that will be used to display the items,

1. The applications receives a request, in the form of a REST operation, and returns its items;
2. A set of Abstract Interface Selection rules is evaluated, determining an Abstract Interface instance, among those defined by the designer, which is able to display the items. These rules can take into account not only the data returned, but also any other context information, such as device being used, network bandwidth available, user information, etc....;
3. The selected Abstract Interface instance is assembled. Each Abstract Interface is a composition of widgets, each of which may have a condition associated with it. This condition is evaluated also based on the data and the context information; only those widgets with enabled conditions are included in the actual assembled Abstract Interface instance. Some widgets may not have an associated condition and will be always included.
4. A second set of rules is evaluated to determine the mapping between each Abstract Interface widget in the selected Abstract Interface instance and a corresponding Concrete Interface widget. The final Concrete Interface is also a composition of widgets. Each widget may encapsulate complex interface behaviors, and depends on the actual runtime environment under which the interface will be displayed.

The first step is the selection of the abstract interface, determined by its own set of rules. The result of executing these rules is a ranked list of candidate Abstract Interfaces, based on a weighting function defined by the UI designer.

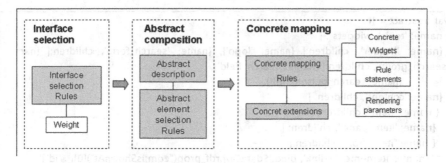

Fig. 5. Interface generation flow.

The highest-ranking Abstract Interface is then chosen. Its own composition is again determined by executing another set of rules, which may include or exclude widgets from the initial base Abstract Interface composition defined by the designer.

Next, a third set of rules is executed to determine how each Abstract Interface widget will be mapped onto concrete interface widgets.

This rule-driven approach has several advantages:

1. It allows taking into account actual runtime data and context information in determining which interface should be used. Since the rules can refer to actual input data to be exhibited through it, as well as to the Domain Model, it is fair to say that the interface definition is now Semantic, in the sense of being aware of the data types and values of the data it is exposing;
2. It allows adapting the interface to both the user and to the execution environment, allowing a user experience that is in tune with the user's device and environment capabilities. Once again, such rules may take into account the semantics of the user or context model to alter the concrete interface.
3. It becomes a design choice whether the adaptation process will be run only at design time, or also during runtime. Running them during the application execution provides maximum flexibility, as the interface can change dynamically in reaction to several context changes, such as change of device, reduced bandwidth, loss of modality due to either circumstantial reasons (e.g., no visual access during driving) or due to hardware failure (e.g., display failure).

3.2 Abstract Interface Definition

The Abstract Interface is a composition of elements, forming a hierarchy of widgets. Each element may have conditions associated to it, which determine if that element will be included in the final Abstract Interface composition or not. This conditional inclusion allows defining variations of the same basic interface that share common elements.

Below we show part of the Abstract Interface specification for the interfaces in Figs. 2 and 3.

```
var abstract = [{
 name: 'topic', widgets : [
 {name: 'header', children:[ {name: 'logo'}, {name: 'search_form', children:[ {name:
'search_group', children:[ {name: 'search_field'},
        {name:'search_button'} ]}]}]},
 {name:'content', children: [
  { name: "item", children: [
   {name: 'item_panel', children: [
   { name:"item-box", children:[
    {name: 'item-media-link', bind:'$dataObj.rdf_prop("edm:isShownAt")[0]["@id"]'
      children: [
      {name: "item-media", bind:'$dataObj.rdf_prop("edm:object")[0]["@id"]' }] },
    { name:"item-title", bind:'$dataObj.rdf_prop("dc:title")[0]' },
    { name:"item-contributor"},
    { name:"item-contributor-value", bind:'$dataObj.rdf_prop("dc:contributor")' },
    { name:"item-date"},
    { name:"item-date-value", bind:'$dataObj.rdf_prop("dc:date")[0]' },
    { name:"item-format"},
    { name:"item-format-value", bind:'$dataObj.rdf_prop("dcterms:extent")[0]' },
    { name:'item-player', when:'isSound,hasPreview',
       bind:'$dataObj.rdf_prop("edm:isShownBy")[0]["@id"]' },
    { name:"item-extra-info", children:[
     { name:"item-subject"},
     { name:"item-subject-value", bind:'$dataObj.rdf_prop("dc:subject")[0]' },
     { name:"item-identifier"},
     { name:"item-identifier-value", bind:'$dataObj.rdf_prop("dc:identifier")[0]' },
     { name:"item-language"},
     { name:"item-language-value", bind:'$dataObj.rdf_prop("dc:language")[0]' },
     { name:"item-provider"},
     { name:"item-provider-value"}, bind:'$dataObj.rdf_prop("edm:dataProvider")[0]'},
     { name:"item-country" },
     { name:"item-country-value", bind:'$dataObj.rdf_prop("edm:country")[0]' }]}]}]},
   { name: 'sidebar-dbpedia', when: 'hasDbpedia', datasource:
'url:<%= $env.methods.get_datasource_dbpedia_uri($dataObj.rdf_prop(
"dc:contributor")) %>', children:[ { name:"dbpedia-item"},
/* ... */
     }] }] }],
 {name: 'footer'} ]}
```

Each widget has a "name" and may have a sub-tree of widgets, indicated by the array "children". The element "bind" binds a value from the data (Domain Model) to an abstract widget. In the example, several widgets have values bound to RDF properties using the MIRA built-in auxiliary function "rdf_prop", which has been defined to ease handling Json-LD structures. For the widget "sidebar-dbpedia" to be included, the condition named "hasDbpedia" (highlighted in the text) is satisfied. This condition is specified in the Conditions section detailed in Sect. 3.3, and tests whether a DBPedia link is present in the triples having "dc:contributor" as property. The widget "item-player" also has a condition, which causes it to be included only when there is an audio file linked to the entry (as in the case of interface in Fig. 3).

3.3   Conditions and Interface Definition Parameters

MIRA uses condition-action rules for selecting the Abstract Interface, for including widgets (or not) in the selected Interface, and for deciding on the mapping to apply to generate the concrete widget.

To ease the specification, conditions are declared separately, and can thus be reused within different rules. These conditions can test

- Any expression involving the Domain Model. For instance, it can test the type and value of a data item (e.g., datatype property), or whether the element being exhibited is a hypertextual link (or an Object Property).
- Hypertextual parameters received in an http request;
- Browser header information, including browser, platform, operating system, etc.
- Environment variables, e.g., date and time of day, location.

Some of the conditions used in the example are shown below.

```
var conditions = [
{name: 'isItem', validate: '$data.action == "search.json"'},
{name: 'isJsonLD', validate: '$data["@context"] != null'},
{name: 'hasDbpedia', validate:
'$env.methods.get_datasource_dbpedia_uri($dataObj.rdf_prop(
"dc:contributor")) != null'},
{name: 'hasPreview', validate: '$dataObj.rdf_prop("edm:isShownBy").length >
0'},
{name: 'isSound', validate: '$dataObj.rdf_prop("edm:type")[0] == "SOUND"'}];
```

Each condition specification has the general form {name: <name>, validate: <expression>}, where <expression> is the Boolean function corresponding to the condition itself.

In the example, the condition "isItem" tests if the action executed was a search operation; the condition "isJsonLD" tests if the response from the request contains a "@context" element; "hasDbpedia" tests if there are DBPedia URLs in the "dc:Contributor" property; and "isSound" tests if the "edm:type" property has value "Sound".

These condition expressions also illustrate some of the built-in functions and variables available in MIRA, such as "$data.object", used to access complex JSON-LD structures; "rdf-prop", which extracts RDF properties from JSON-LD structures.

3.4 Abstract Interface Selection Rules

The first step in defining the Interface is establishing the selection rules for the Abstract Interface. The pre-condition in these rules define when each Abstract Interface is applicable, allowing, for instance, to

- Select the interface only if the user is logged in;
- Select the interface only if the application is being accessed from a mobile device;
- Select the interface only for certain types of data passed as input during runtime. Notice that this is often necessary if one wants to deal with "raw" data in RDF, which may not have any schema or vocabulary information associated with it.

In our example, the Abstract Interface selection rules are

```
var selection = [
{ when: 'isItem',  abstract: 'items' },
{ when: 'isJsonLD', abstract: 'topic' }
];
```

The first rule selects the abstract interface "items" if the condition "isItem" (defined in Sect. 3.3) is satisfied. Similarly, the abstract interface "topic", illustrated in and specified in Sect. 3.2 is selected if the "isJsonLD" condition (defined in Sect. 3.3) is true.

3.5 Concrete Interface Mapping Rules

For each Abstract Interface widget, there is a mapping rule that determines how it is mapped onto concrete widgets. As a consequence, the Concrete Interface's nesting structure is defined by the Abstract Interface's own structure, since it is assumed that this structure is determined by the application's semantics. In addition, the Concrete Interface may further detail the Abstract Interface by refining any abstract widget with additional levels of composition.

Abstract Interfaces may be mapped to more than one Concrete Interface, in which case they must include a "maps" element in their specification. By default, if no explicit mapping is given, MIRA matches both by having the same name.

Each Concrete Widget has a "name", a "widget" type, and a series of optional "tags", which depend on the type of widget. MIRA includes a *SimpleHTML* predefined type that maps to HTML, and a *Bootstrap* type, which maps to Bootstrap framework[12] primitives. A condition may be specified in the optional "when" element; when present, the mapping is applied only if the condition is true. Widgets are processed in the order of the specification; if there is more than one specification for the same widget, that last one evaluated is used.

---

[12] http://getbootstrap.com/.

Below we show some of the rules that map the Abstract Interface "topic" shown in Sect. 3.2 into the interfaces shown in Fig. 2, followed by some comments.

```
1.   var concrete = [{
2.   name: 'topic',head:head, maps: [
3.   { name: 'header', widget: 'SimpleHtml', tag:'div', class:'container-fluid text-center
         fundo' },
4.   { name: 'logo', widget: 'SimpleHtml', tag:'img', src:'"imgs/europedia.png"' },
5.   { name: 'search_form', widget: 'SimpleHtml', tag:'form',
         onsubmit:'do_search(event);' },
6.   { name: 'search_group', widget: 'SimpleHtml', tag:'div', class:'input-group
         form_center col-sm-8' },
7.   { name: 'search_field', widget: 'SimpleHtml', tag:'input', class:'form-control input-
         lg', placeholder:'"Please type search term"' },
8.   { name: 'search_button', widget: 'BootstrapFormGroupButton', class:'btn-warning',
         value:'"Search"', events:{'click': 'do_search'} },
9.   { name: 'content', widget: 'SimpleHtml', tag:'div', class:'container' },
10.  { name: 'item', widget: 'SimpleHtml', tag:'div', class:'row' },
11.  { name: 'item_panel', tag:'div', md:'12' },
12.  { name: 'item_panel', when:'hasDbpedia,isDesktop', tag:'div', xs:'12', sm:12, md:8,
         lg:8 },
13.  { name: 'item-box', tag:'div', class:'well' },
14.  { name: 'item-extra-info' },
15.  { name: 'item-extra-info', when:'isMobile', widget:'Collapsed', title:{value:'Click for
         more info'} },
16.  { name:"item-title", tag:'h2', value:$bind},
17.  { name:"item-media-link", tag:'a', pull:'right', href:$bind, xs:12, sm:12, md:4,
         lg:4},
18.  { name:"item-media", tag:'img', img:'thumbnail', src:$bind},
19.  { name:"item-contributor", tag:'h4', value: 'Contributor'},
20.  { name:"item-date", tag: 'h4', value:'@Date'},
21.  { name:"item-type", tag: 'h4', value:'Type'},
22.  /*...*/
23.  { name:"item-contributor-value", value:'$dataObj.rdf_prop("dc:contributor")[0]' },
24.  { name:"item-contributor-value", value:'$dataObj.rdf_prop("dc:contributor")[1]',
25.  /*...*/
26.  { name:"item-player", when:'isSound,hasPreview', widget:'AudioPlayer',
         source:$bind},
27.  { name:"sidebar-dbpedia", xs:12, sm:12, md:4, lg:4},
28.  /*...*/
29.  { name: 'footer', widget: 'TecWebRodape'}]}
```

Lines 3–9 show the specification for the header of the page and the search box, mapping to plain HTML tags. Lines 10–26 show the mappings for the details of each "item". In line 12 a widget has a condition specifying that it will be mapped only if "hasDBPedia, isDesktop" (see Sect. 3.3) is true. Since the same element is also mentioned in line 11, the item that is a link to DBPedia will be shown only when present. Lines 14–15 achieve an analogous effect; the element "items-extra-info" will be included only if the application is running on a mobile device. Lines 23–24 illustrate the use of built-in function "rdf_prop" to retrieve property values to be exhibited. Line 26 shows the conditional inclusion of an audio player widget if there is an "edm: isShownBy" property value of type "sound" (see Fig. 3).

These examples illustrate how MIRA can leverage schema and data information to adapt both the form and the content of the generated interface. Notice that it would be similarly easy to change the concrete widgets used based also on meta-properties of the data, for example, changing from a pull-down menu widget to a check-box list widget depending on the number of items returned by a request. Such a change cannot be achieved by simple changes in CSS.

As illustrated in the examples for the mapping rules, concrete widgets are treated as software components outside the model itself; different concrete widgets should be defined for different runtime platforms. In this sense, we diverge from the Cameleon model, as Concrete Widgets are rendered directly to the Final User Interface.

A Concrete Widget should be self-contained, and capable of self-rendering based only on their input parameters. In addition to the built-in concrete widget types, MIRA provides an interface that allows the developer to add new concrete widgets whenever necessary[13].

3.6   Interface Events

A common behavior found in rich interfaces is the inter-dependence among widgets, such that changes in the value assigned to one widget (either capture or exhibition) will trigger changes in other widgets. For example, when booking a flight, once the departure date has been entered, the widget showing the return date is updated for instance, disabling dates earlier than the departure date.

MIRA provides the "event" primitive as part of conditions, that allowing widgets to react to events and take action when needed, taking the semantics of the data into account. In the flight reservation dialog, for example, the action can query the Domain Model for the earliest return date given a departure date for a flight in a given fare code. Alternatively, this value can be informed via an "Exhibitor" abstract interface widget, bound to the appropriate Domain Model element. This would be an example of a value present in the Abstract Interface that is consumed by the interaction logic, and not presented directly to the user.

---

[13] Several examples can be found in the Flickr application example at MIRA website.

4 Implementation

MIRA has been implemented in Javascript, following the UMD standard[14], allowing it to be executed in both client browser and servers using Node.js. This flexibility allows MIRA to access sources that block "cross-site" scripting on the client (as is the case in several RDF repositories) by running this part of the code in a server environment. In addition, running on a server may be desirable in cases where the clients are expected to be mobile devices with limited computing and power consumption capabilities. MIRA also follows the SOUI/SOFERA architectural style, and can be used with any api providing a REST interface to some service, including non-semantic applications.

We did several code complexity analysis of MIRA's source code (see [2] for details). For reasons of space, we don't include them here, but it we can say that MIRA is of similar complexity as popular Javascript Interface Frameworks such as Backbone. js, Angular.js and JQuery.

MIRA is open source and publicly available at https://github.com/TecWebLab/mira.

5 Evaluation

There are at least two aspects we considered important in assessing MIRA. The first is its "expressive power", in the sense of being able to allow implementation of really complex, sophisticated interfaces.

The second, and most important one, is whether it actually brings benefits to the development of application interfaces, including ones with characteristics discussed in Sect. 1. We next discuss each.

5.1 Expressive Power

MIRA is intended to be used by practitioners developing web applications, including but not limited to linked-data applications. Most proposed frameworks and corresponding documentation present simple examples destined to illustrate each approach, but are far simpler than real life applications.

We have used MIRA to implement a wide range of applications, from simple straightforward to more sophisticated ones. The most complex application mimics some of the interfaces found in the well-known Flickr website, which is very complex and highly sophisticated. We have found that MIRA allows implementing such interfaces with simpler code.

One example application provides an interface to Flickr can be accessed in the MIRA website. The Flickr photo page is quite sophisticated, with several conditions dictating its appearance and behavior, including the screen size, whether the user is logged in or not, whether it is the author of the photo or not, and previous browsing history.

---

[14] https://github.com/umdjs/umd.

A second example is the Europeana interface used as an example in this paper, also accessible in the website.

It should also be noted that in all examples, rules were used to generate mobile-friendly versions without requiring changes in the Abstract Interface definition, supporting our hypothesis that such decompositions are indeed viable and useful.

5.2   Qualitative Evaluation

Given the complexity of carrying out a complete evaluation of the benefits of MIRA in interface development, we did a detailed qualitative evaluation with a small number of individuals. Our goal was to assess if developers would be able to use MIRA, and it would be more effective (for them) than any of the tools they were already used to.

We defined two applications with essentially the same functionality, but in different domains. The first required the developer to present a list of ads for real estate properties, where the presentation depended on the type of real estate property. Clicking on a property presents a new interface with its details also with different properties depending on its type.

The second required the developer to present a list of items for soccer matches, with different presentations depending on the previous winning records of each team, and whether it was a home or away game. Clicking on a team presents the detailed items about its latest games, with different presentations depending on the item and location (home or away).

Each individual was given an hour-long introduction to MIRA, which included a complete walkthrough of an example application, and access to the complete detailed online documentation, with examples. They were also asked to fill in a questionnaire to allow us to assess their prior professional experience and background, particularly with respect to interface development.

Subjects were given the option to choose one of the applications using any interface development framework they were already familiar with, if any. After finishing developing using the familiar framework, they developed the other application using MIRA.

For each application, they were given the documentation of the REST interface, including the format of the data returned, an HTML wireframe, a natural language specification of the business rules they should implement.

We used the "think out loud" approach during de development of each application, asking the subject to say out lout their doubts, thought processes, decisions, etc...., which were videotaped.

The details of these tests are summarized in Table 1.

All users were able to complete both tasks, with the exception of user 3, who had little prior programming knowledge and had never implemented an interface. For this user, it is actually remarkable that he was able to implement the interfaces using MIRA.

All subjects were able to develop also a mobile version of each application.

The development times in Table 1 show that developing using MIRA, a framework that was previously unknown to the subjects, was of the same order, and sometimes less, than the time taken using familiar frameworks.

Table 1. Summary of development times using MIRA and known frameworks. Circled numbers indicate the order of examples chosen.

	Background	Framework used	Conventional	MIRA
1	Database developer	Jquery	1h35 ①	1h55 ❷
2	Junior Frontend Developer	Backbone	1h31 ❶	1h41 ②
3	Systems Analyst, very little programming experience	N/A	N/A	1h57 ❶
4	Senior Frontend Developer	Jquery + Underscore	1h57 ②	1h26 ❶
5	Senior Frontend Developer	Angular	1h18 ②	1h07 ❶

Key:
① Soccer game items first ② Soccer game items second
❶ Classifieds first ❷ Classifieds second

Post-test interviews confirmed that the users were satisfied with their solutions and would consider using MIRA in their daily tasks. They also stated that it would be much simpler to change the implementation if the requirements changed.

Details of the whole evaluation process can be found in [2].

These preliminary observations give us strong evidence that MIRA can indeed improve the development process for Web applications, including Semantic ones. In addition, this qualitative evaluation indicates that we should indeed test with a population of users already familiar with MIRA, and that we should also include maintenance tasks, which in most cases entails changing a declarative specification vs. changing code. A third indication from this evaluation is that we should conduct a separate evaluation with non-developers (of interfaces), as there was some evidence that they can still develop interfaces with MIRA even if they have no programming experience.

6 Discussion and Ongoing Work

We have described a data- and model-driven rule based model and runtime architecture to specify interfaces to applications, including semantic ones according to Karger's definition. It is data-driven since the actual interface is self-assembled as a item of the execution of the various rule-sets that use the instance data. It is model-driven in the sense that it can use schema information if it is available as data, as in the case of RDF, RDFS and OWL repositories, as illustrated in the example.

The work presented here is related to a very large number of models and approaches that have been proposed in the literature (see, for example, [11]. Several of the Interface Models in SHDM, e.g., the Abstract Interface and the Concrete, have counterparts in the many proposed models, e.g., Maria [14], UsiXML [10] UIML [8], among many, as well as those in WebML [6]. Space reasons prevent us from making a

comparison with each one of them here, but we can say that MIRA differs fundamentally from all in the nature of the Abstract Interface Model – it is more abstract and
focuses only on the flow of information between interface and user. A second difference is in the way adaptation occurs – in selecting the applicable Abstract Interface, in
selecting the component widgets within an Abstract Interface, and in the mapping rules
to concrete widgets. None of them show this degree of adaptability. Another less
critical difference lies on the underlying formalism (e.g., XML vs. RDF) used by each.

For RDF-based applications, there are a few frameworks for application development, such as Graphity[15] and Callimachus[16], but none have interface-specific models
beyond HTML. There are several frameworks for exhibiting RDF data, such as Exhibit
[9] and Fresnel [15], but they do not allow developing full-fledged interfaces, focusing
on presentation and visualization instead.

The main contribution of this work is the update of the original SHDM Interface
Models [13] to be applicable to any application providing a REST interface, independently of other SHDM models (viz. Domain and Navigation). Specifically, the use
of the Abstract Interface has been generalized to include not only script Domain Model
information, but also Domain-dependent interaction information (e.g., error messages).
In addition, rule definitions were simplified and modularized. A completely new
implementation was developed, including a new event architecture that allows sim-
plifying the Concrete Interface Mapping specification.

MIRA provides also a standards-based implementation framework that leverages
the Interface models to generate running, adaptable interfaces. In addition, extensions
were defined to smoothen the use of MIRA specifically with RDF data, using Json and
Json-LD formats.

MIRA was used to provide adaptive, data-driven interfaces to third-party publicly
available REST apis with complex data, indicating its expressive power in terms of
Qualitative evaluations indicate that MIRA can effectively ease the development of
adaptive interfaces of the kind required by Semantic Applications.

We have also identified some potential shortcomings of MIRA, the main one being
the difficulty to incorporate previously existing designs, unless they are previously
described using the MIRA models. This is a further area of research.

A second challenge is the management of rules when the size and complexity of the
interface grows, as complex interactions between a large set of rules can lead to
unexpected or undesirable behavior. A third shortcoming lies in the lack of authoring
tools, and appropriate concrete libraries that map to commonly used frameworks.

We are continuing this work in several directions. The first is to continue the evaluation of the approach, both in terms of performance, but also in terms of its expressivity
and usability for developers. Second, we continue building tools and components to ease
using MIRA. Third, we want to explore the design trade-offs for multi-platform applications, as well as for distributed, multi-device interfaces.

---

[15] https://github.com/Graphity.
[16] http://callimachusproject.org/.

Acknowledgments. D. Schwabe was partially supported by CNPq (WebScience INCT proj. 557.128/2009-9). E. Bertti was partially supported by a grant from NIC.br and the W3C Office Brazil. This work also had partial support from the Microsoft Open Source Initiative.

References

1. Voida, A., Harmon, E., Al-Ani, B.: Homebrew databases: complexities of everyday information management in nonprofit organizations. In: Proceedings of the ACM SIGCHI Conference on Human Factors in Computing Systems (CHI 2011), Vancouver, BC, 7–12 May. ACM Press, New York, pp. 915–924 (2011)
2. Bertti, E.: MIRA – a model-driven interface framework for REST applications. MSc dissertation, Department of Informatics, PUC-Rio, March 2015 (in Portuguese)
3. de Souza Bomfim, M.H., Schwabe, D.: Design and implementation of linked data applications using SHDM and Synth. In: Auer, S., Díaz, O., Papadopoulos, G.A. (eds.) ICWE 2011. LNCS, vol. 6757, pp. 121–136. Springer, Heidelberg (2011)
4. Calvary, G., et al.: The CAMELEON Reference Framework, CAMELEON Project, September 2002 (2002). http://giove.isti.cnr.it/projects/cameleon/pdf/CAMELEON%20D1. 1RefFramework.pdf
5. Coutaz, J., Calvary, G.: HCI and software engineering for user interface plasticity. In: Jacko, J. (ed.) Human Computer Handbook: Fundamentals, Evolving Technologies, and Emerging Applications, 3rd edn. Taylor and Francis Group Ltd., New York (2012)
6. Ceri, S., Fraternali, P., Bongio, A.: Web modeling language (WebML): a modeling language for designing web sites. In: Proceedings of the WWW9 Conference, Amsterdam, May 2000
7. Lima, F., Schwabe, D.: Application modeling for the semantic web. In: Proceedings of LA-Web 2003, pp. 93–102, Santiago, Chile. IEEE Press, November 2003
8. Helms, J., Schaefer, R., Luyten, K., Vermeulen, J., Abrams, M., Coyette, A., Vanderdonckt, J.: Human-centered engineering with the user interface markup language. In: Seffah, A., Vanderdonckt, J., Desmarais, M.C. (eds.) Human-Centered Software Engineering. Springer, London (2009)
9. Huynh, D.F., Karger, D.R., Miller, R.C.: Exhibit: lightweight structured data publishing. In: Proceedings of the 16th International Conference on World Wide Web, Banff, Canada, pp. 737–746 (2007)
10. Limbourg, Q., Vanderdonckt, J., Michotte, B., Bouillon, L., López-Jaquero, V.: USIXML: a language supporting multi-path development of user interfaces. In: Feige, U., Roth, J. (eds.) DSV-IS 2004 and EHCI 2004. LNCS, vol. 3425, pp. 200–220. Springer, Heidelberg (2005)
11. Meixner, G., Paternó, F., Vanderdonckt, J.: Past, present, and future of model-based user interface development. i-com **10**(3), 2–11 (2011)
12. Myers, B., Rosson, M.B.: Survey on user interface programming. In: Proceedings of 10th Annual ACM CHI Conference on Human Factors in Computing Systems, pp. 195–202 (2000)
13. Nascimento, V., Schwabe, D.: Semantic data driven interfaces for web applications. In: Daniel, F., Dolog, P., Li, Q. (eds.) ICWE 2013. LNCS, vol. 7977, pp. 22–36. Springer, Heidelberg (2013). ISBN 978-3-642-39199-6
14. Paterno, F., Santoro, C., Spano, L.D.: MARIA: a universal, declarative, multiple abstraction level language for service-oriented applications in ubiquitous environments. ACM Trans. Comput.-Hum. Interact. (TOCHI) **16**(4), 19 (2009)

15. Pietriga, E., Bizer, C., Karger, D.R., Lee, R.: Fresnel: a browser-independent presentation vocabulary for RDF. In: Cruz, I., Decker, S., Allemang, D., Preist, C., Schwabe, D., Mika, P., Uschold, M., Aroyo, L.M. (eds.) ISWC 2006. LNCS, vol. 4273, pp. 158–171. Springer, Heidelberg (2006)
16. Silva de Moura, S., Schwabe, D.: Interface development for hypermedia applications in the semantic web. In: Proceedings of WebMedia and LA-Web, 2004, Ribeirão Preto, Brazil, pp 106–113. IEEE Press, October 2004
17. Tsai, W.T., Huang, Q., Elston, J., Chen, Y.: Service-oriented user interface modeling and composition. In: IEEE International Conference on e-Business Engineering, 2008, ICEBE 2008, Xi'an, pp. 21–28 (2008). doi:10.1109/ICEBE.2008.114

Volatile Functionality in Action: Methods, Techniques and Assessment

Darian Frajberg[1,2(⊠)], Matías Urbieta[2,3], Gustavo Rossi[2,3],
and Wieland Schwinger[4]

[1] Dipartimento di Elettronica, Informazione e Bioingegneria,
Politecnico di Milano, Milan, Italy
darian.frajberg@polimi.it

[2] LIFIA, Facultad de Informática, UNLP, La Plata, Argentina
{murbieta,gustavo}@lifia.info.unlp.edu.ar

[3] Conicet, Buenos Aires, Argentina

[4] Department of Cooperative Information Systems,
Johannes Kepler University Linz, Linz, Austria
wieland.schwinger@jku.ac.at

Abstract. One of the main features of most Web applications today is their great dynamism. They are undoubtedly characterized by a continuous evolution. After implementing and performing the first deployment of a Web application, some new requirements are bound to arise, which involve the need to incorporate new functionalities, generally unknown during the design stage. This type of functionalities, which arise as a response to unexpected requirements of the business layer, have the peculiarity that they eventually need to be removed due to the expiration of their commercial value. The continuous incorporation and removal of these functionalities, which we will call "volatile functionalities", usually has a negative impact on some important aspects of the Web application. Volatile Functionality meta-framework is a conceptual framework that permits to support the lifespan of volatile functionalities in Web applications. We have developed diverse techniques enabling full support of volatile functionalities for enterprise application. Moreover, we have performed an evaluation for assessing developers' experience and solutions' performance.

Keywords: Volatile functionality · Evolutionary architecture · Web application · Approach · VF framework · Event scheduling

1 Introduction

One of the main features of most Web applications today is their great dynamism. They are undoubtedly characterized by a continuous evolution. After implementing and performing the first deployment of a Web application, some new requirements are bound to arise, which involve the need to incorporate new functionalities, generally unknown during the design stage. Sometimes said functionalities are tested during a specific period and are then discarded as consequence of not having resulted to be useful enough for the users. Some other times, they appear as a response to determined events and/or conditions. Finally, it is quite common for certain functionalities to be

© Springer International Publishing Switzerland 2016
A. Bozzon et al. (Eds.): ICWE 2016, LNCS 9671, pp. 59–76, 2016.
DOI: 10.1007/978-3-319-38791-8_4

periodically activated at a specific moment of the year, and then be deactivated. That is to say, they are repeatedly introduced and removed from an application. This type of functionalities, which arise as a response to unexpected requirements of the business layer, have the peculiarity that they eventually need to be removed due to the expiration of their commercial value.

The continuous incorporation and removal of these functionalities, which we will call "volatile functionalities" (VFs), usually has a negative impact on some important aspects of the Web application. This occurs because usually the task is carried out manually and is quite prone to errors. Therefore, both the quality of the application code as well as its performance are harmed, requiring extra work for the developers during the maintenance stage, and probably a project cost overrun. It is well worth mentioning that VFs can be extremely complex and involve changes in all the application layers (business layer, navigation layer and presentation layer).

A clear example can be seen in the Web applications of companies engaged in online commercialization of products and services. The Black Friday launched by Amazon.com case is a marketing term employed to refer to the day following Thanksgiving in the United States, but has been adopted worldwide. Big companies created this event in order to encourage online shopping by applying great discounts and the same marketing strategy has been adopted for other promotion such as Cyber Monday case. Figure 1 shows the "Black Friday" promotions. On top of the image you can see several Black Friday banners notifying the availability of promotions. In the middle, there is a carousel showing products that have big discounts. Finally, there is another banner with the remaining time for the promotion, and one of the advertised products with its corresponding discount.

These components allow the navigation towards specific products on sale. Amazon's customization for "Black Friday" not only required the modification of Web pages through the introduction of images and links. Some other things also needed to be considered, such as the addition of new specific business rules in order to make the

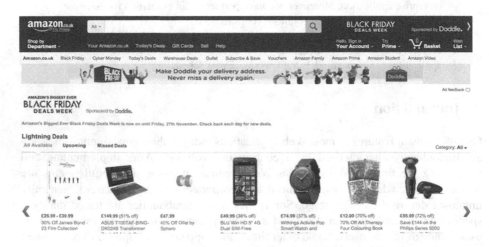

Fig. 1. Black Friday in Amazon.co.uk.

advertised discounts, the record of the sales with their corresponding promotions, and the specific definition of discounts for the different products involved, among others.

Considering the unforeseen and unexpected characteristic of volatile functionality (VF), its design and implementation introduce challenges to software engineers, as they were not considered during application design. Nowadays there are several approaches and tools for tackling challenges introduced by VFs, but they face the problem only partially. Aspect Oriented Programming (AOP) [4] allows the introduction of new variables and methods to classes, but does not consider its weaving and unweaving based on business events. On the other hand, Web pages can be augmented using document transformation technologies (XSLT [30]) but those available do not replace AOP for classes modification. In this work, we complement our approach for designing VF [17] with a meta-framework for instrumenting a new functionality modeled with the approach. This meta-framework defines the requirements that a platform must meet for supporting unexpected and unforeseen requirements with a seamless solution.

To cope with the above mentioned problems, we present as novel contribution:

- A set of basic requirements an application that supports VF lifecycle must meet. All the minimum fundamental concepts which software solutions are required to satisfy in order to make use of such framework.
- A discussion about how those requirements were introduced into two applications, one of them based on a static type binding language and the other one on a dynamic type binding language. This meta-framework proposes the decoupling of VFs from the original application, thus maintaining the integrity and independence of the latter, where the type of binding determines the implementation strategy.
- Finally, an experiment has been conducted in order to evaluate and obtain feedback from impartial developers regarding the presented framework.

The rest of the paper is structured as follows: in Sect. 2, we discuss some related work; in Sect. 3, we introduce the approach; in Sect. 4, we present the VF Framework and an evaluation using Java and Smalltalk technologies; and in Sect. 5 we describe an evaluation for assessing developers' experience and solutions' performance; finally in Sect. 6, we present the conclusions of our work.

2 Related Work

Systems evolution has been largely studied in order to avoid common mistakes, predict costs of maintenance and reduce changes' impact. In [7], a study of variability is presented as the ability to change software artifacts for specific context. Small and Medium Enterprises were surveyed resulting as outcome an enumeration of challenges such as documentation, change traceability, change extent, among others when facing changes in a system. Unfortunately, change impact analysis was not deepened in products' source code and quality.

An outstanding trend to deal with transparent evolution is the use of Aspect-oriented technologies as mentioned some paragraphs above. In the specific area of Web applications, an interesting approach can be read in [1]. In this work the authors propose to tackle evolution using Aspect-oriented Design Patterns. The approach is sound and powerful as the authors identify a set of possible types of changes in a Web application and associate an Aspect Pattern to solve each specific situation. However, it is geared towards implementation more than design and therefore it loses part of its power; nevertheless, as discussed throughout this paper, the underlying ideas behind Aspect orientation are key concepts to use with VF.

Another related work in which we found similar problems and ideas to ours is Web application adaptation. A Web modeling framework with orthogonal facilities for extending functionality in a seamless way is AMACONT [11]. This framework provides means for addressing adaptation in Web applications by implementing AOP concepts. Using aspect-oriented adaptation and semantics-based adaptation for different adaptation granularity, it allows specifying changes in a component-based model. The work provides a useful framework but lacks of means for specifying presentation aspects as well as describing aspects lifecycle.

The traceability of changes in the lifecycle of evolution/maintenance requirements has been combined with Impact Analysis (IA) in [6]. It provides an integrated approach that gives traceability support from the change request, going through model artifacts, source code changes and execution behavior. This approach can be used for tracing any Volatile Requirement, but its removal is still compromised and should be studied.

Model Driven Engineering aims at providing methods and tools for designing Web applications, where developers abstract from source code aspects and focus on functional requirements instead. In [9], authors studied how maintenance tasks, in both OOHRIA approach and code centric approach, were perceived by practitioners. The experiment was performed by 26 students and their perception was captured by questionnaires. The results showed that OOH4RIA improved efficiency and effectiveness of maintenance tasks over the same tasks when using .NET technology. However, the abovementioned evaluations were focused on subjective metrics gathered from students' perception and they did not cover source code's metrics in order to assess internal quality such as object-oriented metrics [2] for code centric solution and model metrics. Additionally, most of the empirical research works focused on the development from the scratch study case whereas we study maintenance challenges.

Technical debt has been studied largely in industry projects [3] and how to manage it [14] as it highly relates with an application's budget. In this field we can find plenty of tools that enable to measure technical debt from source code [21, 24, 25, 29], but also taking into account other points of view such as architecture-sourced debt [12] on components coupling [10] or database schemas' technical debt [18]. Technical debt must be analyzed using different approaches in order to gain as much information as possible. In [20], Hadoop an open source No-sql database was processed using code smells, automatic static analysis issues, grime buildup, and modularity violations taking into account several application versions. The outcome remarks that techniques are loosely coupled and therefore a Technical debt analysis should combine several techniques.

Feature Oriented Programming has been an approach for facing those developments that compose functionality mainly focused on Software Families. In [15], authors introduce the relevant factors in variability realization of Software product families. As part of the work, they proposed taxonomy of variability introducing different realization techniques for software changes. The presented techniques were mapped to surveyed and/or studied software companies that adapt their software to changes.

Maintenance effort was studied in [8], where ten PhD and Master students were asked to maintain a desktop application. The work studied the processes and tools used by students for solving the problem in depth. The outcome was a characterization of problems, relevant code and APIs, and testing processes.

Though transparent improvement of conceptual and navigational models has been treated in the literature, we are not aware of any approach supporting oblivious [4] composition of interface design models in such a way that different concerns keep orthogonal. In the XML field, the AspectXML project [22] has ported some concepts of aspect-orientation to XML technology by allowing the specification of point-cuts and advices similarly to Aspect Java. The project is still in a research stage.

3 Approach

In most mature Web design approaches, such as UWE, WebML, UWA, Hera, OOWS or OOHDM (see [13] for description and examples of each approach), a Web application is designed with an iterative process comprising at least conceptual and navigational modeling. Most of these design methods produce an implementation-independent model that can be later mapped to different run-time platforms. For the sake of clarity we will concentrate on the conceptual, navigational and interface models, as they are rather similar in different design approaches.

As most of the problems discussed so far apply to all development approaches, we will first describe the philosophy underlying our technical solutions in such a way that it can be reused. In [17] we describe its usage with OOHDM design models and briefly discuss how each part of our approach could be adapted to other methods.

Our approach is based on the idea that even the simplest VF (e.g., a discount available for a period of time, as in Fig. 1) should be considered as a first-class functionality and, as such, designed accordingly. At the same time, their design and implementation have to be taken separately and as much as possible decoupled from that of core and stable functionalities.

Building on the above ideas, our approach can be summarized with the following design guidelines, which are shown schematically in Fig. 2:

- We decouple volatile from core functionalities by introducing a design layer for VFs (called Volatile Layer), which comprises a requirements model, a conceptual model, a navigational model, and an interface model.
- Volatile requirements are modeled using the same notation used to model core requirements (e.g., use cases, class diagrams, user interaction diagrams, etc.) and separately mapped onto the following models using the heuristics defined by the design approach. Notice that, as shown in Fig. 2, volatile requirements are not integrated into the core requirements model, therefore leaving their integration to further design activities.
- New behaviors, i.e. those which belong to the VF layer, are modeled as first class objects in the volatile conceptual model; they are considered as a combination of

Commands and Decorators [5] of the core classes. This strategy applies also to slight variants of business rules (such as adding a price discount to a product). In this case, the decoration is applied at the method level more than at the class level. Notice that this strategy can be applied to any object-oriented method, i.e., any method using a UML-like specification approach.

- We use inversion of control to achieve obliviousness; i.e., instead of making core conceptual classes aware of their new features, we invert the knowledge relationship. New classes know the base classes on top of which they are built. Core classes, therefore, have no knowledge of the additions. This also stands for aspect-oriented approaches.
- Nodes and links belonging to the volatile navigational model may or may not have links to the core navigational model. The core navigational model is also oblivious to the volatile navigational classes, i.e., there are no links or other references from the core to the volatile layer. This principle can be applied in any Web design approach.
- We use a separate integration specification to specify the connection between core and volatile nodes. As we show later in the paper, the integration is achieved at run-time. In other model-driven approaches, the integration can be performed during model transformation by implementing the corresponding transformations.
- We design (and implement) the interfaces corresponding to each concern (core and volatile) separately; the interface design of the core classes (described in OOHDM using Abstract Data Views (ADV) [16]) are oblivious with respect to the interface of volatile concerns. As in the navigational layer this principle is independent of the design approach.
- Core and volatile interfaces (at the ADV and implementation layers) are woven by executing an integration specification, which is realized using XSL transformations. Again, the idea of model weaving is generic and therefore the same result can be obtained using another technical solution.

In the next section we introduce methods and approaches for supporting VF in Enterprise Web applications.

4   VF Framework

In order to implement a system supporting VF, a set of non-functional requirements must be met. These requirements, when satisfied by the underlying technology of either a new or legacy application, permit to configure VF abstracting from activation/ deactivation rules, seamless entities enrichments and Web page augmentations. We have already discussed how to manage VF in MDWE in [17].

We present this sort of checklist in Table 1, which helps architects to introduce new unforeseen and unexpected requirements on in-production systems. The approach used in this work aims at adopting new requirements, even though the involved architecture did not consider them while it was designed. Such approach is available for Object-Oriented systems that implement the MVC pattern.

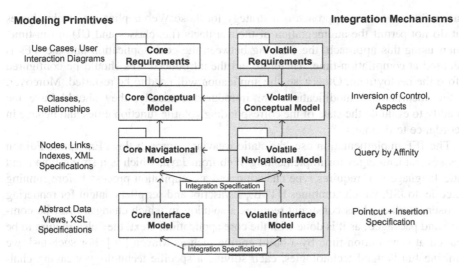

Fig. 2. A schematic representation of our approach

Two prototypes[1] were implemented in order to test the presented framework. One of them was developed by using Java and Java Enterprise Edition (JEE) frameworks, and the other one through Smalltalk. Their implementation pursued not only a concrete and practical demonstration of VF Framework, but also the analysis and testing of diverse strategies in order to achieve the incorporation and manipulation of VFs in Web applications. The selection of these programming languages was based on the fact that they have important differences with each other. While Java is a static typed language, Smalltalk is a dynamic typed and pure Object-Oriented one.

4.1 Weaving Approach

Architecture plays a main role, as it must support the VF's approach artifacts. Any new unexpected and unforeseen requirement must be thought independently from the core application and specify the weaving mechanisms for its compromised application layer. That is, the core application's code must be kept untouched and any augmentation must be automated. Depending on the underlying technology there are two possible weaving approaches, which are presented next:

Dynamic: Dynamic weaving approach is a strategy available for powerful and dynamically Web applications technologies, which are capable of executing the weaving between the core application and the VFs on the fly. It permits introducing changes at run-time without need of recompiling.

The Smalltalk implementation uses the dynamic weaving approach for the incorporation of VFs. The code corresponding to a VF is located in a package of the running Virtual Machine image and the code weaving is indeed performed dynamically by modifying the application model at run-time.

---

[1] Source code, demo video and used questionnaires are available at https://goo.gl/J7C2WV.

Static: Static weaving approach is a strategy for those Web applications technologies that do not permit the augmentation of their artifacts (i.e. classes and UI) at run-time. When using this approach, the weaving between the core application and the VFs is executed at compilation-time. Therefore, all the introduced VFs should be configured before the deployment. Otherwise, the application will need to be restarted. Moreover, as the incorporated modifications are introduced statically, they should have the capacity to evaluate the state of the corresponding volatile functionalities and behave in accordance to them.

The JEE implementation uses the static weaving approach. Java Enterprise Edition uses several languages for implementing Web from Java, which is a strong typed and static language that requires type checking and a compilation process before running the code, to JSP, which combines HTML, Javascript and scriptlet content for rendering the user interface. This constraint requires a solution in which changes must be compiled and packaged, as it is done with the core application. Next, they also require to be weaved at compilation-time by a build engine such as Maven [26]. For such task we combine full-fledged technologies, each solving a specific technology weaving challenge. For example, the VFs are added mainly by defining a set of XSL transformations and aspects, which are all applied by Maven on the compiled original application. Thus, the VFs are not intrusive with the original application and can be added within the compilation cycle. The volatile code is packaged in a War file with the new classes, Web pages and artifacts.

Table 1. Features required for supporting VF approach

Feature	Strategies	Applicability conditions	Implementation examples
Weaving approach	Dynamic	Dynamic type binding	Reflection
	Static	Static type binding	Maven
Business & Navigation model enhancement	AOP	Methods interception	AspectJ, PHANtom
	Regex modifications	Interpreted code execution	Pharo native support
Presentation model enhancement	Documents transformation	Document-based UI	XSLT
	AOP	Methods interception	AspectJ, PHANtom
	Regex modifications	Interpreted code execution	Pharo native support
Lifespan management	Rules-engine based	Mature enterprise solutions	Drools
	Scheduler and AOP based	Restricted development kit	Quartz

Conclusions: The approach implements an architecture that keeps core application oblivious from new changes, which must be integrated and managed as corresponds. The adoption of any of the weaving approaches is a decisive factor, which will have a direct impact regarding the applicability of the strategies to cover the other framework's basic features. Undoubtedly, the dynamic weaving approach provides a more flexible and simple solution in order to accomplish the goal of supporting VFs.

4.2 Business and Navigation Models Enhancement

The modification of the business layer includes matters such as the injection and Object-Relational Mapping (ORM) of variables and relations, and the injection and modification of methods. On the other hand, the modification of the navigation layers comprises the injection of dependencies, and also the injection and modification of methods. The techniques to perform these changes are presented next:

AOP: Aspect Oriented-Programming [4] is a paradigm that aims at modularizing crosscutting concerns. This technology can be used for the enhancement of business and navigation models for those cases in which their implementations are defined by classes. AOP provides the capability to modify classes' structures by adding new variables and methods and also their behaviors by intercepting and modifying methods with associated pointcuts and advices. However, there is an important difference regarding how AOP is used depending on the programming languages' type systems. For dynamically typed languages, aspects can be enabled and disabled at run-time as needed, while for statically typed languages, this is not possible as aspects have to be incorporated during compilation time. Therefore, the modification of methods for static languages must be controlled by wrapping the advices' code within conditional sentences based on the current state of certain VF. Thus, the involved classes will behave as appropriate. It is not mandatory to perform the same treatment for injected methods due to the fact that when their corresponding VFs are disabled they should not even be invoked.

Both developed implementations use aspects. The JEE implementation uses AspectJ framework and, as it is a statically typed programming language, it incorporates the modifications at compilation time. As for the ORM of injected variables, the Java prototype has covered it perfectly through Hibernate annotations. The Smalltalk implementation uses PHANtom [27] framework and the ORM of variables has not been taken into account for it. This is due to the fact that it does not employ a real database, but is managed as from instances created in memory. Nevertheless, it has been analyzed and should be covered perfectly by using the Glorp [19] ORM technology. Code 1 and Code 2 present examples of business model enhancement for JEE and Smalltalk implementations, in which a variable that holds a discount, as well as a getter and a setter for it, are injected into a class. Moreover, they both modified the computation of the final price by intercepting it and applying the corresponding discount.

Regex Modifications: Regex modifications aim at using regular expressions for the identification of fragments of source code corresponding to certain classes' methods.

Afterward, the defined modifications for them can be effected in run-time. Logically, regex modifications can only be implemented for interpreted or dynamic type binding programming languages such as Smalltalk and PHP, which must be capable of modifying the classes' model with dynamic code generation.

The Smalltalk implementation also uses regex modifications to alter the original flow of existing methods. These modifications are executed within the framework's provided predefined methods used to fill the VFs' hotspots.

Conclusions: AOP demonstrated to be capable enough to support the features corresponding to the business and navigation layers for languages in which their implementations are defined by classes. Nonetheless, languages with interpreted code execution have some important advantages towards those that do not, provided that they have two options in order to modify the flow of existing methods. The first one is the interception with associated pointcuts and advices; and the second one is the use of regex modifications. Although interception through aspects can be sufficient in some cases, it can be inconvenient when multiple VFs involve modifications of coincidental code sections. Advices can be defined to be executed before, after or at the time of accessing a determined pointcut. Therefore, the correct execution of a method intercepted by multiple VFs is limited by the degree of modularization that it possesses. On the other hand, regex modifications can deal much better with this issue since with them it is able to identify and modify fragments of source code within methods.

```
public aspect DiscountVFAspect {
@NotNull
private int   Product.discount = 0;

public int Product.getDiscount()
    {return this.discount;}

public void Product.setDiscount(int  d)
    {this.discount =d;}

pointcut getFinalPricePointcut(Product p) : exe-
cution(* Product.getFinalPrice()) && target(p);

int around(Product p):getFinalPricePointcut(p) {
    return proceed() * p.getDiscount(); }
}
```

```
AddVars
self addInstVar:'discount' toClass:'Product'.

addMethods
self addInstMethod:'discount
     ^discount ' toClass: Product.
self addInstMethod:'discount:aFloat
     discount:=aFloat ' toClass: Product.

addPointcuts
self add:(PhAdvice new pointcut:
(PhPointcut new receivers: Product;
selectors: 'finalPrice'; context: #(#receiver
#arguments #selector #proceed));
advice: [:context | context proceed * self
discount.]; type: #around).
```

Code 1. Aspect definition using AspectJ in JEE implementation.

Code 2. Ad-hoc framework in Smalltalk for supporting VF features.

4.3   Presentation Models

The modification of the presentation layer implies the alteration of the views that comprise the Web application interface. Once the changes to the model have been made, it is essential for said changes to be reflected in the interface to be consumed by the final user. This task consists of effecting the corresponding transformations in each view and visualization, depending on the state of the VFs included in the application (activated or deactivated). The resulting application must be capable of showing or hiding the changes introduced at run-time. In order to achieve this aim, there are three possible strategies, which are the following ones:

Documents Transformation: The documents transformation implies the use of transformation pipeline, in which a document used as UI is augmented by a set of transformations. These transformations are an option for those languages that use documents such as XHTMLs for the views. It is important to consider the capacity of the used technologies to modify the processing pipeline of each request, as it will define if the transformations can be executed in run-time as necessary. For example, in order to introduce transformations in Servlet-based technology, we need to introduce Servlet-filters responsible for transforming documents. In that case, each time a VF is activated or deactivated, the views engaged must be modified in the act. Otherwise, changes should be incorporated during compilation-time. For that purpose, the modifications should include a conditional visualization of the modifications, which implies the introduction of conditional sentences (present throughout the whole execution of the application) responsible for visualizing or not the modifications belonging to the VFs. Logically, for this to be possible the views need to have the capacity to process information on the server side so as to make decisions based on it. Thus, the state of each VF is evaluated at the moment a modified view is invoked. If the VF is activated, all the changes introduced in the view will be presented. Otherwise, the original view will be shown.

The JEE implementation uses XSLT transformations of XHTML documents, which are executed in compilation-time through conditional visualizations. An example of this can be seen in Code 3, where a banner is displayed depending on the VF's state.

AOP: There are technologies such as GWT or Seaside that permit to specify UI programmatically using an API. As discussed previously, AOP perfectly fits in this scenario for enriching interface aspects by executing a piece of code (advice) before, after or both a given method is invoked.

The Smalltalk implementation uses aspects in order to incorporate new styles for the views.

Regex Modifications: As mentioned above, UI defined programmatically with an API can be modified by changing the source code, when coded with interpreted languages. The Smalltalk implementation uses regex modifications to introduce new elements to views and styles at run-time. In Code 4 there is an example of regex modification for the augmentation of Seaside user interface by adding a promotion banner.

Conclusions: The modification of the presentation layer in dynamic typed languages where the enhancement targets are classes turns out to be a much simpler, powerful and scalable solution than in those that use view documents. On one hand, aspects and regex modifications are easy to define (being regex modifications the most convenient option). On the other hand, documents transformations are much more complex and may become a bit cumbersome when they are implemented. Moreover, high complexity can also bring great difficulty regarding the modifications' scalability.

Nevertheless, it should also be taken into account that executing transformations at run-time might turn out to be slow and inefficient if the employed architecture does not count with the adequate processing speed.

`<xsl:template match="node()[@id='banner']">` `<xsl:text><![CDATA[<c:choose>` `<c:when test="#{vf.enabled}">]]></xsl:text>` `<h1 id="banner" Promotion 2x1</h1>` `<xsl:text><![CDATA[</c:when>` `<c:otherwise>]]></xsl:text>` `<xsl:copy-of select ="."/>` `<xsl:text><![CDATA[</c:otherwise>` `</c:choose>]]></xsl:text></xsl:template>`	**addMethodsModifications** self addInstMethodModification: (InstMethodModification instMethod: 'renderContentOn:' forClass: Store beforeRegex: 'html div id\: "body"' insert: 'html table id: banner; with: [html tableRow: [html tableData: [html div id: "title"; with:"Promotion 2x1" .]]].').

Code 3. An example of JSP augmentation using XSLT.   Code 4. An example of Seaside user interface augmentation using regex modification.

4.4   Lifespan Management

The lifespan management is one of the main features of the framework because it is responsible for VFs' activation and deactivation scheduling. It is required to count with a suitable technology for configuring three different types of events, which are: temporal events, business events and temporal business events. For example, a specific date, for enabling a promotion, and business based events, such as "Out of Stock", for disabling a promotion.

VF's orchestration manages the VF's activation/deactivation, but does not imply weaving as that is constrained to the underlying technologies introduced in Sects. 4.2 and 4.3. Nonetheless, if the platform allows it, then it may include the execution of hot deploys and weaving of VFs in real-time. This possibility is only available for certain technologies, which provide certain flexibility and avoid stopping and re-compiling the application in order to introduce a new VF.

For such purpose, the following strategies can be applied:

Rules-Engine Based: The activation and deactivation scheduling is perfectly achieved by using a rules engine. It makes it possible to configure all the types of events in a very simple and natural way.

The JEE implementation uses Drools [23] rules engine, which effectively enables to define any kind of rules for the activation and deactivation of VFs. In Code 5 an example for temporarily activating product discounts in such rules engine is presented. The rule will enable the VF on Feb 12th at 00:00 and will be online for two days. Said implementation does not allow hot-deploy of VFs, but needs to be compiled and deployed again in order to do add them. However, this constraint could be removed if VF is built on top of OSGI architecture.

Scheduler and AOP Based: The activation and deactivation events can also be covered by using a Scheduler and AOP. Temporal events can be configured with a

Scheduler such as Quartz [28], business events with aspects' interception and temporal business events with a combination of both Scheduler and aspects.

The Smalltalk implementation used this strategy provided that no good and well documented rules engine was found for this programming language. This approach required more work, but got similar final results to the Rules-engine based. Code 6 shows a Smalltalk-based sentence for enabling a VF, which will be enabled 10 min after its deployment. This implementation clearly covered the hot deploy without any complication due to its dynamism and flexibility.

Conclusions: We need to manage the activation of VF available in a given application as it distinguishes our approach from an ad-hoc one. The hot deploy of VFs is not a mandatory feature for the framework. Conversely, the activation and deactivation scheduling must definitely be covered. And we can assure that the usage of rules engines for scheduling activation and deactivation events seems to be the simplest and most suitable solution. However, if it is not possible to use one of them, the same results can be achieved with the Scheduler and AOP based approach.

rule "discountVF activation rule"	setUpScheduler
date-effective "12-Feb-2016 00:00"	self scheduleEnableOnceAt:
date-expires "14-Feb-2016 00:01"	(DateAndTime now + 10 minute).
when eval(true);	
then vfService.enable("discountVF");end	
Code 5. Drools' rule for temporarily activating product discounts.	**Code 6**. Smalltalk-based sentence for enabling VF.

4.5   Discussion

The implementation of prototypes by using different programming languages as Java and Smalltalk was very important for the development of this research. These prototypes allowed us not only to put the VF Framework concepts into practice, but also to consider different alternatives and strategies for their implementation.

Although both prototypes covered the most important VF Framework concepts satisfactorily (and might as well cover the remaining ones), a better result has been obtained with the Smalltalk prototype. Unlike Java, Smalltalk is a dynamically typed language, which makes it a very powerful alternative, and is very easy to handle. These characteristics have a great impact, as they enable a much more dynamic implementation and with more and better options to be carried out.

Furthermore, a white box framework has been developed for Smalltalk, which greatly facilitates the implementation process of VFs according to the VF Framework concepts. Simply from the extension of certain classes and the implementation of certain hotspots, it is possible to incorporate VFs in a decoupled manner and to schedule the activation and deactivation events for them. This task results more costly for Java, where the modifications and programming of events corresponding to the varied VFs are scattered without a clear separation from each other.

Besides, the use of AspectJ and Drools in Java obtained highly positive results and their incorporation was relatively simple. In the case of the Smalltalk implementation, it was necessary to search for new and more complex alternatives (combining different technologies) in order to achieve similar final results.

5 Evaluation

5.1 Experiment Planning

We have designed two experiments in order to study how different approaches perform at maintaining VF. Each experiment assesses the developers' perception of the development process as well as the software internal quality. Software components of code-based applications are affected by the introduction and later removal of VFs, we evaluate a set of representative quality metrics that covers business model and controller tiers, usually coded using programming languages such as Java, Python, C#, etc., and interface tier implemented with HTML, JavaScript and CSS.

By the introduction and later removal of such VF, Web applications pass through different development stages. The application was modified twice and, for each version, a snapshot was captured so as to evaluate its quality. We will call Original Version (OV) the starting stable version that resolves core business requirements. Next, we will have a version that introduces a set of VFs extending the application, which will be outlined later, called Volatile Version (VV); and finally we have a version that will be the result of removing such VFs, named Maintenance Version (MV), that presents the set of requirements served by OV. At first sight, MV should be alike OV and we will study any difference found focusing on those that are detrimental to the overall quality. The transition of Web applications' versions is shown in Fig. 3.

We have selected a hotel booking site, as a running example, which has been modified in order to introduce two VFs: Long weekend promotion (that includes the application of discounts and promotional interface enhancements) and Notification (that informs the authorities if a booking cost exceeds a predefined limit). We tackle

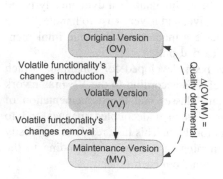

Fig. 3. Application's evolution scheme.

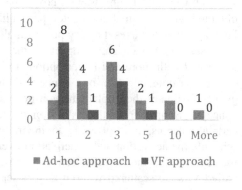

Fig. 4. Testing cycles per approach.

VF Implementation and maintenance by using both an ad-hoc application and VF approach. The first one requires manual management of VF lifecycle and code belonging to VF software artifacts, and the latter requires the use of the presented framework that fully supports VF's characteristics. For this application we have conceived VFs like those already discussed in [17].

Besides, we perform a tier-focused semi-automatic analysis of source code to assess internal quality. Variances between OV and MV will be analyzed and discussed.

5.2 Participants

The two experiments were performed by independent groups of developers. In the first one, we evaluated the maintenance by using an ad-hoc approach with 17 developers, and in the second one we used a VF approach with 14 developers. We aim at capturing VF maintenance challenges from the performers' point of view. They were students attending the last year at the National University of La Plata's bachelor degree (comparable to European Master Degree). Developers were mostly students with programming experience (about at least 4 years), who received the target applications in VV and were later asked to remove the VFs on their own, without any extra guide other than removing the deprecated functionality. After the developers removed the VFs and got the MV, we performed a quality evaluation of each version (OV, VV and MV) in order to detect whether changes were detrimental to the overall quality. Students were motivated and committed to the experiment, as it was part of their final examination earning education credit.

5.3 Research Questions

In order to evaluate VF approach performance against ad-hoc approach, we have defined research questions. Next, we present a summary of Research Questions, considered metrics and statistical methods.

(a) Is ad-hoc approach more prone to have application external quality issues?

Ad-hoc maintenance of VF showed in 76 % of the samples that perceivable changes (labels, library imports, message containers, etc.) were overlooked, leaving evidence of functionality associated to the VF. Using our VF Framework, the introduction and removal of VF did not modify core application and, as a result, there are not perceivable changes pending or quality issues.

(b) Is VF approach more productive than ad-hoc approach?

Yes, on average removing VF from applications with an ad-hoc (5.2 h) approach took almost five times more than removing with the VF approach (0,9 h). On the other hand, as confirmed before, using an ad-hoc way is prone to leave overlooked changes, being detrimental to internal software quality. By using a full-fledge framework for removing functionality, no line of code is left unattended. As we do not have enough samples, it is not possible to perform statistical analysis for significance.

(c) Is application's internal quality more negatively affected by Ad-hoc approach than VF approach?

Both business and controller layers were affected by quality issues. By running SonarQube tool, we detected several quality[2] issues from unused methods to commented code. This situation is detrimental to software quality as deprecated VF artifacts get tangled and scattered in the application making it more complex to understand by developer. Moreover, 94.12 % and 70 % of samples left unattended changes (variables, methods and metadata) at model and controller layers. As mentioned before, our framework permits to model new changes at business and controller layer without modifying code corresponding to the core application. When needed, it is removed by a tool ensuring that the core application's code is kept untouched.

(d) Is the developers' confidence affected by VF approach?

We measured the developers' confidence through survey questions that consider stability, complexity and maintenance. The results show that 86,7 % consider that using VF approach the application was equally or more stable than ad-hoc approach.

On the other hand, we also evaluated the required testing to complete the maintenance task. As presented in Fig. 4, the VF approach required less testing to check whether the VF has been completely removed. Most of the developers using VF approach claimed that one test allowed them to verify the correctness of the application, whereas with the ad-hoc approach developers needed 10 or more testing cycles.

5.4   Conclusions

Evidence shows that applications based on modern MVC and ORM frameworks may suffer from the discussed problems and this research sets the basis for further work considering other kinds of Web applications. The result shows that using a VF Framework avoided introducing errors when removing deprecated functionality, saved time and effort, and improved developer's experience skipping sloppy tasks. We were able to validate not only perceivable quality, but also internal one that compromised the technical debt. Additionally, developers involved found that development process was positively improved from experience and perception.

6   Conclusions

To sum up, we may highlight some interesting issues, which have arisen throughout the development of this research.

The proposed framework definitely improves the lifespan of VFs in Web applications. Moreover, it has been contributed with evidence that the latter fits and might perfectly be applied to enterprise Web applications, devoted to the marketing of products and services. This type of applications is very dynamic and often suffer modifications during certain special dates responding to business requirements, when

---

[2] Java rules http://dist.sonarsource.com/reports/coverage/rules_in_squid.html (Mar 15 2016).

all kinds of offers are launched. Using the proposed framework might be very useful for this type of events, as it would ease, improve and automate the management of VFs.

As shown, this approach has not limited itself to the theoretical and conceptual definition, but has been satisfactorily taken into practice by implementing two prototypes that exploit methods and techniques outlined by the framework, which overcomes VF implementation challenges. Just as this was possible, the same could be achieved with other languages capable of covering the defined requirements.

It is also important to mention that after having carried out an experiment to measure the acceptance and performance of the presented approach, the obtained results have been highly positive. The framework has indeed shown great advantages over the traditional approach for the management of VFs. The quality of the original application's source code is not degraded, no errors are introduced and time and costs are reduced. Furthermore, most of the participants showed interest and issued good reviews regarding the presented approach, highlighting the improvements and convenience of its utilization.

The future of the approach basically consists of deepening each of the concepts in order to obtain better results. So far, the two prototypes obtained a very positive outcome. However, these prototypes should continue to be improved, optimizing their performance, facilitating their implementation and undertaking some tasks left aside such as the testing of OSGI for the Java implementation and the study of different persistence frameworks. Furthermore, the development of new prototypes with new underlying technologies would be definitely meaningful for the research, as it could lead to the emergence of new strategies to support the defined framework's features.

Once solid and mature implementations have been consolidated, the next step might aim at the creation of frameworks that facilitate the support of VFs within Web applications. This point would be vital for the approach to be positioned and to start being used by the community in the industry.

Finally, the framework does not currently consider a graphic environment for the configuration of the activation and deactivation events. On the contrary, it uses mechanisms that can only be implemented by developers. The implementation of an intuitive environment would be important, as it would allow users without much IT knowledge to define their own activation and deactivation rules.

References

1. Bebjak, M., et al.: Evolution of web applications with aspect-oriented design patterns. In: Proceedings of ICWE, pp. 80–86 (2007)
2. Chidamber, S.R., Kemerer, C.F.: A metrics suite for object oriented design. IEEE Trans. Softw. Eng. **20**(6), 476–493 (1994)
3. Curtis, B., et al.: Estimating the size, cost, and types of technical debt. In: Proceedings of the 2012 3rd International Workshop on Managing Technical Debt, MTD 2012, pp. 49–53 (2012)
4. Filman, R.E.: Aspect-Oriented Software Development. Addison-Wesley, Boston (2005)
5. Gamma, E., et al.: Design patterns: elements of reusable object-oriented software (1995)

6. Gethers, M., et al.: An adaptive approach to impact analysis from change requests to source code. In: 2011 26th IEEE/ACM International Conference on Automated Software Engineering (ASE 2011), pp. 540–543 (2011)
7. Ihme, T., et al.: Challenges and industry practices for managing software variability in small and medium sized enterprises. Empir. Softw. Eng. 1–25 (2013)
8. Ko, A., et al.: An Exploratory study of how developers seek, relate, and collect relevant information during software maintenance tasks. IEEE Trans. Softw. Eng. **32**(12), 971–987 (2006)
9. Martínez, Y., et al.: Empirical study on the maintainability of Web applications: Model-driven Engineering vs Code-centric (2013)
10. Morgenthaler, J.D., et al.: Searching for build debt: experiences managing technical debt at Google. In: Proceedings of the 2012 3rd International Workshop on Managing Technical Debt, MTD 2012, pp. 1–6 (2012)
11. Niederhausen, M., van der Sluijs, K., Hidders, J., Leonardi, E., Houben, G.-J., Meißner, K.: Harnessing the power of semantics-based, aspect-oriented adaptation for AMACONT. In: Gaedke, M., Grossniklaus, M., Díaz, O. (eds.) ICWE 2009. LNCS, vol. 5648, pp. 106–120. Springer, Heidelberg (2009)
12. Nord, R.L., et al.: In search of a metric for managing architectural technical debt. In: Proceedings of the 2012 Joint Working Conference on Software Architecture and 6th European Conference on Software Architecture, WICSA/ECSA 2012, pp. 91–100 (2012)
13. Rossi, G.: Web Engineering: Modelling and Implementing Web Applications. Springer, London (2008)
14. Seaman, C., Guo, Y.: A portfolio approach to technical debt management. In: Proceedings - International Conference on Software Engineering, pp. 31–34 (2011)
15. Svahnberg, M., et al.: A taxonomy of variability realization techniques. Softw. Pract. Exp. **35**, 705–754 (2005)
16. Urbieta, M., et al.: Designing the interface of rich internet applications. In: 2007 Latin American Web Conference (LA-WEB 2007), pp. 144–153. IEEE (2007)
17. Urbieta, M., et al.: Modeling, deploying, and controlling volatile functionalities in web applications. Int. J. Softw. Eng. Knowl. Eng. **22**, 129–155 (2012)
18. Weber, J.H., et al.: Managing technical debt in database schemas of critical software. In: 2014 Sixth International Workshop on Managing Technical Debt, pp. 43–46. IEEE (2014)
19. Whitney, R.: Glorp Tutorial (2005)
20. Zazworka, N., et al.: Comparing four approaches for technical debt identification (2013)
21. Application quality benchmarking repository - Appmarq – CAST. http://www.castsoftware.com/products/appmarq
22. Aspectxml - An Aspect-Oriented XML Weaving Engine (AXLE) - Google Project Hosting. https://code.google.com/p/aspectxml/
23. Drools - JBoss Community. http://drools.jboss.org/
24. FindBugs™ - Find Bugs in Java Programs. http://findbugs.sourceforge.net/
25. HP Static Analysis, Static Application Security Testing, SAST. http://goo.gl/qtRf0X
26. Maven – Welcome to Apache Maven. https://maven.apache.org/
27. phantom @ pleiad.cl
28. Quartz Scheduler | Documentation | Quartz 1.x Tutorials: crontrigger. http://goo.gl/D0tNbO
29. SonarQube™. http://www.sonarqube.org/
30. XSL Transformations (XSLT). http://www.w3.org/TR/xslt

Abstracting and Structuring Web Contents for Supporting Personal Web Experiences

Sergio Firmenich[1], Gabriela Bosetti[1], Gustavo Rossi[1], Marco Winckler[2(✉)], and Tomas Barbieri[1]

[1] LIFIA, Facultad de Informática, Universidad Nacional de La Plata and Conicet, La Plata, Argentina
{sergio.firmenich,gabriela.bosetti, gustavo}@lifia.info.unlp.edu.ar
[2] ICS-IRIT, University of Toulouse 3, Toulouse, France
winckler@irit.fr

Abstract. This paper presents a novel approach for supporting abstraction and structuring mechanisms of Web contents. The goal of this approach is to enable users to create/extract Web contents in the form of objects that they can manipulate to create Personal Web experiences. We present an architecture that not only allows the user interaction with individual objects but also supports the integration of many objects found in diverse Web sites. We claim that once Web contents have been organized as objects it is possible to create many types of Personal Web interactions. The approach involves end-users and developers and it is fully supported by dedicated tools. We show how end-users can use our tools to identify contents and transform them into objects stored in our platform. We show how developers can use of objects to create Personal Web applications.

Keywords: Personal web · Web augmentation · Mashups

1 Introduction

Current Web personalization approaches usually suffer a boundary problem, since most, if not all, work in an individual application basis. When a user needs to deal with two or more applications for performing a particular task, he will face differences in the personalization approach for each of them (if any). Another drawback of personalization mechanisms is that, specified by application's developers, do not necessarily may foreseen the requirements of every single application user. These problems have been the base for the Personal Web, defined in [2] as a "collection of technologies that confer the ability to reorganize, configure and manage online content rather than just viewing it". This generic definition might be realized in different ways such as: (1) PIMs and object manipulation which allow users to collect information objects and make them available for performing operations [16], e.g. to collect scientific work's titles relevant for a researcher to perform further tasks. (2) Mashups, to integrate and combine information objects from different resources into a specialized application [11, 12, 12], e.g. to combine multimedia search results from different resources in a single view. (3) Web

© Springer International Publishing Switzerland 2016
A. Bozzon et al. (Eds.): ICWE 2016, LNCS 9671, pp. 77–95, 2016.
DOI: 10.1007/978-3-319-38791-8_5

augmentation, where users are able to enrich information objects in-situ, i.e. in the same Web page they appear [1] e.g. to add information to each movie in the IMDB's Top250 list. (4) Reactive Web which allows users to obtain reactive feedback from information objects under certain events that these objects are able to detect automatically [14], e.g. to inform the user that a new movie was presented. (5) Creation of specific applications: for example, running specific client-side applications that using existing information objects, use them to build a domain specific application, such as a personal agenda, e.g. a personal application for managing scientific literature.

These approaches, altogether, provide users with the possibility of interacting with Web objects (information items from the existing Web) in different ways. However, all the approaches work isolated, with specific and dedicated information models, which makes very complicated to have a complete Personal Web experience supporting arbitrary combinations of these kinds of interactions, given that several different and specialized tools should be developed and maintained which moreover hinders reuse (of contents and behaviors).

In this paper we present a platform for supporting the abstraction of domain objects from Web sites with the goal of creating applications (Mashups, Web augmentation, independent applications, etc.) providing a full interactive Personal Web experience supporting the reuse of structure definition and behavior. The main contributions of our approach are that (1) it supports all the kinds of interactions mentioned above and new ones that could be envisioned in the future; (2) it achieves this goal by using a uniform and rich underlying object-oriented model and (3) the possible combinations of application types (e.g. mashups and augmentations) makes the overall result much richer than the mere sum of these individual approaches.

The paper is organized as follows. Section 2 presents the motivation and an overview of the approach. Section 3 presents the related works. Section 4 introduces our approach. Section 5 describes the tool support and in Sect. 6 several case studies for illustrating the approach are explained. Finally, Sect. 8 concludes and presents the future works.

2   Motivation and Approach Overview

Imagine a journalist who must be informed constantly. With this aim, too many contents might be got from different Web sources, and even different kind of interactions could be needed for achieving a real Personal experience: (I1). *Interact with information objects directly from an object representation space*: if the user needs to store preferred news that he wants to follow, then a PIM with those news could be good for starting any interaction with them. (I2) *Merge objects from different sources into specialized apps*: in this case he would need a mash-up application that integrates the daily news from the preferred media Web sites, allowing him to browse several sources at one time. *(I3) Interact with objects when they are presented in the visited pages*: when visiting a media Web sites, the user could take advantage of Web augmentation capabilities, and then augment the news in specific Web sites with behavior to obtain related news, multimedia resources, look for reactions on social networks, etc. (I4) *Get reactive interaction from the Web*: when there is a hot topic, the user could be interested in some kind of reactive experience, for instance to have immediate notifications informing him the last news. (I5) *Domain Specific application experience:* this user may appreciate a specialized news and journalist tracker application that allows him to follow specific journalists, recommend news, etc. This is similar to mashups, but the underlying application behavior is specific for the news domain.

For providing a full Personal Web experience like this, we must use several applications: a Web augmentation script, a Mashup tool, a PIM, an environment for client-side domain specific applications, etc. In this context, all approaches listed before tackle only a "portion" of the Personal Web. This situation presents some challenges to end-users, who could need to deal with different kind of artifacts at different moments and circumstances. To obtain all these tools for a single domain could be time consuming for end-users, or simply not possible because the required programming skills.

In this paper, we propose a layer for identification and abstraction of information objects; we call these objects *Instance Object (IO)* when they are specific and static instances and *Class Object (CO)* when they refer to the type of those instances and will help to retrieved *IO* dynamically (we explain how both are collected by users in Sect. 4.1). In Fig. 1 we give an overview of the approach showing how *IO* are extracted from Web sites and put on a specific ambient, that we named Web Object Ambient (WOA). Once there, *IO* can be decorated with specific and varied behaviors. These decorations are basically set of messages that the object may response. Some of the messages could be eventually sent by end-users and answers to that messages might have a UI effect correlation. Together with the WOA, we developed a default application (WOA application), that similar to a PIM, presents the *IO* to the user with different menus to send these messages directly to them. This first WOA application allows users to interact directly with the abstracted objects, without the need of visiting the corresponding Web site, as we will show later. Users can determine the relevance of *IO* over the Web and then deal or interact with them in different contexts, but reusing the same model and implemented behavior. This layer is transversal to all the mentioned approaches (mashups, Reactive Web, Web Augmentation, etc.), which impact directly on the maintenance of the client-side artifacts used. Similar to other approaches related to the Personal Web, end-users are responsible of managing the data model (i.e. giving structure to Web objects and collet them into the WOA), while advanced users with some programming skills may create and share complex applications using the data model specifications. The approach offers the WOA functionality through an API over which any kind of application, and even combinations of these (such as Reactive Web Augmentation) may be developed. All these applications are thought to be ran on client-side, but if any communication with a specific server is needed, the approach does not limit it. Supporting different kinds of applications with the same underlying model makes much easier sharing artifacts among users; both *IO* specifications and applications (since they run on top of the same underlying data models). In this approach, we envision two kind of user roles: (a) Developers: they may create specific behavior for *IO* (called decorators) as well as new data collectors, and domain-specific applications. (b) End-Users: they may either consume *IO* or produce *CO*, which consist of specifications for creating *IO,* by using visual tools. When a DOM element is collected and a *CO* is specified, then WOA can instantiate *IO* enhanced with some basic operations, either

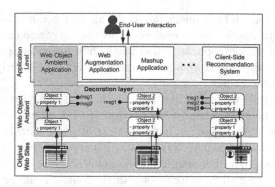

Fig. 1. Web ambient object layer

through the WOA Viewer or in-situ modality. However, end-users may use any product created by developers in order to use *IO* in advanced ways.

3   Related Works

The idea of object extraction is similar to Web Scraping [4]. Web scraping is the process of non-structured (or with some weak structure) data extraction, usually emulating the Web browsing activity. Normally, it is used to automate data extraction in order to obtain more complex information, which means that end-users are not usually involved on determining what information to look for and still less about what to do with the abstracted objects. When Web content has not an underlying structure, Web scraping would be a good option in order to retrieve information from Web sites.

Some Web sites already tag their contents allowing other software artifacts (for instance a Web Browser plugin) to process those annotations and improve interaction with that structured content. A well-known approach for giving some meaning to Web data is Microformats [5]. Some approaches leverage the underlying meaning given by Microformats, detecting those objects present on the Web page and allowing users to interact with them in new ways [6]. A very similar approach is Microdata [7]. Considering Semantic Web approaches, and an aim similar to our proposal, [9] presents an approach for mashups based on semantic information; however, it depends too heavily on the original application owners, something that is not always viable.

However, when analyzing the Web, we see that a huge majority of Web sites do not provide structured data. According to [8], only 5,64 % among 40.6 million Web sites provide some kind of structured data (Microformats, Microdata, RDFa [13], etc.). This reality raises the importance of empowering users to add semantic structure when it is not available. Several approaches let users adding structure to existing contents to ease the management of relevant information objects. For instance, HayStack [16] offers an extraction tool that allows users to populate a semantic-structured. Atomate it! [14] offers a reactive platform that could be set to the collected objects by means of rule definitions. Then the user can be informed when something interesting (such as a new movie, or record) happens. [15] allows the creation of domain specific applications that work over the objects defined in a PIM.

Web augmentation is a popular approach that lets end-users improve Web applications by altering original Web pages with new content or functionality not originally contemplated by developers. Nowadays, users may specify their own augmentations by using end-user programming tools. Very interesting tools have emerged [2], to manipulate DOM (Document Object Model) objects in order to specify the adaptation. However, the costs associated to specifying similar functionality in different Web applications sharing the same underlying domain may be high. Reutilization in Web Augmentation has been confined to reusing scripts. For example, Scripting Interface [10] is oriented to support better reutilization by generating a conceptual layer over the DOM, specifically for GreaseMonkey scripts. Since the specification of a Scripting Interface could be defined in two distinct Web sites, the augmentation artifacts written in terms of that interfaces could be reused.

Another well-known approach for integrating content and services are mashups. Very popular tools such as Yahoo Pipes! [11] allowed users to combine different resources and present a specific result. Yahoo Pipes! is strongly based on the existence of APIs, but other approaches propose in-situ composition, i.e. without generating a new independent application [12]. Although MashMaker allows to abstract widgets with their properties, the way in which the widgets are used is always the same and extending the use implies modifying the application.

It must be noted that if we consider the interactions mentioned before (I1-I5), we can see that they may be supported individually by one of the mentioned approaches. Nevertheless, none approach supports these interactions altogether; therefore, the Personal Web experience might be restricted. Moreover, how future kind of interactions could be contemplated is not taken into account in most of the approaches. The main reason for that, is that the underlying data models seems to be specifically defined for supporting a particular kind of interaction.

4 Our Approach

Our approach proposes using a reusable object layer to build any kind of Personal Web application. This is achieved by giving end-users the possibility to structure *CO* from existing content, to import them into the WOA and to interact with their instances either from our WOA viewer, using in-situ Web Augmenters, or in domain-specific applications. Applications and decorators are created by developers, who profit from a reusable layer of specifications of *CO* and their behavior.

4.1 Abstracting and Collecting Objects

Most Web users' tasks involve looking for information objects (news, papers, movies, hotels, books, etc.). We focus on the problem of identifying and abstracting information objects as *IO* and *CO* that can be used in different contexts. For doing this, our approach first adds a meaning layer to any Web content, similarly to other PIM approaches [16].

For each object type that the user wants to import into the ambient (e.g. books), he should create a *CO*, which is a template that will allow producing instances of such concept. Although this kind of content structuring is not new, our approach is different at the end of the process. The process ends on the object materialization, i.e. generating live objects with internal state and intrinsic behavior that can be used in different contexts. Such process is composed of three steps, as shown in Fig. 2: (1) Class Identification, (2) Conceptual abstraction and class structuring, and (3) Instances Extraction and materialization.

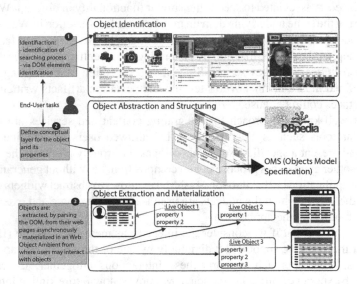

Fig. 2. Object materialization process

Class identification (1), consists of identifying relevant DOM elements on the context of any Web site, yielding either a single or a list of occurrences of the same element (such as a resulting list of products in Amazon). Implementation details are presented in Sect. 5, but it is worth mentioning that users are enabled to select DOM elements, and decide between extracting only such element or collecting all similar occurrences. For instance, in Fig. 4, although the collection task is made with the Carrie Fisher actor, users may choose to collect all similar detected objects, such as Harrison Ford, etc. Either collecting only one instance or a collection of them, WOA can manage both the Actor *CO* and its individual *IO*.

Concerning *conceptual abstraction and class structuring (2)*, the semantic type and the internal state of a *CO* should be set. The user might provide some required data for defining the *CO*: the generic name, a tag and if it should be statically stored or not. The most outstanding step consists in associating the identified element with a concrete tag, which preferably corresponds with a class in the DBPedia's ontology and will be used for further matching decorators with proper functionality. For example if the user defines a Book, it could be matched and wrapped (in the following step) with behavior that allow looking for the book in multiple stores, looking for movies based on it, etc. Although the user can manually add these data, our tool can auto fill some values at extraction time. For those Web sites that provide some semantic structure via DOM annotation, the tool suggests certain values for tagging the authored *CO*; otherwise, the user should write a tag, which better represents the identified element. Values are also suggested when the user input data at the sidebar, but it is not mandatory to choose one of them. The benefit of using these tags is that our repository contains many decorators associated with the classes of such ontology (the suggested tags). Regarding the extraction techniques, an *IO* can be obtained by parsing one or different DOM elements, including plain text. The component enabling the objects harvesting activity is called *ObjectCollector*. When the identification is based on structured DOM elements, we can create the meaning layer for that object either consuming DOM annotations (e.g. RDFa [13] or Microformats [5] annotations) or asking the user for a tag. We also differentiate–at least– three ways for abstracting and structuring objects, which we describe below. Our goal is to define the same transversal model layer for any of these possibilities, and then to generate instances of that model independently of how the meaning is either added or extracted from DOM elements. Our approach is not tied to any implementation of annotations and new types can be supported by extending the *ObjectCollector*. At the left of Fig. 3, we show a generic example of extraction based on an existing semantic layer; by analyzing the DOM, we can detect the concept definition and then extract it for creating the *CO*, which will allow instantiating "live" objects. At the right of Fig. 3, we show two different examples. At the top, a RDFa-based example where the concept Person and some of its properties are nested into the HTML. At the bottom, a similar example is presented, based on Microformats.

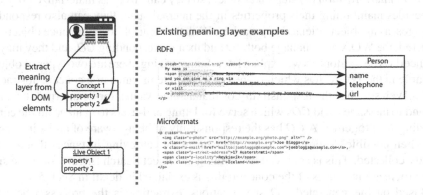

Fig. 3. Examples of existing semantic layers

Regarding the internal structure, a *CO* may be composed of some properties that require similar identification and abstraction steps than concepts, but also implies defining a mapping to its corresponding *CO*. When a concept is abstracted from existing DOM elements, the properties associated to the object may be more than one. For instance, at the right of Fig. 4, the concept Actor is defined with two properties (picture and name). In cases where there are many instances available, the properties should be obtained from children elements of each DOM element representing a whole Actor instance. In this way, by defining how to get the properties for a specific instance should be enough for inferring other instances existing in the same Web page. In the center of Fig. 4, we show how the same concept could also be abstracted from different Web sites with different strategies. Each particular instance has different properties related to the information available in each Web site. When the object is abstracted from plain text, only one property might be available. For example in the concept Actor (Fig. 4), the property "name" acquires the value from the selected text.

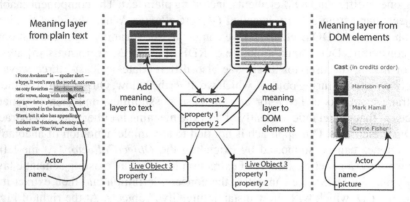

Fig. 4. Examples of semantic layer addition

Finally, all the abstracted objects are stored into the WOA and the *instances extraction and materialization (3)* step takes place, so they can "live" as materialized objects; i.e. besides maintaining their properties in the internal state, they can also respond to messages, as in object-oriented approaches. With the same philosophy, once objects are collected, the WOA may manage both *IO* and their corresponding *CO*, and they may be enhanced via decorators, as we explain later. Summarizing, there are two types of objects available in the WOA: *IO*s which represent a concrete instance of a concept abstracted from a Web site, has the responsibility of maintaining values for its internal state, and respond to messages, and *CO*s which serve for letting end-users to manage all the corresponding *IO* altogether. A *CO* has the responsibility of being aware of all its instances, and when possible, to provide some mechanism for retrieving instances that are not already collected. This is achieved by defining an Object Search Engine for those sites where there are instances of the concept; this is explained in detail in Sect. 5.

Based on the generated *CO* specifications, extraction is the process where the concrete information about the specified DOM elements is obtained. The *CO* may contain the specification for extracting a single object from a Web page (for instance the main news from a media portal), or all the news from the same site. For each object to be extracted, the *CO* contains–at least– the corresponding URL and XPath. In this way, the extraction step includes the task of obtaining a DOM (from that URL), parsing it and getting each information piece to extract all the required for setting the instances internal state (e.g. the title of the last news). Regarding materialization, it implies creating an *IO*; setting its internal state and wrapping it with some behavior.

4.2   Enhancing Objects

In the WOA, users may deal with *CO* or *IO*. Both of them has some basic behavior, which is automatically inherited. For example any *CO* responds to messages such as *getInstances()*, *removeInstance()*, etc. An *IO* inherits automatically some behavior such as *showInContext()*, *getDOMImage()*, *getPropertyByName()*, etc. Besides this default behavior, an object can be enhanced either with behavior for the specific object type or with behavior that can be applied over any kind of object (i.e. behavior independent of the application domain). These enhancements are called decorators, inspired in the Decorator design pattern [3] and are developed by advanced users. For instance, if a journalist has collected News objects in the WOA, then an instance decorator could add *getRelatedMultimedia()*, *getRelatedTweets()*, etc. Regarding to the News *CO*, a domain-specific class decorator could add *getCurrentEconomyNews()*, etc. A decorator adds new messages that can be sent to the object from different contexts (from a WOA viewer, augmentation scripts, etc.). Decorators may be generic or even domain specific when these are specifically defined for a type of object from an ontology in DBpedia. When a new *IO* is obtained, then available decorators may be automatically applied. Since decorators specify meta-information related to the type of objects over which it can be applied and also related to the needed properties to work properly, the WOA may discard those decorators that do not fit with an OMS.

End-users may add existing decorators in their browsers and then decide which decorators to apply over the WOA objects (See Sect. 5). Decorating an object requires identifying the desired decorator and choose the target objects. This can be done from the WOA Viewer, which helps end-users in this task by filtering decorators and *CO* analyzing their compatibility. Decorators must specify (a) the needed object structure: to which kind of objects the decorator may be applied. When the decorator is domain-specific, the target objects may be a particular *CO* or its *IO*. When the decorator is generic, then the target objects may be any *CO* or any *IO*. (b) The messages with which target objects will be enhanced: decorators must be able to define which are the messages for enhancing objects, which also includes if the messages have or not a UI effect that the end-user may perceive.

Decorators may use (a) WOA objects (*CO* and *IO*): although the behavior is going to be added to particular objects, decorators may consume any other objects existing into the WOA for accomplishing that behavior; (b) Any Web content: decorators may need to consume other content besides WOA objects. This can be done in two ways. First, decorators may consume any Web content via the use of APIs or ad-hoc DOM parsing. However, decorators may also reuse other OMS and obtain objects from different Web sites, without the need that these objects already exist in the WOA. For instance the *getRelatedNews()* decorator could parse a media Web site by applying (on the fly) an OMS to GoogleNews, etc., in order to obtain other objects.

Section 4 presents further technical details, but it is important to note at this point that the fact of separating decorator development from the underlying object in which it is going to be applied, implies that these behaviors are intrinsically reusable among Web sites sharing the same domain model in different contexts or applications.

4.3 Interacting with Objects

The reason for collecting information objects into the WOA, is that end-users may interact with them in different ways and contexts in order to obtain personal experiences. Such interaction may be performed in two basic ways, which are illustrated in Fig. 5: (1) by interacting in a Web page context or (2) in the WOA viewer or any other application. In the first case, it is achieved through Web Augmentation decorators, and the context could be the Web page from which the object was extracted, or any other where the object was added. In the second case, the Viewer (which is the default WOA application), lets end-users to directly send messages to the *IO* and obtaining a visual feedback in response. For interacting from both, the WOA viewer or any other WOA application, the reader should note that the Web site from where these objects are extracted is retrieved transparently by WOA, based on the corresponding *CO*, which does not necessary implies the user opening that site. For instance, if the user has defined the object DRNews (a news *CO* collected from an online media called DiarioRegistrado.com–DR–), and he wants to interact with that object for obtaining the titles of the last news, it is not necessary to open the Web site.

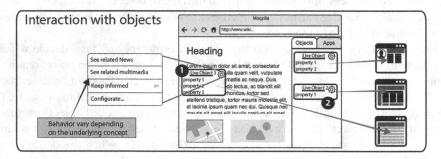

Fig. 5. Interaction patterns with materialized objects

By interacting directly with objects, end-users may send messages (provided by their chosen decorators) to the objects. For instance, a journalist may send the *getRelated-Multimedia( )* message when he wants; this message may return a list of Yooutube Videos and Google Images, while other similar decorators may consume content form other sources. All the messages shown in the menu are dynamic, because this behavior is implemented by decorators, as explained in Sect. 4.4.

Besides interacting directly with objects, end-users may install further WOA applications (created by developers), which might provide different ways to interact with objects. For instance, if the journalist wants to be informed about news related to a particular topic (economy, sports, etc.), he could use a WOA application for Reactive News, which alerts the user when a news appears. Other kind of applications such as one for integrating news related to a map could be also possible, as Sect. 6 shows.

4.4   Programming WOA Objects and Applications

A decorator is a JavaScript object developed by extending an existing class, *Abstract-Decorator*; see line 5 of the code in Fig. 6. Several behaviors are inherited from AbstractDecorator, and two abstract methods must be implemented in order to allow WOA to manage decorators. One, called *getDisplayName*, to return the Decorator's name in order to be visualized by users. A second one, called *getMessages*, returns a collection of associative arrays describing each of the messages (each new behavior) that the decorator adds to the target object, as the simple example from Fig. 6 shows. For each of these associative arrays, four properties are needed. The first describes the name of the corresponding decorator's method that will be executed when messages are sent; the second one that is the display name of the message, the third one indicates if that message returns a UI feedback to recognize which are the messages that can be sent under demand directly by end-users. The last attribute lists the properties that the object must have in order to be compatible with the message.

```
1    function GenericDecorator(concept){
2        AbstractDecorator.call(this, concept);
3        this.tags.push('*');
4        this.getSelectedMessages = function(){}
5        this.highlight = function(){ ... }
6        this.orderByName = function(){ ... }
/        ...
8    }
9    GenericDecorator.prototype = new AbstractDecorator();
10   GenericDecorator.getDisplayName = function(){ return "Generic"; }
11   GenericDecorator.getMessages = function(){
12       return [
13           {id:"highlight", name:"Highlight in Web page", showInUI:true },
14           {id:"orderByName", name:"Order by name", showInUI:true, properties:[{"id": "name", "name": "Name"}]},
15           ...
16       ];
17   }
```

Fig. 6. Decorator implementation

WOA applications meanwhile are Web pages with embedded JavaScript code. Basically a WOA application has an associated UI layout (implemented with HTML), and from the JavaScript code it is possible to interact with the WOA, since in the context of a WOA application a WOA library is available allowing to make queries to the materialized objects. The use of this library is shown in Fig. 7. At the left, we show the specification of a WOA application in a special package.json file needed for importing the application. The required fields are an ID for resolving the file in the system, a name for displaying at management time, and the name of the entry point file. At the right we can see the pure JavaScript code defined under a script tag, using the WOA library (this code could be included in both decorators and WOA applications). Note that besides the use of our library, the layout of the application is also defined using HTML. With this approach, domain-specific application such as a News dashboard can be implemented in a straightforward way. Besides, this allows working with several kinds of objects in the same application, allowing powerful relationships among different WOA objects.

```
1  {
2      "id": "dash@lifia.info.unlp...",
3      "name": "DR News Dashboard",
4      "version": "1.0.3",
5      "description": "A dashboard ...",
6      "author": "LIFIA",
7      "homepage": "http://www.lifia...",
8      "license": "MPL 2.0",
9      "index": "index.html"
10 }
```

```
1  <!DOCTYPE html>
2  <html lang="en">
3      <head>
4          <title>DR News Dashboard</title>
5          <meta charset="UTF-8"/>
6          <!-- ... -->
7          <script type="text/javascript">
8              window.addEventListener("DOMContentLoaded", function(){
9
10                 this.initWOAScript = function(){
11                     WOA.initSubset();
12                     WOA.filterByTag('news');
13                     WOA.filterByOrigin('http://www.diarioregistrado.com/*');
14                     WOA.filterByAttribute('title', 'ARSAT');
15                     WOA.decorate('News');
16                     var news = WOA.getInstances();
17
18                     for (var i = 0; i < news.length; i++) {
19                         drawInDashboard(news[i].getRepresentation());
20                     };
21
22                     WOA.clearFilters();
23                     ...
24                 }
25             });
26         </script>
27     </head>
28     <body onload=""> <!-- ... --> </body>
29 </html>
```

Fig. 7. Using WOA objects from WOPs

5 WOA Supporting Tools

The complete tool is deployed as a Firefox browser extension, including the WOA, the WOA application runner, and the Object Collectors. More Object Collectors, WOA applications and decorators may be added in a plug-in-like style.

5.1 Tool Support for Collecting and Structuring Objects

As shown in Fig. 8, our tool adds the necessary controls that let users creating objects, no matter what Web resource has been loaded in the browser.

Fig. 8. Identifying and abstracting concepts

First, we added a toolbar button with two options: opening WOA, and enabling the concept selection. Clicking the second option (step 1 in the picture), every DOM element is highlighted on a mouse-over event, so the user can clearly appreciate what is the current target element to collect. Then, as shown in step 2, he can access via a context menu to the options for extracting an element in the current DOM. Options are dynamically loaded according to the selected target element. This behavior is provided by a set of *ObjectCollectors* explained later. Once one of the options is clicked, a sidebar is opened for completing the remaining data required for the abstraction and structuring stage. The contextual menu is populated with those *ObjectCollectors* that match with the selected element. This is carried out by asking the set of collectors to analyze the target DOM element, and rendering just the ones that accomplish the required characteristics for being created with such extraction technique. Our tool currently supports collecting elements from Microformats, DOM element selection and text highlighting. New collectors can be incorporated by extending the framework. Each collector must be capable of analyzing a target HTML element and, if applicable, rendering a context-menu item with their description and associating some behavior to it, in order to return the created object.

Back to the materialization process, once the DOM element is selected, a UI form is opened at the sidebar, which lets the user selecting a name for the *CO*, a semantic tag, the saving method and the number of *IO* in the original Web page. The saving method determines if the extracted element should be stored as a static definition or to be retrieved from its context every time an *IO* is created. Concerning the occurrences, a combo is filled with different XPaths applicable to such element, and allow to univocally reference it or to reference a set of elements instead. For example, it is possible to identify an element by its type of node at certain level of the document tree, or by the CSS class it has applied. This allows the user to choose one or more elements, according to his needs. As shown at left in Fig. 9, he is asked to name the *CO* and tag it, then to select one of the possible selectors in the DOM, so, e.g. he can choose multiple DOM elements by changing the selector. Properties can be added in the same way; the only difference is the addition of a combo for linking such property to an existing concept. The result of this process is the definition of a set of *CO* specifications which allow to obtain one or multiple *IO* according to the selector the user has chosen during the authoring process: if it refers to a single element in the DOM or to several of them. As WOA is a browser extension, it counts on the necessary privileges to retrieve external and even third party content, to manipulate it and then use it into the required context (e.g. in the sidebar, WOA application or augmented Web page).

Fig. 9. Structuring a concept with WOA

5.2   WOA Viewer

Once saved into the WOA, users may see the *CO* and *IO* in the WOA viewer, as shown at the right of Fig. 9. We show the view of a *CO*, whose contextual menu allows to manage the properties, edit the *CO*, wrap it with some behavior and define an Object Search Engine for retrieving *IO* that may not be present as a result in the current DOM. If there are class decorators enabled, then the messages that can be sent directly by the user are shown under the submenu "Available Messages".

5.3   Decorating Objects

In Fig. 10, we show how the user associates the DR News concept with the *ReactiveNews* decorator (1). He selects the messages he wants to use for enhancing such concept instances (2), link the required decorator's messages parameters with the properties of the created concept (3). He can return to the WOA viewer for interacting with the functionality provided by the decorator (4).

Fig. 10.   Wrapping an object with specialized behavior

5.4   Object Search Engines

To support different ways of searching objects, we take into advantage original Web applications engines, allowing end-users to abstract that searching engine UI similarly to the way in which they can abstract content into objects. These ObjectSearchEngine are search APIs, each of them containing the searching URL, the form where the user would enter the text to search, and the button for performing the action. Also searching modifiers (such as filter or ordering options) and pagination managers are supported. Then, for example, a decorator may easily search for news in Google News given a particular news title from an object extracted from DiarioRegistrado.com and materialized into the WOA, assuming that an Object Search Engine for Google News was defined. Finally, a *CO* that was added into the WOA may have associated several ObjectSearchEngine defined in different Web sites. For the sake of space we omit further explanation on creating custom search engines, which can be found in an online documentation site (see footnote on page 17th).

6   Case Studies

In this section we present some case studies demonstrating the power of the approach. Here several examples show how CO and IO materialized into the WOA may be enriched with decorators and then used in different contexts.

6.1   A Web Augmentation Approach Based on Domain-Specific Models

Another possible scenario for using directly materialized concepts is in-situ Web Augmentation. When the concept has been wrapped with a decorator with Web Augmentation capabilities, every DOM element related to an *IO* is enhanced with a floating-menu in its original context. Such menu is placed at the top-right corner of the element and makes it possible to interact with the decorator messages, in the original context of the structured data.

Consider a scenario in which a radio journalist frequently accesses a set of Web sites that allow him to be informed about what is happening outside while he is producing his live broadcast, and also to provide their listeners with additional updated information. He uses a news portal as his main source of information. Once he has read the last entries in the portal, he navigates to other sites looking for the concrete topics he read about. As his program concerns political and society issues, he also uses to read people opinions on social networks. In this sense, he has a particular interest in Twitter, because of the public visibility of its messages. It would be highly desirable for this user to create a custom WA application, that takes the news portal as background information and that add functionality for easily retrieving each portal's entry with a set of related news and tweets. For achieving such goal by using WOA, the user should identify the "News" concept, then abstract and structure *a CO* by using any available WOA collector. During the structuring process, he finds a matching tagged decorator available for the "News", but it is required that the user defines, at least, the "Title" property. Once done, this decorator augments the news portal site with a floating menu at the right-top corner of the main HTMLElement related to each *IO*. When the user clicks on it, he is offered with the configured messages for interacting with such *IO*. Figure 11 shows a screenshot of a WOA application satisfying the journalist's needs.

Until this point, creating a personal solution does not require any programming skills. However, if the needed functionality is not being contemplated by any of the existing decorators, a developer should implement it. Developers can create not only decorators

Fig. 11. Web augmentation decorators enhancing entries of a news portal

but also applications. In both cases, the WOA library is accessible for also querying instances of existing templates, concepts and decorators.

6.2   A Personal Dashboard Based on Composition of Abstracted Objects

When the journalist needs to be informed with the news from several portals at the same time, he can use an application that uses the news defined for both sites and have an integrated experience, as shown in Fig. 12. This application has an HTML page for the application's content structure and the *initWoaScript()* function to initialize after the WOA library was loaded, so the application can start making requests about the *IO* available for each portal and Twitter. He can ask the decorator the representation to display of every *IO*; and wrap them to present them with a unified style. As we can see, the main advantage of implementing this dashboard instead of creating a mashup is that it allows to embed its own domain-specific behavior. Finally, the user should specify the application data in package.json file, place in the root directory of the application and import it with WOA.

Fig. 12.   A dashboard application integrating entries from two news portals

6.3   Using Decorators with Reactive Web Capabilities from WOPs

Finally, consider the fact that the consumed news of the previous example were retrieved from certain subsection of both Web portals–e.g. economics–. Both portals have other sections that, under certain circumstances may have news of interest for the journalist, either because the subject is directly related with his interests or because they have reached high level of popularity. Generally, the main entry of news portals usually owns such qualities, so a considerable feature for the journalist's application could be tracking changes of such main entries. This is possible to implement through reactive programming, making elements capable of propagating their changes. As WOA decorators are instantiated in a high privileged context (our browser extension's main code), it is possible to retrieve and manipulate external documents for achieving this goal.

Back to the example, the developer should define such "Main News" as a new *CO*, because even they are also news from the same portals, these are in different contexts and have a different structure, which are unknown for WOA. Then, he can use a *ReactiveNews* decorator for wrapping such *CO*. This decorator allows retrieving the concept's owner document and tracking changes on its proper elements. As a result, notifications can be shown in any context, by defining a target place where the notification should be displayed as a property in the *CO* definition. At the left of Fig. 13, you can see a notification as the result of integrating the "Main News" decorated-concept in the Personal Dashboard example. At the right, you can see the same decorator displaying a notification in the Google News site, under the in-situ modality.

Fig. 13. A notification as result of the reactive news decorator's message

7 Evaluation

We have performed an expert-oriented evaluation, to measure te power of the approach. Based on the motivational examples presented in Sect. 2, we identified the dimensions or aspects that an approach must support for letting users obtain such Personal Web experience. We found more than 10 dimensions of interest in the evaluation namely Consumes static data, Consumes dynamic data (Web services or extractors), Consumes structured data, Consumes unstructured data, No technical skills needed, Content authoring, Reusable information objects, Individual information objects shareability, Tracks changes in the original Web content, Allows augmenting existing Web content, Integrates content from multiple sources, Integrates and displays services from multiple sources, Objects can live in background.

We used these dimensions for comparing how each type (e.g. mashup) and individual approach (for instance Marmite) support personal experiences. For reasons of space, we cannot include the full comparison table here, but it can be read in the WOA documentation Web site[1]. As a result, we found that none of these approaches supports all experience at the same time. In some cases, the problem is data structuring. In other cases, the changes in Web pages (where an object was abstracted) are not tracked (and consequently some interactions such as reactive ones are not possible). Others do not support the enhancement of objects when they are visualized in their corresponding Web page. Our approach, in contrast, supports altogether the interaction kinds listed in Sect. 2 (and further ones, such as client-side recommender systems) since its underlying object-oriented data model is, in our opinion, the best way to implement such a layer, given its intrinsic properties such as reuse and extensibility makes the approach application-agnostic. Over these models, applications may be run in different scopes but always using the same client-side web technologies.

---

[1] WOA Website Comparison table: https://sites.google.com/site/webobjectambient/comparison.

8   Conclusions and Future Works

The constant evolution of Web and their users have shown the need of more personal Web applications. Web Mashups, Web Augmentation and other approaches have emerged to reach this goal; however these approaches are usually not integrated and underlying domain models are not easy to reuse. We believe that, for reaching a more Personal Web, the kinds of interaction experiences supported by these approaches should be composable, in such a way that information object models and their behavior could be reused. In this paper we presented an approach for adding an object-oriented layer over Web contents, that serves as a platform for the development of third-party software. Solutions can be created from existing contents, and focused on existing content and decorators–therefore behavior– reusability. We presented our tools and several case studies that demonstrate the power of the approach. We are currently developing a WOA application and Decorators repository. In this way, we are increasingly covering functionality needs of diverse end-users in the process of decorating the objects they materialize. The same repository is being designed to support collaboration in the creation of OMS and also as a communication platform for sharing them. We are also developing an end-user tool for creating WOA applications, such as the dashboard presented in the case studies section. Finally, we plan to perform experiments with end-users for further validating our approach.

References

1. Díaz, O., Arellano, C.: The augmented web: rationales, opportunities, and challenges on browser-side transcoding. ACM Trans. Web 9(2), 8 (2015)
2. Díaz, O., Arellano, C., Aldalur, I., Medina, H., Firmenich, S.: End-user browser-side modification of web pages. In: Benatallah, B., Bestavros, A., Manolopoulos, Y., Vakali, A., Zhang, Y. (eds.) WISE 2014, Part I. LNCS, vol. 8786, pp. 293–307. Springer, Heidelberg (2014)
3. Gamma, E., Helm, R., Johnson, R., Vlissides, J.: Design Patterns: Elements of Reusable Object-Oriented Software. Pearson Education, Upper Saddle River (1994)
4. Ferrara, E., De Meo, P., Fiumara, G., Baumgartner, R.: Web data extraction, applications and techniques: a survey. Knowl.-Based Syst. 70, 301–323 (2014)
5. Khare, R., Çelik, T.: Microformats: a pragmatic path to the semantic web. In: Proceedings of the 15th International Conference on WWW, pp. 865–866. ACM, May 2006
6. Operator Firefox Extension. https://addons.mozilla.org/es/firefox/addon/operator/?src=search
7. Microdata. http://www.w3.org/TR/microdata/
8. Bizer, C., Eckert, K., Meusel, R., Mühleisen, H., Schuhmacher, M., Völker, J.: Deployment of RDFa, microdata, and microformats on the web– a quantitative analysis. In: Alani, H., et al. (eds.) ISWC 2013, Part II. LNCS, vol. 8219, pp. 17–32. Springer, Heidelberg (2013)
9. Kalou, A.K., Koutsomitropoulos, D.A., Papatheodorou, T.S.: Semantic web rules and ontologies for developing personalised mashups. Int. J. Knowl. Web Intell. 4(2–3), 142–165 (2013)
10. Díaz, O., Arellano, C., Iturrioz, J.: Interfaces for Scripting: Making Greasemonkey Scripts Resilient to Website Upgrades, pp. 233–247. Springer, Heidelberg (2010)
11. Pruett, M.: Yahoo! Pipes. O'Reilly, California (2007)

12. Ennals, R., Garofalakis, M.: Mashmaker: mashups for the masses (demo paper). In: Proceedings of the 2007 ACM SIGMOD International Conference on Management of Data (SIGMOD 2007) (2007)
13. RDFa. https://rdfa.info
14. van Kleek, M., Moore, B., Karger, D.R., André, P.: Atomate it! end-user context-sensitive automation using heterogeneous information sources on the web. In: Proceedings of the 19th International Conference on World Wide Web, pp. 951–960. ACM, April 2010
15. van Kleek, M., Smith, D.A., Shadbolt, N.: A decentralized architecture for consolidating personal information ecosystems: The WebBox (2012)
16. Karger, D.R., Bakshi, K., Huynh, D., Quan, D., Sinha, V.: Haystack: a customizable general-purpose information management tool for end users of semistructured data. In: Proceedings of the CIDR Conference, January 2005

CTAT: Tilt-and-Tap Across Devices

Linda Di Geronimo[✉], Maria Husmann, Abhimanyu Patel,
Can Tuerk, and Moira C. Norrie

Department of Computer Science, ETH Zurich, 8092 Zurich, Switzerland
{lindad,husmann,norrie}@inf.ethz.ch, {apatel,can.tuerk}@student.ethz.ch

Abstract. Motion gestures have been proposed as an interaction paradigm for pairing, and sharing data between, mobile devices. They have
also been used for interaction with large screens such as semi-public
displays where a mobile phone can be used as a form of remote control
in an eyes-free manner. Yet, so far, little attention has been paid to their
potential use in cross-device web applications. We therefore decided to
develop a framework that would support investigations into the use of a
combination of touch and tilt interactions in cross-device scenarios. We
first report on a study that motivated the development of the framework
and informed its design. We then present the resulting Cross-Tilt-and-
Tap (CTAT) framework for the rapid development of applications that
make use of various motion gestures for communication between two or
more devices. We conclude by describing an applications developed using
CTAT.

Keywords: Web interaction framework · Cross-device · Motion sensors

1 Introduction

In 1991, Mark Weiser envisioned a world in which people would be surrounded by
devices of different sizes, technologies and goals [1]. Years later, this scenario has
become our everyday life. Typically, people now own several personal devices,
possibly sharing some of them with family and friends [2]. At the same time,
public and semi-public screens are now to be found throughout our places of work
and study as well as in public places such as train stations, airports, shopping
malls and even in the street. Hence, as Weiser imagined two decades ago and has
been confirmed by GSMA Intelligence[1], we are currently living a multi-device
era, where the number of mobile devices has surpassed the world population.

In such an environment, Weiser assumed that all of these devices would
be interconnected in a vast network to drastically improve the user experience
when shifting from one device to another, or when using two or more devices
together, despite their intrinsic differences in terms of hardware and goals. While
the spread of mobile devices was correctly predicted by Weiser, the vision of a
stable cross-device and cross-platform network is still some way off. It remains an

---

[1] http://gsmaintelligence.com.

© Springer International Publishing Switzerland 2016
A. Bozzon et al. (Eds.): ICWE 2016, LNCS 9671, pp. 96–113, 2016.
DOI: 10.1007/978-3-319-38791-8_6

everyday challenge for users to interact with their set of devices and cross-device applications are still in their infancy [3].

Researchers have explored several ways of supporting interaction in multi-device settings. One is to make use of the motion sensors in mobile devices to pair devices as well as to interact with cross-device applications [4,5]. Specific cases involve using tilting gestures on mobile phones to interact with large screens. This allows users to retain their focus of attention on the large screen while using the mobile phone in an eyes-free manner as a form of remote control.

Despite their advantages, motion gestures have mainly been used in native apps and little attention has been paid to their potential use in web applications as a whole, and cross-device web applications in particular. One reason may be the lack of support offered to web developers as well as portability issues caused by device-dependent sensor APIs. We therefore set out the goal to develop a framework to support the rapid development of cross-device web applications that use a combination of tilt and touch interactions. The resulting Cross-Tilt-and-Tap (CTAT)[2] framework is built on top of two frameworks previously developed in our group: XD-MVC[3] and Tilt-and-Tap [6]. XD-MVC is a framework for cross-device web applications that provides a simple and intuitive API for communication between devices, while Tilt-and-Tap supports the development of web applications that use motion-based interaction. By combining the functionality of both frameworks, there is no need for CTAT developers to handle motion interactions on each device, since they can simply specify one or more senders of the tilting gesture and the corresponding receiver/s.

Before developing the framework, we performed a preliminary study to investigate the potential benefits of using motion gestures in cross-device web applications and inform the design of the framework. For this study, we were able to use the existing Tilt-and-Tap framework with some extensions to cater for a simple cross-device setting. We report on this study in Sect. 3.

The new CTAT framework is able to support a wide-variety of cross-device applications that may span over many different devices. We present the main features of CTAT in Sect. 4 and give details of the implementation in Sect. 5. In Sect. 6, we describe an application that was designed to demonstrate and test the different forms of interaction supported. Finally, we give some concluding remarks and outline future work in Sect. 7.

2   Background

It is now common for mobile devices such as smartphones and tablets to have motion sensors such as accelerometers and gyroscopes that can be used to detect motion gestures. As discussed by Baglioni et al. [7], tilting gestures are a good alternative when touch interactions are not suitable due to users wearing gloves or having dirty fingers. They proposed JerkTilts, a set of toggle gestures where

---

users move the mobile device rapidly in some direction. Hinckley et al. [8] further point out that tilting interactions, possibly combined with touch, have the advantage of being eyes-free, single-handed gestures.

Given the potential benefits of motion gestures, we previously decided to study the use of tilting interactions in web applications. This led to the development of Tilt-and-Tap, a jQuery framework for the rapid development of motion-based interaction on the web. Tilt-and-Tap supports combinations of tilt gestures with touch gestures such as tap, double tap and hold tap, together with various feedback modes [6]. Two types of tilting gestures are distinguished: jerk tilting as proposed by Baglioni et al. [7] and continuous tilting where the user interacts with their handheld device by continuously moving it, for example to perform scrolling.

Motion sensors have been applied to cross-device applications for various purposes. Boring et al. [5] employed motion gestures to improve and increase interactions with public screens. In their work, users can remotely control a cursor shown on a large screen by moving their handheld device where the speed of the cursor depends on the tilt angle of the mobile device. The use of mobile phones to interact with large screens was also proposed by Seifert et al. in their PointerPhone project [9]. Making use of a laser pointer mounted on a smartphone, they were able to explore Point-and-Interact techniques where users can point to objects on a large display and then interact with them using their mobile device. For example, a user could rotate a selected object by simply moving their phone. Dachselt et al. [10] have studied the use of jerk and continuous tilting gestures for direct interaction with large displays in detail using applications such as browsing a music library and a map on Google Earth.

Other common uses of motion sensors concern the pairing of devices and sharing of information among devices [4,11–13].

Pering et al. [12] used jerk tilting to play a particular song on a stereo or to turn on lights in a room. While Pering et al. were one of the few to consider jerk tilting in a one-many environment where one handheld device is used to interact with many devices, they do not cover scenarios where multiple smartphones, tablets or screens are involved. As discussed by Kray et al. [14], gestures such as touch or motion interactions may vary depending on several factors including the type of the device which can play an important role. Also, as noticed by Marquardt et al. [15], some interactions may be better suited to smartphone-tabletop communications, while others are better for smartphone-smartphone or smartphone-public display and so on. The amount of possible combinations and scenarios in cross-device applications introduces a challenge that developers need to tackle and could be one of the reasons why cross-device applications are not yet in common usage. In recent years, researchers have tried to solve these problems by proposing a number of frameworks and tools [16–19].

Nebeling et al. proposed XDStudio [16], a visual tool to easily distribute UI elements among devices with the focus on providing different authoring modes for the design of web applications. Chi et al. developed Weave [17] which is a set of high level JavaScript APIs designed to handle different interaction modes over multiple and diverse devices. Weave offers API support for touch gestures, rotation-change and shake events. For example, multiple users can pair their devices by shaking them at the same time. Without the support of Weave, developers would have to manage the shaking interaction as well as their timestamps on each device. While these works gave us inspiration for our framework, none of them support jerk or continuous tilting interactions.

Moreover, previous research on the use of motion gestures tends to either focus only on native apps, as discussed in our previous work [6], or is very limited in terms of the cross-device settings supported. For example, many researchers have focused on one-to-one scenarios where smartphones are used as remote controls, ignoring the potential use of other mobile devices such as tablets. For these reasons, we decided to take our work on Tilt-and-Tap [6] further by investigating the use of tilting interactions in cross-device web applications. Working with web technologies allowed us to study motion interaction techniques in scenarios where multiple and diverse devices can be involved, giving developers and researchers the opportunity to study and personalize motion interactions in their web application.

3   Preliminary Study on Tilt-and-Tap Across Devices

To better understand the benefits and issues of Tilt-and-Tap style interaction in cross-device settings, we conducted a preliminary study based on a simple, handcrafted cross-device web gallery application that uses tilting gestures on either a smartphone or tablet as a means of interaction. The study involved 12 participants (9 males and 3 females). All participants stated that they to use mobile devices as well as desktop or laptop machines several times a day.

As shown in Fig. 1, users can navigate through a grid of pictures shown on both the smaller screen of a mobile device and a larger desktop screen by continuously moving the mobile device. A ball which plays the role of a cursor is shown on both screens and its movements are influenced by the orientation and speed of the device. When the ball is positioned over an image, that image becomes selected and is highlighted with a red border as feedback on the mobile device and enlarged on the desktop screen. By tapping anywhere in the page, the selected image will be displayed full screen on the desktop screen and its metadata shown on the mobile screen. Users can return to the grid page at any time by rapidly rotating the mobile device counterclockwise. The recognition of tilting gestures is handled by the Tilt-and-Tap framework, while the communication among devices is implemented using Node.js[4] and Socket.IO[5].

To compare tilting interactions to touch gestures, we also developed a touch-only version of the same application. We asked participants to find a particular image in the grid and display it full screen. The task was repeated in four different ways: *smartphone tilt*, *smartphone touch*, *tablet tilt* and *tablet touch*. In the *tilt* versions for both tablet and smartphone, the user could interact with the

---

[4] https://nodejs.org/.
[5] http://socket.io/.

Continuously move the device to browse

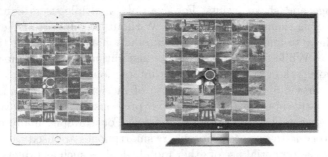

Tap anywhere to select

Fig. 1. Tilt-Gallery application and its interaction flow

applications only via motion gestures, while during *touch* tasks, motion gesture weres disabled and only touch interactions allowed.

The grid of images is scaled to display full screen size. We then classify the images according to their position on the mobile screen which reflects how hard it would be to reach them with a thumb. As seen in Fig. 2, and as similarly done by [20], we identified three main areas on the smartphone and four on the tablet. The areas labeled with A have been categorized as hard to reach when the user holds the device in portrait mode, with one hand in the case of the smartphone, and with two hands in the case of the tablet. The B zones were identified as easier to reach. However, participants were unaware of this categorization. The setup of the study is shown in Fig. 3. The devices involved in the study were: a 24 inch. TV as the desktop display, an iPad Air, and an iPhone 6. In addition, a laptop was used to show the image that the user was required to select.

Users were given a brief explanation of the study and a training phase on a test page, before starting the tasks. They first had to select nine images using the *smartphone touch* version with the images distributed evenly across the three areas labelled A or B. The same task was then repeated on the *smartphone tilt* version. Similarly, for the tablet, the users had to select eight different pictures, with two in each of the areas labeled A or B, performing this first for the touch-only version and then for the tilt-only version. To avoid a learning effect on

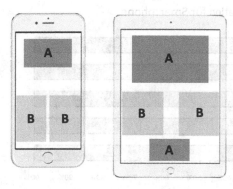 

Fig. 2. Identified areas on smartphone and tablet

Fig. 3. Study environment

the position of the pictures, a completely different set of images was shown for each task. Moreover, half of the participants started with the smartphone tasks, while the rest started with the tablet tasks. At the end of the study, participants filled out a questionnaire that involved background information as well as qualitative questions about the study. We recorded the study on video in order to analyse particular user behaviours during the tasks and keep track of the time to complete a task.

As can be seen in Fig. 4, participants enjoyed using tilting interactions. More than 80 % of users agreed or strongly agreed that motion gestures were enjoyable on the smartphone, while around 70 % of participants found it enjoyable on the tablet.

Generally, motion sensors performed better on smaller mobile devices with 70 % of participants finding it easy or very easy to use them on smartphones, with the corresponding figure for tablets being 50 %. This trend is also mirrored in the question where participants were asked to rate efficiency of motion gestures. 40 % of participants did not find tilting interactions particularly efficient on tablets, while only 20 % were of the same opinion for smartphones.

The velocity of the indicator was the same for both the mobile and tablet tasks. Therefore, to move the ball to a particular position, the user either had to use a higher tilt angle on the tablet or tilt the device for a longer period of time. Some participants perceived the *tablet tilt* task to be slower than the *smartphone tilt*. This factor could have been one of the reasons why users preferred tilting interactions on smartphones. However, tilting interactions on tablets have their advantages since some participants felt that motion gestures were more suited to the iPad where they appreciated the ease of controlling the ball on the larger screen.

When compared to touch only gestures, around 50 % of participants found tilting gestures on both tablet and smartphone (50 % and 59 % respectively) comparable to, or less demanding than, touch. The average time to complete a task was similar for all four versions at around 7 seconds per image. Moreover,

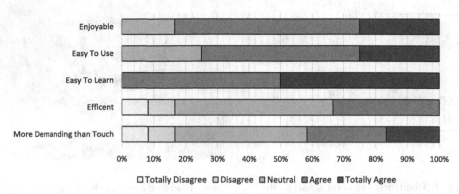

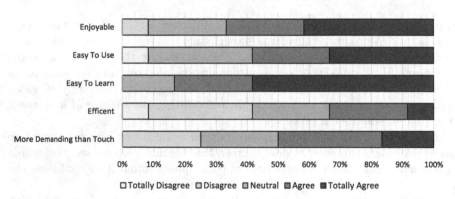

Fig. 4. User evaluation for tilting interactions on smartphone (top) and on tablet (bottom)

there was no significant statistical difference between times to select images located in different areas. We note however that the main focus of the study was not to directly compare motion-based interaction against touch, but rather to receive feedback in order to improve and design a version of Tilt-and-Tap better suited to cross-device applications.

One interesting finding concerns the focus of attention of the participants during tasks. In the case of tilting interactions, most users concentrated exclusively on the desktop screen which was not true in the case of touch. One participant commented on this behaviour by saying: *"[...] during the tapping I could not use the TV at all since I would have to search for the image twice."* During the *tablet touch* task, only one participant started by paying attention to the TV screen but, after few moments, he changed his focus to the mobile device and said: *"Why look at the TV, I need to select it from the iPad anyways."*.

These findings motivated us to pursue our research on the use of motion sensors in cross-device applications. Based on the feedback from users regarding the limitations as well as the potential of our tilting interactions, we were able to design and develop our cross-device framework CTAT which pays more attention to the intrinsic differences among devices and adjusts tilting interactions accordingly.

4   The CTAT Framework

Taking into account user feedback as well as our experience of using Tilt-and-Tap in a cross-device environment, we developed the new CTAT framework, which is specifically designed for the rapid prototyping of applications with cross-device tilting interactions.

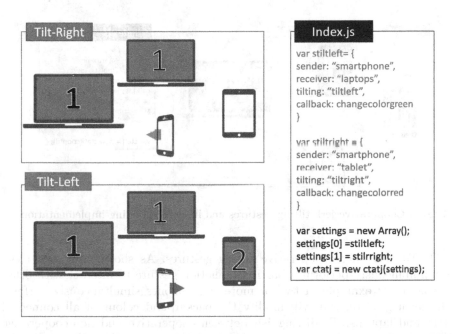

Fig. 5. Cross-device jerk tilting interactions and their implementation

CTAT offers support for the two main forms of motion-based interaction used in Tilt-and-Tap, namely jerk and continuous tilting. Since many applications tend to use only one of the two forms of tilt interaction, we decided to actually produce two variants CTATJ (CTAT-Jerk) and CTATC (CTAT-Continuous). The resulting reduction in size and complexity of the framework required in many cases, can significantly improve performance. However, in cases where both forms of tilting interactions are used in an application, the two frameworks can be used together.

In the example shown in Fig. 5, jerk tilting gestures are used to change the background colour of other devices connected to the same web page. By rapidly rotating their smartphone to the left, the colour on the two laptops will change, while rapidly tilting to the right will change the colour on the tablet. The code to achieve this behaviour using the CTATJ variant of the framework is shown on the right of Fig. 5.

As the names suggest, the variables `stiltleft` and `stiltright` correspond to the tilt left right and tilt left gestures. These two objects contain all the information that CTAT needs to manage motion interactions among devices. The `sender: "smartphone"` setting indicates the actor in the tilting interaction, while `receiver: "laptops"` and `receiver: "tablet"` specify the target devices for the tilt left and tilt right gestures, respectively. The function specified in the callback option will be executed on the receivers whenever the corresponding tilting interaction is performed on the sender.

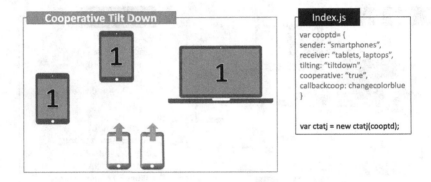

Fig. 6. Cooperative jerk tilting gestures and its corresponding implementation

CTATJ also offers cooperative tilting gestures. As shown in Fig. 6, users can simultaneously perform a particular motion gesture to interact with other devices. In our example, if two or more smartphones simultaneously perform a tilt down gesture, this will modify the background colour of all connected tablets and laptops. To distinguish between cooperative and non-cooperative jerk tilting gestures, the `cooperative` option inside the settings object has to be set to `true`. Moreover, the `callbackcoop` option defines the callback function for only cooperative executions of the gesture.

A cross-device continuous tilting example implemented with CTATC is shown in Fig. 7. Similar to the web gallery application developed for our preliminary user study, users can interact with a large screen by moving their smartphone. The red ball shown on the laptop simulates a cursor. When the ball is over one of the elements, that element becomes selected and is enlarged on the laptop screen. As with CTATJ, developers can define a sender, one or more receivers, possible touch interactions and a callback function for when an element becomes selected. In addition, with the `ball: "laptop"` option, the developer specifies

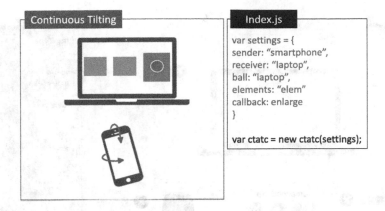

Fig. 7. Cross-device continuous tilting interactions and their implementation

on which device the ball will be shown, in this case, the laptop screen. Any number and types of devices can be specified under this option.

While it is very easy to specify interactions using these settings variable, the lines of code necessary to define motion gestures increases with the number of interactions that the developer wants to recognize on each device. For this reason, we have developed a visual tool that automatically generates the CTAT objects.

The tool is shown in Fig. 8. Developers can add devices as well as creating new communications among them in step 1. When a new connection has been added, the corresponding settings can be modified in the *Connection Manager* menu shown in step 2. If developers save the connection (step 3), icons will be displayed for each device involved in the communication (step 4). The direction of the arrow indicates if the device is a sender or receiver of that specific tilting interaction. The tool is implemented as a web applications in HTML, CSS and JavaScript.

5 Implementation

From our preliminary study, we recognised two main problems of using Tilt-and-Tap for cross-device applications. The first of these concerned the development process and the second the lack of support for adapting interactions to different devices, especially in continuous tilting interactions.

Managing tilting interactions on every device required us to develop tedious and long code, making our applications more prone to errors. Socket.IO allowed communication among devices, but, for each interaction, it also required an exchange of messages between the sender, the server and finally the receiver. Moreover, continuous tilting interactions in cross-device applications revealed some challenges that were not originally considered by Tilt-and-Tap.

Cross-Tilt-and-Tap was developed specifically with cross-device applications in mind and therefore a primary goal was to overcome these issues. As previously

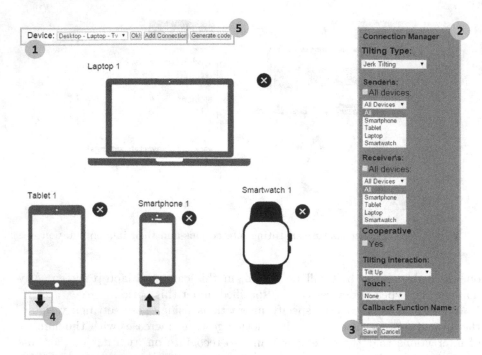

Fig. 8. Visual tool for the generation of CTAT objects

mentioned, one of the first decisions made was to split responsibilities for jerk and continuous tilting between the two sub-frameworks CTATJ and CTATC.

To share real-time messages among devices, CTAT uses the communication module of XD-MVC, a cross-device framework previously developed in our group. XD-MVC includes a Node.js server, and uses Socket.IO and Peer.js for cross-device communications. When supported by the browser, peer-to-peer communication is used, resulting in lower latency which is crucial, especially for continuous tilting. As a fallback, client-server communication can also be used and this allows us to support a wide range of devices. XD-MVC abstracts this mechanism from the developer, thus allowing direct communications among clients to be easily managed.

We note that since CTAT can involve many different devices, developers have to include the client as well as the server side of our framework in their web application. A Node.js installation is then required on the machine that will act as the server. Other than this, no particular installations are required on the client nor on the server.

Figure 9 indicates some of the APIs supported by CTAT and its two sub-frameworks CTATJ and CTATC.

We currently support four categories of devices: laptop-screens, tablets, smartphones and smartwatches. These devices are recognised by making use of user agent information. Developers can use these types of devices to specify a particular

CTATJ and CTATC

Option	Description	Default Value	Possible Values
sender	Indicates the sender(s) of the interaction. Multiple senders available only for CTATJ.	null	"all"; "tablet(s)"; "smartphone(s)"; "smartwatch(es)" "laptop(s)" and combination
receiver	Indicates the receiver(s) of the interaction.	null	"all"; "tablet(s)"; "smartphone(s)"; "smartwatch(es)" "laptop(s)" and combination
touch	Indicates if the jerk tilting interaction needs to be performed with a touch gesture	null	"tap"; "double tap"; "tap hold"
callback	Callback function executed on receiver when jerk tilting interaction performed or when ball selects an element	null	any existing function

CTATJ

Option	Description	Default Value	Possible Values
tilting	Indicates the jerk tiling interaction	null	"tiltup"; "tildown"; "tiltleft"; "tiltrigh"; "tiltse"; "tiltsw"; "tiltnw"; "tiltne"; "tiltclockwise"; "tiltcounterclockwise"
cooper ative	Indicates if the jerk tilting interaction is cooperative	false	true, false
callback coop	Callback function executed on receiver when cooperative jerk tilting interaction performed	null	any existing function

CTATC

Option	Description	Default Value	Possible Values
ball	Indicates if ball is visible and where.	null	""; "sender"; "sender-receiver"; "receiver"
elements	Indicates the class name of elements that the ball will select	null	any existing class

Fig. 9. List of main APIs supported by Cross-Tilt-and-Tap

client or set of clients for their tilting interactions. As seen in Fig. 9, CTATJ allows many-to-many communications, meaning that the same tilting interaction can be performed by more than one client and these events will trigger the execution of a callback function on one or more receivers. Developers can indicate a set of devices by using its plural form such as "laptops", "smartphones" and so on. Similarly, to target one specific client, developers can simply use the singular form of the device name. In this case, our framework will assign the first client connected to the page of the set specified by the developer. When the selected device disconnects, the next client will be assigned to the interaction.

In contrast to non-cooperative gestures, when a developer indicates that a particular communication is cooperative, all the senders specified should perform the tilting interaction simultaneously.

While CTATJ allows many-to-many connections, CTATC only considers one-to-many communications since it is counterintuitive to have more than one device able to remotely control a cursor on another client.

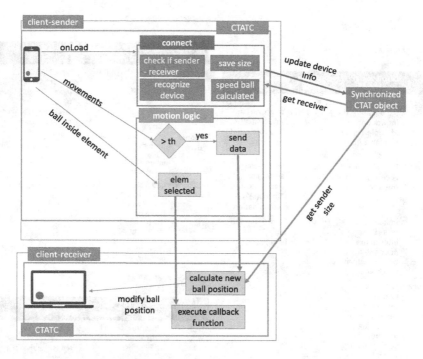

Fig. 10. Example of CTATC execution flow

To explain in detail how continuous tilting interactions among devices are managed we show the execution flow in Fig. 10. In our example, a smartphone device is used to remotely control a large screen represented as a laptop. We assume that the larger device is already connected to the web page, and the mobile device initiates a connection. Every time a new client connects, the device type is first checked. If it is involved in a tilting interaction as a sender or receiver, we save its width and height. All this information is stored in an object that is shared among all the connected devices with our framework ensuring that these shared objects are synchronised across devices. For example, if a device that is currently a sender for a tilting interaction disconnects, CTAT needs to modify the corresponding shared object and assign a new sender to the tilting interaction if possible. As indicated in Fig. 10, whenever a device is assigned to be the sender for a tilting interaction, the speed of the ball cursor is calculated dynamically depending on the screen size of the sender device. By default, the speed of the ball increases slightly as the dimension of the sender screen size increases. This parameter can also be adjusted by the developer using the corresponding setting.

In Tilt-and-Tap, the movement of the ball is managed on the sender side. In the case of CTAT, the framework has the role of communicating changes to all the receivers. For performance reasons, we first filter the movements performed by the mobile device on the client side and only send the new ball coordinates to the receivers if the movement performed is larger than a threshold. At this point, the receiver has all the necessary information to update the position of the ball. The new position is calculated by multiplying the ball position sent from the sender with the quotient of the receiver and sender width and height. This proportion allows the user to have a good match between the two devices despite their differences in resolution.

When the ball moves inside one of the elements, the framework wraps the event triggered on the sender side and sends this information to all the receivers involved in the interaction. We note that while the motion logic module is only present in CTATC, the overall behaviour of the jerk tilting version of our framework, CTATJ, is similar.

6 Demonstrator Application

To define, demonstrate and test the capabilities of the CTAT framework, we designed an advanced gallery application that featured the various forms of interaction and device configuration that we aimed to support.

The application was designed to engage users with semi-public and public displays throughout our university and promote social interaction among viewers. As mentioned earlier, many cross-device applications have been based around the use of mobile phones as a sort of remote control device for large displays. We wanted to take this idea further by considering multiple displays and multiple mobile devices and allowing them to take different roles. Also, there should be some form of interaction between mobile devices as well between mobiles and the displays.

The resulting application, called aCrossETH, was inspired by 500px[6] a well known image sharing website for photographers. Similar to 500px, users upload images and other users can then like or favourite them, with the most highly-rated images making it onto a "Popular" page[7]. All tilting interactions included in the aCrossETH application were developed making use of CTAT, while the GUI was implemented with HTML, CSS and JavaScript.

Figure 11 shows the three display categories in aCrossETH: slideshow-screen, voting display and mobile devices. The slideshow screen shows the six most popular images uploaded by users where the popularity takes into account the number of likes and favourites together with its freshness. In the example setting shown in Fig. 11, this role is taken by a projected display in a social area. All the most recent uploaded images are shown in a grid layout on one or more voting displays.

By scanning a QR code shown on both the slideshow and voting displays, users can interact with voting displays using their mobile device. The first connected mobile user is assigned the role of controller which allows them to browse images on the voting display by simply swiping left and right on their mobile device. Additional information about a selected image will be shown on all of the connected mobile devices which have the role of viewers. The selected image will also be enlarged on the voting display. A different version of the same application

---

[6] https://500px.com/.
[7] 500px recently merged likes and favourites into a single Twitter-style heart.

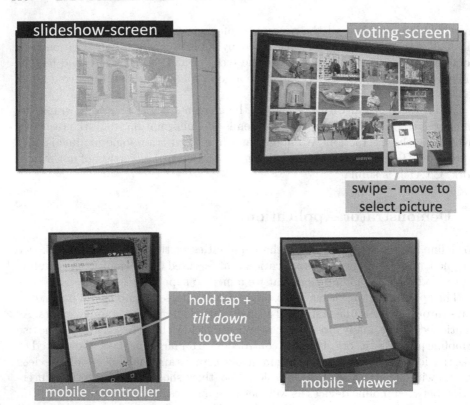

Fig. 11. Overview of aCrossETH on the three different categories of screens: slideshow, voting and mobile displays

allows the controller to browse the gallery of images using continuous tilting. In this version, the ball is shown only on the voting screen.

Detailed views of the mobile user interface for the controller and viewers is shown in Fig. 12. Users can vote for the current selected image using a hold tap on the rectangular area at the bottom of their mobile screen and rapidly tilting the device down. While the viewer device can only see the current selected image, the controller has an overview of all images visible on the voting screen. To improve user engagement, if the vote gesture is performed simultaneously by two or more devices, the number of votes added is doubled. This means that, the more users cooperate, the greater the chances that the images they vote for will be among the most popular shown on the slideshow screen.

By tapping on the upload button displayed on mobile devices, users can upload new images. Once they have selected an image from their local gallery, the system shows a preview of the selected image in full screen mode. To receive immediate feedback, users can decide to share the image with other connected mobile devices by simply performing a tilt left gesture as shown in Fig. 13. At this point, all the connected devices can see the new image and choose to like or

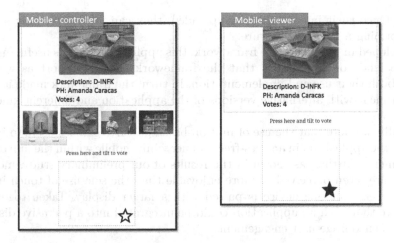

Fig. 12. User interface of aCrossETH on mobile controller and viewer devices

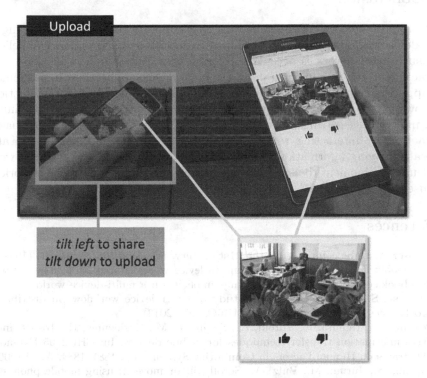

Fig. 13. User interface of aCrossDevice when user uploads a new image and shares it with other devices

unlike it. The owner can see how users have voted on their mobile device and, based on that, decide whether or not to go ahead and upload the image to the system. Once their image has been uploaded, they can view the voting screen by performing a tilt down gesture.

Developed in parallel to the framework, this application gave us useful insight into the kinds of interactions that the framework should support as well as testing both their use and implementation. In turn, the framework made it easy to experiment with alternative versions of the application and different kinds of interactions.

Finally, we note that the use of motion-based gestures enables users to interact with the application in an eyes-free manner while mobile within the university environment. Further, as shown in the results of our preliminary study, motion gestures are often perceived as more enjoyable than the sole use of touch interactions when a mobile device is paired with a larger display. Taken together, we believe that such an application could be integrated into a pervasive display system to encourage user engagement.

7   Conclusion

We have presented CTAT, a framework that supports the rapid prototyping of cross-device web applications that employ motion-based interaction. We believe that such a framework is necessary to push forward research in motion-based interaction on the web in general, and in cross-device applications in particular, by supporting experimentation with novel applications and modes of interaction.

Now that we have the framework, we plan to experiment further with multi-user, multi-device settings, investigating the potential benefits of motion-based interaction for interacting with public displays, sharing information and also generally moving information between devices. We also plan to take the work on visual development tools further, by building on ideas from previous work in end user development [21].

References

1. Weiser, M.: The computer for the 21st century. Sci. Am. **265**(3), 94–104 (1991)
2. Facebook: Finding simplicity in a multi-device world, March 2014. https://www.facebook.com/business/news/Finding-simplicity-in-a-multi-device-world
3. Santosa, S., Wigdor, D.: A field study of multi-device workflows in distributed workspaces. In: Proceedings of the UbiComp. (2013)
4. Yatani, K., Tamura, K., Hiroki, K., Sugimoto, M., Hashizume, H.: Toss-it: intuitive information transfer techniques for mobile devices. In: CHI 2005 Extended Abstracts on Human Factors in Computing Systems, pp. 1881–1884. ACM (2005)
5. Boring, S., Jurmu, M., Butz, A.: Scroll, tilt or move it: using mobile phones to continuously control pointers on large public displays. In: Proceedings of the 21st Annual Conference of the Australian Computer-Human Interaction Special Interest Group: Design: Open 24/7, pp. 161–168. ACM (2009)
6. Di Geronimo, L., Aras, E., Norrie, M.C.: Tilt-and-Tap: framework to support motion-based web interaction techniques. In: Cimiano, P., Frasincar, F., Houben, G.-J., Schwabe, D. (eds.) ICWE 2015. LNCS, vol. 9114, pp. 565–582. Springer, Heidelberg (2015)

7. Baglioni, M., Lecolinet, E., Guiard, Y.: Jerktilts: using accelerometers for eight-choice selection on mobile devices. In: Proceedings of the 13th International Conference on Multimodal Interfaces, pp. 121–128. ACM (2011)
8. Hinckley, K., Song, H.: Sensor synaesthesia: touch in motion, and motion in touch. In: Proceedings of the SIGCHI Conference on Human Factors in Computing Systems, pp. 801–810. ACM (2011)
9. Seifert, J., Bayer, A., Rukzio, E.: PointerPhone: using mobile phones for direct pointing interactions with remote displays. In: Kotzé, P., Marsden, G., Lindgaard, G., Wesson, J., Winckler, M. (eds.) INTERACT 2013, Part III. LNCS, vol. 8119, pp. 18–35. Springer, Heidelberg (2013)
10. Dachselt, R., Buchholz, R.: Natural throw and tilt interaction between mobile phones and distant displays. In: CHI 2009 Extended Abstracts on Human Factors in Computing Systems, pp. 3253–3258. ACM (2009)
11. Aumi, M.T.I., Gupta, S., Goel, M., Larson, E., Patel, S.: Doplink: using the doppler effect for multi-device interaction. In: Proceedings of the 2013 ACM International Joint Conference on Pervasive and Ubiquitous Computing, pp. 583–586. ACM (2013)
12. Pering, T., Anokwa, Y., Want, R.: Gesture connect: facilitating tangible interaction with a flick of the wrist. In: Proceedings of the 1st International Conference on Tangible and Embedded Interaction, pp. 259–262. ACM (2007)
13. Hassan, N., Rahman, M.M., Irani, P., Graham, P.: Chucking: a one-handed document sharing technique. In: Gross, T., Gulliksen, J., Kotzé, P., Oestreicher, L., Palanque, P., Prates, R.O., Winckler, M. (eds.) INTERACT 2009. LNCS, vol. 5727, pp. 264–278. Springer, Heidelberg (2009)
14. Kray, C., Nesbitt, D., Dawson, J., Rohs, M.: User-defined gestures for connecting mobile phones, public displays, and tabletops. In: Proceedings of the 12th International Conference on Human Computer Interaction with Mobile Devices and Services, pp. 239–248. ACM (2010)
15. Marquardt, N., Hinckley, K., Greenberg, S.: Cross-device interaction via micro-mobility and f-formations. In: Proceedings of the 25th Annual ACM Symposium on User Interface Software and Technology, pp. 13–22. ACM (2012)
16. Nebeling, M., Mintsi, T., Husmann, M., Norrie, M.: Interactive development of cross-device user interfaces. In: Proceedings of the SIGCHI Conference on Human Factors in Computing Systems, pp. 2793–2802. ACM (2014)
17. Chi, P.Y.P., Li, Y.: Weave: Scripting cross-device wearable interaction. In: Proceedings of the 33rd Annual ACM Conference on Human Factors in Computing Systems, pp. 3923–3932. ACM (2015)
18. Krug, M., Wiedemann, F., Gaedke, M.: SmartComposition: a component-based approach for creating multi-screen mashups. In: Casteleyn, S., Rossi, G., Winckler, M. (eds.) ICWE 2014. LNCS, vol. 8541, pp. 236–253. Springer, Heidelberg (2014)
19. Kovachev, D., Renzel, D., Nicolaescu, P., Klamma, R.: DireWolf - distributing and migrating user interfaces for widget-based web applications. In: Daniel, F., Dolog, P., Li, Q. (eds.) ICWE 2013. LNCS, vol. 7977, pp. 99–113. Springer, Heidelberg (2013)
20. Wolf, K., Henze, N.: Comparing pointing techniques for grasping hands on tablets. In: Proceedings of the 16th International Conference on Human-Computer Interaction with Mobile Devices & Services, pp. 53–62. ACM (2014)
21. Paternò, F., Santoro, C., Spano, L.D.: Model-based design of multi-device interactive applications based on web services. In: Gross, T., Gulliksen, J., Kotzé, P., Oestreicher, L., Palanque, P., Prates, R.O., Winckler, M. (eds.) INTERACT 2009. LNCS, vol. 5726, pp. 892–905. Springer, Heidelberg (2009)

Revisiting Web Data Extraction
Using In-Browser Structural Analysis
and Visual Cues in Modern Web Designs

Alfonso Murolo[(⊠)] and Moira C. Norrie

Department of Computer Science, ETH Zurich, 8092 Zurich, Switzerland
{alfonso.murolo,norrie}@inf.ethz.ch

Abstract. Recent trends in website design have an impact on methods used for web data extraction. Many existing methods rely on structural analysis of web pages and, with the introduction of CSS, table-based layouts are no longer used, while responsive design means that layout and presentation are dependent on browsing context which also makes the use of visual clues more complex. We present DeepDesign, a system that semi-automatically extracts data records from web pages based on a combination of structural and visual features. It runs in a general-purpose browser, taking advantage of direct access to the complete CSS3 spectrum and the capability to trigger and execute JavaScript in the page. The user sees record matching in real-time and dynamically adapts the process if required. We present the details of the matching algorithms and provide an evaluation of them based on the top ten Alexa websites.

Keywords: Data extraction · Wrapper induction · Browser

1 Introduction

As the web rapidly evolved into a vast data source covering any and every topic, it was natural that researchers strove to develop efficient ways of programmatically extracting data from web pages. Thus, the research area of web data extraction emerged and many different techniques have been proposed over the last two decades. As more and more web pages started to be generated dynamically based on queries to underlying content management systems and application databases, the term *deep web* was introduced to refer to the huge amounts of dynamic data contained in web pages that could not be indexed by traditional search engines. Web data extraction involved generating wrapper code that could generate queries and extract that data from the resulting web pages.

Instead of hard-coding wrappers, *wrapper induction* techniques were developed to enable wrappers to be generated based on patterns detected within dynamically generated web pages. These wrappers typically enabled data to be gathered from sets of web pages and converted into a tabular structure which could then be handled as relational data. Wrapper induction systems can be divided into two general categories: those which attempt to extract entities at

© Springer International Publishing Switzerland 2016
A. Bozzon et al. (Eds.): ICWE 2016, LNCS 9671, pp. 114–131, 2016.
DOI: 10.1007/978-3-319-38791-8_7

the page level, and those which extract records from lists of entities contained within a page using similarity measures [1].

While most previous work has focused on the use of structural cues for detecting patterns within and across sets of web pages, some techniques have combined structural cues with visual ones such as the coordinates of bounding boxes, the width and height of elements, and the use of different font faces and sizes [2–4]. However, with the introduction and evolution of the CSS standards in recent years, the information that can be gleaned from CSS stylesheets in conjunction with HTML markup has increased enormously. At the same time, CSS has enabled designers to move away from table-based layouts and many of the structural cues used in previous web data extraction techniques have been eradicted from HTML due to the separation of concerns supported by the new HTML and CSS standards. Further, the widespread adoption of responsive design techniques to enable websites to adapt to different viewing contexts means that previous techniques that made use of visual cues such as the position or size of elements to locate data or labels may no longer function in all contexts since these are no longer fixed but rather controlled by CSS media queries. Last but not least, the extensive use of JavaScript nowadays also needs to be taken into account as it may be responsible for generating or updating data, structure and presentation and can therefore have a major impact on data extraction.

Our goal was to develop a tool that would enable users to extract data as they browse. One possible use of such a tool would be for users to collect and add data to their personal libraries while browsing as proposed in Sift [5], but without requiring the presence of semantic markup. It has also been shown that such a tool can support web development by enabling database code plus data to be generated based on data extracted from digital mockups of a website [6].

We therefore decided to revisit web data extraction techniques with a view to developing methods that could not only cope with modern standards and practices, but also exploit them in wrapper induction. The main contributions of this paper are the following:

- We propose a hybrid approach that performs extraction at the record level using a combination of structural, content and visual features based on current web technologies and design practices. The approach requires users to label parts of an example record but this was kept to a minimum.
- The approach can be implemented as a web application that runs in a general-purpose browser and takes advantage of direct access to the page, the DOM and the CSS3 rules applied at runtime as well as the capability to trigger and execute JavaScript in a page. We present a specific tool, called DeepDesign, which was implemented as a browser extension for Chrome which allows users to see the matching process in real-time, adjusting the input if necessary until they are satisfied with the results. The extraction process is executed in each page directly, rather than delegating it to an external system, and therefore is completely realized with web technologies.

- An evaluation of our approach based on the top ten websites according to the Alexa[1] ranking and a comparative evaluation against previous work.

The methods presented are based on earlier work where we showed how custom post types for WordPress[2] could be generated based on sample content used in digital mockups [6]. As well as adapting the approach to allow data to be extracted from any website, we have improved the algorithms by taking more visual cues into account so that data record detection is more reliable.

We first provide a review of related work on web data extraction in Sect. 2 before going on to present an overview of our approach in Sect. 3. Details of our matching algorithm and its reliability improvements are presented in Sect. 4 and we discuss the implementation of the DeepDesign tool in Sect. 5. We then present an evaluation of our algorithm in Sect. 6. Concluding remarks and an outline of future work are given in Sect. 7.

2   Related Work

There has been a lot of research on the problem of extracting data records and performing *wrapper induction* from web pages in the past two decades. A wrapper embeds some form of extraction rules to match content based on a pattern detected in a web page. The detection of the patterns may involve different features: most use structural cues [1], while others use visual indicators, content-related measurements or some combination of these. We will outline the various approaches used, focussing on those closest to our own work.

The survey by Chang et al. [7] classifies methods using many different dimensions including the degree of automation and the difficulty of the task addressed. Here, we choose to classify techniques based on two dimensions: the level at which data extraction is performed and the integration with the browser. The level of data extraction can be either at the page level or the record level. Techniques that work at the page level typically take multiple pages containing data records of the same type as input and infer patterns for extracting data records from individual pages. Those that work at the record level typically take one or more pages containing multiple occurrences of data records of the same type and try to detect repeating patterns in individual pages that can be used to extract records from that page.

Among the most important systems that work at the page level is *NoDoSE* [8], which can generate wrappers and extract content to be stored in a database in a supervised way. The tool needs user-provided oracles to decompose entire web pages. Then, according to an inferred grammar, NoDoSE computes the field delimiters and extracts the attributes of each data record. This system is demanding for users as they have to provide various inputs to guide the creation of the extraction rules. NoDoSE was implemented as a separate system and is not integrated in any web-based system.

---

[1] http://www.alexa.com.
[2] https://wordpress.org/.

RoadRunner [9] also works at the page level, but data extraction is instead formulated as a decoding process. It requires a set of similar pages as input and assumes that the dynamic content will be different across pages. All dynamic parts are taken into account in guiding the generation of a wrapper. RoadRunner is divided into two modules. The *classifier* module clusters similar pages together and generates a wrapper based on their similarities and differences. The *labeller* module then tries to discover attribute names for data records within similar pages. While this is an interesting approach, it requires a set of similar pages rather than a single page as input. For the labeller to work, it requires the coordinates of the bounding boxes of the text nodes in the pages. It is a Java-based system and, although it tries to rebuild and re-render pages to locate the bounding boxes of candidate labels, it mainly performs a structural analysis.

An example of a record-level system is *IEPAD* [10] which uses so-called PAT trees to discover repeating patterns in pages. It implements a semi-automated approach and was later extended by *DeLa* [11] to remove the need for user interaction. Computation starts by detecting a *data-rich section* of the web page and then patterns in the DOM tree to generate regular expressions for future data extraction. As an extension of IEPAD, DeLa also works at the record level, aiming to detect multiple records from search page results. Again, the DeLa approach differs from our own in its requirement to have multiple input pages in order to detect data-rich sections. Moreover, it does not use any visual features, focusing only on content and structural analysis. DEPTA [12] also works at the record level to detect repeating patterns, but parses only the HTML tag strings verifying that the repeated record's tags have the same parent in the HTML tag tree. Using an algorithm called MDR-2, DEPTA processes the pages in three steps: first, it builds a DOM tree of the page, using the visual features of bounding boxes to compare those of child and parent elements. Second, a tree is built based on which bounding boxes contain those of other elements. Finally, data records are identified by analysing structural cues and the containment relationships of elements represented in the tree. DEPTA was integrated with the MSHTML API, which provides a rendering of each HTML element and builds the DOM tree for the system with the results in a spreadsheet.

A different approach that processes a document with similarly structured data without supervision is the one by Lu et al. [13]. This system performs alignment, clustering and annotation of sets of data records that appear as the results of queries to websites performed through forms. The alignment step at the start of their process identifies the data records. Then their fields are clustered in groups with different semantic meanings, for example names and titles. The second step attempts to automatically annotate the fields with labels based on heuristics. For example, if the data is in a table, the column headings are used as labels. While their method also takes into account some features considered in our system such as the contiguity and presentation style of data units, it only looks at six visual properties of text elements. The system accesses the rendered properties using a ViNTs [14] component as a browser renderer and extracting two critical cues to their system: the first is a tree structure that maps elements to the original page DOM tree and the second is the coordinates of the bounding boxes for the elements along with the other visual properties.

ViWER [15] is another work that uses visual as well as structural features, also focussing on the sizes of the bounding boxes of elements, in conjunction with a tree matching algorithm, to detect data records. In contrast to these works which use visual cues alongside structural analysis, *ViDE* [16] mainly relies on visual features. ViDE first builds a so-called visual block tree using the coordinates of the bounding boxes of the data regions and of the contained elements. Second, each region in the tree is analysed based on a group of features such as content-related features, positioning, layout and a limited number of appearance features such as font faces and sizes. By doing block grouping and clustering, it then constructs the records and their fields. ViDE retrieves the rendered information through a programming interface that allows their system to be interfaced with an external browser renderer, in their case Internet Explorer. Unlike ViDE's approach which moves radically away from structural cues, we aim to exploit both structural and visual cues, but to make more extensive use of visual cues and content-based features than in the combined methods proposed previously. Our approach is to first group elements by structural similarity and only then use visual cues to reconstruct records in the propagation of the labels.

Another important characteristic of methods for web data extraction is the role that the user plays in terms of interacting with the system and guiding the extraction process. DEByE [17] specifies an approach to user interaction which we share: a user provides example data records and the system then tries to find similar data records. In the case of DEByE, wrappers are generated from examples and these are then used to extract data from other web pages. Similar to our approach, DEByE works at the record level. However, our approach differs in a number of ways. First, we have tried to minimise the input required by the system by requiring users to mark up only parts of at most 2 examples. Second, our tool is in-browser while DEByE runs as a separate system. Third, and most important, our record extraction process works in the opposite way, first detecting the records and then propagating the fields.

OLERA [18] also operates based on user-specified examples. It runs as an independent system with an embedded browser. OLERA learns extraction rules at the record level from the example by first finding the information block of interest by interaction with the user, and then looking for similar blocks using approximate matching techniques and creating extraction patterns through string alignment techniques. The data is shown to the user through spreadsheets in the OLERA interface, and they can drill-down or roll-up through the data, allowing them to further manipulate the results. A third stage allows attribute names for the extracted data to be specified in the spreadsheet.

Previous work such as Sift [5] has also targeted the use case of extracting records from a web page while browsing. However, the Sift approach relies on semantic markup specified by Schema.org[3] or microformats to aid the extraction process.

---

[3] http://www.schema.org.

Finally, Thresher [19] is a previous project that also integrated a web induction system in a browser. Specifically, it was integrated in the Haystack information client, which acts as a browser for the semantic web. The system uses structural cues that take advantage of a user-assisted labelling procedure to perform the semantic web annotations. The user achieves two different goals at the same time: the first being the generation of the requested wrapper and the second the semantic annotation of content not previously annotated, thereby promoting the spread of semantic web technologies. Our approach differs by not only taking DOM-based features into account, but also content-related measurements and especially visual-based features, introducing the complete CSS3 spectrum to extract the data records.

3   DeepDesign

DeepDesign has been implemented as a Chrome extension and can therefore be loaded and executed in any page that the browser opens. Users can quickly access the tool while browsing whenever they find data of interest that they want to extract as structured data records. To do so, they simply click on the DeepDesign button which triggers the opening of a control panel for our tool as shown on the right of Fig. 1.

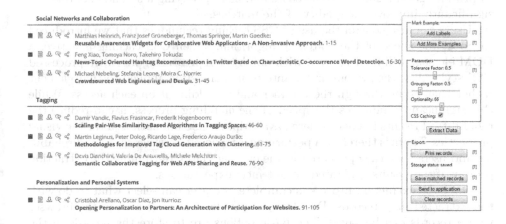

Fig. 1. A page from DBLP with the control panel of the matcher.

From the control panel, the user can start and fine-tune the detection process. The first button allows users to start the labelling process of a single example that will guide the matching process. Users annotate examples by clicking on any element that they consider to be part of the data record and giving it a label. We have tried to minimise the amount of annotations that users have to perform by letting them annotate only one element of a repeating field. Further, they do not need to specify whether a field may be repeating or optional. For example, in the publications list from DBLP shown in Fig. 1, a user would be required to annotate just one author, one title and the pages in the proceedings. The system will propagate the annotations to similar fields in each record automatically, for example all authors of a publication.

Once an example has been annotated, the user can start the extraction process. Data records are matched based on a similarity metric that takes both structural and visual cues into account. Moreover, the annotations get propagated to all records and all similar fields that have been matched, within and across different records. The system dynamically highlights records in the page as the matching process proceeds so users can see results produced in real-time. Elements labelled by the system are underlined in green and the user can check these by hovering over the element to display the propagated label. This enables the user to quickly evaluate the quality of the matching process. If the results show the matching process has had limited success, they can stop the process and either adjust threshold parameters or annotate a second example before restarting the extraction process. The three thresholds used in our algorithms will be explained in Sect. 4 where we describe the matching process in detail. For users who do not have a good understanding of the algorithm and the effect of these thresholds, they can easily experiment with different values on the sliders based on some general help guidelines.

In Sect. 4, we also explain in detail why a single example may not be sufficient to produce good results in some cases and how specifying a second example can significantly improve the quality of the matches.

Users can also control the use of CSS caching techniques that we introduced to boost the speed of the matching algorithm. When CSS caching is active, a DOM element will be decorated with an object representing its entire processed CSS style when the system first wants to find the style applied to that element rather than going through the browser and rebuilding it on each access. While this significantly improves the speed of the matching process, it can reduce the reliability of results in pages where JavaScript or CSS animations alter the visual properties. There is therefore a performance trade-off between speed and reliability and users have the option to disable caching before re-running the extraction process if the results generated do not meet expectations.

Once the extraction process is complete, the user can select what to do with the extracted data records. DeepDesign provides a storage area in the browser where records can be saved. The basic options are to store the records in the extracted format or send these to a web application using a message-based system that allows Chrome extensions to send content to any web page that is open. The web application might process the data directly or map it to another format before storing it. In this way, users can open another web application and send the matched records to it by reading them from the storage area in which they were saved. Additionally, the control panel allows the JSON representation of the matched records to be obtained which can then be read from external applications. In the case of the first scenario presented in the introduction, the external application could store it in the user's personal library of data gathered from

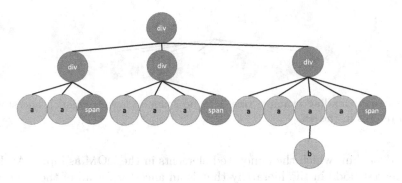

Fig. 2. A tree representing a list of some example publications.

websites. For the second scenario where data is extracted from a digital mockup as part of the process of developing a website, an external application could, for example, generate custom post types for the WordPress platform based on the schema of the extracted data as described in [6]. In the latter case, populating instances of those custom post types with the actual data used in the mockup and extracted by DeepDesign would be optional. The control panel interface to DeepDesign was implemented using HTML, CSS and JavaScript since Chrome allows extensions to have web-based interfaces that can communicate with the tool being executed in the page through message-based communication.

4   Matching Algorithm

The matching algorithm uses structural as well as visual cues. The input elements are the annotated fields of an example data record as discussed in the previous section and the DOM of the web page as well as the set of tuning parameters which we explain in detail later in this section. To explain how the algorithm works, we will use the example in Fig. 2 which represents a possible DOM for a list of publications similar to that shown in Fig. 1. The anchor elements, a, represent authors and link to their individual web pages. The span elements include the titles of the publications. We will assume that the only annotations provided initially by the user are the label *"author"* for the first anchor to the left, and the label *"title"* for the first span element.

Our algorithm works in four steps. We first aim to detect the boundaries of the annotated record, then look for subtrees with a similar structure in the page. Once these have been found, we propagate the labels from the example record to each of the matched records and then propagate them locally within the records. This means that the author and title labels of our example would be propagated to an author and title of all subtrees before detecting the co-authors within each record in a second step and propagating the author label to them. We will now discuss the details for each of these steps.

1. Record Boundaries Detection. The algorithm starts by detecting the boundaries of the annotated example record using a lowest common ancestor

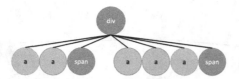

Fig. 3. A corresponding example tree with no common lowest common ancestor for the two records in the list.

(LCA) algorithm, which the annotated elements in the DOM as input. An LCA is the nearest node in the hierarchy that is an ancestor for all of the annotated elements. In Fig. 2, this corresponds to the first of the three div elements which is on the left branch and wraps the first publication.

However, this cannot always be guaranteed. There are cases where the records are siblings of the same parent, such as the example presented in Fig. 3. Here, the two publications are not wrapped by an LCA. First of all, we need to be able to detect such a case and, second, we have to be able to identify the record boundaries once such a case has been detected. This is an example where it is necessary for the user to provide two examples in order to detect that such a situation occurs and be able to demarcate records. The LCA of both records will be the same node, namely the one enclosing the entire list of records, which we will call $L2$. In Fig. 3, $L2$ would be the div element enclosing the two publications. Once we have detected such a situation, we can trigger our fault correction. Since there should be exactly one LCA per record, we need to locate the first and last nodes in the children of $L2$, which act as delimiters for the first data record. To do so, we traverse the elements of the first annotated example and their parents up to $L2$ and assign them a specific marker. Then the children of $L2$ are re-examined knowing what the start and end of a record look like from the perspective of its children. This is necessary because it is possible that the annotated elements are not direct children of $L2$. In the example of Fig. 3, it would be clear based on two examples that the first a element is the start of the first example annotated by the user and the first span element is the end of that record since they are direct children.

Making the assumption that all records start and end in the same way, we look for similar nodes among the children of $L2$ so we can find the boundaries of all records. The similarity is assessed according to the distance function $dist(x, y)$ which is a weighted sum of various distances, the style distance ratio Δ_s; the tree edit distance, the ratio between the length of the longest common subsequence in the text of nodes and their maximum length, and finally the Levenshtein distance [20] between the XPaths of the two elements. The style distance ratio is defined as:

$$\Delta_s = \frac{\Delta_{css}}{max(\Delta_{css} + S, 1)}$$

where Δ_{css} is the number of CSS rules which differ between the two elements being considered, and S is the number of CSS rules which are similar. The style distance ratio Δ_s is also used in the later step of local label propagation. To achieve the maximum reliability of this measurement, the CSS rules for the two elements being compared are retrieved from the computed style, which returns all the CSS properties, including the non-standard ones computed by the browser for each DOM element. The tree-edit distance instead is calculated through an approximation algorithm called pq-gram distance [21].

Once we have found candidates close enough to be matched with the start and end of the example record, respectively, we process these candidates to mark them as boundaries of records, enclosing them with a wrapper node which provides an LCA in cases where none is present.

2. Finding Similar Records. After the boundaries of the example record have been found, we have a DOM subtree similar to all other data records of the same type present in the page. To allow for variability across data records, we rely on the approximated tree edit distance provided by the pq-gram distance. To consider records as candidates, their distance has to be smaller than a threshold called the *tolerance factor*. This is the first of the thresholds that can be specified in the control panel of DeepDesign. At this stage, the middle and the right branch of Fig. 2 would be detected as possible candidates for record matching.

Up to this point, there is no information about the internal fields of the newly detected data records. For this reason, we now need to propagate user annotations automatically to the matched records.

3. Cross-Record Propagation. In general, this step aims at locating the elements that correspond to those annotated by the user in each of the matched data records. Once these have been located, the corresponding annotations can be migrated from the original example record to all of the matched records.

We introduce an intermediate step of candidate detection for each label, and a candidate selection step among those previously found. Candidate detection and selection make extensive use of visual cues, content-based measurements and structural analysis to ensure that only the most suitable nodes are considered for cross-record propagation. In our previous work [6], we addressed this step using an XPath-based approach where, for each annotation, we inferred the XPath of an annotated element relative to a data record, and accessed the corresponding element in each candidate data record. While this tree-to-tree mapping of XPaths is a fallback technique when not enough labels could be propagated with the candidate detection, this implementation assumes a regularity of record structures that is not always present in practice. For example, in the case of publications, fields can be optional and even variable in structure. We therefore decided on an alternative approach that could cope with record-related peculiarities that impact on the DOM structure and/or order of elements and could lead to faulty cross-record propagation.

We introduced a candidate detection step that locates which elements of the subtree are the best matches for an annotated element. This step starts by looking for all the elements in the local subtree, filtering out the non visible ones. For each label, the algorithm computes a list of candidates with the closest distance from the originally annotated element according to the previously presented distance function $dist(x, y)$. For text nodes, since visual cues can be fewer, also the text and style similarities of the surrounding elements is considered.

Since multiple elements can have the same distance from the originally labelled one, the candidate detection step returns, for each label annotation, at most three sets of elements in the current subtree with the lowest distances to the labelled element in the example record. Thus, we obtain sets of candidate elements for each label, together with the corresponding distance from the original annotated element, that are good candidates for the cross-record propagation of that label. However, various issues can still affect these candidate elements. It is possible that some of these are ancestors or parents of other elements in the list. Even worse, it could be possible that some elements appear in more than one set, being a candidate for different labels, possibly with different distances. This is likely to happen when there are elements which should be assigned different labels, but have a very small difference in visual styling.

To tackle these two issues, we first perform a cleaning step to remove ancestors from the list of candidates. We decorate each possible parent of all candidate elements with a specific marker and, after all elements of the list have been processed, remove marked elements from the list.

After the cleaning step, we select a single element from each of the candidate lists to be associated with the corresponding label. Note that, since an element can appear in more than one candidate list, it is actually possible that all the candidate lists contain the same elements, which means that we may not be able to propagate some of the labels if there are more labels than elements.

Our goal is to minimise the sum of the distances of the elements selected from the sets, while maximising the number of sets from which a candidate is picked. We call this problem *LABEL-ASSIGN*, and have found it easily convertible to the *minimum weighted maximum independent set* problem. We will provide more information on the rationale and conversion in Sect. 5. Based on previous research [22], we have implemented a greedy algorithm that returns an approximated solution.

The algorithm starts by building a list E of objects for all the nodes from the candidate lists associated with their label and distance. It first sorts them in ascending order according to the following function, as proposed by Sakai et al. [22]: $f(e) = W(e)/[O(e) + 1]$ where $W(e)$ is the distance of the element e and $O(e)$ is its number of occurrences in the candidate lists S_i.

It then builds a map of solutions that associates a label to an element from the candidates, iterating the following: The first element in the list E is selected as part of the solution, with its label as key and the node as a value, and is removed from E. At this stage, all the elements that belonged to the same set, as well as those from other sets that are competing for the same label, are removed from E together with all the other occurrences of the selected element. The current element is also removed from all the other candidate lists in which it appears. Now the element list E is again sorted and the loop repeated until there are no more candidates.

At the end of this stage, we have a map that associates an annotation label to one DOM element of the current record's subtree. We also know which distances each element in the map had. We discard the record if the average distance between all the selected elements and the corresponding ones in the original example is above a threshold, or if we have matched a number of labels which is smaller than the 66 % of the total amount of labels in the original example. However, the user can modify these values via the control panel. The optionality parameter which has the default setting of 66 % allows for records with optional fields. If records have optional fields, it could cause the algorithm to mistakenly discard fully matched records because these records lack optional attributes that the user annotated in the example. In general, the optionality parameter allows the system to be tuned to deal with the variability that may be present in records due to optional fields as well as controlling how strict the system should be about the possibility of false positives since it forces the algorithm to only accept records which have a higher number of assigned labels.

4. Local Label Propagation. The next step is to replicate the labels to all of the elements within a matched data record with a similar meaning, for example all authors of a publication. Consider our example where, so far, only one of the anchor tags in both the second and third branch of the tree in Fig. 2 would have been selected as an author. We want to propagate this label to the other elements that also represent authors within the respective subtrees. To do so, we take all the visible descendants d of the record node with the same tag name (for example `div`) and all of the node's visible children that do not contain any d. Using agglomerative hierarchical clustering, we group these descendants of the record node according to a *distance function*. As a stopping criterion for the hierarchical clustering, we check the distance between the clusters against a threshold called the *grouping factor*. This is the second threshold bar that can be configured by the user in the control panel. The clustering distance function takes into consideration various factors, which can be both visual and structural cues. The structural cues currently considered are: the tag equality, the *style distance ratio* mentioned in the previous stage, and two discontinuity scores, namely the structural tag discontinuity and the field discontinuity score. The former increases as the elements are further away (separated by elements of different tags), while the latter increases as the elements between those being compared received a different label from the previous step. While the tag equality is trivial to understand and the style distance ratio has already been presented, the two discontinuity scores accommodate arbitrary scenarios in subtrees, and therefore deserve some more explanation. All subtree elements are projected into a linear vector in the order in which they appear in the document, starting from the root of the record. In this linear vector, all elements will be compared in their contiguity for each individual contiguity function. Sequences of different types of elements between two compared elements over this line will increase their structural tag discontinuity, while sequences of elements with different *assigned* labels will increase the field discontinuity. The reason why we need the distinction of assigned labels is that many nodes in each record subtree may not be selected for the cross-record propagation step, and therefore their label may be undefined. These nodes do not contribute to discontinuity in the context of record fields.

Once the two discontinuities have been summed up, we divide them by the maximum depth of the record subtree to mitigate the effect of the projection on a linear vector. As a result, the elements which are considered to be similar in structural and visual terms, or which happen to be presented in a contiguous fashion, will be put into the same cluster. Majority voting is used to decide which label should be applied to each cluster and it is then applied to all elements of the cluster.

5 Implementation Challenges

Implementing the DeepDesign tool using only web technologies introduced a number of challenges arising from both the technical limitations of the technologies and the complexity of the problems to be solved in the different steps of the algorithm. For example, browsers still do not offer a way to retrieve which rules from the stylesheets apply to an element. Although there are libraries to do so, they require expensive processing and cannot be used for complex computations.

Also, improving the runtime of the algorithm through parallelisation is very hard since the JavaScript Web Workers do not allow parallel access to the DOM, which is required in our case at every step.

Another challenge is the cross-record propagation step described in Sect. 4, where our tool needs to solve the *LABEL-ASSIGN* problem. We used an algorithm for *minimum-weighted maximum independent set* (*mWMIS*). This means having to convert instances of *LABEL-ASSIGN* into instances of *mWMIS* by building a graph G in such a way that, for every element in every candidate set, we create a node in the graph. If an element appears in more than one candidate set, we still add a different node to the graph. Every node corresponding to an element in a candidate set is connected to every other node from the same candidate set, meaning that they are in a clique. The clique also includes all elements from other candidate sets with the same label. Moreover, if an element appears in more than one candidate set, all the other nodes corresponding to that element need to be connected. Finally, the weights to the elements are the distances with which their set has been labelled.

Now let S be a solution for the *LABEL-ASSIGN* problem where its elements maximise the number of candidate sets covered and are those of minimum weight. Given how the graph has been constructed and the constraint that an element can only be picked once from any set and any label, S will be an independent set, and the nodes in S are those that make it of minimum weight. Conversely, let S now be a maximum independent set of minimum weight. Then we can pick the corresponding elements in the candidate sets, having guaranteed that at most one element per set is selected, and the element is not selected in more than one set. Since S had minimum weight, and weights are the same as in the instance of *LABEL-ASSIGN*, we will also have the minimum-weighted solution in this case. Unfortunately, for the *minimum weighted maximum independent set*, we cannot have an approximated algorithm within a ratio independently from the weights, unless $P = NP$ [23]. Therefore we have chosen a greedy algorithm for deriving the *minimum-weighted maximum independent set* proposed in previous research that tries to approximate within a ratio that is dependent on the weights [22]. Finally, the cross-propagation algorithm was designed to find the solution with the smallest distance from the annotated elements, while maximising the number of labels that can be assigned in order to minimise the chance of having false negatives. This can however increase the occurrence of errors in the case where there is a high chance that some of the fields will be missing in the records to be detected. If the visual or structural differences between these fields according to $dist(x, y)$ is very low, it could happen that the LABEL-ASSIGN prefers to assign a label to the wrong element rather than keeping it unassigned. This can especially occur with pure text nodes which, having less styling information than usual elements, can more easily be marked as a candidate for the wrong label.

6   Evaluation

We have performed a preliminary evaluation of DeepDesign. To make sure that there was no bias in the websites and content used in the evaluation, we decided to base it on the top ten websites in the Alexa ranking[4]. Note that since Google occupied both positions 1 and 10 (with its Indian version), we selected the eleventh in the ranking as a replacement for the tenth. For each selected website, we identified the most important content to retrieve independent of whether it was statically or dynamically loaded. The pages used in this dataset contained a total of 212 records. We performed multiple labelling operations on different pages of each website, trying to capture different data elements that the website could offer in different HTML structures. For the sake of space we provide all the details on the labelling operations and the dataset in an archive.[5]

We selected four evaluation metrics: the *time* elapsed to perform the automatic matching expressed in seconds, the number of misplaced labels (labelling errors), the *precision* and *recall* over the dataset, and the *precision* and *recall* where partial matches are counted as positives. By partial matches, we refer to data records which were extracted by DeepDesign, but with some repeating fields not completely propagated. The tests were run on an i7-4770 with 16 GB of RAM using Chrome 45. The use of the matching tool involves two main factors: the tolerance factor and the grouping factor. The former acts as a threshold for the pq-gram approximation algorithm, while the latter acts as threshold for the hierarchical clustering, considering two clusters 'far enough' when their distance is above the grouping factor. This means that the higher these two thresholds are, the more expensive the computation will be. For example, setting a tolerance factor of 1.0 implies considering any element in the DOM tree as a possible candidate record since 1.0 is the highest possible distance provided by the implementation of the pq-gram approximation[6]. Thus, the only way these can be discarded is if the cross-record propagation fails to propagate

[4] http://www.alexa.com/topsites - 15.10.2015.

[5] http://dev.globis.ethz.ch/deepdesign/DDpreliminaryeval.zip.

[6] https://github.com/hoonto/jqgram - 15.10.2015.

Website	Pos.	T (sec)	TF	GF	TR	MR	PMR	LE	FP	FN	TM	Prec.	Prec.(PM)	Recall	Recall (P.M.)	TMR	DOM
Google	1	0.46	0.8	0.5	9	9	0	0	0	0	9	1		1		9	946
Facebook	2	4.2	0.95	0.5	8	5	0	4	0	3	5	1		0.625	0.625	5	3839
Youtube#1	3	1.6	0.75	0.5	15	15	0	0	0	0	15	1		1		15	2349
Youtube#2	3	6.4	0.8	0.1	27	27	0	0	51	0	78	0.34615	0.346154	1		27	5278
Baidu	4	1.6	0.9	0.65	9	7	2	2	1	0	10	0.7	0.9	0.778		9	747
Yahoo	5	1	0.65	0.5	20	19	1	1	0	0	20	0.95		0.95		20	1790
Amazon	6	5.7	1	0.2	16	7	9	8	0	0	16	0.4375		0.438		16	4076
Wikpedia	7	0.1	1	0.5	19	19	0	0	0	0	19	1		1		19	970
qq	8	1.3	0.95	2.5	22	17	2	0	0	1	19	0.89474		0.85	0.95	19	2435
Twitter	9	3.52	0.9	0.15	19	19	0	0	0	0	19	1		1		19	4201
Taobao	11	4.7	0.55	0.5	48	48	0	0	0	0	48	1		1		48	3062

Pos. - Position in the alexa ranking PMR - Partially Matched Records Prec. - Precision   TM - Total Matches
T - Time elapsed (sec)   P.M. - including Partial Matches FP - False Positives DOM - Size of DOM
TF - Tolerance factor   TMR - Total Matched Records   FN - False Negatives
GF - Grouping factor
TR - Total Records
MR - Matched Records
LE - Labeling errors

	Dataset 1 (Alexa)		Dataset 2	DeepDesign	RoadRunner
Precision	0.85				
Precision PM	0.93		Precision	0.92	0.67
Recall	0.88		Recall	0.98	0.6
Recall PM	0.96				

Fig. 4. Results of the evaluations. At the top we see detailed results from the websites from Alexa (Dataset 1). In the bottom-right corner, aggregated results are shown from both datasets.

labels to their descendants. Setting the grouping factor value too high instead forces the algorithm to go through more clustering procedures, implying more calls to the clustering distance function. Moreover, the DOM structure of each site will have an impact on the overall processing time. In Fig. 4, we report the size of the DOM of each web page used in our tests.

The evaluation for each site involved the following steps:

1. Identification of the data records in the page.
2. Labelling the fields of an example record.
3. Activation of data record matching.
4. Check against the number of examples: If every data record that we expected to match was not successfully matched, we would raise the tolerance or the grouping factors to repeat the matching.

We show the data collected during the evaluation in Fig. 4. For YouTube, we showcase two different relevant results, which involved different matching processes. The two sessions on YouTube were performed to extract video details from the subscription feed (#1) and from the "Advertised videos" (#2).

The median time for execution was 1.6 s. For some pages, the processing took considerably longer: YouTube #2 (6.4 s), Facebook (4.2 s), Taobao (4.7 s) and Amazon (5.7 s). However, it is important to note that the count of the elements in the DOM and the tolerance factor for these matchings were rather high. In the case of Facebook, this can probably be related to the high variability between different posts which can include link sharings, videos or status updates.

As true positives for our tool, we only considered those matches whose label assignment was handled correctly. If any element that should have received a label was assigned a different one or none, we considered them as partially matched. On the other hand, any element that should not have been assigned a label but was assigned one is considered a labelling error if the rest of the record was correctly matched. The average precision without taking into account any partial matches was 0.85 (std. dev. 0.23), while it increases to 0.93 (std. dev. 0.18) if we consider partial matches. This is a good result, with one outlier in YouTube #2, where the tool matched 51 data records which were considered false positives, even though these were not visible on the screen. However, since these were indeed matched by the tool, even if they were not visible, they have to be taken into account. The average recall without taking partial matches into account is 0.88 (std. dev. 0.18), while the average with partial matches is slightly higher at 0.96 (std. dev. 0.11). The worst results were seen on YouTube #2 (51 false positives out of 27 total records to match). In all of the experiments, there were a total of 15 labelling errors, which include labels placed on elements that should not have been considered, giving 0.07 labelling errors per correctly matched data record. The fact that the tolerance factor needed to be high in the majority of the captures ($TF > 0.75$) might mean that the current implementation would benefit from an improvement in the subtree matching phase, with an algorithm that could potentially better discriminate between different subtrees. However, due to the constraints in the label propagation step explained in Sect. 4, the overall algorithm is still robust and offers good precision most of the time, especially when considering partial matches. Partial matches occur in four cases: Yahoo, Baidu, Amazon, and qq.com. Having partial matches can mean that the cross-record propagation step has failed to identify the best candidate element to migrate its label, or that the clustering phase has failed to group all of the similar fields together, for example all the authors within a publication.

We ran a second evaluation to compare DeepDesign against a tool from previous work. Although quite an old system, we chose RoadRunner [9] in our comparative evaluation since, to the best of our knowledge, it is the only tool from previous research that is still available for download. For the comparison, we decided to collect a set of pages that mixed different design practices so there was not an unfair bias towards DeepDesign which was designed to cater for modern designs. For this reason, we collected a set of 10 pages from 10 different websites which cover quite different design structures. Some of them have a table-based layout and some involve structures where the records do not have their own LCA. This dataset included a total of 223 records. It has to be noted that RoadRunner works at the page level so, in order to be able to feed the 10 pages to RoadRunner, we had to manually split each page to make them contain exactly one record per page. Another task that was handled manually (and therefore can be prone to error) was the configuration of RoadRunner, which involved an XML tool that allows many parameters to be specified to fine tune the extraction process. RoadRunner does not perform a record detection step since the records are already split across pages. We therefore compare only the quality of the alignment process, which in our tool is handled by the cross-record propagation and local-label propagation steps. Therefore, the granularity of this second evaluation is not at the record level, but at the field level. After manually establishing the ground truth, we recorded the number of correctly separated fields by the two tools, together with the false positives and false negatives. As shown in Fig. 4, RoadRunner achieved 67 % precision and 60 % recall, with DeepDesign achieving better performance with 92 % precision and 98 % recall. However, RoadRunner was much faster, always completing the extraction process in less than a second, whereas DeepDesign has a median time of 6.3 s and a very high average running time of 14.2 s due to three pages of the dataset where the runtime reached approximately 14, 17 and 23 s, respectively. In two of these pages, records did not have an LCA and so required the additional processing for this case described in Sect. 4. Note that the times reported only include the execution of the algorithm and not the time for labelling. In the last case, each record had a unique LCA, but our hypothesis is that, since the records had very long text descriptions, the analysis of these descriptions for the cross-propagation step required a much longer time. It is important to note that while these are both systems for data extraction, the tools were designed to be used in different ways and hence the difference in runtimes was expected. Road-Runner is a system that runs as a batch algorithm with a list of input files and it visualises the results only at the end. DeepDesign extracts data while browsing, incrementally showing the matched results while the process is running by using the rendering engine of the browser to dynamically update the page.

7   Conclusion

We have presented DeepDesign, a tool for extracting data from web pages while browsing. Users guide the extraction process by performing a minimal labelling of fields within an example record and can fine tune the process as it runs based on an incremental, real-time visualisation of results. The evaluations performed are very encouraging and we plan to integrate it in a system that supports the development of websites based on digital mockups in order to carry out studies with developers and end-users. We have also started working on support for the detection of complex schema structures that involve relationships or aggregations over the data. Additionally, we are considering ad-hoc formulations of the tree-edit distance problem that can allow for more variability in the subtrees of data records. Finally, we plan to improve the support for HTML text nodes.

References

1. Zheng, S., Song, R., Wen, J., Giles, C.L.: Efficient record-level wrapper induction. In: Proceedings of the 18th ACM Conference on Information and Knowledge Management. ACM (2009)
2. Liu, W., Meng, X., Meng, W.: Vision-based web data records extraction. In: Proceedings 9th International Workshop on the Web and Databases (2006)
3. Manabe, T., Tajima, K.: Extracting logical hierarchical structure of HTML documents based on headings. Proc. VLDB Endowment 8(12), 1606–1617 (2015)
4. Pembe, F., Canan, F., Güngör, T.: A tree learning approach to web document sectional hierarchy extraction. In: Proceedings of the 2nd International Conference on Agents and Artificial Intelligence (2010)

5. Geel, M., Church, T., Norrie, M.C.: Sift: an end-user tool for gathering web content on the go. In: Proceedings of the 2012 ACM Symposium on Document Engineering, pp. 181–190. ACM (2012)
6. Murolo, A., Norrie, M.C.: Deriving custom post types from digital mockups. In: Cimiano, P., Frasincar, F., Houben, G.-J., Schwabe, D. (eds.) ICWE 2015. LNCS, vol. 9114, pp. 71–80. Springer, Heidelberg (2015)
7. Chang, C., Kayed, M., Girgis, M.R., Shaalan, K.F.: A survey of web information extraction systems. IEEE Trans. Knowl. Data Eng. 18(10), 1411–1428 (2006)
8. Adelberg, B.: NoDoSE a tool for semi-automatically extracting structured and semistructured data from text documents. In: Proceedings of the 9th ACM SIG-MOD International Conference on Management of Data (SIGMOD). ACM (1998)
9. Crescenzi, V., Mecca, G., Merialdo, P.: Roadrunner: towards automatic data extraction from large web sites. In: Proceedings of the 27th International Conference on Very Large Data Bases (VLDB). Morgan Kaufmann (2001)
10. Chang, C., Lui, S.: IEPAD: information extraction based on pattern discovery. In: Proceedings of the 10th International Conference on World Wide Web (WWW). ACM (2001)
11. Wang, J., Lochovsky, F.H.: Data extraction and label assignment for web databases. In: Proceedings of the 12th International Conference on World Wide Web (WWW). ACM (2003)
12. Zhai, Y., Liu, B.: Structured data extraction from the web based on partial tree alignment. IEEE Trans. Knowl. Data Eng. 18(12), 1614–1628 (2006)
13. Lu, Y., He, H., Zhao, H., Meng, W., Yu, C.: Annotating search results from web databases. IEEE Trans. Knowl. Data Eng. 25(3), 514–527 (2013)
14. Zhao, H., Meng, W., Wu, Z., Raghavan, V., Yu, C.: Fully automatic wrapper generation for search engines. In: Proceedings of the 14th International Conference on World Wide Web. ACM (2005)
15. Hong, J.L., Siew, E., Egerton, S.: ViWER-Data extraction for search engine results pages using visual cue and dom tree. In: Proceedings of the 1st International Conference on Information Retrieval & Knowledge Management (CAMP). IEEE (2010)
16. Liu, W., Meng, X., Meng, W.: Vide: a vision-based approach for deep web data extraction. IEEE Trans. Knowl. Data Eng. 22(3), 447–460 (2010)
17. Laender, A.H., Ribeiro-Neto, B., da Silva, A.S.: DEByE - data extraction by example. Data Knowl. Eng. 40(2), 121–154 (2002)
18. Chang, C., Kuo, S.: OLERA: semisupervised web-data extraction with visual support. IEEE Intell. Syst. 19(6), 56–64 (2004)
19. Hogue, A., Karger, D.: Thresher: automating the unwrapping of semantic content from the world wide web. In: Proceedings of the 14th International Conference on World Wide Web. ACM (2005)
20. Levenshtein, V.: Binary codes capable of correcting deletions, insertions, and reversals. Sov. Phys. Dokl. 10, 707–710 (1966)
21. Augsten, N., Böhlen, M., Gamper, J.: Approximate matching of hierarchical data using Pq-Grams. In: Proceedings of the 31st International Conference on Very Large Data Bases (VLDB), VLDB Endowment (2005)
22. Sakai, S., Togasaki, M., Yamazaki, K.: A note on greedy algorithms for the maximum weighted independent set problem. Discrete Appl. Math. 126(2), 313–322 (2003)
23. Demange, M.: A note on the approximation of a minimum-weight maximal independent set. Comput. Optim. Appl. 14(1), 157–169 (1999)

Clustering-Aided Page Object Generation
for Web Testing

Andrea Stocco[1(✉)], Maurizio Leotta[1], Filippo Ricca[1], and Paolo Tonella[2]

[1] DIBRIS – Università di Genova, Genova, Italy
andrea.stocco@dibris.unige.it, {maurizio.leotta,filippo.ricca}@unige.it
[2] Fondazione Bruno Kessler, Trento, Italy
tonella@fbk.eu

Abstract. To decouple test code from web page details, web testers adopt the *Page Object* design pattern. Page objects are facade classes abstracting the internals of web pages (e.g., form fields) into high-level business functions that can be invoked by test cases (e.g., user authentication). However, writing such page objects requires substantial effort, which is paid off only later, during software evolution. In this paper we propose a clustering-based approach for the identification of meaningful abstractions that are automatically turned into Java page objects. Our clustering approach to page object identification has been integrated into our tool for automated page object generation, APOGEN. Experimental results indicate that the clustering approach provides clusters of web pages close to those manually produced by a human (with, on average, only three differences per web application). 75 % of the code generated by APOGEN can be used as-is by web testers, breaking down the manual effort for page object creation. Moreover, a large portion (84 %) of the page object methods created automatically to support assertion definition corresponds to useful behavioural abstractions.

1 Introduction

Web applications are among the most challenging software systems to test [27]. On one side, developing web applications is becoming easier thanks to recent frameworks (e.g., AngularJS[1]), which hide the complexity behind an expressive and readable web programming environment, and allow even newbie programmers to quickly develop highly interactive and complex applications. On the other hand, this comes at a price, because the programmers' inexperience with error-prone languages like Javascript, and the combination of new technologies may introduce new kinds of faults, which have unpredictable effects and are hard to detect [18].

End-to-end (E2E) test automation is commonly adopted in such context, often justified by continuous integration and test driven approaches. Test scripts simulate typical end-users' interactions by delivering mouse clicks and keystrokes

---

[1] https://angularjs.org/.

© Springer International Publishing Switzerland 2016
A. Bozzon et al. (Eds.): ICWE 2016, LNCS 9671, pp. 132–151, 2016.
DOI: 10.1007/978-3-319-38791-8_8

to the browser at a pace that would be likely infeasible to perform manually. The GUI responses are recorded and validated through assertions to check the web application for functional correctness.

A disadvantage of test automation is the poor maintainability of the test code throughout the development process. In fact, test scripts are often highly customised and coupled with the technical details of the underlying web pages, which make them quite difficult to read and maintain when features are added or altered in the web application under test. Web testers try to prevent these issues by using the *Page Object* design pattern, which provides a simplified interface towards the web application. All the technicalities the test scripts refer to, such as low-level operations or web elements locators (e.g., an XPath to select an input field [14]), are moved to the page objects. The test code is thus separated from the implementation details, because test scripts interface with page objects methods, rather than directly with web page elements.

Building page objects for web applications is an activity which is performed manually [25]. Our prototype tool APOGEN [24] is the first solution able to provide a considerable degree of automation, hence reducing the effort for the creation of page objects. However, the initial version of APOGEN [25] suffered two major limitations: (1) in the presence of highly dynamic web pages, it creates a huge number of page objects that should be conceptually regarded as a single page object; (2) it does not support the creation of getter methods in any way. A getter method retrieves textual portions of a web page that can be used to verify the behaviour of the web application (e.g., with assertions) through the results displayed to the user.

In this paper, we overcome such limitations with the following novel contributions, implemented in the new version of the tool APOGEN:

- the automatic detection of cloned and semantically similar web pages, based on clustering, to be associated with the same page object;
- the Cluster Visual Editor (CVE), a web-based interactive cluster visualiser and editor, allowing the tester to inspect and modify the clustering results;
- the automatic creation of page object getter methods, capable of detecting and reporting Document Object Model (DOM) differences observed between web pages within the same cluster.

We have applied APOGEN to six web applications and we have studied how different clustering algorithms, working on different syntactic features (e.g., DOM), are able to group similar web pages that should be conceptually mapped onto a single page object. Our results indicate that: (1) hierarchical clustering provides clusters of web pages close to those manually produced by a human, (2) 75 % of the code generated by APOGEN can be used as-is by the tester, reducing the manual effort for page object creation and (3) 84 % of the automatically generated getter methods correspond to methods the tester needs when creating test case assertions.

The paper is organised as follows: Sect. 2 provides some background on the *Page Object* design pattern, our original tool APOGEN, and the challenges in the automatic creation of page objects for web applications. Section 3 describes

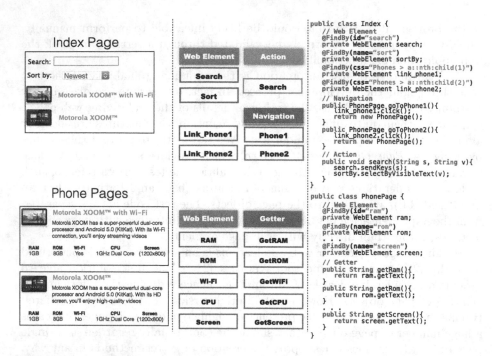

Fig. 1. AngularJS Phonecat web application **(left)**, with its abstract representation in terms of Web Elements and Functionalities (Navigations, Actions, Getters) **(center)**, and associated Java page objects **(right)**

the clustering-aided version of APOGEN and the features we evaluated in our experiment. Section 4 presents the quantitative and qualitative results of the experiment we conducted to evaluate the effectiveness of our approach. Section 5 describes the related work, while conclusions and future work are drawn in Sect. 6.

2   Background

In web development, E2E functional testing is a widely adopted practice thanks to the increased popularity of powerful test automation tools, such as Selenium[2]. Automated tests created with these tools operate by instructing a browser to click or type on page elements. Whereas the biggest advantage is an accurate simulation of the user's behaviour, one of the major drawbacks is that such tests tend to be fragile and highly coupled with the web pages. To prevent this, testers use the *Page Object* design pattern.

A page object is a class that abstracts a web page hiding the technical details about how the test code interacts with the underlying web page behind a more readable and business-focused facade. This brings two main advantages: (i) tests

---

[2] http://www.seleniumhq.org/.

```
1  public class TestAddOwnerWithoutPageObjects {          1  public class TestAddOwnerWithPageObjects {
2    @Test                                                 2    @Test
3    public void testAddOwner(){                           3    public void testAddOwner(){
4      WebDriver driver = new FirefoxDriver();             4      WebDriver driver = new FirefoxDriver();
5      driver.get("http://localhost:8080/phonecat/");      5      driver.get("http://localhost:8080/phonecat/");
6      driver.findElement(By.id("sort")).selectByVisibleText("Newest");   6      Index indexPage = new Index(driver);
7      driver.findElement(By.id("search")).sendKeys("Motorola");          7      indexPage.search("Motorola", "Newest");
8      driver.findElement(By.css("Phones > a::nth:child(1)")).click();    8      PhonePage phone1 = indexPage.goToPhone1();
9      AssertThat(driver.findElement(By.css("#ram")).getText(), is("1 GB"));   9      AssertThat(phone1.getRam(), is("1 GB"));
10     AssertThat(driver.findElement(By.css("#rom")).getText(), is("8 GB"));   10     AssertThat(phone1.getRom(), is("8 GB"));
11     AssertThat(driver.findElement(By.css("#wifi")).getText(), is("Yes"));   11     AssertThat(phone1.getScreen(), is("Yes"));
12     driver.quit();                                      12     driver.quit();
    }}                                                         }}
```

Fig. 2. Two test cases created to test the Add Owner functionality of PETCLINIC. On the left is the test code without the adoption of page objects, whereas on the right is the same test case, using the automatic page objects generated by APOGEN

are more readable, and (ii) the page access logic is centralised in one place, making test suite maintenance easier [9,10].

Let us consider the running example in Fig. 1, based on the AngularJS Phonecat web application[3], one of the experimental objects considered in this work. On the top-left part there is the home page, displaying a list of phones (we limited the figure to two), whereas in the bottom-left part are shown the web pages obtained after clicking on the links in the home page. In the central part there are the web page abstractions that the page objects should provide, showing the web elements test cases may interact with, and the functionalities the two pages offer (action, navigation, and getter functionalities). The right part shows the page object representations of such pages, written in Java. We can notice how the two web pages displaying phone details for two phones (bottom-center part) have exactly the same abstract representation: only their textual content varies. Correspondingly, only one Java page object can represent both of them (class *PhonePage*, bottom-right).

In Fig. 2 we can see an example of how page objects improve the readability of the test cases by encapsulating functionalities. The test steps shown on the left (without page objects) are directly coupled with the web page internals, while the steps on the right (with page objects) map directly to human-readable, use case scenario's steps (e.g., open the index page, go to the first phone page, etc.).

2.1 First Steps in the Automatic Generation of Page Objects

Our tool APOGEN is the first effective prototype able to generate automatically a set of page objects for a web application. APOGEN consists of three main modules: a Crawler, a Static Analyser, and a Code Generator. The input is a web application, together with the data (e.g., login credentials) required to navigate it. The output is a set of Java files, representing a code abstraction of the web application, organised using the *Page Object* and *Page Factory*[4] design patterns, as supported by the Selenium WebDriver framework.

---

[3] https://github.com/angular/angular-phonecat/.
[4] https://code.google.com/p/selenium/wiki/PageFactory.

The Crawler generates a state-based model (graph) of the web application, in which nodes are dynamic states of the web pages and edges are event-based transitions between nodes. In particular, we use Crawljax [17], a state of the art open source Java tool for automatically crawling highly-dynamic web applications. The Static Analyser of APOGEN takes the Crawler outputs and for each dynamic state builds an abstract state object-based representation. The graph and the DOMs are parsed to collect the necessary information for building comprehensive and readable classes. The class name is generated from the URL, whereas the web elements stimulated by the Crawler are inserted as WebElement instances in the page object class. For each of them, a meaningful variable name and a locator (XPath or CSS) are generated. For what concerns the methods, each transition in the graph is turned into a navigational method between pages, and every data-submitting form is parsed to acquire information about its web elements and the associated functionality. The output of the Static Analyser is an abstract representation of the web pages and their interactions. In the last step, the Code Generator transforms such model into a set of Java page objects, tailored for the Selenium WebDriver framework.

2.2 Major Limitations

While experimenting with the initial version of APOGEN, we noticed two major issues that limit its applicability [25]. The *first issue* depends on the default state abstraction of the Crawler, which is affected by minor UI changes. Indeed, Crawljax was designed to perform an extensive exploration and when it visits the same page filled with different input data, it often creates different dynamic states, even though the page is conceptually the same. We refer to these duplicate pages as "clones" (e.g., the two phone detail pages of the running example of Fig. 1 bottom-left). As a direct consequence, when crawling a non-trivial application, the size of the extracted model is often huge, with APOGEN generating a high amount of page objects, some of which are conceptually clones of each other. The *second issue* is the lack of assistance in the automatic creation of getter methods, necessary when defining test case assertions.

3 Clustering-Aided Page Object Generation

In order to address the limitations discussed in Sect. 2.2, we applied clustering as a post-processing technique (after the crawling phase) for a triple aim: (1) grouping pages related to the same functionality, e.g., all the pages concerning user authentication; (2) grouping clone pages, i.e., different versions of the same page, only differing by minor, dynamic details, as the textual content (see, for instance, those in Fig. 1 bottom-left); (3) exploiting the differences between clones to retrieve information useful for getter methods.

We extended APOGEN with an additional module, the Clusterer, which runs a clustering algorithm over the Crawler output. We opted for three popular clustering algorithms from the literature: K-means++ [1], Hierarchical Agglomerative [7], and K-medoids [6]. For the first two we used the implementations available from the popular Java machine learning library WEKA [30], whereas K-medoids was not available, thus we implemented it from scratch. The Clusterer is able to automatically calculate different kinds of syntactic feature matrixes from the web pages (e.g., tag frequency), that are then used by the clustering algorithms to compute the similarities.

Since there is no perfect clustering technique working for all web applications, the result might be somehow imprecise and might need to be manually refined. To this aim, APOGEN supports the tester with the Cluster Visual Editor (CVE), an interactive cluster visualisation and editor facility, allowing testers to inspect and modify the clustering results, as shown in Fig. 3.

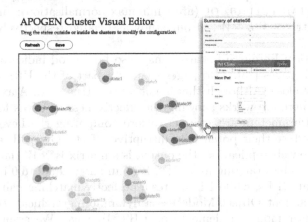

Fig. 3. Cluster Visual Editor (CVE), a web-based tool developed using the D3 library

3.1 Feature Extraction and Matrix Creation

Clustering algorithms rely on the concept of similarity between web pages. There exist a number of works studying the factors affecting web page similarity [2,23,26], in which authors observed that structural features are related with semantic properties of the data and provide meaningful means of comparison between web pages. The Clusterer considers the following features: Tag Frequency, Word Frequency, URL and Document Object Model (DOM).

Tag Frequency (TF) measures the frequency at which tags occur in a web page. The general intuition is that such frequency provides an indication of the general layout and structure, and may be effective for detecting structurally similar web pages. TF for a web application W is calculated as follows: (1) extract a Tag List TL of the tags from all the pages in W, (2) for each page $p \in W$ and for each tag $t \in TL$, calculate $TF(t,p)$, as the normalised frequency of occurrence of tag t in page p (after min-max normalisation); and (3) create the output matrix $TL \times W$ of the normalised TF values.

Word Frequency. The textual content of a page captures information that may be salient for such web page. We assume that two web pages sharing similar textual content shall have some degree of topical relatedness and thus should be grouped together. The Clusterer can calculate the word frequency in two ways, considering: (1) only words within the tag BODY (WF1); (2) only words within the tags TITLE, H1–H6, TABLE, LI–UL–OL (WF2). With the former we take into account the full main content of the page, whereas with the latter we follow the intuition that these tags may contain a succinct representation of the page semantic content [26]. WF1 and WF2 for a web application W are calculated as follows: (1) extract the Word List WL including the words from all pages in W; (2) remove stop-words[5] from WL; (3) for each page $p \in W$ and for each word $w \in WL$, calculate WF1(w, p) and WF2(w, p), as the normalised frequency of occurrence of word w respectively found in the page p within tag BODY or tags TITLE, H1–H6, TABLE, LI–UL–OL (after min-max normalisation); and (4) create two output matrixes $WL \times W$, in our study associated respectively with WF1 and WF2.

URL (Uniform Resource Locator) may also be a good indicator of similarity between web pages [23]. Two pages sharing a part of the URL are likely to be semantically close. Although this is not always true (e.g., Ajax single page applications), there are works showing the effectiveness of URLs for structural clustering [2]. Parameters are stripped before computing the Levenshtein distance [15], to reduce their potentially disruptive effects. Given W as the set of web pages of the web application, the output is a matrix $W \times W$ (later indicated as URL-Lev) of values ranging in $[0..1]$, where an entry equal to 0 indicates two totally dissimilar URLs, while 1 indicates a perfectly matching pair of URLs.

DOM (Document Object Model) is a dynamic hierarchical structure representing the user interface elements of a HTML page. We assume that two web pages sharing similarities between their DOMs are likely to represent pages having analogous functionalities and that they should be grouped in the same cluster. The DOM can be treated either (1) as a tree-like structure, or (2) as a string. Given W, the set of web pages of the web application, two distance matrixes $W \times W$ can be calculated, in the first case using the Robust Tree Edit Distance (RTED) algorithm [19], whereas in the second case using the Levenshtein distance between the string representation of the DOM (after word/text removal, to preserve only the structure). In our study, we refer to these two matrixes as DOM-RTED and DOM-Lev, respectively.

Summary. To wrap up, the Clusterer extracts raw features (TF, WF1, WF2) from the web pages, or features representing distance measures (URL-Lev, DOM-RTED, DOM-Lev), to be given in input to the clustering algorithms. It is important to highlight that K-means++ needs to compute the mean feature vector (centroid) from the set of feature vectors in the same cluster. This is not possible in the case of URL-Lev, DOM-RTED, DOM-Lev, since feature vectors represent distance measures.

---

[5] Retrieved from http://www.lextek.com/manuals/onix/stopwords1.html.

3.2 Potential Getter Methods Detection

In the Static Analyser of APOGEN we have integrated a differencing engine, based on XMLUnit[6], that takes into account the results of clustering and supports the automatic creation of getter methods based on the DOM differences between web pages within the same cluster (e.g., clones). We believe that such intra-cluster differences point to dynamic portions of web pages, on top of which a tester might be interested in creating an assertion. For instance, in Fig. 1, getter methods are created for the phone details fields that vary across web pages in the same cluster. In order to minimise the number of false positives (i.e., irrelevant differences), the differencing engine ignores case sensitivity, white spaces, attribute value order and white-spaces between values, retaining only the differences in the textual node elements which were modified or added.

3.3 From Web Page Clusters to Page Objects

We use hard clustering, i.e., each web page is a member of exactly one cluster, because we want to map each cluster into a page object and each web page must be represented by a unique page object. Let us consider Fig. 4, showing a cluster of web pages $C = \{state35, state39, state44\}$ from the PetClinic web application, one of the experimental objects considered in our study. $State35$ and $state39$ contain the same navigation web element (e.g., a link that can be clicked) and two different textual elements, while $state44$ contains the same navigation web element and an action (e.g., a text field that can be filled in).

Without considering the results of clustering, APOGEN would generate three page objects PO_1, PO_2, PO_3 for $state35$, $state39$ and $state44$. The same navigation method $navigation1$ is replicated three times in all page objects; no getter

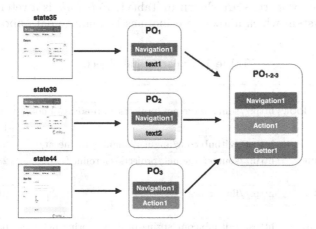

Fig. 4. Pictorial view of APOGEN page object merging strategy, applied to PetClinic web pages

---

[6] http://www.xmlunit.org/.

methods are available for *text1* and *text2*, and the third page object has one
method, to perform *action1*. For the web tester would be quite difficult to decide
when to use PO_1, PO_2 or PO_3. Moreover, manual corrections and adjustments
to the automatically generated page objects should be repeated three times.

By using clustering, instead, APOGEN generates a sole page object, corresponding to the entire cluster. The navigation method *navigation1* appears only
once in such page object. The action method *action1* is also included. For what
concerns getter methods, only textual elements belonging to structural clones
and differing across such clones are turned into getters. In our example, *state35*
is a clone of *state39* (i.e., their DOMs are structurally equivalent) and *text1*
differs from *text2*. Hence, a getter method to retrieve the value of the dynamically changing textual element, namely *getter1*, is generated. The result is a
merged page object $PO_{1-2-3} = \{navigation1, action1, getter1\}$, exposing all
functionalities of *state35*, *state39* and *state44* relevant for web test creation.

4   Empirical Evaluation

We present the empirical study conducted to evaluate the effectiveness of clustering in grouping similar web pages conceptually associated with the same page
object, and the quality of the page objects generated by APOGEN. We follow the
guidelines by Wohlin et al. [31] on designing and reporting empirical studies in
software engineering. Our tool and demo videos are available at: http://sepl.
dibris.unige.it/APOGEN.php.

4.1   Experimental Objects

We selected six real-world web applications covering different application
domains, whose properties are shown in Table 1. *PetClinic* is a veterinary clinic
information system which allows veterinarians to manage data about pets and

Table 1. Experimental objects

Id	Name	Source	LOC
WA1	ADDRESSBOOK (8.2.5)	http://sourceforge.net/projects/php-addressbook	30.1K (PHP) 1.1K (JS)
WA2	PHONECAT	https://github.com/angular/angular-phonecat/	0.4K (JS)
WA3	CLAROLINE (1.11.5)	http://sourceforge.net/projects/claroline/	285K (PHP) 36K (JS)
WA4	FLUXBB (1.5.8)	http://fluxbb.org/	21K (PHP)
WA5	PETCLINIC	https://github.com/spring-projects/spring-petclinic	6.1K (JAVA) 432 (JSP)
WA6	PPMA (0.2)	http://sourceforge.net/projects/ppma/	9K (JS) 3.5K (PHP)

their owners. It has been developed using Java Spring Framework and makes use of technologies as JavaBeans, MVC presentation layer and Hibernate. *Address-Book* is a PHP/MySQL-based address and phone book, contact manager, and organiser. *PPMA* is a web based password manager. *Claroline* is a collaborative learning environment which allows teachers or education institutions to administer courses online. The software provides group management, forums, document repositories, calendar. *Phonecat* is a web-based phone catalog using the AngularJS framework. *FluxBB* is a fast and light PHP forum application.

4.2   Research Questions

We conducted our empirical study to address the following research questions:

RQ1 (effectiveness): *What clustering algorithm provides the best result and how do different algorithms compare with each other?*

RQ2 (reduction): *What is the maximum reduction achievable in the number of generated Page Objects when using clustering with* APOGEN *?*

RQ3 (quality): *How successful is the clustering-aided* APOGEN *in generating high quality Page Objects, i.e., Page Objects similar to those a developer would write?*

4.3   Metrics

A human expert has manually defined the Gold Standard for clusters and page objects, i.e., the ideal grouping of web pages into clusters (Clusters Gold Standard, C-GS) and the ideal page object classes associated with the clusters (Page Objects Gold Standard, PO-GS).

Both Gold Standards require the intervention of a human for their construction. To limit any bias or subjectivity, we asked an external third party (hereafter referred as EXP) to define the Gold Standards. EXP is a programmer with strong professional experience in developing and testing web applications using page objects. EXP has substantial industrial experience and was not involved in the development of APOGEN.

The metric we used *to answer RQ1* is the Partition Edit Distance (PED), which in our case measures the minimum number of web pages that must be moved between clusters to make two web page partitions (i.e., the output of clustering and C-GS) the same. We chose PED because it provides a direct measure of the tester's manual actions necessary to produce the target clustering (i.e., C-GS) starting from the output produced by any of the considered clustering algorithms. In fact, a high value of PED means that many web pages need to be reassigned, whereas a low value of PED means that the clusters are close to C-GS (with few moves required). In the following, we introduce the concepts behind PED and how to calculate it. Let us assume to have a set of six web pages $W = \{p_1, p_2, p_3, p_4, p_5, p_6\}$ and that we want $k = 4$ separate clusters (gs_0, gs_1, gs_2, gs_3). Suppose we have the following C-GS:

$$gs_0 \rightarrow \{p_1\} \qquad gs_1 \rightarrow \{p_3, p_4\} \qquad gs_2 \rightarrow \{p_2\} \qquad gs_3 \rightarrow \{p_5, p_6\}$$

whereas a hypothetical clustering algorithm C gives the following partitions:

$$c_0 \rightarrow \{p_1, p_2\} \qquad c_1 \rightarrow \{p_3\} \qquad c_2 \rightarrow \{p_4, p_6\} \qquad c_3 \rightarrow \{p_5\}$$

We first compare each cluster gs_i from C-GS with each cluster c_j from C using the Jaccard similarity coefficient:

$$J(c_i, gs_j) = \frac{|c_i \cap gs_j|}{|c_i \cup gs_j|}$$

where 0 indicates no element in common; 1 total agreement. For instance, the Jaccard similarity between c_0 and gs_0 is $J(c_0, gs_0) = |\{p_1\}| / |\{p_1, p_2\}| = 0.5$.

The Jaccard similarity matrix for all possible pairs $\langle c_i, gs_j \rangle$ is shown in Table 2. Given the similarity matrix between two partitions, PED can be obtained by solving the following linear assignment problem:

Given two partitions C and C-GS, find the partial bijection between the elements of C and C-GS (i.e., partial, unique assignment of elements from C to elements of C-GS) that maximises the total similarity between paired elements.

In our example, a linear assignment algorithm (we used the Hungarian Method [8]) would produce the following best pairs BP (highlighted in bold in Table 2):

$$BP = \{\langle c_0, gs_0 \rangle, \langle c_1, gs_1 \rangle, \langle c_2, gs_3 \rangle, \langle c_3, gs_2 \rangle\}$$

Table 2. Jaccard similarity matrix. The best pairs that a linear assignment algorithm would produce are highlighted in bold

C-GS \ C	gs_0	gs_1	gs_2	gs_3
c_0	**0.50**	0.00	0.50	0.00
c_1	0.00	**0.50**	0.00	0.00
c_2	0.00	0.50	0.00	**0.50**
c_3	0.00	0.00	**0.00**	0.50

Given BP, the asymmetric set difference cardinality between each pair gives us the number of pages that must be moved to unify the two partitions. Formally, PED is computed as follows:

$$PED(C, C\text{-}GS) = \sum_{\langle c_i, gs_j \rangle \in BP} |c_i \setminus gs_j| + |\text{unassigned}(C, BP)|$$

If there are unassigned clusters in C, due to the size of C being different from that of C-GS, the total number of pages contained in such unassigned clusters are also added in the formula given above. Although the asymmetric set difference operator ($\setminus$) has been used in the formula to compute PED, it can be easily shown that PED is symmetric: $PED(C, C\text{-}GS) = PED(C\text{-}GS, C)$. In our example: $PED(C, C\text{-}GS) = |c_0 \setminus gs_0| + |c_1 \setminus gs_1| + |c_2 \setminus gs_3| + |c_3 \setminus gs_2| = 1 + 0 + 1 + 1 = 3$. Thus, a tester would need to move three web pages from the clusters of C to obtain C-GS: p_2 from c_0 to c_2, p_4 from c_2 to c_1 and p_6 from c_2 to c_3. This gives a rough estimate of the effort required for the manual correction of the clustering output.

To answer RQ2, we counted the number of generated page objects first disabling and then enabling the clustering in APOGEN.

To answer RQ3, for each page object of PO-GS, we manually inspected all methods: (i) classifying the kind of functionality as *navigational, action* or *getter*; (ii) determining whether the method has a semantically equivalent counterpart in the automatic page objects (we tag such methods as *Equivalent*); (iii) determining whether the method has a counterpart in the automatic page objects that needs minor modifications (we tag such methods as *To Modify*); (iv) determining any missing methods (we tag such methods as *Missing*). Further, we are interested in determining if APOGEN leads to the generation of extra methods, e.g., methods not contained in PO-GS. The number of *Equivalent, To Modify, Missing* and *Extra* methods allows us to estimate the possibility to use the code produced by APOGEN as-is, and the effort needed to manually correct the methods to be modified, or to be added/deleted.

4.4   Experimental Procedure

To answer RQ1, we proceeded as follows:

(i) We ran the Crawler over each web application to infer its model. We fed the Crawler with the data necessary to explore each application, such as login credentials. EXP manually inspected the crawling outcomes and created a C-GS for each web application.

(ii) Clustering algorithms need the specification of the number of clusters k as input. Such a value can be either provided manually or can be obtained by automated methods, such as the Silhouette method [22]. We have compared the optimal number of clusters, k_{opt} available from the C-GS, with the number produced by the Silhouette method and the two are very close to each other in all experimental objects (with median difference 3, maximum difference 5 and minimum 0). Hence, we ran APOGEN on each web application with each *(algorithm, feature)* pair searching for exactly k_{opt} clusters. We compared the clusters obtained from APOGEN with C-GS.

(iii) We calculated PED for all *(algorithm, feature)* pairs, in order to assess: (1) what is the best *(algorithm, feature)* pair, and (2) how far the best algorithm is from the C-GS.

To answer RQ2, we ran APOGEN on each web application twice, both enabling and disabling the Clusterer, and we counted the number of generated page objects.

Table 3. Comparison between automatic clusters and gold standard (PED)

Clustering Algo (Feature)	WA1	WA2	WA3	WA4	WA5	WA6	Tot
Hierarchical (DOM-RTED)	4	0	6	7	0	1	18
Hierarchical (URL-Lev)	1	3	4	8	2	6	24
K-means++ (TF)	2	5	8	8	0	3	26
Hierarchical (DOM-Lev)	4	0	9	5	7	3	28
K-means++ (WF2)	4	4	8	7	6	3	32
K-means++ (WF1)	2	3	9	9	7	3	33
K-medoids (TF)	5	6	11	10	6	4	42
K-medoids (DOM-RTED)	6	5	12	9	6	4	42
K-medoids (WF1)	5	2	11	10	11	3	42
K-medoids (WF2)	5	3	12	10	10	4	44
K-medoids (DOM-Lev)	5	5	14	10	7	5	46
K-medoids (URL-Lev)	5	9	12	10	7	6	49

To answer RQ3, we proceeded as follows. For each web application:

(i) EXP manually created PO-GS from the optimal clusters in C-GS;
(ii) we inspected and compared PO-GS with the page objects automatically generated by APOGEN. In detail, for each page object, we manually classified all methods as *navigational, action* or *getter*, and as *Equivalent, To Modify, Missing*, or *Extra*.

4.5   Results

Table 3 reports the values of PED for the admissible combinations of *algorithm* (Hierarchical, K-means++, K-medoids) and *feature* (TF, WF1, WF2, DOM-RTED, DOM-Lev, URL-Lev).

Globally, the best algorithm is *Hierarchical*, which occupies the first, second and fourth positions of the rank. It scores 18 (DOM-RTED), 24 (URL-Lev), and 28 (DOM-Lev). *K-means++* has variable performances: it is ranked third with a value of 26 (TF) but also fifth with a value of 32 (WF2) and sixth with a value of 33 (WF1). *K-medoids* stabilises in the worse positions of the rank, independently from the input data matrix. Its values range between 42–49.

RQ1 (effectiveness): considering all the applications, Hierarchical clustering resulted to be the optimal choice, being in the first, second and fourth position of the PED rank and undergoing little oscillations in its performance across different web applications. In our experiment, the effort to align its clusters with C-GS consists on average of two–four page moves per application. K-means++ also proved to be a good choice when used with the data matrix representing the tag frequencies. Indeed, its performance is aligned with that of the Hierarchical algorithm on WA5 (*PetClinic*). To summarise:

> *Hierarchical clustering applied to the DOM tree distance matrix has the best performance, producing clusters of web pages very close to those manually defined by a human tester.*

RQ2 (reduction). Table 4 shows data about the reduction in the number of generated page objects when using clustering in APOGEN. The first column shows the experimental objects, whereas in the second column are the number of page

Table 4. Reduction of generated page objects when using clustering

Web Application	No Clustering	Clustering	% Reduction
PETCLINIC	26	10	61.54
ADDRESSBOOK	20	10	50.00
PPMA	16	8	50.00
CLAROLINE	63	15	76.19
PHONECAT	21	2	90.48
FLUXBB	55	13	76.19
Total	201	58	67.43

objects generated by APOGEN without considering clustering, which is equal to the number of dynamic states retrieved by the Crawler. The third column displays the number of clusters defined in the C-GS, which is equal to the number of page objects produced by APOGEN, since k_{opt} was provided as input to the clustering algorithm (the value of k obtained from Silhouette would be only slightly different).

To summarise, in our experiment:

> *When using clustering, the reduction in the number of generated page objects ranges between 50–90 % (average 67 %).*

Beyond the mere quantitative data, the substantial reduction achieved by clustering gives an idea of the reduction in page object maintenance that is expected to occur during software and testware evolution. Empirical studies that assess human costs associated with test maintenance are required, however, to substantiate our belief.

RQ3 (quality): Table 5 shows the number of methods (navigational, action or getter) that we tagged as Equivalent (Eq), that need to be modified (TM), missing (Mis) and extra (Extra) w.r.t. PO-GS. The first column shows the experimental objects. The second, third and fourth macro-columns show the cardinality of navigational, action and getter methods generated by APOGEN (macro-columns are split into Eq, TM, Mis and Extra). The fifth macro-column shows the amount of methods contained in PO-GS (i.e., the key functionalities a web tester would put as methods in the page objects). The sixth macro-column reports the sum over all kinds of methods.

Based on the data, we can notice that on average about 75 % of the methods are equivalent, 7 % are to modify, and 18 % are missing. Looking at results by type, for what concerns navigational methods, most are directly usable, as produced by APOGEN, (about 80 %), none is to be modified and 16 % are missing. About the actions, we can notice that roughly 51 % are equivalent, 28 % need to be manually modified and 21 % are missing. For the getter methods, which are generated on top of intra-clusters differences (see Sect. 3), we can notice that 84 % are equivalent, none is to be modified and 16 % are missing. Concerning the methods tagged as extra, i.e., methods that are not explicitly present in the C-GS, we have a total of 53 methods, all falling in the getter category.

> *About 75 % of the generated methods are equivalent to those defined by a human tester, 7 % need to be manually refined, and 18 % are missing.*

Table 5. Comparison between automatic and manual page objects

Web Application	# Navigational				# Action				# Getter				Total (GS)	# Methods			
	Eq	TM	Mis	Extra	Eq	TM	Mis	Extra	Eq	TM	Mis	Extra	Eq+TM+Mis	Eq	TM	Mis	Extra
PETCLINIC	9	0	0	0	6	0	3	0	8	0	3	0	29	23	0	6	0
ADDRESSBOOK	10	0	3	0	4	3	4	0	6	0	1	23	31	20	3	8	23
PPMA	4	0	8	0	4	1	1	0	1	0	2	11	21	9	1	11	11
CLAROLINE	15	0	2	0	7	4	0	0	6	0	3	15	37	28	4	5	15
PHONECAT	1	0	0	0	0	0	1	0	27	0	0	4	29	28	0	1	4
FLUXBB	14	0	0	0	1	4	0	0	6	0	3	0	32	26	4	2	0
Total	53	0	13	0	22	12	9	0	59	0	11	53	179	134	12	33	53

4.6 Qualitative Analysis

For space reasons, we focus the qualitative analysis on the main page of the FluxBB web application (Fig. 5 top). This example is representative because the page object automatically generated by APOGEN (Fig. 5 bottom) for such page includes all the cases (Equivalent, ToModify, Missing, Extra) described in Sect. 4.3.

The navigational method goToUserlist() is an example of Equivalent method (**a**). In fact, it replicates exactly what the tester would do while performing a navigation from the current page toward the user list page: click on the menu item and change the state by instantiating a new proper page object (Userlist) and by passing it the WebDriver instance.

The action method qjump(), instead, is an example of method ToModify (**b**). First, the name retrieved from the form attributes is not very expressive (the label "Jump To" would have been a better choice for the name, in this case). Second, the return parameter with the target object is missing. The reason is that static analysis misses the next dynamic state. The returned page object should be a TestForum page object, whereas if an incorrect parameter is passed as args0, the page object should manage the error. The second getter method is an example of Extra method (**c**), because it refers to a web element within the page representing the same information targeted by the first getter (see the two SPAN "Pages: 1" fields in Fig. 5). In this case, the tester may keep only one of the two getters (e.g., the first one), deleting the second. On the other hand, the tester may check for any inconsistency between the two values, so having two separate methods might be regarded as useful. We decided to leave this choice to the tester. In fact, we believe that the generation of extra getter methods does not impact so negatively the readability of the page objects. On the other hand, no clones in the cluster exposed any differences, while some variability might occur, for instance, in the Replies field (**d**). Thus, we marked such field as a Missing getter.

4.7 Discussion

Hierarchical agglomerative clustering offered stable performance across all web applications, possibly because of the single linkage (min) method, which aggregates clusters when their minimum similarity is the highest among all possible

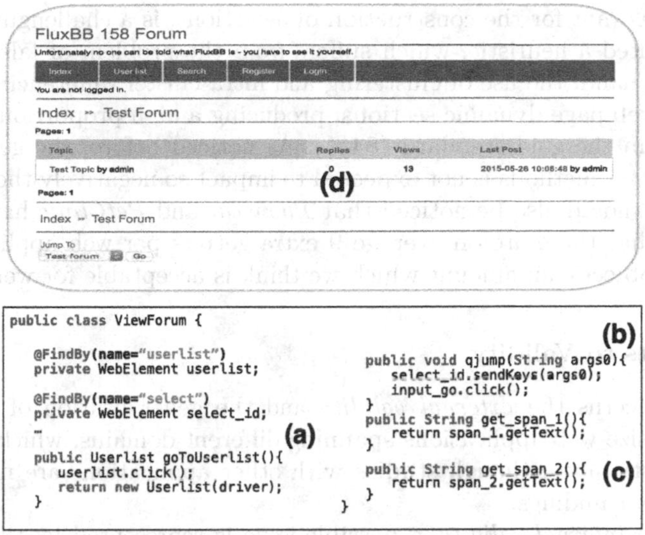

```
FluxBB 158 Forum
Unfortunately no one can be told what FluxBB is - you have to see it yourself.

  Index      User list      Search      Register      Login

You are not logged in.

  Index  »  Test Forum

Pages: 1

  Topic                          Replies      Views        Last Post
  Test Topic by admin               0           13          2015-05-26 10:05:48 by admin
Pages: 1                                    (d)

  Index  »  Test Forum

  Jump To
    Test forum   ▢  Go
```

```
public class ViewForum {
                                                                        (b)
    @FindBy(name="userlist")
    private WebElement userlist;            public void qjump(String args0){
                                                select_id.sendKeys(args0);
    @FindBy(name="select")                      input_go.click();
    private WebElement select_id;           }
    ¯                              (a)      public String get_span_1(){
                                                return span_1.getText();
    public Userlist goToUserlist(){         }
        userlist.click();
        return new Userlist(driver);        public String get_span_2(){  (c)
    }                                           return span_2.getText();
}                                           }
                                    }
```

Fig. 5. The main page of FluxBB web application (**top**), and a portion of the page object generated by APOGEN (**bottom**)

pairs of clusters being aggregated, hence leading to aggregation choices that we think are close to those made by a human when defining the Gold Standard. Content-based features (WF1 and WF2) seem to capture a significant amount of information related to the semantic content and sometimes improve the effectiveness of clustering, though they are not the best choice, according to our study. The features calculated over the DOM (RTED and Lev) work best with Hierarchical clustering, while they perform quite poorly with K-medoids. Thus, we can conclude that structural properties have the best performance, in particular DOM-RTED, TF and DOM-Lev, especially if coupled with Hierarchical clustering.

Concerning the results for RQ3, we can notice that there were no methods to be modified in the navigational and getter categories. This is mainly due to the code transformation phase, in which the mapping is 1-1 for these kinds of methods (see Sect. 2.1). On the other hand, 28 % of action methods needed a manual refinement, usually to add some complex interaction pattern (e.g., a mandatory click on a checkbox before triggering a form submission). These patterns cannot yet be captured by the current version of APOGEN, which is not able to automatically add the missing statements. Although this is an interesting challenge for future work, it represents a minor issue, since the majority of the actions are correctly generated and ready for use by developers.

For similar reasons (static analysis of the DOM and 1-1 model to code transformation), we have a complete absence of Extra action and navigational methods. Concerning the getters, instead, there are 53 extra getter methods. This result is not surprising, since the problem of identifying the getters that are potentially relevant for the construction of assertions, is a challenging problem. We implemented a heuristic, which suffers from the problem of false positives. On the other hand, the use of clustering and intra-cluster differencing captured most of the web page dynamic sections, producing a high proportion of the getter methods in the gold standard (84 %). As noticed before, the generation of additional getter methods is not expected to impact so negatively the activity of the tester. It should also be noticed that *Phonecat* and *PetClinic* have no extra getters and that there are on average 9 extra getters per web application over all the page objects, an amount which we think is acceptable for web testers.

4.8 Threats to Validity

For what concerns the *external validity* and the generalisation of results, we selected real size web applications spanning different domains, which makes the context realistic, even though studies with other applications are necessary to corroborate our findings.

About the *internal validity*, a possible issue is represented by the manually created gold standards, both for the clusters and the page objects. It should be noticed that we must necessarily rely on a *manual* gold standard for evaluating the output of APOGEN, because no automated method can provide us with the ideal clusters and page objects. We minimised this threat by having the gold standards produced by a third subject independent from us and from APOGEN.

For what concerns the *construct validity*, for the evaluation metrics used to answer RQ3 we did not adopt Precision-Recall measures, because they rely on a boolean classification of the output (either correct or incorrect), while in the case of page object methods labelled as To Modify or Extra it is not completely appropriate to deem them as incorrect (neither as correct). We preferred to present the data as they are, split into four categories (Equivalent, To Modify, Missing, Extra), and to discuss them in terms of usability, benefits and expected manual actions required for the refinement of the automatically generated page objects.

5 Related Work

The automated creation of page objects for E2E web testing is a completely new research field, so, to the best of our knowledge, there are no strictly related previous works. However, there are related works that deal with applications of clustering techniques to support web testing and engineering [3–5,16,20,21,28].

State Objects. *Van Deursen* [29] describes a state-based generalisation of page objects. From a testing viewpoint, moving a page object to the state level makes the design of test scenarios easier. Besides the mere terminological difference, the work by van Deursen describes a series of guidelines and good practices (e.g., let each state correspond to a state object) that we share and tried to incorporate in the development of APOGEN, since our ultimate goal is the automatic generation of meaningful page/state objects.

Clustering. *Crescenzi et al.* [5] present an algorithm to cluster web pages, exploiting the structural similarities of the DOMs. In this paper, we studied several structural similarity measures beyond the DOM, with the aim of supporting the clustering of web pages from a testing perspective. *Tonella et al.* [28] provide two methods for web clustering evaluation, the gold standard and a task oriented approach, together with guidelines and examples for their implementation. In our paper, we compared the results of web page clustering against a gold standard, in order to ensure its meaningfulness from the web testing viewpoint. In another work, *Ricca et al.* [20] utilise keyword-based clustering to improve the comprehension of web applications. In our paper, we did not limit ourselves to content-based metrics. Actually, structural properties (e.g., DOM or TF) showed to be more effective.

Crawling/Differencing. *Choudhary et al.* [4] present a dynamic technique based on differential testing to automatically detect cross-browser issues (XBI) and assist developers in their diagnosis. The approach operates on single web pages and focuses on visual analysis, whereas we perform intra-cluster DOM-differencing. *Mesbah et al.* [16] analyses an entire web application, using dynamic crawling, also for the retrieval of XBIs. Similarly, we adopt crawling and web page differencing, but our approach is constrained to finding textual differences between intra-cluster web pages, on top of which a tester can build meaningful assertions. *Choudhary et al.* [3] combined and extended the two above-mentioned approaches for XBI detection in the tool CROSSCHECK. Even though this paper shares some methods with us, such as the reverse engineering of a web application model with a crawler, and performs DOM differencing between web pages, we use clustering, which is an unsupervised machine learning technique, instead of a classifier, and we target a completely different goal, automated page object construction.

6   Conclusions and Future Work

We presented a novel approach, based on web page clustering, to automatically generate page objects for web testing. The tool APOGEN, which implements the approach, has been applied to six existing web applications. Experimental results indicate that our clustering approach is effective to group semantically related web pages. Furthermore, the page objects obtained from the output of clustering are very similar to the page objects that a developer would create manually. Indeed, 75 % of the code generated by APOGEN can be used as-is by a tester, breaking down the manual effort for page object creation. Moreover, a large part (84 %) of the page object methods created to support assertion definition corresponds to meaningful and useful behavioural abstractions.

As future work, we plan to improve the heuristics used to create the getter methods, which cannot be applied to single page clusters. We will investigate a complementary approach, for input data generation, capable of exposing the variable part of multiple as well as single pages in each cluster. We will also study visual mechanisms, based on image processing, to retrieve dynamic page portions [3] and produce visual page objects [11]. Finally, we plan to improve the maintainability of the page objects by enhancing APOGEN with robust web element localisation techniques [12–14].

References

1. Arthur, D., Vassilvitskii, S.: K-means++: the advantages of careful seeding. In: Proceedings of SODA, pp. 1027–1035. Society for Industrial and Applied Mathematics (2007)
2. Blanco, L., Dalvi, N., Machanavajjhala, A.: Highly efficient algorithms for structural clustering of large websites. In: Proceedings of WWW, pp. 437–446 (2011)
3. Choudhary, S.R., Prasad, M.R., Orso, A.: Crosscheck: combining crawling and differencing to better detect cross-browser incompatibilities in web applications. In: Proceedings of ICST, pp. 171–180 (2012)
4. Choudhary, S.R., Versee, H., Orso, A.: Webdiff: automated identification of cross-browser issues in web applications. In: Proceedings of ICSM, pp. 1–10 (2010)
5. Crescenzi, V., Merialdo, P., Missier, P.: Clustering web pages based on their structure. Data Knowl. Eng. **54**(3), 279–299 (2005)
6. Kaufman, L., Rousseeuw, P.: Clustering by means of medoids. In: Statistical Data Analysis Based on the L1-Norm and Related Methods, pp. 405–416. North-Holland (1987)
7. Kaufman, L., Rousseeuw, P.J.: Finding Groups in Data: An Introduction to Cluster Analysis. Wiley Series in Probability and Mathematical Statistics. Wiley, Hoboken (1990)
8. Kuhn, H.W.: The hungarian method for the assignment problem. Naval Res. Logistics Q. **2**, 83–97 (1955)
9. Leotta, M., Clerissi, D., Ricca, F., Tonella, P.: Capture-replay vs. programmable web testing: an empirical assessment during test case evolution. In: Proceedings of 20th Working Conference on Reverse Engineering, WCRE 2013, pp. 272–281. IEEE (2013)
10. Leotta, D., Clerissi, D., Ricca, F., Tonella, P.: Approaches and tools for automated end-to-end web testing. Adv. Comput. **101**, 193–237 (2016)
11. Leotta, M., Stocco, A., Ricca, F., Tonella, P.: Automated generation of visual web tests from DOM-based web tests. In: Proceedings of 30th ACM/SIGAPP Symposium on Applied Computing, SAC 2015, pp. 775–782. ACM (2015)
12. Leotta, M., Stocco, A., Ricca, F., Tonella, P.: Meta-heuristic generation of robust XPath locators for web testing. In: Proceedings of 8th IEEE/ACM International Workshop on Search-Based Software Testing, SBST 2015, pp. 36–39. IEEE (2015)
13. Leotta, M., Stocco, A., Ricca, F., Tonella, P.: Using multi-locators to increase the robustness of web test cases. In: Proceedings of 8th IEEE International Conference on Software Testing, Verification and Validation, ICST 2015, pp. 1–10. IEEE (2015)
14. Leotta, M., Stocco, A., Ricca, F., Tonella, P.: ROBULA+: an algorithm for generating robust XPath locators for web testing. J. Softw. Evol. Process **28**(3), 177–204 (2016)
15. Levenshtein, V.: Binary codes capable of correcting deletions, insertions and reversals. Sov. Phys. Dokl. **10**, 707 (1966)
16. Mesbah, A., Prasad, M.R.: Automated cross-browser compatibility testing. In: Proceedings of ICSE, pp. 561–570. ACM (2011)

17. Mesbah, A., van Deursen, A., Lenselink, S.: Crawling ajax-based web applications through dynamic analysis of user interface state changes. TWEB **6**(1), 3:1–3:30 (2012)
18. Ocariza, F., Bajaj, K., Pattabiraman, K., Mesbah, A.: An empirical study of client-side JavaScript bugs. In: Proceedings of ESEM, pp. 55–64. IEEE Computer Society (2013)
19. Pawlik, M., Augsten, N.: Efficient computation of the tree edit distance. ACM Trans. Database Syst. **40**(1), 3:1–3:40 (2015)
20. Ricca, F., Pianta, E., Tonella, P., Girardi, C.: Improving web site understanding with keyword-based clustering. J. Softw. Maintenance **20**(1), 1–29 (2008)
21. Ricca, F., Tonella, P.: Detecting anomaly and failure in web applications. IEEE Multimedia **13**(2), 44–51 (2006)
22. Rousseeuw, P.: Silhouettes: a graphical aid to the interpretation and validation of cluster analysis. J. Comput. Appl. Math. **20**(1), 53–65 (1987)
23. Sampath, S.: Advances in user-session-based testing of web applications. Adv. Comput. **86**, 87–108 (2012)
24. Stocco, A., Leotta, M., Ricca, F., Tonella, P.: APOGEN: automatic page object generator for web testing. Softw. Qual. J. (under review)
25. Stocco, A., Leotta, M., Ricca, F., Tonella, P.: Why creating web page objects manually if it can be done automatically? In: Proceedings of 10th IEEE/ACM International Workshop on Automation of Software Test, AST 2015, pp. 70–74. IEEE (2015)
26. Tombros, A., Ali, Z.: Factors affecting web page similarity. In: Losada, D.E., Fernández-Luna, J.M. (eds.) ECIR 2005. LNCS, vol. 3408, pp. 487–501. Springer, Heidelberg (2005)
27. Tonella, P., Ricca, F., Marchetto, A.: Recent advances in web testing. Adv. Comput. **93**, 1–51 (2014)
28. Tonella, P., Ricca, F., Pianta, E., Girardi, C.: Evaluation methods for web application clustering. In: Proceedings of WSE, pp. 33–40. IEEE (2003)
29. van Deursen, A.: Testing web applications with state objects. Commun. ACM **58**(8), 36–43 (2015)
30. Witten, I.H., Frank, E., Hall, M.A.: Data Mining: Practical Machine Learning Tools and Techniques, 3rd edn. Morgan Kaufmann Publishers Inc., San Francisco (2011)
31. Wohlin, C., Runeson, P., Höst, M., Ohlsson, M.C., Regnell, B.: Experimentation in Software Engineering. Springer, Heidelberg (2012)

Coverage Patterns-Based Approach to Allocate Advertisement Slots for Display Advertising

Vaddadi Naga Sai Kavya[✉] and P. Krishna Reddy

Kohli Center on Intelligent Systems (KCIS) IIIT Hyderabad,
Gachibowli, Telangana, India
saikavya.vaddadi@research.iiit.ac.in, pkreddy@iiit.ac.in

Abstract. Display advertising is one of the predominant modes of online advertising. A publisher makes efforts to allocate the available ad slots/page views to meet the demands of the maximum number of advertisers for maximizing the revenue. Investigating efficient approaches for ad slot allocation to advertisers is a research issue. In the literature, efforts are being made to propose approaches by extending optimization techniques. In this paper, we propose an improved approach for ad slot allocation by exploiting the notion of coverage patterns. In the literature, an approach is proposed to extract the knowledge of coverage patterns from the transactional databases. In the display advertising scenario, we propose an efficient ad slot allocation approach by exploiting the knowledge of coverage patterns extracted from the click stream transactions. The proposed allocation framework, in addition to the step of extraction of coverage patterns, contains mapping, ranking and allocation steps. The experimental results on both synthetic and real world click stream datasets show that the proposed approach could meet the demands of increased number of advertisers and reduces the boredom faced by user by reducing the repeated display of advertisements.

Keywords: Internet monetization · Computational advertising · Display advertising · Coverage patterns

1 Introduction

Banner advertising or display advertising is one of the predominant modes of online advertising along with contextual and sponsored search advertising [3]. The three major entities involved in display advertising scenario are advertiser, publisher (or ad server) and user (or visitor to the website). In the guaranteed contract of display advertising scenario, an advertiser demands certain number of views for his/her display ad. A publisher manages the available ad slots on web pages of the website through ad server and makes an effort to allocate appropriate sets of ad slots to meet the demands of advertisers. A user visits a set of web pages and the corresponding display ads which are placed in the ad slots. In this scenario, given the budget constraints, an advertiser aims to reach the maximum number of distinct potential users. That is, it may not be beneficial

© Springer International Publishing Switzerland 2016
A. Bozzon et al. (Eds.): ICWE 2016, LNCS 9671, pp. 152–169, 2016.
DOI: 10.1007/978-3-319-38791-8_9

for the advertiser if the same user sees the advertisement multiple number of times. A publisher aims to meet the demands of increased number of advertisers to maximize the revenue. Also, a user who visits multiple web pages and the corresponding ads wants to have a good browsing experience [2,7,9,17]. The user is annoyed if the advertisement is displayed repeatedly. The research problem is to develop efficient allocation approaches to help the publisher in maximizing the revenue by satisfying the demands of increased number of advertisers and help the advertiser to reach the maximum number of distinct users without causing annoyance to users.

In the literature [13,19,26], the problem of display ad allocation is being studied by modeling it as a bipartite graph in which ad slots, advertisers and allocations between ad slots to advertisers are represented as supply nodes set, demand nodes set, and edges respectively. Efforts [7,12,15,17] are being made to develop efficient ad allocation approaches using optimization techniques by mathematically formulating the ad serving scenario. These approaches have modeled the problem of display ad allocation as a stochastic optimization problem and attempted to develop optimal or near optimal allocation plans.

In this paper, we have made an effort to propose a different approach for efficient allocation of ad slots by extending the notion of coverage. In the literature, an effort has been made to extract the knowledge of coverage patterns from transactional databases [21,22]. Each coverage pattern (or set) covers certain percentage of transactions. So, a large number of coverage patterns can be extracted from the transactional databases such that each pattern covers certain percentage of transactions. In the display advertising scenario, there is an opportunity to use the knowledge of coverage patterns which can be extracted from the click stream data of a website to efficiently identify the supply of user visits for various ad slots to meet the goals of both publisher and advertiser. Further, the boredom to the user can be reduced.

For display advertising, in this paper, we have explored how the knowledge of coverage patterns extracted from click stream transactions could be exploited in developing the efficient ad slot allocation approach. We have exploited the fact that a coverage pattern gives certain coverage/percentage of visitors and it contains a distinct set of visitors. We have proposed a framework to allocate ad slots to advertisers based on the knowledge of coverage patterns. The experimental results on both synthetic and real world click stream datasets show that the proposed allocation approach could allocate increased number of advertisers by reducing the repeated display of the same ad as compared to the baseline approach.

In this approach, it is assumed that the transactions formed from click stream data could be used to identify the set of ad slots that cover a given percentage of visitors. Such knowledge could be used to allocate ad slots to the advertisers by assuming similar access behaviour. The related issues will be investigated as a part of future work.

The rest of the paper is organized as follows. In Sect. 2, we present related work. In Sect. 3, we present an overview of coverage patterns and explain the framework of display ad allocation. In Sect. 4, we explain proposed allocation framework. In Sect. 5, we present experiments. In Sect. 6, we present conclusion and future work.

2   Related Work

Regarding display advertising, research efforts are being made in the literature to propose efficient approaches for scheduling of display ads, allocation of display ads, preserving privacy, auction mechanisms and charging schemes [5,11,15,20]. We discuss the related work concerning allocation of display ads. As we employ approaches related to click stream data and coverage patterns in the proposed approach, we also discuss the corresponding related work.

Efforts have been made to study the problem of display ad allocation by modeling it as a bipartite graph matching between the advertisers with demands and ad slots with supply of user visits with an objective of maximizing the revenue. Feldman et al. [13] have considered the online ad allocation problem by modeling it as an ad matching problem and generated upper bounds for the optimum allocation. Vee et al. [26] have formulated the optimization problem of ad allocation and described primal compact sample allocation plan which might generalize to a near optimal solution. Vahab et al. [19] have studied the problem of simultaneous approximations for the adversarial and stochastic online budgeted allocation problem and provided mathematical approximation bounds based on the arrival orders of nodes in the bipartite graph. Bharadwaj et al. [7] have considered the impression based mathematical formulation that minimizes the under delivery rate in a bipartite graph framework of ad allocation. Hojjat et al. [17] assign each user a predefined fixed stream of ads from a pool of simulated ad streams and use a column generation scheme to select a small set of ad streams that optimize the defined ad allocation problem.

Research in click stream mining is mainly focused on the development of knowledge discovery techniques specifically designed for the analysis of web usage data. Web log databases provide rich information about web dynamics [16,24]. In [18], several measures of interest to evaluate the association rules mined from web usage data were proposed and compared.

An approach to extract coverage patterns from transactional database has been proposed in [21]. Alternative approaches to extract coverage patterns have also been proposed in [22,23]. In [25], a methodology to extract content-specific coverage patterns from transactional database has been proposed. It was shown that the knowledge of coverage patterns can be extracted from relatively large transactional databases and the potential application of coverage patterns to the display advertising and sponsored search advertising scenario was described. In [8], a framework has been proposed to improve the efficiency of adwords by considering a set of queries of a user as a transaction.

It can be noted that the preceding allocation approaches estimate the supply of user visits for ad slots. In addition, an objective function is modeled mathematically by simulating display ad serving scenario for maximizing the revenue.

The solution sets are generated based on the mathematical bounds for the specified constraints. The solutions produced require predicting the user visits in a concrete way to start with the ad allocation plans.

The ad allocation approach proposed in this paper is different from preceding approaches as we have extended the knowledge of coverage patterns extracted from click stream transactions to improve the performance of ad allocation in display advertising.

3   Background

In this section, we briefly explain the concept of coverage patters and explain the problem of display ad allocation.

3.1   Overview of Coverage Patterns

In the literature, the concept of coverage has been used to the solve set cover problem in set theory [10] and node cover problem in graph theory [14]. By extending the notion of coverage to transactional databases, a model to extract coverage patterns (CPs) was proposed to extract transactional coverage value of distinct sets of data items [21] or patterns.

Given a transactional database C, a pattern is a set of items. We attach the following notions to coverage patterns: coverage set, coverage support and overlap ratio. Given a pattern, the coverage set denotes the set of all distinct transactions n such that every transaction in n contains at least one web page of a pattern. The coverage support indicates the coverage i.e., the extent of the coverage of the pattern. It is the ratio of coverage set and total number of transactions. Another important parameter is overlap ratio. Consider a set of two items appearing in n transactions out of C transactions. If the two items are appearing in every transaction of n transactions, then the coverage support is n/C. But, this pattern is uninteresting with respect to coverage point of view. It would be more interesting, ideally, if each item in it appears from every different transaction of n transactions so that the coverage can be maximized. So, given the pattern, the degree of overlap of individual items coverage is captured by overlap ratio. So, a pattern is interesting if it has high coverage support and low overlap ratio.

Formally, given a transactional database, the CPs can be extracted based on the threshold values specified for relative frequency, coverage support and overlap ratio parameters. We briefly explain the three parameters as follows.

Let $I = \{i_1, i_2, \cdots, i_n\}$ be a set of items and C be a set of transactions such that each transaction T is a set of items where $T \subseteq C$. P is a pattern of items such that $P \subseteq I$ and $P = \{i_p, \cdots, i_q, i_r\}$ where $1 \leq p \leq q \leq r \leq n$ and T^{i_k} denotes a set of transactions containing the item i_k and its cardinality is denoted by $|T^{i_k}|$.

– **Relative Frequency:** The fraction of transactions containing the item, i_k is called relative frequency of i_k. It is denoted by $RF(i_k)$ and measured as follows.

$$RF(i_k) = \frac{|T^{i_k}|}{|C|} \tag{1}$$

– **Coverage Support:** Coverage support of a pattern, P is the ratio of number of transactions which contains at least one item in P to the size of the transactional database, $|C|$ such that $|T^{i_p}| \geq \cdots \geq |T^{i_q}| \geq |T^{i_r}|$. It is denoted by $CS(P)$ and measured as follows.

$$CS(P) = \frac{|(T^{i_p} \cup \cdots \cup T^{i_q} \cup T^{i_r})|}{|C|} \tag{2}$$

– **Overlap Ratio:** Overlap ratio of a pattern, P, where $|T^{i_p}| \geq \cdots \geq |T^{i_q}| \geq |T^{i_r}|$, is the ratio of the number of transactions common in $P - \{i_r\}$ and $\{i_r\}$ to the number of transactions in i_r (i.e., minimum number of transactions in either $P - \{i_r\}$ or $\{i_r\}$). It is denoted by $OR(P)$ and measured as follows.

$$OR(X) = \frac{|(T^{i_p} \cup T^{i_{p+1}} \cup \cdots \cup T^{i_q}) \cap (T^{i_r})|}{|T^{i_r}|} \tag{3}$$

Let $minRF$, $minCS$ and $maxOR$ be the threshold values specified for RF, CS and OR parameters respectively to extract CPs from a transactional database. A pattern P is said to be a CP, if $RF(i_k) \geq minRF$ where $i_k \in P$, $CS(P) \geq minCS$ and $OR(P) \leq maxOR$.

Example 1: We explain the notion of CPs on an example transactional database C where $|C| = 10$ as shown in Table 1. Let us consider $minRF = 0.4$, $minCS = 0.7$ and $maxOR = 0.5$. From C, the set of items, $I = \{a, b, c, d, e, f\}$, $T^a = \{1, 2, 3, 4\}$ and $T^b = \{1, 5, 6, 7, 8, 9, 10\}$. Thus, $RF(a) = \frac{4}{10} = 0.4$ and $RF(b) = \frac{7}{10} = 0.7$. Similarly, RF will be calculated for all other items in the set I. The items whose $RF \geq minRF$ will be considered and the rest will be removed. Here in this example, $RF(f) = 0.3 \leq minRF$, hence it will be removed. As a,b satisfy the $minRF$ constraint, $\{b, a\}$ can be an item set. We need to measure CS and OR parameters of $\{b, a\}$ to check whether it can be a CP. $CS(\{b,a\}) = \frac{|(T^b \cup T^a)|}{|C|} = \frac{|\{1, 2, 3, 4, 5, 6, 7, 8, 9, 10\}|}{10} = \frac{10}{10} = 1$. $OR(\{b,a\}) = \frac{|(T^b) \cap (T^a)|}{|T^a|} = \frac{|\{1\}|}{4} = \frac{1}{4} = 0.25$. As $CS(\{b, a\}) \geq minCS$ and $OR(\{b, a\}) \leq maxOR$, $\{b, a\}$ is a CP. Similarly, all other valid CPs are extracted from C.

In the literature, an effort has been made to propose apriori-like approach [21] to extract complete sets of CPs from transactional database. A pattern growth-like approach [22,23] is also proposed to extract the complete set of CPs in an efficient manner.

Table 1. Example transactional database

TID	items	TID	items
1	a, b, c	6	b, d
2	a, c, e	7	b, d
3	a, c, e, f	8	b, e, f
4	a, c, d	9	b, e, f
5	b, d	10	c, b, d

3.2 Framework of Display Ad Allocation

In the guaranteed contract of display advertising scenario, an advertiser aims to reach the potential users and demands certain number of views (or impressions) for his/her advertisement on the publisher's website. The publisher who manages the ad space through the ad server, guarantees the supply of demanded impressions to the display ad, and generates revenue under appropriate revenue model. Cost per impression (CPI) is the most commonly used revenue model [17]. In this scenario, major components include ad slots on web pages of the website which supply certain number of impressions, advertisers who demand impressions and the publisher who allocates the ad slots that matches demands of advertisers through the ad server and generates revenue under CPI revenue model.

The entire scenario of display ad allocation naturally fits into a bipartite graph in which one set of nodes represent ad slots, another set of nodes represent advertisers and edges represent allocations [7,17,26,27]. Figure 1(a) shows a bipartite graph $G(S, D, E)$ in which S contains five supply nodes (ad slots) on the left and D contains three demand nodes (advertisers) on the right. Here, each ad slot is modeled as a supply node and each advertiser (advertising contract) is modeled as a demand mode. Each supply node $S_i \in S$ supplies s_i impressions (weight of the node S_i) and each demand node $D_j \in D$ demands d_j impressions (weight of the node D_i). Th edge set E represents the eligible allocations between the supply and demand nodes. The problem is to achieve fair and optimal allocation between the supply nodes and demand nodes so as to maximize the publisher revenue, minimize the under-delivery of impressions to advertisers, and achieve desired user-level diversity.

Figure 1(b) shows the existing ad allocation framework. It contains the following steps.

1. **Identification of User Visits:** The input to this module is the available ad slots. In this step, the probability of user visits to different ad slots is computed. The arrival of users to the different pages of the website is unpredictable. It would require identifying the arrival of specific user visits to the website to implement the ad allocation solutions. The output of this module is the supply nodes set (probability of user visits to ad slots). In the literature [7,17,26], several efforts have been made to predict or estimate the user visits for available ad slots using sampling procedures.

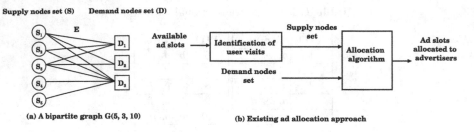

(a) A bipartite graph G(5, 3, 10)

(b) Existing ad allocation approach

Fig. 1. Existing ad allocation framework

2. **Allocation Approach:** The input to this step is the supply nodes and demands from advertisers. Based on the objective function, appropriate allocation algorithm is employed to allocate supply nodes to advertisers. Approaches to generate optimum ad allocation plans to achieve the objectives of the defined problem is an important research issue. Research efforts [7,17,26] have also been made to develop theoretical solutions by modeling the ad allocation problem as a stochastic optimization problem.

4   Proposed Allocation Framework

In this section, given a website, we first present the analysis of potential revenue from the impressions. Next, we explain the basic idea. Subsequently, we present the proposed ad allocation approach.

4.1   Analysis of Potential Revenue

Given a website which contains W web pages, the maximum revenue that can be generated from W is bound by the total number of page views ensured in a unit duration. The total number of pages views is equal to the summation of all individual page views of the website. It can be observed that, given a website, the revenue that can be extracted under the Cost Per Impressions (CPI) revenue model will be proportional to the total impressions served by all the ad slots associated with the web pages of the website in a unit duration. The ideal case would be when all the advertisers are allocated ad slots such that no two web pages in their allocated sets of ad slots are visited by the same user, and demanded impressions are exactly satisfied. This scenario is mathematically represented as follows.

If an advertiser D_i demands d_i impressions and a pattern of ad slots $S_i = \{s_j, s_{j+1}, \cdots, s_k\}$ is allocated, then the maximum revenue is obtained when the following conditions are satisfied.

$$Conditions = \begin{cases} T^{s_p} \cap T^{s_q} = \phi, \forall s_p, s_q \in S_i, p \neq q & \text{(4a)} \\ \sum_{s_i \in S_i} |T^{s_i}| = d_i & \text{(4b)} \end{cases}$$

Here, given an ad slot x, T^x represents the set of transactions in which x has occurred.

The revenue of the publisher would be the maximum over the considered period of time when the preceding conditions are satisfied for all the advertisers and no web page is left unallocated. So, the maximum revenue is proportional to the total number of page views which is represented as follows.

$$\text{Maximum revenue} \propto \text{total number of page views} \tag{5}$$

$$\propto \sum_{i=1}^{|C|} |T^i| \tag{6}$$

$$= \beta \times \sum_{i=1}^{|C|} |T^i| \tag{7}$$

The proportionality constant β (> 0) depends on various factors. Some predominant factors include number of ad slots on each web page, ad geometry, ad frequency, ad pacing and bid of the advertisers [6]. Web pages with more advertising space yield more revenue. Bigger the size of the advertisement, it occupies more space and hence yields more revenue. Since the space is finite, each ad is displayed multiple times with pacing in line with the time spent on the web pages which helps in multiplying the revenue.

4.2   Basic Idea

Website click stream data provides rich information about various dynamics of users who visit the website. It is possible to extract coverage patterns from a transactional database extracted from the website log files. A web page contains a set of ad slots. The notion of coverage support of a CP indicates distinct sets of ad slots, which ensures a certain percentage of views. Also, the overlap ratio of a CP indicates the degree of co-occurrence of ad slots in the same session of the user which can be exploited to achieve desired user-level diversity of ads by reducing the repeated display of the same ad. Most importantly, it can be noted that several low traffic ad slots can be part of a CP which can be used by the publisher to meet the demands of advertisers.

For example, consider an e-commerce website in which popular pages such as home page and frequently answered questions (FAQ) pages draw more users when compared to other product pages of the website. A typical user may visit more than one page, say p_1, p_2,..., p_n in a given session. If the publisher allocates p_1 and p_2 to the same advertiser and place the corresponding ad, the user encounters the same ad several times which leads to boredom. The coverage patterns extracted from click stream data allow the allocation of the ad slots of home page and FAQ page which are visited by the same group of users to different advertisers. The coverage patterns also allow combining the ad slots of frequently accessed web pages with ad slots of less popular web pages such that the overlap is minimal, would result in displaying advertisement to a wide spectrum of website users and at the same time due to lesser overlap, repeatability can be minimized. As a result, the publisher would get an opportunity to satisfy demands of increased number of advertisers.

Since the coverage pattern contains ad slots with minimum overlap of click stream transactions, the impressions of a single user can be assigned to different advertisers. As a result, maximum number of impressions can be exploited for banner advertising. By carrying out allocations using coverage patterns having maximum coverage support and minimum overlap ratio, it is possible to maximize the revenue as given in Eq. 4.

It can be noted that, in display advertising scenario, estimation of user visits to the ad slots is crucial for effective allocation. An improvement in the estimation of user visits to the website could improve the performance of allocation which in turn helps in realizing the objectives of both publisher and advertisers. Based on the knowledge of coverage patterns extracted from click stream transactions, it is possible to improve the performance of ad allocation. This is under the assumption that the knowledge of coverage patterns will be helpful to estimate the user visits. It can be observed that the patterns from click stream transactions are widely employed to recommend products in e-commerce environments. However, the investigation about predicting user visit behaviour using coverage patterns is investigated as a part of future work.

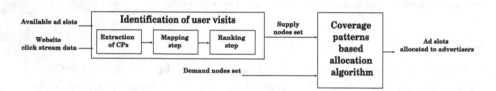

Fig. 2. Proposed ad allocation framework

4.3   Proposed Ad Allocation Approach

The following assumptions are defined in the proposed allocation framework. We consider one ad slot per each web page and an advertiser's bid is a constant value predefined per impression. Advertisers demand the ad impressions to be shown and the publisher allocates a set of web pages (or ad slots) by considering the expected impressions in a unit duration. The duration can be fixed in terms of hours or days based on the user and advertiser dynamics [17].

In the proposed framework, the bipartite graph of display ad allocation is similar to the existing one shown in Fig. 1(a). However, in the proposed framework, the supply nodes set S is formed and allocation will be carried out by exploiting the knowledge of coverage patterns from click stream data of a website.

Several issues need to be handled to form the supply nodes set using CPs in advertising scenario. Under the considered revenue model CPI, advertisers demand in terms of impressions. Hence, we propose a mapping methodology to convert coverage pattern with coverage support and overlap ratio into impressions. Also, a huge set of CPs are extracted from the click stream data of a website. Hence, we propose a ranking step to rank the CPs. Finally, an allocation algorithm is proposed to allocate appropriate set of ad slots to each advertiser.

The proposed approach is shown in Fig. 2. It contains the following steps.

1. **Identification of User Visits:** Available ad slots and the website click stream data are inputs to this step and output is supply nodes set. It performs the following sub steps to identify the supply nodes set from the click stream data of a website. We explain the steps in detail as follows.

    (a) **Extraction of CPs:** The input to this step is website click stream data considered over a period of time. From the website log data, click stream transactional database is generated in such a way that each transaction represents a user and the items in the transaction represents the pages visited by that user in a session. Complete set of CPs can be extracted from the click stream transactional data by employing the *CPPG* algorithm [23] with specified thresholds for *RF*, *CS* and *OR* parameters. The output of this step is a set of CPs extracted from the click stream transactional data. Each CP is a set of web pages. As we assume one ad slot is available on each web page, each CP can be referred as a set of ad slots along with the corresponding *CS* and *OR* values.

    (b) **Mapping Step:** The *CS* of a CP provides the proportional value of number of transactions (unique visitors). The advertisers demand in terms of impressions. So, to facilitate the allocation, we need to estimate the number of impressions ensured by a CP to match with the demands of the advertisers for facilitating the allocation. We associate the value of impressions with each CP in this step. The number of impressions (I) ensured by a CP is equal to the summation of individual frequencies of the web pages in the CP multiplied with the respective number of ad slots available on each web page. The formula is as follows.

    $$\text{Impressions}(S_i) = \text{I}(S_i) = \sum |T^{w_i}| * n_i, \forall w_i \in S_i \qquad (8)$$

    where $S_i = \{s_j, s_{j+1}, \cdots, s_k\}$ is a supply node which is a CP of web pages, $|T^{w_i}|$ is the number of transactions in which the web page w_i occurred in the click stream transaction, n_i is the number of ad slots on the web page w_i and $I(S_i)$ is the number of impressions mapped to S_i. The output of this step is CPs with the corresponding value of impressions.

    (c) **Ranking Step:** A large number of CPs are extracted from the click stream transactional data. It is possible that several hundreds of CPs match an advertiser demand. In such a case, it is important to allocate the most interesting CP first to the advertisers. A CP is interesting if it has high coverage support and low overlap ratio. This is due to the fact that high *CS* value reflects more unique users and low *OR* value reflects less repetition or together occurrence of the web pages in the same session. We define the interestingness measure *Uniqueness (U)*, to capture both the aspects of high CS and low OR of a CP which is equivalent to the difference between CS and OR parameters. The difference gives a proportional measure which is equal to the number of unique visitors visiting the corresponding ad slots of a CP. The formula is as follows.

$$\text{Uniqueness}(S_i) = \text{U}(S_i) = |CS(S_i) - OR(S_i)| * |C| \tag{9}$$

where S_i is a CP, $|C|$ is the transactional database size, CS and OR is the overlap ratio and.

2. **Allocation Step:** Supply nodes set generated from the preceding step and demand nodes set is the input to this step. The approach first sorts the S set in the increasing order of impressions. Next, the patterns with equal number of impressions are sorted based on uniqueness measure. The algorithm considers each D_i in D set to identify eligible appropriate supply nodes. Out of eligible supply nodes, the supply node with weight close to the demand of D_i is allocated and an edge is formed between the demand node D_i and eligible supply node S_k. The procedure is repeated by considering the remaining supply nodes till no demand node is left or remaining supply nodes are unable to satisfy any demand further. The allocation algorithm (CPs-based allocation) is given in Algorithm 1.

Table 2. Extracted CPs with CS, OR, $Impression(I)$, $Uniqueness(U)$

ID	CPs	CS	OR	I	U	ID	CPs	CS	OR	I	U
1	{b}	0.7	0.0	7	7	11	{d}	0.5	0.0	5	5
2	{b, a}	1.0	0.25	11	7.5	12	{d, a}	0.8	0.25	9	5.5
3	{b, c}	1.0	0.4	12	6	13	{d, a, e}	1.0	0.5	13	5
4	{b, e}	0.9	0.5	11	4	14	{d, a, f}	1.0	0.3	12	7
5	{c}	0.5	0.0	5	5	15	{d, e}	0.9	0.0	9	9
6	{c, e}	0.7	0.5	9	2	16	{d, f}	0.8	0.0	8	8
7	{c, d}	0.8	0.4	10	4	17	{a}	0.4	0.0	4	4
8	{c, d, e}	1.0	0.5	14	5	18	{a, e}	0.6	0.5	8	1
9	{c, d, f}	1.0	0.3	13	7	19	{a, f}	0.6	0.3	7	3
10	{c, f}	0.7	0.3	8	4	20	{e}	0.4	0.0	4	4

Example 2: We explain the proposed approach by considering the click stream transactional data of the Table 1. We consider a set of three advertisers D_1, D_2, D_3 coming with impressions demands of $d_1 = 8$, $d_2 = 11$, $d_3 = 9$ respectively. Here d_1, d_2, d_3 are the weights associated with D_1, D_2, D_3 in the set D.

The algorithm of $CPPG$ [23] is employed with the parameters $RF=0.3$, $CS=0.4$ and $OR=0.5$ on the Table 1 to extract CPs. The CPs which satisfy the specified threshold requirements are given in Table 2. The algorithm has

Algorithm 1. CPs based allocation algorithm

Input: D: Demand nodes set, W: Website click stream data
Output: O: Ad slots allocated to advertisers.
1: **procedure** ALLOCATION(D, W)
2:    $S \leftarrow CoveragePatterns(W)$ ▷ S is a supply nodes set
3:    **for** $i \leftarrow 1, |D|$ **do**
4:        $C \leftarrow \arg\min_{C \in S} |Supply(C) - D_i|$ ▷ C is a supply node
5:        $O[i] \leftarrow O[i] \cup \{C\}$
6:        $\mathcal{R} \leftarrow \{r \in S : \exists w \in W\{w \in C\}\}$ ▷ R is an allocated supply nodes set
7:        $S \leftarrow S \backslash \mathcal{R}$
8:    **end for**
9:    **return** O
10: **end procedure**

---

extracted 20 CPs from Table 1 with the length of the patterns varying from 1 to 3 for the specified parameters.

As the advertisers demand in terms of impressions in the considered model, we need to estimate and map the impressions ensured by each extracted CP. We associate the value of impressions to each extracted CP using the formula given in the mapping step. For example, consider the CP $\{d, a, e\}$ from the extracted CPs. The number of impressions ensured by $\{d, a, e\}$ using the above mentioned formula is the summation of individual frequencies of web pages appearing in the CP. Hence impressions ensured by $\{d, a, e\}$ is $|T^d + T^a + T^e| = 13$. Similarly, the number of impressions are mapped to each extracted CP which forms the supply set S with respective mapped impressions as weights.

The uniqueness measure for each CP is calculated using the formula given in the ranking step of the algorithm. For example, consider the CP $\{c, d, e\}$ from the extracted CPs. The uniqueness measure of $\{c, d, e\}$ using the above mentioned formula is the difference between the CS and OR values associated with it and multiplied by $|C|$. From the Table 2, the CS and OR of $\{c, d, e\}$ are 1.0 and 0.5 respectively and $|C|$ is the total number of transactions in Table 1. Hence uniqueness measure of $\{c, d, e\}$ is $|1.0 - 0.5| * 10 = 5.0$. The values of impressions (I) and uniqueness measure (U) for the rest of the extracted CPs are calculated similarly and given in the Table 2.

The proposed algorithm allocates the demands in first-come-first-serve basis. In the first iteration, the algorithm identifies an eligible subset of S with weights able to satisfy the demand $d_1 = 8$ of the first advertiser D_1. The patterns or the supply nodes $\{c, f\}$, $\{d, f\}$ and $\{a, e\}$, all ensure 8 impressions, are eligible to satisfy the demand and hence picked by the algorithm. From Table 2, the uniqueness values of $\{c, f\}$, $\{d, f\}$ and $\{a, e\}$ are 4, 8 and 1 respectively. Hence, the CP $\{d, f\}$ is allocated to the advertiser D_1. In the second iteration, the algorithm identifies a possible subset of S with weights eligible to satisfy the demand $d_2 = 11$ of the second advertiser D_2. The patterns or the supply nodes $\{b, a\}$, $\{b, e\}$ are eligible to satisfy the demand and hence picked by the algo-rithm. The CP $\{b, a\}$ has high uniqueness measure and hence allocated to the advertiser D_2. In the third iteration, the algorithms picks and allocates the CP $\{c, e\}$ close to the demand $d_3 = 9$ to the third advertiser D_3 similarly. The algorithm terminates as no advertiser is left to allocate in this example.

5   Experiments

In this section, we explain datasets, approaches implemented, performance metrics and results.

5.1   Description of Datasets

To evaluate the proposed approach, three types of click stream datasets and simulated advertiser dataset are being used.

T40I10D100K Dataset (TIK) [1]: It is a synthetic dataset. The format of the dataset is {Item ID1, Item ID2,..., Item IDk}. Each record corresponds to one distinct transaction. We consider each record as distinct session and the items comprise each distinct session as the web pages visited by the visitor during that session. We consider 100000 transactions.

Kosarak Dataset (KSK) [1]: It is an anonymized click stream transactional dataset of a Hungarian online news portal. The format of the dataset is {Item ID1, Item ID2,..., Item IDk}. Each record corresponds to one distinct session where the items are the web pages visited by the visitor during that session. We consider 20000 sessions of the dataset for the experiment.

Yoochoose Dataset (YCT) [4]: It is a real world click stream dataset of an e-commerce website provided by a retailer. The dataset comprises of click-through transactions in the form of web sessions. The format of the dataset is ⟨ *Session ID, Timestamp, Item ID, Category* ⟩. We consider 10000 sessions of the dataset for the experiment.

The statistics of the datasets are given in the Table 3. It should be noted that the three datasets used in the experiments capture different aspects of click-through behaviour.

Simulated Advertisers Dataset: The datasets available are either click-stream datasets of websites or individual advertiser datasets for sponsored search advertising. So we have created an advertiser dataset to run experiments on both the datasets. For each dataset, five advertiser datasets were simulated containing 20, 40, 60, 80 and 100 advertisers. For creation of the dataset, impressions required by each advertiser were generated randomly satisfying the condition that every advertiser in the corresponding dataset can be satisfied within the available impressions of the respective click stream data. For example, in the 4th column of Table 3, the average impressions in the dataset 20 is 1325.55. The impressions demanded by the 20 advertisers are generated around that average between the maximum and the minimum impressions available in the respective

Table 3. Statistics of click stream transactions and Advertisers demands data

Dataset	Page views	Average transaction length	Advertisers demands dataset				
			20	40	60	80	100
TIK	131530	13.15	1325.55	1328.35	1344.02	1294.30	1310.30
KSK	162513	8.12	1746.95	1675.10	1710.50	1728.20	1607.27
YCT	62861	6.28	1045.65	1003.75	1013.86	725.42	626.66

click stream datasets. Similarly, the impressions are generated for the rest of the datasets. The statistics of the average impressions demands are provided in Table 3 for TIK, KSK and YCT datasets respectively. The upper bound on the advertisers demands data size is set by analyzing the website click stream data of respective datasets such that we can exploit all available page views to achieve a comparison between both the approaches. For each advertisers dataset, the impressions demands are uniformly generated around the average impressions ensured in the respective click stream transactional dataset. This indicates that the advertising load on the system is increasing with a uniform distribution of advertisers demands.

5.2 Approaches Implemented

In the literature [7,17,27], the work on display advertising is focused upon mathematical formulations of display ad scheduling by defining parameters and carried out experiments by randomly generated numerical values that simulate appropriate scaled versions of a real world data instances of a website. CPs based allocation is the first allocation approach proposed using click stream transactional database of a website. Consequently, there are no concrete existing benchmarks for comparing the performance. As the earlier approaches dealt the problem by considering simulated user visit frequencies, we compare the proposed approach with the same underlying notion as our baseline approach and hereafter referred as visit frequency based allocation approach (VF-based allocation).

For the experiment, the VF-based allocation approach is implemented in the following manner. Each advertiser comes with a demand of certain impressions. The visit frequency of a web page is the number of times the web page has appeared in the click stream transactional data considered over a period of time. Thus, visit frequency of each web page gives the number of impressions ensured by that web page. VF-based allocation allocates web pages by considering the visit frequency of individual web pages. Given an advertisers impressions demand d_i, the approach selects a set of web pages such that the total number of expected visits (or impressions) is greater than or equal to the request made by the advertiser. This approach is repeated for every advertiser till there are no advertisers left or it is not possible to identify a set of web pages that meet the requests of rest of the advertisers.

For the experiment, to extract CPs from the click stream transactional database, we have set $minRF = 0$ to engage every web page. Also, we set $minOR = 0.5$ and $minCS$ = average value of $minRF$ in the respective datasets. The CPPG [23] algorithm is employed to extract CPs with the respective thresholds.

5.3   Performance Metrics

We employ two measures to compare the performance.

- **Allocated Advertisers:** It is equal to the number of allocated advertisers per unit time duration. At most, the number of allocated advertisers is equal to the number of advertisers who have requested the ad slots. The approach which gives the high value of allocated advertisers is better as it meets the demands of more number of advertisers which helps in maximizing the revenue.
- **Ad Repeatability (AR):** Ad repeatability measure indicates how many times the same advertisement appeared in the same session of a user. It is measured by considering a set of ad slots in which at least two occur in the same session of a user. It captures the maximum co-occurrence of ad-slots on which the same ad is being displayed to the same user. For the advertiser, less ad repeatability is preferred to maximize the reach. In addition, the boredom of the visitor is directly proportional to the value of the metric i.e., higher the value of ad repeatability more the boredom of the visitor. The lower value of the metric signifies the efficient utilization of ad slots which indicates improved user-level diversity (displaying diverse set of ads to users). For a pattern $P_i = \{a_i, a_{i+1}, \cdots, a_j\}$, where $a_i's$ are ad slots, the metric is defined as follows:

$$AR(P_i) = \begin{cases} 0 & \text{if } |P_i| = 1 \\ |T^{a_i} \cap T^{a_j}| & \text{if } |P_i| = 2 \\ \max_{a_i, a_j \in P_i, a_i \neq a_j} AR(\{a_i, a_j\}) & \text{if } |P_i| > 2 \end{cases}$$

5.4   Results

Figure 3a, b and c show the performance results of allocated advertisers for the experiments conducted on TIK, KSK and YCT datasets respectively. It can be observed that initially both the approaches could meet the demands of advertisers. However, as the number of advertisers is increasing, it can be observed that the VF-based allocation could not allocate more number of advertisers whereas CPs-based allocation is meeting the demands of increased number of advertisers. This is because the VF-based allocation carries out allocation based on user visit frequencies and by arbitrarily combining the web pages. As a result, there is a high possibility that the same user will see the advertisement multiple times which leads to under utilization of user views. The CPs-based allocation carries out allocation based on the interesting coverage patterns which has maximum

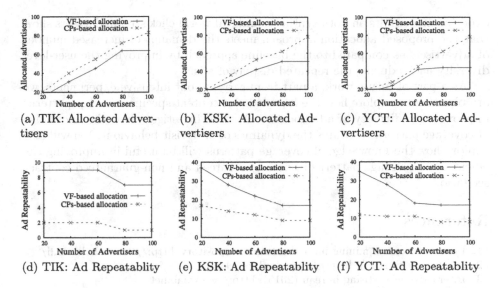

(a) TIK: Allocated Advertisers

(b) KSK: Allocated Advertisers

(c) YCT: Allocated Advertisers

(d) TIK: Ad Repeatablity

(e) KSK: Ad Repeatablity

(f) YCT: Ad Repeatablity

Fig. 3. Performance results on TIK, KSK and YCT datasets

coverage support and minimum overlap ratio. As a result, multiple advertisements are shown to the same visitor which leads to an efficient utilization of user views.

Figure 3d, e and f show the performance results of ad repeatability for the experiments conducted on TIK, KSK and YCT datasets respectively. It can be observed that, the average ad repeatability of the both approaches is decreasing with the number of advertisers. This is due to the fact that as the number of advertisers increases, the user may encounter the same advertisement multiple times. However, it can be observed that the ad repeatability reduced significantly in the proposed approach as compared to the VF-based allocation. The proposed allocation approach ensures that there is less user overlap among the web pages of a CP by carrying out the allocation based on the coverage patterns with high value of uniqueness measure thereby leading to more unique visits to a web page. As a result, ad repeatability is significantly reduced in the proposed allocation approach.

6   Conclusion and Future Work

In display advertising scenario, the objective of publisher is to maximize the revenue by meeting the advertising demands of increased number of advertisers. In this paper, we have proposed an improved allocation framework for display advertising scenario by exploiting the knowledge of coverage patterns extracted from the click stream transactions of the website. We have discussed how the nature of coverage patterns could improve the efficiency of ad slots allocation to the advertisers. We have developed the allocation framework based on coverage patterns by adding mapping, ranking steps and allocation algorithm. The experimental results on both synthetic and real world click stream datasets show that the proposed allocation approach meets the demands of increased number of advertisers as compared to the baseline approach by improving the user-level diversity and reducing the repeated display of ads.

As a part of future work, a part from carrying out intensive experiments, we are planning to explore how the knowledge of content-specific coverage patterns improves the efficiency of ad allocation. We will investigate how the knowledge of coverage patterns captures the dynamics of user visit behaviour. We will also explore how the knowledge of coverage patterns will be useful in improving the efficiency of coverage patterns in both guaranteed and non-guaranteed contract scenario.

References

1. Frequent itemset mining implementations repository. http://fimi.cs.helsinki.fi/
2. Double click (2015). http://www.doubleclick.net
3. Interactive advertising bureau (2015). http://www.iab.net
4. Recsys challenge 2015 (2015). http://2015.recsyschallenge.com/challenge.html/
5. Right media (2015). https://en.wikipedia.org/wiki/Right_Media
6. Adler, M., Gibbons, P.B., Matias, Y.: Scheduling space-sharing for internet advertising. J. Sched. **5**(2), 103–119 (2002)
7. Bharadwaj, V., Chen, P., Ma, W., Nagarajan, C., Tomlin, J., Vassilvitskii, S., Vee, E., Yang, J.: Shale: an efficient algorithm for allocation of guaranteed display advertising. In: The 18th International Conference on Knowledge Discovery and Data mining. pp. 1195–1203. ACM (2012)
8. Budhiraja, A., Reddy, P.K.: An approach to cover more advertisers in adwords. In: The 2nd International Conference on Data Science and Advanced Analytics. pp. 1–10. IEEE (2015)
9. Caruso, F., Giuffrida, G., Zarba, C.: Heuristic Bayesian targeting of banner advertising. J. Optim. Eng. **16**(1), 247–257 (2015)
10. Chvatal, V.: A greedy heuristic for the set-covering problem. Math. Oper. Res. **4**(3), 233–235 (1979)
11. Feige, U., Immorlica, N., Mirrokni, V., Nazerzadeh, H.: A combinatorial allocation mechanism with penalties for banner advertising. In: The 17th International Conference on World Wide Web. pp. 169–178. ACM (2008)
12. Feldman, J., Henzinger, M., Korula, N., Mirrokni, V.S., Stein, C.: Online stochastic packing applied to display ad allocation. In: Berg, M., Meyer, U. (eds.) ESA 2010, Part I. LNCS, vol. 6346, pp. 182 194. Springer, Heidelberg (2010)
13. Feldman, J., Mehta, A., Mirrokni, V., Muthukrishnan, S.: Online stochastic matching: beating 1–1/e. In: The 50th Annual Symposium on Foundations of Computer Science. pp. 117–126. IEEE (2009)
14. Garey, M.R., Johnson, D.S., Stockmeyer, L.: Some simplified NP-complete problems. In: The 6th Annual ACM Symposium on Theory of Computing. pp. 47–63. ACM (1974)
15. Ghosh, A., McAfee, P., Papineni, K., Vassilvitskii, S.: Bidding for representative allocations for display advertising. In: Leonardi, S. (ed.) Internet and Network Economics. LNCS, vol. 5929, pp. 208–219. Springer, Heidelberg (2009)
16. Han, J., Chang, C.C.: Data mining for web intelligence. Computer **35**(11), 64–70 (2002)

17. Hojjat, A., Turner, J., Cetintas, S., Yang, J.: Delivering guaranteed display ads under reach and frequency requirements. In: The 28th AAAI Conference on Artificial Intelligence. pp. 2278–2284. AAAI Press (2014)
18. Huang, e., Cercone, N., An, A.: Comparison of interestingness functions for learning web usage patterns. In: The 11th International Conference on Information and Knowledge Management. pp. 617–620. ACM (2002)
19. Mirrokni, V.S., Gharan, S.O., Zadimoghaddam, M.: Simultaneous approximations for adversarial and stochastic online budgeted allocation. In: The 23rd Annual Symposium on Discrete Algorithms. pp. 1690–1701. ACM-SIAM (2012)
20. Nakamura, A., Abe, N.: Improvements to the linear programming based scheduling of web advertisements. J. Electron. Commer. Res. 5(1), 75–98 (2005)
21. Srinivas, P.G., Reddy, P.K., Sripada, B., Kiran, R.U., Kumar, D.S.: Discovering coverage patterns for banner advertisement placement. In: Tan, P.-N., Chawla, S., Ho, C.K., Bailey, J. (eds.) PAKDD 2012, Part II. LNCS, vol. 7302, pp. 133–144. Springer, Heidelberg (2012)
22. Srinivas, P.G., Reddy, P.K., Trinath, A.V., Sripada, B., Kiran, R.U.: Mining coverage patterns from transactional databases. J. Intell. Inf. Syst. 45(3), 423–439 (2015)
23. Srinivas, P.G., Reddy, P.K., Trinath, A.V.: CPPG: efficient mining of coverage patterns using projected pattern growth technique. In: Li, J., Cao, L., Wang, C., Tan, K.C., Liu, B., Pei, J., Tseng, V.S. (eds.) PAKDD 2013 Workshops. LNCS, vol. 7867, pp. 319–329. Springer, Heidelberg (2013)
24. Srivastava, J., Cooley, R., Deshpande, M., Tan, P.N.: Web usage mining: discovery and applications of usage patterns from web data. SIGKDD Explor. News Lett. 1(2), 12–23 (2000)
25. Trinath, A., Gowtham Srinivas, P., Krishna Reddy, P.: Content specific coverage patterns for banner advertisement placement. In: The 1st International Conference on Data Science and Advanced Analytics. pp. 263–269. IEEE (2014)
26. Vee, E., Vassilvitskii, S., Shanmugasundaram, J.: Optimal online assignment with forecasts. In: The 11th Conference on Electronic Commerce. pp. 109–118. ACM (2010)
27. Yang, J., Vee, E., Vassilvitskii, S., Tomlin, J., Shanmugasundaram, J., Anastasakos, T., Kennedy, O.: Inventory allocation for online graphical display advertising. Computing Research Repository, CoRR (2010)

Enabling Fine-Grained RDF Data Completeness Assessment

Fariz Darari[✉], Simon Razniewski, Radityo Eko Prasojo, and Werner Nutt

Free University of Bozen-Bolzano, Bolzano, Italy
fariz.darari@stud-inf.unibz.it

Abstract. Nowadays, more and more RDF data is becoming available on the Semantic Web. While the Semantic Web is generally incomplete by nature, on certain topics, it already contains complete information and thus, queries may return all answers that exist in reality. In this paper we develop a technique to check query completeness based on RDF data annotated with completeness information, taking into account data-specific inferences that lead to an inference problem which is Π_2^P-complete. We then identify a practically relevant fragment of completeness information, suitable for crowdsourced, entity-centric RDF data sources such as Wikidata, for which we develop an indexing technique that allows to scale completeness reasoning to Wikidata-scale data sources. We verify the applicability of our framework using Wikidata and develop COOL-WD, a completeness tool for Wikidata, used to annotate Wikidata with completeness statements and reason about the completeness of query answers over Wikidata. The tool is available at http://cool-wd.inf.unibz.it/.

Keywords: RDF · Data completeness · SPARQL · Query completeness · Wikidata

1 Introduction

Over the Web, we are witnessing a growing amount of data available in RDF. The LOD Cloud[1] recorded that there were 1014 RDF data sources in 2014, covering various domains from life science to government. RDF follows the Open-World Assumption (OWA), assuming data is incomplete by default [1]. Yet, given such a large quantity of RDF data, one might wonder if it is complete for some topics. As an illustration, consider Wikidata, a crowdsourced KB with RDF support [2]. For data about the movie Reservoir Dogs, Wikidata is incomplete, as it is missing the fact that Michael Sottile was acting in the movie.[2] On the other hand, for data about Apollo 11, it is the case that Neil Armstrong, Buzz Aldrin, and Michael Collins, who are recorded as crew members on Wikidata, are indeed *all*

---

[1] http://lod-cloud.net/.

[2] By comparing the data at https://www.wikidata.org/wiki/Q72962 with the complete information at http://www.imdb.com/title/tt0105236/fullcredits.

© Springer International Publishing Switzerland 2016
A. Bozzon et al. (Eds.): ICWE 2016, LNCS 9671, pp. 170–187, 2016.
DOI: 10.1007/978-3-319-38791-8_10

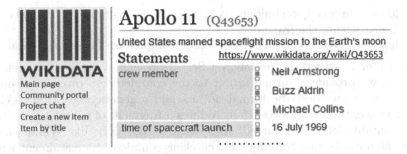

Fig. 1. Wikidata is actually complete for all the Apollo 11 crew

the crew (see Fig. 1).[3] However, such completeness information is not recorded and thus it is left to the reader to decide whether some data on the Web is already complete.

Nevertheless, the availability of explicit completeness information can benefit data access over RDF data sources, commonly done via SPARQL queries. To illustrate, suppose that in addition to the complete data of Apollo 11 crew, Wikidata is also complete for the children of the three astronauts. Consequently, a user asking for the children of Apollo 11 crew should obtain not only query answers, but also the information that the answers are complete.

Motivated by the above rationales, we argue that it is important to describe completeness of RDF data and provide a technique to check query completeness based on RDF data with its completeness information. Such a check is called *completeness entailment*. In previous work, Darari et al. [3] proposed a framework to describe completeness of RDF data and check query completeness based on completeness information. One fundamental limitation of this work is that the completeness check is agnostic of the content of the RDF data to which the completeness information is given, which results in weaker inferences. In the next section, we show that incorporating the content of RDF data may provide stronger inferences about query completeness. From the relational databases, Razniewski et al. [4], proposed wildcard-based completeness patterns to provide completeness information over databases. To check query completeness, they defined a pattern algebra, which works upon database tables enriched with completeness patterns. The work incorporated database instances in completeness check, which are conceptually similar to the content of RDF data. However, only a sound algorithm was provided for completeness check.

In this work, we make the following contributions:

1. We provide a formalization of the completeness entailment problem for RDF data, and develop a sound and complete algorithm to solve the completeness entailment problem.
2. We identify a practically relevant fragment of completeness information suitable for crowdsourced, entity-centric RDF data sources like Wikidata, and

---

[3] http://www.space.com/16758-apollo-11-first-moon-landing.html.

develop an indexing technique to improve the feasibility of completeness entailment within the fragment.
3. We develop COOL-WD, a tool to manage completeness over Wikidata.

Our paper is structured as follows: Sect. 2 presents a motivating scenario. In Sect. 3, we provide a formalization to the completeness problem, followed by Sect. 4 where we describe formal notions and a generic algorithm to check completeness entailment. Section 5 introduces a fragment of completeness information, suitable for crowdsourced, entity-centric RDF KBs like Wikidata, and presents an optimization technique for checking completeness entailment within this fragment. Section 6 reports our experimental evaluations. In Sect. 7, we describe COOL-WD. Related work is given in Sect. 8, whereas further discussion about our work is in Sect. 9. Section 10 concludes the paper and sketches future work.

2   Motivating Scenario

Let us consider a motivating scenario for the main problem of this work, that is, the check of query completeness based on RDF data with its completeness information. Consider an RDF graph about the crew of Apollo 99 (or for short, A99), a fictional space mission, and the children of the crew, as shown below.

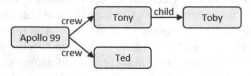

Consider now the query Q_0 asking for the crew of A99 and their children:

$$Q_0 = (W_0, P_0) = (\{\,?crew, ?child\,\}, \{\,(a99, crew, ?crew), (?crew, child, ?child)\,\})$$

Evaluating Q_0 over the graph gives only one mapping result, where the crew is mapped to Tony and the child is mapped to Toby. Up until now, nothing can be said about the completeness of the query since: (i) there can be another crew member of A99 with a child; (ii) Tony may have another child; or (iii) Ted may have a child.

Let us now consider the same graph as before, now enriched with completeness information, as shown below.

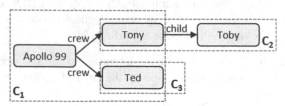

Informally, the above figure contains three completeness statements: C_1, which states that the graph contains all crew members of A99; C_2, which states the graph contains all Tony's children; and C_3, which states the graph contains all Ted's children (i.e., Ted has no children). With the addition of completeness information, let us see whether we may answer our query completely.

First, since we know that all the crew of A99 are Tony and Ted, the query Q_0 then becomes equivalent to the following two queries:

- $Q_1 = (W_1, P_1) = (\{\,?child\,\}, \{\,(a99, crew, tony), (tony, child, ?child)\,\})$
- $Q_2 = (W_2, P_2) = (\{\,?child\,\}, \{\,(a99, crew, ted), (ted, child, ?child)\,\})$

where the variable $?crew$ is instantiated with Tony and Ted, respectively.

Moreover, for Q_2 according to our graph and completeness information, Ted has no children. Thus, there is no way that Q_2 will return an answer, so Q_2 can be safely removed. Now, only Q_1 is left. Again, from our graph and completeness information, we know that Toby is the only child of Tony. Thus, Q_1 in turn is equivalent to the following boolean query:

$$Q_3 = (W_3, P_3) = (\{\}, \{\,(a99, crew, tony), (tony, child, toby)\,\})$$

with the variable $?crew$ is instantiated to Tony and $?child$ to Toby. However, our graph is complete for Q_3 as it contains the whole body of Q_3. Since from our reasoning the query Q_3 is equivalent to our original query Q_0, we conclude that our graph with its completeness information can guarantee the completeness of Q_0, that is, Toby is the only child of Tony, the only crew member of A99 having a child.

Note that using the data-agnostic approach from [3], it is not possible to derive the same conclusion. Without looking at the actual graph, we cannot conclude that Ted and Tony are all the crew members of Apollo 99. Consequently, just having the children of Tony and Ted complete does not help in reasoning about Apollo 99. In the rest of the paper, we discuss how the intuitive, data-specific reasoning from above can be formalized.

3   Formal Framework

In this section, we remind the reader of RDF and SPARQL, and provide formalization to our completeness problem.

RDF and SPARQL. Assume three pairwise disjoint infinite sets I (*IRIs*), L (*literals*), and V (*variables*). A tuple $(s, p, o) \in I \times I \times (I \cup L)$ is called a triple, while a finite set of triples is called an RDF graph.

The standard query language for RDF graphs is SPARQL [5]. At the core of SPARQL lies triple patterns, which are like triples, but also variables are allowed in each position. In this work, we focus on the conjunctive fragment of SPARQL, which uses sets of triple patterns, called basic graph patterns (BGPs). Evaluating a BGP P over G gives the set of mappings $[\![P]\!]_G = \{\,\mu \mid \mu P \subseteq G \text{ and } dom(\mu) = var(P)\,\}$. Over P, we define *a freeze mapping* $\tilde{id}$ that maps each variable $?v$ in P to a fresh IRI $\tilde{v}$. From such a mapping, we construct *the prototypical graph*

$\tilde{P} := \tilde{id}P$ that encodes any possible graph that can satisfy the BGP. A query $Q = (W, P)$ projects the evaluation results of a BGP P to a set W of variables. Moreover, a CONSTRUCT query has the abstract form (CONSTRUCT P_1 P_2) where both P_1 and P_2 are BGPs. Evaluating a CONSTRUCT query over G results in a graph where P_1 is instantiated with all the mappings in $[\![P_2]\!]_G$.

Completeness Statements. A completeness statement describes which parts of an RDF graph are complete. We adopt the definition of completeness statements in [3].

Definition 1 (Completeness Statement). *A completeness statement C is defined as $Compl(P_C)$ where P_C is a non-empty BGP.*

Example 1. The completeness statements in our motivating scenario are as follows: $C_1 = Compl(\{\,(a99, crew, ?c)\,\})$, $C_2 = Compl(\{\,(tony, child, ?c)\,\})$, and $C_3 = Compl(\{\,(ted, child, ?c)\,\})$.

To serialize completeness statements in RDF, we refer the reader to [3]. Now, let us define the semantics of completeness statements. First, we associate the CONSTRUCT query $Q_C = ($CONSTRUCT P_C $P_C)$ to each statement C. From now on, we fix a graph G upon which we describe its completeness. Given a graph $G' \supseteq G$, we call (G, G') *an extension pair.* In general, with no completeness statement, every extension pair is a valid extension pair, that is, G' is a possible state of the ideal world where all the information is complete. For instance, without completeness statement, in the motivating scenario, all of the following would be valid extensions: That there are more crew members of A99; that Tony has more children; and that Ted has children. Completeness statements restrict the valid extensions of a graph.

Definition 2 (Valid Extension Pairs). *Let G be a graph and C a completeness statement. We say that an extension pair (G, G') is valid wrt. C, written $(G, G') \models C$, if $[\![Q_C]\!]_{G'} \subseteq G$.*

The above definition naturally extends to sets of completeness statements. Over a set $\mathcal{C}$ of completeness statements and a graph G, we define *the transfer operator* $T_{\mathcal{C}}(G) = \bigcup_{C \in \mathcal{C}} [\![Q_C]\!]_G$. We have the following characterization: for all extension pairs (G, G'), it is the case that $(G, G') \models \mathcal{C}$ iff $T_{\mathcal{C}}(G') \subseteq G$.

Query Completeness. We write $Compl(Q)$ to denote that a query Q is complete. Over an extension pair, a query is complete iff it returns the same results over both the graphs of the extension pair.

Definition 3 (Query Completeness). *Let (G, G') be an extension pair and Q be a query. We define that: $(G, G') \models Compl(Q)$ iff $[\![Q]\!]_{G'} = [\![Q]\!]_G$.*[4]

---

[4] Since in this work we focus on conjunctive queries which are monotonic, the direction $[\![Q]\!]_{G'} \supseteq [\![Q]\!]_G$ comes for free.

Completeness Entailment. We now define the main problem of our work, the completeness entailment.

Definition 4 (Completeness Entailment). *Given a set C of completeness statements, a graph G, and a query Q, we define that C and G entail the completeness of Q, written as $C, G \models Compl(Q)$, if for all extension pairs $(G, G') \models C$, it holds that $(G, G') \models Compl(Q)$.*

In our motivating scenario, we have seen that the graph about the crew of A99 and the completeness statements there entail the completeness of the query Q_0 asking for the crew of A99 and their children.

In this work, we assume bag semantics for query evaluation, which is the default of SPARQL.[5] Consequently, this allows us to focus on the BGPs used in the body of conjunctive queries for completeness entailment.

4   Checking Completeness Entailment

In this section, we present an algorithm for performing the completeness check as demonstrated in our motivating scenario.

4.1   Preliminaries

Before presenting the algorithm, we introduce important notions.

First, we need to have a notion for a BGP with a stored mapping from variable instantiations. Let P be a BGP and μ be a mapping such that $dom(\mu) \cap var(P) = \emptyset$. We define the pair (P, μ) as a *partially mapped BGP*, which is a BGP with a stored mapping. Over a graph G, the evaluation of (P, μ) is defined as $[\![(P, \mu)]\!]_G = \{\mu \cup \nu \mid \nu \in [\![P]\!]_G\}$. It is easy to see that $P \equiv (P, \emptyset)$. Furthermore, we define the evaluation of a set of partially mapped BGPs over a graph G as the union of evaluating each of them over G.

Example 2. Consider our motivating scenario. Over the BGP P_0 of the query Q_0, instantiating the variable $?crew$ to $tony$ results in the BGP P_1 of the query Q_1. Pairing P_1 with this instantiation gives the partially mapped BGP $(P_1, \{?crew \mapsto tony\})$. Moreover, it is the case that $[\![(P_1, \{?crew \mapsto tony\})]\!]_G = \{\{?crew \mapsto tony, ?child \mapsto toby\}\}$.

Next, we would like to formalize the equivalence between partially mapped BGPs wrt. a set C of completeness statements and a graph G.

Definition 5 (Equivalence under C and G). *Let (P, μ) and (P', ν) be partially mapped BGPs, C be a set of completeness statements, and G be a graph. We define that (P, μ) is equivalent to (P', ν) wrt. C and G, written $(P, \mu) \equiv_{C,G} (P', \nu)$, if for all $(G, G') \models C$, it holds that $[\![(P, \mu)]\!]_{G'} = [\![(P', \nu)]\!]_{G'}$.*

The above definition naturally extends to sets of partially mapped BGPs.

---

[5] http://www.w3.org/TR/sparql11-query/.

Example 3. Consider all the queries in our motivating scenario. It is the case that $\{(P_0, \emptyset)\} \equiv_{C,G} \{(P_1, \{?crew \mapsto tony\}), (P_2, \{?crew \mapsto ted\})\} \equiv_{C,G} \{(P_3, \{?crew \mapsto tony, ?child \mapsto toby\})\}$.

Next, we would like to figure out which parts of a query contain variables that can be instantiated completely. For this reason, we define

$$cruc_{C,G}(P) = P \cap \tilde{id}^{-1}(T_C(\tilde{P} \cup G))$$

as *the crucial part* of P *wrt.* C *and* G. It is the case that $C, G \models Compl()$ $cruc_{C,G}(P)$, that is, we are complete for the crucial part. Later on, we will see that the crucial part is used to 'guide' the instantiation process during the completeness entailment check.

Example 4. Consider the query $Q_0 = (W_0, P_0)$ in our motivating scenario. We have that $cruc_{C,G}(P_0) = P_0 \cap \tilde{id}^{-1}(T_C(\tilde{P_0} \cup G)) = \{(a99, crew, ?crew)\}$ with $\tilde{id} = \{?crew \mapsto \widetilde{crew}, ?child \mapsto \widetilde{child}\}$. Consequently, we can have a complete instantiation of the crew of A99.

The operator below implements the instantiations of a partially mapped BGP wrt. its crucial part.

Definition 6 (Equivalent Partial Grounding). *Let* C *be a set of completeness statements,* G *be a graph, and* (P, ν) *be a partially mapped BGP. We define the operator* equivalent partial grounding:

$$epg((P, \nu), C, G) = \{(\mu P, \nu \cup \mu) \mid \mu \in [\![cruc_{C,G}(P)]\!]_G\}.$$

The following lemma shows that such instantiations produce a set of partially mapped BGPs equivalent to the original partially mapped BGP, hence the name equivalent partial grounding. The lemma holds since the instantiation is done over the crucial part, which is complete wrt. C and G.

Lemma 1 (Equivalent Partial Grounding). *Let* C *be a set of completeness statements,* G *be a graph, and* (P, ν) *be a partially mapped BGP. We have that*

$$\{(P, \nu)\} \equiv_{C,G} epg((P, \nu), C, G).$$

Example 5. Consider our motivating scenario. We have that:

- $epg((P_2, \{?crew \mapsto ted\}), C, G) = \emptyset$
- $epg((P_3, \{?crew \mapsto tony, ?child \mapsto toby\}), C, G) = \{(P_3, \{?crew \mapsto tony, ?child \mapsto toby\})\}$
- $epg((P_0, \emptyset), C, G) = \{(P_1, \{?crew \mapsto tony\}), (P_2, \{?crew \mapsto ted\})\}$

Generalizing from the example above, there are three cases of $epg((P, \nu), C, G)$:

- If $[\![cruc_{C,G}(P)]\!]_G = \emptyset$, it returns an empty set.
- If $[\![cruc_{C,G}(P)]\!]_G = \{\emptyset\}$, it returns $\{(P, \nu)\}$.

– Otherwise, it returns a non-empty set of partially mapped BGPs where some variables in P are instantiated.

From these three cases and the finite number of triple patterns with variables of a BGP, it holds that the repeated applications of the epg operator, with the first and second cases above as the base cases, are terminating. Note that the difference between these two base cases is on the effect of their corresponding epg operations, as illustrated in Example 5: for the first case, the epg operation returns an empty set, whereas for the second case, it returns back the input partially mapped BGP.

We define that a partially mapped BGP (P, ν) is *saturated* wrt. $\mathcal{C}$ and G, if $epg((P, \nu), \mathcal{C}, G) = \{ (P, \nu) \}$, that is, if the second case above applies. Note that the notion of saturation is independent from the mapping in a partially mapped BGP: given a mapping ν, a partially mapped BGP (P, ν) is saturated wrt. $\mathcal{C}$ and G iff (P, ν') is saturated wrt. $\mathcal{C}$ and G for any mapping ν'. Thus, wrt. $\mathcal{C}$ and G we say that a BGP P is saturated if $(P, \emptyset)$ is saturated.

The completeness checking of saturated BGPs is straightforward as we only need to check if they are contained in the graph G.

Proposition 1 (Completeness Entailment of Saturated BGPs). *Let P be a BGP, $\mathcal{C}$ be a set of completeness statements, and G be a graph. Suppose P is saturated wrt. $\mathcal{C}$ and G. Then, it is the case that: $\mathcal{C}, G \models Compl(P)$ iff $\tilde{P} \subseteq G$.*

Based on the above notions, we are ready to provide an algorithm to check completeness entailment. The next subsection gives the algorithm.

4.2   Algorithm for Checking Completeness Entailment

Now we introduce an algorithm to compute all saturated, equivalent partial grounding results of a BGP wrt. $\mathcal{C}$ and G. Following from Proposition 1, we can then check whether all the resulting saturated BGPs are contained in the graph G to see if the completeness entailment holds.

ALGORITHM 1. $sat(P_{orig}, \mathcal{C}, G)$

Input: A BGP P_{orig}, a set $\mathcal{C}$ of completeness statements, a graph G

Output: A set Ω of mappings

1 $\mathbf{P}_{working} \leftarrow \{ (P_{orig}, \emptyset) \}$
2 $\Omega \leftarrow \emptyset$
3 **while** $\mathbf{P}_{working} \neq \emptyset$ **do**
4 $\quad (P, \nu) \leftarrow \texttt{takeOne}(\mathbf{P}_{working})$
5 $\quad \mathbf{P}_{equiv} \leftarrow epg((P, \nu), \mathcal{C}, G)$
6 $\quad$ **if** $\mathbf{P}_{equiv} = \{ (P, \nu) \}$ **then**
7 $\quad \quad \Omega \leftarrow \Omega \cup \nu$
8 $\quad$ **else**
9 $\quad \quad \mathbf{P}_{working} \leftarrow \mathbf{P}_{working} \cup \mathbf{P}_{equiv}$
10 $\quad$ **end**
11 **end**
12 **return** Ω

Consider a BGP P_{orig}, a set C of completeness statements, and a graph G. The algorithm works as follows: First, we transform our original BGP P_{orig} into its equivalent partially mapped BGP $(P_{orig}, \emptyset)$ and put it in $\mathbf{P}_{working}$. Then, in each iteration of the while loop, we take and remove a partially mapped BGP (P, ν) from $\mathbf{P}_{working}$ via the method takeOne. Afterwards, we compute $epg((P, \nu), C, G)$. As discussed above there might be three result cases here: (i) If $epg((P, \nu), C, G) = \emptyset$, then simply we remove (P, ν) and will not consider it anymore in the later iteration; (ii) If $epg((P, \nu), C, G) = \{(P, \nu)\}$, that is, (P, ν) is saturated, then we collect the mapping ν to the set Ω; and (iii) otherwise, we add to $\mathbf{P}_{working}$ a set of partially mapped BGPs instantiated from (P, ν). We keep iterating until $\mathbf{P}_{working} = \emptyset$, and finally return the set Ω.

The following proposition follows from the construction of the above algorithm and Lemma 1.

Proposition 2. *Given a BGP P, a set C of completeness statements, and a graph G, the following properties hold:*

- *For all $\mu \in sat(P, C, G)$, it is the case that μP is saturated wrt. C and G.*
- *It holds that $\{(P, \emptyset)\} \equiv_{C,G} \{(\mu P, \mu) \mid \mu \in sat(P, C, G)\}$.*

From the above proposition, we can derive the following theorem, which shows the soundness and completeness of the algorithm to check completeness entailment.

Theorem 1 (Completeness Entailment Check). *Let P be a BGP, C be a set of completeness statements, and G be a graph. It holds that*

$$C, G \models Compl(P) \quad iff \quad for\ all\ \mu \in sat(P, C, G)\ .\ \widetilde{\mu P} \subseteq G.$$

Example 6. Consider our motivating scenario. We have that $sat(P_0, C, G) = \{\{?crew \mapsto tony, ?child \mapsto toby\}\}$. It is the case that for all $\mu \in sat(P_0, C, G)$, it holds that $\widetilde{\mu P_0} \subseteq G$. Thus, by Theorem 1 the entailment $C, G \models Compl(P_0)$ holds.

By reduction from validity of $\forall\exists$3SAT formula, one can show that the complexity of the completeness entailment is Π_2^P-complete.

Corollary 1 (Complexity of Completeness Check). *Deciding whether the entailment $C, G \models Compl(P)$ holds, given a set C of completeness statements, a graph G, and a BGP P, is Π_2^P-complete.*

In what follows, we provide optimization techniques for the algorithm, which work for generic cases of completeness entailment.

Early Failure Detection. In our algorithm, the containment checks for saturated BGPs are done at the end. Indeed, if there is a single saturated BGP not contained in the graph, we cannot guarantee query completeness. Thus, instead of having to collect all saturated BGPs and then check the containment later on, we can improve the performance of the algorithm by performing the containment check right after the saturation check (Line 6 of the algorithm). So, as soon as there is a failure in the containment check, we stop the loop and conclude that the completeness entailment does not hold.

Completeness Skip. Recall the definition of the operator $epg((P, \nu), \mathcal{C}, G) = \{ (\mu P, \nu \cup \mu) \mid \mu \in [\![cruc_{\mathcal{C},G}(P)]\!]_G \}$, which relies on the **cruc** operator. Now, suppose that $cruc_{\mathcal{C},G}(P) = P$, that is, we are complete for the whole part of the BGP P. Thus, we actually do not have to instantiate P in the **epg** operator, since we know that the instantiation results are contained in G as the consequence of it being complete wrt. $\mathcal{C}$ and G. In conclusion, whenever $cruc_{\mathcal{C},G}(P) = P$, we just remove (P, ν) from $\mathbf{P}_{working}$ and thus skip its instantiations.

Despite these optimizations, for a large number of completeness statements, the completeness entailment check may take long. In the next section, we identify a practically relevant fragment of completeness statements, for which we develop an indexing technique to make the entailment check feasible.

5   A Practical Fragment of Completeness Statements

This section identifies *SP-statements*, a fragment of completeness statements possessing several properties that are suitable to be used in practice. In the next sections, we show by experimental evaluations the feasibility of this fragment with an indexing technique we describe below, and demonstrate a completeness tool for Wikidata using the fragment.

5.1   SP-Statements

An SP-statement $Compl(\{ (s, p, ?v) \})$ is a completeness statement with only one triple pattern in the BGP of the statement, where the subject and the predicate are IRIs, and the object is a variable.[6] In our motivating scenario, all the completeness statements are in fact SP-statements. The statements possess the following properties, which are suitable for practical use:

- Having a simple structure, completeness statements within this fragment are easy to create and to be read. Thus, they are suitable for *crowdsourced* KBs, where humans are involved.
- An SP-statement denotes the completeness of all the property values of the entity which is the subject of the statement. This fits *entity-centric* KBs like Wikidata, where data is organized into entities (i.e., each entity has its own data page).
- Despite their simplicity, SP-statements can be used to guarantee the completeness of more complex queries such as queries whose length is greater than one (as illustrated by our motivating scenario).

5.2   SP-Indexing

We describe here how to optimize completeness entailment check with SP-statements. Recall our generic algorithm to check completeness entailment:

---

[6] We do not allow the subject to be a variable as it is not practically reasonable (e.g., complete for all the entities and values of predicate **child**).

In the *cruc* operator within the *epg* operator (Line 5 of Algorithm 1), we have to compute $T_C(\tilde{P} \cup G)$, that is, evaluate all CONSTRUCT queries of the completeness statements in C over the graph $\tilde{P} \cup G$. This may be problematic if there are a large number of completeness statements in C. Thus, we want to avoid such costly T_C applications. Given that completeness statements are of the form SP-statements, we may instead look for the statements having the same subject and predicate of the triple patterns in the BGP. The crucial part of the BGP P wrt. C and G are the triple patterns with the matching subject and predicate of the completeness statements.

Proposition 3. *Given a BGP P, a graph G, and a set C of SP-statements, it is the case that*

$$cruc_{C,G}(P) = \{\, (s,p,o) \in P \mid there\, exists\, a\, statement\, Compl(\{\, (s,p,?v)\,\}) \in C \,\}.$$

From the above proposition, to get the crucial part, we only have to find an SP-statement with the same subject and predicate for each triple pattern of the BGP. In practice, we can facilitate this search using a standard hashmap, providing constant-time performance, also for other basic operations such as **add** and **delete**. The hashmap provides a mapping from the concatenation of the subject and the predicate of a statement to the statement itself. To illustrate, the hashmap of the completeness statements in our motivating scenario is as follows: $\{\, a99\text{-}crew \mapsto C_1, tony\text{-}child \mapsto C_2, ted\text{-}child \mapsto C_3 \,\}$.

6   Experimental Evaluation

Now that we have an indexing technique for SP-statements, we want to see the performance of completeness check. To do so, we perform experimental evaluations with a realistic scenario, where we compare the runtime of completeness entailment when query completeness can be guaranteed (i.e., the success case), completeness entailment when query completeness cannot be guaranteed (i.e., the failure case), and query evaluation.

Experimental Setup. Our reasoning algorithm and indexing modules are implemented in Java using the Apache Jena library.[7] We use Jena-TDB as the triple store of our experiment. The SP-indexing is implemented using the standard Java **hashmap**, where the keys are strings, constructed from the concatenation of the subject and predicate of completeness statements, and the values are Java objects representing completeness statements. All experiments are done on a standard laptop with a 2.4 GHz Intel Core i5 and 8 GB of memory.

To perform the experiment, we need three ingredients: a graph, completeness statements, and queries. For the graph, we use the direct-statement fragment of the Wikidata graph, which does not include qualifiers nor references and consists of 100 mio triples.[8] The completeness statements and queries of this experiment are constructed based on the following pattern queries:

---

[7] https://jena.apache.org/.
[8] http://tools.wmflabs.org/wikidata-exports/rdf/index.php?content=dump_download.php&dump=20151130.

1. Give all mothers of mothers of mothers.
   $P_1 = \{ (?v, P25, ?w), (?w, P25, ?x), (?x, P25, ?y) \}$
2. Give the crew of a thing, the astronaut missions of that crew, and the operator of the missions.
   $P_2 = \{ (?v, P1029, ?w), (?w, P450, ?x), (?x, P137, ?y) \}$
3. Give the administrative divisions of a thing, the administrative divisions of those divisions, and their area.
   $P_3 = \{ (?v, P150, ?w), (?w, P150, ?x), (?x, P2046, ?y) \}$

To generate queries, we simply evaluate each pattern query over the graph, and instantiate the variable $?v$ of each pattern query with the corresponding mappings from the evaluation. We record 5200 queries instantiated from P_1, 57 queries from P_2, and 475 queries from P_3. Each pattern query has a different average number of query results: the instantiations of P_1 give 1 result, those of P_2 give 4 results, and those of P_3 give 108 results on average.

To generate completeness statements, from each generated query, we iteratively evaluate each triple pattern from left to right, and construct SP-statements from the instantiated subject and the predicate of the triple patterns. This way, we guarantee that all the queries can be answered completely. We generate in total around 1.7 mio statements, with 30072 statements for P_1, 484 statements for P_2, and 1682263 statements for P_3. Such a large number of completeness statements would make completeness checks without indexing very slow: Performing just a single application of the T_C operator with all these statements, which occurs in the cruc operator of the algorithm without SP-indexing, took about 20 min. Note that in a completeness check, there might be many T_C applications.

Now we describe how to observe the behavior when queries cannot be guaranteed to be complete, that is, the failure case. In this case, we drop randomly 20 % of the completeness statements for each pattern query. To make up the statements we drop, we add dummy statements with the number equal to the number of dropped statements. This way, we ensure the same number of completeness statements for both the success and failure case.

For each query pattern, we measure the runtime of completeness check for both the success case and the failure case, and then query evaluation for the success case.[9] We take 40 sample queries for each pattern query, repeat each run 10 times, and report the median of these runs.

Experimental Results. The experimental results are shown in Fig. 2. Note that the runtime is in log scale. We can see that in all cases, the runtime increases with the first pattern query having the lowest runtime, and the third pattern query having the highest runtime. This is likely due to the increased number of query results. We observe that in all pattern queries, completeness check when queries are guaranteed to be complete is slower than those whose completeness cannot be guaranteed. We suspect that this is because in the former case, variable

---

[9] We do not measure query evaluation time for failure case since query evaluation is independent of the completeness of the query.

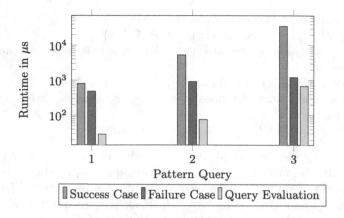

Fig. 2. Experiment results of completeness entailment

instantiations have to be performed much more than in the latter case. In the latter case, as also described in Subsect. 4.2, as soon as we find a saturated BGP not contained in the graph, we stop the loop in the algorithm and return `false`, meaning that the query completeness cannot be guaranteed.

In absolute scale, completeness check runs relatively fast, with 796 μs for P_1, 5264 μs for P_2, and 35130 μs for P_3 in success case; and 485 μs for P_1, 903 μs for P_2, and 1209 μs for P_3 in failure case. Note that as mentioned before, completeness check without indexing is not feasible at all here, as there are a large number of completeness statements, making the T_C application very slow (i.e., 20 min for a single application). For all pattern queries, however, query evaluation runs faster than completeness checking. This is because completeness checking may involve several query evaluations during the instantiation process with the `epg` operator.

To conclude, we have observed that completeness checking with a large number of SP-statements can be done reasonably fast, even for large datasets, by the employment of indexing. Also, we observe a clear positive correlation between the number of query results and the runtime of completeness checking. Last, performing completeness check when a query is complete is slower than that when a query cannot be guaranteed to be complete.

7   COOL-WD: A Completeness Tool for Wikidata

In this section, we introduce COOL-WD, a **CO**mpleteness to**OL** for **Wik**i**D**ata. The tool implements our completeness framework with SP-statements and focuses to provide completeness information for direct statements of Wikidata. While our implementation is based on Apache Jena, our approach can be applied also via other Semantic Web frameworks like Sesame.[10] Our tool is inspired by

---

[10] http://rdf4j.org/.

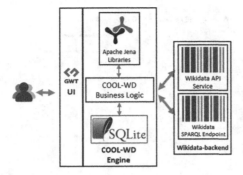

Fig. 3. COOL-WD architecture

real, natural language completeness statements on Wikipedia, where completeness statements are given in a crowdsourced way.[11] The tool is available at http://cool-wd.inf.unibz.it/.

7.1 System Architecture

As shown in Fig. 3, COOL-WD consists of three main components: user interface (UI), COOL-WD engine, and Wikidata-backend.

The first component is the UI, developed using GWT.[12] The UI provides the front-end interface for COOL-WD users, enabling them to search for Wikidata entities, look at facts about them enriched with completeness information, add/remove completeness statements, and check the completeness of a Wikidata query.

The second component is the engine, responsible for storing completeness statements using SQLite and performing completeness checks. We use optimization techniques as described in Subsect. 4.2 and SP-indexing as described in Sect. 5 to improve the performance of completeness checks.

The last component is the Wikidata-backend. It consists of two subcomponents: Wikidata API and Wikidata SPARQL endpoint. The API is used for the suggestions feature in searching for Wikidata entities, while the Wikidata SPARQL endpoint serves as the source of Wikidata facts to which completeness statements are given, and of query evaluation.

7.2 Tool Usage

Here, we describe how one can use COOL-WD. From the landing page, the user is provided with a search bar for Wikidata entities. The search bar features autocomplete search suggestions, matching user keywords with the English labels of Wikidata entities. Clicking on a search suggestion gives the users the entity

---

[11] https://en.wikipedia.org/wiki/Template:Complete_list.
[12] http://www.gwtproject.org/.

Fig. 4. The COOL-WD page of Apollo 11. Complete property values are with checkmarks.

page, consisting of Wikidata facts about the entity with its completeness information. An example is shown in Fig. 4, which is the Apollo 11 page with the complete crew. Complete properties are distinguished by the checkmark symbol. To add a completeness statement, a user simply clicks a question mark next to the respective properties of an entity. Additionally, it is possible to add provenance information about authors, timestamps, and references of the statement. Suppose the user would also like to add completeness statements for the astronaut missions of Neil Armstrong, Buzz Aldrin, and Michael Collins. Therefore, she may perform an analogous operation: go to the entity pages, and click the question mark next to the respective properties. We also have a feature to see all stored completeness statements over Wikidata filtered by properties on the aggregation page.

If a user would like to evaluate a query and check its completeness, she has to go to the query page. Suppose she wants to know the crew of Apollo 11 and their astronaut missions. The user then specifies her query, and executes it. Instead of having only query answers, she can also see the completeness information of the answers.

8   Related Work

Data completeness concerns the breadth, depth, and scope of information [6]. In the relational databases, Motro [7] and Levy [8] were among the first to investigate data completeness. Motro developed a sound technique to check query completeness based on database views, while Levy introduced the notion of local completeness statements to denote which parts of a database are complete. Razniewski and Nutt [9] further extended their results by reducing completeness reasoning to containment checking, for which many algorithms are known, and characterizing the complexity of reasoning for different classes of queries. In terms of their terminology, our completeness entailment problem is one of QC-QC entailment under bag semantics, for which so far it was only known that it is in Π_3^P [10]. In [4], Razniewski et al. proposed completeness patterns and defined a pattern algebra to check the completeness of queries. The work incorporated database instances, yet provided only a sound algorithm for completeness check.

We now move on to the Semantic Web. Fürber and Hepp [11] distinguished three types of completeness: ontology completeness, concerning which ontology classes and properties are represented; population completeness, referring to whether all objects of the real-world are represented; and property completeness, measuring the missing values of a specific property. In our work, SP-statements can be used to state the property completeness of an entity. Mendes et al. [12] proposed Sieve, a framework for expressing quality assessment and fusion methods, where completeness is also considered. With Sieve, users can specify how to compute quality scores and express a quality preference specifying which characteristics of data indicate higher quality. In the context of crowdsourcing, Chu et al. [13] developed KATARA, a hybrid data cleaning system, which not only cleans data, but may also add new facts to increase the completeness of the KB; whereas Acosta et al. [14] developed HARE, a hybrid SPARQL engine to enhance answer completeness.

Galárraga et al. [15] proposed a rule mining system that is able to operate under the Open-World Assumption (OWA) by simulating negative examples using the Partial Completeness Assumption (PCA). The PCA assumes that if the dataset knows some r-attribute of x, then it knows all r-attributes of x. This heuristic was also employed by Dong et al. [16] to develop Knowledge Vault, a Web-scale system for probabilistic knowledge fusion. In their paper, they used the term Local Closed-World Assumption (LCWA).

9   Discussion

We discuss here various aspects of our work: sources of completeness statements, completeness statements with provenance, and no-value information.

Sources of Completeness Statements. As demonstrated by COOL-WD, one way to provide completeness statements is via crowdsourcing. For domain-specific data like biology and archeology, domain experts may be a suitable source of completeness statements. An automated way to add completeness statements can also be leveraged by using NLP techniques to extract natural language completeness statements already available on the Web: around 13000 Wikipedia pages contain the keywords "complete list of" and "list is complete", while IMDb provides complete cast information with the keywords "verified as complete" for some movies like Reservoir Dogs.[13]

Completeness Statements with Provenance. Just as data can be wrong, completeness statements can be wrong, too. Moreover, as data may change over time, completeness statements can be out-of-date. As a possible solution, one can add provenance information. Adding information about the author and reference of completeness statements may be useful to check the correctness of the statements, while attaching timestamps would provide timeliness information to the statements.

---

[13] http://www.imdb.com/title/tt0105236/fullcredits.

No-Value Information. Completeness statements can also be used to represent the non-existence of information. For example, in our motivating scenario, there is the completeness statement about the children of Ted with no corresponding data in the graph. In this case, we basically say that Ted has no children. As a consequence of having no-value information, we can be complete for queries despite having the empty answer. Such a feature is similar to that proposed in [17]. The only difference is that here we need to pair completeness statements with a graph that has no corresponding data captured by the statements, while in that work, no-value statements are used to directly say that some parts of data do not exist.

10   Conclusions and Future Work

The availability of an enormous amount of RDF data calls for better data quality management. In this work, we focus on the data quality aspect of completeness. We develop a technique to check query completeness based on RDF data with its completeness information. To increase the practical benefits of our framework, we identify a practically relevant fragment of completeness information upon which an indexing can be implemented to optimize completeness check, and develop COOL-WD, a completeness management tool for Wikidata.

For future work, we would like to investigate indexing techniques for more general cases. One challenge here is that how to index the arbitrary structure of completeness statements. Another plan is to develop a technique to extract completeness statements on the Web. To do so, we in particular want to detect if a Web page contains completeness statements in natural language, and transform them into RDF-based completeness statements. Last, we also want to increase the expressivity of queries, say, to also handle negations. Queries with negations are especially interesting since negation naturally needs complete information to work correctly.

Acknowledgments. We would like to thank Sebastian Rudolph for his feedback on an earlier version of this paper. The research was supported by the projects "CANDy: Completeness-Aware Querying and Navigation on the Web of Data" and "TaDaQua - Tangible Data Quality with Object Signatures" of the Free University of Bozen-Bolzano, and "MAGIC: Managing Completeness of Data" of the province of Bozen-Bolzano.

References

1. Hayes, P.J., Patel-Schneider, P.F. (eds.): RDF 1.1 Semantics. W3C Recommendation, 25 February 2014
2. Vrandecic, D., Krötzsch, M.: Wikidata: a free collaborative knowledgebase. Commun. ACM **57**(10), 78–85 (2014)
3. Darari, F., Nutt, W., Pirrò, G., Razniewski, S.: Completeness statements about rdf data sources and their use for query answering. In: Alani, H., Kagal, L., Fokoue, A., Groth, P., Biemann, C., Parreira, J.X., Aroyo, L., Noy, N., Welty, C., Janowicz, K. (eds.) ISWC 2013, Part I. LNCS, vol. 8218, pp. 66–83. Springer, Heidelberg (2013)

4. Razniewski, S., Korn, F., Nutt, W., Srivastava, D.: Identifying the extent of completeness of query answers over partially complete databases. In: ACM SIGMOD 2015, pp. 561–576 (2015)
5. Harris, S., Seaborne, A. (eds.): SPARQL 1.1 Query Language. W3C Recommendation, 21 March 2013
6. Wang, R.Y., Strong, D.M.: Beyond accuracy: what data quality means to data consumers. J. Manage. Inf. Syst. **12**(4), 5–33 (1996)
7. Motro, A.: Integrity = Validity + Completeness. ACM Trans. Database Syst. **14**(4), 480–502 (1989)
8. Levy, A.Y.: Obtaining complete answers from incomplete databases. In: VLDB 1996, pp. 402–412 (1996)
9. Razniewski, S., Nutt, W.: Completeness of queries over incomplete databases. PVLDB **4**(11), 749–760 (2011)
10. Razniewski, S., Nutt, W.: Assessing query completeness over incomplete databases. In: VLDB Journal (submitted)
11. Fürber, C., Hepp, M.: SWIQA - a semantic web information quality assessment framework. In: ECIS 2011 (2011)
12. Mendes, P.N., Mühleisen, H., Bizer, C.: Sieve: linked data quality assessment and fusion. In: EDBT/ICDT Workshops, pp. 116–123 (2012)
13. Chu, X., Morcos, J., Ilyas, I.F., Ouzzani, M., Papotti, P., Tang, N., Ye, Y.: KATARA: a data cleaning system powered by knowledge bases and crowdsourcing. In: ACM SIGMOD 2015, pp. 1247–1261 (2015)
14. Acosta, M., Simperl, E., Flöck, F., Vidal, M.-E.: HARE: a hybrid SPARQL engine to enhance query answers via crowdsourcing. In: K-CAP 2015, pp. 11:1–11:8 (2015)
15. Galárraga, L.A., Teflioudi, C., Hose, K., Suchanek, F.M.: AMIE: association rule mining under incomplete evidence in ontological knowledge bases. In: WWW 2013, pp. 413–422 (2013)
16. Dong, X., Gabrilovich, E., Heitz, G., Horn, W., Lao, N., Murphy, K., Strohmann, T., Sun, S., Zhang, W.: Knowledge vault: a web-scale approach to probabilistic knowledge fusion. In: ACM SIGKDD 2014, pp. 601–610 (2014)
17. Darari, F., Prasojo, R.E., Nutt, W.: Expressing no-value information in RDF. In: ISWC Posters and Demos (2015)

Benchmarking Web API Quality

David Bermbach[1] and Erik Wittern[2(✉)]

[1] ISE Research Group, TU Berlin, Berlin, Germany
db@ise.tu-berlin.de
[2] IBM T.J. Watson Research Center, Yorktown Heights, NY, USA
witternj@us.ibm.com

Abstract. Web APIs are increasingly becoming an integral part of web or mobile applications. As a consequence, performance characteristics and availability of the APIs used directly impact the user experience of end users. Still, quality of web APIs is largely ignored and simply assumed to be sufficiently good and stable. Especially considering geo-mobility of today's client devices, this can lead to negative surprises at runtime.

In this work, we present an approach and toolkit for benchmarking the quality of web APIs considering geo-mobility of clients. Using our benchmarking tool, we then present the surprising results of a geo-distributed 3-month benchmark run for 15 web APIs and discuss how application developers can deal with volatile quality both from an architectural and engineering point of view.

1 Introduction

Nowadays, mobile and web applications regularly include third-party data or functionality through web APIs; often, the application's own back end systems are accessed in a comparable way. Building on technologies like AJAX, runtime environments like the Play Framework[1], and research results, e.g., from service-oriented computing, cloud computing, or mash-ups, this no longer poses a technological challenge. Therefore, we now see thousands of public APIs as well as applications using them [33].

In consequence, though, application developers now heavily rely on third-party entities beyond their control sphere for core functionality of their applications. This can have impacts on applications' user experience. For example, the latency of web API requests may impact application response times. Response times above 1 or 10 seconds have been shown to disrupt users' flow of thought or even cause loss of attention, respectively [25]. Or, a long-term experiment performed by Google showed that increasing response times artificially from 100ms to 400ms did measurably decrease the average amount of searches performed by users [10]. User experience and, hence, application reputation is thus directly affected by actions and non-actions of the API providers. As another example,

---

Author names are in alphabetical order as both authors have contributed equally.
[1] https://www.playframework.com/.

© Springer International Publishing Switzerland 2016
A. Bozzon et al. (Eds.): ICWE 2016, LNCS 9671, pp. 188–206, 2016.
DOI: 10.1007/978-3-319-38791-8_11

APIs may be discontinued or changed without notice, thus disabling applications. A recent analysis of a set of mobile applications finds that they silently fail and in cases even crash when confronted with mutated (e.g., adapted or faulty) web API responses [13]. Another aspect largely ignored yet is quality of web APIs: Due to the black-box nature of web API endpoints[2], applications are directly affected by volatile latencies, throughput limitations, and intermittent availability without having any influence or forewarning. Furthermore, quality of web APIs may vary depending on the geo-origin of requests.

In this work, we aim to shed some light on this issue and propose a number of strategies for dealing with poor quality. For this purpose, we present the following contributions:

1. A measurement approach and its prototypical proof-of-concept implementation for geo-distributed benchmarking of performance and availability of web APIs.
2. The results of a geo-distributed 3-month experiment with 15 web APIs.
3. A number of strategies on the implementation and architecture level for dealing with select observations from our experiments.

This paper is structured as follows: Initially, we give an overview of the request flow for web API calls and discuss how different qualities can be affected at various points in that request flow (Sect. 2). We also describe how we propose to measure select qualities. Next, we describe our experiment design (Sect. 3) and our observations (Sect. 4). Finally, we sketch-out how application developers can deal with lack of quality (Sect. 5), and discuss related work (Sect. 6) before coming to a conclusion (Sect. 7).

2 Quality of Web APIs

In this section, we give an overview of select qualities in web APIs and discuss how they can be measured. For this purpose, we start with a description of individual steps in performing web API requests (Sect. 2.1) and potential root causes of failures (Sect. 2.2). Afterwards, we characterize the qualities which we have studied for this paper (Sect. 2.3) and describe our measurement approach and the corresponding prototypical implementation of our toolkit (Sect. 2.4).

2.1 Interaction with Web APIs

Web APIs expose *data*, e.g., a user profile or an image file, and *functionalities*, e.g., a payment process or the management of a virtual machine through a resource abstraction. This abstraction enables users to manipulate these resources without requiring insight into the underlying implementation.

---

[2] We denote an endpoint to be the combination of a resource, identified by a URL, and an HTTP *method* as proposed in [30].

Developers can access Web APIs through the *Hypertext Transfer Protocol* (HTTP), which again uses the *Transmission Control Protocol* (TCP) for error-free, complete, and ordered data transmission on the transport layer, and the *Internet Protocol* (IP) at the network layer. Figure 1 illustrates the steps involved in a typical HTTP request[3].

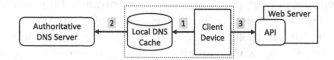

Fig. 1. Overview of the Steps Involved in Sending an HTTP Request

The resources exposed by an API are identified by *unified resource locators* (URLs), describing the scheme to be used for interaction, the server Internet address, and the specific resource identifier. The semantics of interactions with a resource depend upon the HTTP *method*, e.g., GET, POST, or DELETE. Before a client can send a request to the server that offers the web API, client and server need to establish a TCP connection. For this purpose, the client first sends a lookup request for the URL of the server to a *Domain Name Service* (DNS) server which returns the Internet protocol (IP) address and port number of the target host. If available, IP address and port may be returned from a local cache (step 1); otherwise, an external DNS authority is consulted (step 2). Afterwards, the client opens a socket connection to the server, i.e., it initiates TCP's three-way hand-shake, thus, establishing a TCP connection (step 3). Based on this connection, multiple HTTP requests with application data can be sent to the server.

If additional security is required, the client will typically use HTTPS which introduces the *Transport Level Security* (TLS) protocol[4] between HTTP and TCP/IP. TLS has two main phases: a negotiation phase and a bulk data transfer phase. In the negotiation phase, the server authenticates itself through his X.509 certificate. Afterwards, the client sends his list of supported cipher suites (a combination of symmetric encryption algorithm and a message authentication code (MAC)) to the server which then selects a cipher suite supported by both client and server and responds accordingly. Using asymmetric encryption (e.g., RSA) and key exchange protocols (e.g., DHE), client and server also agree on a symmetric key and other TLS sessions parameters.

After this TLS handshake has been completed, the server signals a change to the bulk data transfer phase. During that phase, each HTTP request is broken down into data packets which are – based on the agreed session parameters – encrypted and signed before transmission over the network. Cipher suite and pro-tocol version determine whether encrypt-then-MAC or the reverse order is used.

---

[3] For simplicity's sake, we do not include possible complications like proxies, keep alive connections, caches, or gateways in this figure.

[4] TLS has largely replaced its predecessor SSL which is typically supported only for compatibility with old clients.

The recipient can then reassemble the original request and verify its integrity based on the received MAC.

2.2 Sources of Failures

Considering the typical HTTP request flow described in Sect. 2.1, a number of possible breakpoints emerge at which a request may fail. As we will see, while some of these are in control of a web API provider, others are not.

A **failed DNS lookup** is caused by attempting to look up a host for which no DNS entry exists or by a network partitioning which causes the lookup request to an authoritative DNS server to time out. The first error source is rather unlikely for web API requests with the correct URL, as it would imply the disappearance of the API's host altogether. Typically, a failed lookup results in a timeout error reported to the client. The second error source appears only in case that the network is not available and the DNS entry is not yet cached locally.

A **client connection error** appears if no TCP connection can be established between the client and the server hosting the web API. Reasons for this error are network partitioning or that the server is in a state where it cannot accept connections (for example, because it crashed).

In the case of HTTPS, a request can also fail if authentication of the server is not possible due to certificate issues or if there is no cipher suite supported by both client and server.

A **client error** appears if the request sent by the client cannot be processed by the server. One reason for client errors is that the requested resource cannot be found on the server. Furthermore, users may not be authorized to access the requested resource. The client may not have been aware of authentication mechanism like basic authentication or OAuth or may not own proper credentials. Furthermore, providers may deny authorization for specific clients if their usage of an API exceeds certain thresholds. A broad range of client errors are considered by HTTP and should result in the server sending 4xx status codes. While these errors are attested to the client, it is important to note that their appearance can be tightly related to actions of the web API provider. For example, many changes on the server, e.g., introducing authentication, removing or renaming resources, or changing request formatting, cause existing clients to malfunction, i.e., the client error is in fact caused by the web API provider.

A **server error** appears if the server fails to process an otherwise correct request. Reasons for server errors may include failed lookups for resources in databases or errors in the execution of functionalities. Server errors are, similar to client errors, considered by HTTP and should result in the server sending 5xx status codes.

2.3 Qualities

Systems have a number of properties. These can be functional, i.e., describe the abilities of said system, or non-functional, i.e., describe the quality of said system. Quality describes how "good" or "bad" a system fulfills its tasks along several dimensions[5] – the qualities.

There is a plethora of qualities that we can see in web APIs. Examples range from availability and performance, to security, reliability, scalability, cost, or correctness (of results). All these qualities are inherently connected through complex direct and indirect tradeoff relationships [3]. In this paper, we focus on two qualities: availability and performance.

Availability. Generally, availability describes the likelihood of a system – here, a web API – being able to respond to requests. Providing a concise definition of availability, though, is non-trivial: Does an API have to send correct responses or does it suffice if it is still able to tell about current problems? For this paper, we distinguish three different kinds of availability to consider these questions:

Pingability describes whether there is anything "alive" at the API provider's site. This may be a load balancer or even a fault endpoint. For a single machine deployment, pingability describes whether said machine is reachable at an operating system level. Pingability is fulfilled if, at the web API's URL, some entity responds to basic low level requests, e.g., ping requests (ICMP protocol).

Accessibility describes whether the resource represented by the web API is still accessible but not necessarily able to fulfill its task. For a single machine deployment, accessibility describes whether the web server component is reachable but does not require the hosted application logic to be accessible. A web API is accessible if it responds to HTTP requests using one of the predefined HTTP status codes.

Successability describes whether the web API is fully functional. For a single host deployment, it requires the application logic to be working[6]. Hence, we define successability to be fulfilled if a web API responds to requests using 2xx or 3xx status codes.

Performance. Performance has two dimensions: *latency* and *throughput*. Latency describes the amount of time between the start of a request at the client and the end of receiving a response, also at the client. Throughput, on the other hand, describes the number of requests a web API is handling at a given point in time. Typically, throughput measurements try to determine the maximum throughput, i.c., the maximum number of requests that a web API is able to handle without timeouts.

Usually, these two dimensions are interconnected: If the load increases towards maximum throughput, then latency will increase. If this is not the case, then the system behind the web API is typically referred to as elastically scalable [20,27].

---

[5] It depends on the respective quality what "good" or "bad" implies.

[6] Please, note, that successability does not say anything about correctness of results.

2.4   Implementation

We have built our measurement system around the quality definitions above: Pingability can be measured by sending a ping request to the respective endpoint; accessability and successability can be measured by sending HTTP or HTTPS requests. This also allows us to track request latencies. Originally, we also planned to measure throughput (and, thus, also scalability since we do not have any insight into the API provider's implementation) by sending large numbers of concurrent requests. For our experiments, we refrained from doing so since most provider's terms of use explicitly rule out any kind of usage which would resemble a DDoS attack. Therefore, we also recommend strongly that application developers who plan to roll out their application to large user groups should contact the respective API providers about throughput limits.

Our measurement toolkit is parameterized with a list of API endpoints. Based on this parameter list, it periodically sends ping, HTTP, and HTTPS requests. The toolkit then logs detailed results which are analyzed when the benchmark run has been completed. Our open source prototype for benchmarking web APIs is publicly available.[7]

3   Experiment Design

In this section, we will give an overview of our experiment setup. We will start with a description of chosen API endpoints (Sect. 3.1) before continuing with the parameters of our experiment setup (Sect. 3.2).

3.1   Analysed Web API Endpoints

Typically, web API endpoints require clients to authenticate to interact with the resources they expose. Authentication mechanisms include *basic authentication*, where a username and password have to be sent with every request, or the more frequently used *OAuth*. OAuth allows clients to access web APIs without having to expose user's credentials. OAuth, however, requires eventual human interaction to authorize client applications for requests and involves additional requests to establish authentication. While this may be an option for actual applications, it is prohibitive for benchmarking purposes. One way to circumvent the need for human interaction is to "automate" it through the use of people services [4], but latency and availability measurements would then become entirely meaningless. Another possibility is to make requests using API-specific *software development kits* (SDKs), which hide such complexities from the client. However, SDKs are not readily available for all APIs. Furthermore, correctly interpreting benchmark results obtained using SDKs would require us to fully understand their inner workings (e.g., through code-reviews) and eventually to align them for comparability. All in all, we, thus, decided to perform our experiments with unauthenticated API endpoints only. Focusing on these endpoints allows us to

---

[7] https://github.com/dbermbach/web-api-bench.

control the parameters influencing our measurements, e.g., as we avoid multiple roundtrips (possibly to third-party entities) for authentication.

We identified unauthenticated API endpoints from a variety of different providers with regards to company sizes, country of origin, local or global target users, public or private sector. We specifically included some of the most well-known providers like Google, Apple, Amazon, and Twitter. Table 1 gives an overview of the web API endpoints which we have selected for our experiments and the respectively supported protocols.

Table 1. Benchmarked API Endpoints and Supported Protocols.

API Name	ICMP	HTTP	HTTPS	Request Meaning
Amazon S3	-	X	X	Get file list for the 1000 genomes public data set
Apple iTunes	X	X	X	Get links to resources on artists
BBC	-	X	-	Get the playlist for BBC Radio 1
ConsumerFinance	X	X	X	Retrieve data on consumer complaints on financial products in the US
Flickr	X	X	X	Get list of recent photo and video uploads
Google Books	X	-	X	Get book metadata by ISBN
Google Maps	X	X	X	Query location information by address
MusicBrainz	X	X	X	Retrieve information about artists and their music
OpenWeatherMap	X	X	-	Get weather data by address
Postcodes.io	X	X	X	Get location information based on UK zip codes
Police.uk.co	-	X	X	Retrieve street level crime data from the UK
Spotify	X	X	X	Get information on a given artist
Twitter	X	X	-	Get the number of mentions for a given URL
Wikipedia	X	X	X	Retrieve a Wikipedia article
Yahoo	X	X	X	Get weather data by address

Please, note: In this work, we want to highlight unexpected behavior and unpredictability of web API quality but we do not aim to discredit individual API providers. For this reason, we decided to anonymize our results and will, for the remainder of this paper, only refer to these API endpoints as API-1 to API-15. There is no correlation between the identifiers and the order of API endpoints in Table 1. However, we will reveal this mapping information upon request if we are convinced that the information will not be used to discredit individual providers.

3.2   Experiment Setup

To analyze whether API quality varies depending on the geo-origin of the request, we deployed our toolkit in several locations. For this purpose, we used one Amazon EC2 instance in each of the following Amazon regions: US East (Virginia), US West (Oregon), EU (Ireland), Asia (Singapore), Asia (Sydney), Asia (Tokyo), and South America (Sao Paulo).

We configured our toolkit to send ping, HTTP, and HTTPS requests every 5 min but each starting at a different timestamp for the first request to avoid interference. Ping was configured to use 5 packets per request and we disabled local caching for HTTP and HTTPS requests.

Our test started on August 20th, 2015 (16:00h CEST) and was kept running for exactly three months; due to detailed logging and extensive prior testing, we can rule out crashes and other issues happening in our prototype.

4   Observations

Within this section, we present select results of our quality benchmarks. First, we summarize findings regarding availability and latency (Sect. 4.1). The partially poor quality revealed by these findings motivates our discussion of mitigation strategies in Sect. 5. Second, we present select cases of observations that reveal interesting behavior and correlations in qualities (Sect. 4.2).

We have uploaded our collected raw data on GitHub so that other researchers can use it as well.[8]

4.1   General Observations

Figure 2 summarizes our findings with regard to collected **availability** measures. For every API endpoint, all measurements from all regions were aggregated to derive the illustrated successability values. Results regarding ping requests allow statements regarding the pingability of the web APIs (cf. Sect. 2.3). For ping requests, the results presented in Fig. 2 reflect the mean values for all ping requests performed (we performed 5 attempts to ping a server per measurement). In cases where no data is presented, the server did not allow ping requests with the ICMP protocol. Results regarding HTTP and HTTPS requests allow statements regarding the accessibility and successability of requests (cf., Sect. 2.3). The results presented in Fig. 2 focus on successability, that is, the success rates relate to the number of requests that return an HTTP status code between 200 and 399. On the other hand, we do not differentiate here between requests failing due to failed DNS lookups, client connection errors, client errors, or server errors. Thus, Fig. 2 reflects the perspective of an application user for whom it is more important *if* a request fails rather than *why* it does. In cases where no HTTPS data is available, the endpoint did not support TLS.

---

[8] https://github.com/ErikWittern/web-api-benchmarking-data.

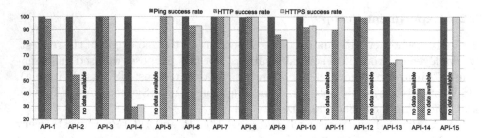

Fig. 2. Aggregated Availability Results.

Table 2. Availabilities of Benchmarked API Endpoints.

End-point	Successability [%]			Days with HTTP/HTTPS Successability <50%							Sum
	Ping	HTTP	HTTPS	Ireland	Oregon	Sao Paulo	Singa-pore	Sydney	Tokyo	US East	
API-1	99.97	97.80	69.73	11/11	-/72	-/-	-/-	3/29	-/-	83/-	14/195
API-2	99.35	54.16	-	43/-	43/-	43/-	43/-	43/-	43/-	43/-	301/-
API-3	99.83	99.98	99.98	-/-	-/-	-/-	-/-	-/-	-/-	-/-	-/-
API-4	99.86	29.43	31.08	64/64	64/64	78/64	64/64	64/64	64/67	64/64	462/451
API-5	-	99.97	99.40	-/4	-/-	-/-	-/-	-/-	-/-	-/-	-/4
API-6	99.88	92.59	92.58	49/49	-/-	-/-	-/-	-/-	-/-	-/-	49/49
API-7	99.96	99.98	99.98	-/-	-/-	-/-	-/-	-/-	-/-	-/-	-/-
API-8	99.33	99.96	99.96	-/-	-/-	-/-	-/-	-/-	-/-	-/-	-/-
API-9	99.75	85.79	81.90	-/-	-/-	-/89	-/-	6/-	57/-	-/-	63/89
API-10	99.94	91.37	92.56	49/49	-/-	-/-	-/-	-/-	-/-	-/-	49/49
API-11	-	89.44	99.13	-/-	66/-	-/-	-/-	3/6	-/-	-/-	69/6
API-12	99.79	98.86	-	-/-	-/-	-/-	-/-	-/-	-/-	-/-	-/-
API-13	99.77	63.81	66.17	-/-	92/92	-/-	-/-	70/70	3/58	71/-	236/220
API-14	-	43.75	-	-/-	91/-	92/-	-/-	92/-	88/-	4/-	367/-
API-15	99.23	-	99.96	-/-	-/-	-/-	-/-	-/-	-/-	-/-	-/-
Sum				216/177	356/228	213/153	107/64	281/169	255/125	265/64	1610/1063

We furthermore depict corresponding figures in the columns "success rates" in Table 2. We find that availability rates, indicated by ping requests, are above 99% for all APIs that support the ICMP protocol. With respect to successability, indicated by HTTP and HTTPS GET requests, a different picture emerges. Of the 14 endpoints tested with HTTP GET requests, 8 have a successability of 90% or higher, 6 have a successability of 95% or higher, and only 4 have a successability of 99% or higher. On the bottom, 4 endpoints even show a successability below 65%. On average, the 12 endpoints tested with HTTPS GET requests performed slightly better than their HTTP counterparts. 6 out of 12 endpoints have a successability of 99%, and 8 have a successability of 90% or higher.

To obtain a more precise picture about the distribution of the availability of API endpoints across regions, we determined for every API in every region the number of days in which successability is below 50%. Note that overall, our experiments ran for 92 days. The results of this analysis are presented in the columns "Days with HTTP/HTTPS Successability <50%" in Table 2.

The results show that even if overall successability is above 90 %, there can be considerable outages across a day in a subset of regions. For example, tested endpoints of API-6 and API-10 are not available for 49 days via HTTP from region Ireland. Furthermore, differences in the overall successability between different regions become visible. Oregon has overall the most and Singapore the least days in which web API calls fail for over 50 % of all requests. Interestingly, considering the successability observations of the 11 API endpoints that accept requests both via HTTP and HTTPS, we find that on average in 73.53 % of all situations where either HTTP or HTTPS requests fail, the other request does succeed during the same time frame.

Next, we also assess **latency** figures for the tested API endpoints. In Fig. 3, we present box plots of the measured latencies for HTTPS requests across regions. We decided to present HTTPS requests only since HTTPS seems to be becoming the default in the web.

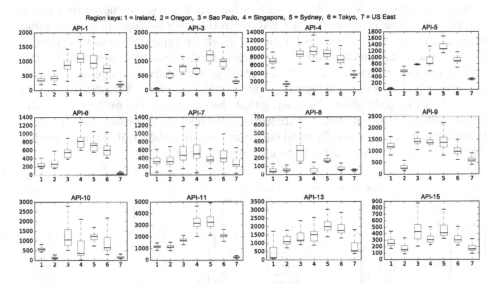

Fig. 3. Summary of HTTPS Request Latencies Across Regions in Milliseconds.

We consider two observations especially significant from the presented figures. First, for a single web API endpoint, latencies can vary tremendously depending on the geographic region from which requests originate. On average per API, the highest mean latency in a region is approximately 9 times higher than the lowest mean latency in another region. Even for the endpoint of API-7, whose performance is the most consistent one, the average latency in Singapore is 1.64 times higher than in Ireland. For 10 out of the 12 presented web API endpoints, the difference between the lowest and highest average latency is above 300 %, for 7 it is above 500 %, and for 4 endpoints, it is even above 1000 %. At the top end, for API-5, the highest average latency is over 27 times higher than the lowest average latency in another region. Second, even within individual regions, latencies can vary tremendously. For example, calls to the endpoint of API-1 from region Sydney have a standard deviation of 6943.63 around a mean value of 1411.61ms. Or, also from region Sydney, calls to the endpoint of API-7 have a standard deviation of 2410.95 around a mean value of 487.39ms. Both cases feature significant outliers (up to 498, 246ms respectively 120, 035ms). So while these endpoints may technically be available, their response times render them unusable in some cases from a practical point of view.

4.2   Select Examples

The first example of interesting behavior is that two API endpoints, the ones of API-2 and API-4, became unavailable in all regions during our experiments and remained that way until we concluded our tests. Figure 4 shows observed status codes of HTTP requests to the endpoint of API-2 over time. For the chart, we assigned a status code of 600 to requests for which the server never returned a response. Possible error sources are failures in the DNS lookup, client connection errors, or network partitionings (cf. Sect. 2.2), which typically result in a timeout of the request. The figure shows that requests predominantly succeed in the first half of our experiments, except for eventual server errors or requests for which we received no answer. At a certain point, however, requests consistently start to return a status code of 401, indicating that the client failed to authenticate, and some infrequent lost requests with status code 600. In this case, it seemed the provider turned the originally open endpoint into an authenticated one, requiring clients to adapt correspondingly to continue working.

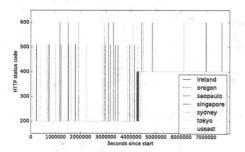
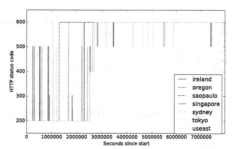

Fig. 4. Availability of API-2 over Time.

Fig. 5. Availability of API-4 over Time.

Figure 5 shows the status codes for HTTP requests to the endpoint of API-4 over time. Here, requests start to fail from one region, Oregon, at first. Then, as in the case of the endpoint of API-2, all regions receive status codes of 401 indicating unauthorized calls, however, shortly after turning into status codes of 600 throughout. This behavior is at odds with the fact that pingability of API-2 succeeded throughout the experiment.

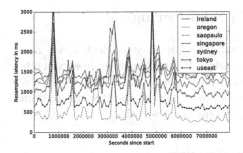
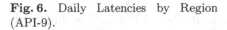

Fig. 6. Daily Latencies by Region (API-9).

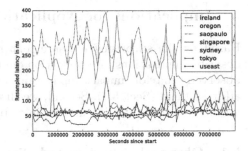

Fig. 7. Daily Latencies by Region (API-8).

Another interesting observation from our experiments is the possibility to infer data center locations. Figures 6 and 7 plot the average daily latency for the endpoints of API-9 and API-8 over the period of our experiment. Figure 6 is an example for a case where latency values across regions follow one pattern. The region from which requests feature the consistently lowest latencies is Oregon, indicating that API-9's endpoints are served from close to that region. There are still differences in latency due to the distance from that region, but the uniformity in the behavior of latencies indicates that all global requests are served from a single geographical location. On the other hand, in Fig. 7, the latencies from the different regions are much less clearly related. Notably, latencies for the regions Sao Paulo and Sydney are significantly higher than in the other five regions. Apart from that, the API seems to serve requests in different regions from different data centers, as there are little notable similarities between latencies.

4.3 Discussion and Threats to Validity

We rule out network partitionings that would disconnect a region completely for a longer period of time. As we see from the results of very well performing APIs (e.g.,. API-8, API-3), successful requests were performed from all regions throughout the duration of our experiments.

Our experiments target select endpoints. The findings from our experiments can, thus, not necessarily be generalized to the overall API from which the endpoint stems. For example, providers may choose to remove an endpoint we benchmarked, while the majority of the API is still available. Another aspect is that we only used GET requests – due to caching, actual availabilities may be worse. Nonetheless, we deem our results valid examples of how web API qualities can impact applications, which ultimately rely on specific endpoints.

We, furthermore, limited our experiments to endpoints that do not require authentication. One might argue that these endpoints may be of less importance to their providers and may, thus, undergo less scrutiny than other endpoints. Nonetheless, these endpoints may well be used by applications and the here presented findings can, hence, be considered relevant to application developers.

5   Implications for Application Engineering

Based on the surprising measurement results we reported in Sect. 4, we now describe implications for application engineering. First, we outline how concrete observed behaviors impact applications and present possible measures to directly address them (Sect. 5.1). Second, we discuss how different architecture options are able to deal with fluctuations in web API quality (Sect. 5.2).

5.1   Observed Behaviors and Direct Measures

Highly volatile latencies and temporary unavailabilites: All of our benchmarked web APIs show highly volatile latencies and temporary unavailabilities, even for requests originating from the same region. These behaviors lead to equally volatile application non-functionalities, whose impact depends upon the role the web API requests play in the application. If web API requests are a central part of an application's functionality, e.g., showing the user's location based on a maps API, the whole user experience will suffer. On the other hand, some web API calls perform mere supportive functionalities, e.g., advertising APIs, in which cases the perceived experience does not suffer.

Without detailed monitoring, an application provider may not even become aware of these quality problems and will only notice decreasing usage numbers (cf. [10]). While some web APIs expose monitored past and current availability and response times[9], the usefulness of this information is limited because it only focuses on the availability from a API provider perspective. Similarly, web API monitoring services like Runscope[10] only measure the availability of the server. However, unavailability may also be an effect of network partitioning between client and server, which is especially relevant for availability across geographic regions and/or from mobile clients.

In cases where a small degree of data staleness is acceptable, client-side caching can be used to address volatile latencies or unavailabilities, e.g., standard HTTP client-side caching or HTML 5's offline web storage. Recently, Google proposed a service to queue web API requests in case of temporary unavailability of mobile devices [1]. While the device is unavailable, the service queues web API requests and executes them once availability is back. This pattern could be adopted to compensate for temporary unavailability of web APIs in cases where the user does not need the results of the API call, e.g., status posts on social networks will work but requests for coordinates based on a given address will not.

Differences in latency and availability based on geo-origin of requests: Another set of observed behaviors is that some APIs denote stark differences in latency and availability across regions. Thus, developers rolling out globally accessible applications should not expect that web API qualities observed locally are true for every user. One approach to address this issue is, as we do in this paper,

---

[9] For example, http://status.ideal-postcodes.co.uk/.
[10] https://www.runscope.com/.

to perform geographically distributed benchmarking of qualities as part of the API selection process. Existing performance monitoring tools targeting website or web API providers could be used for this purpose[11]. However, the resulting efforts and costs might still render this solution inadequate, especially, since observed behavior may change at any time and without warning. Interestingly, we find that in many cases HTTP endpoints were accessible while HTTPS ones were not and vice versa (cf. Sect. 4.1). If the nature of the resource to interact with permits it, one approach to increase availability is, thus, to simply switch protocol if an API becomes unavailable. An alternative is using another API with comparable functionality as backup, i.e., choosing a strategy comparable to horizontal SaaS federation as proposed in [22].

Long-Lasting Unavailabilities and Disappearance of Endpoints: Finally, we have observed long-lasting unavailabilities or even the disappearance of endpoints based on discontinued or changed APIs in our experiments (cf. Sect. 4.2). This behavior causes a serious risk for application developers as functionalities their application rely on might disappear entirely, potentially even only in regions that developers do not have direct access to. Again, developers can rely on continuous, distributed monitoring of APIs to detect such cases, if they can justify the efforts and cost. A recent service[12] addresses the issue of (parts of) web APIs disappearing by allowing developers to register for notifications in case of API changes.

All in all, developers should not assume that web APIs are a given in their (then) current form or that their performance remains anything close to stable. Sending API requests asynchronously is, from a user experience perspective, probably a good idea for most scenarios.

5.2   Considering Web API Quality at Architecture Level

Since quality of web APIs is highly volatile, it needs to be considered in engineering of web or mobile applications. We have already discussed some direct measures like client-side caching or geo-distributed benchmarking during the API selection process. However, web API quality can also be considered on an architectural level. Figure 8 gives an overview of three different options.

The first option, on the left, is probably the state of the art for most mobile applications but also for many web applications. Whenever the API is needed, the application directly invokes the API and is, thus, highly dependent on it and mirrors experienced quality to the end user. This architectural style, hence, does not account for variations in quality but is the easiest to implement.

The second option, in the middle, uses a backup API in case of problems (unavailability or high latency) with the original one. To our knowledge, this is not yet done in practice (at least not on a large scale) but may become more and more feasible as dynamic service substitution techniques which have been well

---

[11] For example, https://www.pingdom.com.
[12] https://www.apichangelog.com/.

researched in service-oriented computing (e.g., [14]) can leverage the increased use of machine-readable API descriptions (e.g., Swagger) and corresponding research efforts [30]. This architectural style offers some degree of resilience to API-based problems but obviously introduces additional complexity (and, thus, development cost). For mobile applications, it may also be difficult to account for permanent API changes as new versions will never reach all users and will, in any case, take some time.

When using this architectural style, we propose to add a monitoring component to the app which tracks latency and availability of the API calls based on the current location of the client and periodically forwards aggregations of this information to a back end component of the app developer. Otherwise, it may take really long for the developer to become aware of permanent API changes or long-lasting unavailabilities in some geographical regions.

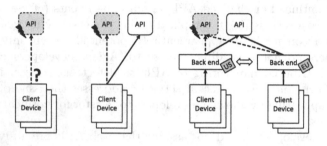

Fig. 8. High-Level Architecture Options for Web and Mobile Applications

The third option, on the right, uses a (geo-distributed) back end controlled by the application provider. Client devices do not invoke APIs directly. Instead, they direct their requests to the back end system which acts as a proxy, making actual API requests on behalf of the application. While this option certainly introduces an additional layer of complexity and cost (operating an additional back end), it also offers a set of unique benefits with regards to dealing with web API quality and resulting user experience:

1. Changing the API which is used becomes rather trivial and can be rolled out quickly on the back end. This is especially helpful as the back end will also be the entity to primarily detect API quality problems and is, through communication with other back end components, also able to interpret these problems (i.e., whether a problem is a temporary or regional issue).
2. Unavailabilities in some regions can be accounted for by tunneling API requests through another region. For instance, in case of problems with API availability for EU clients, the EU back end could send all its API requests through the US back end – at least if higher latencies are preferable over unavailability.
3. This architecture will typically improve user-perceived performance: Client-side caching can be used on both the client device and the back end, thus,

resulting in an additional speed-up and the back end may prefetch data by anticipating future API requests from the client device.
4. The API may not be a perfect fit for the requirements of the application, e.g., by returning excess amounts of data. At least for mobile applications data traffic is often expensive and, depending on the current location, slow. An additional back end can preprocess API call results (e.g., scale down images based on the needs of the client device) and can use custom, highly optimized protocols and data formats for communication with the client device.

All in all, the positive advantages outlined above should always be compared against the required efforts and cost both for building and for operating the back end. Still, the back end-based architecture will be a good solution for many application scenarios.

6 Related Work

To our knowledge, this is the first paper to address quality of web APIs through long-term benchmarking experiments, especially considering geo-distribution. There is, however, a lot of work quantifying quality in other application domains:

Beyond the classical TPC[13] benchmarks, a new set of benchmarks has recently been developed for various kinds of database and storage systems, e.g., [2,5–8,12,17,19,26,27,31,34]. There is also a number of dedicated cloud benchmarks that treat various (cloud) services as black boxes as we have done in our experiments, e.g., [9,15,18,21,23,35], or many SPEC[14] benchmarks, e.g., [28]. There are also a number of approaches trying to measure security or security overheads, e.g., TLSBench [24] for NoSQL databases, [16] for web services, and [11] for web servers.

Some works have studied how web APIs evolve [29] and how this evolution impacts client applications [32]. Others assess how well clients, e.g., mobile applications, are capable of dealing with web API changes [13]. We present specific cases in which web API endpoints changed to require authentication or eventually disappeared in Sect. 4.2. Our work, hence, provides an empirical motivation for these related works and more generally motivates a discussion about how clients can deal with web API imperfections as presented in Sect. 5 – no matter if these imperfections are caused by API evolution or other effects.

7 Conclusion

As the number of web APIs and their usage grows, their quality increasingly impacts application behavior and user experience. In this work, we presented the means to benchmark select qualities of web APIs in a geo-distributed way. Our 3-month study of 15 API endpoints reveals serious quality issues: Availability varies considerably between APIs, ranging from temporary outages to

---

[13] http://www.tpc.org.
[14] https://www.spec.org/.

the complete disappearance of tested endpoints. Furthermore, average latencies vary across regions by a factor of 9. In some cases, the observed latency of requests was so high that it virtually resembles unavailability. These findings show that application developers need to be aware of these issues and need to mitigate them if possible. For that reason, we presented ways for application developers to detect and handle web API unavailabilities and deal with volatile performance.

References

1. Archibald, J.: Introducing Background Sync. https://developers.google.com/web/updates/2015/12/background-sync?hl=en. Accessed: 17 Dec 2015
2. Bermbach, D., Tai, S.: Benchmarking eventual consistency: lessons learned from long-term experimental studies. In: Proceeding of IC2E, pp. 47–56. IEEE (2014)
3. Bermbach, D.: Benchmarking Eventually Consistent Distributed Storage Systems. Ph.D. thesis, Karlsruhe Institute of Technology (2014)
4. Bermbach, D., Kern, R., Wichmann, P., Rath, S., Zirpins, C.: An extendable toolkit for managing quality of human-based electronic services. In: Proceedings of the 3rd Human Computation Workshop HCOMP (2011)
5. Bermbach, D., Kuhlenkamp, J.: Consistency in distributed storage systems. In: Gramoli, V., Guerraoui, R. (eds.) NETYS 2013. LNCS, vol. 7853, pp. 175–189. Springer, Heidelberg (2013)
6. Bermbach, D., Tai, S.: Eventual consistency: how soon is eventual? an evaluation of amazon s3's consistency behavior. In: Proceedings of MW4SOC, pp. 1–6. ACM (2011)
7. Bermbach, D., Zhao, L., Sakr, S.: Towards comprehensive measurement of consistency guarantees for cloud-hosted data storage services. In: Nambiar, R., Poess, M. (eds.) TPCTC 2013. LNCS, vol. 8391, pp. 32–47. Springer, Heidelberg (2014)
8. Binnig, C., Kossmann, D., Kraska, T., Loesing, S.: How is the weather tomorrow?: towards a benchmark for the cloud. In: Proceedings of DBTEST, pp. 1–6. ACM (2009)
9. Borhani, A.H., Leitner, P., Lee, B.S., Li, X., Hung, T.: WPress: an application-driven performance benchmark for cloud-based virtual machines. In: Proceedings of EDOC, pp. 101–109. IEEE (2014)
10. Brutlag, J.: Speed Matters for Google Web Search. Google, Inc, Technical report (2009)
11. Coarfa, C., Druschel, P., Wallach, D.S.: Performance analysis of TLS web servers. ACM Trans. Comput. Syst. (TOCS) 24(1), 39–69 (2006)
12. Cooper, B.F., Silberstein, A., Tam, E., Ramakrishnan, R., Sears, R.: Benchmarking cloud serving systems with YCSB. In: Proceedings of SOCC, pp. 143–154. ACM (2010)
13. Espinha, T., Zaidman, A., Gross, H.G.: Web API Fragility: How robust is your mobile application? In: Proceedings of MOBILESoft, pp. 12–21. IEEE (2015)
14. Fredj, M., Georgantas, N., Issarny, V., Zarras, A.: Dynamic service substitution in service-oriented architectures. In: IEEE Congress on Services - Part I, pp. 101–104. IEEE, July 2008
15. Garfinkel, S.L.: An Evaluation of Amazon's Grid Computing Services: EC2, S3, and SQS. Harvard University, Technical report (2007)

16. Juric, M.B., Rozman, I., Brumen, B., Colnaric, M., Hericko, M.: Comparison of performance of web services, WS-security, RMI, and RMI-SSL. J. Syst. Softw. **79**(5), 689–700 (2006)
17. Klems, M., Bermbach, D., Weinert, R.: A runtime quality measurement framework for cloud database service systems. In: Proceedings of QUATIC. pp. 38–46 (2012)
18. Klems, M., Menzel, M., Fischer, R.: Consistency benchmarking: evaluating the consistency behavior of middleware services in the cloud. In: Maglio, P.P., Weske, M., Yang, J., Fantinato, M. (eds.) ICSOC 2010. LNCS, vol. 6470, pp. 627–634. Springer, Heidelberg (2010)
19. Kossmann, D., Kraska, T., Loesing, S.: An evaluation of alternative architectures for transaction processing in the cloud. In: Proceedings of SIGMOD. pp. 579–590. ACM (2010)
20. Kuhlenkamp, J., Klems, M., Röss, O.: Benchmarking Scalability and Elasticity of Distributed Database Systems. pp. 1219–1230 (2014)
21. Kuhlenkamp, J., Rudolph, K., Bermbach, D.: AISLE: assessment of provisioned service levels in public IaaS-based database systems. In: Barros, A., et al. (eds.) ICSOC 2015. LNCS, vol. 9435, pp. 154–168. Springer, Heidelberg (2015). doi:10. 1007/978-3-662-48616-0_10
22. Kurze, T., Klems, M., Bermbach, D., Lenk, A., Tai, S., Kunze, M.: Cloud federation. Cloud Comput. **2011**, 32–38 (2011)
23. Lenk, A., Menzel, M., Lipsky, J., Tai, S., Offermann, P.: What are you paying for? performance benchmarking for infrastructure-as-a-service offerings. In: Proceedings of CLOUD, pp. 484–491. IEEE (2011)
24. Müller, S., Bermbach, D., Tai, S., Pallas, F.: Benchmarking the performance impact of transport layer security in cloud database systems. In: Proceedings of IC2E, pp. 27–36. IEEE (2014)
25. Nielsen, J.: Usability Engineering. Elsevier, 1st edn. (1994)
26. Patil, S., Polte, M., Ren, K., Tantisiriroj, W., Xiao, L.,López, J., Gibson, G., Fuchs, A., Rinaldi, B.: YCSB++: benchmarking and performance debugging advanced-features in scalable table stores. In: Proceedings of SOCC, pp. 1–14. ACM (2011)
27. Rabl, T., Gómez-Villamor, S., Sadoghi, M., Muntés-Mulero, V., Jacobsen, H.A., Mankovskii, S.: Solving Big Data Challenges for Enterprise Application Performance Management. pp. 1724–1735 (2012)
28. Sachs, K., Kounev, S., Bacon, J., Buchmann, A.: Performance evaluation of message-oriented middleware using the SPECjms2007 benchmark. Perform. Eval. **66**(8), 410–434 (2009)
29. Sohan, S., Anslow, C., Maurer, F.: A case study of web API evolution. In: Proceedings of SERVICES, pp. 245–252. IEEE (2015)
30. Suter, P., Wittern, E.: Inferring web api descriptions from usage data. In: Proceedings of the 3rd IEEE Workshop on Hot Topics in Web Systems and Technologies (HotWeb), pp. 7–12 (2015)
31. Wada, H., Fekete, A., Zhao, L., Lee, K., Liu, A.: Data consistency properties and the trade-offs in commercial cloud storages: the consumers' perspective. In: Proceedings of CIDR, pp. 134–143 (2011)
32. Wang, S., Keivanloo, I., Zou, Y.: How do developers react to RESTful API evolution? In: Franch, X., Ghose, A.K., Lewis, G.A., Bhiri, S. (eds.) ICSOC 2014. LNCS, vol. 8831, pp. 245–259. Springer, Heidelberg (2014)
33. Wittern, E., Laredo, J., Vukovic, M., Muthusamy, V., Slominski, A.: A graph-based data model for api ecosystem insights. In: Proceedings of ICWS, pp. 41–48. IEEE (2014)

34. Zellag, K., Kemme, B.: How consistent is your cloud application? In: Proceedings of SOCC. ACM (2012)
35. Zhao, L., Liu, A., Keung, J.: Evaluating cloud platform architecture with the CARE framework. In: Proceedings of APSEC, pp. 60–69 (2010)

Correlation of Ontology-Based Semantic Similarity and Human Judgement for a Domain Specific Fashion Ontology

Edgar Kalkowski[✉] and Bernhard Sick

University of Kassel, Kassel, Germany
{kalkowski,bsick}@uni-kassel.de

Abstract. Evaluation of semantic similarity is difficult because semantic similarity values are highly subjective. There are several approaches that compare automatically computed similarities with values assigned by humans for general purpose terms and ontologies that contain general purpose terms. However, ontologies should be as domain specific as possible to capture the maximal amount of semantic knowledge about a domain. To evaluate the semantic knowledge captured by a custom fashion ontology we conducted a survey and crowdsourced similarity values for fashion terms. In this article we compare the manually assigned similarities to those computed automatically with several ontology-based similarity measures. We show that our proposed feature-based measure achieves the highest correlation with human judgement and give some insight into why this kind of similarity measure most resembles human similarity assessments. To evaluate the influence of the ontology on similarities we compare the results achieved with our fashion ontology to similarity values computed using a fragment of DBpedia.

Keywords: Feature based similarity · Semantic similarity · Fashion ontology

1 Introduction

Many applications of the semantic web deal with ontologies and use them to assess the semantic similarity of terms. However, since the semantic similarity of terms is highly subjective it is difficult to evaluate whether or not computed similarity values actually make sense. One approach is to compare automatically computed similarities to values assigned by human experts. For example, in [1] 353 and in [2] 3000 word pairs were manually assigned with similarity values based on human judgement. In both cases general purpose words were used and WordNet [3] was used to automatically compute similarities for comparison.

Our application is concerned with search engine marketing where much historical data is aggregated over time for all search keywords entered into the search engine and the advertisement displayed for them. However, since there can be thousands [4] or millions [5,6] of keywords, data for many low traffic

© Springer International Publishing Switzerland 2016
A. Bozzon et al. (Eds.): ICWE 2016, LNCS 9671, pp. 207–224, 2016.
DOI: 10.1007/978-3-319-38791-8_12

keywords is sparse, if existent at all. Since those keywords are rather specific, they are interesting for advertisement, because it is reasonable to assume that a customer is more inclined to buy an advertised product if it fits to their very specific search request.

To derive forecasts for low traffic keywords we propose to aggregate data from similar keywords. These aggregated data can then be used to train machine learning models like ARMA models [7–9], support vector regression [10–12], or generative models such as those presented in [13,14]. To compute similarities between keywords we propose to use ontology-based similarity measures. Because the terms that occur in search engine marketing are highly specific to the domain for which ads are placed we created our own custom ontology that covers those domain specific terms.

The key contribution of this article is an evaluation of the similarity values computed based on our custom ontology. Since the terms are highly domain specific the results of [1,2] cannot be used for comparison since very few terms from our search engine marketing domain occur in these samples. Instead, we gathered similarity values assigned by humans for comparison by conducting our own survey among 183 participants. In this article we evaluate the results of the survey and compare the similarities assigned by humans with similarity assessments computed automatically by similarity measures based on our custom ontology. In addition to the custom ontology we also used a subset of the DBpedia ontology [15] extracted from Wikipedia for the evaluation.

The remainder of this article is structured as follows: In Sect. 2 we give a brief overview of related work. The ontologies we used in our evaluation are described in Sect. 3 and the similarity measures based on those ontologies are defined in Sect. 4. Section 5 is concerned with the survey we conducted and in Sect. 6 we discuss our findings and compare the similarity values obtained with the survey with those computed by our similarity measures. Finally, in Sect. 7 we summarize our findings and give a brief outlook of further research.

2   Related Work

This articles touches on two particular topics for both of which some related work will be presented in this section. Firstly, in this article several graph based similarity measures are used. Secondly, this article is concerned with evaluating the semantics captured by a custom ontology by comparing automatically computed similarity values to those assigned by humans.

There are several approaches to computing similarities based on graphs or ontologies. The article [16] gives an overview of ontology-based similarity measures and categorizes measures as being either *edge counting*, *feature-based*, or making use of *information content*. In case of edge counting measures [17–20] the similarity assessment of two nodes in an ontology is based on the number of hops on a path between the two nodes for edge counting measures. Feature-based similarity measures [21,22] assess the properties of nodes in the ontology, e.g. their taxonomical neighborhood. Finally, measures making use of information content [23–27] are based on a big text corpus and assess the similarity of nodes in an ontology by evaluating the frequencies and positions in which terms of the nodes occur in the text corpus.

In this article we use two edge counting approaches and one feature-based method to compute the similarity of concepts in ontologies. Measures based on information content are not feasible in our application due to the lack of a suitable domain specific text corpus.

As mentioned for example in [28] it is difficult to evaluate whether or not semantic similarity values are reasonable since the semantic similarity of two terms is highly subjective. However, there have been several approaches [1,2,29,30] in which automatically computed similarities have been compared to those assigned by humans. All of these data sets use general purpose terms and only few general purpose terms occur in our domain specific ontology. Thus, in order to evaluate how well our ontology captures semantic information about our application domain we performed a survey to create a new data set with manually assigned similarity values for term pairs taken from the fashion domain.

3   Ontologies

In this section we briefly describe our custom fashion ontology and the fragment of DBpedia we use for similarity measurements.

There already exist many general purpose ontologies like DBpedia [15] or WordNet [3] which are also available in German. However, our application contains many domain specific terms, especially fashion brands and categories, which are not represented in general purpose ontologies. Thus, we created our own ontology which tries to incorporate as many relevant terms as possible by analyzing the website of the online shop doing the advertising, in our case a shop mainly concerned with fashion items.

The main hierarchical structure of our ontology is a tree of 769 fashion categories. Orthogonal to the categories we have several secondary flat hierarchies that describe properties of the fashion items present in each category, e.g., used materials, color, size, etc. The biggest secondary hierarchy is that of fashion brands which contains 1749 entries, even more than we have fashion categories. Table 1 summarizes all concepts in our ontology and additionally states the number of instances of each concept and the number of connections from instances of each concept to other nodes in the ontology.

There are several options to store an ontology. We decided to use Neo4J [31] since this database explicitly supports graph storage and natively supports typical graph queries such as paths of arbitrary lengths between two nodes which is convenient for edge counting approaches.

Our fashion ontology is the first ontology used in this paper. To analyze the influence of the ontology on similarity measurements we compare the results obtained with our fashion ontology to those computed with a fragment of the DBpedia. The nodes of this ontology represent Wikipedia pages and the relationships between nodes represent links between Wikipedia pages. Including further

Table 1. Concepts and relationships in our fashion ontology. For each concept the number of instances in the ontology is stated and the number of connections from those instances to other nodes in the ontology. Where appropriate the concepts were translated from German.

Concept	Instances	Connections	Concept	Instances	Connections
Brand	1749	90748	Pattern	7	1118
Category	769	1520	Clasp	6	872
Size	522	30932	HeelHeight	5	378
Technology	24	1204	ShaftHeight	5	220
OuterMaterial	21	6356	DEN	5	24
Color	18	17162	ShoeTip	4	542
InnerLining	17	1468	ShaftWidth	3	60
Length	15	362	TrouserHeight	3	136
Collar	12	580	Collection	2	1316
HeelForm	10	584			

Wikipedia content such as the info boxes or article abstracts into the ontology is not feasible since the resulting ontology gets too big to be stored in the Neo4J database and query times become unreasonably high and memory intensive. The DBpedia fragment we use consists of 7 149 395 instances of the "resource" concept and 112 453 671 connections between resources each of which represents a link between the two corresponding Wikipedia pages.

The search engine marketing application is concerned with 236 837 keywords which consist of 26 324 unique terms. With our fashion ontology for 201 789 of the keywords at least one matching concept in the ontology can be found. For the DBpedia this number is a little higher since we find at least one concept for 224 102 keywords. When looking directly at the terms, the difference gets even higher: We find at least one concept for only 3 553 terms using our fashion ontology while 15 575 terms can be mapped to at least one concept in the DBpedia ontology. Although the coverage of both keywords and terms is greater in case of the DBpedia ontology we show in Sect. 6 that our fashion ontology better captures the semantics of the application domain in the sense that similarities computed with the fashion ontology have a higher correlation to human judgement.

After we described the used ontologies in this section the following section is concerned with the similarity measures which make use of the semantic information stored in the ontologies to compute the similarities of sets of terms.

4   Similarity Measures

This section presents the ontology-based similarity measures used in this article.

The goal of our measures is to compute the similarity of two sets of terms T_1 and T_2 whose terms belong to one of two keywords that shall be compared.

The comparison is executed in three stages: First, we compare the terms themselves and factor in how many terms the two sets have in common. Secondly, the terms are mapped to concepts in the used ontology and a second factor considers how many concepts are common in both sets. Lastly, we compare the remaining concepts using the structure of the ontology in different ways.

The first factor that considers the common terms is denoted with τ and is computed as

$$\tau = \begin{cases} 0, & T_1 = T_2 = \emptyset \\ \frac{|T_1 \cap T_2|}{|T_1 \cup T_2|}, & \text{otherwise} \end{cases} \tag{1}$$

where $|\cdot|$ denotes the cardinality of a set and T_1, T_2 are two sets of terms whose similarity shall be computed. If both sets have no terms in common or both sets are empty τ becomes 0, if both sets contain exactly the same terms τ is 1.

The remaining terms in each set which are not contained in the other set are mapped to concepts in the ontology. How exactly this is done depends on the used ontology. For our custom fashion ontology each concept node just contains one or more terms as a description. In this case we perform a case insensitive match and check if a term is contained as a substring in any of the terms describing a concept. For the DBpedia fragment each concept is described by a unique URI which always begins with http://de.dbpedia.org/resource. Here, the first common part of the URI is stripped to prevent terms like "http" or "resource" matching all nodes. The remainder of the URI is again searched in a case insensitive manner to check if a term is contained as a substring.

By means of this matching we get a set C_1' of concepts in the ontology for $T_1 \backslash (T_1 \cap T_2)$ and a set C_2' of concepts and for $T_2 \backslash (T_1 \cap T_2)$. The second factor then considers the concepts both sets have in common and is computed as

$$\zeta_\mathcal{O} = \begin{cases} 0, & C_1' = C_2' = \emptyset \\ \frac{|C_1' \cap C_2'|}{|C_1' \cup C_2'|}, & \text{otherwise} \end{cases}. \tag{2}$$

Similar to τ the factor $\zeta_\mathcal{O}$ is 1 if both sets of concepts are identical and becomes 0 if the two sets of concepts are disjoint. The index $\mathcal{O}$ indicates that in contrast to τ the factor $\zeta_\mathcal{O}$ depends on the used ontology $\mathcal{O}$.

For the final comparison of remaining concepts we remove common concepts from each of the two sets and get $C_1 = C_1' \backslash (C_1' \cap C_2')$ and $C_2 = C_2' \backslash (C_1' \cap C_2')$. The remaining concepts in the two disjoint sets C_1 and C_2 are now compared making use of the ontology in different ways. Overall, the similarity $\text{sim}_{\mathcal{O}, s_\mathcal{O}}(T_1, T_2)$ of the two sets of terms is computed as

$$\text{sim}_{\mathcal{O}, s_\mathcal{O}}(T_1, T_2) = \begin{cases} \tau + (1 - \tau)\zeta_\mathcal{O}, & C_1 = \emptyset \vee C_2 = \emptyset \\ \tau + (1 - \tau)(\zeta_\mathcal{O} + (1 - \zeta_\mathcal{O})s_\mathcal{O}(C_1, C_2)), & \text{otherwise} \end{cases} \tag{3}$$

where $s_\mathcal{O}$ is a similarity measure that assesses the similarity of the remaining disjoint sets of concepts C_1 and C_2.

Our main similarity measure is feature-based and considers how many neighbors each pair of concepts has in common and is thus called *direct neighbors*. This idea is inspired by the Google similarity distance [24] which was also adapted to Wikipedia [27]. We already proposed this measure in [32] and compared it to two edge-counting approaches. The idea of the first measure is that two concepts are very similar in case they have many common neighbors and they are very different in case they have few or no neighbors in common. In order to compute the neighborhood of nodes in the ontology graph let $n_\mathcal{O} : \mathcal{C} \to \mathcal{P}(\mathcal{C})$ be a function that maps a concept from the set $\mathcal{C}$ of all concepts to the set of neighbors of that concept which is a subset of the power set $\mathcal{P}(\mathcal{C})$ of all concepts in the ontology. The similarity of $\mathcal{C}_1$ and $\mathcal{C}_2$ is then computed as

$$\mathrm{DN}_\mathcal{O}(\mathcal{C}_1, \mathcal{C}_2) = \frac{1}{|\mathcal{C}_1| \cdot |\mathcal{C}_2|} \sum_{(c_1, c_2)^\mathsf{T} \in \mathcal{C}_1 \times \mathcal{C}_2} \frac{|n_\mathcal{O}(c_1) \cap n_\mathcal{O}(c_2)|}{|n_\mathcal{O}(c_1) \cup n_\mathcal{O}(c_2)|}. \tag{4}$$

The second similarity measure is based on the average number of hops between pairs of concepts and thus counts as an edge-counting measure. This very simple type of similarity measure was e.g. proposed in [17]. The assumption is that concepts are very similar if there exists a very short path between them in the ontology. The longer the shortest path between them the more different two concepts are assumed to be. To evaluate the paths between all remaining concepts in the sets $\mathcal{C}_1$ and $\mathcal{C}_2$ we first compute the sum

$$\mathrm{S}_\mathcal{O}(\mathcal{C}_1, \mathcal{C}_2) = \sum_{(c_1, c_2)^\mathsf{T} \in \mathcal{C}_1 \times \mathcal{C}_2} p_\mathcal{O}(c_1, c_2) \tag{5}$$

and the maximum

$$\mathrm{M}_\mathcal{O}(\mathcal{C}_1, \mathcal{C}_2) = \max_{(c_1, c_2)^\mathsf{T} \in \mathcal{C}_1 \times \mathcal{C}_2} \{p_\mathcal{O}(c_1, c_2) + 1\}. \tag{6}$$

Here, $p : \mathcal{C}^2 \to \mathbb{N}$ is a function that maps two concepts to the length of the path between them. From these values we compute the weighted average path length

$$\overline{\mathrm{len}_\mathcal{O}}(\mathcal{C}_1, \mathcal{C}_2) = \frac{N_1 \, \mathrm{S}_\mathcal{O}(\mathcal{C}_1, \mathcal{C}_2) + N_2 \, \mathrm{M}_\mathcal{O}(\mathcal{C}_1, \mathcal{C}_2)}{|\mathcal{C}_1| \cdot |\mathcal{C}_2|} \tag{7}$$

with the normalizing factors

$$N_1 = \sum_{(c_1, c_2)^\mathsf{T} \in \mathcal{C}_1 \times \mathcal{C}_2} 1_\mathcal{O}(c_1, c_2) \qquad N_2 = |\mathcal{C}_1| \cdot |\mathcal{C}_2| - N_1. \tag{8}$$

The indicator function $1_\mathcal{O}$ becomes 1 in case two concepts are connected by a path in the ontology and is 0 otherwise. With the average path length we define our *graph distance* similarity measure as

$$\mathrm{GD}_\mathcal{O}(\mathcal{C}_1, \mathcal{C}_2) = \exp\left(1 - \overline{\mathrm{len}_\mathcal{O}}(\mathcal{C}_1, \mathcal{C}_2)\right). \tag{9}$$

The exponential scaling ensures that the minimal average path length of 1 also yields a similarity of 1 and for longer paths the similarity decreases towards 0.

The third similarity measure is also based on paths in the ontology graph, however, instead of taking the direct route between pairs of concepts hierarchical substructures in the ontology graph are explicitly considered. This measure is also an edge-counting approach. To consider hierarchical substructures in the ontology graph the path length function $p_{\mathcal{O}}$ is substituted by a function $t_{\mathcal{O}} : \mathcal{C}^2 \to \mathbb{N}^2$ that yields the path lengths of a pair of concepts to their nearest common ancestor. Similar to Eqs. (5) and (6) we then compute the sum

$$S_{\mathcal{O}}(\mathcal{C}_1, \mathcal{C}_2) = \sum_{(c_1, c_2)^{\mathrm{T}} \in \mathcal{C}_1 \times \mathcal{C}_2} (t_1 + t_2 - 2) \tag{10}$$

and the maximum

$$M_{\mathcal{O}}(\mathcal{C}_1, \mathcal{C}_2) = \max_{(c_1, c_2)^{\mathrm{T}} \in \mathcal{C}_1 \times \mathcal{C}_2} \{t_1 + t_2 - 1\} \tag{11}$$

where $(t_1, t_2)^{\mathrm{T}} = t_{\mathcal{O}}(c_1, c_2)$. From these values we compute the average path length according to Eq. (7) and then get the *tree distance* similarity as

$$TD(\mathcal{C}_1, \mathcal{C}_2) = \exp\left(-\overline{\mathrm{len}_{\mathcal{O}}}(\mathcal{C}_1, \mathcal{C}_2)\right). \tag{12}$$

The exponential scaling ensures that the minimal average path length of 0 yields a similarity of 1 and similarity values slowly decrease towards 0 for longer paths.

The last similarity measure is based on the *normalized dissimilarity* from [16]. The motivation behind this measure is that similar concepts are subsumed under the same parent concepts in an ontology. Thus, to assess the dissimilarity of two concepts the sets of their parent concepts are compared. Let $\phi : \mathcal{C} \to \mathcal{P}(\mathcal{C})$ be a function that yields the set of all parent concepts for each concept in the ontology. With the help of this function the normalized dissimilarity in $[0, 1]$ of two concepts $c_1, c_2 \in \mathcal{C}$ can be computed as

$$\mathrm{dis}_{\mathrm{norm}}(c_1, c_2) = \log_2\left(1 + \frac{|\phi(c_1)\backslash\phi(c_2)| + |\phi(c_2)\backslash\phi(c_1)|}{|\phi(c_1)\backslash\phi(c_2)| + |\phi(c_2)\backslash\phi(c_1)| + |\phi(c_1) \cap \phi(c_2)|}\right). \tag{13}$$

To transform this dissimilarity into a similarity we use $1-\mathrm{dis}_{\mathrm{norm}}$ and to compare two sets of concepts we use the average of the individual values. Thus, we get

$$\mathrm{ND}(\mathcal{C}_1, \mathcal{C}_2) = \frac{1}{|\mathcal{C}_1| \cdot |\mathcal{C}_2|} \sum_{(c_1, c_2)^{\mathrm{T}} \in \mathcal{C}_1 \times \mathcal{C}_2} (1 - \mathrm{dis}_{\mathrm{norm}}(c_1, c_2)). \tag{14}$$

Any of the similarity measures defined in Eqs. (4), (9), (12), and (14) can now be substituted for $s_{\mathcal{O}}$ in Eq. (3). More details regarding the first three similarity measures can be found in [32].

After we have now described the ontologies and similarity measures used in this article the next section is concerned with the survey we conducted to evaluate the computed similarity values.

5 Survey

In this section we describe the survey we conducted to gather similarity values from humans.

As mentioned in Sect. 3 our application is concerned with 236 837 keywords which consist of 26 324 unique terms. Since these are too many terms to ask for human similarity assessments for all of them we selected a subset of 74 terms. Doing so we especially considered that many of the 26 324 terms are very domain specific (e.g. small fashion brands) and probably not known to the general public. Thus, we selected terms of which we thought that they are more widely known.

The 74 selected terms can be paired up to 2 701 term pairs. However, we have to consider that for each term there are only a few similar terms and very many completely unrelated terms. When conducting a survey it is tiresome and frustrating for the participants if most of the term pairs they are asked about consist of unrelated terms and they must select the answer "very dissimilar" over and over again. Thus, when selecting term pairs for the survey, pairs of similar terms should be selected with proportionally higher probability than pairs of unrelated terms. To achieve this we ranked the term pairs according to their similarity computed with the DN measure. This should not bias the obtained results since the ranking only influences the probability with which term pairs are selected and does not change the similarity values later assigned by the participants of the survey. We then created 28 buckets of equal width of similarity values and randomly drew pairs from each bucket without replacement. This way terms with high similarity according to DN are selected with higher probability than pairs of completely unrelated terms. In several test subjects this over-sampling of term pairs with relatively high similarity led to considerably less frustration when participating in the survey compared to a uniquely distributed sampling of term pairs.

In total, we drew 135 term pairs which were randomly separated into 3 surveys with 45 questions each. At the beginning of each survey the same four examples of fashion term pairs with suggestions of similarity values were given to each participant to explain what we were looking for. After this introduction we asked some demographic questions to see if correlations to our measures differ between different demographic groups. The first two questions asked about the gender (male/female) and the age (below 18, 18 to 23, 24 to 30, 31 to 40, 41 to 60, 61 to 80, above 80) of each participant. With the next two questions we wanted to ascertain the fashion expertise of the participants. We asked how well they assess their fashion knowledge themselves (very good, good, not so good) and how much money they spend each month on fashion items including shoes (up to 25€, 25 to 50€, 50 to 100€, 100 to 150€, 150 to 200€, more than 200€).

After this introduction and general part each participant was presented with 50 pairs of fashion pairs, one pair at a time. For each pair the similarity should be assessed on a scale from 1 to 7. In case a participant did not know some term or did not feel comfortable evaluating the similarity they were allowed to skip the question. 5 of the 50 similarity questions were control questions. One question contained the same term twice to check whether or not the maximal similarity value of 7 was assigned in this case. Two questions repeated previous term pairs to see whether or not consistent answers were provided and two further questions repeated previous term pairs but with switched term order.

6 Evaluation and Discussion

In this section we evaluate and discuss the results of our survey.

Altogether 183 people participated in our survey. Many of them were students or research assistants but there are also several friends and family members. For the evaluation of the results we first performed several preprocessing steps to eliminate duplicate and unreasonable answers. For the first survey 2 answers were duplicates possibly caused by people clicking the submit button multiple times. 3 further participants failed to assign the maximum similarity value of 7 to the control question that asked for the similarity of a term to itself. For the other control questions that repeated previous term pairs a threshold has to be defined because many people do not assign the exact same similarity value several questions later because they cannot remember the exact value the assigned previously. Thus, we decided to allow a deviation of 1 similarity unit which still eliminated another 19 answers for the first survey. This means that for the first survey 37 answers remain for the final evaluation steps.

For the second survey 3 duplicate entries had to be eliminated. In this case no one failed the control question with identical terms and 14 participants failed the other control questions. This leaves 44 answers of the second survey for final evaluation. In case of the third survey we have 1 duplicate and 1 failure of the identical terms question. 13 answers were excluded due to the control questions with repeated term pairs. Thus, 46 answers remain of the third survey which makes a total of 127 answers over all three surveys.

To compare the survey results with similarities computed with our similarity measures we use Pearson's and Spearman's correlation coefficients. While Pearson's correlation only considers a linear dependency between dimensions Spearman's correlation compares a ranking of points and thus also captures some non-linear correlations. Pearson's correlation coefficient is defined as

$$\frac{\sum_{i=1}^{n}(x_i - \overline{x})(y_i - \overline{y})}{\sqrt{\sum_{i=1}^{n}(x_i - \overline{x})^2}\sqrt{\sum_{i=1}^{n}(y_i - \overline{y})^2}}. \tag{15}$$

Here, the pair $(x_i, y_i)^{\mathrm{T}}$ contains the averaged similarity values assigned by humans and as second entry the automatically computed similarity.

To compute Spearman's correlation coefficient both the automatically computed and manually assigned similarity values are ranked. Then, Spearman's correlation is defined as

$$1 - \frac{6\sum_{i=1}^{n}(r_{x,i} - r_{y,i})^2}{n(n^2 - 1)} \tag{16}$$

where $r_{x,i}$ is the rank of the average of the manually assigned similarity of the i-th term pair and $r_{y,i}$ is the rank of the corresponding automatically computed similarity.

In addition to the correlation coefficients we compute the *Distinguishability* of of each similarity measure. We define the Distinguishability as the fraction of term pairs which are assigned a unique similarity value by a measure among the tested set of term pairs. A high value of Distinguishability close to 1 means that many term pairs can be distinguished by just looking at their similarity values. A low Distinguishability close to 0 means that many term pairs are assigned the same similarity value and cannot be distinguished by the respective measure. We argue that it is desirable to be able to distinguish as many term pairs as possible since a similarity measure should capture even fine grained semantic differences. Also, in our application where we want to aggregate data associated to terms we would like to gradually add data and not add a whole bulk of data from a set indistinguishable terms in one go.

Of course for very large sets of terms the Distinguishability is bound to take values smaller than 1 because the probability for duplicate similarity values increases for very many term pairs. However, Distinguishability values of different similarity measures can still be interpreted relative to each other. Also, the set of 135 term pairs we used in our survey is small enough to allow unique similarity values for all of them.

6.1 Overall Correlations

In Fig. 1 correlation plots are given for all presented similarity measures and the averaged human judgement for the 135 term pairs. In addition to the similarity values the first principal axis is given by a straight line and the 10 similarity pairs with the greatest deviation from the axis are highlighted as solid black circles.

Figure 1(a) shows the results of the direct neighbors measure (DN). It achieves the highest correlation according to both a Pearson's correlation coefficient of 0.6 and a Spearman's correlation coefficient of 0.567. Although not the whole range of values occurs, especially there are no similarities above 0.65, the similarities are well scattered in the remaining range in contrast to some of the other measures where similarities agglomerate around certain values. Also, according to the Distinguishability this DN similarity measure performs best with a value of 0.963 which means that very few term pairs are assigned an identical similarity value.

The highlighted 10 term pairs whose similarities deviate the most from the shown principal axis are given in Table 2. They can be split in two groups, one with term pairs whose similarity is overestimated by the DN measure and one group whose similarity is underestimated by the measure. In cases where one of the terms occurs as a substring in the second term, the similarity gets underestimated. This is due to the fact that there exist many more nodes in the ontology which match to the shorter of the two terms and only some nodes which match to the more specific longer term. This fact leads to the neighborhoods of

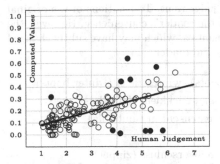

(a) Direct Neighbors: Pearson: 0.6, Spearman: 0.567, Distinguishability: 0.963

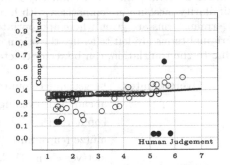

(b) Graph Distances: Pearson: 0.323, Spearman: 0.546, Distinguishability: 0.281

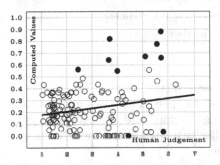

(c) Tree Distances: Pearson: 0.203, Spearman: 0.068, Distinguishability: 0.644

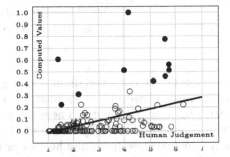

(d) Tree Distances considering only fashion categories: Pearson: 0.424, Spearman: 0.509, Distinguishability: 0.444

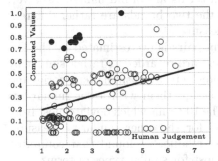

(e) Normalized Dissimilarity: Pearson: 0.296, Spearman: 0.269, Distinguishability: 0.822

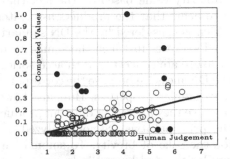

(f) Normalized Dissimilarity considering only fashion categories: Pearson: 0.449, Spearman: 0.515, Distinguishability: 0.474

Fig. 1. Correlation plots of similarity measures with crowdsourced human judgement. In addition to the similarity values the first principal axis is displayed and the 10 values with the greatest deviation from that axis are highlighted as solid circles.

Table 2. Term pairs whose similarity gets most over- resp. underestimated by the DN similarity measure in comparison with human judgement. Translations of the original German terms are given where appropriate for the reader's convenience. However, the original terms are left to assure the original semantics, which may have subtly changed due to the translation, can be reconstructed by the reader.

Overestimated	bergschuhe (mountain boots), winterstiefel (winter boots)
	abendkleid (evening dress), strickkleid (knit dress)
	kopfhörer (headphones), regenschirm (umbrella)
	mütze (cap), hüte (hats)
	klettverschluss (Velcro), reißverschluss (zipper)
Underestimated	calvin klein, nike
	sportbekleidung (sportswear), jack wolfskin
	schuhe (shoes), badeschuhe (flip flops)
	bergschuhe (mountain boots), schuhe (shoes)
	jacke (jacket), lederjacke (leather jacket)

the two terms not overlapping to a great degree and, thus, a low similarity assessment. However, overestimation does not happen in all cases of term pairs with such a characteristic. There are pairs, e.g. "hemd" and "unterhemd" (engl. "shirt" and "undershirt"), for which the similarity assessment of the DN measure more accurately mirrors the human judgement.

The two other cases in which the similarity is underestimated by the DN measure are concerned with names of fashion brands. In the first case two brand names ("calvin klein" and "nike") are compared. Here, humans assign a high similarity value based on the fact that both terms are brand names. However, it appears that the products associated to the two brands are rather different which is considered by the DN similarity measure.

Two cases in which the similarity of term pairs is overestimated by the DN measure are concerned with accessories. These are regarded as rather similar by the DN measure because the corresponding products are in similar categories and have similar properties. Humans, however, assign them with lower similarities because they are rather different products. The 10 terms which deviate most from the principal axis are not analyzed in detail for the other similarity measures for the sake of brevity. To summarize those results, we found that computed similarities and human judgement deviate most for similar types of terms.

Figure 1(b) shows the results of the graph distances measure (GD). Here, Pearson's correlation coefficient takes a distinctly lower value of 0.323 and also Spearman's correlation is a little bit lower with a value of 0.546. When considering the similarity values assigned by the GD measure we see that many pairs get a similarity of approx. 0.38. In fact the GD measure achieves a very low Distinguishability of 0.281. This is due to the fact that the corresponding nodes in the fashion ontology are connected by paths of similar lengths.

In Fig. 1(c) the results of the tree distances similarity measure (TD) are visualized. In comparison to the DN and GD similarity measures the results are much more scattered in this case. Also the TD measure achieves very low correlations of 0.203 (Pearson) and 0.068 (Spearman) which indicates very low or nearly no correlation to the human judgement. While there are some term pairs which are assigned identical similarity values, especially the value 0, the Distinguishability of 0.644 is rather high.

Since the TD similarity measure is based on tree structures it may be useful to restrict it to use only the fashion category hierarchy of the fashion ontology since this is it's main hierarchical structure (cf. Sect. 3). The resulting similarity measure is denoted by TDC and it's results are shown in Fig. 1(d). In comparison to the unrestricted TD measure many term pairs, especially those which are regarded as dissimilar by humans, are assigned distinctly lower similarity values. This leads to higher correlation with the human judgement expressed by a Pearson's correlation coefficient of 0.424 and a Spearman's correlation coefficient of 0.509 which are both higher than their respective counterparts of the unrestricted TD measure but not as high as those of the DN measure. However, restricting the tree distance measure to only the category hierarchy of the fashion ontology lowers the Distinguishability since now many term pairs are assigned with a similarity value of 0. Many of those pairs are concerned with fashion brands which obviously cannot accurately be compared using a hierarchy of fashion categories.

The next similarity measure whose results are visualized in Fig. 1(e) is based on the normalized dissimilarity (ND) measure from [26]. There, it was shown that this measure performs best among several others when applied to the WordNet ontology. The ND measure is similar to the TD measure since it is also based on the tree structure of the used ontology. The obtained results are also similar to those of the TD measure although both correlations and the Distinguishability are a little higher than with the TD measure. We get a Pearson's correlation coefficient of 0.296 and a Spearman's correlation coefficient of 0.269. Although these correlations are higher than those of the TD measure they are nowhere close to those of the DN measure. The Distinguishability of 0.822 is rather high although still smaller than that of the DN measure.

Similar to the TDC measure it is sensible to restrict the ND measure to only make use of nodes belonging to the fashion category hierarchy since they constitute the most hierarchical part of the fashion ontology. This measure is denoted by NDC in the remainder of this article. The results for the NDC measure are visualized in Fig. 1(f). Similar to the TD measure restricting the ND measure to fashion categories increases the correlation with human judgement but decreases the Distinguishability. We get a Pearson's correlation coefficient of 0.449 and a Spearman's correlation coefficient of 0.515. However, the Distinguishability drops from 0.822 to 0.474 due to many term pairs now getting a similarity of 0. These especially are term pairs with at least one brand name which obviously cannot accurately be compared using a hierarchy of fashion categories.

6.2   Correlations for Demographic Groups

In addition to the overall correlation we also evaluated the correlation between the similarity measures and several demographic groups of participants. The most interesting results are presented in Fig. 2.

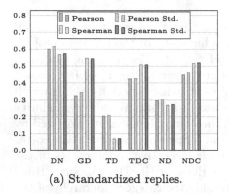

(a) Standardized replies.

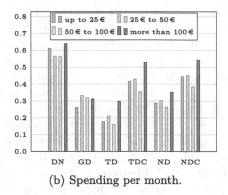

(b) Spending per month.

Fig. 2. Correlations of similarity measures and human judgement grouped by different properties of the participants of the survey. If not stated otherwise Pearson's correlation coefficient is used.

First Fig. 2(a) compares the overall correlations with those obtained by first standardizing the replies of each participant in such a way that their mean reply is 0 with a variance of 1. This makes results of the participants more comparable since different people make different use of the used rating scale and especially many people only make sparse or no use of the extreme value 1 and 7.

In most cases standardization leads to a very slight increase in the correlations with human judgement. Also, Fig. 2(a) visualizes well that in case of the GD measure Spearman's correlation coefficient is much higher than Pearson's coefficient independent of any standardization of replies. In case of the TD measure the opposite is the case. Here, Pearson's correlation coefficient is much higher than Spearman's coefficient. This suggests that in case of the GD measure the dependency between calculated similarities and human judgement has a non-linear component.

The most interesting of the demographic questions we asked (cf. Sect. 5) with regard to the correlation of human judgement and automatically computed similarity values is the amount of money participants spend per month on fashion items (including shoes). We asked this question because we proposed that it is reasonable for someone who spends much on fashion items to have a higher expertise in this area than someone who spends very little. Due to too few answers we had to aggregate all categories with more than 100€ spending volume. After the aggregation we have 26 participants who spend less than 25€ per month on fashion items, 38 participants who spend between 25€ and 50€, 46 participants who spend between 50€ and 100€, and 16 participants spend more than 100€ per month on fashion items. One participant did not answer this question.

Figure 2(b) shows the correlations grouped by monthly spending volume. The most noticeable difference in correlations is between the group spending more than 100€ per month and the other groups. Especially for the TD, TDC, ND, and NDC measures the correlation is distinctly higher for this group than for the other groups. Also, for these measures participants spending 50€ to 100€ per month achieve a slightly lower correlation than the other groups. For the DN measure the correlation is also slightly higher for the group spending more than 100€ whereas for the GD measure it is slightly lower than the correlation for the other groups. This result supports our proposition that, at least with respect to the used similarity measures, a high monthly spending volume indeed signifies a higher fashion expertise.

The results of the remaining demographic questions we asked are not presented in more detail for the sake of brevity. We found that among different age groups, genders, and self-assessed fashion expertise the correlation with the similarity measures is constant apart from small fluctuations.

6.3 DBpedia

To assess the influence of the ontology on the similarities we applied the similarity measures to a fragment of the DBpedia (cf. Sect. 3). Similar to Sect. 6.1 we computed the correlations between the measures applied to the DBpedia fragment and the averaged human judgement. However, in contrast to our rather small fashion ontology the fragment of the DBpedia even though being only a fragment is still too large to evaluate all of our measures. For the GD measure we had to limit the maximal depth for which paths are searched to 4. The tree based measures TD and ND take too long to evaluate even when limiting the search depth. Also, since the DBpedia fragment only contains one type of edge it makes no difference to restrict the tree based measures to only use edges of that type.

The results for the DN measure are visualized in Fig. 3(a) In contrast to the fashion ontology all computed similarity values are much smaller and several term pairs are assigned a similarity of 0. This is partially due to terms for which no matching node exists in the DBpedia fragment and partially due to nodes having no common neighbors in the DBpedia because nodes lie further apart in this large graph and only direct neighbors are considered. The correlation to human judgement is also a lot lower than was the case for the fashion ontology with a Pearson's correlation coefficient of 0.364 and a Spearman's coefficient of 0.304. The Distinguishability is also much lower than in case of the fashion ontology and reaches 0.526.

In Fig. 3(b) the results of the GD measure are shown. When applied to the DBpedia fragment this measure shows nearly no correlation with human judgement with a Pearson's correlation coefficient of 0.074 and a Spearman's coefficient of 0.02. Nevertheless, the Distinguishability of 0.711 is higher than that achieved with the fashion ontology and also than that of the DN measure in

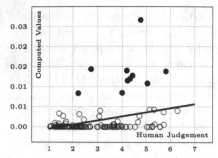
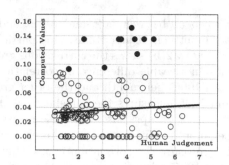

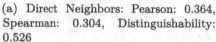

(a) Direct Neighbors: Pearson: 0.364, Spearman: 0.304, Distinguishability: 0.526

(b) Graph Distances: Pearson: 0.074, Spearman: 0.02, Distinguishability: 0.711

Fig. 3. Correlation plots of DBpedia based similarity measures with crowdsourced human judgement. In addition to the similarity values the first principal axis is displayed and the 10 values with the greatest deviation from that axis are highlighted as solid circles.

conjunction with DBpedia. This shows that paths between several node pairs which share no common neighbors can be found in the DBpedia.

7 Conclusion and Outlook

In this article we presented a custom fashion ontology and several similarity measures. The similarity values were compared with the results of a survey we conducted to gather crowdsourced similarity values for a set of 135 term pairs. From preparing the survey we especially learned that it is important to include enough pairs of similar terms in order to not bore and frustrate participants.

We evaluated the results of the survey in several ways. First of all, we showed that our proposed direct neighbors (DN) similarity measure achieved the highest correlation with human judgement compared to several other state of the art similarity measures.

Furthermore, we analyzed which term pairs deviate most from the principal axis of measurements to find out in which cases the automatic similarities fit worst to the human judgement. From this we learned that all measures have problems in case one term is contained as a substring in the other term, if one term describes a fashion category and the other one a brand, and if terms are involved that describe accessories. In these cases human judgement and the knowledge captured by the fashion ontology deviate most.

In addition to the correlation analysis we calculated the Distinguishability to evaluate how many term pairs were assigned unique similarity values by a measure since we argue that it is important to be able to distinguish as many terms as possible with a similarity measure. With regard to the Distinguishability the DN similarity measure achieved the highest ranking since there are only very few term pairs which are assigned identical similarity values.

In our survey we asked several questions to divide participants into different demographic groups. The main result with regard to demographics is that the correlation between automatically calculated similarities and human judgement is higher than average for people that spend much money on fashion items. This can be expected and confirms that our measures reflect the similarity assessment of people who spend much money on fashion items and thus have a high expertise in the domain.

Finally, we applied two of the similarity measures to a fragment of the DBpedia to determine the influence of the ontology on similarity assessments. Due to the size of this ontology the tree based measures could not be evaluated and we could just compare the DN and GD approaches. Of those two, however, the DN measure achieved the highest correlation with human judgement.

In the future we would like to improve the mentioned shortcomings of the DN similarity measure and apply it do further ontologies like WordNet. We also want to actually use the similarity measures in our application to find training data for machine learning models in case no historical data is yet available.

References

1. Finkelstein, L., Gabrilovich, E., Matias, Y., Rivlin, E., Solan, Z., Wolfman, G., Ruppin, E.: Placing search in context: the concept revisited. ACM Trans. Inf. Syst. **20**(1), 116–131 (2002)
2. Bruni, E., Tran, N.K., Baroni, M.: Multimodal distributional semantics. J. Artif. Intell. Res. **49**, 1 47 (2014)
3. WordNet. http://wordnet.princeton.edu/. Accessed 17 Dec 2015
4. Ghose, A., Yang, S.: An empirical analysis of search engine advertising: sponsored search in electronic markets. Manage. Sci. **55**(10), 1605–1622 (2009)
5. Kelly, B., Burka, K.: Enterprise paid media compaign management platforms 2015: a marketer's report. http://downloads.digitalmarketingdepot.com/MIR_1305_PPCamp2013_buyersguidelandingpage.html. Accessed 16 Dec 2015
6. Thumasathit, T.: Wag the dog: the tail of bid management. http://searchenginewatch.com/sew/opinion/2048496/wag-dog-the-tail-bid-management. Accessed 16 Dec 2015
7. Chatfield, C.: Time-Series Forecasting. Chapman and Hall/CRC, Boca Raton (2000)
8. Box, G.E.P., Jenkins, G.M., Reinsel, G.C.: Time Series Analysis: Forecasting and Control, 4th edn. Wiley, Oxford (2008)
9. Brockwell, P.J., Davis, R.A.: Introduction to Time Series and Forecasting, 2nd edn. Springer, New York (2002)
10. Smola, A.J., Schölkopf, B.: A tutorial on support vector regression. Stat. Comput. **14**, 199–222 (2004)
11. Pai, P.F., Hong, W.C.: Forecasting regional electricity load based on recurrent support vector machines with genetic algorithms. Electr. Power Syst. Res. **74**(3), 417–425 (2005)
12. Tay, F.E.H., Cao, L.: Application of support vector machines in financial time series forecasting. Omega **29**(4), 309–317 (2001)
13. Kalkowski, E., Sick, B.: Generative exponential smoothing models to forecast time-variant rates or probabilities. In: Proceedings of the International Work-Conference on Time Series (ITISE 2015), pp. 806–817 (2015)

14. Kalkowski, E., Sick, B.: Probabilistic generative models to; forecast time-variant rates or probabilities. In: Rojas, I., Pomares, H. (eds.) Time Series Analysis and Forecasting. Contributions to Statistics. Springer, New York (2015, to appear)
15. DBpedia. http://wiki.dbpedia.org. Accessed 16 Dec 2015
16. Sánchez, D., Batet, M., Isern, D., Valls, A.: Ontology-based semantic similarity: a new feature-based approach. Expert Syst. Appl. **39**(9), 7718–7728 (2012)
17. Rada, R., Mili, H., Bichnell, E., Blettner, M.: Development and application of a metric on semantic nets. IEEE Trans. Syst. Man Cybern. **19**(1), 17–30 (1989)
18. Leacock, C., Chodorow, M.: Combining local context and WordNet similarity for word sense identification. In: Fellbaum, C. (ed.) WordNet: An Electronic Lexical Database, pp. 265–283. MIT Press, Cambridge (1998)
19. Li, Y., Bandar, Z.A., McLean, D.: An approach for measuring semantic similarity between words using multiple information sources. IEEE Trans. Knowl. Data Eng. **15**(4), 871–882 (2003)
20. Al-Mubaid, H., Nguyen, H.A.: Measuring semantic similarity between biomedical concepts within multiple ontologies. IEEE Trans. Syst. Man Cybern. Part C Appl. Rev. **39**(4), 389–398 (2009)
21. Tversky, A.: Features of similarity. Psycological Review **84**(4), 327–352 (1977)
22. Petrakis, E.G.M., Varelas, G., Hliaoutakis, A., Raftopoulou, P.: X-similarity: computing semantic similarity between concepts from different ontologies. J. Digital Inf. Manage. **4**(4), 233–237 (2006)
23. Resnik, P.: Using information content to evaluate semantic similarity in a taxonomy. In: Proceedings of the 14th International Joint Conference on Artificial Intelligence (IJCAI 1995), vol. 2, Montreal, QC, Canada, pp. 448–453 (1995)
24. Cilibrasi, R.L., Vitányi, P.M.B.: The Google similarity distance. IEEE Trans. Knowl. Data Eng. **19**(3), 370–383 (2007)
25. Zhou, Z., Wang, Y., Gu, J.: A new model of information content for semantic similarity in WordNet. In: Second International Conference on Future Generation Communication and Networking Symposia (FGCNS 2008), vol. 3, Sanya, Hainan Island, China, pp. 85–89 (2008)
26. Sánchez, D., Montserrat, B.: Semantic similarity estimation in the biomedical domain: an ontology-based information-theoretic perspective. J. Biomed. Inform. **44**(5), 749–759 (2011)
27. Milne, D., Witten, I.H.: An open-source toolkit for mining Wikipedia. Artif. Intell. **194**, 222–239 (2012)
28. Bollegala, D., Matsuo, Y., Ishizuka, M.: A relational model of semantic similarity between words using automatically extracted lexical pattern clusters from the web. In: Proceedings of the 2009 Conference on Empirical Methods in Natural Language Processing (EMNLP 2009), pp. 803–812 (2009)
29. Rubenstein, H., Goodenough, J.: Contextual correlates of synonymy. Commun. ACM **8**, 627–633 (1965)
30. Miller, G.A., Charles, W.G.: Contextual correlates of semantic similarity. Lang. Cogn. Process. **6**, 1–28 (1991)
31. Neo Technology Inc: Neo4J. http://neo4j.com. Accessed 17 Dec 2015
32. Kalkowski, E., Sick, B.: Using ontology-based similarity measures to find training data for problems with sparse data. In: Proceedings of the 2015 IEEE International Conference on Systems, Man, and Cybernetics (SMC 2015), pp. 1693–1699 (2015)

Co-evolution of RDF Datasets

Sidra Faisal, Kemele M. Endris, Saeedeh Shekarpour, Sören Auer,
and Maria-Esther Vidal(✉)

University of Bonn and Fraunhofer IAIS, Bonn, Germany
{Faisal,Endris,Shekarpour,Auer,Vidal}@cs.uni-bonn.de

Abstract. Linking Data initiatives have fostered the publication of
large number of RDF datasets in the Linked Open Data (LOD) cloud,
as well as the development of query processing infrastructures to access
these data in a federated fashion. However, different experimental studies
have shown that availability of LOD datasets cannot be always ensured,
being RDF data replication required for envisioning *reliable* federated
query frameworks. Albeit enhancing data availability, RDF data replication requires synchronization and conflict resolution when replicas and
source datasets are allowed to change data over time, i.e., *co-evolution*
management needs to be provided to ensure consistency. In this paper,
we tackle the problem of RDF data co-evolution and devise an approach for conflict resolution during co-evolution of RDF datasets. Our
proposed approach is *property-oriented* and allows for exploiting *semantics* about RDF properties during co-evolution management. The quality of our approach is empirically evaluated in different scenarios on the
DBpedia-live dataset. Experimental results suggest that proposed proposed techniques have a *positive impact* on the quality of data in source
datasets and replicas.

Keywords: Dataset synchronization · Dataset co-evolution · Conflict
identification · Conflict resolution · RDF dataset

1 Introduction

During the last decade, the Linked Open Data (LOD) cloud has considerably
grown [20], comprising currently more than 85 billion triples from approximately
3400 datasets[1]. Further, Web based interfaces such as SPARQL endpoints [9] and
Linked Data fragments [23], have been developed to access RDF data following
the HTTP protocol, while federated query processing frameworks allow users to
pose queries against federations of RDF datasets. Nevertheless, empirical studies
by Buil-Aranda et al. [6] suggest the lack of Web availability of a large number of
LOD datasets, being frequently required the replication of small portions of data,
i.e., slices of an RDF dataset, to enhance reliability and performance of Linked
Data applications [7]. Although RDF replication allows for enhancing RDF data

---

[1] Observed on 17th December 2015 on http://stats.lod2.eu/.

© Springer International Publishing Switzerland 2016
A. Bozzon et al. (Eds.): ICWE 2016, LNCS 9671, pp. 225–243, 2016.
DOI: 10.1007/978-3-319-38791-8_13

availability, synchronization problems may be generated because source datasets and replicas *may change* over time, e.g., *DBpedia Live mirror tool*[2] publishes changes in a public changesets folder[3].

Co-evolution refers to mutual propagation of the changes between a replica and its origin or source dataset, where propagation specially in a mutual way, raises synchronization issues which need to be addressed to avoid data inconsistency. Issues are about how changes should be propagated and in case of *inconsistencies* or *data conflicts*, how these conflicts should be resolved. Thus, our main research problem is to develop a co-evolution process able to exploit the properties of RDF data and solve conflicts generated by the propagation of changes among source datasets and replicas. We propose a two-fold co-evolution approach, comprised of the following components: *(i)* an RDF data synchronization component, and *(ii)* a component for conflict identification and resolution.

Our approach relies on the *assumption* that either the source dataset provides a tool to compute a changeset at real-time or third party tools can be used for this purpose. Another *assumption* is that *slices* of the RDF data from the source dataset are replicated in the replicas or *target datasets*, where a slice[4] corresponds to an RDF subgraph of the source RDF graph [18].

Figure 1 illustrates the co-evolution between two RDF datasets. Initially, a slice of source dataset is used to create a target dataset, i.e., the target dataset T_{t_0} is sliced from the source dataset S_{t_0} of dataset S at time t_0. Both the source and target datasets evolve themselves with the passage of time, e.g., these datasets evolve to S_{t_j} and T_{t_j} during timeframe $t_i - t_j$, while $t_i < t_j$. Changes from S_{t_j}, denoted by $\delta(S_{t_i - t_j})$, are propagated to the target and vice versa by the RDF data synchronization component. For synchronization, changes from both source and target datasets are compared to identify conflicts. The resolved conflicts are applied on the source and target datasets to vanish inconsistencies, for example, at time point t_j, the co-evolution manager identifies the conflicts and resolves them. The conflicts are resolved and final changes are merged in both datasets.

We empirically evaluate the quality of our co-evolution approach on different co-evolution scenarios of data from the DBpedia[5] and changesets from DBpedia-live published from September 01, 2015 to October 31, 2015 using iRap [8]. The goal of the evaluation is to study the impact on data quality of the propose co-evolution process, where quality is measured in terms of completeness, consistency, and consciseness [24]. Observed experimental results suggest that our synchronization, and conflict identification and resolution techniques positively affect the quality of the data in both the source and target datasets.

The paper is structured as follows: Sect. 3 provides formal definitions of the basic notations and concepts used in the proposed co-evolution approach. Section 4 presents detailed problem description and different synchronization

---

[2] https://github.com/dbpedia/dbpedia-live-mirror.

[3] http://live.dbpedia.org/changesets/.

[4] An RDF slice is also known as a fragment in the approaches proposed by Ibañez et al. [10], Montoya et al. [15], and Verborgh et al. [23].

[5] http://wiki.dbpedia.org/.

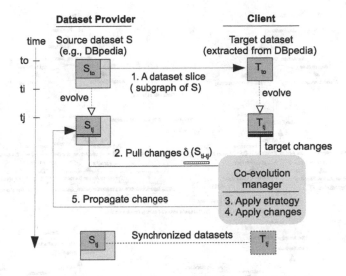

Fig. 1. Co-evolution of linked datasets

strategies. We then present the proposed approach in Sect. 5 followed by evaluation in Sect. 6. Section 7 presents the related work. We close with the conclusion and the directions for the future work.

2   Motivating Example

Let us assume an application which requires information of politicians (e.g., name, birthYear, and spouse). This information can be sliced from the datasets like DBpedia[6], and used locally by the application. We use the following SPARQL query to slice DBpedia for our use case scenario:

```
CONSTRUCT  WHERE {
    ?s      rdf:type       dbo:Politician.
    OPTIONAL {
    ?s      foaf:name      ?name.
    ?s      dbp:birthYear  ?birthYear.
    ?s      dbp:spouse     ?spouse.
    ?s      owl:sameAs     ?sameAs }
    }
```

Our approach is inspired from the scenario described in Fig. 2. Initially, at time t_0, this slice is used to populate target dataset. Both source and target datasets evolve during timeframe $t_i - t_j$, while $t_i < t_j$. Source dataset adds object value *dbo : Agent* for rdf:type, *AdrianSanders* for foaf:name, 1959 for dbp:birthYear, and *Freebase : AdrianSanders* and http://wikidata.org/entity/Q479047 for owl:sameAs to resource dbr:Adrian_Sanders. Target dataset adds object value *dbo : MemberOfParliment* for rdf:type, *Sanders, Adrian* for

---

[6] http://dbpedia.org.

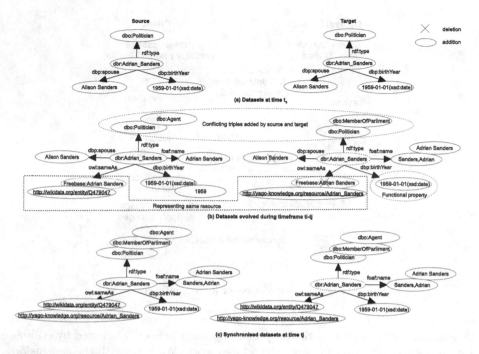

Fig. 2. Motivating example: (a) Target dataset initialization, (b) evolution, and (c) synchronization with source

foaf:conname, and *Freebase* : *AdrianSanders* and http://yago-knowledge.org/resource/Adrian_Sanders for owl:sameAs to resource dbr:Adrian_Sanders.

For resource dbr:Adrian_Sanders, we have two different values for rdf:type in source and target changesets. We need to check which of them is correct. We already know dbr:Adrian_Sanders can be an agent and member of parliment at the same time. However, this check can be made by looking whether the two classes are disjoint or not. Source adds object value 1959 for dbp:birthYear to dbr:Adrian_Sanders. As dbp:birthYear is a functional property, it can have only one value. So, we have to choose one value among the already existing value $1959 - 01 - 01$ in dataset and the new value 1959 in the changeset. One solution can be to randomly select one value among two. Similarly, source adds object value *Freebase* : *AdrianSanders* for owl:sameAs while target dataset deletes this value after adding it. Considering target as a more customized dataset, we prefer the changes of target over source changes. Thus, we delete *Freebase* : *AdrianSanders* in synchronized dataset. We still have two different owl:sameAs values for dbr:Adrian_Sanders. However, as they are representing the same resource, we will keep both values in synchronized dataset.

3   Preliminaries

In this section, we formalize the main concepts required for realizing co-evolution of RDF datasets. The *Resource Description Framework (RDF)*[7] is widely used to represent information on the Web. A resource can be any thing (either physical or conceptual). The RDF data model expresses statements about Web resources in the form of subject-predicate-object (triple). The subject denotes a resource; the predicate expresses a property of subject or a relationship between the subject and the object; the object is either a resource or literal. For identifying resources, RDF uses Uniform Resource Identifiers (URIs)[8] and Internationalized Resource Identifier (IRIs)[9]. The rationale behind is that the names of resources must be universally unique. We assume that both source and target datasets are RDF datasets. An RDF dataset is formally defined as follows:

Definition 1 (RDF Dataset). *Formally, an RDF dataset is a finite set of triples $(s, p, o) \in (I \cup B) \times I \times (I \cup L \cup B)$, where $I, B,$ and L are the disjoint sets of all IRIs, blank nodes, and literals* [8].

Let us assume that the slice contains the following triples

```
dbr:Adrian_Sanders rdf:type      dbo:Politician;
                   dbp:spouse    Alison Sanders;
                   dbp:birthYear 1959-01-01 (xsd:date).
```

Listing 1.1. Content of initial target dataset

This local copy of sliced dataset, referred as *target dataset*, might undergo changes by user feedback (e.g. user can update the restaurant rating or fulfil abstract information). After some time, DBpedia dataset also evolves by adding new restaurants information or updating the existing ones. As a result, *target dataset* might be out of date and need to be synchronized with DBpedia. During synchronization, a conflict (defined in Definition 5) might occur, if the same information was updated by the source (DBpedia) dataset and the target dataset (by the app users).

Definition 2 (Evolving RDF Dataset). *Let us assume that D_{t_i} represents the version of the RDF dataset D at the particular time t_i. An evolving dataset D is a dataset whose triples change over time. In other words, for timeframe $t_i - t_j$, there is a triple x such as either $(x \in D_{t_i} \wedge x \notin D_{t_j})$ or $(x \notin D_{t_i} \wedge x \in D_{t_j})$.*

Definition 3 (Changeset). *Let us assume that D is an evolving RDF dataset. and D_{t_i} is the version of D at time t_i. A changeset which is denoted by $\delta(D_{t_i-t_j})$ shows the difference of two versions of an evolving RDF dataset in a particular timeframe $t_i - t_j$, while $t_i < t_j$. The changeset is formally defined as $\delta(D_{t_i-t_j}) = < \delta(D_{t_i-t_j})^+, \delta(D_{t_i-t_j})^- >$ where,*

---

[7] http://www.w3.org/TR/rdf11-concepts/.
[8] A URI is a string of characters used as unique identifier for a Web resource.
[9] A generalization of URIs enabling the use of international character sets.

– $\delta(D_{t_i-t_j})^+$ is a set of triples which have been added to the version D_{t_j} in comparison to the version D_{t_i}.
– $\delta(D_{t_i-t_j})^-$ is a set of triples which have been deleted from the version D_{t_j} in comparison to the version D_{t_i}.

Example 1 (Changesets). Let the following files are found as changesets at time t_i from the source and target datasets.

```
#(A). Deleted triples
#_____
#(B). Added triples
dbr:Adrian_Sanders rdf:type   dbo:Agent;
                   foaf:name   Adrian Sanders;
                   dbp:birthYear 1959;
                   owl:sameAs  Freebase:Adrian Sanders;
                   owl:sameAs  http://wikidata.org/entity/Q479047.
```

Listing 1.2. Source changeset, (A)=$\delta(S_{t_i-t_j})^-$, and (B) = $\delta(S_{t_i-t_j})^+$

```
#(A) Deleted triples
dbr:Adrian_Sanders dbp:spouse Alison Sanders;
                   owl:sameAs  Freebase:Adrian Sanders.
#_____
#(B) Added triples
dbr:Adrian_Sanders rdf:type   dbo:MemberOfParliment;
                   foaf:name   Adrian Sanders;
                   foaf:name   Sanders, Adrian;
                   owl:sameAs  Freebase:Adrian Sanders;
                   owl:sameAs  http://yago-knowledge.org/resource/Adrian_Sanders.
```

Listing 1.3. Target changeset, (A)= $\delta(T_{t_i-t_j})^-$, and (B) = $\delta(T_{t_i-t_j})^+$

Definition 4 (Synchronized Dataset). *Two evolving datasets, $D^{(1)}$ and $D^{(2)}$, are said to be synchronized (or in sync) iff one of the following is true at a given time t_k: (i) $D_{t_k}^{(1)} \subseteq D_{t_k}^{(2)}$, (ii) $D_{t_k}^{(2)} \subseteq D_{t_k}^{(1)}$, or (iii) $D_{t_k}^{(1)} \equiv D_{t_k}^{(2)}$.*

4   Problem Statement

The core of the co-evolution concept relies on the mutual propagation of changes between the source and target datasets in order to keep the datasets *in sync*. Thus, from time to time, the target dataset and the source dataset have to exchange the changesets and then update the local repositories. Updating a dataset with changesets from the source dataset might cause inconsistencies. Our co-evolution strategy aims at dealing with changesets from either the source or target dataset and provide a suitable reconciliation strategy. Various strategies can be employed for synchronising datasets. In this section we provide requirements and formal definitions for guiding the co-evolution process.

4.1   Synchronization

In the beginning the target dataset is derived (as a slice or excerpt) from the source dataset, thus the following requirement always holds.

Requirement 1 (Initial Inclusion). *At the initial time t_0, the target dataset T is a subset of the source dataset S: $T_{t_0} \subseteq S_{t_0}$, and thus source and target datasets are in sync.*

After some time, both source and target datasets evolve. At time t_i, the target dataset is $T_{t_i} = T_{t_0} \cup \delta(T_{t_0-t_i})$ and the source dataset is $S_{t_i} = S_{t_0} \cup \delta(S_{t_0-t_i})$.

Requirement 2 (Required Synchronization). *At time t_j, a synchronization of both datasets is required iff source and target datasets were synchronised at time t_i, and the changesets applied to source and target datasets differ, i.e. $\delta(S_{t_i-t_j}) \neq \delta(T_{t_i-t_j})$.*

4.2 Conflict

When we synchronize the target T_{t_i} with source S_{t_i}, there may exist triples which have been changed in both datasets. These changed triples may be conflicting.

Definition 5 (Potential Conflict). *Let us assume that a synchronization is required for a given time slot $t_i - t_j$. $\delta(S_{t_i-t_j})$ is the changeset of the source dataset and $\delta(T_{t_i-t_j})$ is the changeset of the target dataset. A potential conflict is observed when there are triples $x_1 = (s, p, o_1) \in S_{t_j} \wedge x_2 = (s, p, o_2) \in \delta(T_{t_i-t_j}) \wedge x_2 \notin S_{t_j} = S_{t_i} \cup \delta(S_{t_i-t_j})$ with $o_1 \neq o_2$.*

Taking $o_1 \neq o_2$ as an indication for a conflict is subjective; in the sense that the characteristics of the involved property p influences the decision. Consider two triples (s, p, o_1) and (s, p, o_2). If p is a functional data type property, two triples are conflicting iff the object values o_1 and o_2 are not equal. However, if the property p is a functional object property, these two triples are conflicting if the objects are or can be inferred to be different (e.g. via `owl:differentFrom`). Another property which needs special consideration is `rdf:type`. For this property it is necessary to check whether o_1 and o_2 belong to disjoint classes. Only then these triples would be conflicting. For example, `s1 rdf:type Person` and `s1 rdf:type Athlete` are not conflicting if `Athlete` is a subclass of `Person` (i.e. not disjoint). Thus, the process of detecting conflicts is considering the inherent characteristics of the involved property.

4.3 Synchronization Strategies

In the following, we list possible strategies for synchronization. We consider the time frame $t_i - t_j$, where in the time t_i, the source and target datasets are synchronised and until time t_j, both source and target datasets have been evolving independently. Before applying synchronization, the state of the source dataset is $S_{t_j} = S_{t_i} \cup \delta(S_{t_i-t_j})$ and the target dataset is $T_{t_j} = T_{t_i} \cup \delta(T_{t_i-t_j})$.

Strategy I: This synchronization strategy prefers the source dataset and ignores all local changes on the target dataset; thus, the following requirement is necessary.

Requirement 3 (Inclusion for Synchronization). *At any given time t_j, after synchronising using selected strategy, the target dataset should be a subset of the source dataset, i.e. $T_{t_j} \subseteq S_{t_j}$.*

Therefore, the target dataset ignores all triples $\{x \mid x \notin \delta(S_{t_i-t_j}) \wedge x \in \delta(T_{t_i-t_j})\}$ and adds only the triples $\{y \mid y \in \delta(S_{t_i-t_j})\}$. After synchronization, the state of source dataset is $S_{t_j} = S_{t_i} \cup \delta(S_{t_i-t_j})$ and the state of the target dataset is $T_{t_j} = T_{t_i} \cup \delta(S_{t_i-t_j})$. Thus, the Requirement 3 is met and $T_{t_j} \subseteq S_{t_j}$. A special case of this strategy is when the target is not evolving.

Example 2. Applying strategy I for synchronization on Example 1 gives the following triples:

```
dbr:Adrian_Sanders rdf:type   dbo:Politician;
                   rdf:type   dbo:Agent;
                   foaf:name  Adrian Sanders;
                   dbp:spouse Alison Sanders;
                   dbp:birthYear 1959-01-01 (xsd:date);
                   dbp:birthYear 1959;
                   owl:sameAs Freebase:Adrian Sanders;
                   owl:sameAs http://wikidata.org/entity/Q479047.
```

Strategy II: With this strategy, the target dataset is not synchronized with the source dataset and keeps all its local changes. Thus, the target dataset is not influenced by any change from the source dataset and evolves locally. After synchronization, at time t_j, the state of the target dataset is $T_{t_j} = T_{t_i} \cup \delta(T_{t_i-t_j})$, and the state of the source dataset is $S_{t_j} = S_{t_i} \cup \delta(S_{t_i-t_j})$. It allows for synchronized replicas only if data is deleted. There is no synchronization if triples in the target dataset are updated or new triples are included.

Example 3. Applying strategy II for synchronization on Example 1 gives the following triples:

```
dbr:Adrian_Sanders rdf:type   dbo:Politician;
                   rdf:type   dbo:MemberOfParliment;
                   foaf:name  Adrian Sanders;
                   foaf:name  Sanders, Adrian;
                   dbp:birthYear 1959-01-01 (xsd:date);
                   owl:sameAs http://yago-knowledge.org/resource/Adrian_Sanders.
```

Strategy III: This synchronization strategy respects the changesets of both source and target datasets except that it ignores conflicting triples.

Here, the set of triples in which conflicts occur is $X = \{x_1 = (s, p, o_1) \in S_{t_j} \wedge x_2 = (s, p, o_2) \in \delta(T_{t_i-t_j}) \wedge x_2 \notin S_{t_j}$ with $o_1 \not\equiv o_2\}$[10]. With Strategy III,

---

[10] Set of conflicting triples selected after considering the inherent characteristics of the involved property. In rest of the paper, we say potential conflict a conflict, unless otherwise specified.

the set of conflicting triples X is removed from the target dataset while the source changeset $\delta(S_{t_i-t_j})$ and the target changeset $\delta(T_{t_i-t_j})$ are added. After synchronization, the state of the source dataset is $S_{t_j} = (S_{t_i} \cup \delta(S_{t_i-t_j}) \cup \delta(T_{t_i-t_j})) \setminus X$ and the state of the target dataset is $T_{t_j} = (T_{t_i} \cup \delta(T_{t_i-t_j}) \cup \delta(S_{t_i-t_j})) \setminus X$. Thus, Requirement 3 is met.

Example 4. Applying strategy III for synchronization on Example 1 gives the following triples:

```
dbr:Adrian_Sanders rdf:type   dbo:Politician;
                   rdf:type   dbo:Agent;
                   rdf:type   dbo:MemberOfParliment;
                   owl:sameAs http://wikidata.org/entity/Q479047;
                   owl:sameAs http://yago-knowledge.org/resource/Adrian_Sanders.
```

Strategy IV: This synchronization strategy also respects the changesets of both source and target datasets. In addition, it includes conflicting triples after resolving the conflicts.

Here, we consider the set of triples in which conflict occurs as $X = \{x_1 = (s, p, o_1) \in S_{t_j} \wedge x_2 = (s, p, o_2) \in \delta(T_{t_i-t_j}) \wedge x_2 \notin S_{t_j}$ with $o_1 \neq o_2\}$. The conflicts over these triples should be resolved. It can be resolved using some resolution policy as described in [4]. Table 1 shows a list of various policies for resolving the conflicts. Conflict resolution results in a new set of triples called Y whose triples are originated from X but their conflicts have been resolved. Then, this new set (i.e. Y) is added to the both source and target datasets. After synchronization, the state of the source dataset is $S_{t_j} = ((S_{t_i} \cup \delta(S_{t_i-t_j}) \cup \delta(T_{t_i-t_j})) \setminus X) \cup Y$ and the state of target dataset is $T_{t_j} = ((T_{t_i} \cup \delta(T_{t_i-t_j}) \cup \delta(S_{t_i-t_j})) \setminus X) \cup Y$. Thus, Requirement 3 is met.

Example 5. Applying strategy IV for synchronization on Example 1 while resolving the conflicts using function 'Any' gives the following triples:

```
dbr:Adrian_Sanders rdf:type   dbo:Politician;
                   rdf:type   dbo:Agent;
                   rdf:type   dbo:MemberOfParliment;
                   foaf:name  Adrian Sanders;
                   foaf:name  Sanders, Adrian;
                   dbp:birthYear 1959-01-01 (xsd:date);
                   owl:sameAs http://wikidata.org/entity/Q479047;
                   owl:sameAs http://yago-knowledge.org/resource/Adrian_Sanders.
```

5   Approach

Our approach allows a user to choose a synchronization strategy (as presented in Sect. 4.3). Below, we describe the status of the source and target datasets after applying each synchronization strategy (see Algorithm 1).

Function CDR is presented in Algorithm 2 which (i) identifies conflicts for the case of strategy III and strategy IV, and then (ii) resolves conflicts only in case of strategy IV. Our approach considers triple-based operations, explained below

Table 1. Conflict resolution policies and functions

Category	Policy	Function	Type	Description
Deciding	Roll the dice	Any	A	Pick random value
	Reputation	Best source	A	Select the value from the preffered dataset.
	Cry with the wolves	Global vote	A	Select the frequently occurring value for the respective attribute among all entities.
	Keep up-to-date	First*	A	Select the first value in order.
		Latest*	A	Select the most recent value.
	Filter	Threshold*	A	Select the value with a quality score higher than a given threshold.
		Best*	A	Select the value with highest quality score.
		TopN*	A	Select the N best values.
Mediating	Meet in the middle	Standard deviation, variance	N	Apply the corresponding function to get value.
		Average, median	N	Apply the corresponding function to get value.
		Sum	N	Select the sum of all values as the resultant.
Conflict ignorance	Pass it on	Concatenation	A	Concatenate all the values to get the resultant.
Conflict avoidance	Take the information	Longest	S, C, T	Select the longest (non-NULL) value.
		Shortest	S, C, T	Select the shortest (non-NULL) value.
		Max	N	Select the maximum value from all.
		Min	N	Select the minimum value from all.
	Trust your friends	Choose depending*	A	Select the value that belongs to a triple having a specific given value for another given attribute.
		Choose corresponding	A	Select the value that belongs to a triple whose value is already chosen for another given attribute.
		Most complete*	A	Select the value from the dataset (source or target) that has fewest NULLs across all entities for the respective attribute.

* - requires metadata, A - all, S - string, C - category (i.e., domain values have no order), T - taxonomy (i.e., domain values have semi-order), N - numeric

```
Data: S_{t_i}, T_{t_i}, δ(T_{t_i-t_j}), δ(S_{t_i-t_j}), strategy
Result: S_{t_j}, T_{t_j}
1  switch strategy do
2     /* Synchronise with the source and ignore local changes        */
3     case Strategy I
4        |  T_{t_j} := T_{t_i} ∪ δ(S_{t_i-t_j});
5        |  S_{t_j} := S_{t_j} ;
6     end
7     /* Do not synchronise with the source and keep local changes    */
8     case Strategy II
9        |  T_{t_j} := T_{t_i} ∪ δ(T_{t_i-t_j});
10       |  S_{t_j} := S_{t_i} ∪ δ(S_{t_i-t_j});
11    end
12    /* Synchronise with the source and target datasets and ignore conflicts */
13    case Strategy III
14       |  S_{t_j}, T_{t_j} := CDR(δ(S_{t_i-t_j}), δ(T_{t_i-t_j}), T_{t_i}, false);
15    end
16    /* Synchronise with the source and target datasets and resolve the conflicts */
17    case Strategy IV
18       |  S_{t_j}, T_{t_j} := CDR(δ(S_{t_i-t_j}), δ(T_{t_i-t_j}), T_{t_i}, true);
19    end
20 end
```

Algorithm 1. Updating the source and target datasets by the chosen synchronization strategy.

using seven cases, to identify conflicts. Consider three triples $x_1 = (s, p, o_1)$, $x_2 = (s, p, o_2)$, and $x_3 = (s, p, o_3)$ which are in conflict with each other $x_1 \in \delta(S_{t_i-t_j}) \wedge x_2 \in \delta(T_{t_i-t_j}) \wedge x_3 \in \{\delta(S_{t_i-t_j}) \wedge \delta(T_{t_i-t_j})\} \wedge o_1 \neq o_2 \neq o_3$. In the following we present seven cases of evolution causing conflicts. For the first three cases (I–III), the conflict resolution is straightforward. But for the cases IV–VII, we have to employ a conflict resolution policy to decide about triples x_1 and x_2:

- **Case I:** x_1 is added to T_{t_j} if x_1 is added by the source dataset and x_2 is deleted from the target dataset: $x_1 \in \delta(S_{t_i-t_j})^+ \wedge x_2 \in \delta(T_{t_i-t_j})^-$.
- **Case II:** x_1 is added to T_{t_j} if x_1 is modified by the source dataset and x_2 is deleted from the target dataset: $x_1 \in \delta(S_{t_i-t_j})^+ \wedge x_2 \in \delta(S_{t_i-t_j})^- \wedge x_2 \in \delta(T_{t_i-t_j})^-$.
- **Case III:** x_2 is added to S_{t_j} if x_1 is deleted from the source dataset and x_2 is modified in the target dataset: $x_1 \in \delta(S_{t_i-t_j})^- \wedge x_2 \in \delta(T_{t_i-t_j})^+ \wedge x_1 \in \delta(T_{t_i-t_j})^-$.
- **Case IV:** if the triple x_1 is added to the source dataset and x_2 is added to the target dataset: $x_1 \in \delta(S_{t_i-t_j})^+ \vee x_2 \in \delta(T_{t_i-t_j})^+$.
- **Case V:** if x_3 is modified by both source and target datasets: $x_2 \in \delta(S_{t_i-t_j})^+ \wedge x_3 \in \delta(S_{t_i-t_j})^- \wedge x_1 \in \delta(T_{t_i-t_j})^+ \wedge x_3 \in \delta(T_{t_i-t_j})^-$.
- **Case VI:** if x_1 is modified by the target dataset: $x_1 \in \delta(S_{t_i-t_j})^+ \wedge x_2 \in \delta(T_{t_i-t_j})^+ \wedge x_1 \in \delta(T_{t_i-t_j})^-$.
- **Case VII:** if x_1 is modified by the source dataset: $x_2 \in \delta(S_{t_i-t_j})^+ \wedge x_1 \in \delta(S_{t_i-t_j})^- \wedge x_1 \in \delta(T_{t_i-t_j})^+$.

Algorithm 2 shows the pseudocode of the procedure for updating the source and target datasets at the end of each timeframe. The function `resolveConflict`

Data: $S_{t_i}, T_{t_i}, \delta(T_{t_i-t_j}), \delta(S_{t_i-t_j}), conflict resolution$
Result: S_{t_j}, T_{t_j}

```
1  T_{t_j} = φ ;
2  S_{t_j} = φ ;
3  temp = φ ;
4  /* step_1                                                          */
5  for all triples x_1 = (s_1, p_1, o_1) ∈ δ(S_{t_i-t_j})^+ do
6  |   /* finding triples which are in conflict with x_1             */
7  |   X = {x_2 = (s_1, p_1, Node.ANY) ∈ δ(S_{t_i-t_j})^- ∪ δ(T_{t_i-t_j})^+ ∪ δ(T_{t_i-t_j})^- ∪ T_{t_i}} ;
8  |   if X == φ then
9  |   |   temp = temp ∪ x_1 ;
10 |   end
11 |   else
12 |   |   x = resolveConflict(x_1, X) ;
13 |   |   temp = temp ∪ x ;
14 |   end
15 end
16 /* step_2                                                          */
17 T_{t_i} := T_{t_i} \ δ(T_{t_i-t_j})^- ∪ δ(S_{t_i-t_j})^- ;
18 S_{t_i} := S_{t_i} \ δ(T_{t_i-t_j})^- ∪ δ(S_{t_i-t_j})^- ;
19 /* step_3                                                          */
20 temp := temp ∪ δ(S_{t_i-t_j})^+ ∪ δ(T_{t_i-t_j})^+ ;
21 /* Updating the target dataset                                    */
22 T_{t_j} := T_{t_i} ∪ temp ;
23 /* Updating the source dataset                                    */
24 S_{t_j} := S_{t_i} ∪ temp ;
```

Algorithm 2. CDR algorithm: conflict detection and resolution

identifies operations described in Case I–VII. In addition, for the cases IV–VII, it resolves conflicts based on the type of involved predicate. As we discussed earlier, whether a conflict between two triple exists depends heavily on the type of property. Consider two triples (s, p, o_1) and (s, p, o_2), if p is `rdfs:label`, we measure the similarity between o_1 and o_2 using the Levenshtein distance. We pick both values of `rdfs:label` if their similarity is below a certain threshold otherwise we treat them as conflicting. The function `resolveConflict` identifies operations containing deleted in the source, deleted/added/modified in the target dataset. In case of deleted in the source dataset and added/modified by the target dataset, it returns a triple to be added in T_{t_j} otherwise null.

Figure 3 illustrates Algorithm 2 for updating the target dataset T_{t_i}. We choose the synchronization strategy IV for the synchronization task. In the first step, we use a tree structure to identify conflicts for the triples in $\delta(S_{t_i-t_j})^+$. Consider the tree structure (a) in $step_1$ for the triple ($dbr : Adrian\_Sanders, rdf : type, dbo : Agent$). We find different object values for ($dbr : Adrian\_Sanders, rdf : type$) in $\delta(S_{t_i-t_j})^+, \delta(T_{t_i-t_j})^+$, and T_{t_i}. Then, we identify the triple based operation. For example, if we find the object value $dbo : Agent$ in $\delta(S_{t_i-t_j})^+$, $dbo : MemberOfParliment$ in $\delta(T_{t_i-t_j})^+$, and $dbo : Politician$ in T_{t_i}, it represents case IV of addition by both source and target. Thus, this case represents a potential conflicting triple. We check if the values in $T_{t_i}, \delta(S_{t_i-t_j})^+$ and $\delta(T_{t_i-t_j})^+$ are disjoint for predicate rdf:type. As $dbo : Politician, dbo : Agent$, and $dbo : MemberOfParliment$ are not disjoint, we pick all these values.

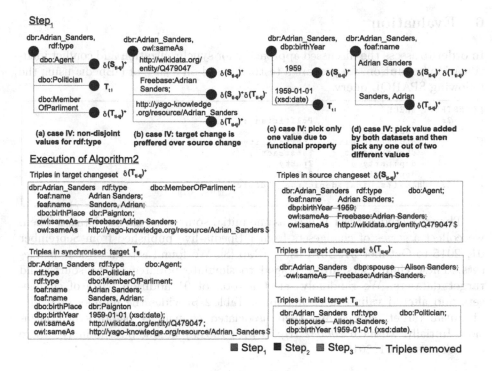

Fig. 3. Execution of Algorithm 2 to synchronize T_{t_i} with S_{t_i}

Now, consider the tree structure (b) in $step_1$ for triple ($dbr : Adrian\_Sanders$, $owl : sameAs$, http://wikidata.org/entity/Q479047). It also represents case IV of addition by both source and target. The triple ($dbr : Adrian\_Sanders$, $owl : sameAs$, $Freebase : AdrianSanders$) is added by source but deleted by target. Considering the target as more customized dataset, we give preference to target change. The tree structure (c) in $step_1$ for the triple ($dbr : Adrian\_Sanders$, $dbp : birthYear$, 1959). It is also handled in case IV. As dbp:birthYear is functional property, we select only one value among already existing value and the new value using resolution function 'Any'.

Furthermore, the user has the opportunity to adopt the manual or automatic selection of resolution functions. The resolution function is oriented to the type of predicates. The list of supported resolution functions is shown in Table 1. For automatic selection of conflict resolution functions for predicates, we check attributes of predicates (e.g., type, cardinality). Based on the usage analysis of different functions in [4], we prefer functions such as first, longest, and maximum for resolving conflicts. For instance, we prefer function longest for strings to avoid loss of information. For numeric data types, we prefer function max to keep the up-to-date value. For URIs, we pick the first value.

6   Evaluation

In order to assess the discussed approaches for synchronization and conflict identification/resolution, we prepare a testbed based on a slice of DBpedia using the following SPARQL query.

```
CONSTRUCT  WHERE   {
    ?s      a                  Politician ;
            foaf:name          ?name ;
            dbo:nationality    ?nationality ;
            dbo:abstract       ?abstract ;
            dbp:party          ?party ;
            dbp:office         ?office
    OPTIONAL {?s   foaf:depiction   ?depiction}
}
```

The extracted dataset is used as the initial source and target dataset. Then, we collect a series of changesets from DBpedia-live published from September 01, 2015 to October 31, 2015 using iRap [8]. We found a total of 304 changesets. These changesets are leveraged to simulate updates of the source and target datasets. We randomly select a total of 91 addition parts of changesets and altered values of their triples. Table 2 provides the number of triples of initial target, source and their associated changesets before synchronization. Initially, we have *200082* triples with *163114* unique objects in T_{t_i} where $t_i = September01, 2015$.

Table 2. Number of triples in the source, target, and changesets for a given timeframe

S_{t_i}	T_{t_i}	$\delta(S_{t_i - t_j})^+$	$\delta(S_{t_i - t_j})^-$	$\delta(T_{t_i - t_j})^+$	$\delta(T_{t_i - t_j})^-$
200082	200082	948	160	11725	81

Given a timeframe $t_i - t_j$[11], the goal is to synchronize source and target datasets. To do that, we define five different scenarios. In four scenarios, we apply subsequently the strategy (I–IV) over all predicates of the changesets and measure the performance. For the last scenario, we apply two strategies in a combined form on the changesets where we select strategy IV for predicate *dbp:office*, and strategy I for predicates *dbp:party*, *dbo:nationality*, *rdf:type*, *foaf:name*, *dbo:abstract*, and *foaf:depiction*. For all predicates using strategy IV, we select the resolution function 'any'. Table 3 provides the number of triples produced as a result of synchronizing S_{t_i} and T_{t_i} in each scenario. The updated changesets are sent back to the source and target for synchronization purpose. The number of conflicting triples found in scenarios 3, 4, and 5 are shown in Table 3.

The running time of the five different scenarios is also shown in Table 3 (These times are recorded only for the execution of synchronization part and do not include data loading time). Evaluation showed that strategy IV (performed

---

[11] 09/01/2015-10/31/2015.

Table 3. Results of synchronization

Scenario	$\delta(S_{t_i-t_j})^+$	$\delta(S_{t_i-t_j})^-$	$\delta(T_{t_i-t_j})^+$	$\delta(T_{t_i-t_j})^-$	Conflicting triples	RunTime (seconds)
1	0	0	948	160	-	0.0
2	0	0	11725	81	-	0.0
3	11682	81	12060	81	343	0.5
4	11800	195	12186	81	343	2.0
5	5227	131	6081	121	186	0.2

in scenario IV) needs more time even from strategy III (performed in scenario III) where all conflicts were detected but not resolved.

Synchronization influences data quality specially in terms of data consistency. To evaluate the usefulness of the synchronization approach, we use three data quality metrics i.e. (1) *completeness*, (2) *conciseness*, and (3) *consistency* described as follows:

1. Completeness refers to the degree to which all required information is present in a dataset [24]. We measure it for source and target changesets to identify which helps more in completeness. We measure it using

$$\frac{Number\,of\,unique\,triples\,in\,synchronised\,dataset}{Number\,of\,unique\,triples\,in\,(initial\,dataset\,\cup\,changeset)}$$

2. Consistency states that the values should not be conflicting. We measure it using

$$\frac{Number\,of\,non\text{-}conflicting\,triples\,in\,synchronized\,dataset}{Number\,of\,triples\,in\,(initial\,dataset\,\cup\,source\,and\,target\,changesets)}$$

3. Conciseness measures the degree to which the dataset does not contain redundant information using

$$\frac{Number\,of\,unique\,triples\,in\,dataset}{Number\,of\,all\,triples\,in\,dataset}$$

Conciseness (before synchronization) is computed using initial target dataset and source and target changesets. We compute these metrics for all the assumed scenarios, the results are shown in Table 4. For our sample case study, we found almost equal contribution of both source and target changesets in reducing the missing information. However, we found minimum *163191* number of unique objects using strategy II and maximum *163591* number of unique objects using strategy IV. Please note that strategy 1 and strategy II may not necessarily increase the number of unique triples as they do not consider about conflicts. It can be observed by analyzing the scenario 1 where the role of source changesets in completeness is 99 % which is less than the target contribution. Through evaluation, we found significant increase in conciseness for all strategies.

Table 4. Synchronization effect on completeness, consistency, and conciseness

Scenario	Completeness (source)	Completeness (target)	Consistency	Conciseness (before synchronization)	Conciseness (after synchronization)
1	99 %	100 %	-	77 %	81 %
2	99 %	99 %	-	77 %	81 %
3	99 %	100 %	94 %	77 %	81 %
4	99 %	100 %	94 %	77 %	81 %
5	99 %	100 %	-	77 %	81 %

7   Related Work

Related work includes synchronization of semantic stores for concurrent updates by autonomous clients [1], synchronization of source and target [22], replication of partial RDF graphs [19], ontology change management [12], and conflict resolution for data integration [3–5, 11, 13, 14, 16, 17, 21]. We discuss related work here along the dimensions change management and conflict resolution.

7.1   Change Management

Efficient synchronization of semantic stores is challenging due to the factors, scalability and number of autonomous participants using replica. *C-Set* [1] is a Commutative Replicated Data Type (CRDT) that allows concurrent operations to be commutative and thus, avoids other integration algorithms for consistency. The approach, proposed in [19], allows to replicate part of an RDF graph on clients. Clients can apply offline changes to this partial replica and write-back to original data source upon reconnection. Table 5 provides a comparative analysis of change management approaches used for synchronization.

A few surveyed approaches [2, 12] are related to ontological change management. In [12], a framework is developed for ontology change management and tested for RDF ontologies. This framework allows to design ontology evolution algorithms. In [2], an approach for the versioning and evolution of ontologies, based on RDF data model, is presented. It considers atomic changes such as addition or deletion of statement and then aggregates them to compound changes to form a change hierarchy. This change hierarchy allows human reviewers to analyze at various levels of details.

7.2   Conflict Resolution

For relational databases, there is much work on inconsistency resolution [3, 4, 16]. The *Humboldt Merger* [3], extension to SQL with a FUSE BY statement, resolves conflicts at runtime. *Fusionplex* [16] integrates data from heterogeneous data sources and resolves inconsistencies during data fusion. For fusion, it uses parameters such as user-defined data utility, threshold of acceptance, fusion functions, and metadata. [4] classifies conflict resolution strategies into three classes: ignorance, avoidance, and resolution. Conflict ignorance strategies are not aware of

Table 5. Synchronization approaches

Approach	Synchronization	Bi-directional	Participants	Conflict handling*
C-Set	✓	✓	n	x
RDFSync	✓	x	source, target	x
Col-graph	✓	✓	n	x
[14]	✓	back to source	n	x
Co-evolution	✓	✓	source, target	✓

* - Triple level conflicts according to Definition 5

conflicts in the data. Conflict avoidance strategies are aware of whether and how to handle inconsistent data. Conflict resolution strategies may use metadata to resolve conflicts. These can be divided into deciding and mediating. A deciding strategy chooses value from already existing values whereas a mediating strategy may compute a new value.

Sieve Fusion Policy Learner [5] uses a gold standard dataset to learn optimal fusion function for each property. The user specifies possible conflict resolution strategies from which the learning algorithm selects the one that gives maximum results within error threshold with respect to the gold standard.

Most relevant approaches to our proposed work are *Sieve* [13] - part of *Linked Data integration framework (LDIF)* [21], data fusion algorithm [14] for *ODCleanStore* [11], *RDFSync* [22], and *Col-graph* [10]. Our approach differs from the previous ones in the scope of the problem (see Fig. 4). RDFSync performs synchronization of two datasets by merging both graphs, deleting information which is not known by source, or making the target equal to source. In contrast to RDF-Sync, our co-evolution approach allows merging of both graphs while ignoring or resolving conflicts and keeping only source or target changes. Col-graph deals with consistent synchronization of replicas and does not tackle conflicts.

Sieve and ODCS are data fusion approaches and thus, are applicable where described data have different schemata. In contrast to both, co-evolution approach is applicable where described data have same schemata. Both approaches define conflicts as RDF triples sharing same subject/predicate with inconsistent values for objects. Sieve uses quality scores to resolve data while, ODCS produces quality scores of resolved data and keeps name of dataset from where the

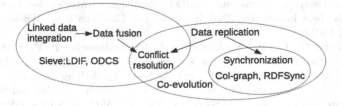

Fig. 4. How co-evolution fits with state-of-the-art

resolved value belongs. We extend the conflict definition by further considering the predicate type, as discussed earlier (see Definition 5).

8 Conclusion and Future Work

In this paper we presented an approach to deal with co-evolution which refers to mutual propagation of the changes between a replica and its origin dataset. Using the co-evolution process, we address synchronization and conflict resolution issues. We demonstrated the approach using formal definitions of all the concepts required for realizing co-evolution of RDF datasets and implemented it using different strategies. We evaluated the approach using data quality metrics completeness, conciseness, and consistency. A thorough evaluation of the approach, using DBpedia changesets, indicates that our method can significantly improve the quality of dataset. In the future, we will extend the concept of conflict resolution at schema level. For example, renaming a class invalidates all triples that belong to it in a dataset. Further, we will evaluate the scalability and performance of our proposed approach using a benchmark dataset.

Acknowledgements. This work is supported in part by the European Union's Horizon 2020 programme for the projects BigDataEurope (GA 644564) and WDAqua (GA 642795). Sidra Faisal is supported by a scholarship of German Academic Exchange Service (DAAD).

References

1. Aslan, K., Molli, P., Skaf-Molli, H., Weiss, S.: C-set: a commutative replicated data type for semantic stores. In: 4th International Workshop on REsource Discovery (RED) (2011)
2. Auer, S., Herre, H.: A versioning and evolution framework for RDF knowledge bases. In: Virbitskaite, I., Voronkov, A. (eds.) PSI 2006. LNCS, vol. 4378, pp. 55–69. Springer, Heidelberg (2007)
3. Bilke, A., Bleiholder, J., Naumann, F., Böhm, C., Draba, K., Weis, M.: Automatic data fusion with hummer. In: 31st International Conference on Very Large Data Bases (VLDB) (2005)
4. Bleiholder, J., Naumann, F.: Data fusion and conflict resolution in integrated information systems. In: International Workshop on Information Integration on the Web (2006)
5. Bryl, V., Bizer, C.: Learning conflict resolution strategies for cross-language wikipedia data fusion. In: 23rd International Conference on World Wide Web (WWW) (2014)
6. Buil-Aranda, C., Hogan, A., Umbrich, J., Vandenbussche, P.-Y.: SPARQL webquerying infrastructure: ready for action? In: Alani, H., et al. (eds.) ISWC 2013, Part II. LNCS, vol. 8219, pp. 277–293. Springer, Heidelberg (2013)
7. Endris, K.M., Faisal, S., Orlandi, F., Auer, S., Scerri, S.: Interest-based RDF update propagation. In: The Semantic Web - ISWC 2015–Proceedings of 14th International Semantic Web Conference, Part I, Bethlehem, PA, USA, pp. 513–529, 11–15 October 2015

8. Endris, K.M., Faisal, S., Orlandi, F., Auer, S., Scerri, S.: IRAP - an interest-based RDF update propagation framework. In: ISWC 2015 Posters and Demonstrations Track Co-located with the 14th Interational Semantic Web Conference (ISWC) (2015)

9. Feigenbaum, L., Williams, G., Clark, K., Torres, E.: SPARQL 1.1 protocol (2013). http://www.w3.org/TR/sparql11-protocol/

10. Ibáñez, L.-D., Skaf-Molli, H., Molli, P., Corby, O.: Col-graph: towards writable and scalable linked open data. In: Mika, P., et al. (eds.) ISWC 2014, Part I. LNCS, vol. 8796, pp. 325–340. Springer, Heidelberg (2014)

11. Knap, T., Michelfeit, J., Daniel, J., Jerman, P., Rychnovský, D., Soukup, T., Nečaský, M.: ODCleanStore: a framework for managing and providing integrated linked data on the web. In: Wang, X.S., Cruz, I., Delis, A., Huang, G. (eds.) WISE 2012. LNCS, vol. 7651, pp. 815–816. Springer, Heidelberg (2012)

12. Konstantinidis, G., Flouris, G., Antoniou, G., Christophides, V.: Ontology evolution: a framework and its application to RDF. In: Joint ODBIS-SWDB Workshop on Semantic Web, Ontologies, Databases (2007)

13. Mendes, P.N., Müleisen, H., Bizer, C.: Sieve: linked data quality assessment and fusion. In: Joint EDBT-ICDT Workshops, pp. 116–123 (2012)

14. Michelfeit, J., Knap, T., Neaský, M.: Linked data integration with conflicts. Web Semant. (2014)

15. Montoya, G., Skaf-Molli, H., Molli, P., Vidal, M.E.: Federated SPARQL queries processing with replicated fragments. In: The Semantic Web - ISWC 2015– Proceedings of 14th International Semantic Web Conference, Part I, Bethlehem, PA, USA, 11 15 October 2015

16. Motro, A., Anokhin, P.: Fusionplex: resolution of data inconsistencies in the integration of heterogeneous information sources. Inf. Fusion 7(2), 176–196 (2006)

17. Paton, N.W., Christodoulou, K., Fernandes, A.A.A., Parsia, B., Hedele, C.: Pay-as-you-go data integration for linked data: opportunities, challenges and architectures. In: 4th International Workshop on Semantic Web Information Management (2012)

18. Saleem, M., Ngonga Ngomo, A.-C., Xavier Parreira, J., Deus, H.F., Hauswirth, M.: DAW: Duplicate-AWare federated query processing over the web of data. In: Alani, H., et al. (eds.) ISWC 2013, Part I. LNCS, vol. 8218, pp. 574–590. Springer, Heidelberg (2013)

19. Schandl, B.: Replication and versioning of partial RDF graphs. In: 7th Interational Conference on The Semantic Web, pp. 31–45 (2010)

20. Schmachtenberg, M., Bizer, C., Paulheim, H.: Adoption of the linked data best practices in different topical domains. In: Mika, P., et al. (eds.) ISWC 2014, Part I. LNCS, vol. 8796, pp. 245–260. Springer, Heidelberg (2014)

21. Schultz, A., Matteini, A., Isele, R., Bizer, C., Becker, C.: LDIF linked data integration framework. In: 2nd International Workshop on Consuming Linked Data (2011)

22. Tummarello, G., Morbidoni, C., Bachmann-Gmür, R., Erling, O.: RDFSync: efficient remote synchronization of RDF models. In: Aberer, K., et al. (eds.) ASWC 2007 and ISWC 2007. LNCS, vol. 4825, pp. 537–551. Springer, Heidelberg (2007)

23. Verborgh, R., et al.: Querying datasets on the web with high availability. In: Mika, P., et al. (eds.) ISWC 2014, Part I. LNCS, vol. 8796, pp. 180–196. Springer, Heidelberg (2014)

24. Zaveri, A., Rula, A., Maurino, A., Pietrobon, R., Lehmann, J., Auer, S.: Quality assessment for linked open data: a survey. Semant. Web J. (2015)

LinkSUM: Using Link Analysis to Summarize Entity Data

Andreas Thalhammer[1]([⊠]), Nelia Lasierra[2], and Achim Rettinger[1]

[1] AIFB, Karlsruhe Institute of Technology, Karlsruhe, Germany
{andreas.thalhammer,achim.rettinger}@kit.edu
[2] University for Health Sciences, Medical Informatics and Technology,
Hall in Tirol, Austria
nelia.lasierra@umit.at

Abstract. The amount of structured data published on the Web is constantly growing. A significant part of this data is published in accordance to the Linked Data principles. The explicit graph structure enables machines and humans to retrieve descriptions of entities and discover information about relations to other entities. In many cases, descriptions of single entities include thousands of statements and for human users it becomes difficult to comprehend the data unless a selection of the most relevant facts is provided.

In this paper we introduce LinkSUM, a lightweight link-based approach for the relevance-oriented summarization of knowledge graph entities. LinkSUM optimizes the combination of the PageRank algorithm with an adaption of the Backlink method together with new approaches for predicate selection. Both, quantitative and qualitative evaluations have been conducted to study the performance of the method in comparison to an existing entity summarization approach. The results show a significant improvement over the state of the art and lead us to conclude that prioritizing the selection of related resources leads to better summaries.

Keywords: Entity summarization · Linked data · Knowledge graph · Information filtering

1 Introduction

A significant part of search engine result pages (SERPs) is nowadays dedicated to knowledge graph panels about entities (e. g., Fig. 1). In that context, a large amount of information about searched entities is often readily available to be presented to the user in a structured way. In its complete form, data about a single entity may involve thousands of statements. This is an overloading amount for humans. Therefore, fact-based information is often filtered and presented with a pre-defined set of predicates, such as *"name, age, and date of birth"* in the case of persons. Such a listing is usually associated with fixed patterns and static type-based orderings. However, as each entity is special in its own way it would be more appropriate to select relevant facts with respect to its

© Springer International Publishing Switzerland 2016
A. Bozzon et al. (Eds.): ICWE 2016, LNCS 9671, pp. 244–261, 2016.
DOI: 10.1007/978-3-319-38791-8_14

Release date: October 14, 1994 (USA)

Director: Quentin Tarantino

Screenplay: Quentin Tarantino

Producer: Lawrence Bender

Production companies: Miramax, A Band Apart, Jersey Films

Cast   View 15+ more

Quentin Tarantino	John Travolta	Uma Thurman	Samuel L. Jackson	Bruce Willis
Jimmie Dimmick	Vincent Vega	Mia Wallace	Jules Winnfield	Butch Coolidge

Fig. 1. Parts of a Google knowledge graph summary of "Pulp Fiction".

individual particularities. In the movie domain, for example, some movies are heavily influenced by their main actor(s) (e. g., in the case of "Terminator") while others are genuine masterpieces by their directors (e. g., in the case of "Pulp Fiction"). It is the goal of entity summarization to distill such individual particularities and present them in a ranked fashion.

In the last five years, the field of entity summarization has gained particular attention by both, industry [1,13] and research [2,4,7,14,16–19]. On the one hand, the commercial approaches are very specific to their individual settings and rely on large amounts of background information. From their interfaces it is also indistinguishable, how much of the approach is automatic and which parts are manually generated or revised. As such, these approaches can neither be generally applied nor reproduced. On the other hand, the approaches from the scientific field are more generic and generally applicable. Among those, we distinguish between *diversity-centered* summaries [7,14] and *relevance-oriented* summaries [4,17,19]:

Diversity-Centered. Summaries focus more on presenting a diverse selection of predicates (i. e. the type of relation). Repetitive lists of the same type of relation (e. g., "*starring* Uma Thurman; *starring* John Travolta; *starring...*") are avoided in this setting. Instead, diversification of the relations aims at providing a more complete overview of an entity.

Relevance-Oriented. Summaries are more focused on the values (i. e. the connected resources). The importance of the connected resource and the relevance for the target entity is prioritized. In this setting, a complete summary could involve only one type of relation, if the respective resources are deemed more important than others with different relations.

Both methods present summaries of entities in a top-k manner, i. e. the k most diverse or relevant facts.

In this paper we present LinkSUM, a new method for entity summarization that follows a relevance-oriented approach to produce generic summaries to be displayed in a SERP. LinkSUM goes beyond the state of the art by addressing the following observed limitations of previously developed methods: lack of general applicability (commercial approaches) and the inclusion of redundant information in a summary (commercial and research approaches).

To address these challenges, LinkSUM combines and optimizes techniques for resource selection with approaches for predicate selection in order to provide a generic method for entity summarization. Like other research and commercial approaches [1,4,7,14,19], LinkSUM is focused on global relevance measures and does not rely on personal or contextual factors like individual interests or temporal trends. Instead, it serves as a foundation which can be extend by such approaches. To study the performance of LinkSUM we compare it with FACES, a recent approach on entity summarization [7] that has been shown to perform better than [4,17].

The contribution of this paper is twofold:

1. We present LinkSUM, a lightweight link-based approach for relevance-oriented entity summmarization. We investigate on different configuration parameters and evaluate them with respect to their effectiveness.
2. In a quantitative and qualitative evaluation setting we show that prioritizing the selection of the related resources (rather than focusing on relation selection) and omitting redundancies within the set of related resources leads to better summaries.

The remainder of the paper is organized as follows: Sect. 2 introduces the key components of our approach. Section 3 presents first the experimental setup and afterwards the results of the configuration of the approach. In Sect. 4 we compare the approach to a diversity-centered summarization approach in a quantitative as well as qualitative evaluation setting. Section 5 discusses the obtained results and Sect. 6 provides an overview of related work. Section 7 presents our conclusions and Sect. 8 addresses open topics that will be part of our future work.

2   Proposed Approach

The proposed entity summarization method comprises two main stages:

Resource Selection. The goal of this stage is to create a ranked list of resources that are semantically connected to the target entity. The output of this step is a set of triples, where the semantic relation is not fixed, e. g.
Pulp Fiction – ?relation → *Quentin Tarantino*. One requirement for a resource to be included in the list of relevant entities is at least one existing semantic relation to the target entity.
Relation Selection. This stage deals with the selection of a semantic relation that connects the resource with the target entity. This step is necessary if more than one relation exists, e. g.
PulpFiction – *starring* → *QuentinTarantino*, and
PulpFiction – *director* → *QuentinTarantino*.

In the entity summarization setting the list of relevant resources is cut-off at k after resource selection. We refer to such summaries as top-k summaries. In the following subsections we will explain each of the two parts. We will refer to the target entity as e (i. e. the entity that needs to be summarized).

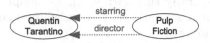

(a) Example: Backlink between the two entities.

(b) **Example:** Multiple semantic relations can exist between two entities.

Fig. 2. Web links (black, solid) and semantic relations (blue, dashed) between "Quentin Tarantino" and "Pulp Fiction" (Color figure online).

2.1 Resource Selection

For the resource selection, we combine two link-measures: one that accounts for the importance of the connected resource (PageRank [3]) and one that accounts for the strength of the connection (Backlink [20]). We consider links between entities as a mean for identifying and ranking relevant resources. The presented method covers scenarios, in which semantic relations are present in addition to textual descriptions that contain Web links to other resources.

Important Related Resources. As a first step, we run the PageRank algorithm [3] on the set of all resources R with their individual directed links $link(r_1, r_2)$ with $r_1, r_2 \in R$ and their individual count of out-going links: $c(r) = |\{r_1|link(r, r_1); r_1 \in R\}|$.

$$pr(r_0) = (1 - d) + d \cdot \sum_{r_n \in \{r|link(r, r_0); r \in R\}} pr(r_n)/c(r_n) \qquad (1)$$

The variable d is called "damping factor". Generally, it accounts for the probability of a jump in the random walk model of PageRank. Like in [3], we set the damping factor to 0.85 in all our experiments. The PageRank algorithm applies the above-given formula incrementally. The number of iterations depends on the general size of the dataset as well as on the density of links. After executing the algorithm, each resource r has its own PageRank score $pr(r)$. The set of resources that have a semantic connection to e is defined as $res(e) \subseteq R$. As a matter of fact, every resource $r \in res(e)$ can be ranked in accordance to its individual PageRank. A basic popularity-based top-k summary of e can be produced with that information [17].

Strongly Connected Resources. PageRank focuses on the general importance of related resources. It does not provide an indication about how the two resources are important for each other. This part is addressed by the Backlink method that was first described in [20]. In this work, the authors analyze a variety of set-based heuristics for identifying related resources in order to feature exploratory search with Linked Data. The analyzed Backlink method performs best in terms of F-measure when the results are compared to their reference dataset. In [20] the method is introduced as follows:

$$bl(e) = \{r|link(r, e) \wedge link(e, r), r \in R\} \qquad (2)$$

For entity summarization, we adapt the Backlink method in order to ensure that a semantic relation exists between e and every r. The adapted formula is as follows:

$$bl(e) = \{r | link(r, e) \wedge link(e, r) \wedge r \in res(e), r \in R\} \tag{3}$$

Figure 2a shows the Backlink method and the additional requirement for a semantic relation between two resources. Backlink can not be used directly for entity summarization as it returns an unranked set of related entities and the size of this set depends on the target entity.

Combined Scores for Resource Selection. In this work, an optimized combination of PageRank with Backlink is proposed. This enables us to select relevant resources with a tight connection to e. For this, we normalize the PageRank score of each entity by the maximum and linearly combine the score with the indicator function of the set $bl(e)$. With $r \in res(e)$:

$$score(e, r) = \alpha \cdot \frac{pr(r)}{max\{pr(a) : a \in res(e)\}} + (1 - \alpha) \cdot \mathbf{1}_{bl(e)}(r) \tag{4}$$

For a top-k summary we rank resources $r \in res(e)$ in accordance to the defined score and cut off at k. We define a top-k list of connected resources with the function $top_k(res(e))$. The α parameter is flexible and lies in the interval $0.5 \leq \alpha \leq 1$. With $\alpha = 0.5$, the top positions of a summary of e first involve all resources contained in the Backlink set $r \in bl(e)$ in the order of their PageRank scores. This listing is followed by the resources that are not in the Backlink set $r \notin bl(e)$ but still semantically connected $r \in res(e)$ in the order of their PageRank scores. This is also the case if α is chosen in the interval $0 < \alpha \leq 0.5$. With $\alpha = 1.0$, all connected resources $r \in res(e)$ are ordered in accordance to their PageRank scores. In this case, the Backlink set does not influence the results. In Sect. 3 we present different configurations of LinkSUM with respect to α.

2.2 Relation Selection

In a knowledge graph, two resources can be linked through multiple semantic connections. We provide an example in Fig. 2b which demonstrates that the entities "Pulp Fiction" and "Quentin Tarantino" are connected in multiple ways. As a matter of fact, it is very common that multiple relations between entities exist. However, in many cases, one relation is more relevant than others. In our approach, the relation selection task identifies the most prominent connection for presentation in order to avoid redundancies among the connected resources in the top-k set.

In order to choose an optimal relation selection method for LinkSUM, the following factors were defined:

Frequency (FRQ). Ranks the candidate relations in accordance to how often a specific relation is used overall in the complete dataset. The relation that is used the most is selected as the most promising candidate.

Exclusivity (EXC). For both entities of a relation, the relation might not be exclusive. For example a movie has commonly more than one starring actor while also an actor is usually starring in more than one movie (N:M). This measure considers the exclusivity of a relation in context to e and $r \in res(e)$ respectively. For both resources, e and r, we add up the number of times the relation is used with each (N+M). We use the inverse of this number $1/(N + M)$, in order to get the exclusivity score (the more exclusive, the better). The upper bound of EXC is 0.5 (for a 1:1 relation).

Description (DSC). Relations are represented by RDF predicates. Those predicates are commonly described with domains, ranges, and labels in different languages. The sum $|labels| + |ranges| + |domains|$ forms a basic method for estimating the quality of the description of the predicate. The relation with the highest quality is chosen.

For each related resource in $r \in top_k(res(e))$, combinations of the above-presented relation selection mechanisms identify the most relevant connection to e.

3   Configuration

As reported in [7], the FACES system (to which we compare) was tuned to its best performance by setting the cut-off level of the cluster hierarchies to 3. Also LinkSUM can be configured with respect to various parameters. First, the α-value for resource selection is flexible in the range of 0.5 to 1 (see Sect. 2.1). Second, the relation selection method can be adjusted or replaced in order to fit one or another scenario (see Sect. 2.2). For finding the best configuration, we considered the following configurations:

α-value. We tested different settings for α in the range of 0.5 to 1 with 0.1 steps.
Relation Selection. We tested different relation selection mechanisms. We considered only combinations based on frequency as it has been proven as a robust popularity measure in [14]. The following setups were considered as promising candidates:

- FRQ – relations are selected by their frequency in the dataset.
- FRQ*EXC – relations are chosen by the product of frequency and exclusivity.
- FRQ*DSC – relations are selected by the product of frequency and description.
- FRQ*EXC*DSC – relations are chosen by the product of frequency, exclusivity, and description.

As a reference dataset, we use the same as the FACES approach [7].[1] The dataset provided in [2] would also serve as reference for evaluation. Unfortunately, we could not obtain summaries of the FACES system for the entities covered by [2].

The dataset provided by FACES involves DBpedia (version 3.9) and features outgoing connections only [7]. Without loss of generality, we also configured

---

[1] FACES reference dataset – http://wiki.knoesis.org/index.php/FACES.

LinkSUM to consider outgoing connections only. We also apply LinkSUM on DBpedia version 3.9. We computed the PageRank [3] scores for each DBpedia entity. As a basis for this, we used DBpedia's Wikipedia Pagelinks dataset in English language. This dataset contains triples of the form "Wikipedia page A links to Wikipedia page B". We only use these Web links, i.e. do not make use of semantic links (e.g., `dbpedia-owl:birthPlace`) for the computation of PageRank. The computed PageRank scores are made available online [15] in Turtle RDF format using the vRank vocabulary [11]. For the Backlink method, we also use the Wikipedia Pagelinks dataset.

3.1   Configuration Setup

Our experimental setup involves a reference dataset as well as measures for computing the agreement and similarity. We use a similar evaluation setup as the FACES approach [7] as we directly compare LinkSUM with the FACES system (see Sect. 4).

Reference Dataset. The dataset includes 50 DBpedia (version 3.9) entities. The dataset contains at least seven top-5 and seven top-10 reference summaries per entity that were created by 15 experts of the Semantic Web field [7]. For each entity, these references describe outgoing connections to other resources. The average number of these relations is 44. In addition, several relations, such as `dcterms:subject` and Wikipedia related links, were filtered out for creating the reference dataset as they do not contain sufficient semantic information [7].

Measures. For computing the agreement and for comparing the produced summaries with the reference dataset, we use the same similarity measures as in [4,7]:

$$Agreement(e) = \frac{2}{n(n-1)} \sum_{i=1}^{n} \sum_{j=i+1}^{n} |Sum_i^E(e) \cap Sum_j^E(e)| \qquad (5)$$

$$Quality(Sum(e)) = \frac{1}{n} \sum_{i=1}^{n} |Sum(e) \cap Sum_i^E(e)| \qquad (6)$$

With n being the number of experts. The expert summaries are denoted as $Sum_i^E(e)$. The agreement measure estimates the agreement of the experts about a top-k summary of the entity e. The *Quality* measure estimates the overlap of the produced summary $Sum(e)$ with all expert summaries. Both values are computed for all entities in the reference dataset and afterwards averaged.[2] The upper and lower bounds for both measures are $0 \le Agreement(e) \le k$ and $0 \le Quality(Sum(e)) \le k$ in the top-k setting. When we reproduced the setting of [7], we found that our results did not match the provided

---

[2] k is fixed to the same value for all summaries, expert and automatically generated ones, before applying the measures.

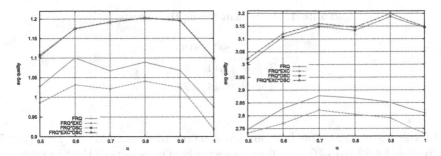

Fig. 3. LinkSUM (SPO) average *Quality* scores with different settings for α and different relations selection approaches for top-5 (left) and top-10 (right) summaries.

values: the *Quality* values of FACES were lower than the provided ones. In order to reproduce the reported values for the FACES system in [7], we found out that only the last part of the URI was used for matching automatically generated summaries with expert summaries for all tested systems. Unfortunately, this setting matches DBpedia predicates with different namespaces (i. e. dbpprop and dbpedia-owl) in an arbitrary way. As an example, on the one hand, dbpprop:party and dbpedia-owl:party are matched while, on the other hand, dbpprop:placeOfBirth and dbpedia-owl:birthPlace remain unmatched because the last parts of the URI are syntactically not the same. As a consequence, we decided not to adopt this basic ontology alignment approach and applied two measures instead:

- Subject–Object (SO): This measure treats a summary as a set of tuples containing only subjects and objects while ignoring the predicate. The full URIs of the subject and the object are used respectively. As a matter of fact, the relation selection method has no impact on this measure.
- Subject–Predicate–Object (SPO): This measure treats summaries as sets of triples. For representing a triple we use the full URI of each, subject, predicate and object. This measure also estimates the performance of the relation selection approach.

3.2 Configuration Results

In [7], the reported agreement among the experts is 1.92 for top-5 and 4.64 for top-10 respectively. Those values were computed with the aforementioned basic ontology alignment approach. We recomputed the values for SO and SPO respectively. The results are displayed in Table 1. The agreement among the experts is not particularly high. According to [7], this can be explained by the high number of facts that were presented to the experts for each entity (in average 44 facts per entity). Although - technically - the average agreement is not an upper bound for the performances of the tested systems, the values can serve as reference points.

Table 1. Agreement among the experts.

	SO	SPO
Top-5	2.14	1.64
Top-10	5.14	3.92

In the SO setting, the best achieved scores of LinkSUM are 1.89 (top-5, $\alpha = 0.8$) and 4.82 (top-10, $\alpha = 0.9$) respectively. The results of the SPO settings are shown in Fig. 3. The FRQ measure provides a good baseline for both, top-5 and top-10. While the combination of FRQ with DSC improves the *Quality* in both settings, the combination with EXC damps the impact of FRQ. In the top-10 setting, the combination of the three measures (FRQ*EXC*DSC) provides best values. In the top-5 settings, FRQ*DSC and FRQ*EXC*DSC provide equally good results. In general, the values for α are best at 0.8 for top-5 and 0.9 for top-10. The impact of the Backlink method on the rankings ($\alpha < 1.0$) in comparison to PageRank-only ($\alpha = 1.0$) is evident. In addition it is noticeable that strictly prioritizing all results of the Backlink method (ranked in accordance to their respective PageRank scores) does also not yield best results ($\alpha = 0.5$). The full blend between importance and strong connectivity produces the best outcomes.

Summarizing, the following configurations performed best for top-5 and top-10 summaries respectively:

config-1 (top-5): $\alpha = 0.8$, FRQ*EXC*DSC
config-2 (top-10): $\alpha = 0.9$, FRQ*EXC*DSC

4   Evaluation

In our evaluation setting, we compare LinkSUM with the FACES entity summarization system [7]. FACES focuses on the diversification of the relation types (i. e. no semantically similar predicates should be occur in the result summary). The system has two stages: partitioning the feature set and ranking the features. The main idea is to partition the semantic links of an entity into semantically diverse clusters of predicates. For resource selection, the approach uses a tf-idf-related popularity measure for the object. In contrast, in our approach we follow the objective to identify the most relevant object first and then select the predicate. In their evaluation, the authors demonstrate that their system provides better results than [4,17]. For 50 DBpedia entities, the authors published the results of FACES for top-5 and top-10 summaries (along with the reference dataset described in Sect. 3.1).[3] The used DBpedia version is 3.9.

We compare LinkSUM and FACES in two evaluation settings, a quantitative and a qualitative one. In the following we will first describe the experimental setup and the obtained results afterwards.

---

[3] FACES summaries – http://wiki.knoesis.org/index.php/FACES.

4.1   Evaluation Setup

Quantitative Analysis. For evaluating the two methods quantitatively, we chose the same setup as described in Sect. 3.1, i. e. the same reference dataset and the same evaluation measures that were used for the evaluation of the FACES system [7]. For comparison, we use the average *Quality* of each method. In addition, in order to prevent influence of strong outliers, we use the *Quality* value of each of the 50 entities per system for computing significance. As a significance test, we use the Wilcoxon Signed-Rank Test with two tails as recommended in [5]. We compare the best configurations of LinkSUM for top-5 and top-10 respectively (see Sect. 3.2) with the published results of FACES.

Qualitative Analysis. For the qualitative evaluation we sent a call for participation to more than 60 people and asked them to compare summaries of different entities. In this setup, we evaluated the top-10 setting with LinkSUM@config-2 (which turned out to perform best for the top-10 setting in the configuration, see Sect. 3.2). We chose a set of ten entities out of the 50 provided summaries of FACES with respect to their types. The types of the selected entities involve the following classes: person, country, football club, TV series, movie, and company. The selection between the entities of a specific type was random.

For each entity, we displayed the summaries of the two systems next to each other (see Fig. 4) without giving indications about which system produced the summaries. The summaries produced by LinkSUM were displayed on the

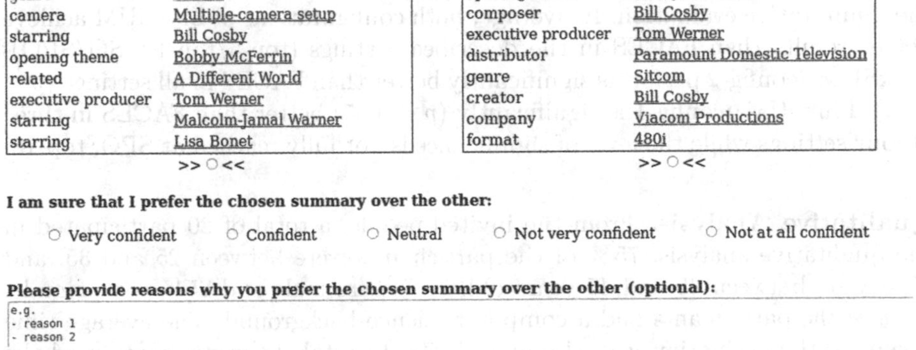

The Cosby Show

I know a lot about this entity:

○ Strongly agree   ○ Agree   ○ Neither agree, nor disagree   ○ Disagree   ○ Strongly disagree

language	English language		network	NBC
network	NBC		language	English language
genre	Sitcom		opening theme	Bobby McFerrin
camera	Multiple-camera setup		composer	Bill Cosby
starring	Bill Cosby		executive producer	Tom Werner
opening theme	Bobby McFerrin		distributor	Paramount Domestic Television
related	A Different World		genre	Sitcom
executive producer	Tom Werner		creator	Bill Cosby
starring	Malcolm-Jamal Warner		company	Viacom Productions
starring	Lisa Bonet		format	480i

>> ○ <<   >> ○ <<

I am sure that I prefer the chosen summary over the other:

○ Very confident   ○ Confident   ○ Neutral   ○ Not very confident   ○ Not at all confident

Please provide reasons why you prefer the chosen summary over the other (optional):

```
e.g.
- reason 1
- reason 2
```

Fig. 4. Excerpt of the interface for qualitative evaluation for the entity "The Cosby Show". The users could choose whether they prefer the summary of LinkSUM (left) or FACES (right) in a SERP setting.

left side in 50 % of the cases with random choice. Below each summary, we provided a radio button for the users to choose their preferred summary. Every user had one vote either for LinkSUM or FACES. We used two 5-point Likert scale questions in order to enable participants to provide information about their previous knowledge about the entity and the confidence with their choice:

- *"I know a lot about this entity"* – [Strongly agree; Agree; Neither agree, nor disagree; Disagree; Strongly disagree]
- *"I am sure that I prefer the chosen summary over the other"* – [Very confident; Confident; Neutral; Not very confident; Not at all confident]

Besides we provided an optional field where comments about their choice could be given. We included the following introductory text in order to instruct the users on how to proceed with the evaluation:

"You have been searching on a Web search engine for an entity. The search engine result page (SERP) is displayed with a picture of the entity, a short textual description, and a box with facts about the entity. For the following ten entities, it is your task to decide which fact box you would like to see in a SERP."

In addition, we asked the participants to assume that all displayed data is correct. This was to avoid influence of data quality on the results. Finally, for statistical classification, we requested the participants to provide the following information: gender, age, whether or not the participants had a background in computer science, and the time taken for evaluation.

4.2 Evaluation Results

In the following, we present the outcomes of both evaluation settings.

Quantitative Analysis. In Table 2, we present the overall *Quality* results of the quantitative evaluation. In average, both configurations of LinkSUM achieve better results than FACES in the described settings (top-5/top-10, SO/SPO). LinkSUM@config-2 performs significantly better than FACES in all settings ($p <$ 0.05). LinkSUM@config-1 is significantly ($p < 0.05$) better than FACES in three of four settings while the level of significance is not fully reached at SPO, top-10.

Qualitative Analysis. From the invited people, a total of 20 participated in the qualitative analysis. 75 % of the participants were between 25 and 35, and 25 % were between 35 and 45 years old. 75 % were male and 25 % were female. 95 % of the participants had a computer science background. The average time taken for the evaluation was 11 min and 27 s. In total, 13 participants used the option to comment about their choice. With respect to these characteristics, we did not find any significant difference within the distribution of the votes. The distribution of the votes is visualized in Fig. 5. 73 % of all votes were given

Table 2. Overall *Quality* results of the quantitative evaluation and their respective standard deviation (SD). Best results are bold. † compared to the best, difference is significant *(p < 0.05)*; ‡ compared with each of the other two settings, difference is significant *(p < 0.05)*.

	SO (top-5)	SPO (top-5)	SO (top-10)	SPO (top-10)
LinkSUM@config-1	**1.89** (SD 0.55)	**1.20** (SD 0.57)	4.78 (SD 1.05)	3.15 (SD 0.89)
LinkSUM@config-2	1.84 (SD 0.60)	**1.20** (SD 0.60)	**4.82** (SD 1.06)	**3.20** (SD 0.87)
FACES	1.66‡ (SD 0.57)	0.93‡ (SD 0.54)	4.33‡ (SD 1.01)	2.92† (SD 0.94)

to LinkSUM, 27 % of the votes were received by FACES. Out of ten entities, LinkSUM system was clearly chosen with more than 15 votes in the case of five entities. For another 2 entities, the LinkSUM system was chosen with votes in the interval 13 to 14. The votes for the remaining three entities were distributed in the interval of 9 to 11 for both systems. Both systems each received in total ten low-confidence votes (*"Not very confident"* or *"Not at all confident"*). This means that 10 out of 146 votes in the case of LinkSUM, and 10 out of 54 votes in the case of FACES were low-confidence votes. With respect to the total number of votes for each system, this means a disproportionate low number of low-confidence votes for LinkSUM. The amount of knowledge of the participants did not influence the preference for either system: the values for high or low knowledge were both in line with the total distribution of the votes.

Another interesting part of the results of the evaluation are the comments of the participants. We group the comments into two categories depending on hints about the decision-making process of the participants. In many cases, the participants gave reason why they selected a summary and/or why they rejected the other. The most-provided reasons for selection/rejection were as follows:

Selection the presented resources are relevant for the entity (e. g., "I like to see Turing machine mentioned for Alan Turing").

Rejection redundancy (e. g., "The same thing twice once with prize and once with award"), the presented resources do not characterize the entity (e. g., "I do not care about technical aspects such as format").

5 Discussion

To select the most relevant facts that characterize an entity is, in many cases, a subjective task. Thus, to produce a generic summary not tailored to any specific background or context the user might have is a challenging task that involves the identification of facts that are deemed important by the majority of the users. In order to address this challenge, the LinkSUM method combines and optimizes methods that enable to select relevant facts about entities and at the same time reduce the amount of redundant information. In our experiments and evaluation we assessed and analyzed the efficiency of the mentioned aspects

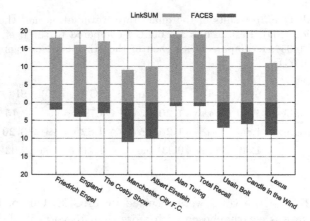

Fig. 5. Results of the qualitative evaluation. The x-axis denotes the respective entities and the y-axis accounts for the number of user votes per system. (Color figure online)

of the LinkSUM method. In a quantitative as well as qualitative setting we compared LinkSUM to the FACES system. In both setups, we demonstrated that LinkSUM exhibits significantly better results than FACES. The comments of the participants of our qualitative experiment suggest that the relevance of the related resources should be of importance and at the same time characterize an entity. We cover this by the combination of PageRank with Backlink. Our experiments with the SO-measure demonstrate that the produced *Quality* values are close to the agreement of the expert summaries (cf. Table 1).

We have tested four different methods for relation selection. The combination of the frequency of the relation, its exclusivity, and the its description has been shown to perform best in the top-10 setting, while in the top-5 setting the exclusivity score did neither contribute positively, nor negatively in that setup. The introduced measures should be considered as baselines for future evaluation settings in context to the relation selection step.

With regard to the qualitative evaluation, in the cases of the entities "Manchester City F.C.", "Albert Einstein", and "Lexus" we could not find any clear majority for either of the two systems. In the case of "Lexus" the set of presented facts has a very high overlap between the systems (with different ordering). In the case of "Manchester City F.C." and "Albert Einstein" the choices are subjective as the provided comments suggest: some users liked the listing of players ("Machester City F.C.") or children ("Albert Einstein") while others stated they did not. Contrary to the claims in [7], we could not find evidence that repetitive relations have a negative impact on the quality of the summaries. For example, the entity "The Cosby Show" contains a listing of various actors with the "starring"-relation in the LinkSUM summary while in the output of FACES this information is missing (see Fig. 4). This led to 17 vs. three votes for the LinkSUM method. In this case many of the participants provided the "inclusion of the actors" in the LinkSUM method as the main reason for their choice. The FACES system does not filter redundancies on the object level: it happens that the set of relations is diverse while on the object side, a connected resource is re-occurring multiple times (linked through different relations). An example is the entity "Total Recall (1990 film)" where FACES included the following information: *director Jerry Goldsmith; Artist Jerry Goldsmith; music Jerry Goldsmith; music composer Jerry Goldsmith; screenplay David Cronenberg; writer David Cronenberg*. Those and similar repetitions in the summaries of other entities were commented as "redundant" by a high number of participants (in total ten out of 13 participants with comments mentioned redundancy as a problem).

At http://km.aifb.kit.edu/services/link, a deployment of LinkSUM is available online. It implements the SUMMA entity summarization API [18].

6   Related Work

To the best of our knowledge, Hogan et al. first mentioned the concept of "summaries of the relevant entities" in [8].

The authors of [4] introduce RELIN, a summarization system that supports quick identification of entities. The approach applies a "goal directed surfer" which is an adapted version of the random surfer model that is also used in the PageRank algorithm. The main idea of the contribution is to combine textual notions of informativeness and relatedness for the ranking of features. As a major effect, the concise presentation of retrieved entities for quick identification by users after search is one of the scenarios that RELIN supports. In [7], the system is shown to perform significantly worse than FACES.

Google "Knowledge Graph" [13] is an example for an entity search system. The main idea is to enrich search results with summarized information about named entities. While the details of the approach are not public, Amit Singhal, the author of [13], outlines that for summarization, the system goes back to user data in order to "... study in aggregate what they've been asking Google about each item". This indicates, that Google uses additional data sources for the summaries, i.e. the queries of the users. In addition, this also provides reason to assume that the analysis focuses on informal and partial statements of the subject + predicate or subject + object kind. Our approach is similar to this methodology and follows the pattern of identifying important objects first and then select a predicate.

TripleRank by Franz et al. introduces a tensor-based approach for ranking RDF triples [6]. The approach uses the PARAFAC tensor decomposition method for deriving authority and hub scores as well as information about the importance of the link type. In contrast, in our contribution we separate the steps of deriving importance of the resource and the importance of the link as we put additional focus on the context that the target entity brings (while TripleRank addresses a more general ranking of triples). However, our general PageRank importance scores can be easily augmented or replaced by the scores produced by the TripleRank method.

The authors of [14] discuss the notion of diversity for graphical entity summarization. Two algorithms are introduced, of which one is diversity-oblivious (called PRECIS) and the other is diversity-aware (called DIVERSUM). The evaluation of the algorithms is shaped towards the movie domain and involved expert-based assessments as well as crowd-sourced experiments. The results suggest that the DIVERSUM algorithm was favored over the PRECIS algorithm. A drawback of the method is that both algorithms treat the predicate-value pairs on a per-predicate basis without measures on the object.

Also with respect to diversity, Schäfer et al. detect anomalies about entities in accordance to their different types [12]. At the current state, the system needs also the specific type as an input. However, if the main type of an entity is detected reliably, the method can be regarded as an entity summarization system that points out hidden or interesting facts.

Blanco et al. introduce Yahoo!'s Spark system [1], an entity recommendation system that suggests related entities based on a learning approach employing gradient boosted decision trees. The utilized features range from co-occurrence information over popularity features (such as the click frequency) to graph-theoretic features (such as PageRank). The system focuses on related entity recommendation in the domains of locations, movies, people, sports, and TV shows. The types of entities as well as the type of their relation play an important role in the recommendation process. Connecting predicates are not considered by Spark. The system is currently applied in the Yahoo! search system.

In another contribution [19], Thalhammer et al. exemplify a summarization approach for movie entities that utilizes rating data from the MovieLens dataset. For this, an item neighborhood is established through an item-based collaborative filtering approach. The approach is based on the idea that the semantic background that connects a movie with its neighbors can be found and extracted by making use of structured data. Similar to [4], the authors treat the object and the predicate as predicate-value compounds. The method introduces a tf-idf-based weighting scheme in order to penalize features that occur commonly in the whole dataset.

Waitelonis and Sack explain in their paper [20] how different heuristics can be used for discovering related entities in order to support exploratory search. The tested Backlink heuristic achieves the best results in terms of F-measure. In our contribution, we adopted this method and adapted it in order to fit the scenario of entity summarization. Like all tested heuristics of [20], Backlink provides an unranked set of related entities that is not directly useable in top-k settings. As a consequence, for our resource selection approach, we combine Backlink with PageRank [3].

In this work, we extended on the state of the art in the field of relevance-oriented entity summarization systems [4,19] and fact ranking in general [6]. Our contribution provides a clear cut between relevance-oriented and diversity-centered systems. We demonstrate that relevance-oriented systems provide a better foundation for displaying summaries in search engine result pages.

7 Conclusions

We presented LinkSUM, a generic relevance-centric summarization method for entity summarization. LinkSUM works with a lightweight two-stage approach in order to produce summaries for entities. In the first step, the method identifies relevant connected resources. In the second step, the system selects the most promising semantic relation for each of the connected resources. We also investigated on the most efficient configuration parameters for LinkSUM.

The results of our quantitative and qualitative evaluation, where we compared LinkSUM to the state-of-the-art system FACES [7], lead us to the following conclusions:

- For SERP scenarios, summarization systems should primarily focus on the relevance and the strength of the connection to the related resources. As a second factor the selection of an appropriate semantic relation is of importance.
- Redundancies in the set of related resources should be avoided (e. g., see Fig. 1). Commonly, if two entities are related, there is one relation that is more relevant to be mentioned. Summaries should focus on this relation and then present relations to other interesting resources.

We demonstrated applicability of the LinkSUM method for the DBpedia and Wikipedia datasets and provide results that significantly improve the state of the art. The LinkSUM system is relevant to many other tasks, like e.g.,

Semantic MediaWiki. Semantic MediaWiki (SMW) [9] is a popular extension of the MediaWiki software (used by Wikipedia). In SMW, (hyper-) textual information about entities is combined with structured information about them. Using the hyperlinks of the MediaWiki articles in combination with the semantic links of the SMW, LinkSUM can be used to provide structured summaries of entities in SMW.

Microdata/RDFa. The number of Web pages that include semantic information about entities is on the rise [10]. In many sites that focus on specific entities, hyperlinks and semantic links are occurring side by side. A prominent example for such co-occurrence is IMDb[4]. Applied in a Web data setting, LinkSUM can use plain hyperlinks in combination with the hidden semantic information for providing structured summaries of entities that occur on the Web.

LinkSUM is applicable to both of the above-mentioned scenarios and it remains a technical task to implement prototypes. With respect to research, the DBpedia/Wikipedia setting is the most suitable scenario for evaluation as other researchers can also use the same datasets for providing their own summaries and compare them to LinkSUM (that is available online).

Note that the field of entity summarization is not limited to SERPs. As the availability of structured data is growing, applications for different domains and purposes emerge. Examples include business intelligence, e-learning, health

---

[4] IMDb – http://www.imdb.com/.

information systems, news pages, data sheets, recipes etc. In fact, this includes all domain-specific cases where it is necessary for users to efficiently comprehend large information resources. In addition, entity summarization systems may adapt to user-context factors such as geo-location, cultural background, or time. As entities are retrieved without a specific information demand (like it is the case in question answering) the full personalization/contextualization of entity summaries remains an open challenge.

The above and further challenges need to be addressed in the emerging field of entity summarization. The LinkSUM method can serve as a generic foundation for such domain and/or user-centric scenarios.

8   Future Work

LinkSUM provides high-quality summaries and improves on the performance of existing solutions in the literature. In order to further improve its performance, to address limitations, and account for new features, we plan investigate on the following open points:

- While in this paper we have presented the evaluation of LinkSUM for the case of generic search in the Web, the performance of the LinkSUM method is planned to be evaluated in specific domain settings (e. g., health information).
- LinkSUM can be combined with a learning-to-rank approach with respect to the α-value and different linear combinations of the predicate selection methods.
- In future versions of LinkSUM, we plan to include literal values - such as strings or dates - as descriptors of the entities. The blending of entity-literal and entity-entity relations into a single summary will receive specific attention.

Acknowledgments. The research leading to these results has received funding from the European Union Seventh Framework Programme (FP7/2007-2013) under grant agreement no. 611346 and by the German Federal Ministry of Education and Research (BMBF) within the Software Campus project "SumOn" (grant no. 01IS12051).

References

1. Blanco, R., Cambazoglu, B.B., Mika, P., Torzec, N.: Entity recommendations in web search. In: Alani, H., et al. (eds.) ISWC 2013, Part II. LNCS, vol. 8219, pp. 33–48. Springer, Heidelberg (2013)
2. Bobić, T., Waitelonis, J., Sack, H.: FRanCo - a ground truth corpus for fact ranking evaluation. In: Joint Proceedings of SumPre and HSWI 2015, Co-located with the 12th Extended Semantic Web Conference, vol. 1556. CEUR-WS (2016)
3. Brin, S., Page, L.: The anatomy of a large-scale hypertextual web search engine. In: Proceedings of the 7th International Conference on World Wide Web 7. Elsevier (1998)

4. Cheng, G., Tran, T., Qu, Y.: RELIN: relatedness and informativeness-based centrality for entity summarization. In: Aroyo, L., Welty, C., Alani, H., Taylor, J., Bernstein, A., Kagal, L., Noy, N., Blomqvist, E. (eds.) ISWC 2011, Part I. LNCS, vol. 7031, pp. 114–129. Springer, Heidelberg (2011)
5. Demšar, J.: Statistical comparisons of classifiers over multiple data sets. J. Mach. Learn. Res. **7**, 1–30 (2006)
6. Franz, T., Schultz, A., Sizov, S., Staab, S.: TripleRank: ranking semantic web data by tensor decomposition. In: Bernstein, A., Karger, D.R., Heath, T., Feigenbaum, L., Maynard, D., Motta, E., Thirunarayan, K. (eds.) ISWC 2009. LNCS, vol. 5823, pp. 213–228. Springer, Heidelberg (2009)
7. Gunaratna, K., Thirunarayan, K., Sheth, A.P.: FACES: diversity-aware entity summarization using incremental hierarchical conceptual clustering. In: Proceedings of the 29th AAAI Conference Artificial Intelligence, 2015, Austin, Texas, USA (2015)
8. Hogan, A., Harth, A., Umrich, J., Decker, S.: Towards a scalable search and query engine for the web. In: Proceedings of the 16th International Conference on World Wide Web, WWW 2007, pp. 1301–1302. ACM, New York, NY, USA (2007)
9. Krötzsch, M., Vrandečić, D., Völkel, M.: Semantic mediaWiki. In: Cruz, I., Decker, S., Allemang, D., Preist, C., Schwabe, D., Mika, P., Uschold, M., Aroyo, L.M. (eds.) ISWC 2006. LNCS, vol. 4273, pp. 935–942. Springer, Heidelberg (2006)
10. Meusel, R., Petrovski, P., Bizer, C.: The WebDataCommons microdata, RDFa and microformat dataset series. In: Mika, P., et al. (eds.) ISWC 2014, Part I. LNCS, vol. 8796, pp. 277–292. Springer, Heidelberg (2014)
11. Roa-Valverde, A., Thalhammer, A., Toma, I., Sicilia, M.-A.: Towards a formal model for sharing and reusing ranking computations. In: Proceedings of the 6th International Workshop on Ranking in Databases in conjunction with VLDB 2012 (2012)
12. Schäfer, B., Ristoski, P., Paulheim, H.: What is special about Bethlehem, Pennsylvania? identifying unusual facts about DBpedia entities. In: Proceedings of the ISWC 2015 Posters and Demonstrations Track (2015)
13. Singhal, A.: Introducing the knowledge graph: things, not strings (2012). http://goo.gl/kH1NKq
14. Sydow, M., Pikuła, M., Schenkel, R.: The notion of diversity in graphical entity summarisation on semantic knowledge graphs. J. Intell. Inf. Syst. **41**(2), 109–149 (2013)
15. Thalhammer, A.: DBpedia PageRank dataset (2016). http://people.aifb.kit.edu/ath#DBpedia_PageRank
16. Thalhammer, A., Knuth, M., Sack, H.: Evaluating entity summarization using a game-based ground truth. In: Cudré-Mauroux, P., et al. (eds.) ISWC 2012, Part II. LNCS, vol. 7650, pp. 350–361. Springer, Heidelberg (2012)
17. Thalhammer, A., Rettinger, A.: Browsing DBpedia entities with summaries. In: Presutti, V., Blomqvist, E., Troncy, R., Sack, H., Papadakis, I., Tordai, A. (eds.) ESWC Satellite Events 2014. LNCS, vol. 8798, pp. 511–515. Springer, Heidelberg (2014)
18. Thalhammer, A., Stadtmüller, S.: SUMMA: a common API for linked data entity summaries. In: Cimiano, P., Frasincar, F., Houben, G.-J., Schwabe, D. (eds.) ICWE 2015. LNCS, vol. 9114, pp. 430–446. Springer, Heidelberg (2015)
19. Thalhammer, A., Toma, I., Roa-Valverde, A.J., Fensel, D.: Leveraging usage data for linked data movie entity summarization. In: Proceedings of the 2nd International Ws. on Usage Analysis and the Web of Data (USEWOD2012) (2012)
20. Waitelonis, J., Sack, H.: Towards exploratory video search using linked data. Multimedia Tools Appl. **59**, 645–672 (2012). doi:10.1007/s11042-011-0733-1

Beyond Established Knowledge Graphs-Recommending Web Datasets for Data Linking

Mohamed Ben Ellefi[1(✉)], Zohra Bellahsene[1], Stefan Dietze[2], and Konstantin Todorov[1]

[1] LIRMM, University of Montpellier, Montpellier, France
{benellefi,bella,todorov}@lirmm.fr
[2] L3S Research Center, Leibniz University Hannover, Hannover, Germany
dietze@l3s.de

Abstract. With the explosive growth of the Web of Data in terms of size and complexity, identifying suitable datasets to be linked, has become a challenging problem for data publishers. To understand the nature of the content of specific datasets, we adopt the notion of dataset profiles, where datasets are characterized through a set of topic annotations. In this paper, we adopt a collaborative filtering-like recommendation approach, which exploits both existing dataset profiles, as well as traditional dataset connectivity measures, in order to link arbitrary, non-profiled datasets into a global dataset-topic-graph. Our experiments, applied to all available Linked Datasets in the Linked Open Data (LOD) cloud, show an average recall of up to 81%, which translates to an average reduction of the size of the original candidate dataset search space to up to 86%. An additional contribution of this work is the provision of benchmarks for dataset interlinking recommendation systems.

1 Introduction

The web of data, in particular Linked Open Data (LOD) [1], is growing constantly both in terms of size and impact. This growth introduces a wide variety and heterogeneity of datasets with respect to represented resource types, currentness, coverage of topics and domains, size, used languages, coherence, accessibility [2] or general quality aspects [3]. The wide variety and heterogeneity of these dataset characteristics pose significant challenges for data consumers when attempting to find useful datasets without prior knowledge of available datasets. Dataset registries such as Datahub[1] or DataCite[2] aim at addressing this issue, for instance, by enabling users and data providers to annotate their datasets with some basic metadata, for instance, descriptive tags and access details. However, due to the reliance on human annotators, such metadata are often sparse and outdated [4]. This has contributed to the fact that, the majority of data consumption, linking and reuse focuses on established datasets and knowledge

---

[1] http://datahub.io.
[2] http://datacite.org.

© Springer International Publishing Switzerland 2016
A. Bozzon et al. (Eds.): ICWE 2016, LNCS 9671, pp. 262–279, 2016.
DOI: 10.1007/978-3-319-38791-8_15

graphs such as DBpedia [5] or YAGO [6], while a long tail of datasets has hardly been reused and adopted.

For these reasons, dataset recommendation is becoming an increasingly important task to support challenges such as entity interlinking [7], entity retrieval or semantic search [8]. In line with [9], dataset recommendation is the problem of computing a rank score for each of a set of datasets $\mathcal{D}$ so that the rank score indicates the relatedness of a dataset from $\mathcal{D}$ to a given dataset, D_0. In turn, this allows to determine the likelihood of datasets in $\mathcal{D}$ to contain linking candidates for D_0.

While our approach is agnostic to the underlying data sharing principles, entity and data interlinking are of particular concern when considering Linked Open Data [1], not least because its essential principles and reliance on IRIs for identifying any term or entity facilitates Web-scale linking of data. Here, the current topology of the LOD cloud underlines the need for practical and efficient means to recommend suitable datasets, as only very few, well established knowledge graphs show a high amount of inlinks with DBpedia being the most obvious target, while a large amount of datasets is largely ignored, often due to a lack of understanding of their content and characteristics and consequently, the challenge to identify suitable linking candidates.

For the dataset recommendation problem, one has to consider both schema-level features, to take into account the overlap and complementarity of the actual schemas, as well as instance-level features, to consider the overlap and complementarity of described entities. Given the scale of available datasets, exhaustive comparisons of schemas and instances or some of their features are not feasible as an online process. Descriptive and reliable metadata, i.e. an index is required, which allows the efficient computation of suitable recommendations.

Some approaches exist, which obtain such an index through topic modeling approaches. For instance, [4] generates a weighted bipartite graph, where datasets and topics represent the nodes, related through weighted edges, indicating the relevance of a topic for a specific dataset.

However, while computation of such *topic profiles* is costly, it is usually applied to a subset of existing datasets only, where any new or so far unannotated datasets require the pre-computation of a dedicated topic profile.

In our work, we provide a recommendation method which not only takes into account the direct relatedness of datasets as emerging from the topic-dataset-graph produced through the profiling in [4], but instead, we adopt established *collaborative filtering* practices by considering the topic relationships emerging from the global topic-dataset-graph to derive specific dataset recommendations. We exploit dataset connectivity measures to relate non-profiled datasets to datasets in the dataset-topic-graph, enabling us to consider arbitrary datasets as part of our recommendations. This approach on the one hand significantly increases the recall of our recommendations, but at the same time improves recommendations through considering dataset connectivity as another relatedness indicator. The intuition is that this leads to more robust and less error-prone recommendations, since the consideration of global topic connectivity provides reliable connectivity indicators even in cases where the underlying topic profiles might be noisy. Our assumption is that even poor or incorrect topic annotations will serve as reliable relatedness indicator when shared among datasets.

While we adopt the topic profile graph in [4] for our experiments, we would like to emphasize that our approach is agnostic to the underlying topic index. Topic profiles which are obtained by annotating samples of instances as in the chosen method, are shown to reflect both, instance-level as well as schema-level characteristics of a specific dataset. Even though topics are derived from instances, resources of particular types show characteristic topic distributions, which significantly differ across different types [10].

In our experiments, we apply our approach to the LOD cloud as one scenario and use case, where dataset recommendation is of particular relevance. Our experiments show superior performance compared to three simple baselines, namely based on shared key-words, shared topics, and shared common links. In a series of experiments, we demonstrate the performance of our technique compared to the current version of the LOD as an evaluation data, achieving a reduction of the original (LOD) search space of up to 86 % on average.

We proceed to present the theoretical grounds of our technique in Sect. 2, which contains *two* of the contributions of the paper – an efficient approach of propagating dataset profiles over the LOD cloud by starting off with a small set of profiled datasets and a dataset recommendation technique based on topic-profiles. Section 3 defines the evaluation framework that has been established and reports on our experimental results, providing a comparison to a set of baseline recommendation approaches, made available, as a *third* contribution of this work, to the community as a benchmark. Related approaches are presented and discussed in Sect. 4 before we conclude in Sect. 5.

2   Dataset Recommendation Framework

The current section introduces a novel approach to dataset recommendation based on dataset profiles with an aimed application in the entity interlinking process. In the current setting, the datasets profiles are generated by a topic modeling paradigm, which is briefly introduced in the following subsection together with some notation and basic definitions. A computationally efficient approach of propagating existing profiles towards new arbitrary datasets is presented in Subsect. 2.2. Our recommendation technique is given in detail in Subsect. 2.3. Figure 2 provides an overview of the main steps of the approach that will be discussed in the sequel.

2.1   Preliminaries

We start by introducing notation and definitions. Let $T_1, \ldots, T_N$ be a number of topics from a set of topics $\mathcal{T}$ and let $\mathcal{D} = \{D_1, \ldots, D_M\}$ be a set of datasets.

Dataset Topic Profile. Topic modeling algorithms such as Latent Dirichlet allocation [11] are used to discover a set of topics from a large collection of documents, where a topic is a distribution over terms that is biased around those associated under a single theme. Topic modeling approaches have been applied to tasks such as corpus exploration, document classification, and information retrieval. Here, we will look into a novel application of this group of approaches, exploiting the topic structure in order to define and construct dataset profiles for dataset recommendation.

As a result of the topic modeling process, a bipartite—*profile*—graph is built, providing a relation between a document and a topic. Documents in our setting are the datasets to be considered, therefore the profile graph is induced by the relation between a dataset, D_i, and a topic, T_k, expressed by a weight, $w_{ik} \in [0, 1]$, for all $i = 1, \ldots, M$ and $k = 1, \ldots, N$. Formally, a profile graph is defined as follows.

Definition 1 (Dataset Topic Profile Graph). *A dataset topic profile graph is a weighted directed bipartite graph $\mathcal{P} = (\mathcal{S}, \mathcal{E}, \Delta)$, where $\mathcal{S} = \mathcal{D} \cup \mathcal{T}$, $\mathcal{E}$ is a set of edges of the form $e_{ik} = (D_i, T_k)$ such that $D_i \in \mathcal{D}$ and $T_k \in \mathcal{T}$ and*

$$\Delta \colon \mathcal{E} \to [0, 1]$$
$$e_{ik} \mapsto w_{ik}$$

is a function assigning weights to the edges in $\mathcal{E}$.

The bipartite property of $\mathcal{P}$ allows to represent a given dataset by a set of topics—its *profile*. For the purposes of this study, it is worth noting that, inversely, a topic can be represented by a set of weighted datasets—what we will call the *signature* of a topic (see Fig. 1). We will denote by Profile(D_i) the function returning the topic profile of D_i, i.e., the set of topics together with their weights with respect to D_i. Inversely, we will denote by $\mathcal{D}_{T_k}$ the set of datasets together with their weights with respect to a topic T_k, derived again from the graph $\mathcal{P}$.

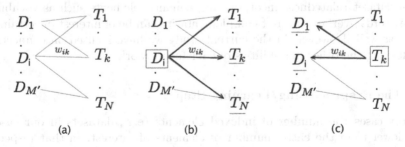

(a)   (b)   (c)

Fig. 1. (a) An example of a bipartite profile graph with topics and datasets linked by weighted edges. (b) Representing a dataset, D_i, as a set of topics. (c) Representing a topic, T_k, as a set of datasets.

Datasets Connectivity. The connectivity behavior of datasets is a central concept within the proposed recommendation framework. We consider the following definition of a measure of the strength of dataset connectedness.

Definition 2 (Dataset Inter-connectivity Measure). *Let $D_i, D_j \in \mathcal{D}$ be two datasets. We define a measure of their common degree of connectivity as follows.*

$$\mathcal{C}(D_i, D_j) = \frac{shared(D_i, D_j) \times [total(D_i) + total(D_j)]}{2 \times total(D_i) \times total(D_j)} \tag{1}$$

where $shared(.,.)$ returns the number of links between two datasets and $total(D_i)$ returns the total number of links between D_i and any other dataset in $\mathcal{D}$.

Note that (1) is the symmetric version of the measure of connectivity of D_i to D_j given by

$$\mathcal{C}'(D_i, D_j) = \frac{shared(D_i, D_j)}{total(D_i)}.$$

Explicitly, (1) is obtained by taking the mean

$$\frac{\mathcal{C}'(D_i, D_j) + \mathcal{C}'(D_j, D_i)}{2} = \mathcal{C}(D_i, D_j).$$

The measure $\mathcal{C}$ is in the interval $[0, 1]$ and has the advantage of considering the relative connectivity between datasets instead of simply looking at the number of links. In our experimental setting, $shared(D_i, D_j)$ is taken as the sum of the links between two datasets in both directions: $D_i \rightarrow D_j$ and $D_j \rightarrow D_i$, resulting in the number of incoming and outgoing links between the datasets. A specific version of the measure $\mathcal{C}$ can be defined by taking only certain types of links (or predicates) in consideration (in our application scenario, we have considered LOD datasets, therefore an example of a specific predicate can be owl:sameAs).

In a more general manner, it is possible to use any dataset connectivity measure of our choice. The measure given above is one that worked well in our experiments (see Sect. 3). In addition, one can define in a broader sense a measure of dataset relatedness incorporating semantic elements such as vocabulary and keywords overlap. Dataset complementarity can be of interest in certain scenarios, as well. However, in the current study we have focused on connectivity only, leaving the other possibilities out for future work.

2.2   The Preprocessing/Learning Step

In many cases the number of indexed elements (e.g., datasets in our case) is much lower than the entire number of elements of interest. In that respect, it is interesting to consider a procedure that allows inexpensively to include novel elements in the index. As a preprocessing step of our recommendation workflow, we adopt a learning approach that consists of assigning topics to datasets by linking them into the dataset-topic-graph after computing their connectivity with already indexed (profiled) datasets. This step is useful in order to include in the recommendation pipeline datasets that have not been initially indexed, in an inexpensive manner, keeping in mind that the indexing process can be often quite costly and time-consuming.

Let $\mathcal{P}$ be a topic profile graph and let $D_j \in \mathcal{D}$ be a random dataset, which is not necessarily included in the original topic profile graph $\mathcal{P}$. We assign topic weights to D_j considering its degree of connectivity with respect to datasets from the topic profile graph by using the following measure of relatedness between linked datasets and topics (see Fig. 2, steps 1 and 2).

Definition 3 (Connectivity-Based Dataset and Topic Relatedness Measure). *Let $D_j \in \mathcal{D}$ and $T_k \in \mathcal{T}$. We define the following dataset and topic relatedness measure.*

$$\sigma(D_j, T_k) = \max_{D_i \in \mathcal{D}} \mathcal{C}(D_i, D_j) * w_{ik}. \tag{2}$$

Recall that w_{ik} is the weight of the topic T_k with respect to D_i as given in Definition 1, taking a zero value in case T_k is not in Profile(D_i). $\mathcal{C}(D_i, D_j)$ is the connectivity measure between two datasets, as defined in (1). The dataset and topic relatedness measure σ is a way to measure the datasets connectivity behavior using their profiles. We will use the notation $\sigma_{jk} = \sigma(D_j, T_k)$ as a shortcut. Note that σ is in the $[0, 1]$ interval.

This new weighting scheme allows to propagate inexpensively the profile of D_i to datasets that are connected to it. Hence, a new graph is created between target datasets and source datasets topics. Precisely, a topic $T_k \subset$ Profile(D_i) will be assigned to a dataset D_j that has a non-zero value of $\mathcal{C}(D_i, D_j)$. The weight of this novel topic-dataset relation is now based on the connectivity order of D_j with respect to D_i, scaled by the weight w_{ik} of T_k with respect to D_i. In that sense, w_{ik} plays a penalization role: the novel weight σ_{jk} of T_k with respect to D_j is penalized by the weight of T_k in the original topic graph, i.e., datasets with high degree of connectivity to D_i will get relatively low weights with respect to a topic, if that topic has a relatively low weight with respect to D_i. We consider the maximum value over all datasets in $\mathcal{D}$, the set of the originally profiled datasets. In this way, we avoid ambiguity when a non-indexed dataset D_j is connected to a single topic T_k via multiple already indexed datasets, assuring that the highest value of relation between T_k and D_j is preserved. Thus, the choice of a topic to be assigned to a dataset is not influenced, only its weight is, and no connectivity information is lost.

The topic-dataset relatedness measure (3) allows to construct a novel profile graph by computing σ_{jk} for all possible values of j and k ($j = 1, \ldots, M$ and $k = 1, \ldots, N$). The novel graph, that we call *the Linked Dataset Topic Profile Graph (LDPG)*, includes new datasets and the original topics as its nodes and is defined as follows (see Fig. 2, step 2).

Definition 4 (Linked Dataset Topic Profiles Graph (LDPG)). *The LDPG is a weighted directed bipartite graph $\mathcal{P}_l = (\mathcal{S}_l, \mathcal{E}_l, \Delta_l)$, where $\mathcal{S}_l = \mathcal{D} \cup \mathcal{T}$, $\mathcal{E}_l$ is a set of edges of the form $e'_{jk} = (D_j, T_k)$ such that $D_j \in \mathcal{D}$ and $T_k \in \mathcal{T}$ and*

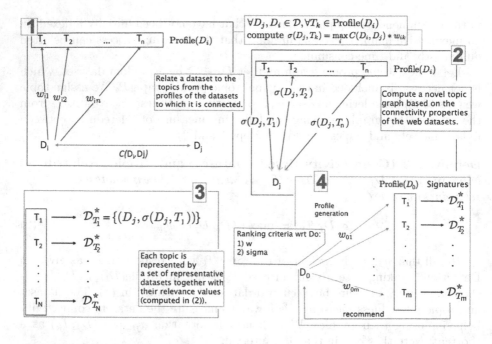

Fig. 2. The four main steps of the profile-based dataset recommendation framework.

$$\Delta_l : \mathcal{E}_l \to [0,1]$$
$$e'_{jk} \mapsto \sigma_{jk}$$

is a function assigning weights to the edges in $\mathcal{E}_l$.

As this was the case within the original profiling scheme, the inherently bipartite nature of the graph $\mathcal{P}_l$ allows for a two-fold interpretation — either a dataset is modeled as a set of topics (a dataset's *profile*), or, inversely, a topic is modeled as a set of datasets assigned to it (a topic's *signature*). Therefore, it is easy to define a set of **significant** datasets with respect to a given topic, by thresholding on their weights in the Linked profiles graph with respect to the topic of interest. Note again that for the purposes of the recommendation task, we will be interested in keeping the weights of every dataset in the resulting topic representations and thus model every topic by a set of *(dataset, weight)* couples.

Definition 5 (Dataset Significance for a Topic. Topic Signature).
*A dataset $D_j \in \mathcal{D}$ is **significant** with respect to a topic $T_k \in \mathcal{T}$ if its weight in the LDPG $\sigma_{jk} = \sigma(D_j, T_k)$ is greater than a given value $\theta \in (0,1)$.*

A topic T_k is modeled by the set of its significant datasets together with their respective weights, given as

$$\mathcal{D}^*_{T_k} = \{(D_j, \sigma_{jk}) | \sigma_{jk} > \theta\}_{j=1,\dots,M}, \tag{3}$$

*for $k = 1, \ldots, N$. We will call $\mathcal{D}^*_{T_k}$ the **signature** of the topic T_k.*

With this definition, the profile of a given dataset, Profile(D_i), is modeled as a number of sets of significant datasets – one per topic in Profile(D_i) coupled with their weights with respect to each topic (see Fig. 2, step 3), or otherwise – a set topic signatures.

For sake of generality, we draw the readers attention to the fact that the learning approach resulting in index extension applies to any dataset profile definition that one might like to consider and not exclusively to the one based on the topic modeling paradigm.

2.3 Profile-Based Dataset Ranking

Let D_0 be a new dataset to be linked. The aim of the recommendation task is to provide the user with an ordered list of datasets, potential candidates for interlinking with D_0, which narrows down considerably the original search space i.e., the web of data. Thus the dataset recommendation can be seen as the problem of computing a rank score for each $D_j \in \mathcal{D}$ that indicates the likelihood of D_j to be relevant to a dataset D_0. In the context of using topic-based dataset profiles for linking recommendation, we restate the problem in the following manner.

For a given non-linked dataset D_0, profile-based dataset recommendation is the problem of computing a rank score r_{0j} for each $D_j \in \mathcal{D}$ based on topic overlap between D_j and D_0, so that r_{0j} indicates the relevance of D_j to D_0 for the entity linking task.

We start by generating the topic profile of D_0, Profile$(D_0) = \{(T_1, w_{01}), \ldots, (T_m, w_{0m})\}$. Then, we extract from the result of the learning step the set of *target* datasets for each topic in Profile(D_0) together with their corresponding relevance values σ, namely the set of m topic signatures $\{\mathcal{D}^*_{T_k}\}^m_{k=1}$. These datasets constitute the pool, from which we will recommend interlinking candidates to D_0. We will use n to denote their number, that is $n = \sum_{j=1}^{m} |\mathcal{D}^*_{T_j}|$, or the sum of the numbers of datasets in each topic signature. The aim is to serve the user with the most highly ranked datasets from that pool. There are two ranking criteria to consider: the weight w of each topic in Profile(D_0) and the weight σ of each dataset in each of the topic signatures in $\{\mathcal{D}^*_{T_k}\}^m_{k=1}$ (step 4 in Fig. 2). Since the ranking score in our setting depends on topic overlap, we define the interlinking relevance of a dataset D_j with respect to D_0 in the following manner.

Definition 6 (Dataset Interlinking Relevance). *For all $j = 1, \ldots, n$, the relevance of a dataset $D_j \in \mathcal{D}$ to a dataset D_0 via the topic T_k is given by*

$$r^0_j = w_{0k} * \sigma_{jk}, \tag{4}$$

with $k = 1, \ldots, m$.

Note that j covers the total number of datasets in the set of m topic signatures, therefore the relevance value depends on j only (i.e., a single relevance value per dataset from the pool of candidates). Similarly to the definition of σ in Definition 6, w has a penalization function, decreasing the ranks of datasets that have high values of their σ weights, but are found in topic signatures of a low relevance to D_0 (expressed by a low value of w).

It is easy to define a mapping $f : \mathcal{R} \to \mathbb{N}$ from a space of interlinking relevance values $\mathcal{R}$ to the natural numbers such that $f(r_{j_1}^0) > f(r_{j_2}^0) \iff r_{j_1}^0 \leq r_{j_2}^0$, for any $j_1, j_2 \in [1, n]$ and $1 = \max_j f(r_j^0)$. With this definition, since there is a relevance value r_j^0 per dataset $D_j \in \mathcal{D}$, $f(r_j^0)$ returns the rank of the dataset D_j with respect to D_0. The results of the recommendation process are given in a descending order with respect to these ranks.

3 Experiments and Results

In this section, we start by a discussion on the evaluation setting then we proceed to report on the experiments conducted in support of the proposed recommendation method.

3.1 Evaluation Framework

The quality of the outcome of a recommendation process can be evaluated along a number of dimensions. Ricci *et al.* [12] provide a large review of recommender system evaluation techniques and cite three common types of experiments: (i) offline setting, where recommendation approaches are compared without user interaction, (ii) user studies, where a small group of subjects experiment with the system and report on the experience, and (iii) online experiments, where real user populations interact with the system.

In our approach, we assume that the dataset connectivity behavior when data were collected (i.e., steps 1, 2 and 3 in Fig. 2) is similar enough to the profile connectivity behavior when the recommender system is deployed (i.e., step 4 in Fig. 2), so that we can make reliable decisions based on an *offline evaluation*. The offline experiment is performed by using pre-collected data as evaluation data (ED). Using these data, we can simulate the profiles connectivity behavior that impacts the recommendation results.

The most straightforward, although not unproblematic (see the discussion that follows below) choice of ED for the entity linking recommendation task is the existing link topology of the current version of links between web datasets. Since this evaluation data are the only available data that we have for both training (our preprocessing steps 1, 2 and 3 in Fig. 2) and testing (the actual recommendation in step 4 of Fig. 2), we opted for a *5-fold cross-validation* [13] to evaluate the effectiveness of the recommendation system. In 5-fold cross-validation, the ED was randomly split into two subsets: the first one, containing random 80 % of the linked datasets in the ED, was used as training set while the second one, containing the remaining linked datasets (i.e., random 20 % of the ED), was retained as the validation data for tests (i.e., the test set). We repeated these experiments five times changing at each time the 20 % representing the test set in order to cover 100 % of the whole data space. The evaluation is based on the capacity of our system to *reconstruct* the links from the ED in the recommendation process.

The most common measures of the efficiency of a recommendation system are Precision, Recall and F1-Score, formalized as functions of the true positives (TP), false positives (FP), true negatives (TN) and false negatives (FN) as follows.

$$Pr = \frac{TP}{TP + FP}; \quad Re = \frac{TP}{TP + FN}; \quad F1 = \frac{2TP}{2TP + FN + FP}. \quad (5)$$

In addition, [12] present a measure of the false positive overestimation, particularly important in our offline evaluation case:

$$FalsePositiveRate = \frac{FP}{FP + TN}. \quad (6)$$

A small value of the false positive rate means that every time you call a positive, you have a high probability of being right. Conversely, a high value of the false positive rate means that every time you call a positive, you have a high probability of being wrong.

3.2 Experimental Setup

Since our recommendation is based on **the connectivity** of the $\mathcal{D}$ graph as well as **the topic profiles** of indexed datasets, the Linked Open Data (LOD) [1] is clearly our best use case to experiment our recommendation. As a topic modeling approach, we adopt the dataset profiles index provided by [4] since it generates accurate profiles and outperforms established topic modeling approaches such as ones based on the well known Latent Dirichlet Allocation[3]. Using the topic profiles approach from [4] it is easy to produce a weighted bipartite graph as described in 1, where datasets and topics represent the nodes, related through weighted edges, indicating the relevance of a topic for a specific dataset. A *dataset profile* is represented through *topics*, which in this case are DBpedia categories[4] derived through a processing pipeline[5] analyzing representative resource samples from specific datasets. For example, the $\mathcal{T}$ profile of the **Semantic Web Dog Food Corpus**[6] dataset includes the following DBpedia categories: *Data management, Semantic Web, Information retrieval, World Wide Web Consortium standards, etc.*.

In the following, we distinguish between the set $\mathcal{D}$ of datasets in the entire LOD and the datasets indexed by the profiling approach [4], denoted by $\mathcal{D}'$. Explicitly, we consider:

---

[3] http://mallet.cs.umass.edu/.
[4] dbpedia.org/page/Category.
[5] http://data-observatory.org/lod-profiles/profiling.htm.
[6] http://data.semanticweb.org/.

- $\mathcal{D}$: All datasets in the LOD cloud group on the Data Hub[7], which will be considered as target datasets (to be recommended) in the testing set, $|\mathcal{D}| = 258$.
- $\mathcal{D}'$: All the datasets indexed by the topics profiles graph[8], which will be considered as source datasets (to be linked) in the testing set, $|\mathcal{D}'| = 76$ and $|\mathcal{D}'| \subset |\mathcal{D}|$.

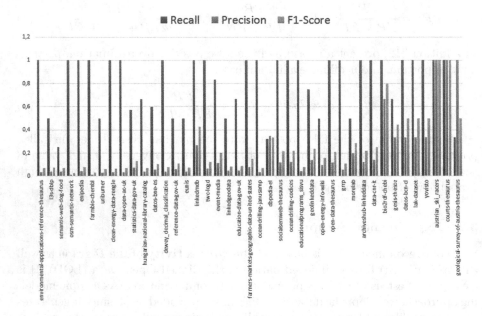

Fig. 3. Recall/Precision/F1-Score over all recommendation lists for all source datasets in $\mathcal{D}'$ and all target datasets in $\mathcal{D}$.

We trained our system as described in steps 1, 2 and 3 in Fig. 2. We started by extracting the topic profiles graph from the available endpoint of Data Observatory[9]. Then we extracted VoID descriptions of all LOD datasets, using the *datahub2void* tool[10]. The constituted **evaluation data (ED)** corresponds to the outgoing and incoming links extracted from the generated VoID file (it is made available on http://www.lirmm.fr/benellefi/void.ttl).

Note that in the training set we used the actual values of VoID:triples (see Sect. 1) to compute dataset connectivity, while in the test set we considered binary values (two datasets from the evaluation data are either linked or not). For example, $shared(tip, linkedgeodata) = 6$, so in the training set we considered

---

[7] http://datahub.io/group/lodcloud.
[8] http://data-observatory.org/lod-profiles/profile-explorer/.
[9] http://data-observatory.org/lod-profiles/sparql.
[10] https://github.com/lod-cloud/datahub2void.

6 as the number of links in Eq. (1), while in the test set we only consider the information that *tip* is connected to *linkedgeodata* and vice versa. Training is performed only once.

3.3   Results and Analysis

We ran our recommendation workflow as described in step 4 in Fig. 2. Using 5-fold cross-validation, for each dataset in $\mathcal{D}'$, we recommended an ordered list of datasets from $\mathcal{D}$. The results are given in Fig. 3.

The results show a high average recall of up to 81 %. Note that the recommendation results for 59 % of the source datasets have a recall of 100 % and two of them have an F1-score of 100 %. As mentioned in Sect. 3.2, we considered only the binary information of the existence of a link in the LOD as evaluation data in the testing set. This simplification has been adopted due to the difficulty of retrieving all actual links in the LOD graph (implying the application of heavy instance matching or data linking algorithms on a very large scale). Certainly, the explicit currently existing links are only a useful measure for recall, but not for precision. In our experiments, we measured an average precision of 19 %. We explain that by the fact that the amount of explicitly declared links in the LOD cloud as ED is certain but far from being complete to be considered as ground truth. Subsequently, we are forced to assume that the false positive items would have not been used even if they had been recommended, i.e., that they are uninteresting or useless to the user. For this reason, based on our evaluation data, a large amount of false positives occur, which in reality are likely to be relevant recommendations. In order to rate this error, we calculated the false positive rate over all results, shown in the Fig. 4. The small values of this rate indicate that every time you call a positive, you have a probability of being right, which provide support to our hypothesis with an average FP-Rate of 13 %.

To further illustrate the effect of false positives overestimation, we included in the ED new dataset links based on the shared keywords of the datasets. Precisely, if two datasets share more then 80 % of their VoID tags, they are considered as linked, and are added to the ED. For example, *linkedgeodata* is connected to 4 datasets in the main ED: *osm-semantic-network, dbpedia, tip et dbpedia-el*. However, we found that *linkedgeodata* shared more than 80 % of its tags with *fu-berlin-eurostat* and *twarql*[11]. By adding both links to the original ED, we noted a gain in precision of 5 % for the *linkedgeodata* dataset with no impact on recall. Thus, we believe that our system can perform much better on more complete ED.

The current version of the topic dataset profile graph from [4] contains 76 datasets and 185 392 topics. Working with this already annotated subset of existing datasets is not sufficient and limited the scope of our recommendations significantly. In addition, the number of the profiled datasets, compared to the number

---

[11] Example: *linkedgeodata* has 11 tags and *twarql* has 9 tags. We considered as connected since they shared 8 tags which is higher than the 80 % of the average amount, i.e., $8 < (0.8 * (11 + 9)/2)$.

of topics is very small, which in turn appeared to be problematic in the recommendation process due to the high degree of topic diversity leading to a lack of discriminability. One way of approaching this problem would be to index all LOD datasets by applying the original profiling algorithm [4]. However, given the complexity of this processing pipeline—consisting of resource sampling, analysis, entity and topic extraction for a large amount of resources—it is not efficient enough, specifically given the constant evolution of Web data, calling for frequent re-annotation of datasets. Also we note that this profiles propagation technique can be of interest for any dataset profile-based application, providing an inexpensive way of computing a profile of an arbitrary dataset. As one of the original contributions of this paper, the preprocessing step in our recommendation pipeline can be seen as an efficient method for automatic expansion of the initial profiles index over the entire linked open data space based on dataset connectivity measures.

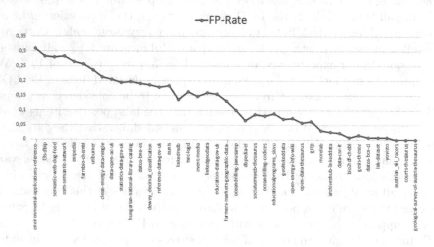

Fig. 4. False positive rates over all recommendation lists over all $\mathcal{D}'$ datasets.

The main goal of a recommender system is to reduce the cost of identifying candidate datasets for the interlinking task. Some systems may provide recommendations with high quality in terms of both precision and recall, but only over a small portion of datasets (as is the case in [14]). We obtain high recall values for the majority of datasets over *the entire set of LOD datasets* with a price to pay of having relatively low precision. Here, low precision/high recall systems still offer significant contributions by narrowing the size of the search space. Therefore, we highlight the efficiency of our system in reducing the search space size. Figure 5 depicts the reduction of the original search space size (258 datasets) in percentage over all source datasets to be linked. The average space size reduction is of up to 86 %.

As mentioned previously, our system can cover 100 % of the available linked datasets, since the topics-datasets profiling approach [4] as well as our profile expansion approach presented in Sect. 2.2 are able to profile any arbitrary dataset.

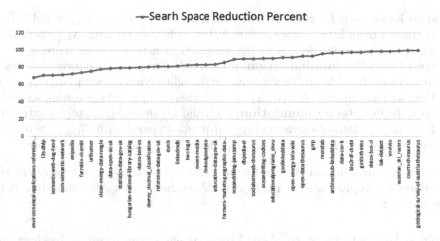

Fig. 5. Search space reduction in percent over all recommended sets and over all $\mathcal{D}'$ datasets.

Our system is also capable of dealing with the well-known cold-start problem (handling correctly newly published and unlinked datasets), since not linked datasets are handled by using the indexing technique in [4], which does not rely on dataset connectivity. Based on the learning step, our system is able to recommend a sorted list of candidate datasets to these not linked datasets.

3.4 Baselines and Comparison

To the best of our knowledge, there does not exist a common benchmark for dataset interlinking recommendation. One of the contributions of this paper is the provision of three simple baseline approaches for this problem. Given two datasets, D_0 and D_j, we define the following baseline recommendation methods.

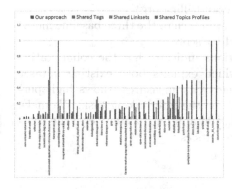

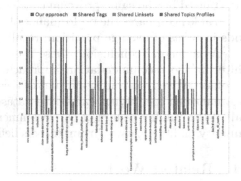

Fig. 6. F1-Score values of our approach versus the baselines overall $\mathcal{D}'$ datasets.

Fig. 7. Recall values of our approach versus the baselines overall $\mathcal{D}'$ datasets.

Shared Keywords Recommendation: if D_0 and D_j share N_{tags} of VoID:Tags extracted from http://www.lirmm.fr/benellefi/void.ttl with $N_{tags} > 0$, then we recommend (D_j, N_{tags}) to D_i, where N_{tags} acts as a rank score.

Shared Links Recommendation: if D_0 and D_j have N_{links} connected datasets in common from http://www.lirmm.fr/benellefi/void.ttl with $N_{linksets} > 0$, then we recommend (D_j, N_{links}) to D_0, where N_{links} acts as a rank score.

Shared Topics Recommendation: if D_0 and D_j share N_{topics} topics extracted from http://data-observatory.org/lod-profiles/sparql with $N_{topics} > 0$, then we recommend (D_j, N_{topics}) to D_0, where N_{topics} acts as a rank score.

The recommendation results for all LOD datasets (D_0 covering D) of the three baseline approaches are made available on http://www.lirmm.fr/benellefi/Baselines.rar.

Table 1. Average precision, recall and F1-score of our system versus the baselines over all $\mathcal{D}'$ datasets based on the ED.

	Our approach	Shared keywords	Shared linksets	Shared topics profiles
AVG Precision	**19 %**	9 %	9 %	3 %
AVG Recall	**81 %**	47 %	11 %	13 %
AVG F1-Score	**24 %**	10 %	8 %	4 %

Figures 6 and 7, respectively, depict detailed comparisons of the F1-Score and the Recall values between our approach and the baselines over all $\mathcal{D}'$ datasets taken as source datasets. From these figures, it can be seen that our method largely outperforms the baseline approaches, which even fail to provide any results at all for some datasets. The baseline approaches have produced better results than our system in a limited number of cases, especially for source and target datasets having the same publisher. For example, the shared keywords baseline generated an F-Score of 100 % on *oceandrilling-janusamp*, which is connected to * *oceandrilling-codices*, due to the fact that these two datasets are tagged by the same provenance (data.oceandrilling.org).

Table 1 compares the performance of our approach to the three baseline methods in terms of average precision, recall and F1-score.

As a general conclusion, these observations indicate that the collaborative filtering-like recommendation approach, which exploits both existing dataset profiles as well as traditional dataset connectivity measures, shows high performance on identifying candidate datasets for the interlinking task. We make all of the ranking results of our recommendation approach available to the community on http://www.lirmm.fr/benellefi/results.csv.

4   Related Work

With respect to finding relevant datasets on the Web, we cite briefly several studies on discovering relevant datasets for query answering have been proposed.

Based on well-known data mining strategies, the works in [15] and [16] present techniques to find relevant datasets, which offer contextual information corresponding to the user queries. A used feedback-based approach to incrementally identify new datasets for domain-specific linked data applications is proposed in [17]. User feedback is used as a way to assess the relevance of the candidate datasets.

In the following, we cite approaches that have been devised for the datasets interlinking candidates recommendation task and which are directly relevant to our work.

Nikolov and d'Aquin [18] propose a keyword-based search approach to identify candidate sources for data linking. The approach consists of two steps: (i) searching for potentially relevant entities in other datasets using as keywords randomly selected instances over the literals in the source dataset, and (ii) filtering out irrelevant datasets by measuring semantic concept similarities obtained by applying ontology matching techniques.

Leme et al. [14] present a ranking method for datasets with respect to their relevance for the interlinking task. The ranking is based on Bayesian criteria and on the popularity of the datasets, which affects the generality of the approach (cf. the cold-start problem discussed previously). The authors extend this work and overcome this drawback in [9] by exploring the correlation between different sets of features—properties, classes and vocabularies— and the links to compute new rank score functions for all the available linked datasets.

Mehdi et al. [19] propose a method to automatically identify relevant public SPARQL endpoints from a list of candidates. First, the process needs as input a set of domain-specific keywords which are extracted from a local source or can be provided manually by an expert. Then, using natural languages processing techniques and queries expansion techniques, the system generates a set of queries that seek for exact literal matches between the introduced keywords and the target datasets, i.e., for each term supplied to the algorithm, the system runs a matching with a set of eight queries: {original-case, proper-case, lower-case, upper-case} * {no-lang-tag, @en-tag}. Finally, the produced output consists of a list of potentially relevant SPARQL endpoints of datasets for linking. In addition, an interesting contribution of this technique is the bindings returned for the subject and predicate query variables, which are recorded and logged when a term match is found on some particular SPARQL endpoint. The records are particularly useful in the linking step.

In contrast to the approaches described above, our method is the first to be based on topic overlap and collaborative filtering. To the best of our knowledge, the current paper is also the first study to provide simple baseline recommendation techniques that can serve as a benchmark (cf. Sect. 3.4).

In comparison with all the work discussed above, our approach has the potential to overcome a series of complexity related problems. Precisely, considering the complexity to generate the matching in [18], to produce the set of domain-specific keywords as input in [19] and to explore the set of features of all the network datasets in [9], our recommendation results are much easier to obtain since we only manipulate the already generated topic profiles (or inexpensively propagated profiles).

Since the majority of used datasets in the papers discussed above were not yet indexed by the topic profiles graph, a direct comparison of the performance of the different recommendation methods to our system seems unfair. In addition, none of the authors have shared data, except for [9]. However, the evaluation of this approach in its first version [14] concludes on one dataset only. In its second version [9], while they provide the data used in their experiments, the authors do not give details on the resulting rank scores.

5   Conclusion and Future Work

We have presented an interlinking candidate dataset recommendation approach, based on the connectivity behavior learning of topic-profiles datasets. We demonstrate that our technique allows to reduce considerably the original search space and that it outperforms the results obtained by three baseline recommendation approaches, developed for the purposes of this study and made available to the community. Since dataset topic profiling is a key component in the recommendation pipeline, we show a simple way of propagating dataset profiles to the entire set of linked open datasets, starting off with a limited number of profiled datasets.

In the future, we plan to improve the evaluation framework by developing a more reliable and complete ground truth for dataset recommendation, possibly by using crowdsourcing techniques, in order to deal with the false positives overestimation problem. Our method could potentially benefit from combining it with machine learning techniques. We plan to conduct a thorough evaluation of the efficiency of our profiles propagation technique for the dataset recommendation task.

Acknowledgements. This research has been partially funded under the Datalyse project (http://www.datalyse.fr/) and by the European Commission as part of the DURAARK project, FP7 Grant Agreement No. 600908.

References

1. Bizer, C., Heath, T., Berners-Lee, T.: Linked data - the story so far. Int. J. Semant. Web Inf. Syst. **5**(3), 1–22 (2009)
2. Buil-Aranda, C., Hogan, A., Umbrich, J., Vandenbussche, P.-Y.: SPARQL web-querying infrastructure: ready for action? In: Alani, H., et al. (eds.) ISWC 2013, Part II. LNCS, vol. 8219, pp. 277–293. Springer, Heidelberg (2013)
3. Guéret, C., Groth, P., Stadler, C., Lehmann, J.: Assessing linked data mappings using network measures. In: Simperl, E., Cimiano, P., Polleres, A., Corcho, O., Presutti, V. (eds.) ESWC 2012. LNCS, vol. 7295, pp. 87–102. Springer, Heidelberg (2012)
4. Fetahu, B., Dietze, S., Pereira Nunes, B., Antonio Casanova, M., Taibi, D., Nejdl, W.: A scalable approach for efficiently generating structured dataset topic profiles. In: Presutti, V., d'Amato, C., Gandon, F., d'Aquin, M., Staab, S., Tordai, A. (eds.) ESWC 2014. LNCS, vol. 8465, pp. 519–534. Springer, Heidelberg (2014)

5. Auer, S., Bizer, C., Kobilarov, G., Lehmann, J., Cyganiak, R., Ives, Z.G.: DBpedia: a nucleus for a web of open data. In: Aberer, K., et al. (eds.) ASWC 2007 and ISWC 2007. LNCS, vol. 4825, pp. 722–735. Springer, Heidelberg (2007)
6. Suchanek, F.M., Kasneci, G., Weikum, G.: Yago: a core of semantic knowledge. In: Proceedings of the WWW, pp. 697–706 (2007)
7. Pereira Nunes, B., Dietze, S., Casanova, M.A., Kawase, R., Fetahu, B., Nejdl, W.: Combining a co-occurrence-based and a semantic measure for entity linking. In: Cimiano, P., Corcho, O., Presutti, V., Hollink, L., Rudolph, S. (eds.) ESWC 2013. LNCS, vol. 7882, pp. 548–562. Springer, Heidelberg (2013)
8. Blanco, R., Mika, P., Vigna, S.: Effective and efficient entity search in RDF data. In: Aroyo, L., Welty, C., Alani, H., Taylor, J., Bernstein, A., Kagal, L., Noy, N., Blomqvist, E. (eds.) ISWC 2011, Part I. LNCS, vol. 7031, pp. 83–97. Springer, Heidelberg (2011)
9. Rabello Lopes, G., Paes Leme, L.A.P., Pereira Nunes, B., Casanova, M.A., Dietze, S.: Two approaches to the dataset interlinking recommendation problem. In: Benatallah, B., Bestavros, A., Manolopoulos, Y., Vakali, A., Zhang, Y. (eds.) WISE 2014, Part I. LNCS, vol. 8786, pp. 324–339. Springer, Heidelberg (2014)
10. Taibi, D., Dietze, S., Fetahu, B., Fulantelli, G.: Exploring type-specific topic profiles of datasets: a demo for educational linked data. In: Proceedings of the ISWC Posters and Demonstrations Track a Track, pp. 353–356, Riva del Garda, Italy (2014)
11. Blei, D.M., Ng, A.Y., Jordan, M.I.: Latent dirichlet allocation. J. Mach. Learn. Res. 3, 993–1022 (2003)
12. Ricci, F., Rokach, L., Shapira, B., Kantor, P.B.: Recommender Systems Handbook, vol. 1. Springer, Berlin (2011)
13. Weiss, S.M., Kulikowski, C.A.: Computer Systems That Learn: Classification and Prediction Methods from Statistics, Neural Nets, Machine Learning, and Expert Systems. Morgan Kaufmann Publishers Inc., San Francisco (1991)
14. Leme, L.A.P.P., Lopes, G.R., Nunes, B.P., Casanova, M.A., Dietze, S.: Identifying candidate datasets for data interlinking. In: Daniel, F., Dolog, P., Li, Q. (eds.) ICWE 2013. LNCS, vol. 7977, pp. 354–366. Springer, Heidelberg (2013)
15. Wagner, A., Haase, P., Rettinger, A., Lamm, H.: Discovering related data sources in data-portals. In: Proceedings of the 1st IWSS (2013)
16. Wagner, A., Haase, P., Rettinger, A., Lamm, H.: Entity-based data source contextualization for searching the web of data. In: Presutti, V., Blomqvist, E., Troncy, R., Sack, H., Papadakis, I., Tordai, A. (eds.) ESWC Satellite Events 2014. LNCS, vol. 8798, pp. 25–41. Springer, Heidelberg (2014)
17. de Oliveira, H.R., Tavares, A.T., Lóscio, B.F.: Feedback-based data set recommendation for building linked data applications. In: Proceedings of the 8th ISWC, pp. 49–55. ACM (2012)
18. Nikolov, A., d'Aquin, M.: Identifying relevant sources for data linking using a semantic web index. In: WWW 2011 Workshop on Linked Data on the Web, Hyderabad, India (2011)
19. Mehdi, M., Iqbal, A., Hogan, A., Hasnain, A., Khan, Y., Decker, S., Sahay, R.: Discovering domain-specific public SPARQL endpoints: a life-sciences use-case. In: Proceedings of the 18th IDEAS, pp. 39–45, Porto, Portugal (2014)

YABench: A Comprehensive Framework for RDF Stream Processor Correctness and Performance Assessment

Maxim Kolchin[1], Peter Wetz[2(✉)], Elmar Kiesling[2], and A Min Tjoa[2]

[1] ITMO University, Saint Petersburg, Russia
kolchinmax@niuitmo.ru
[2] TU Wien, Vienna, Austria
{peter.wetz,elmar.kiesling,a.tjoa}@tuwien.ac.at

Abstract. RDF stream processing (RSP) has become a vibrant area of research in the semantic web community. Recent advances have resulted in the development of several RSP engines that leverage semantics to facilitate reasoning over flows of incoming data. These engines vary greatly in terms of implemented query syntax, their evaluation and operational semantics, and in various performance dimensions. Existing benchmarks tackle particular aspects such as functional coverage, result correctness, or performance. None of them, however, assess RSP engine behavior comprehensively with respect to all these dimensions. In this paper, we introduce YABench, a novel benchmarking framework for RSP engines. YABench extends the concept of correctness checking and provides a flexible and comprehensive tool set to analyze and evaluate RSP engine behavior. It is highly configurable and provides quantifiable and reproducible results on correctness and performance characteristics. To validate our approach, we replicate results of the existing CSRBench benchmark with YABench. We then assess two well-established RSP engines, CQELS and C-SPARQL, through more comprehensive experiments. In particular, we measure precision, recall, performance, and scalability characteristics while varying throughput and query complexity. Finally, we discuss implications on the development of future stream processing engines and benchmarks.

1 Introduction

Major developments such as the Internet of Things, Smart Cities, and Smart Devices increasingly shift data processing challenges from a static towards a continuous paradigm. In many domains, it is crucial to make sense of frequently changing data flows in order to draw timely conclusions about the state of a system. This necessitates means for the efficient processing of and reasoning over dynamic data while accounting for its temporal dimension. Application examples include decision support in a smart city context, environmental monitoring, public transport management, and pervasive healthcare systems.

M. Kolchin and P. Wetz—These authors contributed equally to this work.

© Springer International Publishing Switzerland 2016
A. Bozzon et al. (Eds.): ICWE 2016, LNCS 9671, pp. 280–298, 2016.
DOI: 10.1007/978-3-319-38791-8_16

The notion of continuous queries, which was introduced by Terry et al. [14] in 1992, is central to dynamic data processing. These queries are issued once and executed continuously to provide up-to-date results as new data arrives [7]. Data stream management systems (DSMSs) and their respective query languages, which make use of continuous queries, have been the topic of intense research since 2002 [2]. More recently, dynamic data streams have attracted considerable interest within the semantic web community. This led to the development of various approaches to enable SPARQL-like data access on flows of incoming data under the labels *stream processing* and *stream reasoning*. The resulting RDF stream processing engines, including C-SPARQL [3], CQELS [10], and SPARQL$_{Stream}$ [6], combine stream data processing with semantic web technologies. By leveraging the explicit semantics of RDF streams, these engines facilitate reasoning over dynamic data. They also allow to integrate and fuse data streams through federated queries and provide a platform for innovative applications in data stream analytics.

Implementations of these engines result in considerable differences in both performance characteristics [8,11,15] and crucial differences in operational semantics. A common benchmarking framework would help to assess differences and limitations of these existing implementations, but also provide a basis for steering future research directions and standardization efforts. The need for such standardization is highlighted by the formation of an *RDF Stream Processing* community group backed by W3C[1]. Design decisions in this context should be informed by comprehensive benchmarks, which this work aims to provide.

Previous studies analyzed isolated aspects such as functional coverage [15], performance [11], or correctness [8] through specialized benchmarks. This work focuses on window-based stream processing engines and compares them along all these dimensions. To this end, we developed YABench (Yet Another RDF Stream Processing Benchmark), an integrated framework to assess both correctness and performance of RSP engines. YABench provides means for the definition of test scenarios, generates reproducible test data streams, performs evaluation runs, and provides analyses of the results. It provides full reproducibility and emphasizes visual presentation of results to foster an understanding of engines' individual characteristics, including correctness under varying input loads, window sizes, and window frequencies.

The remainder of the paper is organized as follows (contributions highlighted):

- Sect. 2 provides an **overview** of related work and differentiates YABench from other RSP benchmarks and work in related domains;
- Sect. 3 introduces our **stream generator** (Sect. 3.2), discusses currently **supported engines** (Sect. 3.3), and outlines the design of the **oracle** component (Sect. 3.4);
- next, we **validate YABench** against CSRBench (Sect. 4), and
- discuss results of our **experiments** (Sect. 5) that analyze engines' correctness under varying input parameters.

---

[1] http://www.w3.org/community/rsp/, Accessed Jan. 12th, 2016.

– We conclude with a **discussion** on implications and an outlook on future work in Sects. 6 and 7, respectively.

2   Related Work

In the traditional data streaming domain, the Linear Road (LR) benchmark [1] is widely used for evaluating DSMSs. It is based on a configurable toll system simulation and consists of a historical data generator, a traffic simulator, a data driver, and a validator. LR provides a comprehensive framework for experiments and served as an inspiration for YABench, where our goal is to provide a similarly comprehensive benchmark for RDF stream processing. Like LR, YABench is capable of testing functional aspects such as window-based queries, joins, filters, and aggregations. In addition, YABench covers RSP-specific aspects not covered by LR, such as the influence of query complexity and varying throughput on precision, recall, and delay per window.

In the semantic web domain, there are several well-established benchmarks, including LUBM [9], FedBench [13], BSBM [4], and DBPSP [12]. These benchmarks, however, operate on static knowledge bases and focus on characteristics such as query execution and load times. They do not address aspects that arise in a streaming context, such as correctness under high load. RSP engines' inconsistent interpretation of streaming operators' semantics poses additional challenges and precludes the reuse of existing (non-streaming) benchmarks.

The RSP research community has also developed a number of specialized benchmarks. LSBench [11] first allowed comparisons between Linked Stream Data processing engines. Using a social network scenario, the benchmark uncovered conceptual and technical differences between CQELS, C-SPARQL, and JTALIS. Furthermore, it highlighted performance differences between these engines and included limited functionality and correctness tests. Because LSBench does not include means to determine the correct output, however, it does not provide absolute correctness figures to RSP engine developers. The benchmark is also not customizable for engines' varying execution strategies. YABench overcomes these limitations by introducing a configurable oracle that allows to emulate the behavior of different engines. This is an essential requirement due to the fact that currently available engines do not agree on common operational semantics. Hence, the oracle represents a means to create reproducible results based on configurable operational semantics allowing to compare results from different engines along different dimensions such as performance and correctness.

SRBench (Streaming RDF/SPARQL Benchmark) [15] defines a set of queries that cover RSP-specific aspects, such as ontology-based reasoning or the application of static background knowledge to streaming data. The authors conduct a functional evaluation of C-SPARQL, CQELS, and SPARQL$_{Stream}$ and conclude that the capabilities of these engines are still fairly limited. Due to the focus on functional aspects, SRBench does not recognize differences in the operational semantics of the benchmarked systems. To validate the query results, the authors propose correctness metrics such as precision and recall. YABench implements these metrics on a per-window basis and thereby makes it possible to quantify engines' retrieval performance on the most granular level.

CSRBench (Correctness checking Benchmark for Streaming RDF/SPARQL) [8] focuses on the correctness of stream query results. To this end, CSRBench evaluates RSP engines' compliance to their respective operational semantics using an oracle that determines the validity (i.e., correct or incorrect) of the query results. It thereby complements functional (SRBench) and performance (LSBench) evaluations. The authors find that none of the tested engines passes all tests and provide a detailed account on why certain engines fail at specific queries. CSRBench takes first steps towards validating RSP engines, but lacks comprehensive correctness evaluations over time. YABench extends the idea of oracle-based validation using more comprehensive correctness metrics (i.e., precision and recall) for each window. Moreover, we relate these correctness metrics directly to performance metrics such as delay in query result delivery or memory consumption and CPU utilization. Thereby, YABench provides insights into throughput and scalability and provides a comprehensive toolset to investigate RSP engine characteristics, including both performance and correctness. In addition, our modular architecture also allows researchers to easily exchange the RSP engines, stream generators, and continuous queries used in the benchmark. To the best of our knowledge, YABench is the first RSP benchmarking framework to provide such functionality.

3   YABench Framework

We define the following requirements for comprehensive RSP benchmarking:

R1 *Scalable and configurable input*: Input data should be scalable and configurable to allow for the flexible definition of benchmark scenarios. This allows researchers to conduct experiments under varying conditions, such as high/low load and varying window sizes.

R2 *Comprehensive correctness checking*: It should be possible to check the correctness of results, despite engines' varying operational semantics. Moreover we aim at measuring *real throughput*, i.e., how does input load affect correctness of results.

R3 *Flexible queries*: Queries should be parameterizable, i.e., it should be possible to create test configurations using the same queries, but varying query parameters.

R4 *Reproducibility*: Experiments need to be reproducible to ensure independent validation of results is possible at a later point in time.

The YABench framework implements these requirements through four elements: (i) a stream generator that create test data streams; (ii) an oracle that tests the correctness of results; (iii) supported engines to be benchmarked; and (iv) a reporting tool that visualizes the results.

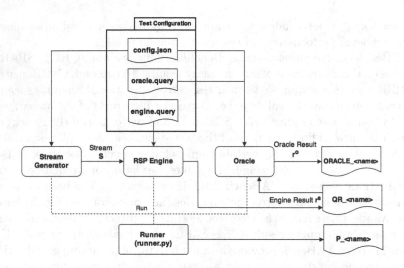

Fig. 1. Architecture of YABench framework

3.1   Architecture

YABench is designed around a modular architecture (Fig. 1) that decouples test configuration from execution. It allows to define tests in a declarative manner and can run complete benchmarking workflows with a single command.

The framework consists of four separately executable modules, i.e., the *Stream Generator*, *RSP engine*, the *Oracle* and the *Runner* which controls the overall execution flow of a test. The test configuration consists of a configuration file (*config.json*) and two query templates, *engine.query* for the engine and *oracle.query* for the oracle. The configuration file defines a set of tests that use the same query templates, but with varying parameters such as window size and slide (*R3*).

Each benchmark yields oracle results ($ORACLE\_ < name >$) and performance measurements ($P\_ < name >$). These results can be visualized by means of a provided reporting web application. More details about the architecture and the test configuration can be found on the wiki of the project's GitHub repository[2].

3.2   Stream Generator

The *Stream Generator* implements *R1* and is used to create input data that is subsequently fed to the respective engines. It turned out to be more practical to separate the steps of creating data, feeding it to the engines, and creating measurements. The stream generator emulates an environmental monitoring scenario and draws on the LinkedSensorDataset[3] which is also used for SRBench [15] and CSRBench [8]. The data set consists of weather observations from hurricanes in the USA. We selected this simple data model for two reasons: (i) it makes our work

---

[2] http://github.com/YABench/yabench, Accessed Jan. 12th, 2016.

[3] http://wiki.knoesis.org/index.php/SSW_Datasets, Accessed Jan. 12th, 2016.

comparable to previous work, particularly to CSRBench (see Sect. 4); and (ii) having such a simple and generic model allows for scenario parameterization, e.g., by changing the *number of simulated weather stations* to vary *load on an engine*.

To simulate more complex data flows, YABench can easily be extended with additional stream generators by extending the class `AbstractStreamGenerator` from the *yabench-generator* module[4]. Note however, that more complex data streams increasingly make it difficult to isolate effects (i.e., which parameter influences which measurable performance indicator).

Figure 2 illustrates the structure of the data model. A central element of the data model is `weather:TemperatureObservation`, which represents a single observation. This observation is connected to actual measure data via `om-owl:result`. The `om-owl:observedProperty` indicates which environmental condition was sensed by the `ssw:system`. The system represents a sensor which is creating measurements. It is connected to the observation via the `om-owl:procedure` relation.[5]

Based on an input function $gen(s, i, d, r, n)$, the process generates an RDF stream $\mathbb{S}$ where s denotes the number of simulated systems, i denotes the time interval between two measurements of a single station, d denotes the duration of the generated output stream, r denotes a seed for randomization to vary the timestamps of initial measurements of each system, and n defines the generator which should be used. Input load for experiments can be varied with the s and i parameters. The combination of parameters s, i, and r ensures reproducibility, because the stream generator guarantees that the exact same stream is generated every time for a given parameter set, hence, this satisfies *R4*.

3.3   Engines

YABench can currently benchmark two engines, i.e., C-SPARQL 0.9.5[6], and CQELS 1.0.0[7]. After a stream has been generated, the YABench engine component calls a function $stream(d, q, s)$, where d denotes the destination of output files, q defines the continuous query which will be registered at the engine, and s defines the input stream, which was previously generated. At this stage output files will be created for performance measurements and query results.

YABench essentially wraps each engine to allow stream data feeding under controlled conditions. The input RDF stream $\mathbb{S}$ consists of a sequence of timestamped triples in non-decreasing time order in the form of $\mathbb{S} = ((\langle s, p, o \rangle, t_0), (\langle s, p, o \rangle, t_1), \ldots)$. The wrapper iterates over the input stream $\mathbb{S}$ and feeds sets of RDF statements with same timestamps to the engine, hence,

---

[4] https://github.com/YABench/yabench/tree/master/yabench-generator,   Accessed Jan. 12th, 2016.

[5] The authors are aware of the fact that at the time of writing, two properties of the used vocabulary for the data model have undergone quasi-standardization as part of the SSN ontology and were changed in the process (`result` changed to `observationResult` and `procedure` changed to `observedBy`).

[6] http://github.com/streamreasoning/CSPARQL-engine, Accessed Jan. 12th, 2016.

[7] https://code.google.com/p/cqels/, Accessed Jan. 12th, 2016.

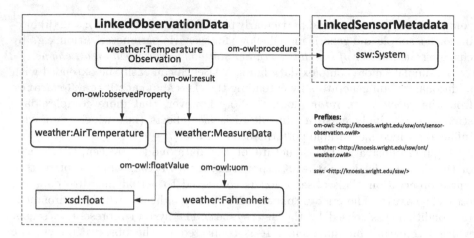

Fig. 2. Data model of generated streams based on LinkedSensorData.

$F_{t_0} = \{(\langle s, p, o \rangle) \mid (\langle s, p, o \rangle, t_0) \in \mathbb{S} \}$ while respecting time intervals $i = t_1 - t_0$ between feeds F_{t_0} and F_{t_1}.

While feeding the engines with the graphs, we continuously take measurements, i.e., absolute and relative memory consumption, cpu usage, and the number of threads spawned. Because YABench is implemented in Java, additional Java-based RSP engines can be easily integrated for benchmarking. To this end, it is sufficient to extend the classes `AbstractEngine`, `AbstractQuery`, `ContinuousListener`, and `AbstractEngineLauncher`, all of which are available in the *yabench-commons* module[8].

3.4 Oracle

To check the correctness of query results and thereby satisfy *R2*, we implemented an oracle. The implementation is inspired by the oracle used in CSRBench [8], but built on top of Jena ARQ[9] and extended with more granular metrics, which are computed for each window: precision and recall, delay of query results, number of triples in the window, and number of tuples in the query results.

The semantics used by the oracle can be configured, i.e., the specification of the oracle can be changed in accordance to the benchmarked engine. Report policy parameters [5] are provided to emulate either CQELS (*OnContentChange*) or C-SPARQL (*OnWindowClose*). Hence, we are able to provide correct results that account for the respective report policy.

The oracle checks the results (recorded in $QR\_ < name >$ file) of a continuous query q by using the same input stream $\mathbb{S}$ and an equivalent, but static, SPARQL query q' (*oracle.query*). It takes into account the report policy which the given

---

[8] https://github.com/YABench/yabench/tree/master/yabench-commons,   Accessed Jan. 12th, 2016.

[9] https://jena.apache.org/documentation/query/, Accessed Jan. 12th, 2016.

engine applies as well as window size α and slide β parameters of the continuous query q. The following report policies are provided by the oracle:

- *Content change*: reporting when the content of the active window changed (used by CQELS).
- *Window close*: reporting when the active window closes (used by C-SPARQL).

The oracle uses the following procedure to check correctness:

1. Determine the *scope* $[t_s, t_e)$ of the next window that will report based on the given window size α, window slide β, and report policy.
2. Use the *scope* $[t_s, t_e)$ to select window *content* from the input stream $\mathbb{S}$ where the relevant triples are $F_{t_s, t_e} = \{(\langle s, p, o \rangle) \mid (\langle s, p, o \rangle, t) \in \mathbb{S}, t_s \leq t < t_e\}$.
3. Compute the expected result by executing the SPARQL query q' on F_{t_s, t_e} on the query engine.
4. Compare the result of this query with the next result of continuous query q and compute precision/recall metrics.
5. Compute remaining metrics, i.e., delay, window size, and result size.

Delay. The delay d of query results is defined as the difference between the end timestamp of the oracle window $t_{e_o}^{\mathrm{W}_i}$ and the actual timestamp $t_{e_s}^{\mathrm{W}_i}$ of the engine's output for this window. The timestamp when the engine output the result is recorded in file $QR\_ < name >$.

Gracious Mode. In addition to the algorithm described above, the oracle implements a new *gracious* mode to reveal issues associated with wrong window content. In the default *non-gracious* mode, the oracle strictly uses the defined window size and range from the registered continuous queries to calculate the content of windows which, in turn, is used to measure precision and recall. However, we found that low precision and recall are often caused by imprecise event processing near windows borders. To determine the magnitude of this effect and isolate incorrect query results that are not caused by window border issues, we implemented a *gracious* mode. In this mode, the oracle iteratively shifts window borders to determine for which borders an engine achieves maximum precision and recall. This method allows to reconstruct the actual window borders which were applied by the engines at the time of running the experiments. By looking at the reconstructed windows (see results of experiment four in Sect. 6) researchers can gain visual and quantifiable insights into the extent and cause of incorrect RSP engine behavior.

4   Validation Against CSRBench

By validating YABench against CSRBench, we ensure that it produces equivalent results. In later experiments (see Sect. 5), we then show that our framework facilitates evaluations that go beyond the scope of CSRBench. The source code and instructions on how to run the validation are published on GitHub[10]. The methodology for the validation is as follows:

- We convert the original data used by CSRBench to N-Triples format, and extend it with timestamps to emulate the input stream load. By doing so, the data stream looks the same as the output of our stream generator.
- For each of the seven CSRBench queries we need to setup tests configurations. These configuration files define parameters such as window size, window slide, and filter parameters, which will be used when registering the queries.
- For each engine and for each of the seven CSRBench queries we then execute the test, i.e., feeding the engines with the input stream and registering queries with the defined parameters.
- After all tests are complete, we compare the results of CSRBench[11] with the results created by YABench.

Table 1. Results of YABench validation against CSRBench results. Cells which include asterisks are referred to in the text.

Query	C-SPARQL		CQELS	
	CSRBench	YABench	CSRBench	YABench
Q1	✓	✓	✓	✓
Q2	✓	✓	✓	✓
Q3	✓	✓*	✓	✓
Q4	✓	✓	✗	✗
Q5	✗	✗	✓	✓
Q6	✓	✓*	✗	✗
Q7	✓	✓*	✗	✗**

Table 1 summarizes the results of the validation. Results were compared and inspected manually. Checkmarks indicate that YABench produced equivalent results to CSRBench. Columns of CSRBench which contain an ✗ denote that the respective engine did not produce correct results. In all such cases, YABench also indicated that the engine did not deliver correct results.

Checkmarks denoted with one asterisk (*) indicate that YABench produced largely identical results, but that some results were missing. This occurred in some cases were triples were very close to a window border. In these cases, we found that in C-SPARQL such triples may fall either into the scope of W_n or W_{n+1}. This can be attributed to timing discrepancies, which we encountered

---

[10] https://github.com/YABench/csrbench-validation, Accessed Jan. 12th, 2016.

[11] Obtained from https://github.com/dellaglio/csrbench-oracle-engines, Accessed Jan. 12th, 2016.

when running benchmarks multiple times and/or on different systems. However, we verified that all results are present, if not in the correct window, then at the latest in the subsequent window.

Crosses in the YABench columns indicate that results did not match those of CSRBench experiments. This is expected behavior, because the same queries did not pass correctness tests of CSRBench in the original tests either. The cross denoted with two asterisks (**) indicates that the query ($Q7$) did not execute successfully on the CQELS engine.[12]

We can conclude that, besides minor, well-explained inconsistencies, YABench reproduces the results of CSRBench. Beyond the scope of previous benchmarks, however, YABench employs a more comprehensive approach that allows (i) to define experiments including test data, input load parameters, and queries, (ii) to perform experiments that consider the varying operational semantics of the tested engines, and (iii) to conduct in-depth analyses based on new throughput, delay, and correctness metrics. These capabilities are used for the experiments discussed in the following section.

5   Experimental Setup

We use YABench and its oracle to perform experiments with two engines, C-SPARQL and CQELS. In particular, we are interested in how the correctness of results is affected by changes in the input data streams. Whereas previous correctness metrics exclusively focused on checking whether engine results are included in the oracle results, i.e., a yes/no evaluation, we provide more granular metrics. To this end, we use precision and recall calculations in combination with performance metrics. These metrics uncover issues that can be caused by, for instance, shifting of window borders under load, leading to lower precision or recall values. Moreover, we measure an engine's delay in delivering results and the amount of RDF statements inside a window's scope to understand and to explain low retrieval rates. Hence, YABench is the first RSP benchmark to provide a comprehensive picture of an engine's behavior under stress.

Generally, we reuse the queries introduced by CSRBench, however, for each query we are able to parametrize window size α, window slide β, and filter values f thereby satisfying $R3$. For the input streams, we control the number of stations s to simulate low, medium, and high load scenarios. The interval time i between measurements will be 1 s and the duration of each experiment is 30s. The experiments are run in *non-gracious* mode, unless otherwise stated.

Performance measurements, such as memory consumption, are taken at regular intervals, i.e., 500 ms. Because all other metrics observe characteristics of the windows, they are taken and displayed on a per window basis. We replicated each experiment ten times and illustrate the distribution of result metrics obtained for precision, recall, and delay as boxplots.

---

[12] The system crashed before returning the query results.

We use the CSRBench queries available on the W3C wiki[13] for our experiments, which were executed on an Intel Core i7-3630QM @ 2.4 GHz, Quad Core, 64bit, 12 GB RAM running Windows 7 Professional. In parantheses we denote which queries of CSRBench are reused in each experiment. Complete results are published on GitHub[14] and can be visualized with our web application *YABench-reports*.

5.1   Experiment 1 (*Q1*)

This experiment uses a simple SELECT statement combined with a FILTER asking for the latest temperature observations above a specified threshold and the sensor which took the measurement. We run the experiment with the following parameters: $\alpha = 5\,s$, $\beta = 5\,s$, $s = 50/1000/10000$ (small/medium/big), $i = 1\,s$.

5.2   Experiment 2 (*Q4*)

The second query makes use of the aggregation function AVG combined with a FILTER to return the average temperature value over a given window. To answer such aggregate queries, depending on the report policy as well as window content and window size, stream processors typically face high resource costs. Because CQELS does not comply with the semantics of AVG as defined by SPARQL 1.1[15], we had to implement a custom AVG operator that returns an empty result if there are no matches. We run the experiment with the following parameters: $\alpha = 5\,s$, $\beta = 5\,s$, $s = 1/1000/10000$, $i = 1\,s$.

5.3   Experiment 3 (*Q6*)

This query returns sensors that made two observations (of different timestamps) with a variation between measurements higher than a given threshold. The query uses the SELECT keyword to ask for shifts of measured values over time from the same sensor. To execute this query, engines must be capable of joining triples over different timestamps. In order to produce meaningful and comparable results for both engines in this experiment, we slightly changed the number of simulated stations (s) and ran the experiment with the following parameters: $\alpha = 5\,s$, $\beta = 5\,s$, $s = 50/200/500$, $i = 1\,s$.

5.4   Experiment 4 (*Q6*)

This experiment is designed to reveal issues of lower precision and recall values encountered for both engines in particular cases. When running experiment three we observed deteriorating precision and recall due to the following reasons: For CQELS the reason is delayed deletion of window content, for C-SPARQL slight

---

[13] http://www.w3.org/wiki/CSRBench, Accessed Jan. 12th, 2016.
[14] http://github.com/YABench/yabench-one, Accessed Jan. 12th, 2016.
[15] http://www.w3.org/TR/sparql11-query/#defn_aggAvg, Accessed Jan. 12th, 2016.

window shifts are responsible. This led us to the development of a so called *gracious* mode where the oracle eliminates these issues resulting in both high precision and recall and the possibility to detect new issues unrelated to potential window delays. Hence, this experiment, shows the effects of the *gracious* mode by comparing its results with the *non-gracious* mode as well as discussing and explaining the differences. In *non-gracious* mode the oracle does not account for any issues and expects ideal behavior of the engines.

We ran two similar tests for both engines with the following parameters, one of them in *gracious* mode and the other one in *non-gracious* mode: $\alpha = 5\,s$, $\beta = 5\,s$, $s = 1$, $i = 1\,s$.

6   Discussion

The YABench framework provides a reporting web application named *YABench-reports*. Based on results of the oracle and performance measurements it displays three graphs, i.e., (i) a precision/recall graph that includes indicators for the windows, (ii) a graph showing delay of result delivery, and expected/actual result size, and (iii) a graph providing performance measurements. For the sake of brevity we only discuss the results of experiments one and four in this paper. Experiments two and three are discussed in an online appendix[16].

Figure 3 illustrates the results of the first experiment; Figs. 3a–c show box-plots of precision and recall values for each of the three load scenarios (small: $s = 50$, medium: $s = 1000$, and big: $s = 10000$); Figs. 3d–f show boxplots of the observed delay; and Figs. 4a–c show line charts of an engine's memory consumption during the stream feeding and query evaluation.

We found that CQELS maintains 100 % precision and accuracy under small load, whereas C-SPARQL achieves slightly lower values (precision is at 100 % except for window three and four, the mean for recall ranges between 97 % and 100 %). Generally, we observe that recall is lower than precision for C-SPARQL. This is due to the shifting of the actual engine windows compared to the ideal expected windows from the oracle due to delays and will be explained in more detail later (see Fig. 5).

We observed similar behavior under medium and high load (see Figs. 3b–c). For this simple query, CQELS still scores perfect precision and recall, whereas we observe deteriorating effects for C-SPARQL. The recall values from window two and three show a particularly higher spread. The mean of all recall measurements is still high. The spread can be explained by the higher delays of the first two windows (see Fig. 3e). Because C-SPARQL delivers results upon the closing of a window, the delay has an effect on precision and recall. This is not the case in CQELS, where delay in result delivery does not necessarily mean that the window content – and consequently the computed results – are incorrect. In fact, for CQELS the opposite is the case, meaning that delayed results still provide correct results. This is also reflected by our oracle.

---

[16] https://github.com/YABench/yabench-one, Accessed Jan. 12th, 2016.

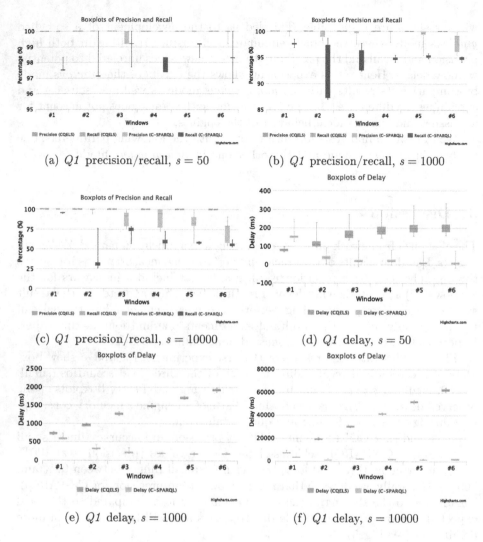

(a) *Q1* precision/recall, $s = 50$

(b) *Q1* precision/recall, $s = 1000$

(c) *Q1* precision/recall, $s = 10000$

(d) *Q1* delay, $s = 50$

(e) *Q1* delay, $s = 1000$

(f) *Q1* delay, $s = 10000$

Fig. 3. Precision/recall results of *Experiment 1* for CQELS and C-SPARQL

Delay of result delivery under low load is depicted in Fig. 3d. For CQELS mean result delivery varies between 81.5 ms and 201.5 ms. The values rise steadily, but even out for the last three windows. Interestingly, delay in C-SPARQL exhibits the opposite characteristics. The first window always yields longer delay (mean = 153.5 ms), whereas the following windows show short delays between 7 ms and 38 ms. Delay can also be negative, when results are delivered earlier than expected.

Figures 3e and 3f show the delay for medium and big load respectively. We observe similar behavior as before, but on a much higher scale. Moreover, CQELS delays do not even out anymore for the last windows, but continue to increase.

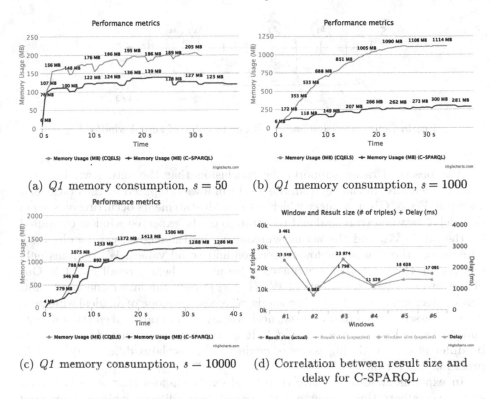

(a) *Q1* memory consumption, $s = 50$

(b) *Q1* memory consumption, $s = 1000$

(c) *Q1* memory consumption, $s - 10000$

(d) Correlation between result size and delay for C-SPARQL

Fig. 4. Performance results of *Experiment 1* for CQELS and C-SPARQL

Finally, we found that YABench reveals a correlation between the result size and delay times, as shown in Fig. 4d, which shows both metrics for a single test run. We see that delay times increase when result size increases. This relation is expected, but YABench allows to quantify the influence of large amount of result bindings on an engine's performance.

Figures 4a–c provide details about both engines' performance. C-SPARQL is more memory efficient and exhibits a moderate increase in memory consumption between low (mean = 123 MB) and medium (mean = 250 MB) load. For both engines, the removal of window content is apparent in the charts – particularly in Fig. 4a– in the form of rapid decreases after every five seconds, i.e., the defined window size. Under medium load, memory consumption of CQELS rises to about 1100 MB where it then flattens out. Both engines show similar behavior under high load (see Fig. 4c), where the charts show a steep increase in memory consumption until ten seconds. Beyond that, the graph flattens out again with a maximum of 1506 MB (CQELS) and 1288 MB (C-SPARQL).

As already noted, for C-SPARQL precision always stays higher than recall, if both values deteriorate. The reason why precision and recall decrease, is given by the fact that higher load leads to bigger delays in query result delivery.

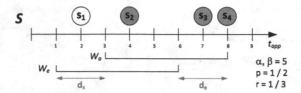

Fig. 5. Lower precision and recall due to delay of actual window $\mathbb{W}_a$

The observed delay supports the conclusion that the actual windows are shifted, therefore, deviating from the ideal windows computed by the oracle as is shown in Fig. 5. Given a query which asks for all statements occurring on stream $\mathbb{S}$, a delay between start and end timestamps of the expected window computed by the oracle $\mathbb{W}_e$ and the actual window $\mathbb{W}_a$ by the engine, can be observed. This is also the reason for lower precision and recall values. $\mathbb{W}_e$ contains only one (s_2) of three relevant statements (blue filling), hence, recall $r = 1/3$. Out of the two selected statements of $\mathbb{W}_e$ ($\{s_1, s_2\}$) only the latter one is relevant, hence, precision $p = 1/2$. In other words, whereas the scope of an ideal window is $[t_s, t_e)$, the scope of shifted windows adds a delay to the start and end timestamps and is denoted as $[t_s + d_s, t_e + d_e)$. It is worth to note that d_s and d_e can be different due to timing issues of engines. This explains different declines in precision and recall.

In experiment four, we investigate and explain issues that we experienced while manually testing the engines. Under certain conditions, which are emulated in this experiment, we observed that precision and recall values are decreasing. For CQELS, which employs a *content change* report strategy, these lower values are caused by delayed purging of active window content. By purging, we mean that all elements are deleted from the content of a window. As time in a streaming setting moves on, elements exit the scope of windows, hence, engines are responsible of correctly maintaining the content of windows. In C-SPARQL, which employs a *window close* report strategy, the values can be explained by the shifting of an engine's active window forward on the timeline (see Fig. 5).

To investigate the root causes of these issues we implemented the *gracious* mode. In this mode, the oracle adjusts its window scope to match the scope of an actual window, even though the actual window may contain incorrect elements (see Sect. 3.4). This has two consequences: First, precision and recall values increase, because *gracious* mode reverts the effects of incorrect window content. This allows us to confirm our assumptions on why low precision and recall values were observed. Second, we are able to reconstruct and visualize the window borders that were actually used internally by the engines. Thereby, we unveil differences between expected and actual windows. Expected windows are windows which we would expect from a correctly implemented engine with zero delays.

Figure 6 shows the oracle results of the tests for CQELS. As we can see in Fig. 6a, precision and recall values decrease after the first window for CQELS in *non-gracious* mode. This confirms the issues we experienced when performing

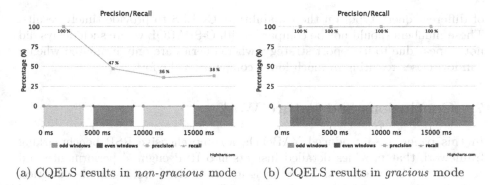

(a) CQELS results in *non-gracious* mode   (b) CQELS results in *gracious* mode

Fig. 6. *Experiment 4* results for CQELS in *gracious* and *non-gracious* mode

manual testing. Figure 6b shows results of the same test, but with *gracious mode* enabled. Here we can see that precision and recall values are both at 100 %. YABench achieves this by shifting the window borders of the oracle until reaching maximum precision and recall values. As a result we can see the adapted window borders at the bottom of the charts. The oracle had to shift the window starts to the left in order to reach high precision and recall. This indicates that the engine forgets to delete outdated elements from the content of the active window for the query which is used in this experiment.

Finally, Table 2 presents observations which we made while executing experiments on CQELS. It shows the time the final result was delivered of the tests for small (S), medium (M), and big (B) load scenarios. One would expect the final result to arrive immediately after the last triple was streamed to the engine, which equals the duration of one test, i.e., 30 s in our case. This is the case when we put CQELS under low load as can bee seen in the columns denoted by an *S*. However, under medium and high load, denoted by *M* and *B* columns, we see that delivery delay of the results grows. The reason for that is that CQELS uses the *OnContentChange* report strategy, where queries are evaluated after each streamed triple. Obviously, more complex queries increase the time needed for computation of query results, resulting in a progressive increase in delay. Hence, by showing the arrival of the last result, we can quantify and infer the influence

Table 2. Arrival time (average, minimum, maximum) of final results in seconds for each conducted experiment (E1, E2, E3) under different loads (S = small, M = medium, B = big) with CQELS.

	E1 (SELECT)			E2 (AVG)			E3 (SELECT + JOIN)		
	S (50)	M (1000)	B (10000)	S (50)	M (1000)	B (10000)	S (50)	M (1000)	B (10000)
AVG	30 s	32 s	98 s	31 s	432 s	12966 s	31 s	62 s	269 s
MIN	30 s	32 s	97 s	31 s	426 s	12305 s	31 s	58 s	263 s
MAX	30 s	33 s	100 s	31 s	440 s	13523 s	31 s	65 s	277 s

of different query types on the capability of CQELS to provide timely results. These numbers should not be compared with C-SPARQL where such delays did not appear due to its report strategy, where queries are only evaluated when a window closes resulting in much lower computational effort.

7 Conclusions and Future Work

In this paper, we introduced YABench, a comprehensive RSP benchmarking framework that provides detailed insights into RSP engines' performance and correctness characteristics. These insights are derived from granular metrics, including those that capture engines' capability to produce correct results under load. The framework supports a complete benchmarking workflow from defining tests, generating suitable test data, executing tests, and finally analyzing the results. We have shown that the framework replicates the basic results of an existing benchmark (i.e., CSRBench) and conducted and discussed four more comprehensive experiments, each of which focused on particluar aspects of RSP engines. The resulting visualizations provide insightful information on the characteristics of the tested engines and highlight key differences. In the process of our benchmarks, we also identified and discussed previously unknown issues.

To sum up our findings, YABench reveals that C-SPARQL operates more memory-efficiently than CQELS in all experiments. Both engines perform similarly in terms of delay, but C-SPARQL outperforms CQELS when more complex queries are used and under increasing input load. This can mainly be attributed to the different report strategies implemented by the engines. Concerning precision and recall, CQELS yields better results for simple queries. However, we identified an issue in CQELS which results in decreasing precision and recall measurements. On the other hand, C-SPARQL suffers from window delays, which increase when load on the engine is raised. By introducing a *gracious* mode for running the oracle, we are able to estimate the extent of these effects.

There are several directions for future research. First, we plan to extend functional coverage of the test cases. It would be interesting to evaluate the influence of multiple windows in one query on an engine. To this end, it would be necessary to extend the oracle to support other window operators and combinations of multiple windows. Second, we aim to support benchmarks that involve background knowledge, multiple input streams, and multiple queries. This will broaden our understanding of how well engines can deal with merging high-frequency data streams with large static data sources, which is one of the promising application scenarios for RSP engines.

Finally, we aim to obtain further insights on how engines cope with variations in inter-arrival times of elements.

Acknowledgments. The work done by Peter Wetz was partially funded by TU Wien through the Doctoral College Environmental Informatics. The work done by Maxim Kolchin was partially funded by the Government of the Russian Federation, Grant 074-U01.

References

1. Arasu, A., Cherniack, M., Galvez, E., Maier, D., Maskey, A.S., Ryvkina, E., Stonebraker, M., Tibbetts, R.: Linear road: a stream data management benchmark. In: Proceedings of the 30th International Conference on Very Large Data Bases, VLDB 2004, VLDB Endowment, vol. 30, pp. 480–491 (2004)
2. Babcock, B., Babu, S., Datar, M., Motwani, R., Widom, J.: Models and issues in data stream systems. In: Proceedings of the 21st ACM SIGMOD-SIGACT-SIGART Symposium on Principles of Database Systems, PODS 2002, NY, USA, pp. 1–16. ACM, New York (2002)
3. Barbieri, D.F., Braga, D., Ceri, S., Della Valle, E., Grossniklaus, M.: C-SPARQL: a continuous query language for RDF data streams. Int. J. Semant. Comput. 4(01), 3–25 (2010)
4. Bizer, C., Schultz, A.: The Berlin SPARQL benchmark. Int. J. Semant. Web Inf. Syst. 5(2), 1–24 (2009)
5. Botan, I., Derakhshan, R., Dindar, N., Haas, L., Miller, R.J., Tatbul, N.: SECRET: a model for analysis of the execution semantics of stream processing systems. Proc. VLDB Endow. 3(1–2), 232–243 (2010)
6. Calbimonte, J.-P., Corcho, O., Gray, A.J.G.: Enabling ontology-based access to streaming data sources. In: Patel-Schneider, P.F., Pan, Y., Hitzler, P., Mika, P., Zhang, L., Pan, J.Z., Horrocks, I., Glimm, B. (eds.) ISWC 2010, Part I. LNCS, vol. 6496, pp. 96–111. Springer, Heidelberg (2010)
7. Cugola, G., Margara, A.: Processing flows of information: from data stream to complex event processing. ACM Comput. Surv. 44(3), 15 (2012)
8. Dell'Aglio, D., Calbimonte, J.-P., Balduini, M., Corcho, O., Della Valle, E.: On correctness in RDF stream processor benchmarking. In: Alani, H., et al. (eds.) ISWC 2013, Part II. LNCS, vol. 8219, pp. 326–342. Springer, Heidelberg (2013)
9. Guo, Y., Pan, Z., Heflin, J.: LUBM: a benchmark for OWL knowledge base systems. Web Semant. 3(2–3), 158–182 (2005)
10. Le-Phuoc, D., Dao-Tran, M., Xavier Parreira, J., Hauswirth, M.: A native and adaptive approach for unified processing of linked streams and linked data. In: Aroyo, L., Welty, C., Alani, H., Taylor, J., Bernstein, A., Kagal, L., Noy, N., Blomqvist, E. (eds.) ISWC 2011, Part I. LNCS, vol. 7031, pp. 370–388. Springer, Heidelberg (2011)
11. Le-Phuoc, D., Dao-Tran, M., Pham, M.-D., Boncz, P., Eiter, T., Fink, M.: Linked stream data processing engines: facts and figures. In: Cudré-Mauroux, P., et al. (eds.) ISWC 2012, Part II. LNCS, vol. 7650, pp. 300–312. Springer, Heidelberg (2012)
12. Morsey, M., Lehmann, J., Auer, S., Ngonga Ngomo, A.-C.: DBpedia SPARQL benchmark – performance assessment with real queries on real data. In: Aroyo, L., Welty, C., Alani, H., Taylor, J., Bernstein, A., Kagal, L., Noy, N., Blomqvist, E. (eds.) ISWC 2011, Part I. LNCS, vol. 7031, pp. 454–469. Springer, Heidelberg (2011)
13. Schmidt, M., Görlitz, O., Haase, P., Ladwig, G., Schwarte, A., Tran, T.: FedBench: a benchmark suite for federated semantic data query processing. In: Aroyo, L., Welty, C., Alani, H., Taylor, J., Bernstein, A., Kagal, L., Noy, N., Blomqvist, E. (eds.) ISWC 2011, Part I. LNCS, vol. 7031, pp. 585–600. Springer, Heidelberg (2011)

14. Terry, D., Goldberg, D., Nichols, D., Oki, B.: Continuous queries over append-only databases. In: Proceedings of the ACM SIGMOD International Conference on Management of Data, SIGMOD 1992, NY, USA, pp. 321–330. ACM, New York (1992)
15. Zhang, Y., Duc, P.M., Corcho, O., Calbimonte, J.-P.: SRBench: a streaming RDF/SPARQL benchmark. In: Cudré-Mauroux, P., et al. (eds.) ISWC 2012, Part I. LNCS, vol. 7649, pp. 641–657. Springer, Heidelberg (2012)

When a FILTER Makes the Difference in Continuously Answering SPARQL Queries on Streaming and Quasi-Static Linked Data

Shima Zahmatkesh[✉], Emanuele Della Valle, and Daniele Dell'Aglio

Department of Electronics, Information and Bioengineering,
Politecnico of Milano, Milan, Italy
{shima.zahmatkesh,emanuele.dellavalle,daniele.dellaglio}@polimi.it

Abstract. We are witnessing a growing interest for Web applications that (*i*) require to continuously combine highly dynamic data stream with background data and (*ii*) have reactivity as key performance indicator. The Semantic Web community showed that RDF Stream Processing (RSP) is an adequate framework to develop this type of applications.

However, when the background data is distributed over the Web, even RSP engines risk losing reactiveness due to the time necessary to access the background data. State-of-the-art RSP engines remain reactive using a local replica of the background data, but such a replica progressively become stale if not updated to reflect the changes in the remote background data.

For this reason, recently, the RSP community investigated maintenance policies (collectively named Acqua) that guarantee reactiveness while maximizing the freshness of the replica. Acqua's policies apply to queries that join a basic graph pattern in a window clause with another basic graph pattern in a service clause. In this paper, we extend the class of queries considered in Acqua adding a FILTER clause that selects mapping in the background data. We propose a new maintenance policy (namely, the *Filter Update Policy*) and we show how to combine it with Acqua policies. A set of experimental evaluations empirically proves the ability of the proposed policies to guarantee reactiveness while keeping the replica fresher than with the Acqua policies.

1 Introduction

The variety and the velocity of Web data is growing. Many Web applications require to continuously answer queries that combine dynamic data streams with quasi-static background data distributed over the Web. Consider, for instance, a Web advertising company; it may want to continuously detect influential Social Network users in order to ask them to endorse its commercials. Such a company can encode its information need in a continuous query like: *every minute give me the ID of the users that are mentioned on Social Network in the last 10* min *whose number of followers is greater than 100,000*.

What makes continuously answering this query challenging is the fact that the number of followers of a user (in the background data) tends to change when

© Springer International Publishing Switzerland 2016
A. Bozzon et al. (Eds.): ICWE 2016, LNCS 9671, pp. 299–316, 2016.
DOI: 10.1007/978-3-319-38791-8_17

she is mentioned (in the social stream). There may be users, whose number of followers was slightly below 100,000 in the last evaluation (and, thus, were not included in the last answer), who may now have slightly more than 100,000 followers (and, thus, are in the current answer).

If the application requires an answer every minute and fetching the current number of followers for a user (mentioned in the social stream) requires around 100 ms[1], just fetching this information for 600 users takes the entire available time. In other words, fetching all the background data may put the application at risk of losing reactiveness, i.e., it may not be able to generate an answer while meeting operational deadlines.

The RDF Stream Processing (RSP) community has recently started addressing this problem. Dehghanzadeh et al. [5] showed that the query above can be written as a continuous query for existing RSP engines. This query has to use the a SERVICE clause[2] which is supported by C-SPARQL [3], $SPARQL_{stream}$ [4] and CQELS-QL [10] and RSP-QL [6].

For instance, Listing 1.1 shows how it can be declared in RSP-QL. Line 1 registers the query in the RSP engine. Line 2 describes how to construct the results at each evaluation. Line 4, every minute, selects from a window opened on the stream S the users mentioned in the last 10 min. Line 5 asks the remote service BKG to select the number of followers for the users mentioned in the window. Line 6 filters out, from the results of the previous join, all those users whose number of followers is below the 100,000 (namely, the Filtering Threshold).

```
1   REGISTER STREAM <:Influencers> AS
2   CONSTRUCT {?user a :influentialUser}
3   WHERE {
4     WINDOW W(10m,1m) ON S {?user :hasMentions ?mentionsNumber}
5     SERVICE BKG {?user :hasFollowers ?followersCount }
6     FILTER (?followersCount > 100000)
7   }
```

Listing 1.1. Sketch of the query studied in the problem

However, Dehghanzadeh et al. [5] also observed that, if many users are mentioned in the window, the SERVICE clause cannot be entirely evaluated every minute or the RSP engine would lose reactiveness. As a solution, they propose to compute the answer at the SERVICE clause at query registration time and to store the resulting mappings in a local replica. Then, they propose several maintenance policies (collectively named Acqua) that guarantee reactiveness while maximizing the freshness of the mappings in the replica.

---

[1] 100 ms is the average response time of the REST APIs of Twitter that returns the information of a user given her ID. For more information see https://dev.twitter.com/rest/reference/get/users/lookup.

[2] http://www.w3.org/TR/sparql11-federated-query/.

Acqua policies were empirically demonstrated to be effective, but the approach focuses only on the JOIN and does not optimize the FILTER clause (at line 6). So, Aqua policies may decide to refresh a mapping that will be discarded by the FILTERING clause. In this case, Acqua policies are throwing away a unit of budget. This paper, instead, investigates maintenance policies that explicitly consider the FILTER clause and exploit the presence of a Filtering Threshold that selects a subset of the mappings returned by the SERVICE clause. By trying to avoid using the refresh budget to update mappings that will be discarded by the FILTER clause, our new policy has the potential to address the limits of Acqua policies.

Let Ω^W be the set of solution mappings returned from a WINDOW clause, Ω^S be the one returned from a SERVICE clause and Ω^R be the one stored in the replica. We formulate our research question as:

Q given a query that joins the set of solution mappings Ω^W returned from a WINDOW clause with Ω^S returned from a SERVICE clause and filters them applying a Filtering Threshold $\mathcal{FT}$ to a variable ?x that appears in Ω^S (i.e., for each mapping $\mu^S \in \Omega^S$ it checks $\mu^S(?x) > \mathcal{FT}$), how can we refresh the local replica of solution mappings Ω^R in order to guarantee reactiveness while maximizing the freshness of the mappings in the replica?

To answer this question, we formulate two hypotheses:

H.1 the replica can be maintained fresher than when using Acqua policies, if we first refresh the mappings $\mu^R \in \Omega^R$ for which $\mu^R(?x)$ is closer to the Filtering Threshold.

H.2 the replica can be maintained fresher than when using Acqua policies by first selecting the mappings as in Hypothesis II.1 and, then, applying the Acqua policies.

To study Hypothesis H.1, we propose a policy (namely, *Filter Update Policy*) for refreshing the replica that selects mappings μ^R for which $\mu^R(?x)$ is closer to the Filtering Threshold and we experimentally demonstrate its effectiveness comparing their performances with those of the Acqua policies. Similarly, to study Hypothesis H.2, we extend Acqua policies combining them with the *Filter Update Policy* and we experimentally demonstrate their efficiency comparing their performance against those of the Acqua policies.

The remainder of the paper is organized as follows. Section 2 defines the relevant background concepts. Section 3 introduces our proposed solution for refreshing the replica of background data. Section 4 provides experimental evaluation for investigating our hypotheses. Section 5 reviews related existing works and finally, Sect. 6 concludes and presents some future works.

2   Background

Data Model. RDF Stream Processing extends the RDF data model and the SPARQL query model in order to take into account the velocity of the data and its evolution over time. The RDF data model is extended in two directions: RDF streams and background data.

An **RDF stream** S is a potentially unbounded sequence of timestamped data items (d_i, t_i):

$$S = (d_1, t_1), (d_2, t_2), \ldots, (d_n, t_n), \ldots,$$

where d_i is a RDF statement, t_i the associated time instant and, for each item i, it holds $t_i \leq t_{i+1}$, i.e. stream items are in a non-decreasing time order. An RDF statement is a triple $(s, p, o) \in (I \cup B) \times (I) \times (I \cup B \cup L)$, where I is the set of IRIs, B is the set of blank nodes and L is the set of literals.

Background data denotes the portion of data that does not change, or changes very slowly w.r.t. the RDF stream, e.g. RDF data exposed through SPARQL endpoints, stored in RDF repositories or embedded in Web pages. In this case, the time dimension is considered through the notions of time-varying and instantaneous graphs. A time-varying graph $\bar{G}$ is a function that relates time instants to RDF graphs; fixed a time instant t, $\bar{G}(t)$ is an instantaneous RDF graph.

Query Model. In the following we present RSP-QL [6], an extension of SPARQL to process RDF streams. The main difference is given by the fact that RSP-QL follows the continuous evaluation paradigm, i.e., every query is issued once (registered) and evaluated multiple times, as the data changes over time, in contrast with the one-time evaluation of SPARQL, i.e. every query is evaluated once. A SPARQL query [12] is defined through a triple (E, DS, QF), where E is the algebraic expression, DS is the data set and QF is the query form. An RSP-QL extends SPARQL by introducing a quadruple (SE, SDS, ET, QF), where SE is an RSP-QL algebraic expression, SDS is an RSP-QL dataset, ET is the sequence of time instants on which the evaluation occurs, and QF is the Query Form.

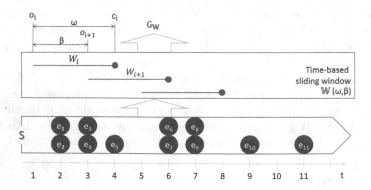

Fig. 1. The time-based sliding window operator dynamically selects a finite portion of the stream.

Key to RSP-QL is the notion of **time-based sliding window** $\mathbb{W}$, depicted in Fig. 1. $\mathbb{W}$ that takes as input an RDF stream S and produces a time-varying graph $\mathbb{W}(S) = G_{\mathbb{W}}$. $\mathbb{W}$ is defined through two parameters ω and β, respectively the width and slide parameters. A sliding window generates a sequence of fixed windows, i.e. portion of the underlying stream defined in a time interval $(o, c]$ that can be queried as RDF graphs. Given a sliding window $\mathbb{W}$ and two generated consecutive windows W_i, W_{i+1} defined respectively in $(o_i, c_i]$ and $(o_{i+1}, c_{i+1}]$, it holds: $c_i - o_i = c_{i+1} - o_{i+1} = \omega$, and $o_{i+1} - o_i = \beta$.

An RSP-QL data set is a set composed by one default time-varying graph $\bar{G}_0$, a set of time-varying named graphs $\{(u_i, \bar{G}_i)\}$, where $u_i \in I$ is the name of the element; and a set of RDF streams associated to named sliding windows $\{(u_j, \mathbb{W}_j(S_k))\}$. Fixed an evaluation time instant, it is possible to determine a set of instantaneous graphs and fixed windows, i.e. RDF graphs, and use them as input data for the algebraic expression evaluation.

An algebraic expression SE is a streaming graph pattern, composed by operators mostly inspired by relational algebra, such as joins, unions and selections. In addition to the ones defined in SPARQL, RSP-QL adds a set of *streaming operators (RStream, IStream and DStream), to transform the query result in an output stream. In addition to I, B and L, let V be the set of variables (disjointed with the other sets); graph patterns are expressions recursively defined as follows:

- a basic graph pattern (i.e. set of triple patterns $(s, p, o) \subset (I \cup B \cup V) \times (I \cup V) \times (I \cup B \cup L \cup V))$ is a graph pattern;
- let P be a graph pattern and F a built-in condition, $P\ FILTER\ F$ is a graph pattern;
- let P_1 and P_2 be two graph patterns, $P_1\ UNION\ P_2$, $P_1\ JOIN\ P_2$ and $P_1\ OPT\ P_2$ are graph patterns;
- let P be a graph pattern and $u \in (I \cup V)$, the expressions $SERVICE\ u\ P$, $GRAPH\ u\ P$ and $WINDOW\ u\ P$ are graph patterns;
- let P be a graph pattern, $RStream\ P$, $IStream\ P$ and $DStream\ P$ are streaming graph patterns.

As in SPARQL, the query semantics rely on the notion of solution mapping, a function that maps variables to RDF terms, i.e., $\mu : V \to (I \cup B \cup L)$. Let $dom(\mu)$ be the subset of V where μ is defined: two solution mappings μ_1 and μ_2 are **compatible** ($\mu_1 \sim \mu_2$) if the two mappings assign the same value to each variable in $dom(\mu_1) \cap dom(\mu_2)$. Let now Ω_1 and Ω_2 be two sets of solution mappings, the join is defined as:

$$\Omega_1 \bowtie \Omega_2 = \{\mu_1 \cup \mu_2 | \mu_1 \in \Omega_1, \mu_2 \in \Omega_2, \mu_1 \sim \mu_2\};$$

Evaluation of a graph pattern produces a set of solution mappings; RSP-QL extends the SPARQL evaluation function by adding the evaluation time instant: let $[\![P]\!]^t_{SDS(\bar{G})}$ be the evaluation of the graph pattern P at time t having $\bar{G} \in SDS$ as active time-varying graph. For the sake of space, in the following we present the evaluation of the operators used in the remaining of the work. The evaluation of a BGP P is defined as:

$$[\![P]\!]^t_{SDS(\bar{G})} = [\![P]\!]_{SDS(\bar{G},t)}$$

where the right element of the formula is the SPARQL evaluation [12] of P over $SDS(\bar{G},t)$. Being a SPARQL evaluation, $SDS(\bar{G},t)$ identifies an RDF graph: an instantaneous graph $\bar{G}(t)$ if $\bar{G}$ is a time-varying graph, a fixed window generated by $\mathbb{W}(S)$ at time t ($\mathbb{W}(S,t) = \bar{G}_{\mathbb{W}}(t)$) if $\bar{G}$ is a time-based sliding window. Evaluations of JOIN, FILTER and WINDOW[3] are defined as follows:

$$[\![P_1 \ JOIN \ P_2]\!]^t_{SDS(\bar{G})} = [\![P_1]\!]^t_{SDS(\bar{G})} \bowtie [\![P_2]\!]^t_{SDS(\bar{G})}$$

$$[\![P \ FILTER \ F]\!]^t_{SDS(\bar{G})} = \{\mu | \mu \in [\![P]\!]^t_{SDS(\bar{G})} \text{ and } \mu \text{ satisfies } F\}$$

$$[\![WINDOW \ u \ P]\!]^t_{SDS(\bar{G})} = [\![P]\!]^t_{SDS(\mathbb{W})} \text{ such that } (u,\mathbb{W}) \in SDS$$

Finally, the evaluation of $SERVICE \ u \ P$ consists in submitting the graph pattern P to a SPARQL endpoint located at u and produces a set Ω^S with the resulting mappings.

Acqua. The challenge given by the Web is the distribution of the data in several sources. RDF Stream Processing offers solutions to integrate and process them. That means, on the one hand, RSP engines can register to RDF stream sources and receive stream items; on the other hand, RSP engines can access background data stored behind SPARQL endpoints by using the federated SPARQL extension [1]. As analyzed in [5], the time to access and fetch the remote background data can be very high, and have a sensible impact on the reactiveness of the RSP engine in answering the query. The solution presented in [5] work applies to queries where the algebraic expression SE contains the graph patterns:

$$(WINDOW \ u_1 \ P_1) \ JOIN \ (SERVICE \ u_2 \ P_2),$$

and consists in introducing a replica $\mathcal{R}$ to store the result of $(SERVICE \ u_2 \ P_2)$.

To keep $\mathcal{R}$ up-to-date, a maintenance process is introduced. It is depicted in Fig. 2, and it is composed by three elements: a proposer, a ranked and a maintainer. (1) The **proposer** selects a set $\mathcal{C}$ of candidate mappings for the maintenance; (2) the **ranker** orders $\mathcal{C}$ by using some relevancy criteria; (3) the **maintainer** refreshes the top γ elements of $\mathcal{C}$ (the elected set $\mathcal{E}$), where γ is named **refresh budget** and encodes the number of requests the RSP engine can submit to the remote services without losing reactiveness. After the maintenance, (4) the join operation is performed.

The paper proposes several algorithms to be used as proposer and ranker; in particular, the one that shows the best performance is the combination of WSJ (proposer) and WBM (ranker). WSJ builds the candidate set by selecting the mappings in $\mathcal{R}$ compatible with the ones from the evaluation of

---

[3] In the following, we assume $u \in I$.

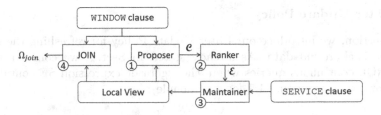

Fig. 2. The framework proposed in [5] to address the problem of joining streaming and remote background data.

($WINDOW$ u_1 P_1). The latter exploits the **best before time**, i.e. an estimation of the time on which one mapping in $\mathcal{R}$ would become stale. That means, WBM orders the candidate set assigning to each mapping $\mu_i \in C$ a score defined as:

$$score_i(t) = \min(L_i(t), V_i(t)),$$

where t is the evaluation time, $L_i(t)$ is the **remaining life time**, i.e. the number of future evaluations that involve the mapping, and $V_i(t)$ is the **normalized renewed best before time**, i.e., the renewed best before time normalized with the sliding window parameters. The intuition behind WBM is to prioritize the refresh of the mappings that contribute the most to the freshness in the current and next evaluations. That means, WBM identifies the mappings that are going to be used in the upcoming evaluations (remaining life time) and that allows saving future refresh operations (normalized renewed best before time). Formally, L_i and V_i are defined as:

$$L_i(t) = \left\lceil \frac{t_i + \omega - t}{\beta} \right\rceil, \tag{1}$$

$$V_i(t) = \left\lceil \frac{\tau_i + I_i(t) - t}{\beta} \right\rceil, \tag{2}$$

where t_i is the time instant associated to the mapping μ_i, τ_i is the current best before time and $I_i(t)$ is the change interval, that captures the remaining time before the next expiration of μ_i. It is worth noting that I_i is potentially unknown and could require an estimator.

Other rankers proposed in [5] are inspired to the random (RND) and Least-Recently Used (LRU) cache replacement algorithms. The former randomly ranks the mappings in the candidate set; the latter orders C by the time of the last refresh of the mappings: the less recently a mapping have been refreshed in a query, the higher is its rank.

3 Proposed Solution

In this section, we introduce our proposed solution. In Sect. 3.1 we discuss the proposed Filter Update Policy as a ranker for maintenance process of replica $\mathcal{R}$. Section 3.2 shows how we can improve the Acqua policies by integrating them with our Filter Update Policy.

3.1 Filter Update Policy

In this section, we introduce our Filter Update Policy for refreshing the replica $\mathcal{R}$ of the background data. As already stated in Sect. 1, we consider a class of SPARQL continuous queries where the algebraic expression SE contains the graph patterns (see Listing 1.1 for an example):

$$(WINDOW\ u_1\ P_1)\ JOIN\ ((SERVICE\ u_2\ P_2)\ FILTER\ F),$$

where F is either $?x < \mathcal{FT}$ or $?x > \mathcal{FT}$, $?x$ is a variable in P_2 and $\mathcal{FT}$ is the **Filtering Threshold** declared in the FILTER clause.

The result of SERVICE clause is stored in the replica $\mathcal{R}$. The maintenance process introduced in Sect. 2 consists of the following components: the proposer, the ranker and the maintainer. In our solution the proposer selects the set $\mathcal{C}$ of candidate mappings for the maintenance. The Filter Update Policy computes the elected set $\mathcal{E} \subseteq \mathcal{C}$ of mappings to be refreshed as a ranker and, finally, the maintainer refreshes the mappings in set $\mathcal{E}$.

For each mapping in the replica define as $\mu^{\mathcal{R}}$, our Filter Update Policy (i) computes how close is the value associate to the variable $?x$ in the mapping $\mu^{\mathcal{R}}$ to the Filtering Threshold $\mathcal{FT}$ and ii) selects the top γ ones for refreshing replica (where γ is the refresh budget). In order to compute the distance between the value of $?x$ in mapping $\mu^{\mathcal{R}}$ and Filtering Threshold $\mathcal{FT}$, we define the Filtering Distance $\mathcal{FD}$ of mapping $\mu^{\mathcal{R}}$ as:

$$FD(\mu^{\mathcal{R}}) = |\mu^{\mathcal{R}}(?x) - \mathcal{FT}| \qquad (3)$$

If the value associated to $?x$ smoothly changes over time[4], then, intuitively, the smaller the Filtering Distance of a mapping in the last evaluation, the higher is the probability to cross the Filtering Threshold $\mathcal{FT}$ in the current evaluation and, thus, to affect the query evaluation. For instance in Listing 1.1, for each user we compute the Filtering Distance between the number of followers and the Filtering Threshold $\mathcal{FT}$=100,000. Users, whose numbers of followers were closer to 100,000 in the last evaluation, are more likely to affect the current query evaluation.

Algorithm 1 shows the pseudo-code of the Filter Update Policy. For each mapping in the candidate mapping set $\mathcal{C}$, it computes the Filtering Distance as the absolute difference of the value $?x$ of mapping $\mu^{\mathcal{R}}$ and the Filtering Threshold $\mathcal{FT}$ in the query (Line 1–3). Then, it orders the set $\mathcal{C}$ based on the absolute differences (Line 4). The set of elected mapping $\mathcal{E}$ is created by getting the top γ ones from the ordered set of $\mathcal{F}$ (Line 5). Finally, the local replica $\mathcal{R}$ is maintained by invoking the SERVICE operator and querying the remote SPARQL endpoint to get fresh mappings and replace them in $\mathcal{R}$ (Line 6–9).

---

[4] With the wording *smoothly changes over time* we mean if $?x = 98$ in the previous evaluation and $?x = 101$ in the current evaluation, in next evaluation it is more likely that $?x = 99$ than jumping to $?x = 1000$.

Algorithm 1. The pseudo-code of the Filter Update Policy

---

1 **foreach** $\mu^{\mathcal{R}} \in \mathcal{C}$ **do**
2 $\quad | \quad FD(\mu^{\mathcal{R}}) = |\mu^{\mathcal{R}}(?x) - \mathcal{FT}|$;
3 **end**
4 order $\mathcal{C}$ w.r.t. the value of $FD(\mu^{\mathcal{R}})$;
5 $\mathcal{E}$ = first γ mappings of $\mathcal{F}$;
6 **foreach** $\mu^{\mathcal{R}} \in \mathcal{E}$ **do**
7 $\quad | \quad \mu^{S} = \text{ServiceOp.next}(\text{JoinVars}(\mu^{\mathcal{R}}))$;
8 $\quad | \quad$ replace $\mu^{\mathcal{R}}$ with μ^{S} in $\mathcal{R}$;
9 **end**

3.2   Integrating Filter Update Policy with Acqua's Ones

It is worth to note that Filter Update Policy can be combined with those proposed in Acqua. In the maintenance process introduced in Sect. 2, first, the proposer generates the candidate set $\mathcal{C}$, then the update policy (ranker) selects a set of mappings $\mathcal{E} \subset \mathcal{C}$ to be refreshed in replica $\mathcal{R}$. We propose to integrate our Filter Update Policy in the maintenance process.

Algorithm 2 shows the pseudo-code that integrates the Filter Update Policy with Acqua ones. It is worth to note that this algorithm requires a parameter, namely Filtering Distance Threshold $\mathcal{FDT}$. For each mapping in the candidate mapping set $\mathcal{C}$, it computes the Filtering Distance (Line 1–2). If the difference is smaller than Filtering Distance Threshold $\mathcal{FDT}$, it adds the mapping to the set $\mathcal{F}$ (Line 3–5). Given the set $\mathcal{F}$, the refresh budget γ, and the update policy name (RND, LRU, WBM), the function UP considers the set $\mathcal{F}$ as the candidate set and applies the policy on it (Line 7).

Algorithm 2. The pseudo-code of integrating Filter Update Policy with Acqua's ones

---

1 **foreach** $\mu^{\mathcal{R}} \in \mathcal{C}$ **do**
2 $\quad | \quad FD(\mu^{\mathcal{R}}) = |\mu^{\mathcal{R}}(?x) - \mathcal{FT}|$
3 $\quad | \quad$ **if** $FD(\mu^{\mathcal{R}}) < \mathcal{FDT}$ **then**
4 $\quad | \quad | \quad$ add $\mu^{\mathcal{R}}$ to $\mathcal{F}$;
5 $\quad | \quad$ **end**
6 **end**
7 UP ($\mathcal{F}$, γ, update policy);

We respectively name the three adapted policies WSJ-RND.F, WSJ-LRU.F and WSJ-WBM.F. In all of them, the candidate set is selected considering the mappings that are closer to the Filtering Threshold $\mathcal{FDT}$.

4 Experiments

In this section, we experimentally verify our hypotheses. In Sect. 4.1 we introduce the experimental setting that we use to check the validity of our hypotheses. In Sect. 4.2 we discuss about the experiments related to our first hypothesis and show the related result. Finally, Sect. 4.3 shows the results related to the second hypothesis.

4.1 Experimental Setting

As experimental environment, we use an Intel i7 @ 1.8 GHz with 4 GB memory and an hdd disk. The operating system is Mac OS X Lion 10.9.5 and Java 1.7.0.67 is installed on the machine. We carry out our experiments by extending the experimental setting of Acqua [5].

The experimental data sets are composed by streaming and background data. The streaming data is collected from 400 verified users of Twitter for three hours of tweets using the streaming API of Twitter. The background data is collected invoking the Twitter API, which returns the number of followers per user, every minute during the three hours we were recording the streaming data. As a result, for each user the background data contain a time-series that records the number of followers.

In order to control the selectivity of the filtering condition, we design a transformation of the background data that randomly selected a specified percentage of the users (i.e., 10 %, 20 %, 25 %, 30 %, 40 % and 50 %) and, for each user, translates the time-series, which captures the evolution overtime of the number of followers, to be sure that it crosses the Filtering Threshold[5] at least once during the experiment. In particular, for each user, first, we find the minimum and maximum number of followers; then, we define the *MaxDifference* equal to the difference of minimum number of followers and Filtering Threshold. We also define the *MinDifference* equal to the difference of maximum number of followers and Filtering Threshold. Finally, we randomly generate a number between *MinDifference* and *MaxDifference* and we add it to each value of the time-series of the number of followers of the selected user.

It is worth to note that this translation does not alter the nature of the evolution over time of the number of followers, it only moves the entire time-series so that it crosses the Filtering Threshold at least once during the experiment. If the original time-series of the number of followers is almost flat (i.e., it slightly moves up and down around a median) or it is fast growing/shrinking; then the translated time-series will have the same trend. The only effect of the translation is to control the selectivity of the filter operator.

In order to reduce the risk to introduce a bias in performing the translation, we repeat the procedure 10 times for each percentage listed above, generating 10 different test data sets for each percentage. We name each group of test data

---

[5] The value of the Filtering Threshold is chosen to guarantee that no one of the original time-series crosses it.

sets using its percentage; for example DS10 % identifies the 10 data sets in which the number of followers of 10 % of the users crosses the Filtering Threshold at least once during the experiment.

We use the query presented in Sect. 1. For each policy we run 140 iterations of the query evaluation.

In order to investigate our hypotheses, we set up an Oracle that, at each iteration i, certainly provides corrects answers $Ans(Oracle_i)$ and we compare its answers with the possibly erroneous ones of the query $Ans(Q_i)$. Given that the answer to the query in Listing 1.1 is a set of users' IDs, we use Jaccard distance to measure diversity of the set generated by the query and the one generated by the Oracle. The Jaccard index is commonly used for comparing the similarity and diversity of overlapping sets (e.g., A and B). The Jaccard index J is defined as the size of the intersection divided by the size of the union of the sets ($J(A,B) = \frac{|A \cap B|}{|A \cup B|}$). The Jaccard distance d_J, which measures dissimilarity between sets, is complementary to the Jaccard index and is obtained by subtracting the Jaccard index from 1 ($d_J(A,B) = 1 - J(A,B)$).

In our experiments, we compute the Jaccard distance for each iteration of the query evaluation. For this reason, we also introduce the cumulative Jaccard distance at the kth iteration $d_J^C(k)$ as:

$$d_J^C(k) = \sum_{i=1}^{k} d_J(Ans(Q_i), Ans(Oracle_i))$$

where $d_J(Ans(Q_i), Ans(Oracle_i))$ is the Jaccard distance of iteration i.

4.2   Experiment 1

This experiment investigates our first hypothesis (H.1). In order to verify the hypothesis, we compare our policy with Acqua's ones. The worst maintenance policy is WST which does not refresh the replica $\mathcal{R}$ during the evaluation and, thus, is an upper bound of errors. We use WSJ as proposer for all maintenance policies. As described in Sect. 2, WSJ selects the mappings from the ones currently involved in the evaluation and creates the candidate set $\mathcal{C}$. For ranker we use RND, LRU, and WBM, which are introduced in Sect. 2. WSJ-RND update policy randomly selects the mappings while WSJ-LRU chooses the least recently refreshed mapping. WSJ-WBM identifies the possibly stale mappings and choose them for maintenance.

In this experiment, we consider the refresh budget γ equal to 3. We select the 10 background data sets DS25 % (those where the number of followers of 25 % of users cross the Filtering Threshold) and run 140 iterations of query evaluation over each of the 10 different background data sets. Figure 3 shows the result of the experiment. Figure 3(a, b) respectively show the best and the worst runs. Figure 3(c) presents the average of the results obtained with the 10 data sets. As the result shows, the Filter Update Policy is the best one in all cases. The WSJ-WBM is better than the WSJ-RND and the WSJ-LRU in average and in the worst case, but the WSJ-LRU is better than WSJ-WBM in the best case. As expected, the WST policy is always the worst one.

Figure 3(d) shows the distribution of cumulative Jaccard distance at the 140*th* iteration obtained with the 10 data sets DS25 %. As the result shows, the Filter Update Policy outperforms other policies in 50 % of the cases. Comparing the WSJ-WBM policy with WSJ-RND and WSJ-LRU policies, WSJ-WBM performs better than WSJ-RND in 50 % of the cases. The WSJ-LRU Policy also perform better than WSJ-RND in average. As expected, the WST policy has always the highest cumulative Jaccard distance.

To check the sensitivity to the filter selectivity (i.e., in the evaluated case, to the percentage of users whose number of followers is crossing the filtering threshold, we repeat the experiment with different data sets in which the percentage is changed. Keeping the refresh budget γ equal to 3, we run experiments with the data sets DS10 %, DS20 %, DS30 %, DS40 %, DS50 %. As for the DS25 %, we generate 10 data sets for each value of percentage and run the experiment on them. For each data set and each policy we compute the average, the first quartile, and the third quartile of cumulative Jaccard distance at the 140*th* iteration over 10 data sets. Figure 4(a) shows the obtained results. The Filter Update

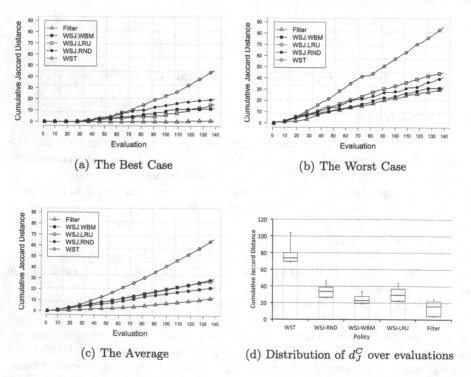

(a) The Best Case

(b) The Worst Case

(c) The Average

(d) Distribution of d_J^G over evaluations

Fig. 3. Result of experiment 1 that investigates Hypothesis H.1 testing our Filter Update Policy and the State-of-the-Art policies proposed in Acqua [5] over the 10 data sets in DS25 %.

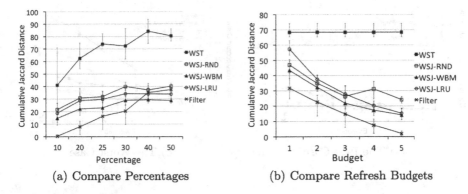

(a) Compare Percentages   (b) Compare Refresh Budgets

Fig. 4. Result of experiment that investigates how the results presented in Fig. 3 change using different percentages and refresh budgets.

Policy has better performance than the other ones for DS10 %, DS20 %, DS25 % and DS30 % . Intuitively, in those data sets, we have fewer users whose number of followers crosses the Filtering Threshold, so we have higher probability of selecting the correct user for updating. The result also shows that the behavior of WSJ-WBM policy is stable over different percentages and performs better than Filtering Update Policy over data sets DS40 % and DS50 %.

In order to check the sensitivity to the refresh budget, we repeat the experiment with different refresh budgets. We set the refresh budget equals to 1, 2, 3, 4, and 5 in different experiments and run them over 10 data set DS25 %. Figure 4(b) shows the average, the first quartile, and the third quartile of cumulative Jaccard distance at the 140th iteration over 10 data sets for different policies and budgets. The cumulative Jaccard distance in WST does not change for different budgets, but for all other policies the cumulative Jaccard distance decreases when the refresh budget increases; this means that higher refresh budgets always leads to fresher replica and less errors.

4.3   Experiment 2

We run a second experiment in order to investigate our second hypothesis (H.2). We compare the performances of WSJ-RND.F, WSJ-LRU.F, and WSJ-WBM.F, which respectively combine our Filtering Update Policy with WSJ-RND, WSJ-LRU and WSJ-WBM, with the Filter Update Policy using data sets DS%25. We set the Filtering Distance Threshold $\mathcal{FDT}$ parameter to 1,000. As explained in Sect. 3, those new policies, first, create the candidate set $\mathcal{C}$, then they reduce the candidate set by omitting the users that have Distance Threshold greater than 1000 and, finally, they apply the rest of the Acqua policy to the candidate set which selects the mappings for refreshing in the replica $\mathcal{R}$.

Figure 5 shows the result of the experiment. In Fig. 5(a) the chart shows the cumulative Jaccard distance across the 140 iterations in the best run. In this case the Filter Update policy performs better in most of the iterations. Figure 5(b)

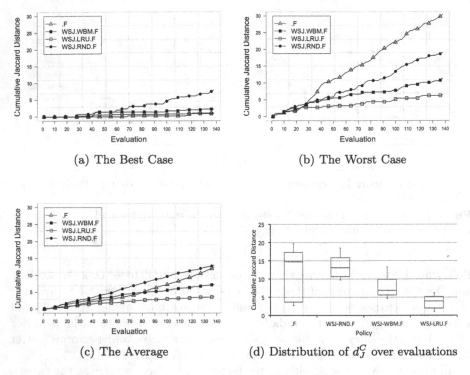

(a) The Best Case

(b) The Worst Case

(c) The Average

(d) Distribution of d_J^C over evaluations

Fig. 5. Result of experiment that combine Filter policy with Acqua's ones to investigate Hypothesis H.2.

shows the worst case, where the WSJ-LRU.F policy is the best one in all the iterations. Figure 5(c) shows the average performance of the policies. The WSJ-LRU.F policy is the best one also in this case. Figure 5(d) shows the distribution of the cumulative Jaccard distance over 10 different data sets DS%25. The WSJ-LRU.F policy performs better than WSJ-RND.F and WSJ-WBM.F in most of the cases. The WSJ-WBM.F Policy performs better than WSJ-RND.F policy in most of the cases.

To check the sensitivity to the filter selectivity, we repeat the experiment with different data sets in which this percentage is changed. We run experiments over the data sets DS10 %, DS20 %, DS25 %, DS30 %, DS40 %, DS50 %, while keeping the refresh budget γ equal to 3. We generate 10 data sets for each value of percentage and run the experiment over them. For each data set and each policy we compute the average, the first quartile, and the third quartile of cumulative Jaccard distance at the last iteration over 10 data sets. Figure 6(a) shows the obtained results. The WSJ-LRU.F policy always has better performance than the other ones. The behavior of WSJ-LRU.F, and WSJ-WBM.F policies are stable over different percentages. The Filter Update Policy has better performance than WBM.F for DS10 %, DS20 %, DS25 % and DS30 % . In those data sets, we have

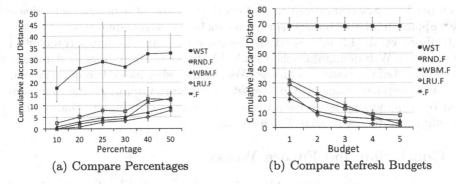

(a) Compare Percentages   (b) Compare Refresh Budgets

Fig. 6. Result of experiment that investigates how the results presented in Fig. 5 change using different percentages and refresh budgets.

fewer users whose number of followers crosses the Filtering Threshold, and with higher probability we select the correct user for updating.

We repeat the experiment with different refresh budgets to check the sensitivity of the result to the refresh budget. We set the refresh budget equals to 1, 2, 3, 4, and 5 in different experiments and run them over 10 data set DS25 %. Figure 6(b) shows the average, the first quartile, and the third quartile of cumulative Jaccard distance at the last iterations over 10 data sets for different policies and budgets. The cumulative Jaccard distance in WST does not change for different budgets, but for all other policies when the refresh budget increases, the cumulative Jaccard distance decreases which means that higher refresh budgets always leads to a fresher replica and less errors.

5   Related Works

Replicas (a.k.a., local views) are used to increase availability and reactiveness, however maintenance processes are needed to keep the freshness of data and reduce inconsistencies. To the best of our knowledge Acqua (presented in Sect. 2) is the only approach that directly targets RSP processing. However, considerable studies exist about maintenance of local views in the database community [2,7,9,14].

Babu et al. [2] proposed an adaptive approach to handle changes of update streams, such as stream rates, data characteristics, and memory availability over time. The approach manages the trade-off between space and query response time. They proposed Adaptive Caching algorithm that estimates cache benefit and cost online in order to select and allocate memory to caches dynamically.

In the context of the Web, view materialization is an appealing solution, since it decouples the serving of access requests from the handling of updates. Labrinidis and Roussopoulos [9] introduced the Online View Selection Problem as how dynamically select materialization views to maximize performance while keeping data freshness at an adequate level. They proposed an adaptive algorithm for Online View Selection Problem that decides to materialize or just cache views. Their approach is based on user-specified data freshness requirements.

Umbrich et al. [13] addressed the response time and freshness trade-off in the Semantic Web domain. Cached Linked Data suffers from missing data as it covers partial of the resources on the Web, on the other hand, live querying has slow query response time. They proposed a hybrid query approach that improves upon both paradigms by considering a broader rang of resources than cashes, and offering faster result than live querying.

6   Conclusion and Future Works

In this work, we studied the problem of the continuous evaluation of a class of queries that joins data streams and background data. Reactiveness is the most important performance indicator for this class of queries. When the background data is distributed over the Web and slowly evolves over time (i.e., it is quasi-static), correct answers may not be reactive, because the time to access the background data may exceed the time between two consequent evaluations.

To address this problem, we brought from the State-of-the-Art of RSP (specifically, from Acqua [5] presented in Sect. 2) the idea to use (*i*) a replica to store the quasi-static background data at query registration time, (*ii*) a maintenance policy to keep the data in the replica fresh and (*iii*) a refresh budget to limit the number of the access to the distributed background data. In this way, accurate answers can be provided while meeting operational deadlines.

In this paper, we contribute to the development of Acqua extending the class of continuous queries for which Acqua policies can refresh the replica. In particular, we investigate queries where (*i*) the algebraic expression is a FILTER of a JOIN of a WINDOW and a SERVICE and (*ii*) the filter condition selects mappings from the SERVICE clause checking if the values of a variable are larger (or smaller) than a Filtering Threshold.

To study this class of queries, we formulate two hypotheses that capture the same intuition: the closer was the value to the Filtering Threshold in the last evaluation, the more probable is that it will cross the Filtering Threshold in the current evaluation and, thus, it is important to refresh the mapping. In Hypothesis H.1, we directly test this intuition defining the new Filtering Update Policy, whereas, in Hypothesis H.2, we test this intuition together with the Acqua policies defining WSJ-RND.F, WSJ-LRU.F and WSJ-WBM.F respectively extending WSJ-RND, WSJ-LRU and WSJ-WBM.

The result of experiments about H.1 shows that our Filter Update Policy keeps the replica fresher than Acqua policies when the number of mappings subject to the filtering condition is below 40 % of the total. Above this percentage Aqua results are confirmed: WSJ-WBM is the best choice. The results of the experiments about H.2 shows that the Filter Update Policy can be combined with Acqua policies in order to keep the replica even fresher than with the Filter Update Policy.

In our future work, we intend to broaden the class of queries that are subject of our study. Our next step is to add multiple FILTER clauses to the SERVICE.

Then, we would like to explore queries where the filtering condition is not as crisp as in this work, but it is formulated as a ranking clause [8] that involves variables present both in the WINDOW and in the SERVICE clauses. In particular, we intend to bring to the RSP domain results already known for SPARQL [11].

Moreover, we intend to further optimize the approach in two ways. On the one hand, we want to explore the static optimization of pushing the FILTER clause(s) into the SERVICE clause. This goes much beyond State-of-the-Art in RSP, because the replica becomes a cache of recent results. On the other hand, we want to explore how to dynamically determine the conditions for switching among policies, e.g., by using the percentage of mappings subject to the filtering condition.

Last but not least, we intend to study the effect of different trends in the data. In the current experiment, we used Twitter data in which (i) the number of mentions in the tweets is correlated to the growth/shrink of the number of followers and (ii) the number of followers does not change drastically. We intend to investigate the effect of the trends in the data using data from other domains (e.g., sensor networks).

Acknowledgment. I would like to acknowledge the support of Soheila Dehghanzadeh and to thank her for the kind help in understanding the code base and the data set of Acqua.

References

1. Aranda, C.B., Arenas, M., Corcho, Ó., Polleres, A.: Federating queries in SPARQL 1.1: syntax, semantics and evaluation. J. Web Seman. **18**(1), 1–17 (2013)
2. Babu, S., Munagala, K., Widom, J., Motwani, R.: Adaptive caching for continuous queries. In: Proceedings of the 21st International Conference on Data Engineering, ICDE 2005, pp. 118–129. IEEE (2005)
3. Barbieri, D.F., Braga, D., Ceri, S., Della Valle, E., Grossniklaus, M.: Querying RDF streams with C-SPARQL. ACM SIGMOD Rec. **39**(1), 20–26 (2010)
4. Calbimonte, J.-P., Jeung, H.Y., Corcho, O., Aberer, K.: Enabling query technologies for the semantic sensor web. Int. J. Seman. Web Inf. Syst. **8**, 43–63 (2012)
5. Dehghanzadeh, S., Dell'Aglio, D., Gao, S., Della Valle, E., Mileo, A., Bernstein, A.: Approximate continuous query answering over streams and dynamic linked data sets. In: Cimiano, P., Frasincar, F., Houben, G.-J., Schwabe, D. (eds.) ICWE 2015. LNCS, vol. 9114, pp. 307–325. Springer, Heidelberg (2015)
6. Dell'Aglio, D., Della Valle, E., Calbimonte, J., Corcho, Ó.: RSP-QL semantics: a unifying query model to explain heterogeneity of RDF stream processing systems. Int. J. Seman. Web Inf. Syst. **10**(4), 17–44 (2014)
7. Guo, H., Larson, P.-Å., Ramakrishnan, R.: Caching with good enough currency, consistency, and completeness. In: Proceedings of the 31st International Conference on Very Large Data Bases, pp. 457–468. VLDB Endowment (2005)
8. Ilyas, I.F., Beskales, G., Soliman, M.A.: A survey of top-k query processing techniques in relational database systems. ACM Comput. Surv. **40**(4) (2008)
9. Labrinidis, A., Roussopoulos, N.: Exploring the tradeoff between performance and data freshness in database-driven web servers. VLDB J. **13**(3), 240–255 (2004)

10. Le-Phuoc, D., Dao-Tran, M., Xavier Parreira, J., Hauswirth, M.: A native and adaptive approach for unified processing of linked streams and linked data. In: Aroyo, L., Welty, C., Alani, H., Taylor, J., Bernstein, A., Kagal, L., Noy, N., Blomqvist, E. (eds.) ISWC 2011, Part I. LNCS, vol. 7031, pp. 370–388. Springer, Heidelberg (2011)
11. Magliacane, S., Bozzon, A., Della Valle, E.: Efficient execution of top-K SPARQL queries. In: Cudré-Mauroux, P., et al. (eds.) ISWC 2012, Part I. LNCS, vol. 7649, pp. 344–360. Springer, Heidelberg (2012)
12. Pérez, J., Arenas, M., Gutierrez, C.: Semantics and complexity of SPARQL. ACM Trans. Database Syst. **34**(3) (2009)
13. Umbrich, J., Karnstedt, M., Hogan, A., Parreira, J.X.: Freshening up while staying fast: towards hybrid SPARQL queries. In: ten Teije, A., Völker, J., Handschuh, S., Stuckenschmidt, H., d'Acquin, M., Nikolov, A., Aussenac-Gilles, N., Hernandez, N. (eds.) EKAW 2012. LNCS, vol. 7603, pp. 164–174. Springer, Heidelberg (2012)
14. Viglas, S.D., Naughton, J.F., Burger, J.: Maximizing the output rate of multi-way join queries over streaming information sources. In: Proceedings of the 29th International Conference on Very Large Data Bases, vol. 29, pp. 285–296. VLDB Endowment (2003)

Aspect-Based Sentiment Analysis on the Web Using Rhetorical Structure Theory

Rowan Hoogervorst[1], Erik Essink[1], Wouter Jansen[1], Max van den Helder[1],
Kim Schouten[1(✉)], Flavius Frasincar[1], and Maite Taboada[2]

[1] Erasmus University Rotterdam,
P.O. Box 1738, 3000 DR Rotterdam, The Netherlands
{369567rh,369723ee,376121mh,357893wj}@student.eur.nl,
{schouten,frasincar}@ese.eur.nl
[2] Simon Fraser University, 8888 University Dr., Burnaby, B.C. V5A 1S6, Canada
mtaboada@sfu.ca

Abstract. Fine-grained sentiment analysis on the Web has received much attention in recent years. In this paper we suggest an approach to Aspect-Based Sentiment Analysis that incorporates structural information of reviews by employing Rhetorical Structure Theory. First, a novel way of determining the context of an aspect is presented, after which a full path analysis is performed on the found context tree to determine the aspect sentiment. Comparing the proposed method to a baseline model, which does not use the discourse structure of the text and solely relies on a sentiment lexicon to assign sentiments, we find that the proposed method consistently outperforms the baseline on three different datasets.

1 Introduction

Being an integral part of most people's lives, the Web is one of the primary outlets for consumers to express their opinions on products and services they feel engaged with. This engagement can stem from the fact that they purchased a certain product or service resulting in a glowing review of that product or service, but it can also come in the form of an outcry on social media against a product or service because of some shortcoming that prevents the consumer from actually buying it. The willingness to freely share these thoughts and emotions is a driving force behind the success of review sites and review sections on e-commerce sites.

The ubiquity of reviews in e-commerce has proven to significantly affect customer decisions [3], as well as to provide a valuable marketing tool for companies [4]. However, to get a robust overview of a certain product or service, a large number of reviews needs to be covered. This calls for an automated method that performs sentiment analysis on consumer reviews.

For more than a decade [19,25], many different methods have been developed that aim to automatically extract consumer sentiment from reviews. Over the years, not only has the accuracy of these methods been improved, its level of detail has also increased. Whereas the first methods computed sentiment with

© Springer International Publishing Switzerland 2016
A. Bozzon et al. (Eds.): ICWE 2016, LNCS 9671, pp. 317–334, 2016.
DOI: 10.1007/978-3-319-38791-8_18

respect to the whole review, later methods analyzed the text at a finer level of granularity, such as at the sentence level (e.g., [11]) or even sub-sentence level (e.g., [26]).

In contrast to methods that compute a sentiment value for a given piece of text, Aspect-Based Sentiment Analysis (ABSA) aims to extract sentiment values for a set of aspects (i.e., characteristics or traits) of the product or service being reviewed [22]. Hence, ABSA considers the joint problem of finding aspects (i.e., what characteristics of the entity under review are discussed?) and computing sentiment for each found aspect (i.e., what sentiment is expressed on that particular trait?). The second task also requires that one must identify the exact part of the text that covers a certain aspect. In this research we focus on the second task only, and thus the aspects that are discussed in the text are considered given. This assumption is valid for many review sites in which the aspects of interest are predefined and the user sentiment is gauged for these particular aspects so that products or services can be easily compared.

An interesting new method that has been introduced at the review level [7] and sub-sentence level [29] is that of using discourse relations in the text to compute sentiment values. More specifically, these approaches use a parser implementing the Rhetorical Structure Theory (RST) [15] to find discourse relations in the text, exploiting those to assign weights to the different discourse elements in the text. Hence, parts that are important for the discourse can be emphasized with a high weight, while parts that are less relevant can be diminished with a lower weight. The application of discourse relations can lead to significant performance improvements, as evidenced by the 15 % increase in F_1-score reported in [7]. Similar results are reported in [29], where using RST at the sub-sentence level is shown to lead to considerable improvements over a Support Vector Machine baseline.

While the application of discourse analysis for sentiment analysis has been successful at both the review and sub-sentence level, its application has, to the best knowledge of the authors, not been considered for ABSA. Unfortunately, a direct extension of the existing methods to the aspect level is non-trivial due to the fact that aggregating text units is not as natural for aspects as it is for text elements. Instead, a crucial step when applying discourse analysis to ABSA is to define a context for the investigated aspect, mapping the aspect to a certain set of text elements. The work presented in this paper aims to extend the application of discourse analysis to the aspect level, where we focus on finding discourse relations through the application of RST. A main contribution in this respect is a novel way of defining the aspect context based on the discourse relations found through the RST analysis. Furthermore, we suggest how to incorporate this new way of defining the aspect context into a larger framework for ABSA.

The organization of this paper is as follows. In Sect. 2, we consider RST and its current application to sentiment analysis. The main processing framework is introduced in Sect. 3, where we present our method of finding aspect context, as well as the weighting scheme and natural language processing steps involved in computing the sentiments associated to the aspects. We then discuss the actual implementation of our framework in Sect. 4. The performance of the proposed method is evaluated in Sect. 5 and in Sect. 6 conclusions and suggestions for future work are presented.

2   Related Work

While many of the suggested methods for sentiment analysis have proven to be successful [22], a possible deficiency of these traditional methods is that they do not make use of structural elements in text. As has been shown by [1], considering such semantic relations in text may have a positive impact on the sentiment mining task. As a result, we have recently seen the development of different sentiment mining methods that take the discourse structure of text into account. A common characteristic of these methods is that they tend to rely on the use of RST [15] for finding the discourse relations in the text.

To find discourse relations in text, an RST analysis first splits the text into clauses, also called elementary discourse units (EDUs). It then postulates relations between these EDUs, selecting from a list of predefined rhetorical relations. One can distinguish between two types of relations: mononuclear relations and multinuclear relations. In mononuclear relations, the two discourse elements have an unequal status, with one element being the more prominent 'nucleus' and the other being the supporting 'satellite'. An example of a mononuclear relation is:

'I bought this laptop, because it has a good processor.'

In this sentence, the clause after the comma is ancillary (and therefore the satellite) to the first clause (the nucleus), as it gives an explanation to the first part. In multinuclear relations, all elements have the same status and are considered nuclei. An example of such a multinuclear relation is:

'This laptop is neither fast nor does it have large storage capacity.'

Here, none of the elements is more prominent than the other and they are thus both considered nuclei.

An important property of an RST analysis is that EDUs can be aggregated to form new clauses, for which we can then again determine the discourse relation they are in. By proceeding in this way, a complete hierarchical structure of the text is obtained, which can be represented as a tree. In RST, the hierarchical structure of a text is referred to as the discourse tree.

Due to the complexity of RST methods, many researchers thought in the 1990s that discourse analysis could only be performed in combination with fully specified clauses and sentence structures [10,12]. However, in [17], the first discourse parser that works with unrestricted text is presented. The proposed parser automatically determines the EDUs in unrestricted text as well as the discourse relations between these EDUs, using several lexicographical rules.

Based on the successful application of RST parsers for unstructured text, RST is a natural candidate for use with online consumer reviews and RST has been applied to sentiment analysis in several different ways. One of the first works to apply RST to sentiment analysis is [24], which suggests to rank words that are contained in a satellite differently than those that are contained in a nucleus. When determining whether a word is contained in a satellite or a nucleus, only the leaf level of the discourse tree is considered. Interestingly, this relatively simple split into nuclei and satellites already leads to an improved performance of their suggested sentiment orientation calculator.

This idea is extended by [7], where, although still functioning at the leaf-level of the discourse tree, not just a distinction between nucleus and satellite is used, but also the rhetorical relations between the discourse elements. For this analysis, the eight relations that are most frequently found in the used dataset are considered, out of the 23 rhetorical relations from [15]. One of the findings is that words that are contained in some relation may be of more importance than others, or it may be the case that a relation indicates the presence of a negation. In the given evaluation setup where sentiment is classified per sentence, applying RST leads to a 15 % improvement in F_1 score compared to a baseline which does not incorporate the discourse structure of the text. Sentence-level sentiment analysis is also the focus of [27], where discourse information is used to formulate constraints for a Conditional Random Field model. It is shown that these discourse-based constraints are especially important in improving sentiment prediction.

In [29], RST is applied at the sub-sentence level through an application of Markov Logic. The main focus is on dividing the relations into contrasting and non-contrasting relations, as a contrasting relation may potentially negate the sentiment found in an EDU. In an experimental evaluation of the proposed method, a considerable improvement is found, compared to a baseline model without discourse information.

Another method that operates at the sub-sentence level is presented in [28], where sentiment is predicted for each EDU. An interesting part of this research is the comparison of RST with the Penn Discourse Treebank (PDTB). The main conclusions are that RST outperforms PDTB and that methods that include discourse information when predicting sentiment for an EDU outperform the baselines that do not have access to this information.

In [13], sentiment is also predicted for each EDU, however, the authors present a Bayesian model that jointly models sentiment, aspects, and discourse markers. Unfortunately, the method assumes that the overall document sentiment is given, which is not the case in ABSA.

The application of discourse analysis can bring significant improvements to the analysis of sentiment. However, it has not yet been applied to sentiment analysis at the aspect level. In order for that to be possible, it is crucial to find the context of a certain aspect within the text, since the sentiment should be computed from that particular context. Next to the actual sentiment analysis method itself, the proposed method for finding this aspect context is one of the main contributions of this paper.

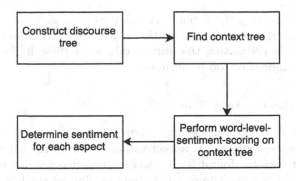

Fig. 1. Outline of framework

3 Framework

In this section we discuss the framework used to find the sentiment with respect to some predefined aspects in online customer reviews. Figure 1 shows the main steps as proposed in the framework and these steps will be elaborated on one-by-one in the coming subsections.

3.1 Constructing the Discourse Tree

To incorporate the structural relations of a review into the analysis, our method relies on the application of RST to analyze the discourse structure in the review text. Two important elements of such an analysis are to determine the type of discourse parser used and the exact set of rhetorical relations considered in the analysis.

In this work, we propose the use of a document discourse parser to construct discourse trees, which has the advantage over sentence level parsers that one can also take inter-sentence relations into account. Since the context of an aspect is expected to be rather small, the use of inter-sentence relations may be advantageous considering that reviews tend to contain rather informal language in which sentences are short. An example would be:

'I like the speed of this laptop. But starting up is terribly slow.'

In such a sentence the actual aspect relating to the speed of the laptop is in the first sentence, but the very positive sentiment in this first sentence is actually reconsidered to some extent in the second sentence. Hence, to properly find the sentiment relating to the aspect, the inter-sentence relationship is of importance, which confirms the need for a document-level discourse parser.

Furthermore, a subset of the 23 discourse relations, as first introduced by [15], is utilized to analyze the discourse structure of the text. For this work, we choose to use the eighteen most frequently found relations, as identified by [8], instead of the small subset of eight relations used by [7], as we hypothesize that

in the supervised setting the framework might still be able to find the correct
impact of a relation, even when a relation is not often encountered. Moreover,
we expect errors in estimating the impact values for these infrequent relations
to have only a minor effect on performance.

3.2   Finding the Context Tree

In order to determine the sentiment associated with a certain aspect, it is important to define the context of that aspect within the text. To that end, a method
is proposed that uses the found RST relations to define which parts of the text
are covering which aspect. The method starts by finding the leaves in the RST
tree that contain aspects. The aspects themselves are given for the data we use.
An example of an annotated sentence from the one of the used datasets is given
below (including the obvious spelling mistakes, as is common in user generated
content on the Web).

```
<sentence id="1028246:1">
    <text>Service was devine, oysters where a sensual as they
        come, and the price can't be beat!!!</text>
    <opinions>
        <opinion target="Service" category="SERVICE#GENERAL"
            polarity="" from="0" to="7" />
        <opinion target="oysters" category="FOOD#QUALITY"
            polarity="" from="20" to="27" />
        <opinion target="NULL" category="RESTAURANT#PRICES"
            polarity="" from="0" to="0" />
    </opinions>
</sentence>
```

For each sentence, the aspects are given together with the position inside
the sentence (i.e., with the from and to values). Some aspects are implicit and
do not have a specific target inside the sentence (i.e., target is NULL and from
and to are zero). In certain cases, including all instances of implicit aspects,
the aspect is not contained in a single EDU, but its description is spread over
multiple leaf nodes. In such a situation, all leaf nodes related to the aspect are
considered separately and the final results are aggregated. The polarity values
are empty, since that is the very thing our method predicts for each aspect.

After finding the leaf nodes that contain the aspect, we determine the relevant
part of the review based on the fact that satellites tend to be complementary to
nuclei. To illustrate this, consider the example:

'I think the hard-drive is good, since it has large storage capacity, so I
bought it.'

Figure 2 shows the rhetorical structure of this example. In this example the
aspect sentiment related to the aspect of the overall quality of the hard-drive is

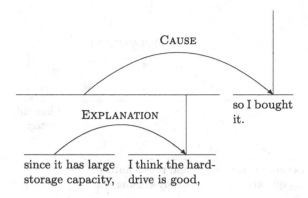

Fig. 2. Full discourse tree of a simple review sentence (the curved lines denote a mononuclear relation between a nucleus and a satellite)

contained in the EDU 'I think the hard-drive is good', but to fully determine the sentiment expressed on the hard-drive we need its corresponding satellite: 'since it has large storage capacity'.

Based on this complementary relation of satellites to nuclei, we argue that a satellite should be taken into account when determining aspect sentiment for the case where the satellite relates back to a nucleus containing the aspect. On the other hand, we argue that nuclei do not add to the understanding of the satellite. Hence, we have a natural definition of context through the asymmetry found in the relation between nucleus and satellite. Relating this back to the discourse tree, it follows that the context defined by this asymmetry is a sub-tree of the original discourse tree. This subtree contains as root the lowest level satellite in which the aspect is contained. More specifically, for the example discussed in Fig. 2, this means that both the satellite and nucleus of the lower level of the tree should be considered, where this nucleus and satellite jointly correspond to the part of the sentence until the junction made by 'so'.

To find the context tree for an aspect, the algorithm looks for the lowest level satellite that contains an aspect. This is done by checking whether the leaf node containing the aspect is a satellite. If this is the case, we stop searching. Otherwise we check whether the parent node (i.e., the linked node one level higher than the leaf node in the discourse tree) is a satellite. If that is not the case, we move up to its parent node and repeat this procedure until we reach a satellite. One can easily verify that this procedure indeed returns the indicated subtree for the example considered in Fig. 2.

In some cases, one aspect can have multiple context trees. Consider the following example for which the discourse tree is given in Fig. 3.

'I like this laptop, because it starts up quickly and reacts immediately to my commands.'

In this example, the aspect relating to the speed of the laptop is described in the second part of the sentence 'because it starts up quickly and reacts immediately

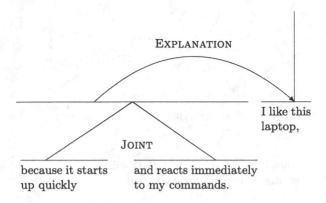

Fig. 3. Full discourse tree for a sentence with multiple context trees (note that the straight lines of the 'Joint' relation denote the fact that this is a multinuclear relation)

to my commands'. However, this sub-sentence consists of two leaves, and thus for both leaves a context-tree is found. In this small example, both leaf nodes will have the same context tree, since they share an immediate parent which is also a satellite. Hence the context tree for both leaves is the tree corresponding to this sub-sentence.

In other cases, the same aspect can be referred to in separate sentences. Since the RST analysis takes inter-sentence relations into account, these cases are naturally dealt with. An example of the RST analysis taking inter-sentence relations into account can be found in the following example, for which the discourse tree is given in Fig. 4.

'I was quite hopeful about the speed. However, it is truly atrociously slow, especially when starting up.'

The aspect 'speed' (e.g., of a laptop), is literally mentioned in the first sentence but without expressing any sentiment. In contrast to this, the second sentence expresses a strong negative sentiment on this aspect, but without literally mentioning the aspect again. The contrasting inter-sentence relation is exploited by our method to combine the sentiment from the second sentence with the aspect in the first sentence.

3.3 Performing Word-Level Scoring

After finding the context tree the next step is to determine the sentiment of the different EDUs contained in the context tree. Note that since EDUs get combined further up the tree, we should compute the sentiment for all leaf nodes in the context tree. To determine the sentiment for the leaves we use a sentiment lexicon-based approach that is constructed around the notion of synsets, which correspond to a set of cognitive synonyms.

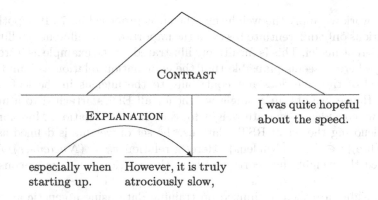

Fig. 4. Full discourse tree showing inter-sentence relation

In this approach all words in the considered reviews are first disambiguated since words can have different meanings in different context. To find a word's meaning, its part-of-speech (POS) and lemma are initially collected. As a lexicon can still have multiple entries for a POS of a word, the information regarding the POS of the word is then complemented by its corresponding word sense as determined by the Lesk algorithm [14]. Using the POS, lemma, and word sense of a word, its sentiment score can be obtained from a sentiment lexicon.

3.4 Determining Aspect Sentiment

Combining the output from the previous steps leads to the calculation of the sentiment for each aspect based on its context tree and sentiment score per EDU. This can be done using either the full-path rhetorical structure model or the partial rhetorical structure model. When using the partial rhetorical structure model, only the relations at the leaf level of the discourse tree are utilized, as these are the most fine-grained. In contrast, using the full-path rhetorical structure will allow the use of the path from the root of the context tree to the leaf level. For this work, the full-path rhetorical structure model is employed, as it has been shown to better capture the expressed sentiment [9].

To introduce this method more formally, we use some relevant notation. Let S be the set of leaf nodes of the context tree, $sent(s_i)$ be the sentiment score corresponding to leaf node $s_i \in S$, and P_{s_i} denote all nodes on the path from the root node of the context tree to leaf node s_i. Furthermore, let $sent(t_j)$ be the sentiment score for word $t_j \in s_i$. Last, let w_{r_n} denote the weight associated with the rhetorical role of node r_n. Then, the sentiment score of a leaf node $s_i \in S$ can be computed as

$$sent(s_i) = \sum_{t_j \in s_i} sent(t_j) \times \prod_{r_n \in P_{s_i}} w_{r_n}, \forall s_i \in S. \tag{1}$$

In addition to the context tree and the model described above, we also need a weighting scheme which determines for each rhetorical role r_n, the weight w_{r_n}. In our framework we apply the weighting scheme as proposed in [7]. It hypothesizes that relations only differentiate between the importance of different satellites and not of different nuclei. This is intuitively illustrated by the example as introduced in Fig. 2, where it seems plausible that the explanation relation as found in the lower level of the tree does not contribute to the nucleus in the leaf level of the tree. Hence, we obtain a single weight for all EDUs attached to a nucleus, whereas we consider a separate weight for each satellite relation. More formally, with R denoting the set of RST relations, the set of weights is defined as $W = \{(r, \text{Satellite}) | r \in R\} \cup \{\text{Nucleus}\}$. Here, a relation $r_n = (Nucleus, r) \ \forall r \in R$ is assigned the weight that corresponds to the relation $Nucleus$ as considered in W.

The weights are then optimized on training data using a genetic algorithm. Starting with an initial population of random weights, the fittest of these are combined in every step to produce a new set of weights. Moreover, each step mutations occur with a certain probability, to ensure variety in the population, lowering the risk of getting stuck in local optima. The chosen fitness measure is the F_1 value that is obtained when running the algorithm with the given weights.

The last step in our framework is to determine the sentiment for each aspect. To that end, the sum is taken of all the sentiment scores belonging to the context trees that we found to relate to the current aspect. A threshold ϵ is then used to categorize the sentiment score into the positive or negative class. As suggested by [7], the threshold ϵ is set as the mean of (1) the average computed sentiment score for the aspects with positive sentiments and (2) the average computed sentiment score of the aspects with a negative sentiment, to avoid the sentiment bias in reviews. In its current form, the proposed algorithm does not predict neutral sentiment values and is limited to positive and negative only.

4   Implementation

Our implementation is done in the Java programming language, using the Senti-WordNet [2,5] sentiment lexicon, the CLULAB [23] processors for RST parsing, and Stanford CoreNLP [16] for various basic natural language processing tasks.

SentiWordNet is used to assign a sentiment score to each disambiguated word, represented as a WordNet synset. For each synset, three scores are available: objectivity, negativity, and positivity. These three scores always sum up to one, hence when knowing two scores, the third can be inferred. To arrive at a single sentiment score for each synsets, we ignore the objectivity score and subtract the negativity score from the positivity score, resulting in a real number in the $[-1, 1]$ interval [9].

CLULAB is a text-level discourse parser which we use to construct a discourse tree for each review. It is primarily based on the HILDA discourse parser [8] and it uses the same discourse relation set as the discourse parser developed by [6]. This means that CLULAB can be used to parse entire texts, whereas sentence level discourse parsers can only be used to construct discourse trees for separate sentences. To break down the input text into EDUs, also called discourse

---

Algorithm 1. *findLeaves(tree, aspect)*

---

    input : The discourse tree and aspect under consideration
    output: List with all leaves that contain the aspect
    `// Find leaves that contain aspects`
    if *tree is leaf* **then**
        if *tree contains aspect* **then**
          | **return** tree;
        else
          | **return** $\emptyset$;
        end
    end
    aspectLeaves $\longleftarrow \emptyset$;
    for *all children of tree* **do**
        | *aspectLeaves* $\longleftarrow$ *aspectLeaves* $\cup$ *findLeaves*(*child*, *aspect*) ;
    end
    return *aspectLeaves*;

---

segmentation, and find the relations between them, support vector machines (SVMs) are used. To specify the different relations between EDUs, CLULAB uses a discourse relation set consisting of 18 different relations. Examples of the considered relations are attribution, condition, and cause. In addition, it specifies whether the specific relation is multinuclear or mononuclear.

4.1 Finding the Context Tree

After constructing the discourse trees, the algorithm presented in Algorithm 1 finds all leaves that contain the aspect under investigation, using as input the aspect to consider, together with the previously constructed discourse tree. The algorithm starts at the root of the discourse tree and recursively checks all the leaf nodes whether they contain the aspect or part of it. If so, that leaf node is added to the list which is the output of the algorithm.

In the previous step we found all leaf nodes that contain the aspect, irrespective of them being a nucleus or a satellite. In the next step, the context tree of each of the selected leaf nodes is determined based on the asymmetry between nucleus and satellite. The algorithm for this task is given by Algorithm 2. The algorithm starts from the position of a leaf node, after which it iteratively evaluates the role of the parent node of the current node. If the parent node is a nucleus, the parent node becomes the current node and the algorithm moves up one step to evaluate its parent node. This procedure is repeated until the evaluated parent node is either a satellite or the root of the discourse tree. Then the algorithm stops and returns the tree that has that node as its root. Hence, every leaf node will get a context tree that is defined as its closest ancestor, that is a satellite, or the top ancestor (i.e., root of the discourse tree), together with all nodes that share this ancestor.

Algorithm 2. *defineContext(aspectLeaves)*

---
input : *aspectLeaves*, the set of leaves that contain the considered aspect
output: *contextTrees*, the set of all context trees for the considered aspect
`// Find closest ancestor that is a satellite`
contextTrees ⟵ ∅;
foreach *leafNode* ∈ *aspectLeaves* **do**
    node ⟵ *leafNode*;
    while *hasParentNode(node)* **and** *typeOf(parentNode(node))* = Nucleus
    do
       | *node* ⟵ *parentNode(node)*;
    end
    `// Context tree, defined by its root` *node*`, is added to set`
    contextTrees ⟵ *contextTrees* ∪ {*node*}
end

4.2 Performing Word-Level Scoring

The next step involves assigning scores to all the nodes that have been previously classified as leaf nodes in the context tree. First, punctuation is removed from the text in the EDUs that correspond to the leaf nodes in the context tree. Then the text is split into separate words. After disambiguating to get the meaning of a word, its sentiment score is retrieved from SentiWordNet. Summing up the sentiment scores yields the sentiment score for each EDU that is linked to a particular aspect.

4.3 Determining Aspect Sentiment

The last step of our algorithm is determining the sentiment score for each context tree. For this purpose, we sum the weighted sentiment of the leaf nodes of a context tree (the RST-based weights are here aggregated by multiplication from leaf to root). The pseudocode for this step is presented in Algorithm 3, where this algorithm should be called with the root node of the context tree as *node* and with a *weightNode* equal to 0. In this algorithm we apply recursion to assign to all leaf nodes a score, which is then weighted as it returns back to the top of the tree. Here we make use of the function *getRelationWeight(node)*, which gives the weight based on the RST relation it is involved in and whether or not this node is a nucleus or satellite.

The last step is now to compare the obtained sentiment score for the aspect to the value of ϵ. If the sentiment score is smaller than ϵ, the returned sentiment for the aspect is negative, otherwise it is positive.

5 Evaluation

This section first introduces the datasets that have been used to evaluate the performance of our proposed methods, after which a comparison of the performance

---

Algorithm 3. *assignScores(nodeTree, weights, weightNode)*

---

    input : the context *tree* under consideration represented by a node, the
               weights for the RST relations, the weights so far built up in the tree
               weightNode
    output: The sentiment score of the context tree
    currentWeight ⟵ *weightNode*;
    if *node is not the root node of the context tree* **then**
       | *currentWeight* ⟵ *currentWeight* ∗ *getRelationWeight(node)*;
    end
    if *node is a leaf node* **then**
       | *score* ⟵ the sentiment for this EDU;
       | **return** *score* ∗ *currentWeight*;
    end
    newScore ⟵ 0;
    foreach *child* **of** *node* **do**
       | *newScore* ⟵ *newScore* + *assignScores(child, weights, currentWeight)*;
    end
    return *newScore*

---

of these methods is made. Additionally, this section introduces a baseline method which we benchmark our method against.

5.1 Data Description

In the evaluation we used three sets of reviews. All of these datasets are from the SemEval ABSA Task [20,21]. We consider here the dataset on restaurant reviews of the SemEval 2014 and the datasets on restaurant and laptop reviews of the SemEval 2015. For the aspects considered for the dataset about laptops, one can think of among others the battery, the screen, and the hard-drive. For the restaurant datasets, aspects relate to for example the atmosphere, taste of the food, and level of service.

An important difference between these datasets is that the SemEval 2014 dataset consists of only single sentence reviews, while the SemEval 2015 datasets consider reviews with multiple sentences. Furthermore, the size of the datasets differs as the restaurants dataset of 2014 contains a total of 3041 reviews and a total of 3693 aspects. The dataset of laptops contains instead 277 reviews, 1739 sentences and 1974 aspects, while the dataset of restaurants of the SemEval 2015 contains a total of 254 reviews, 1315 sentences, and 1654 aspects. The datasets contain mostly positive and negative aspects, but a small number of aspects are annotated as neutral or conflicted. Since our method only predicts positive or negative, the performance with respect to these classes is not reported. Note that for the overall performance measures, these instances are considered incorrect classifications and hence are included in the computation of the performance measures.

Table 1. Performance for the laptops 2015 dataset

(a) Performance of baseline method

	Precision	Recall	F_1
Overall	0.31	0.31	0.31
Positive	0.39	0.34	0.36
Negative	0.24	0.32	0.27

(b) Performance of proposed method

	Precision	Recall	F_1
Overall	0.67	0.67	0.67
Positive	0.67	0.88	0.76
Negative	0.69	0.47	0.56

5.2 Baseline Method

The acquired results are compared against a baseline model in order to evaluate the performance of the suggested method. In this case the baseline method considers a simple natural language processing approach that employs Senti-WordNet and does not account for the discourse structure of the text. For each aspect we consider a fixed size context window of one to three words around the aspect. For aspects that do not have a specific target in the sentence but are implicit, we consider the whole sentence as the context window. Let the set of the words in this context for aspect i be given by c_i, then the baseline method computes the sentiment for aspect i as

$$\text{sent}(i) = \sum_{t_j \in c_i} \text{sent}(t_j). \tag{2}$$

where t_j are the words in the current review j in which i is an aspect. Similar to the proposed method, the sentiment score for each word is retrieved from SentiWordNet.

5.3 Comparison of Methods

The proposed method is evaluated on three datasets using the common 10-fold cross-validation technique. The performance of the baseline and the proposed method are presented in Table 1a and b for SemEval 2015 laptop data. Since this data set does not provide any location within the sentence for aspects, the context window for the baseline is irrelevant.

These tables clearly show that the proposed method outperforms the baseline. An important observation is that the performance is somewhat lower for negative aspects than for positive ones. A possible explanation for this lower performance

Table 2. Performance for the restaurants 2015 dataset

(a) Performance of baseline method

Category	Context window = 1			Context window = 2			Context window = 3		
	Precision	Recall	F_1	Precision	Recall	F_1	Precision	Recall	F_1
Overall	0.57	0.57	0.57	0.54	0.54	0.54	0.50	0.50	0.50
Positive	0.70	0.74	0.72	0.69	0.67	0.68	0.68	0.61	0.64
Negative	0.15	0.15	0.15	0.16	0.20	0.18	0.16	0.23	0.19

(b) Performance of proposed method

	Precision	Recall	F_1
Overall	0.74	0.74	0.74
Positive	0.80	0.86	0.83
Negative	0.52	0.47	0.49

on negative polarities might be found in the fact that negative reviews are often written with many positive words [18]. However, using discourse information mitigates this issue to some extent, as the proposed method is considerably less sensitive to this phenomenon than the baseline.

Table 2a and b show the results for the baseline method and the proposed method for the SemEval restaurant 2015 reviews, respectively. The results found here confirm to a large extent the observations made for the previous dataset. Again, the proposed method outperforms the baseline model.

Last, Table 3a and b show the performance of both methods on the SemEval restaurants 2014 dataset. These tables show that the performance of our method is lower than for the other two datasets. A possible reason for the decrease

Table 3. Performance for the restaurants 2014 dataset

(a) Performance of baseline method

Category	Context window = 1			Context window = 2			Context window = 3		
	Precision	Recall	F_1	Precision	Recall	F_1	Precision	Recall	F_1
Overall	0.50	0.50	0.50	0.47	0.47	0.47	0.43	0.43	0.43
Positive	0.56	0.83	0.67	0.55	0.74	0.63	0.54	0.67	0.60
Negative	0.12	0.07	0.09	0.15	0.15	0.15	0.15	0.20	0.17

(b) Performance of proposed method

	Precision	Recall	F_1
Overall	0.60	0.60	0.60
Positive	0.64	0.91	0.75
Negative	0.42	0.32	0.36

in performance is that this dataset only considers single sentence reviews. As we apply RST analysis at the review level, this implies that we can not use inter-sentence relations in this dataset, as done for the restaurant 2015 dataset. However even in this scenario where the RST analysis cannot be used to its full potential, it is still the better option, yielding higher performance than the baseline method, both for negative and positive aspects.

6   Conclusion

While the application of Rhetorical Structure Theory (RST) in sentiment analysis has already been proven to obtain good performance at higher levels of text granularity, the method has not yet been explored for Aspect-Based Sentiment Analysis (ABSA). For this reason we propose a framework that uses RST for ABSA. In this framework, discourse trees are first created by using a document level discourse parser. The main contribution of this paper is the definition of the aspect context through constructing a context tree based on the asymmetrical relation between satellites and nuclei in RST. This context tree is used for the sentiment scoring, for which we use sentiment lexicon-based word-scoring and a full-path based rhetorical structure processing scheme.

To evaluate the performance of the proposed framework a comparison between the suggested methods and a baseline model that does not incorporate the discourse tree of the review is made. The comparison of the performances of the proposed method to the benchmark is made on the basis of three different datasets, comprised of laptop and restaurant reviews. We find that for all three datasets, the baseline model is clearly outperformed, but the proposed method seems susceptible to negative reviews that use many positive words.

Based on the success of using RST for ABSA as reported in this paper, a next step would be to extend the proposed methodology with additional components. An interesting avenue of research would be to incorporate the found discourse structure and context tree into a classification algorithm such as a Support Vector Machine. This combines the raw power of machine learning with the finesse and detail of discourse analysis.

Acknowledgments. The authors of this paper are supported by the Dutch national program COMMIT.

References

1. Asher, N., Benamara, F., Mathieu, Y.Y.: Appraisal of opinion expressions in discourse. Lingvisticæ Investigationes **32**(2), 279–292 (2009)
2. Baccianella, S., Esuli, A., Sebastiani, F.: SentiWordNet 3.0: an enhanced lexical resource for sentiment analysis and opinion mining. In: Proceedings of the Seventh International Conference on Language Resources and Evaluation (LREC 2010), vol. 10, pp. 2200–2204 (2010)

3. Bickart, B., Schindler, R.M.: Internet forums as influential sources of consumer information. J. Interact. Mark. **15**(3), 31–40 (2001)
4. Chen, Y., Xie, J.: Online consumer review: word-of-mouth as a new element of marketing communication mix. Manage. Sci. **54**(3), 477–491 (2008)
5. Esuli, A., Sebastiani, F.: SentiWordNet: a publicly available lexical resource for opinion mining. In: Proceedings of the Fifth International Conference on Language Resources and Evaluation (LREC 2006), vol. 6, pp. 417–422. European Language Resources Association (ELRA) (2006)
6. Feng, V.W., Hirst, G.: Text-level discourse parsing with rich linguistic features. In: Proceedings of the 50th Annual Meeting of the Association for Computational Linguistics (ACL 2012), pp. 60–68. Association for Computational Linguistics (2012)
7. Heerschop, B., Goossen, F., Hogenboom, A., Frasincar, F., Kaymak, U., de Jong, F.: Polarity analysis of texts using discourse structure. In: Proceedings of the 20th ACM International Conference on Information and Knowledge Management (CIKM, 2011), pp. 1061–1070. ACM (2011)
8. Hernault, H., Prendinger, H., duVerle, D.A., Ishizuka, M., et al.: HILDA: a discourse parser using support vector machine classification. Dialogue Discourse **1**(3), 1–33 (2010)
9. Hogenboom, A., Frasincar, F., de Jong, F., Kaymak, U.: Using rhetorical structure in sentiment analysis. Commun. ACM **58**(7), 69–77 (2015)
10. Kamp, H., Reyle, U.: From Discourse to Logic: Introduction to Modeltheoretic Semantics of Natural Language, Formal Logic and Discourse Representation Theory, vol. 42. Springer Science & Business Media, Berlin (1993)
11. Kim, S.M., Hovy, E.: Determining the sentiment of opinions. In: Proceedings of the 20th International Conference on Computational Linguistics (COLING 2004). Association for Computational Linguistics (2004)
12. Lascarides, A., Asher, N., Oberlander, J.: Inferring discourse relations in context. In: Proceedings of the 30th Annual Meeting on Association for Computational Linguistics (ACL 1992), pp. 1–8. Association for Computational Linguistics (1992)
13. Lazaridou, A., Titov, I., Sporleder, C.: A Bayesian model for joint unsupervised induction of sentiment, aspect and discourse representations. In: Proceedings of the 51th Annual Meeting of the Association for Computational Linguistics (ACL 2013), pp. 1630–1639. Association for Computational Linguistics (2013)
14. Lesk, M.: Automatic sense disambiguation using machine readable dictionaries: how to tell a pine cone from an ice cream cone. In: Proceedings of the Fifth Annual International Conference on Systems Documentation (SIGDOC 1986), pp. 24–26. ACM (1986)
15. Mann, W.C., Thompson, S.A.: Rhetorical structure theory: toward a functional theory of text organization. Text-Interdisc. J. Study Discourse **8**(3), 243–281 (1988)
16. Manning, C.D., Surdeanu, M., Bauer, J., Finkel, J., Bethard, S.J., McClosky, D.: The Stanford CoreNLP natural language processing toolkit. In: Proceedings of 52nd Annual Meeting of the Association for Computational Linguistics: System Demonstrations, pp. 55–60. Association for Computational Linguistics (2014)
17. Marcu, D.: The rhetorical parsing of natural language texts. In: Proceedings of the Eighth Conference on European Chapter of the Association for Computational Linguistics (EACL 1997) pp. 96–103. Association for Computational Linguistics (1997)
18. Pang, B., Lee, L.: Opinion mining and sentiment analysis. Found. Trends Inf. Retrieval **2**(1–2), 1–135 (2008)

19. Pang, B., Lee, L., Vaithyanathan, S.: Thumbs up?: sentiment classification using machine learning techniques. In: Proceedings of the 2002 Conference on Empirical Methods in Natural Language Processing (EMNLP 2002), pp. 79–86. Association for Computational Linguistics (2002)

20. Pontiki, M., Galanis, D., Papageorgiou, H., Manandhar, S., Androutsopoulos, I.: Semeval-2015 task 12: aspect based sentiment analysis. In: Proceedings of the Ninth International Workshop on Semantic Evaluation (SemEval 2015), pp. 486–495. Association for Computational Linguistics (2015)

21. Pontiki, M., Papageorgiou, H., Galanis, D., Androutsopoulos, I., Pavlopoulos, J., Manandhar, S.: Semeval-2014 task 4: aspect based sentiment analysis. In: Proceedings of the Eighth International Workshop on Semantic Evaluation (SemEval 2014), pp. 27–35. Association for Computational Linguistics and Dublin City University (2014)

22. Schouten, K., Frasincar, F.: Survey on aspect-level sentiment analysis. IEEE Trans. Knowl. Data Eng. **28**(3), 813–830 (2016)

23. Surdeanu, M., Hicks, T., Valenzuela-Escárcega, M.A.: Two practical rhetorical structure theory parsers. In: Proceedings of the Conference of the North American Chapter of the Association for Computational Linguistics - Human Language Technologies (NAACL HLT 2015): Software Demonstrations (2015)

24. Taboada, M., Voll, K., Brooke, J.: Extracting sentiment as a function of discourse structure and topicality. Technical report TR 2008–20, Simon Fraser University School of Computing Science (2008). ftp://fas.sfu.ca/pub/cs/TR/2008/CMPT2008-20.pdf

25. Turney, P.D.: Thumbs up or thumbs down?: semantic orientation applied to unsupervised classification of reviews. In: Proceedings of the 40th Annual Meeting on Association for Computational Linguistics (ACL 2002), pp. 417–424. Association for Computational Linguistics (2002)

26. Wilson, T., Wiebe, J., Hoffmann, P.: Recognizing contextual polarity in phrase-level sentiment analysis. In: Proceedings of the Conference on Human Language Technology and Empirical Methods in Natural Language Processing (HLT 2005), pp. 347–354. Association for Computational Linguistics (2005)

27. Yang, B., Cardie, C.: Context-aware learning for sentence-level sentiment analysis with posterior regularization. In: Proceedings of the 52nd Annual Meeting of the Association for Computational Linguistics (ACL 2014), pp. 325–335. Association for Computational Linguistics (2014)

28. Zhou, Y.: Fine-grained sentiment analysis with discourse structure. Master's thesis, Saarland University, Germany (2013). http://lct-master.org/getfile.php?id=783&n=1&dt=TH&ft=pdf&type=TH

29. Zirn, C., Niepert, M., Stuckenschmidt, H., Strube, M.: Fine-grained sentiment analysis with structural features. In: 5th International Joint Conference on Natural Language Processing (IJCNLP 2011), pp. 336–344. Association for Computational Linguistics (2011)

Diversity in Urban Social Media Analytics

Jie Yang$^{(\boxtimes)}$, Claudia Hauff, Geert-Jan Houben, and Christiaan Titos Bolivar

Delft University of Technology, Mekelweg 4, 2628 CD Delft, The Netherlands
{j.yang-3,c.hauff,g.j.p.m.houben,c.titosbolivar}@tudelft.nl

Abstract. Social media has emerged as one of the data backbones of urban analytics systems. Thanks to geo-located microposts (text-, image-, and video-based) created and shared through portals such as Twitter and Instagram, scientists and practitioners can capitalise on the availability of real-time and semantically rich data sources to perform studies related to cities and the people inhabiting them. Urban analytics systems usually consider the micro posts originating from within a city's boundary uniformly, without consideration for the demographic (e.g. gender, age), geographic, technological or contextual (e.g. role in the city) differences among a platform's users. It is well-known though, that the usage and adoption of social media profoundly differ across user segments, cities, as well as countries. We thus advocate for a better understanding of the intrinsic diversity of social media users and contents.

This paper presents an observational study of the geo-located activities of users across two social media platforms, performed over a period of three weeks in four European cities. We show how demographic, geographical, technological and contextual properties of social media (and their users) can provide very different reflections and interpretations of the reality of an urban environment.

Keywords: Social sensing · Urban analytics · User analysis

1 Introduction

A growing number of studies [3,12,20,21,29] have shown the potential of geo-located social media data (microblog posts, images, videos, etc.) as a relevant source to study the spatio-temporal dynamics of urban areas, e.g. a neighbourhood, a city, or an urbanised region. Platforms like Twitter, Instagram, and Sina Weibo can easily provide real-time access to a large volume of social data created by people from all walks of life. It therefore comes as no surprise that social media analysis is now a cornerstone of modern urban analytics solutions [17,30], and advocated as a fundamental component for decision making processes.

A common feature of prior work in this area is the belief that gathering large amount of data is sufficient to derive a detailed and *accurate* description (i.e. a description reflecting the reality) of the spatio-temporal properties of activities that occur within an area. All users contributing social media content are typically treated equally, independent of their origin (citizen or tourist), purpose in the city (e.g. resident or commuter), or demographic characteristics.

© Springer International Publishing Switzerland 2016
A. Bozzon et al. (Eds.): ICWE 2016, LNCS 9671, pp. 335–353, 2016.
DOI: 10.1007/978-3-319-38791-8_19

We argue that in order to draw correct conclusions (and subsequently base decision making on them), it is essential to investigate to what extent the *diversity* of the social media contributing population of users is an influencing factor. Diversity is an intrinsic property of social media platforms, and it is driven by complex socio-economic and socio-technical processes. As such, it represents both a challenge and an opportunity for urban analytics experiments and systems. When neglected, diversity hampers the generalisation and the validity of the obtained results, possibly leading to incorrect interpretations and subsequently erroneous courses of action.

Let us take as an example the case of a municipality monitoring social media to gather insights about the status of the city during a large street festival. The social media feeds may be overwhelmingly positive towards the event and thus the municipality builds a very favourable understanding of event as well. However, by neglecting the demographic distribution of users (or the lack of users from the target population), this understanding is not inclusive – it might miss the point of view of a significant share of the relevant population.

Diversity is not only a challenge though, it can also be a valuable source of information and should be exploited in order to understand, and leverage the intrinsic bias of social media data sources. Awareness of demographic distribution, for instance, helps in providing a sharper perspective, and an unbiased interpretation of an urban environment. Moreover, realising what (or whose point of view) is missing can lead to actions specifically devoted to bridging the existing knowledge gap, i.e. by means of targeted crowd-sourcing campaigns [7,8].

This paper aims to shed light on the entanglement that exists between social media platforms, their user populations, and the observations that can be obtained about an urban environment. We investigate four dimensions of diversity and seek an answer to the following overarching research question:

[**RQ**] How do *technological, geographical, demographic,* and *contextual* diversity impact the reflections of a city environment as perceived through social media?

We explore the influences of these factors in an experimental study performed by observing the social media activities in four different European cities (Amsterdam, London, Paris, and Rome), across two platforms (Twitter and Instagram), over a period of three weeks. We collected a dataset consisting of 1.87M of geolocated micro posts created by 198K of users. By employing state-of-the-art user modelling techniques offered by the `SocialGlass` platform [5,26], we were able to infer properties such as the gender, age, county and city of origin of social media users. We observed differences in population composition across cities and social media platforms, as well as diversity in the spatio-temporal properties of their online activities across roles (i.e. residents vs. tourists), genders, and ages.

Previous studies addressed differences in the composition of social media user populations across platforms and countries as general trends [23,25], or analysed the behaviour of social media users to identify spatio-temporal regularities in urban environments [21,22]. To the best of our knowledge, our work departs from previous efforts by being the first offering a principled analysis of the diverse spatio-temporal characterisations of user activities in urban environments that include demographic and contextual aspects. We are not seeking to validate social media data, our goal is to highlight the diversities. Our findings prove the need for user modelling techniques in urban analytics, as a fundamental component in real-time social data processing pipelines designed for awareness, control, and prediction purposes.

The remainder of this paper is organised as follows. Section 2 presents an overview of the related work. Section 3 describes the applied experimental methodology and includes a set of specific research questions and hypotheses derived from our guiding question introduced in this section. We present our findings in Sect. 4 before turning towards an outlook into the future in Sect. 5.

2 Related Work

Urban Computing [2,3,16,17,30] is a consolidated area of investigation. More recently, the increasing pervasiveness of social media has led to a wealth of research works devoted to the creation of scalable solutions for exploring varied urban dynamics.

Several works have studied the behaviour of citizens by measuring spatio-temporal regularities in geo-located social media traffic for the purpose of event-detection [18], urban area characterisation [12,28], live-tracking and venue recommendation for city-scale events [3], city-scale [9] and global-scale [15] mobility patterns, and community detection [29]. All these works aimed to show that social media sources can be a good approximation to real human behaviour in cities, by measuring user-dependent indicators such as the number of tweets and/or users showing activities in a region of interest, in a specific period of time. [14] exploits geo-referenced data from Facebook and Foursquare to perform venue classification in a city, based on users interest profiling. [12] focuses on discovering the diverse social compositions and dynamics within the city of Pittsburgh, PA, through the analysis of social media data.

Recent studies also analysed the geographical and temporal variability of social media data when used for urban analytics purposes. [21] studied citizens' mobility patterns in Houston, San Francisco and Singapore by exploiting Foursquare data. An earlier study [22] used a large-scale geo-referenced Twitter dataset (with links to Foursquare venues) to identify urban sub-communities within cities. [20] studied the regional variability of categories of point of interests from the point of view of the temporal signature of social media activities.

Despite the abundance of previous works, research on the technical and contextual variability of spatio-temporal social media activities is currently lacking. Previous studies addressed the issue of social media population composition from an ethnographic [23], human computer interaction [25], or marketing perspective. We join the ongoing debate about the issues of big (social) data [4,11,13] by addressing the question of technical, geographical, demographic, and contextual diversity, and by providing evidence on intrinsic demographic and contextual bias in spatio-temporal social media activities.

3   Methodology

The goal of this paper is to investigate the impact of *geographic* (city), *demographic* (age, gender), *technological* (social media platform) and *contextual* (user role – visitor vs. citizen) factors on the perception of urban environments through social media. We are guided by the following three research questions:

RQ1: How does the choice of social media platform affect the spatio-temporal characterisation of an urban environment as observed through social media activities?

We hypothesise that significant differences between the amount and nature of social media activities across cities exist. We postulate an interplay between a social media platform of choice and a targeted urban environment. To test our hypothesis, we target several cities in the same period of time.

RQ2: How does the relationship of social media users with an urban environment affect the spatio-temporal characterisation of their social media activities?

The active population of a city is composed of people having different *roles* with respect to the urban environment. In addition to *residents*, cities temporarily host *local visitors* (i.e. people residing in a different city, but in the same country), and *tourists* (i.e. people residing in a different country). We hypothesise the amount and nature of social media activities to significantly differ across user roles in the targeted urban environment. To test our hypothesis, we infer the roles of our social media users with respect to the four investigated cities and explore the impact of this user partition in urban analytics.

RQ3: How do demographic properties of social media users affect the spatio-temporal characterisation of an urban environment as observed through social media activities?

We hypothesise that user attributes such as gender and age impact the spatio-temporal characterisation of a city. Analogous to **RQ2**, we explore this premise by partitioning our social media users according to these (automatically inferred) demographic properties.

To answer these questions, we crawled geo-located social media activities produced in **four cities** (Amsterdam, London, Paris, and Rome) over a period of **three weeks** (February 20th to March 12th 2014)[1]. For data gathering and exploration, we employ the `SocialGlass` platform, which will be introduced next.

3.1   Data Gathering and Pre-processing

Our study relies on data collected from Twitter and Instagram. We focus on geo-located content, i.e. micro posts augmented with explicit geographic coordinates either as measured by the localisation service of the user device, or inferred by the social network according to the IP address of the user.

---

[1] A motivation for this selection of cities and dates will be provided in Sect. 3.2.

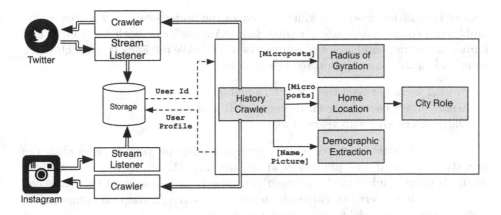

Fig. 1. Data gathering and pre-processing pipeline.

Figure 1 depicts the data gathering and pre-processing pipeline adopted in our study. The streaming APIs of each service push the content and metadata of each geo-located micro post produced in a given area of choice. Two listeners (one for each social network) monitor a stream each and store the content in a centralised repository. To support user-related analyses, the **History Crawler** retrieves, for each new user in the repository, all accessible historic content published by the user. Twitter's API allows the retrieval of the most recent 3,000 tweets of a user, while Instagram allows the retrieval of the entire post history. By taking into account the post history of a user, the **Home Location** module estimates the most likely home area, information which is often not provided in social network user profiles. We use a variation of the method described in [9] where, instead of a custom grid size we make use of geohashes. Once the coordinates of the estimated home location are identified, we use a reverse geocoding service (**Geo-names**) to determine the user's *city* and *country* of origin.

Functional to our study is the characterisation of the *role* a user plays in a city. The **City Role** module classifies users according to the relation of their (estimated) home city and the currently analysed urban area. We assign a user to one of the following three classes:

– *Resident*, if the user's home city is the same as the city under study;
– *Commuter*, if the user's home city is different from the city under study while both are in the same country; and
– *Foreign Tourist*, if the user's home location is in a different country from the city under study.

Lastly, the **Demographic Extraction** module estimates users' *gender* by means of a multi-modal decision tree classifier: starting from the profile picture and the name of a user, we combine the output of a state-of-the-art face detection and analysis component Face++[2] with the output of a dictionary-based

---

[2] Face++, http://www.faceplusplus.com.

gender recognition module[3], which consumes the home location of a user to disambiguate country-dependent names (e.g. "Andrea" can both be a male and female name, depending on the country of origin). We use Face++'s age classifier as-is and classify users into three age groups:

- *Young*: users between the ages of 15 and 30;
- *Middle-aged*: users between the ages of 31 and 45;
- *Older*: users above 45 years of age

We note that this age-based user grouping relies on younger ages than the literature of social and physiological science (e.g. [1,19]) as the use of social media is more familiar to the younger generations [10]. Indeed, in the *Older* age group, very few users are currently active on Twitter/Instagram compared to users of lower ages, yielding sparse data sources.

Whereas home location estimation based on textual evidence is an established research area with known high accuracies, this is yet the case in the inference of demographics from natural images. Thus, in order to determine the quality of the **Demographic Extraction** module we evaluate the face detection output as well as the age and gender classifiers on a manually labelled corpus of 628 culturally diverse Twitter user profiles. We find face recognition to be very precise in the identification of faces when present (*Precision* = 98.5 %). The moderate recall we observe (*Recall* = 65 %) is caused by profile images that portrait the user in a non-standard manner (partial visibility of the face, "artistic" image filters, etc.). Our gender classifier combines face analysis with name analysis and subsequently reaches a higher recall level, with a moderate drop in precision (85 %). Age detection has been performed only on profile pictures for which a face could be detected; there, we observed an age detection accuracy of 88 %.

3.2   Dataset

Our study focuses on four European cities: Amsterdam, London, Paris, and Rome. Their selection is motivated by their commonalities: they are (1) capitals of their respective countries; (2) popular touristic destinations, while being, at the same time, (3) characterised by a very vibrant business ecosystem, and by (4) the presence of a consistent and multi-cultural resident population. It is worth noting that the selection also reflects our intent of excluding profound cultural and economical differences, which might affect technological penetration and usage of social media. The four cities do exhibit differences which we find desirable for our analyses with respect to climate, geography (area and morphology) as well as size of the resident population.

Our window of data collection (February 20, 2014–March 12, 2014), which falls outside of national holidays or large-scale events in the target cities, was chosen to minimise the chances of spurious observations due to exceptional city usage anomalies. Both Stream Listener (cf. Fig. 1) were parameterised with

---

[3] Genderize, https://genderize.io/.

the bounding boxes associated with each of the cities in GeoNames[4], thus ensuring that only micro posts from within the desired city boundaries are added to our storage repository.

We gathered 1.87 million micro posts from 198 thousand users across the three weeks of data collection. Table 1 summarises the amount of geo-located micro posts retrieved for each considered city in the indicated time window. The total number of Twitter users varies between 5,600 (Amsterdam) and 49,200 (London). The total number of micro posts varies between 53,100 (tweets in Amsterdam) and 498,700 (tweets in London). Although the short crawling time window does not allow us to gather millions of micro posts per city, we believe that our data set is robust (and diverse) enough to make our exploratory analysis generalizable across social networks, cities and users.

3.3   Metrics

To compare the frequency and nature of social media activities across cities and diversity factors, we adopt five common measures:

- the absolute number of social media activity performed in the time span of crawling (#**Posts**);
- the unique number of social media users that performed geo-located activities in the observation period (#**Users**);
- the temporal distribution of social media activities in a city, averaged on a 24 h span (**Time**);
- the *temporal diversity* calculated using the *Gini Coefficient* over the temporal distribution of social media activities (#**Gini.Temporal**); and
- the *spatial diversity* calculated using the *Gini Coefficient* over the geographical distribution of social media activities (#**Gini.Spatial**).

The *Gini Coefficient* is a measure of statistical dispersion, commonly used to measure inequality. It is beginning to be used as an important metric in urban analytics as well, e.g. [27]. A coefficient of zero indicates a uniform distribution, while a coefficient of one indicates maximal inequality among values. Intuitively, values at the extreme of the range are very unlikely when analysing social media activities.

4   Findings

We now discuss our findings, and focus on each of the following sections on one particular diversity aspect, while keeping the remaining variables fixed.

---

[4] For instance, the bounding box of the Amsterdam area is available at http://www.geonames.org/2759794/amsterdam.html.

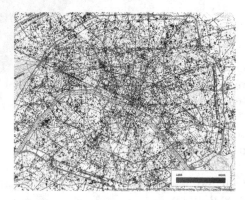

Fig. 2. User activities in Paris through the lens of Twitter.

Fig. 3. User activities in Paris through the lens of Instagram.

4.1 Social Media Diversity

Let us first explore the influence the social media type has on city sensing (**RQ1**). Table 1 contains an overview of the number of users and posts gathered across the four cities on the two platforms. Not surprisingly, a city's size has a significant effect on the absolute number of users and postings made from within the city boundaries: Amsterdam has less than a million inhabitants while London has more than 8 million - this difference in scale can also be found in the total number of users across the two platforms: 17,222 users posted from within Amsterdam while 109,280 users posted from within the city boundaries of London.

Table 1. Overview of the data collected across two platforms and four cities during a three week period. #Users and #Posts are expressed in thousands.

	Amsterdam		Rome		Paris		London	
	Twit.	Inst.	Twit.	Inst.	Twit.	Inst.	Twit.	Inst.
#Users	6.6	10.6	5.7	15.9	17.8	32.4	49.2	60.0
#Posts	53.2	67.4	73.3	108.7	369.4	261.6	498.7	434.9
Gini.Spatial	.630	.772	.538	.615	.224	.499	.439	.588
Gini.Temporal	.255	.330	.313	.341	.310	.327	.286	.321
Inhabitants (in millions)	0.8		2.6		2.2		8.5	

Across the four cities, Instagram is slightly more popular, drawing a larger number of users than Twitter. This is natural, considering that Instagram is a platform focused on images more than on text, and the fact that all four cities are major tourist destinations. As will be covered in more detail later, based on

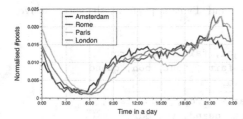

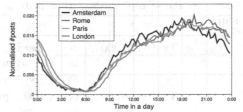

Fig. 4. User activities over time through the lens of Twitter.

Fig. 5. User activities over time through the lens of Instagram.

Table 2. #Users for which demographic and role information are available. #Users and #Posts are expressed in thousands.

		Gender		Age			Role			All
		Male	Female	Young	Mid-aged	Older	Resi.	Loca.	Fore.	
Twitter	Amsterdam	3.0	2.1	1.9	1.3	0.4	2.2	2.0	2.0	6.6
	Rome	1.2	1.0	0.9	0.6	0.2	1.7	0.6	0.9	5.7
	Paris	6.2	6.0	5.3	2.2	0.4	8.2	4.6	3.7	17.8
	London	21.7	17.7	15.4	8.7	1.8	22.7	16.0	7.0	49.2
Instagram	Amsterdam	2.6	3.4	2.4	0.9	0.1	4.0	1.0	4.4	10.6
	Rome	1.1	1.8	1.4	0.5	0.1	3.1	0.9	2.0	15.9
	Paris	7.1	11.0	6.7	2.2	0.3	13.1	3.6	11.6	32.4
	London	14.3	21.0	13.0	4.4	0.5	28.7	10.5	12.8	60.0

the results in Table 4 it is also evident that Instagram has both more tourists and a higher ratio between tourists and residents than Twitter.

Gini.Spatial provides us with an interesting difference between the two platforms in terms of spatial distribution: Instagram posts are clustered spatially much closer together than Twitter postings; most strikingly in Paris. Figures 2 and 3 visualise the spatial distributions of user activities in Paris on Twitter and Instagram, respectively. While Twitter users do not show an obvious preference in posting locations, Instagram users are more in favor of tourism locations such as the Eiffel Tower and Les Champs-Elysees. In addition to the preference of Instagram users towards specific locations, it can also be observed that these users show a higher activity intensity at places close to public transportation hubs. While not shown, similar observations hold for the other cities.

Analogous to *Gini.Spatial*, *Gini.Temporal* shows that Twitter users post more evenly over time than Instagram users. To further inspect the difference of posting time on Twitter and Instagram, Figs. 4 and 5 depict the distributions of #posts over time for all 4 cities on Twitter and in Instagram, respectively. Overall, the distributions based on Instagram data are very similar to each other across the four cities, which is not the case for the Twitter-based distributions. Moreover, the Instagram-based distributions have a single mode, i.e. the time point with locally maximal activities, around 1800; while the Twitter

Table 3. Paris: top words within Instagram and Twitter posts at the most active hours.

Twitter@1200	cest, paris, jai, fait, plus, trop, im, va, bien, faire, tout, bon, quand, vais, comme, ya.
Twitter@2100	cest, jai, paris, trop, plus, fait, bien, tout, va, quand, ya, mdr, demain, faire, bon, comme.
Instagram@1800	paris, love, france, fashion, beautiful, les, show, day, parisfashionweek, art, sunset, louvre, happy, sun, amazing.

distributions have multiple modes, occurring at around 1200 and 2100. To further understand the cause of this difference, Table 3 reports the top words in social media posts at the these hours in Paris. In counting word occurrence, we remove the stop words in French and English, and transform all words into lowercase. While the top words in Twitter are all French words, the top words in Instagram, on the contrary, are in English. This clearly indicates that there are more tourist users using Instagram in Paris, which is also reflected in the semantics of their posts, which include terms such as fashion, art, louvre, sunset etc.

4.2 User Role Diversity

We hypothesised that the role of users w.r.t the city which accommodates their activities is important to be considered in urban analytics (**RQ2**). To investigate this premise, we report the statistics of users' social media activities partitioned by user role in Table 4 – note that we only consider those users in this analysis, for whom we were able to attribute gender, age and user role.

Table 4. Comparative statistics of social media activities across social media and user roles. #Users and #Posts are expressed in thousands.

		Amsterdam			Rome			Paris			London		
		Resi.	Comm.	Fore.	Resi.	Comm.	Fore.	Resi.	Comm.	Fore.	Resi.	Comm.	Fore.
Twitter	#Users	2.2	2.0	2.0	1.7	0.6	0.9	8.2	4.6	3.7	22.7	16.0	7.0
	#Posts	26.9	15.2	10.3	52.2	4.8	9.3	293.4	43.8	26.9	319.1	74.0	59.3
	Gini.Spa	.721	.435	.765	.502	.591	.745	.233	.233	.473	.394	.513	.610
	Gini.Tem	.242	.295	.266	.332	.304	.298	.327	.279	.290	.295	.330	.270
Instagram	#Users	4.0	1.0	4.4	3.1	0.9	2.0	13.1	3.6	11.6	28.7	10.4	12.8
	#Posts	30.3	6.4	26.8	45.4	7.5	21.3	123.7	19.3	93.6	252.3	45.3	92.8
	Gini.Spa	.753	.658	.837	.556	.707	.804	.465	.470	.573	.553	.633	.689
	Gini.Tem	.333	.368	.324	.335	.329	.382	.337	.339	.317	.321	.331	.315

Residents vs. Foreign Tourists: The distribution of Twitter users shows a clear pattern across all four cities: there are more Residents than Foreign Tourists; we find the largest observed difference in London (23K Residents and 7K Foreign Tourists) and the smallest in Amsterdam. With the exception of Amsterdam, the same observation can be made about our Instagram users.

We believe the reason for Amsterdam to behave differently is due to tourists' average length of stay in each city: this metric is shortest in Amsterdam[5].

Commuters vs. Foreign Tourists: the trends we observe are similar to those just described for Residents vs. Foreign Tourists, though their magnitude is lower. Instagram is more popular with Foreign Tourists than Twitter, which in general is more often used by Commuters – in terms of #Users and #Posts. The exception here is Rome. We hypothesise the difference to be due to different demographic distribution of the social media population. However, we lack sufficient information to support our hypothesis, for which a validation will be sought in future work.

Residents vs. Commuters: Interesting to note for these two user groups is the ratio of Commuters and Residents. This ratio is largest in Amsterdam and London, implying that those two cities attract more commuters than Paris or Rome.

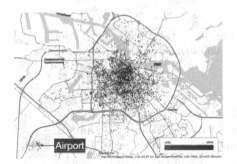 

Fig. 6. Resident activities in Amsterdam through the lens of Instagram.

Fig. 7. Foreign Tourist activities in Amsterdam through the lens of Instagram.

Analysis of Gini.Spatial: Based on the *Gini.Spatial* measure computed over the different user roles, we notice that Foreign Tourists are more clustered in specific areas than the other user roles across all cities.

Figures 6, 7, 8 and 9 show the spatial distribution of activities for the three user roles and the example cities of London and Amsterdam. We hypothesise that Foreign Tourists are also active at airports and thus include Amsterdam's

---

[5] E.g. https://www.rolandberger.com/media/pdf/Roland_Berger_European_Capital_City_Tourism_20120127.pdf.

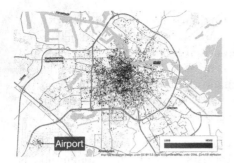

Fig. 8. Resident activities in London through the lens of Instagram.

Fig. 9. Commuter activties in London through the lens of Instagram.

Fig. 10. Temporal distribution of *Resident* activities (Twitter).

Fig. 11. Temporal distribution of *Commuter* activities (Twitter).

Schiphol Airport in the maps. The clusters of Foreign Tourist activities can be clearly distinguished, they are grouped around the city center and the major transportation hub (the airport), as compared in Figs. 6 and 7. Comparing the spatial distribution of Residents and Commuters we find in general the activity areas of Residents to be more balanced than those of Commuters, which can be shown in Figs. 8 and 9.

Analysis of Gini.Temporal: Based on the derived coefficients we find Commuters in Amsterdam and London to have the strongest preference of a posting time, compared to both Residents and Foreign Tourists. An explanation for this finding may be based on the premise that commuters post mostly *during* the commute. Rome and Paris, on the other hand, accommodate most of their workers inside the cities, resulting in a higher *Gini. Temporal* coefficient of Residents Figs. 10, 11 and 12 depict the temporal distributions of activities among the three user roles. Comparing the variation between cities in each of the graph, we conclude that Residents exhibit the largest variations among the four cities: Amsterdam Residents are the most (relatively) active during the day while least active at night; Residents in Paris and Rome, on the other hand, show a much higher number of activities at night. Though with less variation, similar patterns emerge for

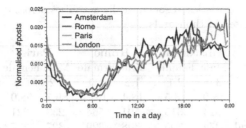

Fig. 12. Temporal distribution of *Foreign Tourist* activities (Twitter).

Foreign Tourists, indicating that each city possesses its individual 'gene', which can influence the temporal preference of Foreign Tourists' social media activities.

We also make the (sensible) observation that Commuters' activity frequencies decay earlier than those of Residents and Foreign Tourists alike — after 1800 most Commuters are likely to move towards their residential places outside the city boundaries. Interestingly, Commuters in Amsterdam have a dramatically higher (relative) number of activities than Commuters in other cities.

Table 5. Top words in Instagram posts of users with different user roles in Amsterdam.

Resident	amsterdam, spring, day, happy, like, morning, fun, today, good, sunday, friends, food, one, holland
Commuter	amsterdam, would, much, life, ever, person, win, blessed, chance, thx, amstelveen, goed, centraal.
Foreign Tourist	amsterdam, love, holland, netherlands, travel, canal, europe, happy, amazing, city, good, morning, museum.

Table 5 lists the most frequent words among users in Amsterdam according to their designated roles (and on the Instagram platform). Clear differences emerge: Residents' posts concern their daily lives (`today`, `fun`, `friends` etc.), Commuters' posts are more high-level (`life`, `ever`) and refer to locations (`amstelveen`, `centraal`), while Foreign Tourists' posts – as expected – revolve around traveling (`holland`, `travel`, `europe`), and tourist attractions (`canal`, `museum`).

4.3 User Demographic Diversity

Lastly we turn to an exploration of **RQ3**, that is, the effect of user demographics on their social media activities in the city.

Table 6. Comparative statistics of social media activities across user genders. #Users and #Posts are expressed in thousands.

		Amsterdam		Rome		Paris		London	
		Male	Female	Male	Female	Male	Female	Male	Female
Twitter	#Users	3.0	2.1	1.2	1.0	6.2	6.0	21.7	17.7
	#Posts	18.0	13.5	18.1	16.7	89.7	98.0	187.2	157.4
	Gini.Spatial	.624	.615	.501	.564	.233	.221	.444	.419
	Gini.Temporal	.274	.305	.308	.329	.327	.297	.291	.291
Instagram	#Users	2.6	3.4	1.1	1.8	7.1	11.0	14.3	21.0
	#Posts	13.6	18.5	12.6	20.3	50.8	78.1	88.7	135.5
	Gini.Spatial	.779	.770	.659	.634	.500	.499	.601	.577
	Gini.Temporal	.335	.348	.338	.349	.319	.343	.319	.331

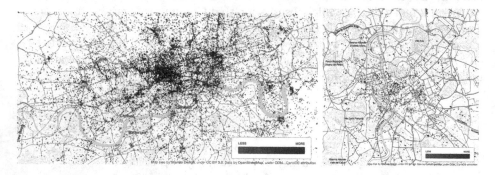

Fig. 13. *Male* user activities in London (Instagram).

Fig. 14. *Male* user activities in Rome (Twitter).

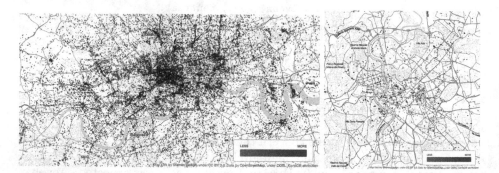

Fig. 15. *Female* user activities in London (Instagram).

Fig. 16. *Female* user activities in Rome (Twitter).

Diversity of User Gender. In Table 6 we report the by now familiar metrics separately for Male and Female users. Across all cities, there are more Male than Female users on Twitter, and more Female than Male users on Instagram, indicating a clear and divergent preference of social media portals. In terms of #Posts this trend is especially strong on Instagram.

Gender also plays a role in the spatial dimension of social media activities. Looking at the Gini.Spatial of user activities in Instagram, one could observe that the social media activities of Male users are in general more geographically clustered. This holds in all four cities, most evidently in London and Rome. Similar phenomenon can also be found in Twitter, with an exception in Rome, where it can be found that the activities of Female users are more clustered than that of Male users. Figures 13, 14, 15 and 16 visualise the different cases in London through Instagram, and Rome through Twitter.

Looking at *Gini. Temporal*, we observe no obvious pattern within our Twitter users, while the Instagram data shows that the temporal activities of Male users are more evenly distributed than that of Female users. Overall, the above observations suggest that Male and Female users are distinct in their social media activities in cities, which calls for a careful separation of user genders in relevant research.

Diversity of User Age. Lastly, we analyze the diversity of social media activities of users in different age groups. As stated before, we classify users into three categories: *Young, Mid-adged* and *Older*. As expected, we find from Table 7 that Young users use social media more than Mid-aged users, who in turn use it more than Older users across all cities and both platforms.

Table 7. Comparative statistics of social media activities across user ages (Young, Mid-aged, and Older). #Users and #Posts are expressed in thousands.

		Amsterdam			Rome			Paris			London		
		Y	M	O	Y	M	O	Y	M	O	Y	M	O
Twitter	#Users	1.9	1.3	0.4	0.9	0.6	0.1	5.2	2.2	0.4	15.4	8.7	1.8
	#Posts	12.6	9.6	2.7	17.0	9.4	2.8	99.6	30.0	5.1	149.0	77.4	17.0
	Gini.Spa	.614	.611	.654	.514	.533	.590	.234	.254	.308	.415	.479	.458
	Gini.Tem	.265	.312	0.333	.322	.316	.357	.311	.323	.318	.290	.288	.307
Instagram	#Users	2.4	0.9	0.1	1.4	0.5	0.1	6.7	2.2	0.3	13.0	4.4	0.5
	#Posts	13.8	5.4	0.9	15.9	6.5	9,7	52,3	18,1	2,8	87,9	29,9	3,6
	Gini.Spa	.790	.778	.813	.661	.679	.729	.502	.514	.474	.589	.605	.606
	Gini.Tem	.334	.353	.449	.351	.364	.363	.332	.334	.340	.324	.332	.350

Gini.Spatial shows for three of the four cities and both platforms that Older users have a more clustered area of social activities. An example is presented in Figs. 17, 18 and 19, where we have visualised the Instagram user activities of the three age groups for the city of Amsterdam. The tendencies for Mid-aged users to be more clustered than Young users exists as well, however, the contrast is less stark. Turning to *Gini. Temporal* we find that Young users post tend to post slightly more evenly over time than Older users who have a work-life schedule to adhere to.

Fig. 17. *Young* user activities in Amsterdam (Instagram).

Fig. 18. *Mid-aged* user activities in Amsterdam (Twitter).

Fig. 19. *Older* user activities in Amsterdam (Instagram).

4.4   Threats to Validity

We have taken a set of users and their social media micro posts and partitioned them along several dimensions to determine the effect (if any) on the urban environment as perceived through social media.

In our exploratory work, we have considered four cities across a period of three weeks, leading to a dataset of 200K users and nearly 2 million posts. These four cities were carefully selected to be different in some dimensions but not others, leading us to believe that the differences we observed will only increase with a wider choice of urban areas.

The main limitation (and threat to validity) of our work is the dataset size: millions of posts are generated on popular social medial portals within a single day. However, on the one hand the 3 week continuous time period is selected in data crawling to exclude large-scale events and national holidays, thus minimises the potential bias; one the other hand, as became evident in this paper, an in-depth and thorough analysis of the various dimensions of interest (contextual, demographic, technological and geographical) can only be conducted for a small number of cities within the scope of a paper.

A second threat that needs to be acknowledged is the exclusive use of geo-located micro posts, which form a small minority among all created micro posts on the social media platforms today. We cannot guarantee that our findings also hold in exactly the same manner for the set of non-geo-located posts. There may be (small) deviations.

Finally, we acknowledge the study to rely on user modelling techniques (i.e. to infer gender, age, and user role) that can be applied only when user profile information is available, and have limitations in terms of accuracy [5,6,24]. While an analysis of the performance of such techniques is outside the scope of this paper, we stress our reliance on state-of-the art and state-of-the-practice solutions.

5   Conclusions

With the increasing value of social media data in urban analytics and decision making, the need for an accurate reflection and representation of the urban environment through the lens of social media is becoming stronger every day.

While past works have commonly treated all social media users in an urban area as one and the same, we have shown that by focusing on different user segments, different reflections of the urban environment surface.

This diversity of users and their impact on urban analytics should not be treated as a problem however. On the contrary, diversity can play a fundamental role analyzing and understanding urban phenomenons. In this paper we have analysed the influence of multiple diversity factors anchored in technology, geography, demographics and context. In future work we plan to expand our analyses across a larger set of users, a larger set of cities and greater urbanised regions across continents as well as across a wider range of diversity factors.

Acknowledgements. This work was carried out on the Dutch national e-infrastructure with the support of SURF Cooperative.

References

1. Al-Zahrani, M.S., Bissada, N.F., Borawski, E.A.: Obesity and periodontal disease in young, middle-aged, and older adults. J. Periodontol. **74**(5), 610–615 (2003)
2. Balduini, M., Bocconi, S., Bozzon, A., Valle, E.D., Huang, Y., Oosterman, J., Palpanas, T., Tsytsarau, M.: A case study of active, continuous and predictive social media analytics for smart city. In: Proceedings of the Fifth International Conference on Semantics for Smarter Cities, S4SC 2014, vol. 1280, pp. 31–46, Aachen, Germany (2014). CEUR-WS.org
3. Balduini, M., Bozzon, A., Valle, E.D., Huang, Y., Houben, G.: Recommending venues using continuous predictive social media analytics. IEEE Internet Comput. **18**(5), 28–35 (2014)
4. Bernaschina, C., Catallo, I., Ciceri, E., Fedorov, R., Fraternali, P.: Towards an unbiased approach for the evaluation of social data geolocation. In: Proceedings of the 9th Workshop on Geographic Information Retrieval, GIR 2015, pp. 10:1–10:2. ACM, New York, NY, USA (2015)
5. Bocconi, S., Bozzon, A., Psyllidis, A., Titos Bolivar, C., Houben, G.-J.: Social glass: a platform for urban analytics and decision-making through heterogeneous social data. In: Proceedings of the 24th International Conference on World Wide Web, WWW 2015 Companion, pp. 175–178 (2015)
6. Bojic, I., Massaro, E., Belyi, A., Sobolevsky, S., Ratti, C.: Choosing the right home location definition method for the given dataset. In: Liu, T.-Y., et al. (eds.) SocInfo 2015. LNCS, vol. 9471, pp. 194–208. Springer, Heidelberg (2015). doi:10.1007/978-3-319-27433-1_14
7. Bozzon, A., Brambilla, M., Ceri, S., Mauri, A., Volonterio, R.: Pattern-based specification of crowdsourcing applications. In: Casteleyn, S., Rossi, G., Winckler, M. (eds.) ICWE 2014. LNCS, vol. 8541, pp. 218–235. Springer, Heidelberg (2014)
8. Bozzon, A., Fraternali, P., Galli, L., Karam, R.: Modeling crowdsourcing scenarios in socially-enabled human computation applications. J. Data Seman. **3**(3), 169–188 (2013)
9. Cheng, Z., Caverlee, J., Lee, K., Sui, D.Z.: Exploring millions of footprints in location sharing services. In: Proceedings of the 5th International AAAI Conference on Weblogs and Social Media, pp. 81–88. AAAI (2011)

10. Correa, T., Hinsley, A.W., De Zuniga, H.G.: Who interacts on the web?: the inter-section of users personality and social media use. Comput. Hum. Behav. **26**(2), 247–253 (2010)

11. Crampton, J.W., Graham, M., Poorthuis, A., Shelton, T., Stephens, M., Wilson, M.W., Zook, M.: Beyond the geotag: situating 'big data' and leveraging the potential of the geoweb. Cartography Geogr. Inf. Sci. **40**(2), 130–139 (2013)

12. Cranshaw, J., Schwartz, R., Hong, J.I., Sadeh, N.M.: The livehoods project: utilizing social media to understand the dynamics of a city. In: Breslin, J.G., Ellison, N.B., Shanahan, J.G., Tufekci, Z. (eds.) Proceedings of the 6th International AAAI Conference on Weblogs and Social Media. The AAAI Press (2012)

13. Boyd, D., Crawford, K.: Critical questions for big data. Inf. Commun. Soc. **15**(5), 662–679 (2012)

14. Del Bimbo, A., Ferracani, A., Pezzatini, D., D'Amato, F., Sereni, M.: Livecities: revealing the pulse of cities by location-based social networks venues and users analysis. In: Proceedings of the 23rd International Conference on World Wide Web, WWW 2014 Companion, Republic and Canton of Geneva, Switzerland, International World Wide Web Conferences Steering Committee, pp. 163–166 (2014)

15. Hawelka, B., Sitko, I., Beinat, E., Sobolevsky, S., Kazakopoulos, P., Ratti, C.: Geo-located Twitter as proxy for global mobility patterns. Cartography Geogr. Inf. Sci. **41**(3), 260–271 (2014)

16. Kindberg, T., Chalmers, M., Paulos, E.: Guest editors' introduction: urban computing. IEEE Pervasive Comput. **6**(3), 18–20 (2007)

17. Kostakos, V., O'Neill, E.: Cityware: urban computing to bridge online and real-world social networks. In: Foth, M. (ed.) Handbook of Research on Urban Informatics: The Practice and Promise of the Real-Time City. Information Science Reference, Hershey, Philadelphia, USA (2008)

18. Lee, R., Sumiya, K.: Measuring geographical regularities of crowd behaviors for Twitter-based geo-social event detection. In: Proceedings of the 2nd ACM SIGSPATIAL International Workshop on Location Based Social Networks, LBSN 2010, pp. 1–10. ACM, New York, NY, USA (2010)

19. Malatesta, C.Z., Izard, C.E., Culver, C., Nicolich, M.: Emotion communication skills in young, middle-aged, and older women. Psychol. Aging **2**(2), 193 (1987)

20. McKenzie, G., Janowicz, K., Gao, S., Gong, L.: How where is when? On the regional variability and resolution of geosocial temporal signatures for points of interest. Comput. Environ. Urban Syst. **54**, 336–346 (2015)

21. Noulas, A., Scellato, S., Lambiotte, R., Pontil, M., Mascolo, C.: A tale of many cities: universal patterns in human urban mobility. PLoS ONE **7**(5), e37027 (2012)

22. Noulas, A., Scellato, S., Mascolo, C., Pontil, M.: Exploiting semantic annotations for clustering geographic areas and users in location-based social networks. In: The Social Mobile Web, Papers from the ICWSM Workshop, Barcelona, Catalonia, Spain, 21 July 2011

23. Palfrey, J., Gasser, U.: Born Digital: Understanding the First Generation of Digital Natives. Basic Books Inc., New York (2008)

24. Paraskevopoulos, P., Palpanas, T.: Fine-grained geolocalisation of non-geotagged tweets. In: Proceedings of the IEEE/ACM International Conference on Advances in Social Networks Analysis and Mining, pp. 105–112. ACM (2015)

25. Pater, J.A., Miller, A.D., Mynatt, E.D.: This digital life: a neighborhood-based study of adolescents' lives online. In: Proceedings of the 33rd Annual ACM Conference on Human Factors in Computing Systems, pp. 2305–2314. ACM, New York, NY, USA (2015)

26. Psyllidis, A., Bozzon, A., Bocconi, S., Titos Bolivar, C.: A platform for urban analytics and semantic data integration in city planning. In: Celani, G., Sperling, D.M., Franco, J.M.S. (eds.) Computer-Aided Architectural Design Futures. The Next City - New Technologies and the Future of the Built Environment. CCIS, vol. 527, pp. 21–36. Springer, Heidelberg (2015)
27. Tranos, E., Nijkamp, P.: Mobile phone usage in complex urban systems: a space-time, aggregated human activity study. J. Geogr. Syst. **17**(2), 157–185 (2015)
28. Wakamiya, S., Lee, R., Sumiya, K.: Crowd-based urban characterization: Extracting crowd behavioral patterns in urban areas from Twitter. In: Proceedings of the 3rd ACM SIGSPATIAL International Workshop on Location-Based Social Networks, pp. 77–84. ACM, New York, NY, USA (2011)
29. Wang, Z., Zhou, X., Zhang, D., Yang, D., Yu, Z.: Cross-domain community detection in heterogeneous social networks. Pers. Ubiquit. Comput. **18**(2), 369–383 (2014)
30. Zheng, Y., Capra, L., Wolfson, O., Yang, H.: Urban computing: concepts, methodologies, and applications. ACM Trans. Intell. Syst. Technol. **5**(3), 38:1–38:55 (2014)

Short Research Papers

Data-Aware Service Choreographies Through Transparent Data Exchange

Michael Hahn[✉], Dimka Karastoyanova, and Frank Leymann

Institute of Architecture of Application Systems (IAAS),
University of Stuttgart, Stuttgart, Germany
{michael.hahn,dimka.karastoyanova,
frank.leymann}@iaas.uni-stuttgart.de

Abstract. Our focus in this paper is on enabling the decoupling of data flow, data exchange and management from the control flow in service compositions and choreographies through novel middleware abstractions and realization. This allows us to perform the data flow of choreographies in a peer-to-peer fashion decoupled from their control flow. Our work is motivated by the increasing importance and business value of data in the fields of business process management, scientific workflows and the Internet of Things, all of which profiting from the recent advances in data science and Big data. Our approach comprises an application life cycle that inherently introduces data exchange and management as a first-class citizen and defines the functions and artifacts necessary for enabling transparent data exchange. Moreover, we present an architecture of the supporting system that contains the Transparent Data Exchange middleware, which enables the data exchange and management on behalf of service choreographies and provides methods for the optimization of the data exchange during their execution.

Keywords: Service choreographies · Transparent data exchange · Decentralized data flow · Data flow optimization

1 Introduction

With the advances in the fields of Big Data and the Internet of Things (IoT) the importance of data in terms of its business value and as a driver for gaining advantages over competitors is increasing significantly. The impact of this development on the domain of Business Process Management (BPM) has already been documented [9,11]. In the domain of eScience data-centric aspects of computations belong to the core requirements [1,12]. In recent years a convergence of approaches from BPM and eScience is taking place and business processes are successfully applied to automate computer-based experiments and scientific calculations. Through our experience in the fields of BPM and eScience, and based on existing literature, we argue that business processes need to reflect this paradigm shift to data-awareness and provide support for the efficient integration and exchange of heterogeneous data through a central role in the BPM life cycle.

© Springer International Publishing Switzerland 2016
A. Bozzon et al. (Eds.): ICWE 2016, LNCS 9671, pp. 357–364, 2016.
DOI: 10.1007/978-3-319-38791-8_20

Business processes implemented through service compositions can be specified by following one of two paradigms: service orchestrations and choreographies [6]. The former ones are also known as workflows and are modeled from the viewpoint of one party which acts as a central coordinator. Service choreographies provide a global perspective of the potentially complex conversations between multiple interacting services, which are often implemented by workflows again. Each party that takes part in the collaboration, a so-called participant, is able to model its conversations with the other parties by specifying corresponding message exchanges with other participants [5]. Participants in a choreography can communicate in a direct, peer-to-peer manner without requiring any central coordinator that controls their interaction. Service choreographies have been successfully applied in both the business and eScience domain [2,6,8,14].

Existing research already shows that conducting the data exchange in a decentralized manner provides valuable performance benefits [3,4,7], however it fails to accommodate all requirements from both BPM and eScience perspective. For example, the model-driven approach presented in [8] introduces capabilities to model and enact data exchange on the level of choreographies, but fails to incorporate mechanisms to decouple the control and data flow since data is still passed through message exchanges between participants. The works of Barker et al. [2,3] introduce a proprietary service choreography language and a framework for its execution, and a framework based on service proxies, respectively. Both works show performance improvements due to decentralized data exchange in a choreography-like manner, but miss other optimization opportunities like transparent data exchange in parallel to the actual control flow of the conversations. Approaches like [7] and [4], rely on the decomposition of service compositions into so-called service proxies or triggers based on analysis of their data dependencies. A central coordinator controls the tightly coupled control and data flow, whereas the decoupling of control commands and data exchange happens only on the level of the invoked services.

In this work we present our vision for an approach towards introducing data as a first-class citizen in service choreographies. With this approach we want to provide support for the specification and handling of data-related aspects throughout the whole BPM life cycle and to resolve the tight coupling of data flow from control flow, which in choreographies results mainly from the fact that data can only be passed through pre-specified conversations between participants. Towards this goal, in Sect. 2 we introduce an extended choreography management life cycle that supports data-related aspects throughout all phases. In Sect. 3 an architecture for a modeling and enactment environment is presented that implements the introduced data-aware life cycle based on a new Transparent Data Exchange (TraDE) middleware layer. The research challenges we face towards achieving our goals are described in Sect. 4. Finally, we present a summary and conclusions in Sect. 5.

2   Approach

To account for data-awareness in service choreographies we use an approach of introducing modeling abstractions, data exchange and management methods to the traditional BPM life cycle. In Fig. 1 we present our proposal for a data-aware service choreography management life cycle that is based on the traditional BPM life cycle [16] and available extensions for choreographies in [6,14]. In the following, we describe the life cycle phases, their relations, the software artifacts they produce or consume and how each of the phases employs the new *TraDE methods* to support data awareness as a separate concern in the development and execution of a choreography.

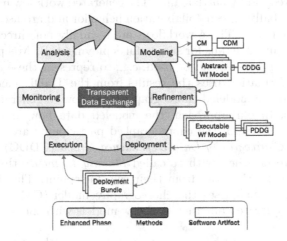

Fig. 1. Data-aware service choreography management life cycle

The *TraDE methods* bundle a set of data-related methods and transformations to support data awareness throughout the whole life cycle and potential optimizations regarding the data perspective of choreographies.

In the *Modeling* phase the different stakeholders, e.g., domain experts of different fields in eScience or business specialists from different companies, who want to collaborate, define their interactions by specifying corresponding participants and their conversations, called also message exchanges, in a choreography model. The choreography model can be seen as a collaboration contract on which all participants agree. The contract contains the definition of visible behavior of the participants that can potentially be realized using executable workflows and the message exchange definitions. BPEL4Chor models [5], BPMN collaboration models or Let's Dance models [18] can be used as underlying modeling notation to represent choreography models. Our approach extends this collaboration contract with the data being exchanged through the conversations between the different partners by introducing an explicit data model and data flow between the participants on the level of the choreography. The resulting *Choreography Data Model* (CDM) provides the foundations for the data awareness in the later life cycle phases and allows us to realize most of the phase transitions and model enhancements in a (semi-)automated manner. Based on the analysis of the specified message exchanges a corresponding CDM can be generated and then manually refined or extended for further use by the TraDE methods in later life cycle phases.

The target of the *Analysis* phase in conjunction with the modeling phase is to produce choreography and workflow models that are optimal with respect to a set of requirements. Additionally, already existing models from earlier life cycle iterations together with their monitoring data are taken into consideration to find optimizations for the models.

As in the classical BPM life cycle at the end of the modeling phase a *Transformation* step takes place and produces an abstract workflow model for each of the specified choreography participants. The generated workflow models together implement the globally agreed collaboration behavior and are used as templates in the refinement phase. These workflows are normally not directly executable since they lack required details for successful deployment. BPMN process models or abstract BPEL processes can be used, e.g., to represent these abstract workflows. The transformation uses the results from the TraDE methods like the defined CDM and the modeled choreography data flow to generate the abstract workflow models. In our approach, the modeled data flow and the resulting data dependencies between the choreographed participants are transformed to a corresponding *Choreography Data Dependence Graph* (CDDG). Furthermore, the workflows are enriched with so-called *Staging Elements* that reflect data exchange between participants from their own viewpoint. The final output of the modeling phase comprises the choreography model (CM), its data model (CDM) and the generated abstract workflow models with the overall CDDG as shown in Fig. 1.

During the *Refinement* phase IT specialists refine the generated abstract workflow models into executable ones. This comprises the specification of the participants internal logic by adding new model constructs like activities, the control flow and data flow between them, as well as the required configuration data for the envisaged run time environment where the choreographed workflows will be executed. When specifying corresponding data flow between the activities the IT specialists have to model where and how the shared data is used in the workflow. After the manual refinement is completed we are analyzing the workflow models to extract the new information about the internal data dependencies and the data flow. For each executable workflow model a so-called *Participant Data Dependence Graph* (PDDG) is generated. For this, the CDDG created during transformation is split into subgraphs where each subgraph represents the data dependencies of one participant (PDDG). Additionally, all activities added during refinement that read or write data from or to a Data Object are added to the PDDG. At the end of the refinement phase a collection of executable workflow models together with their PDDGs is available for deployment (Fig. 1).

In the *Deployment* phase the executable workflow models are packaged in the required *Deployment Bundles* format and deployed to the target workflow middleware. It is the responsibility of the TraDE methods to identify the appropriate static or dynamic deployment strategy based on information like data dependence graphs, monitoring data or manually defined deployment requirements.

After the executable workflow models are deployed they enter the *Execution* phase. By instantiating one or more of the deployed models, e.g., on behalf of a client's requests, the overall choreography is executed through the started interrelated workflow instances which together realize the modeled behavior of the choreography. In the following we use the term *choreography instance* introduced in [15] to describe these groups of interrelated workflow instances without implying that there is a central entity coordinating them. During the execution of the choreography instance each of the participating workflow instances produces a set of events that provide information about executed activities, control and data flow, occurred exceptions or faults and many other aspects. These events are analyzed by the TraDE methods to detect potential data flow optimizations during run time of a choreography instance, e.g., in terms of strategies for optimal data placement, transferring data in advance based on predictions calculated using monitoring information or optimal data life cycle management so that the data is only stored as long as required and as short as possible.

The execution events are collected and analyzed during the *Monitoring* phase. For the monitoring of choreography instances the event data of the involved workflow instances needs to be analyzed, combined and interpreted. For example, the status of the choreography instance has to be calculated based on the status of all workflow instances. The resulting data can be expressed in form of higher-level choreography events, so that the interpretation and combination is done only once and other interested parties are able to directly consume the choreography events. An environment that enables the monitoring of choreographies is introduced in [17]. To support data-awareness, the explicitly modeled data flow and any data flow adaptations during run time triggered by optimization have to be captured.

3   Architecture

Figure 2 shows the overall architecture of the software system enabling the modeling and enactment of data-aware service choreographies. Each participant has a *Choreography and Orchestration Modeling Environment* to model his part of the overall choreography. The modeling environment supports the transformation of the choreography model to a set of abstract workflows where each of the abstract workflows can be further refined to an executable workflow model. The TraDE facilities are integrated into the modeling environment and enable the analysis of the choreography data model (CDM), the generation of the choreography (CDDG) and participant data dependence graphs (PDDG) and the optimization of data-related aspects on the level of both the choreography and the workflow models based on analysis results.

The deployment bundles contain the executable workflow models and their PDDGs. The workflow models (WfM) representing the choreographed services are deployed (depicted by the solid black arrows in Fig. 2) into a corresponding workflow management system (WfMS) for execution and the PDDGs to a TraDE middleware. The deployed WfMs and PDDGs are necessary to conduct the overall choreography and the exchange, placement and staging of the related data in an optimal manner. The TraDE middleware uses the information collected in the PDDGs and the CDDG as well as event data of previously executed choreography

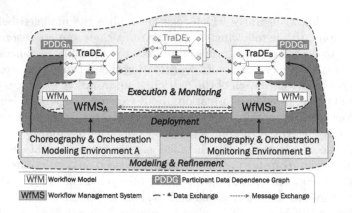

Fig. 2. Architecture of an environment that supports the modeling and enactment of data-aware service choreographies

executions to perform and optimize the data exchange and placement according to the chosen optimization strategy.

As shown in Fig. 2, the TraDE middleware is not a single software component, but rather a network of multiple TraDE nodes in a distributed system. The TraDE middleware clients experience the whole collection of nodes as one single coherent middleware [13]. During choreography execution the WfMSs executing the participant workflows communicate with each other through messages that transport data or trigger corresponding functionality at other participants. In addition, the WfMS and its associated TraDE node are also communicating in terms of handling and optimizing the data exchange between the participants. Based on how the two middleware systems are integrated, this communication looks different. One approach is to extend the WfMS so that it actively invokes corresponding functionality at the TraDE node through its APIs. Alternatively, the TraDE node can be loosely integrated with the WfMS by consuming all emitted execution events of the WfMS to react accordingly based on the information stored in the PDDGs, i.e., reading or writing data through the APIs of the WfMS and transferring it to other TraDE nodes. The TraDE middleware also emits data-related events that allow for the monitoring of the data staging, placement and exchange to ensure that the optimized data flow is still carried out according to the choreography and workflow models.

4   Research Challenges

On the road towards realizing our Transparent Data Exchange vision we face research challenges related to both the modeling aspects of data-aware choreographies and execution and monitoring aspects. The challenges are on the levels of new abstractions, architecture and realization mechanisms.

Through the extension of the traditional BPM life cycle with data management functions we provide a preliminary approach towards rendering data exchange in choreographies and orchestrations as first-class citizen. The architecture we presented accommodates our vision for transparent data exchange and is supported by the newly introduced modeling artifacts like CDM, CDDG, and PDDG. The modeling of choreographies decoupling data exchange from their conversations will require in addition formal definitions of CDM, CDDG, PDDG and corresponding data analysis and optimization algorithms to derive the dependency graphs, suggest improvements, and allow for propagating the data dependencies from the level of the workflow models by refining the PDDGs. Therefore, realizing the transformation step during the modeling and the refinement phase will be one of our major objectives. Addressing the challenges with respect to the modeling aspects is a prerequisite to enable the execution of data-aware choreographies. A major objective of ours is the architecture and realization of the distributed TraDE middleware, the TraDE nodes and the communication protocols among nodes, the most appropriate integration approach with the WfMS as well as enforcing data security. The TraDE middleware will also (a) rely on fault-tolerant, asynchronous data exchange among participants for which we will define models and protocols, (b) will incorporate data shipping mechanisms, which poses the question of how these mechanisms are going to be integrated into the WfMS and ESB middlewares, (c) will enable data reuse across choreographies and services, which is a matter of data identification and mechanisms for their transparent delivery, and (d) will allow for the use of different data sources and formats by using our pluggable data management framework SIMPL [10]. A challenge concerning all components of the execution environment is the correlation of data exchange to the correct instance of a choreography, workflow or service. Monitoring of the data exchange, data staging and placement will require special attention and will provide valuable input to our optimization algorithms and strategies, which are also part of the conceptual work with respect to the execution perspective of our vision.

5   Conclusion

The efficient exchange of data between choreographed services is a crucial factor in classical data-centric domains like eScience. However, with evolving paradigms like Big data or IoT data exchange becomes also an important factor for the business domain. Existing research showed that in terms of data exchange the most promising approach is to decouple the data flow from the control flow definition and handle it in a decentralized manner by exchanging the data directly between the composed services. While most of the existing approaches only utilize the performance benefits from decentralizing the data flow, we want to provide further optimizations throughout all life cycle phases and especially during choreography run time. Towards this goal, we introduced a data-aware service choreography management life cycle that is enriched with so-called TraDE methods for data flow analysis and optimization. Furthermore, a system architecture that implements the extended life cycle was introduced. Based on our experiences and the discussed related work, we presented a set of research challenges that represent our road map for future work.

Acknowledgment. The authors would like to thank the German Research Foundation (DFG) for financial support of the project within the Cluster of Excellence in Simulation Technology (EXC 310/2) at the University of Stuttgart.

References

1. Barga, R., Gannon, D.: Scientific versus business workflows. In: Taylor, I.J., Deelman, E., Gannon, D.B., Shields, M. (eds.) Workflows for e-Science: Scientific Workflows for Grids, pp. 9–16. Springer, Heidelberg (2007)
2. Barker, A., et al.: Choreographing web services. IEEE Trans. Serv. Comput. **2**, 152–166 (2009)
3. Barker, A., et al.: Reducing data transfer in service-oriented architectures: the circulate approach. IEEE Trans. Serv. Comput. **5**, 437–449 (2012)
4. Binder, W., et al.: Decentralized orchestration of composite web services. In: ICWS 2006 (2006)
5. Decker, G., et al.: BPEL4Chor: extending BPEL for modeling choreographies. In: ICWS 2007 (2007)
6. Decker, G., et al.: An introduction to service choreographies. Inf. Technol. **50**, 122–127 (2008)
7. Liu, D., et al.: Data-flow distribution in FICAS service composition infrastructure. In: ICPDCS 2002 (2002)
8. Meyer, A., et al.: Automating data exchange in process choreographies. Inf. Syst. **53**, 296–329 (2015)
9. Meyer, S., et al.: Towards modeling real-world aware business processes. In: WoT 2011 (2011)
10. Reimann, P., et al.: SIMPL-a framework for accessing external data in simulation workflows. In: BTW (2011)
11. Schmidt, R., Möhring, M., Maier, S., Pietsch, J., Härting, R.-C.: Big data as strategic enabler - insights from central European enterprises. In: Abramowicz, W., Kokkinaki, A. (eds.) BIS 2014. LNBIP, vol. 176, pp. 50–60. Springer, Heidelberg (2014)
12. Slominski, A.: Adapting BPEL to scientific workflows. In: Taylor, I.J., Deelman, E., Gannon, D.B., Shields, M. (eds.) Workflows for e-Science: Scientific Workflows for Grids, pp. 208–226. Springer, Heidelberg (2007)
13. Tanenbaum, A.S., Van Steen, M.: Distributed Systems. Prentice-Hall, Upper Saddle River (2007)
14. Weiß, A., Karastoyanova, D.: A life cycle for coupled multi-scale, multi-field experiments realized through choreographies. In: EDOC 2014 (2014)
15. Weiß, A., Andrikopoulos, V., Hahn, M., Karastoyanova, D.: Rewinding and repeating scientific choreographies. In: Debruyne, C., Panetto, H., Meersman, R., Dillon, T., Weichhart, G., An, Y., Ardagna, C.A. (eds.) On the Move to Meaningful Internet Systems: OTM 2015 Conferences. LNCS, vol. 9415, pp. 337–347. Springer, Heidelberg (2015)
16. Weske, M.: Business Process Management: Concepts, Languages, Architectures. Springer Science & Business Media, Heidelberg (2012)
17. Wetzstein, B., et al.: Cross-organizational process monitoring based on service choreographies. In: SAC 2010 (2010)
18. Zaha, J.M., Barros, A., Dumas, M., ter Hofstede, A.: Let's dance: a language for service behavior modeling. In: Meersman, R., Tari, Z. (eds.) OTM 2006. LNCS, vol. 4275, pp. 145–162. Springer, Heidelberg (2006)

Formal Specification of RESTful Choreography Properties

Adriatik Nikaj$^{(\boxtimes)}$ and Mathias Weske

Hasso Plattner Institute, University of Potsdam, Potsdam, Germany
{adriatik.nikaj,mathias.weske}@hpi.de

Abstract. BPM community has developed a rich set of languages for modeling interactions. In previous work, we argue that business process choreographies are suited for modeling REST-based interactions. To this end, RESTful choreographies have been introduced as an extension of business process choreographies. However, RESTful choreographies do not provide information about the validity of interactions. In this paper, we introduce formal completeness properties. These properties support developers to verify REST-based interactions. The approach is motivated by an example of an examination procedure in the context of a massive open online course.

1 Introduction

With the surging use of REST architectural style [1], there is a need to model REST-based interactions from a global perspective. RESTful choreography [2] is a language for modeling RESTful interactions between two or more participants. Additionally, this language is situated as a middle ground between the business perspective of the business process choreography and the implementation perspective of RESTful APIs involved in the interaction. RESTful choreography language itself constitutes an extension of BPMN choreography [3] with REST-specific information.

However, RESTful choreographies lack a formal specification, thus not providing criteria for validating its correctness. To overcome this incompleteness, this paper introduces a formal specification of the RESTful choreography and two properties that each choreography diagram should satisfy for being considered complete. This allows developers to automatically check the validity of a RESTful choreography before using it, e.g., as an skeleton for the development of RESTful APIs.

The rest of the paper is structured as follows. In Sect. 2, RESTful choreographies are briefly explained and a running example is introduced. Section 3 present the reader with related work. Section 4 introduces the formal specification of business process choreography and the RESTful choreography as an extension of the former. Subsequently, Sect. 5 describes two properties of RESTful choreography, which, if satisfied, render it complete. In Sect. 6, we provide an evaluation on the usefulness of the formalizations and the completeness properties. Lastly, we conclude our paper and provide insights about future work in Sect. 7.

© Springer International Publishing Switzerland 2016
A. Bozzon et al. (Eds.): ICWE 2016, LNCS 9671, pp. 365–372, 2016.
DOI: 10.1007/978-3-319-38791-8_21

2   Foundations

RESTful choreography diagram is introduced in [2] with the aim of bridging the conceptual gap between the BPMN business process choreography [3] and its implementation as a RESTful interaction [1]. It is an enhancement of the BPMN choreography diagram with REST-specific annotations.

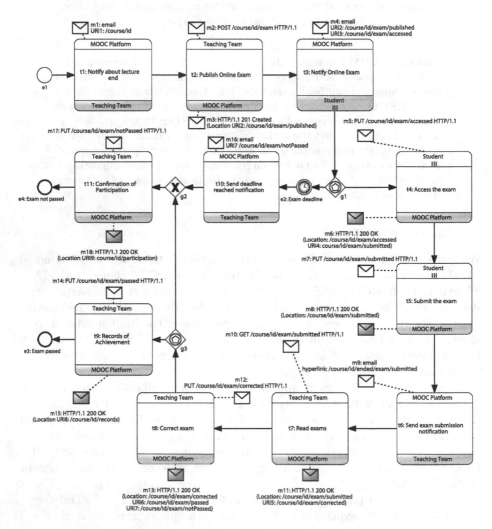

Fig. 1. RESTful choreography for massive open online course

To motivate our approach we introduce a RESTful choreography diagram (see Fig. 1) that models an example of a massive open online course (MOOC) inspired by openHPI (https://open.hpi.de/). We focus only on the online examination procedure taking place after all lectures are published.

The main participants are the teaching team, MOOC platform, and the students. The teaching team is responsible for publishing the exam and correcting the exams submitted by the students. The MOOC platform is a system which facilitates the interaction between the teaching team and the students by providing a web interface and sending emails to coordinate the activities of the participants. Once the teaching team publishes the exam on the MOOC platform, the students are reminded from the latter. Students, then, may access the exam at any time before the deadline. In case the students access the exam, they have to submit it. The teaching team follows up with the exam correction and submits two possible outcomes into the MOOC platform. Either the exam is passed or not passed. If the exam is passed a *Record of Achievement* is created for the students to be accessed. Else, the students can access a *Confirmation of Participation*.

As it can be observed from Fig. 1, the RESTful choreography is a business process choreography with additional REST information. The REST information is embedded in the message exchanged between participants. Each message can represent a REST request or response, or an email in case of server to client updates, e.g., MOOC platform informs the teaching team after an exam is submitted by the student.

3 Related Work

As a language which resides between the business processes collaboration and its platform specific application, RESTful choreography can be compared to BPEL4Chor [4]. BPEL4Chor is an extension of BPEL [5] with choreography-related concepts. It differs from RESTful choreography because it is based on WSDL [6] and SOAP [7].

A similar work is introduced in [8]. The authors use UML sequence diagrams [9] to model REST conversation. However, their approach is limited to the modeling of the interactions between a single client and a single REST API. While, the benefit of our approach is the unlimited restriction of the number of participants and the global view on common REST resources addressed by several participants.

The same limitation holds for the RESTful conversation proposed in [10] i.e. it models the REST-based interaction between one client and one server. Despite being an extension of BPMN choreography diagram, the RESTful conversation differs from our approach in the modeling goal because it omits the textual description of the choreography task. Hence, it focuses only on the REST-based interaction and not in the business logic behind it.

4 Formal RESTful Choreography

In this section we introduce a formal definition of business process choreography, over which the RESTful choreography diagram is subsequently defined. The formalization of business process choreography is not a complete 1 to 1 mapping of the BPMN choreography specification [3] (specified by means of a metamodel) but is limited to only the concepts needed for our extension. E.g., we do not define the call choreography or the sub-choreography.

Definition 1 (Business Process Choreography). *A Business Process Choreography is a tuple* $C = (N, S, P, M, etype, gtype, init, recip, initm, retm)$ *where:*

- $N = T \cup E \cup G$ *is finite set of nodes.* T *is a non-empty, finite set of choreography tasks.* E *is finite set of events. And,* G *is a finite set of gateways. The sets* $T, E, G \subseteq N$ *are all pairwise mutually disjoint.*
- $S \subseteq N \times N$ *is a set of sequence flows.*
- P *is a set of participants.*
- M *is a set of messages.*
- $etype : E \mapsto \{start, intermediate, end\}$ *assigns an event type to each of the events of the choreography.*
- $gtype : G \mapsto \{xor, ebased, or, and\}$ *assigns a gateway type to each of the gateways of the choreography.*
- $init : T \mapsto P$ *assigns a participant as initiator to each of the choreography tasks of the choreography.*
- $recip : T \mapsto P$ *assigns a participant as recipient to each of the choreography tasks of the choreography.*
- $initm : T \mapsto M$ *assigns a message as initiating to each of the choreography tasks of the choreography*
- $retm : T \mapsto M \cup nil$ *assigns a message as return to each of the choreography task of the choreography. nil stands for no return message.*

Moreover, we can formalize the basic rule of the choreography diagram: The initiator of each task is always aware of the immediate previous interactions, hence making the choreography enforceable [11]. In order to formally express the rule of *choreography task sequencing* we need the following notations: $p_a = (n1, n2, \ldots, n_k)$ is a path if $\forall i = 1..k, (n_i, n_{i+1}) \in S$; $\bullet t = \{t' \in T \mid \exists p_a = (t', n_1 \ldots n_k, t) \wedge \forall i = 1..k, n_i \notin T\}$ is the set of all direct-preceding tasks of t; $T^0 = \{t \in T \mid \bullet t = \phi\}$ is the set of all choreography tasks that have no direct predecessor; $T^* = T \backslash T^0$ is the complement of set T^0. Using these notations, we have:

Definition 2 (Choreography Task Sequencing). *Given a choreography diagram* $C = (N, S, P, M, etype, gtype, init, recip, initm, retm)$ *and a participant* $p \in P$, *the basic rule of choreography task sequencing holds iff*

$$\forall t \in T^*, p = init(t) \Rightarrow \forall t' \in \bullet t, p = init(t') \vee p = recip(t')$$

Next, we define RESTful choreography, which extends Definition 1.

Definition 3 (RESTful Choreography). *RESTful choreography* $C_R = (N, S, P, M, U, etype, gtype, init, recip, initm, retm, server, mtype, hyperlink)$ *is an extension of business process choreography with the following concepts:*

- U is a set of URIs.
- $server : P \mapsto \{0,1\}$ marks all participants that have a server role in a RESTful interaction.
- $mtype : M \mapsto \{req, res, email\}$ maps any message exchanged in a RESTful choreography to one of three message types: request; response; and, email. We, then, have $\forall t \in T, server\,(recip\,(t)) = 1 \Leftrightarrow mtype\,(initm\,(t)) = req \Leftrightarrow mtype\,(retm\,(t)) = res$
- $hyperlink : M \mapsto 2^U$ maps each message of the RESTful choreography to set of URIs, which play the role of hyperlinks that the client can use to continue the interaction with the server. We have $\forall m \in M, mtype\,(m) = req \Rightarrow |hyperlink\,(m)| = 1$ because a REST request is composed of a single REST verb and a single URI.

5   Completeness of RESTful Choreographies

In this section we introduce two properties that render a RESTful choreography complete. First we provide the definition of completeness.

Definition 4 (Completeness of RESTful Choreography). *A RESTful choreography C_R is said to be complete, if it is hyperlink complete and it has a correct resource behaviour.*

In a RESTful interactions, hyperlink is the client's main mean of navigation through communication with the server during the conversational flow. The only way to communicate with the server is by sending a request to a specific URI. As a response, the server provides the client with additional hyperlinks for her to follow in future interactions. For server to client direction, an email communication is assumed. We do not explicitly take into consideration RESTful Push Interactions [12] because they are a special case of the normal RESTful interaction, e.g., to notify the client about new updates the role of server and clients are briefly exchanged.

To represent the fundamental importance of the hyperlink, as a steering tool for guiding the RESTful choreography, we introduce the property of hyperlink completeness. A RESTful choreography is hyperlink complete if and only if all the URIs used in the REST requests are introduced previously to the clients in the form of hyperlinks. Naturally, the first occurring choreography tasks are excluded from this criteria because they have no preceding task. Hyperlink completeness also requires that all hyperlinks sent between participants are modelled in the RESTful choreography.

Definition 5 (Hyperlink Completeness). *RESTful choreography is hyperlink complete if a participant p sends a request via URI to the server in task t, then for all execution paths leading to task t the request URI is passed to participant p embedded in a response or email message. Formally:*

$$\forall t \in T^*, server\,(recip\,(t)) = 1 \Rightarrow \forall t^0 \in T^0, \forall p_a = (t_0, .., t), \exists t' \in p_a(t^0, .., t) \mid$$
$$(init\,(t) = init\,(t') \wedge URI\,(req\,(t)) = hyperlink\,(res\,(t')))$$
$$\vee (init\,(t) = recip\,(t') \wedge URI\,(req\,(t)) = hyperlink\,(email\,(t')))$$

The second property is about checking the behaviour of REST resources in that whether or not the resources involved in the choreography behave as expected. Defining this property, assures the users of RESTful choreography that each REST resource does not undergo undesired behaviour. This is particularly useful in case of RESTful choreography due to many participants accessing common resources, e.g., the resource *exam* is accessed by the teaching team and the students multiple times in the choreography.

Definition 6 (Behavioural Correctness). *A RESTful choreography is said to have a correct resource behaviour if all REST resources behave correctly. A resource is said to behave correctly if it:*

- *is created with a POST /resources or PUT /resources/id*
- *changes its state with a PUT /resources/id/newState*
- *is accessed with a GET /resources/id/State yielding no state change*
- *is deleted with a DELETE /resource/id*
- *can only be accessed or modified after it is created and before it is deleted.*

Nevertheless, these conditions apply only when we use a REST request to change the state of a resource. The resource state can also change internally by the server. In this case, we cannot enforce rules as it is out of the interaction scope and it depends on the application logic of the server.

To check the behaviour of the resource, we first derive the resource behaviour, in the form of a UML state machine [9], from the RESTful choreography. The derivation is performed for every REST resource found in the choreography. Then, we check the behaviour of each resource if it is correct or not.

The derivation procedure of the resource behaviour starts with isolating a resource in the choreography diagram, e.g., the resource *exam* in our running example. Then, the REST tasks that are irrelevant to the chosen resource are replaced with a sequence flow. Same is done with all the intermediate events. The gateways are kept untouched because they are needed to determine alternative paths during state transitions of the resource. At last, we have a RESTful choreography which contains only REST tasks addressing only a single resource. Subsequently, we transform the RESTful choreography into a state transition diagram. State naming is based on the URI of the REST request, e.g., exam is published, accessed, submitted. State changes inducted by the REST request are labeled in the state transition diagram with the corresponding request like shown in Fig. 2.

6   Evaluation

In this section we apply the defined properties on the choreography depicted in Fig. 1 and argue about the usefulness of these two properties.

The hyperlink-completeness property of this choreography is checked by identifying the URI used in each REST request, and checking whether or not the URI is sent to client performing the request at some point earlier in the choreography. The automation of this procedure is left as a future work. The diagram from Fig. 1 is hyperlink complete. However, during its design, checking for this property recursively proved to be beneficial because we were able to spot flaws and resolve them, e.g., URI_3, URI_6 and URI_7 were not included respectively in messages m_4, m_{13} and m_{16}.

For checking the resource behavioural correctness of the running example, we identified one main REST resource i.e. the *exam*. Figure 2 depicts the lifecycle of the *exam* resource derived in the manner described in the previous section. Following the definition of resource behavioural correctness we can conclude from Fig. 2 that the *exam* resource has a correct behaviour because it is: created via a POST; accessed via GET and no new state is introduced; edited via PUT leading to a new state; and finally, all requests are performed after the resource is created and before it is deleted (in this example there is no DELETE request).

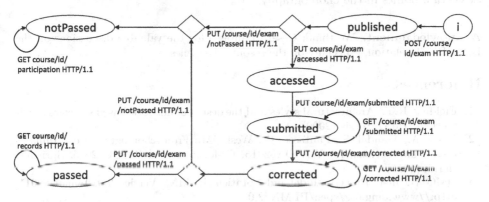

Fig. 2. Exam lifecycle derived from the RESTful choreography in Fig. 1

Additionally, deriving the state transition of the resources helps the developers of RESTful APIs to understand the allowed interactions, e.g., it is not allowed to have a PUT */course/id/exam/accessed* after PUT */course/id/exam/notPassed*. Moreover, GET requests can be easily checked if they are safe i.e. do not introduce side effects. This is realized by making sure that every GET state transition is looped around a single state (see Fig. 2).

Since the MOOC choreography has only one main REST resource that has a correct behaviour, then the choreography has a correct resource behavior. Therefore, the MOOC RESTful choreography is considered complete because it satisfies both properties defined above.

7 Conclusion

In this paper we propose a formal specification of the RESTful choreography diagram together with properties for verifying its completeness. The formalization is realized by: first, formalizing the business process choreography; and second, formalizing the extension that constitutes the RESTful choreography diagram. The proposed specification is applied in an example of examination procedure in the context of a massive open online course.

The two identified properties of the RESTful choreography are hyperlink completeness and behavioural correctness. The former assures that all the hyperlinks used by the client (in the client server context) participants for making a REST request are provided to them prior to their request occurrence. The latter makes sure that all REST resources behave as expected during their lifecycle. For the second property we make use of a different view - a state transition diagram is derived from the RESTful choreography for each REST resource involved in the interaction. This additional view, provides to the user of RESTful choreography a clearer view on each resource behaviour by emphasizing the state transitions induced by REST requests. This is particularly useful in cases when REST resources are accessed and updated by different participants during the course of the interaction because it gives an overview over the allowed changes at certain points in the choreography.

Acknowledgement. We thank Cesare Pautasso for the valuable discussions on the BPM-REST relation, especially on the resource lifecycles.

References

1. Fielding, R.T.: Architectural styles and the design of network-based software architectures. Ph.D. thesis (2000)
2. Nikaj, A., Mandal, S., Pautasso, C., Weske, M.: From choreography diagrams to restful interactions. In: WESOA 2015, Co-located with ICSOC 2015. Springer, Berlin (2015)
3. OMG: Business Process Model and Notation (BPMN), Version 2.0, January 2011. http://www.omg.org/spec/BPMN/2.0/
4. Decker, G., Kopp, O., Leymann, F., Weske, M.: BPEL4Chor: extending BPEL for modeling choreographies. In: IEEE International Conference on Web Services (2007)
5. Jordan, D., Evdemon, J., Alves, A., Arkin, A., Askary, S., Barreto, C., Bloch, B., Curbera, F., Ford, M., Goland, Y., et al.: Web services business process execution language version 2.0. OASIS Stand. **11**, 1–10 (2007)
6. Christensen, E., Curbera, F., Meredith, G., Weerawarana, S.: Web services description language (WSDL) 1.1. W3c note, WWW Consortium, March 2001
7. World Wide Web Consortium: Simple Object Access Protocol (SOAP) 1.2 (2003)
8. Haupt, F., Leymann, F., Pautasso, C.: A conversation based approach for modeling REST APIs. In: Proceedings of the 12th Working IEEE/IFIP Conference on Software Architecture (WICSA 2015), Montreal, Canada, May 2015
9. OMG: Unified Modeling Language (UML), Version 2.0, July 2005. http://www.omg.org/spec/UML/2.0/
10. Pautasso, C., Ivanchikj, A., Schreier, S.: Modeling RESTful conversations with extended BPMN choreography diagrams. In: Weyns, D., et al. (eds.) ECSA 2015. LNCS, vol. 9278, pp. 87–94. Springer, Heidelberg (2015). doi:10.1007/978-3-319-23727-5_7
11. Weske, M.: Business Process Management - Concepts, Languages, Architectures, 2nd edn. Springer, Berlin (2012)
12. Pautasso, C., Wilde, E.: Push-enabling RESTful business processes. In: Kappel, G., Maamar, Z., Motahari-Nezhad, H.R. (eds.) Service Oriented Computing. LNCS, vol. 7084, pp. 32–46. Springer, Heidelberg (2011)

Analysis of an Access Control System
for RESTful Services

Marc Hüffmeyer and Ulf Schreier[(⊠)]

Furtwangen University of Applied Sciences, Furtwangen, Germany
schreier@hs-furtwangen.de

Abstract. RestACL is an access control system for RESTful Services
and describes a policy specification language as well as an architecture
that shows how access control can be integrated with RESTful Services.
The language is based on the ideas of the attribute based access control
model allowing rich variations of security policies with a great diversity of access rules. Its structure utilizes the concepts of REST enabling
a quick identification of security policies that have to be evaluated in
order to find an access decision. This work analyzes the requirements
on such a language and gives a brief introduction over the RestACL
concepts. Evidence is provided that the language enables the implementation of an appropriate and efficient access control system that fulfills
the requirements.

1 Introduction

Attribute Based Access Control (ABAC) is a very generic model that allows
expressing rich variations of security policies [11]. Therefore, it is a suitable
candidate to become the access control model in environments that ship with
great diversity of access rules. ABAC controls access to objects using arbitrary
properties of entities. For example, a subject might have a property *IP address*
and a document a property *privacy level*. A rule could restrict access in a manner
that the conditions *the documents privacy level is secret AND the subjects IP
address is in the range of 10.0.0.1 to 10.0.0.255 AND the access method is read*
must be fulfilled.

Representational State Transfer (REST [5]) defines constraints on distributed
systems enabling high-performing and scalable Web Services. This work analyzes
and evaluates the RestACL language. A brief introduction into the language is
given. An architecture describes how a RestACL system can be integrated in
RESTful environments and how it can enforce access decisions. We explain which
design characteristics of RestACL enable high-performing and scalable access
control. Evaluation is done using two methods: formal performance analysis and
experimental testing.

The remainder of this work is organized as follows: a brief introduction to
the RestACL syntax and semantics is given in Sect. 2. We analyse the language,
the architecture and a reference implementation in Sect. 3. In Sect. 4 we show
the efficiency of our approach using experimental testing. Finally, we refer to
related work in Sect. 5.

© Springer International Publishing Switzerland 2016
A. Bozzon et al. (Eds.): ICWE 2016, LNCS 9671, pp. 373–380, 2016.
DOI: 10.1007/978-3-319-38791-8_22

2   RestACL

The REST Access Control Language (RestACL) enables protection for resources depending on various attributes. This section shows the requirements to such a language and an architecture that describes how an RestACL system can be integrated in RESTful environments.

2.1   Basic Architecture

Figure 1 shows the components in an RestACL access control architecture. A *RESTful Client* application sends resource requests to a *Server*. The *Server* must serve the request including the execution of application and access control logic. Therefore, he formulates access requests and passes them to an *Access Control System* which computes the access decision depending on attributes given in the

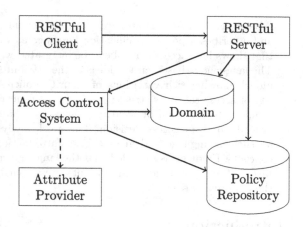

Fig. 1. Access control architecture [8]

access request, attributes collected from an *Attribute Provider*, the *Domain* and a set of polices. The *Domain* and the *Policy Repository* store data objects that determine the security policy. While the *Domain* is used to map between resources and policies, the actual policies are located in a *Policy Repository*. Because a RESTful Service is responsible for the security policy of its resources, the *Server* can modify the mapping between resources and policies (the *Domain*) as well as the policies themself to change the security policy. This enables the adaption of frequent changes to the security policy in an automated fashion. A brief overview over the components is introduced in [8].

2.2   Syntax

In this section we will give an overview over the syntax of RestACL. Note that only a brief introduction is given that explains the main ideas of RestACL. A complete description that includes more details like the application of URI query strings and URI templates can be found in [8].

Domains. Resource orientation and addressability are core concepts of REST. A RestACL *Domain* takes advantage of these concepts and structures the security policy in a resource graph. This enables a key-driven ABAC mechanism with the resource address being the key. The benefit of utilizing resource orientation compared with XACML (discussed in the Sect. 3) is that language interpreters can quickly identify the subset of policies that needs to be evaluated for a single access request. In addition, this approach allows an easy integration with well established modeling tools like Swagger[1]. These tools usually also employ a resource graph. Furthermore, it facilitates the definition and increases the lucidity of resource oriented access policies (if written or read by human users).

Listing 1 shows an example of a *Domain*. The *Domain* is used to do the mapping between resources and policies and administers nested resources represented by their path. The given example expresses the following: access to the user list resource using the GET or PUT method is determined by the policy P1. DELETE access to the user resource with id 1 is determined in policy P2.

This key-driven mechanism allows to utilize well performing data structures.

```
1  {
2    "host" : "http://example.org",
3    "resources" : [{
4      "path" : "/users",
5      "access" : [{
6        "methods" : ["GET, PUT"],
7        "policies" : ["P1"]
8      }],
9      "resources" : [{
10       "path" : "/1",
11       "access" : [{
12         "methods" : ["DELETE"],
13         "policies" : ["P2"]
14       }]
15     }]
16   }]
17 }
```

Listing 1. A RestACL Domain written in JSON

Hash tables are an ideal candidate for such an algorithm because they have offer short search times and perform extremely well in practice [3]. We will show in Sect. 3 that the utilization of a key-driven approach also removes dependencies that interfere scalability.

Policies. RestACL is build on top of the ABAC model because it should support a great diversity of access policies. Therefore, the *Policies* that are referred from the *Domain* declare *Conditions* based on attributes. For example, a *Condition* might demand a subject attribute clearance or a resource attribute privacy level. Therefore, a *Condition* has

```
1  {
2    "policies": [{
3      "id": "P1",
4      "effect": "Permit",
5      "priority": "1",
6      "condition": {
7        "function": "greater",
8        "arguments": [{
9          "category": "subject",
10         "designator": "clearance"
11       },{
12         "value": "9"
13       }]
14     }
15   }]
16 }
```

---

[1] http://swagger.io/.

Listing 2. A RestACL Policy with two conditions

a *Function* that compares *Arguments*. *Arguments* either refer to attributes in a request or they are fixed values. Attributes are demanded from an access request using a *Category* and a *Designator*. *Categories* are used because different entities in an access request might specify the same properties.

3   Comparison with XACML

We compare our approach with the eXtensible Access Control Markup Language (XACML [1]) because XACML is the de facto standard for ABAC. XACML security policies are organized in a tree structure of Policy Sets, Policies and Rules. Each of them has a so called target that expresses attribute conditions. XACML evaluates a Policy Set, Policy or Rule, if the provided attribute values satisfy the target conditions. From a simplified point of view XACML can be seen as a decision tree build by targets [12]. This tree is evaluated in a top-down fashion to find applicable Rules. The access decision is computed in a bottom-up fashion. Therefore, each Policy Set and each Policy uses a so called Combining Algorithm to determine the resulting decision. For example, if one Rule permits access while another Rule prohibits access and both Rules are applicable, the superordinate Policy or Policy Set uses a Combing Algorithm like PermitOverrides or DenyOverrides to determine the resulting decision.

Figure 2 shows a structural example of a XACML security policy. The target of the Policy Set checks an attribute of a resource: the URI. If the URI is equal to the specified value, the Policy Set is applicable and the subordinated Policy is evaluated. The target

> **Policy Set**
> *target*: (resource, URI, http://example.org/users, equal)
> *combining algorithm*: DenyOverrides
>
> > **Policy**
> > *target*: (action, method, GET, equal)
> > *combining algorithm*: PermitOverrides
> >
> > > **Rule**
> > > *target*: (subject, name, alice, equal)
> > > *effect*: Permit

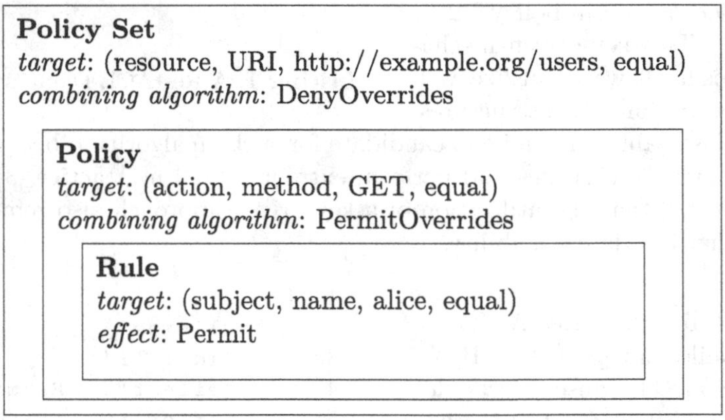

Fig. 2. A XACML security policy protecting a web resource

of the Policy addresses an action attribute: the access method of the resource request. If the access method is equal to GET, the Policy is applicable and the subordinated Rule is evaluated. The target of the Rule addresses an attribute of a subject: the name of the subject. Note that target conditions are quite flexible using a variety of comparison and logical operators. The conditions in XACML do not have to be REST oriented as in the example.

3.1   Analysis of XACML

In larger applications many resources of the same type may occur. For example, an application might serve multiple users identified by the paths /users/1, /users/2, ..., /users/n. All user resources might have different access conditions. Handling all these conditions within one superordinate Policy Set or Policy would be inefficient because a XACML engine would have to sequentially compare all paths during the request evaluation. That would lead to an average target comparison number of $O(n)$ with n being the total number of users. Efficiency can be increased using a transformation into a balanced binary tree of Policy Sets as indicated in Fig. 3. By using the described tree, the identification of the requested resource can be done within $O(log_2(n))$.

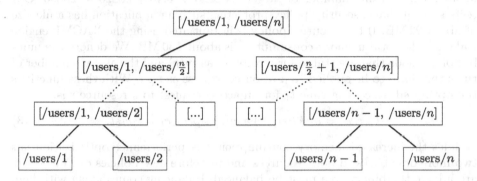

Fig. 3. A binary tree of Policy Sets

In some previous work we have shown that the transformation into a binary tree of Policy Sets is the most efficient way to implement access control for RESTful Services with XACML [7]. The performance optimization is capable to reduce processing times for access requests dramatically, but additional Policy Sets must be added that cause an increased memory consumption. Instead of $n+1$ Policies or Policy Sets (the superordinate Policy Set plus a Policy or Policy Set for each resource) the binary tree has

$$n + \frac{n}{2} + \frac{n}{4} + \frac{n}{8} + \cdots + 1 = \sum_{i=0}^{\log_2(n)} \frac{n}{2^i} \qquad (1)$$

Policies and Policy Sets. From (2) we can derive that the number of Policies and Policy Sets approximately doubles for a large number of resources.

$$\lim_{n \to \infty} \sum_{i=0}^{\log_2(n)} \frac{n}{2^i} = 2n \qquad (2)$$

That means, the optimization to reduce the average processing time from $O(n)$ to $O(log_2(n))$ ships with a doubling of memory consumption.

Now imagine an online photo community with an addressing scheme like /users/{*user_id*}/albums/{*album_id*}/photos/{*photo_id*} and 10 users. Each user has 10 albums containing 10 photos resulting in a total of 1110 resources (10 users, 100 albums, 1000 photos). Because processing resources sequentially takes too much time, we transform the security policy to quickly identify the requested resources as indicated in Fig. 3. From (2) we know that the amount of Policy Sets doubles which means we have 2220 Policy Sets just to identify the requested resource. A security policy for a resource should address at least one access method plus several other conditions that are compared against the attributes of an access request. If we expect an average of two declared access methods handled in Policies and five Rules that determine the access decision, than we have 2220 Policy Sets, $2220 * 2 = 4440$ Policies and $4440 * 5 = 22220$ Rules. That means, the resulting number of targets is $2220 + 4440 + 22220 = 28880$. Our tests showed that a security policy protecting such an application has a file size of about 22 MB. If this security policy is instantiated using the XACML engine Balana[2], the total memory consumption is about 130 MB. We denote the number of methods that are stated for a resource as $m(r)$ and the average number of rules that have to be applied to a resource request as $p(r)$. With these functions the optimized processing time t_1 for an access request to a resource r is:

$$t_1(r, n) = c_1 * log_2(n) * m(r) * p(r), c_1 = const. \tag{3}$$

Besides the increased memory consumption, the performance optimization has two more drawbacks. If new resources and therefore new Policies or Policy Sets are added, the binary tree must be balanced. Balancing comes along with high additional costs [3] which should be avoided for frequently occurring events. In addition administration efforts increase dramatically if the security policy is managed or debugged manually because of an intransparent set of policies. An automatic transformation by the XACML system to an efficient resource oriented form is not reasonable, due to the wide scope of conceivable target conditions.

3.2   Analysis of RestACL

The RestACL system can use a hash table to identify resources due to its resource oriented design resulting in search times of $O(1)$. In consequence, the most significant part of processing time is related to the evaluation of attributes. If we assume again that two access methods and five rules/policies per access method are declared, the complete evaluation of an access request is reduced to an evaluation of at most ten elements. This is a huge reduction compared to the potential 28880 elements for the same security policy written in XACML. The processing time t_2 for an access request can be computed as:

$$t_2(r) = c_2 * m(r) * p(r), c_2 = const. \tag{4}$$

Comparing (3) and (4) shows a dependency on n in (3) that is not present in (4). This makes RestACL a much better scaling solution than XACML.

[2] https://github.com/wso2/balana.

RestACL has two characteristics that reduce also the memory consumption substantially. Firstly, generic ABAC solutions have to reformulate domain specific data using policy sets, defined already elsewhere as REST service definition. RestACL reuses domain specific data.

Secondly, the differentiation between the mapping of resources to policies and the policies themselves makes policies much more reusable, modular and readable, because they are referred instead of explicitly written. Only the reference occurs multiple times. A functionally equal policy that protects the resources as described in the previous section therefore has a file size of only about 1 MB and instantiated with the reference implementation a size of about 10 MB.

4 Experimental Results

The major drawback of XACML is that processing times for access requests depend on how the security policy is written [12]. We compare the RestACL reference implementation with an performance optimized version of XACML as described in the previous section.

Table 1 lists the average processing time for an access request and the memory consumption. As one can see, the processing times for both approaches remains at a constant level. For the XACML implementation the reason is that there is an initialization overhead that is great against the optimized processing time of the access request. For RestACL the reason is the application of hashing to identify policies that have to be evaluated. The price for an increased XACML performance can be found in the memory consumption column. The RestACL implementation can support 100 times more resources with a memory consumption in the same dimension when compared with XACML.

Table 1. Processing time and memory consumption for optimized XACML and RestACL

Approach	Resources	Process.	Memory
XACML	10	14.1 ms	11 MB
XACML	100	14.5 ms	21 MB
XACML	1000	14.7 ms	112 MB
XACML	10000	14.7 ms	731 MB
RestACL	10	0.3 ms	6 MB
RestACL	100	0.2 ms	6 MB
RestACL	1000	0.4 ms	8 MB
RestACL	10000	0.3 ms	30 MB
RestACL	100000	0.4 ms	133 MB
RestACL	1000000	0.3 ms	850 MB

5 Related Work

Several approaches try to optimize XACML performance [10,12]. The approaches have in common that they optimize an generic ABAC solution without utilizing the constraints that are given in dedicated environments. Policy implementation and management can be very challenging [4] and can be simplified with a well structured policy. The drawback of this approach is that the already high memory consumption of XACML is increased again.

The need for an efficient access control system for Web Services is proven by research activity in this area. But the majority of approaches targets specific use cases and can not offer the support for a great diversity of access rules because they rely on different models other than the attribute based model. A role based approach to protect RESTful Services is described in [2]. Access matrices are used to create a mapping between subjects and resources in [9]. We created a first version of the RestACL language that targets ABAC for REST in [6]. In this approach we utilized resource orientation to reduce processing times of access requests to a logarithmic order and to make the approach more intuitive for REST experts. We proposed a second version of the language as a draft including details of the implementation but without a detailed analysis in [8].

References

1. Extensible Access Control Markup Language (XACML) Version 3.0. Organization for the Advancement of Structured Information Standards (OASIS) (2013)
2. Brachmann, E., Dittmann, G., Schubert, K.-D.: Simplified authentication and authorization for RESTful services in trusted environments. In: De Paoli, F., Pimentel, E., Zavattaro, G. (eds.) ESOCC 2012. LNCS, vol. 7592, pp. 244–258. Springer, Heidelberg (2012)
3. Cormen, T., Leiserson, C., Rivest, R., Stein, C.: Introduction to Algorithms, 3rd edn. Massachusetts Institute of Technology, Cambridge (2009)
4. Ferraiolo, D., Kuhn, R., Hu, V., Lei, Y., Kacker, R.: Implementing and managing policy rules in attribute based access control. In: IRI 2015 - IEEE International Conference on Information Reuse and Integrity (2015)
5. Fielding, T.R.: Architectural Styles and the Design of Network-Based Software Architectures. University of California, Irvine (2000)
6. Hüffmeyer, M., Schreier, U.: An attribute based access control model for RESTful services. In: SummerSOC 2015 - Proceedings of the 9th Symposium on Service-Oriented Computing (2015)
7. Hüffmeyer, M., Schreier, U.: Designing efficient XACML policies for RESTful services. In: Lecture Notes in Computer Science - Web Services and Formal Methods. Springer (2016) (Accepted for Publication)
8. Hüffmeyer, M., Schreier, U.: RestACL - an attribute based access control language for RESTful services. In: ABAC 2016 - Proceedings of the 1st Workshop on Attribute Based Access Control (2016) (Accepted for Publication)
9. Oh, S.W., Kim, H.S.: Decentralized access permission control using resource-oriented architecture for the Web of Things. In: ICACT 2014 - International Conference on Advanced Communication Technology (2014)
10. Ros, S., Lischka, M., Marmol, F.: Graph-based XACML evaluation. In: SACMAT 2012 - Proceedings of the 17th ACM Symposium on Access Control Models and Technologies (2012)
11. Sandhu, R.: The authorization leap from rights to attributes: maturation or chaos? In: SACMAT 2012 - Proceedings of the 17th ACM Symposium on Access Control Models and Technologies (2012)
12. Stepien, B., Felty, A., Matwin, S.: Challenges of composing XACML policies. In: ARES 2014 - Ninth International Conference on Availability, Reliability and Security (2014)

Operating System Compositor and Hardware Usage to Enhance Graphical Performance in Web Runtimes

Antti Peuhkurinen[1]([⊠]), Andrey Fedorov[1], and Kari Systä[2]

[1] Huawei Technologies Oy, Helsinki, Finland
{antti.peuhkurinen,andrey.fedorov}@huawei.com
[2] Tampere University of Technology, Tampere, Finland
kari.systa@tut.fi

Abstract. Web runtimes are an essential part of the modern operating systems and their role will further grow in the future.Many web runtime implementations need to support multiple platforms and the design choices are driven by portability instead of optimized use of the underlying hardware.Thus, the implementations do not fully utilize the GPU and other graphics hardware.The consequence is reduced performance and increased power consumption. In this paper, we describe a way to improve the graphical performance of Chromium web runtime dramatically. In addition, the implementation aspects are discussed.

Keywords: Graphics · Web runtimes · Performance

1 Introduction

Performance of the graphics rendering in web runtimes becomes more important when the web applications get more visual and dynamic. Many design decisions in current web runtimes aim at portability and are done before the current enablers like graphical processing units were common. In addition, some of the design decisions have been made poorly in the very beginning in the web runtimes. Examples include the design of the graphical scene graph and lack of using shared buffers between the processes.

In this paper we describe design and prototype of a web runtime that can use the latest hardware enablers to achieve maximum performance. The proposed design is suitable also to other web runtime implementations. Details of texture compression algorithms, driver level buffer update synchronization, display hardware, hardware compositor and graphics processing unit internal design are beyond the scope of this paper.

The rest of this paper is structured as follows. Section 2 discusses background of this work, including a typical architecture designs in mobile terminals and an introduction to the prototype we are implementing. Section 3 describes the principles of the prototype we have implemented, together with an overview

© Springer International Publishing Switzerland 2016
A. Bozzon et al. (Eds.): ICWE 2016, LNCS 9671, pp. 381–388, 2016.
DOI: 10.1007/978-3-319-38791-8_23

of the implementation. Section 4 discusses lessons we have learned during the testing of the implemented prototype. Section 5 concludes the paper with some final remarks.

2   Background

Figure 1 we show an example from common graphics pipeline where output of two applications are rendered by the *operating system compositor* to the device screen. With an operating system compositor we mean the lowest level graphical compositor that combines graphics and visuals from several running applications to a single display. For example, in a mobile device the status bar, user interface of the running applications and pop-up notifications are most probably output of different processes. Initially the applications draw to their own frame buffers. The application's frame buffers are then moved through a ring buffer to the compositor process. Ring buffering is used to create double or triple buffering. With multiple buffers the application can draw to a frame buffer simultaneously with a compositor reading another frame buffer from same ring buffer without blocking happening. This ensures fast throughput.

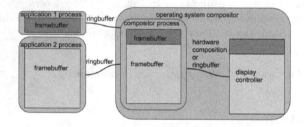

Fig. 1. Common graphics pipeline from application to display controller

The compositor process is responsible of moving the application surface data to the display controller. The connection between a compositor and a display controller is done either with a straight hardware composition in the display controller or with a second ring buffer between the compositor and the display controller. In simplest case the content of a frame buffer can be directly copied to a certain area of a display frame buffer. Ring buffer is used in cases where the compositor process needs to process the application frame buffer and enable simultaneous and non-blocking operation of the display controller.

In our earlier research, we have created a prototype of a 3D volume manager which serves in a similar function as a traditional window manager and operating system compositor but works in a 3D context [1–3]. One of the key contributions of that research was the graphics protocol between the applications and the operating system compositor.

Figure 2 shows the new pipeline that was enabled by our earlier work. In our pipeline application can have multiple shared buffers in use without need of an

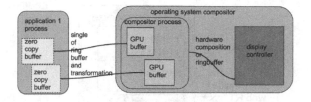

Fig. 2. Single pass compositor and zero copy GPU buffers

intermediate ring buffering. In addition, application can map it's buffer straightly to specific area on display. In this paper, we call a buffer which had a copying removed between processes as a *zero copy buffer*. The zero copy means in this context that the application does not need to copy the buffer to the compositor, but instead the compositor can use the same shared buffer straightly. In addition, the compositor buffers can be mapped to be exact part of a display which can relax the graphics pipeline even more. When a buffer is mapped to a certain display area we say that the buffer is using a *hardware layer*.

In the research reported in this paper we wanted to study feasibility of this protocol with an existing web runtime. One suitable web runtime candidate for the research was the Chromium web runtime. Chromium has a multi-process architecture and moves graphical data between it's processes. The Chromium's development roadmap did not have any similar work planned so we saw this as a good area to continue our research [6].

To make the Chromium to use our graphics pipeline, several technological aspects related to the operating system compositor required some special considerations. To begin with, an attention must be paid to management of graphics drawing within the web runtime. We need to control the textures and their life time, format and transformation. Moreover, when creating the textures we need to control the amount of needed buffers and use of hardware layers. All these elements are addressed in the following.

Figure 3 depicts typical processes running in Chromium. In the internal graphics processing of Chromium it is normal to copy graphical data from a process to another. In addition, Chromium composites most of it's own graphical data to a surface given by the operating system compositor. Chromium treats this as the main interface to adapt to different operating systems and hardware. In some custom cases, like video playing, Chromium can use platform specific adaptations for better performance.

3   Implementation

3.1   Graphics Protocol

In our earlier prototype applications were able to move their graphical scene to the operating system compositor. Instead of each application drawing themselves to single rectangular frame buffers, the applications moved their textures

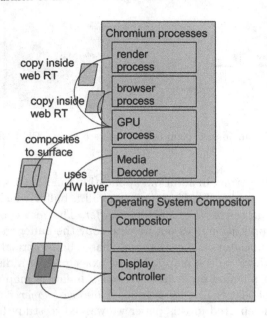

Fig. 3. Default Chromium graphics stack

and texture transformation data to the compositor which then composites the graphical scene to a final screen buffer [2]. The benefits from this kind of protocol are the possibility to use directly lower level graphics buffers and the enablers for more hardware dependent and multi-application (or multi-process) drawing optimization. In addition, when application scene changes it is possible to move only the changes instead of drawing the whole surface again for the compositor. For example in case of animation, the graphic libraries can send the transformation data that is being applied to a texture. This way only the needed transformation information is sent to the compositor instead of first drawing a texture with the transformation being applied to it and then sending this whole new texture to the compositor.

For the transfer of the graphical data over the process boundaries we have defined four types of objects: (1) a render object combining the other three object types, (2) a transformation matrix that defines the transformation of the render object in application space, (3) a mesh that defines the vertex data, and (4) a texture which is a bitmap.

3.2   Graphics Protocol Data Formats

Figure 4 visualizes the atomic 3D data objects in our graphics protocol and the objects the following features. (1) The *mesh* supports shading and texture UV mapping. Each vertex has X, Y, Z values for position, X, Y, Z values for normal and U, V values of texture mapping. The prototype presented in this paper use only rectangular meshes. (2) The *textures* are based on rectangular

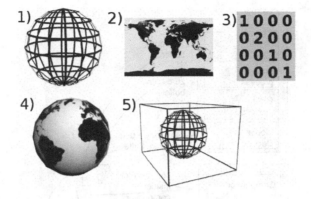

Fig. 4. Graphics protocol data formats

bitmaps. The textures can be in different formats and have single or multiple buffers. Textures with multiple buffers can work as a ring buffer. (3) Our *Transformation Matrix* is a 4×4 matrix that presents a transformation of the render object in the application space. Transformation contains location, rotation and scale. For example the meshes animated with CSS can use transformation matrix to control the animation instead of full using a series of rasterized bitmaps. (4) The *Render Object* connects the above three literals - mesh, texture and transformation matrix - and makes the combination drawable in the compositor. (5) *Application Volume* is the cuboid application space where the render objects of the application can be drawn into. We use a cuboid 3D volume to replace the old rectangular window from the old 2D application paradigm. This is because the graphics stack was originally designed for the augmented and virtual reality 3D application use cases [2].

3.3 Chromium with Enhanced Graphics

Our solution has been depicted in Fig. 5. The main difference to the Chromium's default architecture shown earlier in Fig. 3 is that now the processes of a single Chromium instance can share the buffers between themselves and with the compositor. In addition, Chromium can easily map multiple buffers to be hardware layers. There is no need to composite the website and the Chromium's user interface to a single framebuffer offered by the compositor anymore. This reduces the amount of drawing and buffering needed, thus reducing memory usage and GPU usage.

4 Evaluation

4.1 Power and Performance

The measurements where done by using Huawei P8 device [4]. We tested version 45 of Chromium using our own graphics stack against default P8 Android

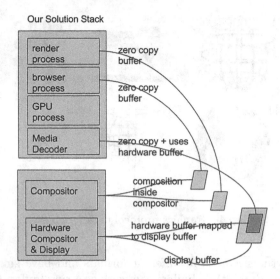

Fig. 5. Chromium with enhanced graphics

Chromium. For the initial tests we have used a Chinese website www.taobao.com as test content [5]. This website has some simple CSS animations, lot of CPU based text bitmap creation and lot of image data. The test was started by loading the page completely, then the page was scrolled down for a length of full screen height for five times waiting 2.0 s between the scrolls and then up five times. We measured scroll times and speeds so that they would as similar as possible in repeated tests. During the testing we measured the CPU, GPU load and clock speeds, memory consumption and total voltage over and amperes drawn from the battery. Agilent 66319D power supply was used as a battery replacement in our testing. Clock speeds and load where measured with sysfs for memory, CPU and GPU. During the tests we also took the screen brightness, device temperature, other processes run and all similar noise factors into account to make the test results more comparable. We call this test case as Taobao test case.

Figure 6 shows the initial test results from the Taobao test case. The test results got are averages over the time and ten test runs. The default Chromium measurements are placed on the left side and our solution's measurements are placed on the right side in each twin bar. The measurements show that the CPU usage is about the same 30 % load with all of the four cores running at 1200 MHz with both of the tested solutions. The GPU load is slightly smaller with our solutions. The GPU clock speed was between 280–480 MHz with our solution and 280–680 MHz with the default Chromium solution. The memory usage is about 20 % smaller with our solution. The power consumption is 17 % less with our solution compared to the default Chromium solution. In the drawing performance we achieved constant 60 frames per second with both of the solutions. It is possible to show heavier content with our system than with the default Android browser still achieving the constant maxed frame rate. This is because our system uses the hardware resources - mainly memory and GPU - more efficiently.

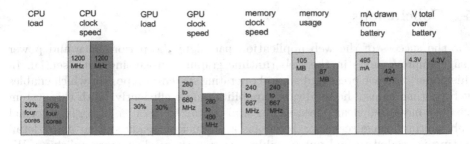

Fig. 6. Test results

4.2   Portability

We believe that our design could be easily ported also to other web runtimes and operating systems. Most portable component is the underlying compositor technology. To enable the web runtime side enhancements operating system compositor must have a similar flexible interface to access the hardware capabilities and to move the application graphical scene to the compositor side. The implementation of the compositor is done top of standard interfaces found from Android compatible hardware. This makes the compositor code portable to other up-to-date platforms. However, the portability of our concrete browser related code is Chromium specific but the general idea behind the changes is easy to adopt also in other web runtimes than Chromium. When porting the technology to other web runtimes it is essential to understand where the web runtime is allocating buffers and how it is managing them internally and between processes.

4.3   Robustness

Robustness of the implementation is being tested currently. It seems that we do not have any major flaws in the design and implementation. We have discovered some small corner cases during the implementation and fixed them.

4.4   Security

When using a GPU it is always possible to introduce flaws in security when multiple processes access the GPU memory at the same time like shown for example by Lee et al. [8]. Our design has not removed this threat completely but it makes it smaller. This is because the web runtime processes are using the GPU much more less than in the earlier web runtime implementation. This means that most of the GPU usage takes place in the operating system compositor. In the operating system compositor we have a better control from the GPU usage because the compositor is one of the vendor controlled system applications. This isolation enhances the security and makes the overall security better.

5   Conclusions

For the success of the web application paradigm the performance and power usage improvements in the web runtime graphics processing are essential. In this paper, we have presented a novel operating system compositor which enables web runtime to use the hardware capabilities more efficiently. With this system we have measured clear power saving and optimized resource usage in a normal web runtime usage scenario. To create a production ready system more detail testing is needed to find out possible corner cases needing more polishing. We will continue this work to enhance the graphical performance of the Chromium browser even more. Next we focus to test the system overall robustness and do some more performance improvements at the same time.

References

1. Peuhkurinen, A., Mikkonen, T., Terho, M.: Using RDF Data as Basis for 3D Window Management in Mobile Devices. MobiWIS, Niagara Falls (2011)
2. Peuhkurinen, A., Mikkonen, T.: Three-dimensional volume managers replacing window managers in augmented reality application paradigm. Poster presented at Mobilesoft, Florence (2015)
3. Peuhkurinen, A.: Method for Displaying a 3D Scene on a Screen. US Patent US20140313197
4. Huawei P8 Mobile Phone. https://en.wikipedia.org/wiki/Huawei_P8. Accessed 13 Feb 2016
5. Taobao Website. https://www.taobao.com/. Accessed 15 Feb 2016
6. Chromium Graphics Roadmap. https://www.chromium.org/developers/design-documents/gpu-accelerated-compositing-in-chrome/gpu-architecture-roadmap. Accessed 13 Feb 2016
7. Android Graphics Components. https://source.android.com/devices/graphics/#android_graphics_components. Accessed 14 Feb 2016
8. Lee, S., Kim, W., Kim, J., Kim, J.: Stealing webpages rendered on your browser by exploiting GPU vulnerabilities. In: IEEE Symposium on Security and Privacy, San Jose (2014)

QwwwQ: Querying Wikipedia Without Writing Queries

Massimiliano Battan and Marco Ronchetti[✉]

DISI, Università degli Studi di Trento, 38123 Povo di Trento, Italy
massimiliano.battan@gmail.com, marco.ronchetti@unitn.it
http://latemar.science.unitn.it

Abstract. Wikipedia contains a wealth of data, some of which somes in a struc-tured form. There have been initiatives to extract such structured knowledge, incorporating it in RDF triples. This allows running queries against the body of knowledge. Unfortunately, writing such queries is an unfeasible task for non-technical people, and even those who are familiar with the SPARQL language face the difficulty of not knowing the logical data schema. The problem has been attacked in many ways, mostly by attempting to provide user interfaces which make it possible to graphically navigate the see of RDF triples. We present an alternative user interface, which allows users to start from a Wikipedia page, and to simply express queries by saying "find me something like this, but with these properties having a value in the [A-B] range".

1 Introduction

The Sematic Web effort has opened the way to the Web of Data initiative. Based on the notion of RDF triplets, every single chunk of data is connected to something else. These connections transform simple data into precious information, and today Linked Data offers a wealth of such. Sometimes however too much information is equal to no infor-mation: we need to be able to find and harness information that is relevant to us and to our goals. Having a gigantic database is of no use if we do not know its schema and what the relations mean, but if we know, we can write queries and extract knowledge that is relevant to us. Likewise, making sense of Linked Data without some base knowl-edge is extremely difficult. This problem has spawned a whole research field: exploration and visualization of Web of Big Linked Data. A review of it has been recently presented by Bikakis and Sellis [1]. Most responses are given in terms of graph visualization and exploration, with no less than 20 different systems having been proposed. Although such approach is certainly useful and valuable, bringing the data to the final, generic user requires something more. Creating a generic user interface that makes it possible to easily find and extract relevant information for non-technical and inexperienced users is an extremely difficult task. Restricting to a subset of data may help, even though is does not respond to the more general problem. A particularly relevant subset of Linked Data is the one collected by the DBPedia by exploiting the structured part of information, which is collected by the Wikipedia project. An example of such an approach is the Spacetime visualizer [2], where the final user can implicitly write queries about those DBPedia data, which have geographic and temporal attributes. They can be queried, and responses are returned in a context-rich interface. For instance, the system allows finding

© Springer International Publishing Switzerland 2016
A. Bozzon et al. (Eds.): ICWE 2016, LNCS 9671, pp. 389–396, 2016.
DOI: 10.1007/978-3-319-38791-8_24

all the poets born in France in the XVII century, or all the battles fought during World War II, visualizing their geographic location in a temporal sequence. Along with this line, we present a novel approach, which deploys the user context to allow her/him to express queries against DBPedia [3] in a simple way and without limitation to specific data types. The interface is presented as a Chrome plug-in that can be activated on any Wikipedia page. The page define the context, and the user can start from the structured data present in it to express queries by analogy, in the form "find me something like this, but with such and such different parameters". No need of knowing any query language is needed, empowering hence generic, non-skilled users.

In this paper we first set the ground, by recalling the DBPedia project and its relations with Wikipedia, then we present our approach, and finally discuss and conclude.

2   From Wikipedia to DBPedia

DBPedia project offers a structured and machine-readable representation of a subset of Wikipedia knowledge. Started in 2007 with its first release, the dataset is currently at the base of the Linked Data effort, connecting and linking to almost any available dataset over the web such as Freebase, Linked MDB1, Linked Geo Data2, Proside and many others. It allows performing semantic queries over entities and relationship, which are directly connected to Wikipedia itself and other dataset.

Information is written in Wikipedia in natural language, so how can DBPedia extract it and put it in a machine-readable form?

The main trick is that a part of the information present in Wikipedia pages is actually coded into the so-called infoboxes. An infobox is a template used to collect and present a subset of information about its subject. The template contains a list of attributes: for instance, the "settlement" infobox, which is used to describe populated areas, lists properties such as "Name", "image_skyline", "governing_body", "area_total_sq_mi", "elevation_ft" etc. A Wikipedia author, who wants to create a page about a city, will include this template and add all the known values for the attributes. In this way content-uniformity is improved, as well as content-presentation. In fact, originally infoboxes were mostly devised for page layout purposes, the original intent being to improve the appearance of Wikipedia articles. When the MediaWiki software parses the document, infobox(es) are processed by a template engine, which applies to it a web document and a style sheet. Such design allows separating content from presentation, so the template rendering can be modified without affecting the information. Usually, infoboxes appear in the top-right corner of a Wikipedia article in the desktop view, or at the top in the mobile view.

Although the infobox idea was mainly related to presentation issues, it had the effect of including some structured data into a relevant portion of Wikipedia pages: about 44.2 % of Wikipedia articles contained an infobox in 2008 [4]. The infobox is usually compiled by the page authors, but there have been attempts to populate them by automatically extracting knowledge from the natural text contained in the page [5].

DBPedia uses machine-learning algorithms to extract structured data from infoboxes. It creates triples consisting of a subject (the article topic), predicate (the parameter name), and object (the value). Each type of infobox is mapped to an ontology class, and each property (parameter) within an infobox is mapped to an ontology property.

DBpedia dataset is regularly (but not frequently) updated, syncing it with the Wikipedia source. There are localized versions of it (so as there are versions of Wikipedia in many languages). Any entity contained in DBpedia (say "the thing"), is associated to an unique URI reference in the form http://dbpedia.org/resource/thingName, where things must always coincide with the URL of the relative Wikipedia article which has the form http://en.wikipedia.org/wiki/thingName; in this way it is possible to have a simple mapping between DBpedia and Wikipedia. Any thing can have various properties, some of which are mandatory. Every DBPedia resource is always described by a label, a link to the relative Wikipedia page, a link to an image representing it (if any) and a short and long abstract. If the resource is available for different Wikipedia languages, corresponding abstracts and labels are added accordingly to the language.

The knowledge contained in DBPedia is far from being complete and fully correct, as it is derived from infoboxes, which are far from being perfect: for instance there is no control on the inserted values. It may happen that pages sharing the same infobox structure show strings, which include numeric values together with a symbol expressing the measure units (and sometimes different units are used), so that it may be difficult to (automatically) make sense of the value. In other cases, different textual expression are used to indicate the same entity, as for instance when the "ruling party" is associated with values such as "Democratic Party", "Democrats" or "D.P.": although for humans the three expression may carry the same meaning, the same cannot hold for automatic processing. It may also happen that a field is left blank by the authors, either because they do not know, or because the forget filling it. In property value sometimes there are even comments! Lacks of standards, typing errors etc. restrict the usefulness of infoboxes as source of machine-readable data.

In spite of this problem, which limits the completeness and usefulness of the harvested data, DBPedia offers the possibility to navigate the data and to express queries, which can extract "hidden" information from the Wikipedia body. For instance, it is possible to find all settlements in a give region, and to select the subset having a population within certain bounds. Further, from the result set we can select only those location being ruled by a certain political party: "find all the towns in Tuscany having more than 10.000 inhabitants, which are ruled by the Democratic Party". Such information is contained in Wikipedia, but extracting it by hand is extremely difficult and time-consuming, while asking that to DBPedia can be "easily" done. Easily, provided that one is familiar with SPARQL, and that one knows the underlying data structure! Hence, not only unskilled, non-technical people are excluded because they are unable to use query languages, but also SPARQL expert may not find the task easy, unless they are familiar with the (gigantic) schema. In this case, rather than a database schema, one needs to be familiar with the ontology, knowing its classes and properties. The focus on this last problem has driven the research towards "exploration tools", which in most cases are graph explorers. LODlive [6] is one such tool: In order to use the system, user have to insert a keyword or a URI to be searched on a selected DBPedia endpoint; if the resource is present, a graph will be drawn with a single node representing the found DBPedia concept. The node is surrounded by small circles, which represent the properties associated to it. For each concept it is then possible to open different types of panels showing a summary of all the properties, abstracts, external links for the concept and its ontology classes. Many similar instruments have been presented in literature: discussing them here would be too long, and hence we refer the reader to the comprehensive survey recently written by Bikakis and Sellis [1].

3   QwwwQ (pron.: "qiuck")

In this scenario, we attempted to devise a quick method for allowing generic users to perform queries on Wikipedia without knowing query languages and ontology structure. It is somewhat similar to the "Query by example" paradigm suggested by Zloof over 40 years ago [7] and later refined by the same author [8]. Zloof's goal was remarkably similar to ours: the idea was to enable the non-professional user who has little or virtually no computer or mathematical background to extract information from the (at that time young) relational data model. Users could provide an example (giving one value per column) where some of the data were considered invariant, and other were variables. Hence, in a table having "TYPE", "ITEM", "COLOR" and "SIZE" columns the user could specify ITEM = P.PEN and COLOR = RED. The underline values meant "variable", and the not-underlined ones meant "constant", so that the query would return a set of items, having the property of being "RED": e.g. {LIPSTICK, PENCIL}. Specifying ITEM = PEN and COLOR = P.RED would return the set {GREEN, BLUE}, i.e. all the available colors for pens. The attributes "TYPE" and "SIZE" are considered irrelevant in the query. A psychological study demonstrated experimentally the ease and accuracy with which nonprogrammers learned and used this Query By Example language [9].

In our case, the user starts from an example, instantiated in a Wikipedia page, which defines the context: for instance s/he could start from the "Berlin" page. The unexpressed statement is "I am interested in (German ?) towns – or in (European ?) state capitals – or in German states (Länder)", as Berlin is both a city and a state, and also an European Capital. Next, the user makes the intention explicit of finding "something like this": s/he does so by invoking QwwwQ, which comes in the form of a Chrome plug-in. QwwwQ presents an interface, where all the known properties of Berlin are shown, in the form of a table. The properties are what DBPedia knows about Berlin, which in turn derives from the Wikipedia page infobox.

Figure 1 shows such example. The right hand side shows a part of the infobox of the "Berlin" Wikipedia page. On the upper left side, a portion of pop-up called by the Chrome extension shows some of the fields present in the infobox, in the form of attribute-value pairs. The user can select the ones s/he deems relevant: for instance "population" and "leader_party". The selection is done by ticking the row. A condition is expressed by selecting an operator: for numbers = , > , ≥ , ≤ , < ; for strings "starts with", "ends with", "contains", "equal". For numbers it is possible to express also ranges, and operators are provided also for dates.

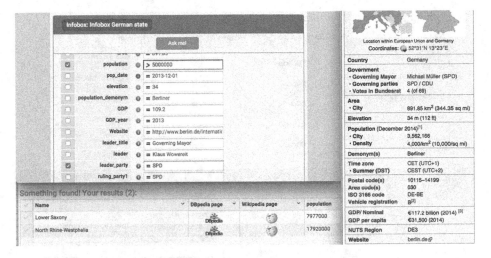

Fig. 1. On the right hand side, a part of the infobox of the "Berlin" Wikipedia page. On the upper left hand side, the pop-up for expressing the query. On the lower left hand side, the results.

The example in Fig. 1 expresses the query: we're looking for items similar to the current one (Berlin), having a population larger than five millions, and lead by the SPD party. We do not put any restriction on the other (non-selected) fields.

On the lower right hand side, the found results are shown: it's Lower Saxony and North Rhine-Westfalia. The variable(s) properties (in this case only the population, as the party is fixed) are shown in a table along with the results, and the table can be ordered on any of the fields. Links also allow opening the corresponding Wikipedia or DBPedia page for the found results (e.g. for Lower Saxony in this case).

Had we have started from "Elizabeth I of England" and asked for House = "House of Tudor", and Religion = anything, we would had found the result set shown in the upper part of Fig. 2 (5 results). These results can be filtered on a pop-up, using two different options: we can use DBPedia similarity class or Wikipedia categories. The applicable classes, given the starting example we have chosen, would be: "Royalty", "Person" and "Agent". In the example the available categories are many (it depends on how the Wikipedia page has been catalogued by its authors), and one possible choice would be "16-century women". Such choice and its results are shown in the lower part of Fig. 2, where also the results are shown: they are now reduced to only 3 values.

Other examples of questions, which can be easily asked to the system include:

1. *Starting from "Avatar (Movie)" page, give me all the films directed by James Cameron where James Horner is the music producer.*
2. *Starting from the "NCSOFT" page, give me all the organization in Computer and Video Games industry founded after January 2000 with Headquarters located in South Korea.*
3. *Starting from the Italian town "Trento" page, give me all the Italian cities that falls in the 4th seismic zone, have an elevation greater than 200 m, a total population larger than 100.000, and whose patron day falls in the first half of the year.*

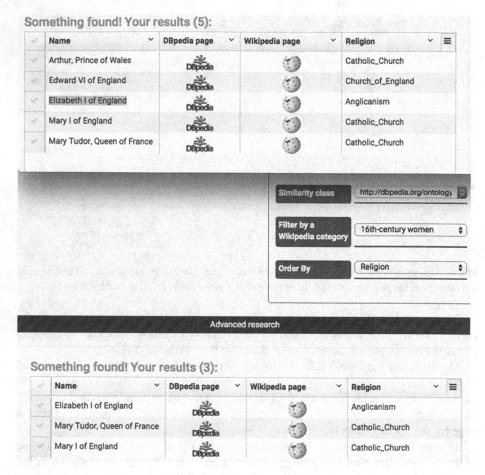

Fig. 2. On the upper part, the result set of the unfiltered query. In the middle, the filtering by Wikipedia category. In the lower part, the filtered results are shown.

3.1   Implementation

The system is composed by four components:

(1) *The core library*: a library written in Java which is responsible of implementing all the features of the system. It is composed of a **Wikipedia Parser module** and a **SPARQL query builder** module, along with several utility classes. The library is responsible to provide the interconnection between DBpedia and the system and between Wikipedia and the system. All the other components never contact directly these services but they rely on the library in order to access either DBpedia or Wikipedia. Wikipedia is replicated on the server for efficiency reasons (first of all to have access to the wikicode, from which the templates can be easily extracted), and to make sure that we refer to the same version of Wikipedia, on which DBPedia is based.

(2) *RestFUL web services.* A component that exposes the core library services, so that they can be called via Ajax from the client component.

(3) *AngularJS application:* implements the client side component. In order to develop a Chrome Extension it was mandatory to use Javascript. The GUI had to meet Chrome plugin requirements and usability. The application has been developed using the Google AngularJS framework.

(4) *Chrome extension:* to integrate the Javascript application in the Chrome Browser, a Chrome plugin was developed, with the duty of detecting user navigation and bootstrapping the JS application with the correct parameters.

A more detailed account of the implementation will be given elsewhere, and can be found a Master Thesis [10].

4 Discussion and Conclusions

We proposed a system that allows inexperienced, non-technical users to query DBPedia, starting from a generic Wikipedia page, expressing interrogations of the type "find something like this, constrained by these parameters". The interface is fully integrated, as it presents itself as a pop-up on a Wikipedia page, and hence enhances the Wikipedia initiative with a set of functionalities, which were missing.

The system is not without problems, which mostly stem from Wikipedia shortcomings. We already mentioned the problems that infoboxes exhibit, and which in good part derive from the poor quality of data control. Another problems comes from Wikipedia categories, which we use for optional filtering of the results. They present several issues: for instance they are not an acyclic graph. Also, not all pages correctly include the suitable categories. For instance, Hanover belongs to the "University towns in Germany", while Berlin does not (which is obviously wrong). Not all pages include the suitable infoboxes: for instance Berlin is both a town and a state (Land), and its page presents only the "State of Germany" infobox, while Hanover presents four infoboxes: "German location", "Historical population", "Weather box" and "Geographic location". This makes the two "things" incomparable. The situation is similar if we examine the DBPedia ontology classes: Hanover is "Town", "Place", "Populated place", "Settlement", while Berlin is "Administrative Region", "Place", "Populated place" and "Region" (so here we have a partial overlap).

Although these shortcomings are general, and affect the whole DBPedia initiative, QwwwQ certainly suffers from them. Improving the QwwwQ Parser Module, e.g. by automatically recognizing measure units so as to convert to a standard would not help, as the data would not match the ones contained in DBPedia. The same happens for specific types of property values such as lists, because user is not able to really make use of them in a query. A possible solutions would be recognizing unusable properties and remove them from the parsing result, so that the user then would never use them when building a query: it is better to have less options having the guarantee that they work rather than a wider spectrum of uncertain possibilities. Of course, the silver bullet would be a better quality control in the Wikipedia initiative.

QwwwQ has not yet undergone a validation with a large enough number of users, which we plan to run soon. The system has been tested with English and Italian versions of DBpedia and Wikipedia and it has been implemented to support multi-language, however parsing issues may arise when dealing with languages other than the ones supported at the moment. Another improvement, which we plan to tackle in future, is the possibility to express the equivalent of a join operation, i.e. to transvers DBPedia relations.

References

1. Bikakis, N., Sellis, T.: Exploration and visualization of web of big linked data: a survey of the state of the art. In: Workshop Proceedings of the EBTD/ICDT 2016 Joint Conference, Bordeaux, France, arXiv:1601.08059v1 [cs.HC] (2016)
2. Valsecchi, F., Ronchetti, M.: Spacetime: a two dimensions visualization engine based on Linked Data. In: 8th International Conference on Advances in Semantic Processing (SEMAPRO 2014), Red Hook, NY 12571: IARIA, pp. 8–12 (2014). ISBN: 9781634392631
3. Bizer, C.: Dbpedia - a crystallization point for the web of data. Web Semant. Sci. Serv. Agents World Wide 7(3), 154–165 (2007)
4. Baeza-Yates, R., King, I. (eds.): Weaving services and people on the World Wide Web. Springer, Heidelberg (2009). ISBN: 9783642005695. LCCN: 2009926100
5. Lange, D., Böhm, C., Naumann, F.: Extracting structured information from wikipedia articles to populate infoboxes. Technische Berichte des Hasso-Plattner-Instituts für Softwaresystemtechnik an der Universität Potsdam, Hasso-Plattner-Institut für Softwaresystemtechnik Potsdam (Universitätsverlag Potsdam) (2010). ISBN: 9783869560816
6. Mazzini, S., Camarda, D.V., Antonuccio, A.: Lodlive, exploring the web of data. In: Proceedings of the 8th International Conference on Semantic Systems, pp. 197–200 (2010)
7. Zloof, M.M.: Query by example. In: Proceedings of the May 19–22, 1975, National Computer Conference and Exposition (AFIPS 1975), pp. 431–438. ACM, New York (1975). doi:http://dx.doi.org/10.1145/1499949.1500034
8. Zloof, M.M.: Query-by-example: a data base language. IBM Syst. J. 16(4), 324–343 (1977)
9. Thomas J.C., Gould J.D.: A psychological study of query by example. In: Proceedings of the May 19–22, 1975, National Computer Conference and Exposition (AFIPS 1975), pp. 439–445. ACM, New York (1975). doi:http://dx.doi.org/10.1145/1499949.1500035
10. Battan, M.: Querying Wikipedia: A Linked Data System for exploring it. Università di Trento, Italy, Master Thesis (2015)

A Quality Model for Linked Data Exploration

Cinzia Cappiello[1(✉)], Tommaso Di Noia[2], Bogdan Alexandru Marcu[1],
and Maristella Matera[1]

[1] Politecnico di Milano - DEIB, Piazza Leonardo da Vinci, 32, 20133 Milano, Italy
{cinzia.cappiello,alexandru.marcu,maristella.matera}@polimi.it
[2] Politecnico di Bari - DEI, via E. Orabona, 4, 70125 Bari, Italy
tommaso.dinoia@poliba.it

Abstract. Linked (Open) Data (LD) offer the great opportunity to interconnect and share large amounts of data on a global scale, creating added value compared to data published via pure HTML. However, this enormous potential is not completely accessible. In fact, LD datasets are often affected by errors, inconsistencies, missing values and other quality issues that may lower their usage. Users are often not aware of the quality and characteristics of the LD datasets that they use for various and diverse tasks; thus they are not conscious of the effects that poor quality datasets may have on the results of their analyses. In this paper we present our initial results aimed to unleash LD usefulness, by providing a set of quality dimensions able to drive the selection and evaluation of LD sources. As a proof of concepts, we applied our model for assessing the quality of two LD datasets.

Keywords: Linked Data (LD) · Data quality · Quality models for LD

1 Introduction

In the last decade we have been facing with the transition of the Web towards a gigantic distributed knowledge base. Nowadays, we share knowledge in the Web by publishing documents, blog posts, reports as well as by deploying services and APIs. At the same time, all this information can be integrated to create new services able to aggregate data and to transform them in new knowledge.

Among the different obstacles to the development of these new breed of services we may identify two main elements: *(i)* information/data are exposed in different formats and made available with reference to diverse data models; *(ii)* it is hard to estimate the quality of a data source. As for the first point, the Linking Open Data initiative has given a big boost in the direction of a unified model to publish data on the Web. In fact, the hyperlinked structure of a Linked Data (LD) dataset looks the perfect nominee to distribute and connect data and resources by exploiting well known and established technologies such as HTTP. Nevertheless, since they are conceived to publish and distribute data in an open environment (as the Web is), LD datasets are affected by all the related issues: incompleteness of the information, inconsistency and, more generally, unknown

© Springer International Publishing Switzerland 2016
A. Bozzon et al. (Eds.): ICWE 2016, LNCS 9671, pp. 397–404, 2016.
DOI: 10.1007/978-3-319-38791-8_25

quality. In order to develop a Web application, the selection of the right data source may impact on the effectiveness of the application itself. The same is if one wants to perform data analysis. Thus, understanding the quality of a LD dataset may be a key factor in the selection of a data source among all the ones publicly available on the Web.

In this paper, we frame the problem of characterizing the quality of LD sources by providing a set of quality dimensions able to drive the evaluation and the selection of Linked Data sources. The literature extensively discusses in general the quality of data; however, there is a lack of contributions focusing on the peculiar nature of LD. This paper is an initial attempt to fill this gap and proposes a quality model that leverages traditional data quality dimensions but extends and specializes them in order to cover the peculiarities of Linked Data. After illustrating the main motivations that led us to define a new data model and analyzing the few contributions so far proposed in the literature (Sect. 2), we introduce our quality model for LD (Sect. 3). Then we show how it has been exploited for the evaluation of two small datasets gathered from two Linked Data sources, DBpedia and LinkedMDB (Sect. 4). In Sect. 5 we draw our conclusions and outline our future work.

2   Rationale and Background

The current Web has moved from a distributed base of interlinked documents to a distributed base of data. In the last years we have been confronting with the publication of data on the Web in diverse and heterogeneous formats, spanning from simple CSVs up to HTML tables. More recently, various data providers have also started to allow direct access to their datasets via Web APIs.

Thanks to the development of the Semantic Web technological stack and to the publication of the LD principles, we are also witnessing the ever increasing availability of a new breed of datasets on the Web. Linked (Open) Data relate to a set of best practices for providing an infrastructure that facilitates, encourages and promotes sharing data across the Web. The result is a distributed model that allows any data provider to publish data and also link them with other information sources on the Web.

The LD model was conceived in 2006 by Tim Berners-Lee as a set of rules and common practices on how to publish data on the Web in a semantics-aware, machine readable way. Since then, Linked Data sources have proliferated; their large volume and especially their interconnected nature have motivated researchers to define methods and tools to access and aggregate data from different LD sources [3,7,8,11].

2.1   Linked Data Technology

LD provide a generic and flexible publishing paradigm, which makes it easier for data consumers to discover and integrate data from a large number of sources. Indeed, by using URIs as global identifiers for resources, it is straightforward to set hyperlinks between entities in different datasets. As a result, in the current Web we find many Linked Data datasets connected with each other in a single global data space thus creating the so called Linked Open Data (LOD) cloud which somehow overcomes the incompleteness that often characterizes single data sources.

LD technology is characterized by the following elements:

- *A unifying data model.* Linked Data rely on RDF as a single, unifying data model. As it bases on the notion of triple, RDF is a perfect candidate to mimic the graph-based nature of the current Web thus allowing a smooth transition towards an interconnected network of entities.
- *Hyperlink-based data discovery.* By using URIs as global identifiers for entities, Linked Data allow to navigate and explore data spaces as well as to connect them with each other in a single global data space (the LOD cloud);
- *Self-descriptive data.* Linked Data ease the integration of data from different sources by relying on shared vocabularies and OWL ontologies.
- *A powerful query language.* Following their inspiring principles, LD are accessible through SPARQL endpoints. SPARQL is the standard query language to get data from a dataset. Its syntax is based on graph-pattern matching thus making it a perfect tool to retrieve data from RDF repositories.

In general, semantic applications based on LOD exploit the two major properties of the LOD architecture: the first one is the standardized data representation and access, as LD rely on a standardized data model (RDF); the second property is the openness of the Web of Data which enables the discovery of new data at runtime, in line with the LOD principles. The knowledge graph, represented through a set of RDF triples, is an ideal candidate for exploratory tasks whose aim can be manyfold. Just to cite the most frequent ones:

- Browsing a linked data space will ease the discovery of serendipitous entities;
- Via the exploration of a dataset starting from a seed node, a system can learn which are the top-k most similar or related entities thus allowing the user to perform approximate retrieval tasks;
- In case of an encyclopedic dataset, such as DBpedia, Freebase or Wikidata, one might partition the knowledge graph by considering reachability criteria.

Moreover, the interlinked nature of LOD dataset makes it possible to perform federated queries among different datasets. By leveraging the links between datasets, the user is allowed to integrate on the fly data that are retrieved from diverse knowledge sources.

All this exploration and integration tasks aim to generate new knowledge through the interlinking of already existing but distributed data. However, the usefulness of the resulting knowledge depends very much on the quality of each single LD dataset. This aspect can be pursued if specific quality models able to capture the novel aspects introduced by LD are considered.

2.2 LD Quality

Despite the potential of LD and the interest they received by the scientific community, recent studies have shown that the majority of Linked Data datasets suffer from data quality problems [9,14] that still limit their adoption in real applications. In the last years some models and related methodologies have been proposed to assess the quality of data (a comprehensive survey is reported in [2]). Some papers concentrate on Web data sources [1,4–6]. However, very few contributions have specifically addressed the LD quality. Among them, in [11] the authors present a framework for assessing the Linked Data quality with focus on the fusion of LD datasets. They start from the definition of quality as "fitness for use" [10], and then pose emphasis on the importance of the task for which Linked Data are used. Thus, they present a framework supporting the specification and the automatic assessment of quality metrics for the specific task of data fusion. The paper, however, does not provide a quality model, while it concentrates on methods and technologies to support the automatic assessment of "any" quality metric within a framework for LD access. Similarly to the previous work, in [12] the authors propose a methodology for Linked Data quality assessment, outlining detailed phases and activities, but they do not clarify which quality dimensions are worth to be considering when LD have to be exploited.

A notable contribution towards the definition of a comprehensive quality model for LD is reported in [14]. This work exhaustively discusses the quality of Linked Data and motivates the need of methods for assessing it. It considers any single dimension of traditional data quality and tries to reformulate it for application to LD usage. The resulting model is comprehensive and valuable, but it can be cumbersome to apply, especially if one's goal is to assess Linked Data quality through the automatic computation of metrics. As explained in the following section, we adopt a minimalist approach, trying as much as possible to *(i)* specialize only the most relevant traditional quality dimensions to the LD nature, *(ii)* identify new dimensions (e.g., navigability) that are specific for exploratory tasks that characterize Linked Data and *(iii)* define measures that can be objectively assessed through automatic methods.

3 Quality Model

As discussed in Sect. 2.1, LD rely on the RDF model, which provides mechanisms for describing groups of related *resources* and the relationships among them. More formally, the model is based on the notion of triple as "`subject-predicate-object`" expressions where the `subject` and the `object` are resources and the `predicate` defines the *properties* for the subject of the statement. *Nodes* are sets of subjects and objects. The subject is a URI or a blank node, the predicate is a URI and the object is a URI, a literal or a blank node. Literals and blank nodes are known as *RDF terms*.

In order to support the users in selecting the most suitable LD datasets for their tasks, we propose to annotate the different sources with a set of quality metadata that can make the users aware of their quality level. We identify a minimal set of dimensions, and related metrics, built by considering and redefining some dimensions gathered from the literature (i.e., [14]), and adding some new concepts. The resulting quality model is composed of five dimensions: *Amount of Data, Conciseness, Completeness, Navigability* and *Interlinking*. Amount of data, Conciseness and Completeness focus on the richness and redundancy of the LD dataset, while Navigability and Interlinking provide a measure for the possibility to explore respectively the considered dataset or different data sources starting from a specific resource. A thorough description of these dimensions is provided in the following.

Amount of Data. It refers to "the extent to which the quantity or volume of data is appropriate for a particular task" [13]. When using LD to feed an application, it is important to have an idea of the richness of the dataset we are using. A simple metric that can help assess such a dimension is related to the average number of properties that characterize an entity in the considered data source.

Conciseness. In data quality literature, it is defined as "the extent to which data are compactly represented without being overwhelming" [13]. For the quality of LD datasets, we restrict the focus on the *intensional conciseness*, which refers to the degree to which a resource is characterized by a set of properties that is free of redundancy. A metric to measure such dimension for a LD entity is given by the ratio of the number of non-redundant properties and the total number of properties. Conciseness for a dataset that includes more resources is calculated by evaluating the average of the different conciseness measures.

Completeness. It refers to the degree to which all required information is present in a particular dataset. In general, completeness is "the extent to which data are of sufficient depth, breadth and scope for the task at hand" [13]. We measure LD completeness as the ratio of the number of retrieved properties of an entity and the number of required properties for a specific resource. The required properties are the ones included in an ideal list of properties that we consider as complete.

Navigability. It refers to the degree to which the different resources in the same dataset are linked. In particular, it highlights how much it is possible to navigate the dataset starting from a specific node. For assessing navigability, we start from a specific resource and all the triples in which it is involved as subject, and we then consider the percentage of objects that are URIs with respect to the total number of objects.

Interlinking. It refers to the degree to which resources in the dataset are linked with the same resource of an external dataset. For the assessment of this dimension, the statements with the predicate `owl:sameAs` are considered as it states that a resource of the graph is the same resource of another dataset. The metric to evaluate the Interlinking dimension of a whole dataset is the total number of `owl:sameAs` links.

Note that Conciseness, Completeness and Navigability metrics are defined as percentages; therefore their values belong to the interval [0,100]. Amount of data and Interlinking have instead values in $\mathbb{N}$.

4   Quality-Aware Source Selection: An Example

In order to start testing the usefulness and effectiveness of the proposed model, we performed some preliminary experiments to evaluate the quality of two datasets gathered from two important LD sources:

- *DBpedia*[1], a dataset containing data extracted from Wikipedia,
- *LinkedMDB*[2], a dataset containing movie-related content.

DBpedia is a project aimed to make Wikipedia data available on the Web in a structured way. It allows one to query Wikipedia data and to integrate them with other Web sources. The English version of DBpedia contains the description of about 4.6 million of resources and most of them (i.e., about 4.2 million) are classified on the basis of the DBpedia ontology. DBpedia is one of the largest LD datasets available; it has the big advantage to cover many knowledge domains and to be always updated, since it evolves as Wikipedia changes.

LinkedMDB publishes the first open semantic Web database for movies, including a large number of interlinks to several datasets on the open data cloud and references to related webpages.

For our experiments, we assume to be interested in developing an application for searching and exploring data about movies. We can rely on DBpedia or on a more specialized source as LinkedMDB. In this section, we show how the quality assessment, according to the model presented above, can be a good driver in the source selection and thus it can support users in understanding which is the source to prefer for their tasks.

Every resource in DBpedia is accessible through the URI pattern: `http://dbpedia.org/resource/<name_of_resource>`. Analogously, movies in LinkedMDB can be accessed via the URI `http://data.linkedmdb.org/directory/film/<movie_id>`. Before thoroughly analyzing the two sources, we just compared two descriptions of the same movie. We considered the movie "Minority Report" and compared information published at http://dbpedia.org/page/Minority_Report_(film) and http://data.linkedmdb.org/page/film/333. We noticed that LinkedMDB contains all the important data (e.g., *director, language, editor, music, producers, writers*, etc.) and also contains the actor list, which is instead missing in DBpedia. As regards conciseness, LinkedMDB does not contain any redundant value while in DBpedia there are four properties that are listed twice (i.e., budget, director, editing and gross). However, LinkedMDB is characterized by a lower interlinking value since it provides the external links only to DBpedia, Freebase, IMDB and RottenTomatoes pages of the movie. In DBpedia, Minority Report has instead 15 `owl:sameAs` links (out of which 11 refer to localized versions of DBpedia in different languages). This first analysis highlights that LinkedMDB has a richer content while DBpedia is less specialized but it has a good interlinking with the LOD cloud.

---

[1] http://wiki.dbpedia.org/.
[2] http://www.linkedmdb.org/.

Table 1. Quality metrics for DBpedia and LinkedMDB datasets

Quality metric	DBpedia	LinkedMDB
Amount of data	51.21	39.22
Conciseness	96.07 %	100 %
Completeness	68.11 %	72.85 %
Navigability	83.66 %	61.40 %
Interlinking	20	0.74

Considering the subgraph related to movies, we calculated the metrics described in Sect. 3. The results are shown in Table 1. Note that for assessing the completeness dimension we identified a set of mandatory properties, which are the most popular ones used in Wikipedia Web pages to describe a movie, that are: starring, writer, director, producer, music composer, distributor, language, cinematography, editing, country, realase date. All these properties are modeled in both data sets but cinematography.

Looking at Table 1, we can notice that DBpedia features a higher amount of data, navigability and interlinking, while LinkedMDB is preferable for completeness and conciseness. This might depend on the fact that LinkedMDB is a specialized data set and thus its content on movies is more accurate than in DBpedia. This in turn highlights that the selection of sources might depend on the target application domain. Therefore, LinkedMDB has to be preferred if high content quality on movies is required, while DBpedia has the capability to provide in general more information and to enable navigation along multiple and multi-language sources.

5   Conclusions

This paper has presented some preliminary results on the definition of a quality model for LD. Our model tries to capture the peculiar nature of Linked Data, considering those dimensions that are more significant for tasks typical of a LD-based application, and with a specific focus on metrics that can foster automatic quality assessment. Some preliminary experiments demonstrated that the model can be effectively used to evaluate LD datasets. Future work will be devoted to refine the model, through a systematic identification of possible tasks on Linked Data and the definition of corresponding dimensions and metrics. Model validation will be also conducted on larger datasets.

Acknowledgments. We are grateful to the students that helped us validate the model by developing tools to download and analyze the DBpedia and LinkedMDB datasets.

References

1. Barbagallo, D., Cappiello, C., Francalanci, C., Matera, M.: Reputation-based selection of information sources. In: Proceedings of ICEIS 2010 (2010)
2. Batini, C., Cappiello, C., Francalanci, C., Maurino, A.: Methodologies for data quality assessment and improvement. ACM Comput. Surv. **41**(3), 1–52 (2009)
3. Bianchini, D., De Antonellis, V., Melchiori, M.: A linked data perspective for effective exploration of web APIs repositories. In: Daniel, F., Dolog, P., Li, Q. (eds.) ICWE 2013. LNCS, vol. 7977, pp. 506–509. Springer, Heidelberg (2013)
4. Bizer, C., Cyganiak, R.: Quality-driven information filtering using the WIQA policy framework. Web Semant. Sci. Serv. Agents World Wide Web **7**(1), 1–10 (2009). The Semantic Web and Policy
5. Cappiello, C., Daniel, F., Matera, M.: A quality model for mashup components. In: Gaedke, M., Grossniklaus, M., Díaz, O. (eds.) ICWE 2009. LNCS, vol. 5648, pp. 236–250. Springer, Heidelberg (2009)
6. Cappiello, C., Daniel, F., Matera, M., Pautasso, C.: Information quality in mashups. IEEE Internet Comput. **14**(4), 14–22 (2010)
7. Desolda, G.: Enhancing workspace composition by exploiting linked open data as a polymorphic data source. In: Damiani, E., Howlett, R.J., Jain, L.C., Gallo, L., De Pietro, G. (eds.) Intelligent Interactive Multimedia Systems and Services. Smart Innovation, Systems and Technologies, vol. 40, pp. 97–108. Springer, Heidelberg (2015)
8. Di Noia, T., Ostuni, V.C., Rosati, J., Tomeo, P., Di Sciascio, E., Mirizzi, R., Bartolini, C.: Building a relatedness graph from linked open data: a case study in the IT domain. Expert Syst. Appl. **44**, 354–366 (2016)
9. Hogan, A., Umbrich, J., Harth, A., Cyganiak, R., Polleres, A., Decker, S.: An empirical survey of linked data conformance. J. Web Sem. **14**, 14–44 (2012)
10. Juran, J.M.: The Quality Control Handbook. McGraw-Hill, New York (1974)
11. Mendes, P.N., Mühleisen, H., Bizer, C.: Sieve: linked data quality assessment and fusion. In: Srivastava, D., Ari, I. (eds.) Proceedings of the Joint EDBT/ICDT Workshops, Berlin, Germany, 30 March 2012, pp. 116–123. ACM (2012)
12. Rula, A., Zaveri, A.: Methodology for assessment of linked data quality. In: Knuth, M., Kontokostas, D., Sack, H. (eds.) Proceedings of the 1st Workshop on Linked Data Quality Co-located with 10th International Conference on Semantic Systems, LDQ@SEMANTiCS. CEUR Workshop Proceedings, vol. 1215, Leipzig, Germany, 2 September 2014. CEUR-WS.org (2014)
13. Wang, R.Y., Strong, D.M.: Beyond accuracy: what data quality means to data consumers. J. Manage. Inf. Syst. **12**(4), 5–33 (1996)
14. Zaveri, A., Rula, A., Maurino, A., Pietrobon, R., Lehmann, J., Auer, S.: Quality assessment for linked data: a survey. Semant. Web **7**(1), 63–93 (2016)

Please Stay vs Let's Play: Social Pressure Incentives in Paid Collaborative Crowdsourcing

Oluwaseyi Feyisetan[(⊠)] and Elena Simperl

University of Southampton, Southampton, UK
{oof1v13,e.simperl}@soton.ac.uk

Abstract. Crowdsourcing via paid microtasks has traditionally been approached as an individual activity with units of work created and completed independently. Other forms of crowdsourcing have however, embraced a mixed model that further allows for interaction and collaboration. In this paper, we expand the model of collaborative crowdsourcing to explore the role of social pressure and social flow generated by partners, as sources of incentives for improved output. We designed experiments wherein a worker could request their partner to collaboratively complete more tasks than required, either not to be abandoned and lose money (social pressure), or for fun (social flow). Our experiments reveal that these socially motivated incentives can act as furtherance mechanisms improving output by over 30 % and accuracy by about 5 %.

Keywords: Paid microtask crowdsourcing · Collaboration · Social pressure · Social flow · Incentives engineering

1 Introduction

Microtask crowdsourcing is one of the most prominent forms of online crowdsourcing [5]. It is primarily used when the work to be outsourced is highly parallelizable and can be divided into smaller pieces down to a micro level, which takes only seconds to minutes to complete. It brings together two sets of actors: requesters (the persons or institutions seeking help from the crowd) and workers (individuals or teams taking on tasks advertised via an open call).

In its most typical instance, microtask crowdsourcing is understood as an aggregation of individual contributions that have been created independently of each other [5]. While this model has some advantages, allowing large numbers of people to take on tasks and complete significant amounts of them quickly,[1] there are also situations in which allowing for social interaction or collaboration is preferred [1,11]. This is a function of many factors: from the complexity of the work to be outsourced [12]; to using synchronicity of crowd answers as a means to

---

[1] For instance, the citizen science project Subspotter achieved 350000 classifications in 20 h with the help of their community of volunteers, see http://blog.zooniverse.org/2015/08/31/. For paid microtasks requesters expect answers in their thousands or more within hours or days.

© Springer International Publishing Switzerland 2016
A. Bozzon et al. (Eds.): ICWE 2016, LNCS 9671, pp. 405–412, 2016.
DOI: 10.1007/978-3-319-38791-8_26

drive participation [16]; or giving the crowd a place to self-organize, share ideas and experiences, and discuss [15]. In this paper, we present results of experiments on paid crowdsourcing, carried out on a bespoke platform - *Wordsmith*, featuring elements of interaction and collaboration. We study the effect of social pressure and social flow on the task quality and output of workers carrying out tasks in this setting.

2   Background and Related Work

Some GWAPs (Games with a purpose), for example, von Ahn's ESP game [16] have a strong element of interaction among contributors. These games employ various strategies such as output agreement between players to generate useful work results and drive engagement. However, in microtask models that involve financial payment, which do not employ these strategies, it becomes important to understand and leverage on these factors (such as collaboration) that might drive participation.

2.1   Factors Affecting Collaborative Work

Several works have looked at the effect of peer and social pressure in incentivising work output collaboratively online and in business enterprises. The effects of peer pressure on contributions to enterprise social media were studied by [2] where they observed that, the participation of a worker's manager is a key source of social pressure in initiating contribution while, comments fuel the pressure for sustained contributions. From their work, we observe that most of the social pressure effects that are seen in the offline world are present, and amplified in the online world.

Social flow stemmed out of an extension of Csikszentmihalyi's 'theory of optimal experience' [4] where flow (or individual/solitary flow), was presented as an intrinsically rewarding, highly absorbing state, which is attainable when individuals freely choose an activity with: clear goals, immediate feedback, and a balance between challenge and skills. Despite the freedom and pleasure that comes from immersive individualistic activities, it has been observed that some of the most gratifying flow experiences occur in social circumstances [7], leading to the concept of *social flow*. Walker [17] presented the conditions and indicators of *social flow*. Some conditions stated include: immediate and clear feedback from the task and group members, interdependence and cooperation, and the challenges being important to the whole group.

2.2   Our Contribution

We look at the impact of socially motivated incentives of pressure and flow as drivers for improved quality and task output in paid collaborative microtask crowdsourcing. We show that beyond basic collaborative crowdsourcing, we can improve task and performance results by employing empathy-centric social pressure and the desire for social fun.

3 The Wordsmith Platform

The Wordsmith microtask crowdsourcing platform consists of an image labelling task to be carried out either by a single worker, or collaboratively by two workers. The collaborative mode in Wordsmith is reminiscent of the ESP game [16] which was designed for voluntary unpaid players who were not primarily motivated by money. The heart of Wordsmith consists of images displayed either sequentially to a single worker, or displayed in-sync to two workers. The workers are in turn, required to input multiple informative keywords (also referred to as labels or tags), which describe the image into a text field. Each keyword is accepted as *valid* based on a simple computed measure of quality: the keyword must be in English (validated via a dictionary web service) and it must not have been used by the worker to describe either that image or repeatedly for previous images - else, all the images could be labeled as *cat, cat, cat*.

We incorporated social and non-social feedback elements to Wordsmith to provide workers with real-time and longitudinal information on their progress in the task. Providing feedback has been shown to improve retention and engagement by enhancing intrinsic feelings of accomplishment as people advance in a task [4,14]. The platform included visual feedback on the number of images annotated, the number of tags generated and how each worker's output compares with that of others. More details on Wordsmith's gamification features and design philosophy can be found in our earlier work here [6].

Fig. 1. Wordsmith interface

4 Social Pressure in Wordsmith

When the *social pressure* setting is activated in the collaborative mode in Wordsmith, a worker is given a heads up when their partner is about to quit the task.

The worker can then select one of two options: *tell them to stay* or *allow them to go*. Choosing to request their partner to remain in the task represents the cost of exerting social pressure as presented by [3]. The message which is then automatically conveyed to the partner is dependent on the sending worker's current level in the task: the message either appeals to the partner to continue till the requesting worker reaches the level where they receive a payoff (*please stay*) or, the message requests that both workers continue annotating for fun if the payoff has been received by the requesting worker (*let's play*).

5 Experimental Design

We carried out a study in which a number of workers were recruited from a large pool, and required to annotate images either in the traditional single worker mode (**SP**) or the collaborative mode (**MP**) of Wordsmith. Within each task mode, workers were required to annotate a certain number of images in order to get paid: annotate 1 image (**LT** - *low threshold*) or annotate 11 images (**HT** - *high threshold*) based on earlier work [6]. Finally, in the collaborative, high-threshold mode (**MP-HT**), we carried out sub studies as follows: in one condition, a partner attempting to exit the task was allowed to leave, in another condition, a partner attempting to exit the task could be shown a **please stay**, or **let's play** message at the request of their partner.

5.1 Research Questions

1. Does collaboration work as an effective model for paid microtask?
2. What is the role of social pressure incentives in collaborative tasks?

6 Results

We recruited participants from CrowdFlower[2]: 600 workers for the single worker experiments modes and 600 workers for the collaborative experiments.

6.1 Social Pressure: Please Stay vs Let's Play

When Wordsmith senses that a worker's partner is about to exit the task, the worker is alerted. The worker can then request their partner to remain in the task. If the worker has tagged less than the requisite number of images in order to get paid, the worker can send a *please stay* request, else, the worker can send a *let's play* request. The receiving worker can then decide to stay (*i will stay*) or to leave the task (*i will go*) Table 1.

Social Pressure Requests. From the results in Fig. 2 with its accompanying table, we observe that workers are more likely to initiate a request of any kind

---

[2] https://crowdflower.com.

Table 1. *Experiment results* - summary of experiment results

Experiment results					
	Low threshold		High threshold		
	Traditional	Collaborative	Traditional	Collaborative	Soc'l pressure
Total workers	402	365	514	499	508
Total tags	21,538	48,171	27,652	108,950	158,716
Unique images tagged	200	200	2,196	2,200	2,200
Inter-annotator agreement	29.44 %	**34.55%**	14.26 %	25.82 %	**29.35%**
ESP tags agreement	41.26 %	25.39 %	43.96 %	37.94 %	40.11 %
Avg images tagged/person	26.68 (SD = 38.21)	9.77 (SD = 13.23)	26.75 (SD = 42.07)	25.05 (SD = 17.92)	29.00 (SD = 28.30)
Avg tags/person	53.57	**131.97**	53.80	218.34	**312.43**
Avg new tags/person	2.78 (1,117/402)	**8.69** (3,172/365)	1.80 (925/514)	11.83 (5,903/499)	**16.21** (8,236/508)

when they have not been paid. When a worker has not yet been paid, they are more likely to request that their partner stay (*please stay request*) than permitting their partner to leave. After the workers had been paid, they were also more likely to request their partner to stay (*let's play request*) than permitting them to leave. The *please stay* requests (*Requests* = 1,023) were used more frequently as a social incentive than the *let's play* request (*Requests* = 151), suggesting that workers are more inclined to put pressure on their partners when there is financial reward at stake than just fun. Figure 2 also reveals that some workers would actually release their partner to leave and wait to be connected to another partner. It shows that on the average, as expected, fewer workers (20 % *vs* 35 %) who haven't been paid would opt for this option.

Social Pressure Responses Figure 3 summarises the results (in a logarithmic scale) of a worker's responses to both *please stay* and *let's play* requests. When a worker receives a *please stay* request (signifying that the requesting partner has not yet been paid), they can respond by choosing either to stay (*I will stay*) or to leave (*I will go*). The choice to stay or to leave also varies depending on whether

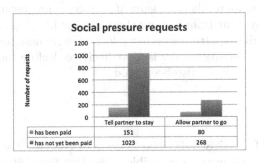

Fig. 2. Social pressure requests made by workers before and after payment (Color figure online)

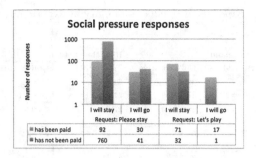

Fig. 3. Worker responses to *please stay* and *let's play* requests (on log scale) (Color figure online)

the receiving worker has been paid or not. The results indicate that, a worker who has not been paid, receiving a *please stay* message from a fellow unpaid is more likely to stay, with 95 % probability, than to exit the task (760 *vs* 41). This is in line with workers being incentivised by having shared circumstances (i.e., the need to both get paid), as stated by [9]. Similarly, a worker receiving a *please stay* request from an unpaid worker, after they have been paid, is also likely to respond by staying, albeit, with a slightly less probability of 75 % (92 *vs* 30). Furthermore, a worker receiving a *let's play* request (from a worker that has been paid) can also choose to stay or to leave, depending on whether the receiving worker has been paid or not. The results illustrate that, a worker who has not been paid, previously intending to exit the task, would almost certainly remain in the task after being sent a *let's play* message with 97 % probability (32 *vs* 1). The result also reveals the response to social flow incentives: a worker who has been paid would return to continue playing with another worker with 80 % certainty, even more likely than they would help a partner get paid (although, the results suggest that these requests occur less frequently). This is also another form of incentivisation by having shared circumstances (i.e., the desire to re-experience social flow).

Figure 3 also gives insights into when workers decide to leave their partners, despite receiving either a *please stay* or *let's play* request. The results reveal that, after receiving a *please stay* request from a worker who has not been paid, a receiving worker is more likely to leave if they have not been paid also. Hence they do not feel any guilt from leaving their partner hanging since they haven't been paid also. Similarly, after receiving a *let's play* request from a partner who has been paid, the receiving worker is more likely to decline the offer and choose to exit the task if they have also been paid.

7   Discussion

Collaboration Must Pay Off. The benefits of collaborative participation in the image labelling task were more visible in the *high threshold* conditions. In the traditional mode, workers annotated, on average, the same number of images (and generated the same number of tags) in the high and low threshold conditions. In other words, without the restriction of partner agreements, the task threshold did not really make a difference. In the low task threshold condition of the collaborative mode, workers tagged more than the requisite number of images, nevertheless, this positive delta was not sufficient to match up to the individual freedom afforded in the traditional mode. The high task threshold on the other hand indicates in the collaborative setting, how the power of (and aspiration towards) social concordance, propped up by a higher payment cutoff can be leveraged to generate more and better results. Workers in this condition, initially motivated by the need to get paid, worked together to realise improved results. This finding contributes to the larger discussion around motivation and paid microtask crowdsourcing. Surveys such as [6,10,13] have observed that financial incentives are just one, though important, part of a much more refined story of motivation of workers. The present work offers evidence on the effects of social pressure and flow, but it also raises new questions regarding the implications of the findings for incentives design that take into account particular types of workers (e.g., top contributors vs casual visitors).

Workers Behave Empathically. Social pressure incentives could be harnessed to attain speedy task completion and encourage empathic collaboration. Our analysis revealed that workers on realising that their partners have not reached the task threshold for payment, would be willing to annotate a few more images to help them get paid. This is in contrast to the individualistic thinking model which has been enshrined in traditional paid micro task platform settings. Our results show that paid workers would be willing, not only to work together, but to go the extra mile to ensure that their partner also gets paid. Workers respond not only to the need to help their partner get paid, they also respond to their partner's desire to continue annotating just for the fun of it. As noted earlier, while these results are encouraging, to develop a theory of incentives for paid microtask platforms, one would need additional experiments that take into account worker behavior patterns, as well as other tasks and possibly more complex collaboration models.

Ethics and Compensation. We understand the negative effects extended gameplay can have on people [8], especially on those who might depend on crowdsourcing as a supplementary income source. We attempted to keep our payments at the fair amount of $0.10 per minute and our low threshold condition paid up to $7.2 per hour ($0.02 for 1 image).

8   Conclusion

This paper presents results showing that social incentives could be used to boost the performance of participants in collaborative crowdsourcing. These results are in line with findings from GWAPs and multi-actor crowdsourcing systems, and could be used to inform the re-design of paid microtask platforms such as Crowd-Flower and Mechanical Turk which do not integrate collaborative workflows as first-class citizens.

References

1. Bernstein, M.S., Brandt, J., Miller, R.C., Karger, D.R.: Crowds in two seconds: enabling realtime crowd-powered interfaces. In: Proceedings of the 24th Annual ACM Symposium on User Interface Software and Technology
2. Brzozowski, M.J., Sandholm, T., Hogg, T.: Effects of feedback and peer pressure on contributions to enterprise social media. In: Proceedings of the ACM International Conference on Supporting Group Work (2009)
3. Calvó-Armengol, A., Jackson, M.O.: Peer pressure. J. Eur. Econ. Assoc. **8**(1), 62–89 (2010)
4. Csikszentmihalyi, M.: Flow: The Psychology of Optimal Experience, vol. 41. Harper Perennial, New York (1991)
5. Dawson, R., Bynghall, S.: Getting Results from Crowds. Advanced Human Technologies, San Francisco (2012)
6. Feyisetan, O., Simperl, E., Van Kleek, M., Shadbolt, N.: Improving paid microtasks through gamification and adaptive furtherance incentives. In: Proceedings of the 24th International Conference on World Wide Web (2015)
7. Jackson, S.A., Csikszentmihalyi, M.: Flow in Sports. Human Kinetics, Champaign (1999)
8. Joukhador, J., Blaszczynski, A., Maccallum, F.: Superstitious beliefs in gambling among problem and non-problem gamblers: preliminary data. J. Gambl. Stud. **20**(2), 171–180 (2004)
9. Kandel, E., Lazear, E.P.: Peer pressure and partnerships. J. Polit. Econ. **100**, 801–817 (1992)
10. Kaufmann, N., Schulze, T., Veit, D.: More than fun and money. worker motivation in crowdsourcing-a study on mechanical turk. In: AMCIS, vol. 11, pp. 1–11 (2011)
11. Kittur, A.: Crowdsourcing, collaboration and creativity. ACM Crossroads **17**(2), 22–26 (2010)
12. Kittur, A., Smus, B., Khamkar, S., Kraut, R.E.: Crowdforge: crowdsourcing complex work. In: Proceedings of the 24th Annual ACM symposium on User Interface Software and Technology, pp. 43–52. ACM (2011)
13. Mason, W., Watts, D.J.: Financial incentives and the performance of crowds. ACM SIGKDD Explor. Newsl. **11**(2), 100–108 (2010)
14. McGonigal, J.: Reality is Broken: Why Games Make Us Better and How They Can Change the World. Penguin Group, London (2011)
15. Tinati, R., Van Kleek, M., Simperl, E., Luczak-Rösch, M., Simpson, R., Shadbolt, N.: Designing for citizen data analysis: a cross-sectional case study of a multi-domain citizen science platform. In: Proceedings of the 33rd Annual ACM Conference on Human Factors in Computing Systems (2015)
16. von Ahn, L.,Dabbish, L.: Labeling images with a computer game. In: Proceedings of the SIGCHI Conference on Human Factors in Computing Systems, CHI 2004, pp. 319–326. ACM, New York, NY, USA (2004)
17. Walker, C.J.: Experiencing flow: is doing it together better than doing it alone? J. Positive Psychol. **5**(1), 3–11 (2010)

On the Invitation of Expert Contributors from Online Communities for Knowledge Crowdsourcing Tasks

Jasper Oosterman(✉) and Geert-Jan Houben

Delft University of Technology, Mekelweg 4, 2628 CD Delft, The Netherlands
{j.e.g.oosterman,g.j.p.m.houben}@tudelft.nl

Abstract. The successful execution of *knowledge crowdsourcing* (KC) tasks requires contributors to possess knowledge or mastery in a specific domain. The need for *expert* contributors limits the capacity of online crowdsourcing marketplaces to cope with KC tasks. While online social platforms emerge as a viable alternative source of expert contributors, how to successfully *invite* them remains an open research question. We contribute an experiment in expert contributors invitation where we study the performance of two invitation strategies: one addressed to the individual expert contributors, and one addressed to communities of knowledge. We target reddit, a popular social bookmarking platform, to seek expert contributors in the *botany* and *ornithology* domains of knowledge, and to invite them to contribute an artwork annotation KC task. Results provide novel insights on the effectiveness of direct invitations strategies, but show how soliciting collaboration through communities yields, in the context of our experiment, more contributions.

1 Introduction

Crowdsourcing is now an established research topic and domain of practice. By exploiting Web-mediated communication (e.g. social networks) and labour (e.g. Amazon Mechanical Turk) platforms, *requesters* engage with individuals and communities in order to find *contributors* willing to execute a given activity.

Knowledge Crowdsourcing (KC) is a type of crowdsourcing where the tasks to be executed require contributors to possess knowledge or mastery in a given domain of knowledge, in order to successfully contribute. Artwork annotation is a known example of KC task, as it demands for contributors to understand the abstract, symbolic, or allegorical interpretation of the reality depicted in the artwork, and to identify and recognise the occurrences of visual classes (e.g. plants, animals, objects) in the artwork. We refer to these individuals as *expert contributors* (or *experts*), to highlight their familiarity with the targeted domain of knowledge.

Online marketplaces provide continuous access to large amount of contributors that are engaged by monetary rewards, and therefore willing to quickly perform the proposed activities. As the suitability of these contributors to

© Springer International Publishing Switzerland 2016
A. Bozzon et al. (Eds.): ICWE 2016, LNCS 9671, pp. 413–421, 2016.
DOI: 10.1007/978-3-319-38791-8_27

the task at hand is typically unknown in advance, recent research proposed several strategies, e.g. worker self-selection and preliminary assessments, to identify expert contributors [4,11,12] within a marketplace. While being effective, these solutions showed an intrinsic limitation of using paid crowdsourcing for KC tasks: the variety of expertise available in online marketplaces is limited by the socio-economical composition of their workforce, which inevitably limits the amount of expert contributions that could actually be identified[1]. In this context, online social platforms emerge as a viable alternative source of contributors [1]. They (i) enable the interaction with large amount of individuals – potentially orders of magnitude larger than the ones available in online marketplace; and, given their general purpose, (ii) they are more likely to host expert contributors. Previous work focused on the identification of expert contributors for KC tasks, building on approaches that exploited social ties [2], topic-based profiling [6], contextual properties (e.g. geographical location) [5], or Web content consumption [9]. How to *invite* expert contributors to KC tasks? How to *engage* them with appropriate rewards? How to create engaging and viral KC campaigns in a replicable manner is still an open research question.

Original Contribution. We advocate the need for a better understanding of how expert contributors could be *invited* to participate in KC campaigns, as a first step towards their long-term engagement with the requesters' goals. To this end, we contribute an experiment in expert contributors invitation focused on KC tasks. We seek answer to the following research question:

How can expert contributors drawn from online social platforms be successfully invited to participate in knowledge crowdsourcing tasks?

We depart from previous work by focusing on the crowd invitation problem. Our ultimate goal is to distill robust invitation strategies to be used by requesters in order to tap the latent workforce readily available in open communities. We focus on `reddit`, a popular social bookmarking platform where users organise in communities to engage in discussions about a broad spectrum of knowledge domains. There, we seek expert contributors in two distinct domain of knowledge – namely *botany* and *ornithology*, to contribute an artwork annotation KC task. We study the performance of two invitation strategies: one addressed to the individual expert contributors, and one addressed to communities of knowledge. We measure their effectiveness in terms of (i) engagement with the requester, (ii) interest in the proposed task, and (iii) engagement with the task. Our findings show that direct invitation messages can result in more interest from expert contributors, while community invitations yields, in the context of our experiment, greater amount of contributions.

The remainder of the paper is organised as follows. Section 2 describes our experimental methodology; Sect. 3 reports the result of the study, and discusses our findings; and Sect. 4 concludes.

---

[1] Studies in behavioural economics show that monetary rewards can act as disincentive both to intrinsically motivated and expert individuals [8].

2   Experimental Methodology

The experiment is organised in three steps. First, we identify communities and expert contributors in `reddit` that are knowledgeable in the two targeted domains of interest, namely *botany* and *ornithology*. This process is described in Sect. 2.1. Then, we dispatch messages of invitation to a knowledge crowdsourcing campaign. We study the performance of two strategies (described in Sect. 2.2), one directly addressed to individual expert contributors, and one collectively addressed to members of relevant communities. The content annotation platform set up for the experiment is presented in Sect. 2.2, while the performance evaluation metrics are introduced in Sect. 2.3.

2.1   Identification of Expert Contributors and Communities

Users in `reddit` contribute by creating their own *submissions*, or by *commenting* and *voting* existing submissions or comments. `reddit` is organised in more than 853 K collections called *subreddits*, each themed to a specific topic, e.g. `/r/flowers`. Moderators (community voted administrators) keep collections on-topic, according to both general and collection specific rules. Submissions are described by a title and a textual content. A message is directed to a `reddit` user, and it allows a message (formatted in Markdown, no images) with up to 10 K characters.

We capitalised on the `reddit` dataset[2] described in [10], which includes 1.367.276 resources from 491.572 active users. With the aim of including only qualified candidates, we first filtered the original set of resources by preserving the ones (i) featuring at least 20 distinct words and 5 sentences; and (ii) having a domain matching score [10] greater than 0.2 for the two investigated domains. This resulted in 170 K resources, produced by 38 K users in 6 K *subreddits*.

To identify communities relevant to the targeted knowledge domains, we assigned a score to each *subreddit* by calculating the cumulative sum of domain matching scores of their resources; we then considered the top 50 *subreddits* in the resulting ranks, granted that they contained at least 10 contributions from more than one user.

The final pool of candidate experts was composed as follows. We downloaded the full set of resources[3] created by each of the 38 K users. Then, using the same definition of *affinity score* as in [10], we calculated the score of each resource, and assigned to each user the highest score amongst the ones in her set of resources. Finally, preserved users that: (i) had at least one submission in one of the top 50 relevant *subreddits* identified in the previous step; and (ii) possess a score higher than 0.2. The process produced in 1301 expert contributors in the botany domain, and 1111 expert contributors in the ornithology domain.

---

[2] http://www.wis.ewi.tudelft.nl/sac2015.
[3] `reddit` APIs – https://www.reddit.com/dev/api – limit this set to the 100 most recent resources.

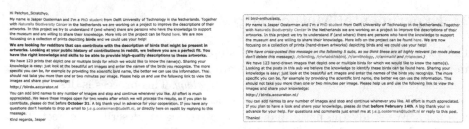

(a) Expert contributor invitation.   **(b)** Community invitation.

Fig. 1. Invitation messages. *Best viewed in the electronic version*

2.2 Invitation Strategies

An invitation strategy operationalises in the dispatch of a message, inviting an expert contributors to perform a domain-specific knowledge crowdsourcing task, namely the annotation of flowers and birds in artworks.

The invitation messages sent to individuals and to communities are depicted in Fig. 1. The message contains a description of the sender (the first author of the paper), the ongoing research project, the required task, and time constraints. The message also contains a link to a page describing the project in more details, and a link to the content annotation platform.

Each expert contributor received a *direct* invitation message, personalised on the targeted domain of knowledge, in her `reddit` inbox. Community invitation messages have been published as a contribution in selected *subreddits*, for all the community members to see and react upon (i.e. via voting and commenting).

We performed a study on the CrowdFlower human computation platform, aimed at validating the quality of the invitation messages w.r.t. its intended purpose. Crowd workers were asked to imagine themselves as **knowledgeable** in the targeted domain of knowledge, and to express their evaluation about the message on a 5-point Likert scale. The evaluation included the following dimensions: *Friendliness*; *Clarity*; *tone* (colloquial or formal; perceived *emotion* of the invitation (impersonal, personal); *likeliness to respond* (How likely is it that you, as someone [...], will react to the invitation?) *likeliness to contribute* (How likely is it that you, as someone [...], will start the task and contribute you knowledge, based on this invitation?).

The task was addressed to high quality USA workers (Level 3), to acquire truthful responses from speakers of the same language as our target platform. We paid \$0.05 per evaluated message, and set up 120 executions. On average, workers perceived the message as friendly ($\mu = 4.4$, $\sigma = 0.73$) and clear ($\mu = 4.6$, $\sigma = 0.60$), moderately personal ($\mu = 3.5$, $\sigma = 0.99$), but with a slightly formal tone ($\mu = 3.7$, $\sigma = 0.92$). Given the invitation message, workers would be inclined to respond ($\mu = 3.9$, $\sigma = 1.16$) and contribute ($\mu = 3.9$, $\sigma = 1.13$). Workers left useful feedback – (i) explain the benefit for contributors; (ii) to explain the required amount of time; (iii) expand the project description – that we incorporated in the final version of the message.

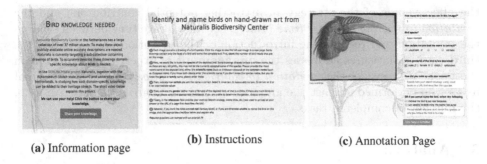

(a) Information page

(b) Instructions

(c) Annotation Page

Fig. 2. Content annotation platform. *Best viewed in the electronic version*

Content Annotation Platform: Accurator. We built upon the `Accurator` content annotation framework [7]. We included an introduction page, containing a detailed explanation of the goals of our research project (including a video), a short description of the task, and a button to start the task (Fig. 2a). The page was used to record statistics about users following up on the invitation. The `Accurator` annotation page contained instructions (Fig. 2b), optional field for users to self-report their username and knowledge level, and artworks to be annotated (Fig. 2c). Each direct invitation message contained a personalised link, unique for each user, to the introduction page. Both the invitation message and the information page contained a personalised link to the annotation page. The community invitation messages contained anonymous links. For both strategies, a user could perform any number of artwork annotations, and stop and continue non-completed tasks any time, using the provided link, until the deadline (two weeks) mentioned in the invitation.

2.3 Evaluation Metrics

To study the performance of two invitation strategies, we measure their effectiveness using three classes of metrics. In the case of communities, we assume the amount of potential users to be the number of subscribers to a given *subreddit*. This is indeed an overestimation, as not all users subscribed to a *subreddit* are also active users.

First, we measure the **engagement** of expert contributors with the *requester* in terms of *number of replies* from invited users (`#Res`). We use this metric to quantify if and when users feel compelled to interact with the requester, to engage in discussions about the invitation itself, or about the task at hand. We also provide qualitative observations about the obtained replies. Second, we address the **interest** of candidate experts **in the proposed task**. We consider the *invitation read conversion rate* (`IRCR`), i.e. the ratio of invited users who read the invitation, to measure the effectiveness of the strategy in terms of stimulated "curiosity" in proposed activity; the *invitation execution conversion rate* (`IECR`), i.e. the ratio of users who opened the execution page, to measure the effectiveness of the strategy in attracting potential contributors; and the *invitation to reading response time* (IRRT), i.e. the average time between sending the invitation and reading the introduction or the execution page. Finally, the third class of measures addresses the **engagement** of expert contributors with the task. We consider the *invitation to contribution ratio* (ICR), i.e. the ratio of users who performed at least one annotation; and the *contribution size* (CS), i.e. the number of completed tasks.

3   Analysis

The experiment took place in two distinct time phases. The first phase addressed the first invitation strategy, i.e. the dispatch of individual, personalised invitation message, and took place between August 22nd and September 26th 2015.

To account for the limitations of Reddit API[4], messages were sequentially delivered, in decreasing order of candidate expert's matching score, and with a random delay between each other. The second invitation strategy, targeting communities, was experimented on January 31st 2016, and we gathered log data for a period of two weeks. The long delay between the two experimental phases was planned to minimise learning effects within the selected population. We selected 5 *subreddits* from each domain, picked from the list of top 50 candidate domains, and reported in Table 1. We found no user overlap between the invited usernames in the first strategy and the self-reported usernames in the second strategy. Table 2 summarises obtained results. We report distinct figures for each considered domain and invitation strategy.

Table 1. Selected *subreddits* for community invitation, rank, and # of subscribed users.

Flowers			Birds		
Name	*Rank*	*# Sub.*	*Name*	*Rank*	*# Sub.*
/r/whatsthisplant	1	20,896	/r/birding	1	5,831
/r/BackyardOrchard	5	1,150	/r/animalid	4	2,634
/r/houseplants	6	874	/r/whatsthisbird	5	7,115
/r/gardening	11	121,223	/r/species	6	5,075
/r/plants	22	3,152	/r/Ornithology	17	5,294

Engagement with the Requester. The invitation messages triggered diverse responses, both according to the domain of knowledge and invitation strategy. Individuals contacted about a flower-related tasks replied the most, while birds-related community members expressed more interest in our contribution to their *subreddits*. To better explain such differences, we manually classified each reply

---

[4] The API policy poses limitations on the amount and frequency of HTTP requests (GET and POST) that could be issued.

Table 2. Experimental results. Metrics are described in Sect. 2.3.

	Flowers		Birds	
	Individual	Community	Individual	Community
#Res	46	3	14	6
IRCR	0.130	0.7e-3	0.032	4.0e-3
IECR	0.101	0.7e-3	0.023	3.7e-3
IRRT(min)	$\mu: 1634, \sigma: 3348$	$\mu: 347, \sigma: 1585$	$\mu: 67, \sigma: 258$	$\mu: 866, \sigma: 1534$
ICR	0.007	7.7e-5	0.002	4.8e-4
CS	55	144	5	179

into one or more categories, including: (issues with) the selection process; questions about the project; questions about the annotation task; and intentions to contribute. All replies were friendly and constructive, indicating a good attitude towards our initiative. No reply asked for additional information about the project or about the annotation task. 15 % of users in the flower domain and 0.07 % in the birds domain acknowledged the reception of the message, and promised to inspect the task; interestingly, all visited the introduction page, and none visited the annotation page.

The majority of replies related to the selection process (70 % in the flower domains, 57 % in the birds domain), where the major concern was about the wrong attribution of expert capabilities. An inspection of the matching domain scores for these users shows their belonging to the whole spectrum of the users rank. This result provides two interesting observations: (i) users felt compelled about being misclassified as experts; and (ii) a mistake from our side was sufficient to establish a communication channel, despite the unsolicited nature of our message. The remaining replies consisted of responses that were not related to the project, and did not hint to an opinion/interest from the user (e.g. a polite "no thank you").

Comments and replies to our community invitation messages were less frequent, but mostly focusing on more details about the project and the annotation task. The limited number of responses does not allow for relevant observations. However, as we will see in the next section, the lack of replies did not translated into a lack of interest in the task: simply put, users were not compelled to interact with us on **reddit**, but were triggered by our call for contribution.

Interest in the Proposed Task. The conversion rates of our strategies are promising both for invitation read and invitation execution: 10 % of experts contributors from the flower domain accessed the introduction page, the annotation page, or both; the number drops to 3 % in the birds domain, although the number of identified expert contributors was 15 % lowers. Community invitations were also successful, despite the lower percentages in Table 2. Respectively, 100 and 119 users from the targeted flower and birds communities visited the introduction page, and 93 and 110 respectively visited the annotation page. Given the unique nature of our study, it is not possible to compare our results to previous work[5]. Finally a note about the *invitation to reading* response time. While we observe great variability, average values are at least in the order of hours; this result suggests that this sort of expert contributors invitations is not suitable for applications requiring low latency and quick response times.

Engagement with the Task. Invitation conversion rates were relatively low. No more than 20 users – in each configuration of strategy/domain – actually performed at least one annotation task. These numbers, however, yield a $10 - 20\%$ conversion rate from users entering the execution page to users actually annotating an artwork. This result is promising, when compared to the one reported in [9], where authors adopted target advertising for recruiting, and monetary incentives to keep contributors engaged. Community invitation strategies provided a considerably higher amount of complete annotations, hinting toward the ability to attract more productive users. We hypothesis this difference to be mainly due to the characteristics of the `reddit` platform, which facilitates community behaviour in favour of direct communications between members. The validation of this hypothesis is left to future work.

Threats to Validity. The target platform (reddit), due to unknown spam detection mechanisms, could have removed direct messages we have send. Only when users responded, i.e. clicked a link or replied, we are sure this did not occur. The chosen dataset and identification model used in the first strategy affects the outcome of this strategy. Using a larger dataset and optimizing the model will most likely increase the response rate of the first strategy but will have a no effect on the second strategy. Researchers repeating this experiment should take this into account.

4 Conclusion and Future Work

This paper contributes an experiment aimed at assessing two invitation strategies for expert contributors. We discuss the performance of a strategy directly addressing individual contributors, and of a strategy addressing communities of knowledge. We provide several novel insights. For instance, we observed how an individual invitation strategy yields more interest to a knowledge crowdsourcing task, while higher amount of task executions were obtained from community invitations.

This work shows how future work can develop in multiple directions. Our ultimate goal is to distill robust invitation strategies to be used by requesters in order to tap the latent workforce readily available in open communities. In this respect, we will investigate how to account for the expert contributor's level of knowledge in the creation of personalised messages. We will also investigate the performance of similar strategies in other online platform (e.g. Quora, Stack-Exchange), and conduct experiments involving domains of knowledge of diverse diffusion in the general population.

---

[5] The closest comparison we could outline is with the average click through rate in social media, which is reported to be up to 2% [3]; The two forms of interaction are, however, intrinsically different.

References

1. Arolas, E.E., González-Ladrón-de-Guevara, F.: Towards an integrated crowdsourcing definition. J. Inf. Sci. **38**(2), 189–200 (2012)
2. Bozzon, A., Brambilla, M., Ceri, S.: Answering search queries with crowdsearcher. In: Proceedings of WWW, pp. 1009–1018, 16–20 April 2012, Lyon, France (2012)
3. Chaffey, D.: Display advertising clickthrough rates. http://www.smartinsights.com/internet-advertising/internet-advertising-analytics/display-advertising-click through-rates/. Accessed 10 Feb 2016
4. Chandler, D., Kapelner, A.: Breaking monotony with meaning: motivation in crowdsourcing markets. CoRR, abs/1210.0962 (2012)
5. Cheng, Z., Caverlee, J., Barthwal, H., Bachani, V.: Who is the barbecue king of texas?: a geo-spatial approach to finding local experts on twitter. In: Proceedings of SIGIR, SIGIR 2014, pp. 335–344, New York, NY, USA. ACM (2014)
6. Difallah, D.E., Demartini, G., Cudré-Mauroux, P.: Pick-a-crowd: tell me what you like, and i'll tell you what to do. In: Proceedings of WWW, pp. 367–374 (2013)
7. Dijkshoorn, C., et al.: Personalized nichesourcing: acquisition of qualitative annotations from niche communities. In: Proceedings of UMAP Workshops, 10–14 June 2013, Rome, Italy (2013)
8. Gneezy, U., Rustichini, A.: Pay enough or don't pay at all. Q. J. Econ. **115**(3), 791–810 (2000)
9. Ipeirotis, P.G., Gabrilovich, E.: Quizz: targeted crowdsourcing with a billion (potential) users. In: Proceedings WWW, WWW 2014, pp. 143–154, New York, NY, USA. ACM (2014)
10. Kassing, S., Oosterman, J., Bozzon, A., Houben, G.: Locating domain-specific contents and experts on social bookmarking communities. In: Proceedings of SAC 2015, pp. 747–752, 13–17 April 2015, Salamanca, Spain (2015)
11. Rogstadius, J., Kostakos, V., Kittur, A., Smus, B., Laredo, J., Vukovic, M.: An assessment of intrinsic and extrinsic motivation on task performance in crowdsourcing markets. In: Proceedings of ICWSM, 17–21 July 2011, Barcelona, Catalonia, Spain (2011)
12. Yu, L., André, P., Kittur, A., Kraut, R.: A comparison of social, learning, and financial strategies on crowd engagement and output quality. In: Proceedings of CSCW, pp. 967–978. ACM (2014)

Analysis of a Cultural Heritage Game with a Purpose with an Educational Incentive

Irene Celino[✉], Andrea Fiano, and Riccardo Fino

CEFRIEL – Politecnico di Milano, Via Fucini 2, 20133 Milano, Italy
{irene.celino,andrea.fiano,riccardo.fino}@cefriel.com

Abstract. In this paper, we present Indomilando, a Cultural Heritage Game with a Purpose (GWAP) with the aim of ranking the photos of the architectural assets in the city of Milan, according to their recognizability. Besides evaluating the ability of Indomilando to achieve its ranking purpose, we also analyze the effect of an educational incentive on the players' engagement. Indeed, discovering new cultural assets appeared to be a valuable reason to continue playing.

1 Introduction

Cultural heritage collections are maintained by public and private institutions and described in digital catalogues, often constituted by Web-based anthologies, The advent of digital photography have led to a significant increase – and Web availability – of the wealth of images depicting cultural heritage assets. However, given a large image collection of cultural heritage assets, the issue arises to analyze and process the set of photos without resorting to expensive manual work. Human Computation [1] has emerged as a successful paradigm to face this challenge in a cheaper way. Therefore, the following questions emerge regarding the adoption of a Human Computation approach: (1) given a set of images of a cultural heritage asset, is it possible to identify the most representative or the most recognizable photo? (2) given a collection of images of different cultural heritage assets, is it possible to tell apart the most popular assets and those that could benefit from promotion campaigns?

This paper contributes the design, implementation and evaluation of Indomilando, an application aimed to rank a quite heterogeneous set of images, depicting the cultural heritage assets of Milan. Indomilando is designed as a Web-based Game with a Purpose that involves players in guessing an asset from a set of photos. We evaluate the ability of Indomilando to achieve its ranking purpose and to engage users. Moreover, given the cultural flavour of our game, we also investigate whether Indomilando achieves the "collateral effect" of giving back new knowledge to users.

2 Related Work

Human Computation [1] and Crowdsourcing [2] are different approaches to involve people in mixed human-machine computational systems to collect and

© Springer International Publishing Switzerland 2016
A. Bozzon et al. (Eds.): ICWE 2016, LNCS 9671, pp. 422–430, 2016.
DOI: 10.1007/978-3-319-38791-8_28

process information. In the cultural heritage field, there are studies and surveys [3,4] that explore how to apply crowdsourcing-like methods to achieve different tasks [5]. Games with a Purpose (GWAP [6]) emerged as an interesting Human Computation method to collect information from game players that are often unaware that their playful activities hide the achievement of a task. Among possible purposes, ranking items in a collection is explored in some GWAP cases [7–9]. Several GWAPs in literature are based on multimedia elements [7,10]; among those, some applications are specifically related to the cultural heritage domain [11]. In this paper, we describe a GWAP aimed to rank images of cultural heritage assets.

The main challenge in those Human Computation applications is modeling and predicting user engagement [12,13]. Therefore it is important to design suitable incentive schemes to foster user participation [14]; it is demonstrated that gamification and furtherance incentives improve both quality and quantity of task execution [15]. One possible incentive can be represented by an educational stimulus [16]: users are encouraged to participate because not only they get fun and/or are paid, but also because they acquire new interesting knowledge. This type of incentive is particularly interesting in our cultural heritage case. However, balancing the purpose of a GWAP with educational-style incentives seems to be far from trivial: either an expensive training effort is needed to ensure results quality [17] or the learning stimulus negatively impacts on the purpose quality [18]. In our work, we aim to analyze and evaluate the interplay of purpose achievement, user engagement and educational-like incentives in a cultural heritage GWAP.

3   Design and Development of the Indomilando Game

We developed Indomilando (cf. http://bit.ly/indomilando), a GWAP [6] that engages players in a game to leverage their human contributions to rank cultural heritage photos. Indomilando makes use of Lombardy region's SIRBeC data related to the architectural assets of the city of Milan: 2,104 photos depicting 685 cultural heritage assets of Milan. The purpose of Indomilando is to rank the assets' photos according to their *popularity*; by popularity we mean both how famous an assets is (with respect to the other assets) and how recognizable or representative a photo is (with respect to the other photos of the same asset). To achieve this purpose, we show some photos of different assets and ask the players to guess which one corresponds to a given asset.

Indomilando can be played in rounds composed by levels; in each level, the player is presented with the name of an architectural asset and 4 photos. The game goal is to identify the correct photo for the given asset; for every right choice, the player score increases and it increases more for consecutive right answers. Gaining points in levels and rounds let the player climb the leaderboard and obtain badges. Every time a user completes a level by making a choice, Indomilando highlights the correct/incorrect answer and shows the 4 names of the assets depicted in the photos. Moreover, the game lets the user learn more

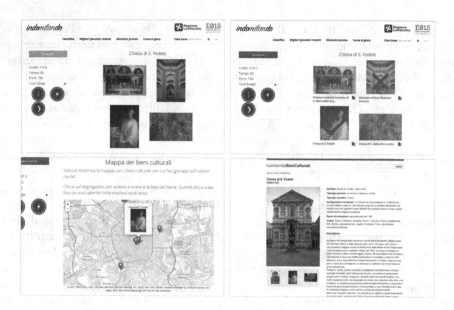

Fig. 1. Screenshots of the Indomilando game.

about the assets: each photo is associated to a link to the corresponding SIRBeC catalogue report. At the end of the round, the player can also explore a map of Milan showing the location of all the assets the user played with. Figure 1 shows some screenshots of Indomilando gameplay.

Indomilando was published online in mid October 2015 and promoted via social media campaigns. A link to the game was recently added to several culture-related official portals of Lombardy Region. In the following sections, we present our analysis and evaluation of Indomilando based on the data collected in the last three months. Further details and graphics regarding this evaluation are available at http://swa.cefriel.it/urbangames/indomilando/icwe2016.html.

4   Game Purpose Analysis

Since Indomilando is a GWAP [6], we first analyze its ability to achieve its goal: ranking the full set of photos and ranking the depicted assets.

4.1   Photo Ranking

Whenever an asset photo is presented to a player to be guessed, the user can either correctly choose it or wrongly select one of the distracting images. To create a numeric score to rank the photos, instead of relying on the ratio between the number of times the photo was correctly chosen and the number of times the photo was visualized to be guessed (in the following simply named chosen/visualized ratio), we assign a score to the photos by using the Wilson score confidence interval [19] for a Bernoulli parameter; in our case, a trial is the visualization of a photo to be guessed, and its possible outcomes are that the photo is correctly chosen (success) or wrongly discarded (failure). We choose the lower bound of the Wilson interval as a conservative measure of the score w. We compute the w score for each asset photo.

Given that a player has to identify the correct image in a set of four photos, the success (or failure) is not only dependent on the "correct" picture, but also on the three distracting ones. The distracting options are selected among the assets belonging to the same category of the one to be guessed, but some categories are more recognizable than others. We correct the w score to take this effect into account, by applying a standardization by asset type, as follows: $\widetilde{w} = (w - \bar{X}_t)/S_t$, where t indicates the photo asset type, $\bar{X}_t$ and S_t the sample mean and the sample standard deviation, respectively, of the w scores of the same type t. We adopt $s_{photo} = \widetilde{w}$ as the metrics to rank Indomilando asset photos.

4.2   Asset Ranking

The score of an asset could be defined as $\bar{s}_{photo}$, the average score of all the photos depicting that asset, but a simple mean is sensitive to the characteristics of the set of images. Experimentally, we observe that the mean score of the asset's photos $\bar{s}_{photo}$ increases with the number N_a of photos in the set. This result could be caused by the "learning" effect that a high number of photos has on the players: a user over time could learn to identify an asset he/she had to recognize or discard in multiple previous game rounds. We introduce an adjustment for the number of photos derived from the linear regression line, as follows: $adj_{num} = \beta_0 + \beta_1 \cdot N_a$.

To take into account the effect of the inhomogeneity of the photo set, we consider the variance v_a of the chosen/visualized rate across the same photos belonging to the asset and we introduce the following adjustment: $adj_{set} = (v_a - \bar{X})/S$, where the variance v_a is standardized with regards to the mean $\bar{X}$ and the standard deviation S of v across all photos.

We finally define the asset score as: $s_{asset} = \bar{s}_{photo} - adj_{num} - adj_{set}$.

4.3   Results

We collect the game log information and compute the s_{photo} score and the s_{asset} score, taking into consideration only the images that were played by at least three players. The results are shown in the following table.

No. of players	Total effective played time	Completed photos	Completed assets	Throughput (tasks/hour)	ALP (time/player)
72	8 h 58 m 20 s	1397 (66.4 %)	524 (76.5 %)	155.22	7 m 29 s

The total effective time includes only the time needed to choose an image in each game level; thus in around 9 h 72 players were able to complete the ranking of 66.40 % of photos and 76.50 % of assets. The main metrics for GWAP evaluation [6] are also displayed: the average life play (ALP) is 7.5 min and measures the time spent on average by each user playing the game: it is a measure of the Indomilando engagement; the throughput is a measure of how many "tasks" are completed in the unit of time. The latter metrics are used to estimate how much time and how many users are needed to complete the tasks at hand. In the Indomilando case, we can therefore estimate that the whole set of 2,104 photos and 685 assets could be ranked in around 13.5 h by less than 110 players.

4.4 Ground Truth Evaluation

To evaluate the ability of Indomilando to achieve its purpose, we need to evaluate the photo ranking and the asset ranking. From our manual inspection of rankings, we can say that indeed the photos depicting the same asset, as well as the assets belonging to the same type, are indeed ordered from the most to the least representative.

To have a more objective evaluation of our scores, we set up a term of comparison for our rankings. We search the cultural heritage assets in the Italian version of Wikipedia, checking if they have a dedicated page: among the 685 assets of Milan, we find 111 pages. Then, we derive a rank by sorting the set of assets by decreasing number of Wikipedia visits (cf. http://stats.grok.se/), which can be interpreted as a measure of the "fame" of the asset. We first evaluate Indomilando with the rank correlation between the asset score computed by the game and the Wikipedia visits. We compute both the Spearman ρ and Kendall τ rank correlation indicators [20]. There is indeed a positive correlation ($\rho = 0.20$, $\tau = 0.15$) that is stronger when focusing on the 10 most visited pages in Wikipedia ($\rho = 0.60$, $\tau = 0.556$).

We build a second reference "ground truth" by manual ordering of the first ten assets in the Wikipedia visits by involving a set of 12 participants who are asked to rank them by their recognisability. Then we aggregate the manual ranks using a weighted brute force algorithm [21]; the weighting is applied both to users (incorporating the level of familiarity with Milan) and to individual ranks (considering the possible lack of knowledge about any asset). We again compute the rank correlation ρ and τ indicators between the Indomilando asset rank and the ordering obtained by the aggregation of the manual tests. In this case, the correlation values are much higher ($\rho = 0.806$, $\tau = 0.60$), indicating that Indomilando is able to approximate the reference ranking with a high level of accuracy.

5 Game Engagement Analysis

We propose two types of evaluation: an objective analysis of played time and a subjective survey of participants' experience.

5.1   Analysis of Played Time

In the experimentation period, a total of 72 users played the Indomilando game for an average ALP of 7.5 min. Figure 2 shows the distribution of the total effective played time, i.e. the time actually spent trying to guess the right answer, from the beginning to the end of a level. This specific left-skewed shape is recurring in casual games' engagement measures. Despite the curve decreases very quickly, we can distinguish a group of players characterized by a different behaviour, corresponding to the little rise between 10 and 20 min.

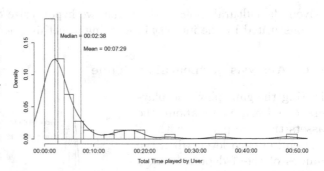

Fig. 2. Distribution of the total time per user.

We therefore suppose the existence of two sets of players: the first and larger one including the users with a total played time around 2.5 min, and a less numerous set with the users who played approximately 7–8 times more. The empirical distribution of the total number of levels played per user displays a very similar behaviour to the played time distribution and confirms our analysis, also on the existence of different groups of players.

5.2   Subjective Analysis of Engagement

We conduct also a second type of engagement assessment, by setting up an online evaluation questionnaire and asking the Indomilando players to compile it. Some of the questions were explicitly directed to understand the game reception (cf. Fig. 3). The results prove that Indomilando is indeed perceived as a fun game with a simple and intuitive gameplay. We can conclude that Indomilando has a good engagement capability.

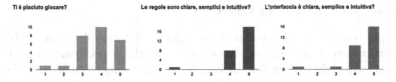

Fig. 3. Survey questions related to the game engagement; from left to right: "did you like playing?", "are the rules clear, simple and intuitive?", "is the user interface clear, simple and intuitive?"; scores range from 1 (not at all) to 5 (very much).

6   Game Cultural Incentive Analysis

Given the cultural topic of the game, we hypothesize that an incentive to play is constituted by the interest in learning something new about Milan.

6.1   Analysis of "Learning" Time

During the gameplay, the players can learn more about the
assets they are playing with: at
the end of each level, when the
names of the 4 depicted assets
are displayed, and at the end of
the round, when the assets are
visualized on a map. We analyze the time spent between levels of the same round and the
time spent between consecutive
rounds; we can consider those
intervals as the actual learning
time. Figure 4 shows the distribution of the time between levels (summed on the round); the

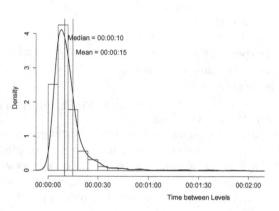

Fig. 4. Distribution of the time spent between levels of the same round per user.

graph is cut at 2 min, but the between-levels time goes up to almost 7 min. The curve decreases very quickly, in most cases only 2–3 s are spent between levels, but we can notice that sometimes users spent a considerable longer time. We can speculate that in those cases, the players exploited the links to the catalogue records.

Whenever a user plays two game rounds within an interval of 15 min, we consider those rounds are consecutive. The time-between-rounds distribution shows the already observed tendency, with a visible group of between-rounds intervals around 40 s, which we can attribute to the most "curious" users that spent some time to explore the asset map.

6.2   Analysis of Learning Effect

It is worth noting that, at the end of each game level, the player not only learns if his/her answer was correct but can also see the asset names for the four photos (cf. top-right screenshot in Fig. 1). Since it can happen that the same image appears more than once as distracting option, over time this can cause the player to learn recognizing some of the assets. We evaluate this possible learning effect by measuring the average number of correct guesses per round as a function of the number of played round. We notice that the players' precision actually improves along with the game rounds; using a simple linear regression model, we can estimate this improvement in 1.1 % per played round.

6.3   Subjective Analysis of the Educational Incentive

Some of the questions in the already mentioned survey are aimed to evaluate the educational incentive of the game, as shown in Fig. 5. The question displayed on the left investigates the incentives to continue playing as perceived by the users. While the main game features are among the highly rated incentives, it is interesting to notice that 27 % of players stated that learning new things is a stimulus to play the game. This is further proved by the question on the right in Fig. 5, asking the participants whether they learned anything new about Milan while playing. The responses distribution clearly shows that an "educational" effect was strongly perceived by Indomilando players. We can conclude that Indomilando has an evident educational "collateral effect" that makes players acquire new knowledge about cultural heritage assets.

Fig. 5. Survey questions related to the game incentives; on the left "what motivated you to play the game?"; on the right "did you learn anything new about Milan?" (1 = not at all, 5 = very much).

7   Conclusions

In this paper, we presented the design, development and evaluation of Indomilando, a cultural heritage GWAP aimed to rank the assets and the photos of the collection of historical-artistic architectures of Milan. Our evaluation results support our claims that: (1) the game is effective in achieving its ranking purpose, because the resulting rank is highly correlated to a ground truth and this outcome is achieved in a very limited time; (2) Indomilando shows a good engagement potential, because most players find the game fun and we also notice a user group that spent a significantly high time in playing; and (3) the game also leads to a learning/educational effect, because players are motivated to acquire new knowledge about the Milan cultural heritage. The interplay of the ranking purpose and the educational incentive, however, is to be further investigated.

Acknowledgments. This work was supported by the SmartCulture project co-funded by Regione Lombardia (POR-FESR 2007-2013, id 40393840).

References

1. Law, E., von Ahn, L.: Human computation. Synth. Lect. Artif. Intell. Mach. Learn. **5**(3), 1–121 (2011)
2. Howe, J.: The rise of crowdsourcing. Wired Mag. **14**(6), 1–4 (2006)
3. Ridge, M.: From tagging to theorizing: deepening engagement with cultural heritage through crowdsourcing. Curator Mus. J. **56**(4), 435–450 (2013)
4. Holley, R.: Crowdsourcing: how and why should libraries do it? D-Lib Mag. **16**(3), 4 (2010)
5. Oomen, J., Aroyo, L.: Crowdsourcing in the cultural heritage domain: opportunities and challenges. In: Proceedings of C&T 2011, pp. 138–149. ACM (2011)
6. von Ahn, L.: Games with a purpose. IEEE Comput. **39**(6), 92–94 (2006)
7. Hacker, S., Von Ahn, L.: Matchin: eliciting user preferences with an online game. In: Proceedings of CHI 2009, pp. 1207–1216. ACM (2009)
8. Hees, J., Khamis, M., Biedert, R., Abdennadher, S., Dengel, A.: Collecting links between entities ranked by human association strengths. In: Cimiano, P., Corcho, O., Presutti, V., Hollink, L., Rudolph, S. (eds.) ESWC 2013. LNCS, vol. 7882, pp. 517–531. Springer, Heidelberg (2013)
9. Celino, I., Della Valle, E., Gualandris, R.: On the effectiveness of a mobile puzzle game UI to crowdsource linked data management tasks. In: CrowdUI (2014)
10. Von Ahn, L., Dabbish, L.: Labeling images with a computer game. In: CHI 2004, pp. 319–326. ACM (2004)
11. Wieser, C., Bry, F., Bérard, A., Lagrange, R.: ARTigo: building an artwork search engine with games and higher-order latent semantic analysis. In: HCOMP (2013)
12. de Vreede, T., Nguyen, C., de Vreede, G.-J., Boughzala, I., Oh, O., Reiter-Palmon, R.: A theoretical model of user engagement in crowdsourcing. In: Antunes, P., Gerosa, M.A., Sylvester, A., Vassileva, J., de Vreede, G.-J. (eds.) CRIWG 2013. LNCS, vol. 8224, pp. 94–109. Springer, Heidelberg (2013)
13. Mao, A., Kamar, E., Horvitz, E.: Why stop now? predicting worker engagement in online crowdsourcing. In: HCOMP (2013)
14. Mao, A., et al.: Volunteering versus work for pay: incentives and tradeoffs in crowdsourcing. In: HCOMP (2013)
15. Feyisetan, O., Simperl, E., Van Kleek, M., Shadbolt, N.: Improving paid microtasks through gamification and adaptive furtherance incentives. In: WWW 2015 (2015)
16. von Ahn, L.: Duolingo: learn a language for free while helping to translate the web. In: IUI 2013, pp. 1–2. ACM (2013)
17. Beal, C.R., Morrison, C.T., Villegas, J.C.: Human computation as an educational opportunity. In: Michelucci, P. (ed.) Handbook of Human Computation, pp. 163–170. Springer, Heidelberg (2013)
18. Garcia, I.: Learning a language for free while translating the web. Does duolingo work? Int. J. Engl. Linguist. **3**(1), 19 (2013)
19. Wilson, E.B.: Probable inference, the law of succession, and statistical inference. J. Am. Stat. Assoc. **22**(158), 209–212 (1927)
20. Fagin, R., Kumar, R., Sivakumar, D.: Comparing top k lists. SIAM J. Discrete Math. **17**(1), 134–160 (2003)
21. Pihur, V., Datta, S., Datta, S.: Weighted rank aggregation of cluster validation measures: a monte carlo cross-entropy approach. Bioinformatics **23**(13), 1607–1615 (2007)

Semantic Measures: How Similar? How Related?

Teresa Costa[✉] and José Paulo Leal

CRACS and INESC-Porto LA, Faculty of Sciences,
University of Porto, Porto, Portugal
{zp,teresa.costa}@dcc.fc.up.pt

Abstract. There are two main types of semantic measures (SM): similarity and relatedness. There are also two main types of datasets, those intended for similarity evaluations and those intended for relatedness. Although they are clearly distinct, they are similar enough to generate some misconceptions.

Is there a confusion between similarity and relatedness among the semantic measure community, both the designers of SMs and the creators of benchmarks? This is the question that the research presented in this paper tries to answer. Authors performed a survey of both the SMs and datasets and executed a cross evaluation of those measures and datasets. The results show different consistency of measures with datasets of the same type. This research enabled us to conclude not only that there is indeed some confusion but also to pinpoint the SMs and benchmarks less consistent with their intended type.

Keywords: Semantic similarity · Semantic relatedness · Semantic measures · Linked data

1 Introduction

Semantic measures are an attempt to quantify and compare pairs of concepts, words or sentences. They can be regarded as a kind of distance in a semantic space [1]. The object of semantic measures is inherently psychological, making an objective analysis more difficult. To complicate matters, there are two main kinds of semantic measures: similarity and relatedness. Similarity measures the amount of common features and relatedness ponders other kinds of relationships. Although these two kinds of semantic measures are distinct, are they defined and benchmarked in acceptable terms, so that they effectively measure different things?

Similarity and relatedness are indeed distinct concepts. The similarity of two concepts depends on size of the smallest class that contains them. Relatedness depends on any relationships connecting the two concepts, including but not restricted to class membership and inclusion. For instance, the concepts of dog and cat are similar insofar they are both mammals; the same can be said about ant and flee since they are both insects. An ant and a dog are similar insofar as they are both animals, but less similar than cats and dogs. This is so since

© Springer International Publishing Switzerland 2016
A. Bozzon et al. (Eds.): ICWE 2016, LNCS 9671, pp. 431–438, 2016.
DOI: 10.1007/978-3-319-38791-8_29

the class of animals contains both the classes of mammals and insects. Flees are related to cats and dogs since they parasite them, thus flees are more related to dogs than ants. This is not because of the features they share, and they do share some since they are all animals, but because of other relationships, in this case parasitism. Thus, the similarity of dogs and flees may be the same as the similarity of dogs and ants, but the relatedness of dogs and flees is greater than that of dogs and ants. There is a clear difference between similarity and relatedness but people often confuse the two, or they value them in different ways. Based on a classical example [2], one could argue that some people value more similarity than relatedness.

There is growing evidence that the confusion between similarity and relatedness exists also among the researchers of semantic measures [1]. There are cases of semantic measures that are designed for similarity and then validated using relatedness datasets benchmark [3–5]. Arguably the source of this confusion is the perception that similarity is particular case of relatedness [1] (page 15). In fact, similarity is based on *is-a* relationships and these are a particular kind of the relationships that may be considered in relatedness. However, this does *not* entail that a similarity measure is a particular case of a relatedness measure. As a metaphor, consider the routes available on a digital map between 2 given points a and b by different means of transport – walking, public transportation or car – and their respective times. These can be named $t_w(a, b)$, $t_p(a, b)$ and $t_c(a, b)$. One can add a fourth route – the quickest one, or $t_q(a, b)$ – which can be obtained with a different means of transport according to each pair of points. Although the car is a particular means of transport, that in some cases is the quickest means of transport, that does not entail that $t_c(a, b)$ is a particular case of $t_q(a, b)$.

By the same token a similarity measure using only *is-a* relationships is not a particular case of a relatedness measure considering all kinds of relationships, including the former. In particular, it does not make sense to use a relatedness dataset as benchmark for a similarity measure. The respondents of the questionnaires used to create a dataset received a clear set of instruction (we hope) stating what is similarity, what is relatedness, and how they differ. Thus a measure should not be compared with a estimation of a different type.

To better understand the tension between similarity and relatedness in semantic measures and benchmarks, the authors surveyed several path-based semantic measures and datasets, described on Sect. 2. Details of the implementation of these measures are provided on Sect. 3 and the results of the cross evaluation are described on Sect. 4. Section 5 summarizes the presented work, showing evidences of a misconception between similarity and relatedness.

2   Background

Semantic measures evaluate the strength of the semantic relationships between elements (words, concepts, phrases). This evaluation relies on the analysis of information extracted from semantic sources.

The type of the semantic measure depends on the type of semantic source. There are two kinds of semantic sources, the unstructured or semi-structured ones (plain texts and dictionaries, for instance) that are used by Distributional measures and the structured ones, that are used by Knowledge-based measures.

Knowledge-based measures rely on knowledge representations, namely semantic graphs. They estimate the semantic measures by taking advantage of the structural properties of the graph, comparing elements by studying their interconnections and the semantics carried in those relationships. These measures follow three different approaches: the structural approach (e.g. [6–8]), the featured-based approach (e.g. [9]) and the Information Theoretical approach (e.g. [10]).

Path-based measures follow the structural approach. They take advantage of several graph traversal strategies, such as shortest path, random walks or other interaction analysis. These measures focus on the analysis of the interconnections between nodes and use it to estimate the similarity (or relatedness) between them.

Several semantic similarity [5–8] and semantic relatedness [4,11] measures were evaluated on this work. These measures rely on the definition of *shortest path* and *least common subsummer*.

The accuracy of a semantic measures is usually evaluated on how well it mimics the human capacity of comparing things. Datasets used in this validation process average human ratings for a set of words [1]. Those scores can be either of similarity or relatedness, as described on the instruction provided to the people that evaluated the dataset.

This work considered 4 semantic similarity datasets [12–14,16] and 5 semantic relatedness datasets [14,17–20].

3 Implementation

In the previous Section, several semantic measures were described. With the exception of the Hirst and St-Onge measure, they were originally designed to measure semantic similarity. However, those measures were adapted to estimate semantic relatedness, as proposed by Strube and Ponzetto [4].

In addition to these measures, Resnik similarity and Hirst and St-Onge relatedness were also adapted, the former to compute relatedness and the later to compute similarity, using an approach similar to that of Strube and Ponzetto. To compute relatedness using Resnik method one must use all the available properties instead only the taxonomic ones. To compute similarity using the Hirst and St-Onge method one must limit the shape of the allowable paths (to up and down), and also limit the properties in the upwards and downwards categories to the taxonomic ones.

All the described measures were implemented to compute both similarity and relatedness. The implementation process considered the following assumptions:

- the value of the semantic measure between a word and itself is its maximum value;

- the value of the semantic measure between two words, if one is not in the semantic proxy, is its minimum value;
- if the semantic proxy has no root or has several ones, a new node is inserted to form a semantic tree with a single root;
- the disambiguation strategy selects the pair of concepts (derived from the two input words) that produces the best measure.

All the semantic measures detailed on Sect. 2 depend on a graph traversal to search the best path connecting two different nodes. This can be a very time consuming process, in particular if a remote source is used. Knowledge bases, such as WordNet[1] [15], usually provide dumps of their data. These dumps were used to preprocess the semantic graph and store it locally. This task was performed using the RDF data dumps available for each version of WordNet.

A testbed to computed semantic measures was developed to support the validation process and is freely available online[2]. It is a Java Web Application created using the Google Web Toolkit, with a back-end server that stores the preprocessed graphs and computes the measures, and a front-end responsible for user interaction. The user interface allows the selection of semantic methods, semantic proxies, and a pair of words. After computation, the best result is displayed for each measure. This consists of the measure value, the pair of concepts associated to the given words, and the path linking them. If available, the user can browse other concept pairs with alternative values.

4   Validation

The cross validation process presented in this section used 10 different semantic measures (5 similarity and 5 relatedness) and 9 semantic datasets (4 similarity and 5 relatedness). As knowledge proxy, the three latest versions of WordNet were used.

The following tables summarize the results obtained for each WordNet version. Each measure as two variants, similarity and relatedness, respectively represented by an S and an R in the table row header. Datasets are also divided into similarity and relatedness. Thus rows are associated with measures and columns with datasets. The values on the cells are Spearman's rank order correlations between the computed values of the row's measure with the column's dataset values. The checkmark symbol ($\checkmark$) means that the obtained result matches the expectations, which means that the semantic measure of a type performs better for a dataset of that type.

Table 1 presents the results obtained for the WordNet 2.1. WUP and HSO similarity measures stand out since they correctly identify the 4 similarity benchmarks. The other measures have mediocre results for datasets of the same type. The dataset with best performance is WS Sim that is correctly identified by all measures while MTurk-287 and MEN are always misidentified.

---

[1] Wordnet.princeton.edu.
[2] http://quilter.dcc.fc.up.pt/smcomp.

Table 1. Cross evaluation of the semantic measures and semantic benchmarks using WordNet 2.1 as semantic source.

		Similarity datasets				Relatedness datasets				
		MC30	RG65	WS Sim	SimLex 999	WS353	WS Rel	MTurk 287	MTurk 771	MEN
Rada	S	0.21	0.28	0.41 ✓	0.20	0.22	0.06	0.27	0.28	0.22
	R	0.26	0.37	0.27	0.22	0.18	0.05	0.22	0.33 ✓	0.15
LCH	S	0.21	0.28	0.41 ✓	0.20	0.22	0.06	0.27	0.28	0.22
	R	0.26	0.37	0.26	0.22	0.18	0.05	0.22	0.33 ✓	0.15
WUP	S	0.20 ✓	0.27 ✓	0.39 ✓	0.10 ✓	0.20	0.03	0.26	0.18	0.18
	R	0.14	0.12	0.17	-0.08	0.12	0.10 ✓	0.17	0.10	0.07
Resnik	S	0.2	0.25	0.35 ✓	0.25 ✓	0.19	0.04	0.25	0.16	0.17
	R	0.26	0.37	0.26	0.22	0.18	0.05 ✓	0.22	0.33 ✓	0.15
HSO	S	0.22 ✓	0.43 ✓	0.40 ✓	0.24 ✓	0.23	0.05	0.31	0.29	0.29
	R	0.18	0.27	0.34	0.14	0.23 ✓	0.11 ✓	0.29	0.18	0.25

Table 2. Cross evaluation using WordNet 3.0 as semantic source.

		Similarity Datasets				Relatedness Datasets				
		MC30	RG65	WS Sim	SimLex 999	WS353	WS Rel	MTurk 287	MTurk 771	MEN
Rada	S	0.15	0.26 ✓	0.34 ✓	0.20	0.20	0.04	0.26	0.27	0.22
	R	0.29	0.23	0.28	0.23	0.20 ✓	0.11 ✓	0.14	0.33 ✓	0.16
LCH	S	0.16	0.26 ✓	0.37 ✓	0.20	0.20	0.05	0.26	0.27	0.22
	R	0.29	0.23	0.28	0.23	0.20 ✓	0.11 ✓	0.14	0.33 ✓	0.16
WUP	S	0.13 ✓	0.23 ✓	0.33 ✓	0.08 ✓	0.18	0.04	0.24	0.16	0.18
	R	0.12	0.19	0.13	-0.09	0.06	0.01	0.11	0.09	0.08
Resnik	S	0.15	0.21	0.31 ✓	0.14	0.16	0.02	0.25	0.15	0.18
	R	0.29	0.23	0.28	0.23	0.20 ✓	0.11 ✓	0.14	0.33✓	0.16
HSO	S	0.16 ✓	0.41 ✓	0.39 ✓	0.24 ✓	0.23	0.06	0.26	0.28	0.3
	R	0.11	0.26	0.32	0.14	0.21	0.09 ✓	0.26 ✓	0.18	0.25

Table 2 presents the results obtained for the WordNet 3.0. WUP and HSO similarity measures stand out again since they identify correctly the 4 similarity benchmarks. The other measures have average results for datasets of the same type. The dataset with best performance is WS Sim that is correctly identified by all measures while MEN is always misidentified.

Table 3 presents the results obtained for the WordNet 2.1. WUP similarity measure stands out since it correctly identify the 4 similarity benchmarks. HSO relatedness measure also stands out by identifying all the relatedness datasets. The other measures have mediocre results for datasets of the same type. The dataset with best performace is WS Rel that is correcty identified by all measures. All benchmarks have their types correctly identified at least once.

The bar graphs of Fig. 1 provide an overview of the accuracy of semantic measures and datasets across the 3 WordNet versions. From the semantic measures perspective, the WUP measures has the best and worst results in similarity and relatedness respectively. It should be noted that the original measure was designed for similarity. All the other measures have mediocre results, with around

Table 3. Cross evaluation using WordNet 3.1 as semantic source.

		Similarity datasets				Relatedness datasets				
		MC30	RG65	WS Sim	SimLex 999	WS353	WS Rel	MTurk 287	MTurk 771	MEN
Rada	S	0.6 ✓	0.76	0.57 ✓	0.37	0.28	-0.04	0.3	0.42	0.3
	R	0.48	0.78	0.46	0.46	0.32 ✓	0.13 ✓	0.25	0.42 ✓	0.45✓
LCH	S	0.6 ✓	0.76	0.57 ✓	0.37	0.28	-0.04	0.3	0.42	0.3
	R	0.48	0.79	0.45	0.47	0.33 ✓	0.12 ✓	0.25	0.42 ✓	0.44 ✓
WUP	S	0.66 ✓	0.7 ✓	0.52 ✓	0.25 ✓	0.27	-0.03	0.28	0.27	0.25
	R	0.58	0.65	0.31	0.12	0.20	0.08 ✓	0.21	0.16	0.21
Resnik	S	0.59	0.73 ✓	0.46	0.3	0.21	-0.08	0.29	0.32	0.24
	R	0.59	0.70	0.70	0.41	0.25 ✓	0.16 ✓	0.24	0.35 ✓	0.34 ✓
HSO	S	0.38	0.52	0.45	0.33	0.23	-0.03	0.32	0.27	0.33
	R	0.62	0.65	0.48	0.43	0.31 ✓	0.11 ✓	0.34 ✓	0.27 ✓	038✓

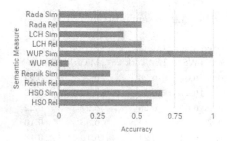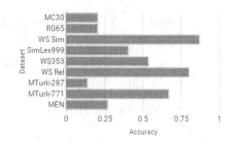

Fig. 1. Datasets accuracy

50 % of accuracy rate. From the dataset perspective, two datasets stand out from the pack with accuracy rate above 75 %: the twin datasets WS Sim and WS Rel.

These results show that there may be some misconception regarding similarity and relatedness among the semantic measure community, both on the measure designers and on the data set creators. However, there are measures and benchmarks that stand out for their accuracy.

5   Conclusions

Semantic measures quantify the relationship between concepts, words and sentences. They try to mimic the human capacity for comparing things, hindering the analysis of artificial SM. There are semantic measures that estimate the amount of features two elements share – similarity – or that estimate all type of relationships between them – relatedness.

Despite being two different concepts, there seems to exist some confusion between them, namely among the semantic measures community. There are cases of semantic datasets that are wrongly categorized and cases of semantic measures that are designed for similarity, but evaluated using semantic relatedness datasets.

This paper surveyed several well known semantic benchmarks and path-based measures. Aiming to understand the tension between similarity and relatedness, a cross evaluation was performed using all measures (and their adaptations) with all surveyed datasets. This process was executed with three different versions of WordNet as semantic proxy. Assuming that there is no confusion between similarity and relatedness, it should be possible to use semantic measures of both types to identify the type of a semantic dataset. It should be also possible to use semantic benchmarks of the two different types to categorize a semantic measure.

The validation showed that this is not the case. In fact, the opposite is more frequent. Most of the SMs do not guess correctly the datasets of their types and vice-versa. This enables us to conclude that some misconception regarding relatedness and similarity may exist among the semantic measure community. Fortunately, this research allowed us to pinpoint a few cases where SMs and datasets are more accurate, namely the WUP similarity measure and the WS-Sim and WS-Rel datasets.

Acknowledgments. This work is partially financed by the ERDF European Regional Development Fund through the Operational Programme for Competitiveness and Internationalisation - COMPETE 2020 Programme and by the FCT within project POCI-01-0145-FEDER-006961 and project "NORTE-01-0145-FEDER-000020" financed by the North Portugal Regional Operational Programme (NORTE 2020), under the POR-TUGAL 2020 Partnership Agreement and through the European Regional Development Fund (ERDF).

References

1. Harispe, S., Ranwez, S., Janaqi, S., Montmain, J.: Semantic similarity from natural language and ontology analysis. Synth. Lect. Hum. Lang. Technol. **8**, 1–254 (2015)
2. Gorodnichenko, Y., Roland, G.: Understanding the individualism-collectivism cleavage, its effects: lessons from cultural psychology. Institutions Comp. Econ. Dev. **150**, 213 (2012)
3. Budanitsky, A., Hirst, G.: Evaluating wordnet-based measures of lexical semantic relatedness. Comput. Linguist. **32**, 13–47 (2006)
4. Strube, M., Ponzetto, S.: WikiRelate! Computing semantic relatedness using wikipedia. In: AAAI (2006)
5. Philip, R.: Using information content to evaluate semantic similarity in a taxonomy. In: IJCAI (1995)
6. Rada, R., Mili, H., Bicknell, E., Blettner, M.: Development and application of a metric on semantic nets. IEEE Trans. Syst. Man Cybern. **19**, 17–30 (1989)
7. Leacock, C., Chodorow, M.: Combining local context and wordnet similarity for word sense identification. WordNet: Electr. Lexical Database **49**, 265–283 (1998)
8. Wu, Z., Palmer, M.: Verbs semantics and lexical selection. In: Proceedings of the 32nd Annual Meeting on Association for Computational Linguistics (1994)
9. Bodenreider, O., Aubry, M., Burgun, A.: Non-lexical approaches to identifying associative relations in the gene ontology. In: Pacific Symposium on Biocomputing (2005)

10. Lin, D.: An information-theoretic definition of similarity. In: ICML (1998)
11. Hirst, G., St-Onge, D.: Lexical chains as representations of context for the detection and correction of malapropisms. WordNet: Electr. Lexical Database **305**, 305–332 (1998)
12. Rubenstein, H., Goodenough, J.B.: Contextual correlates of synonymy. Commun. ACM **8**, 627–633 (1965)
13. Miller, G.A., Charles, W.G.: Contextual correlates of semantic similarity. Lang. Cogn. Proc. **6**, 1–28 (1991)
14. Agirre, E., Alfonseca, E., Hall, K., Kravalova, J., Paşca, M., Soroa, A.: A study on similarity, relatedness using distributional, wordnet-based approaches. In: Proceedings of Human Language Technologies: The 2009 Annual Conference of the North American Chapter of the Association for Computational Linguistics (2009)
15. Fellbaum, C.: WordNet. Wiley, New York (1999)
16. Hill, F., Reichart, R., Korhonen, A.: Simlex-999: evaluating semantic models with (genuine) similarity estimation (2014). arXiv preprint arXiv:1408.3456
17. Evgeniy, G.: The WordSimilarity-353 Test Collection. http://www.cs.technion.ac.il/gabr/resources/data/wordsim353/
18. Radinsky, K., Agichtein, E., Gabrilovich, E., Markovitch, S.: A word at a time, computing word relatedness using temporal semantic analysis. In: Proceedings of the 20th International Conference on World Wide Web (2011)
19. Halawi, G., Dror, G., Gabrilovich, E., Koren, Y.: Large-scale learning of word relatedness with constraints. In: Proceedings of the 18th ACM SIGKDD International Conference on Knowledge Discovery and Data Mining (2012)
20. Bruni, E., Tran, N.-K., Baroni, M.: Multimodal distributional semantics. J. Artif. Intell. Res. (JAIR) **49**, 1–47 (2014)

Design of CQA Systems for Flexible and Scalable Deployment and Evaluation

Ivan Srba$^{(\boxtimes)}$ and Maria Bielikova

Faculty of Informatics and Information Technologies,
Slovak University of Technology in Bratislava, Ilkovičova 2, 842 16 Bratislava, Slovakia
{ivan.srba,maria.bielikova}@stuba.sk

Abstract. Successfulness of Community Question Answering (CQA) systems on the open web (e.g. Yahoo! Answers) motivated for their utilization in new contexts (e.g. education or enterprise) and environments (e.g. inside organizations). In spite of initial research how their specifics influence design of CQA systems, many additional problems have not been addressed so far. Especially a poor flexibility and scalability which hamper: (1) CQA essential features to be employed in various settings (e.g. in different educational organizations); and (2) collaboration support methods to be effectively evaluated (e.g. in offline as well as in live experiments). In this paper, we provide design recommendations how to achieve flexible and scalable deployment and evaluation by means of a case study on educational and organizational CQA system Askalot. Its universal and configurable features allow us to deploy it at two universities as well as in MOOC system edX. In addition, by means of its experimental infrastructure, we can integrate various collaboration support methods which loosely coupled and can be easily evaluated online as well as offline with datasets from Askalot itself or even from all CQA systems built on the top of the Stack Exchange platform.

Keywords: CQA · System design · Flexibility · Scalability · Askalot

1 Introduction and Related Work

Since the emergence of first Community Question Answering (CQA) systems, they became a substantial source of knowledge online. In the most popular and successful CQA systems, such as Yahoo! Answers or Stack Overflow, communities consisting of millions of users share their knowledge by providing answers on questions asked by the rest of the community. This question answering process is based on knowledge sharing between people and builds on theories of collective intelligence and wisdom of the crowd. More specifically, CQA represents a unique example of online community which utilizes principles of crowdsourcing, human computation and social computing.

In the recent time, motivated by many positive outcomes of open CQA systems on the open web, academy as well as industry became interested in a possibility to adapt CQA systems into additional contexts and environments. At first, potential of CQA systems has been recognized not only in the context of the web, but also in educational domain [1], in crowd-based customer services [2] or in integrated development

© Springer International Publishing Switzerland 2016
A. Bozzon et al. (Eds.): ICWE 2016, LNCS 9671, pp. 439–447, 2016.
DOI: 10.1007/978-3-319-38791-8_30

environments (IDE) [3]. Secondly, concepts of CQA systems can be utilized not only by large open communities, but also inside organizations (e.g. as a part of company's social platform IBM Connect [4]). The transferability of CQA systems from the web to these new contexts and environments brings several open problems. Especially, their specifics naturally result in many new opportunities as well as limitations which should be taken into consideration when providing users with:

- *essential features* – core functions related to the question answering process (e.g. in educational domain, it is essential to delay teachers' answers to give students enough time to provide answers by themselves [1]), and
- *collaboration support* (e.g. similarly in educational domain, it is necessary to perform precise expertise matching in new question recommendation as students should not be requested to answer questions which they are not capable to address [5]).

While some initial research approaches address these problems, we recognized that implementation of essential features, and integration as well as evaluation of collaboration support methods lacks sufficient *flexibility* and *scalability*. More specifically, we identified two open problems that direct our research presented in this paper:

1. **Low adaptability of essential features to various settings**. A CQA system adapted to a particular context or environment provides a possibility to be deployed in several different instances at the same time (e.g. in several educational or enterprise organizations). In spite of that, design of essential features is not usually flexible enough to handle various different settings.
2. **Ineffective integration and evaluation of collaboration support methods**. CQA systems without appropriate collaboration support would not be so successful. After ten years long research and development, we can take advantage of many collaboration support approaches (as a part of our previous work, we conducted a comprehensive survey in which we analyzed 265 approaches aimed at CQA systems [6]). Achieving loosely coupled integration of the existing collaboration support methods as well as evaluation of novel ones can be, however, quite difficult. Moreover, adapted CQA systems provide a valuable possibility to perform live experiments which can supplement offline evaluation (in our survey, we found out that only 3 out of 169 approaches were evaluated online [6]). Therefore, there is an open question how to make combination of offline and online experiments as effective as possible.

Despite a number of studies providing design frameworks and design guidelines for applications based on collective intelligence [7], human computation [8] as well as for CQA systems themselves [9], there is not any particular study which would tackle flexibility and scalability of CQA systems, especially with focus on adapted CQA systems. Probably, the most similar design guidelines to our aim, are proposed in study [10] which tackles with adaptability of CQA systems to organizational environment.

In this paper, we propose several design recommendations how to tackle the identified open problems by means of design of our educational and organizational CQA system named Askalot. Thanks to its universal design of essential features, we can deploy it at two universities as well as in MOOC system edX. In addition, its experimental infrastructure allows us to easily implement and experimentally evaluate various research approaches offline as well as online directly in Askalot.

2   Case Study on Educational and Organizational CQA Askalot

In order to achieve our main goal, we draw upon case study on our educational and organizational CQA system named Askalot[1]. Askalot represents a novel concept of an organization-wide educational CQA system that fills the gap between open and too restricted class communities of learners [11].

In contrast to the standard CQA systems (e.g. Yahoo! Answers or Stack Overflow), in the design of Askalot we took into consideration especially educational specifics (e.g. presence of a teacher or different levels of students' knowledge) and organizational specifics (e.g. lower number of users or users' familiarity), for more information see [11]. As a part of our previous work, we provided design recommendations, which reflect these specifics in the adaptation of CQA concepts, and we divided them into five categories: dialogue and action, teachers' assistance, workspace awareness, students' self-regulation or guidance, and finally community level management.

Source code of Askalot is provided as an open source[2]. It is implemented in Ruby on Rails with Bootstrap that ensures a responsive design. The quality of our code is assured by employing test driven development (TDD) and regular code review process.

The first version of Askalot was developed for use at our faculty only. Motivated by positive outcomes as well as feedback from the involved students and teachers, we have recently started a cooperation with:

1. *Harvard University* in order to transform Askalot into a plugin to MOOC system edX, which would be suitable for performing A/B experiments (following MOOClet formalism [12]). Our main goal is to replace the standard unstructured forum with an effective tool that can be used by students to share their knowledge and thus solve various course-related questions.
2. *University of Lugano* in order to deploy Askalot at their university as a part of cooperation project in the SCOPES program.

The original design of Askalot was proposed specifically for our university (e.g. it supported only simple non-hierarchical categorization of questions which reflected our subjects' structure). Therefore, it did not provide sufficient flexibility and scalability which is necessary to deploy Askalot in additional various settings. In spite of the same educational domain, edX differs significantly from university environments as well as both universities differs from each other (in terms of their formal educational process, structure, etc.). As the result, we had to rebuilt the original system design and following this process, we provide several design recommendations in the following section.

---

[1] Demo of Askalot is available at: https://askalot.fiit.stuba.sk/demo.
[2] Source code of Askalot is available at: https://github.com/AskalotCQA/askalot.

3   Designing Essential Features for Various Settings

Some of CQA essential features are natively flexible and scalable. On other side, other ones required to be redesigned what leads to identification of several design recommendations, which we divided into four groups.

Modular System Architecture.   At first, following the requirements, we identified that it is necessary to distinguish two main configurations of our system which we codenamed *Askalot @university* (which is supposed to be deployed at our university and at University of Lugano) and *Askalot @mooc* (which is supposed to be deployed in edX). Consequently, we created three modules. Into the first one, we separated all core features that are common for both configurations (e.g. posting questions and answers or a *global view* containing lists of all questions, categories, tags and users). The remaining two components inherit all features from the core module and add specialized features for a university or MOOC respectively (e.g. in MOOC besides a global view, Askalot provides also a *unit view* – a list of questions asked about a particular learning unit). To achieve the best possible integration with other learning systems (including edX), we adopted LTI (Learning Tools Interoperability) standard. It allows Askalot to obtain data (e.g. information about a student) as well as to provide data back to the learning system (e.g. grades for quality of posts) in the standardized way.

Flexible User Management Integration.   Secondly, to face high diversity of educational environments, Askalot can be integrated with several user authentication services. Many universities have their own LDAP servers, and thus Askalot provides a possibility to configure LDAP authentication. Similarly, users can be authenticated by LTI protocol. In both cases, if a user sings into the system for the first time, his/her account is automatically created and filled with data provided by LDAP/LTI. In other words, Askalot does not require any particular import or configuration of users. Another available possibility is to sign up for an account directly in the system. In this case, a user account can be completely anonymous. This option is important especially in situations when students might hesitate to ask questions because their identity is revealed.

Adaptable Self-managed Content Organization.   Topic structure plays in CQA an essential role for content organization, navigation and collaboration support (e.g. we can analyze in which topics a student is interested in). At the same time, structure of topics differs significantly across universities or MOOC courses. In addition, as topics reflect actual information needs of students, they are really dynamic and cannot be prepared in advance. Therefore, we proposed to create two-level organization of topics.

1. At first, an asker is requested to select a *category* which reflects the formal structure of a university or a MOOC course (e.g. a subject or a course section, see Fig. 1).
2. Secondly, an asker can add any additional *tags* to describe particular question topics.

This solution provides two main advantages in terms of flexibility and scalability. Deploying Askalot in new settings at a university is quite effective, because it is necessary just to prepare a list of subjects what is quite straightforward. Askalot deployed in

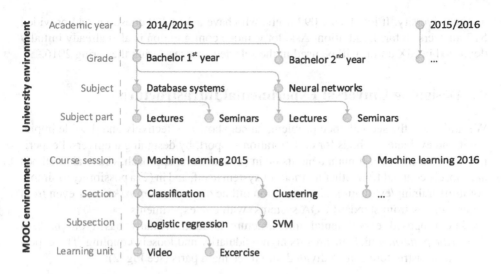

Fig. 1. Example hierarchies of categories in university and MOOC environments.

edX is able to even parse the course structure automatically and create categories on the fly. At the same time, students create a *folksonomy* by means of tags assigned to questions which can be easily adjusted to actual students' needs.

We recognized that categories at universities as well as at MOOC courses need to be organized into a hierarchy. In addition, it is necessary to capture repeating sessions, which are typical for educational domain (i.e. academic years, course sessions), and thus we can easily display user only content from his current user context (e.g. currently opened course session). We solved this requirement by means of a tree structure for each repeating session (an example is provided in Fig. 1). Each node in this tree has four attributes:

1. *domain-specific ID* (e.g. subject code) – to identify the same categories across all academic years or course sessions;
2. *askable flag* – whether students can ask questions in this category (e.g. it is possible to disable asking question for previous academic years);
3. *shareable flag* – whether users with rights to access this category can see also questions from the previous academic years or course sessions (the same categories are identified by means of domain-specific IDs); and finally
4. *roles* – it is possible to give users special roles (i.e. a teacher, an administrator) which assign them special rights, such as assess quality of content or edit/delete posts.

Ubiquitous Activity Awareness and Notifications. As it is necessary to keep students as well as teachers informed about the activity in the system, Askalot provides several ways how to achieve it. Besides notifications displayed directly in the system, users can receive notifications by an email or even let them be sent to their Facebook account.

We have already evaluated the flexibility and scalability of Askalot @university configuration by deploying it as a supplementary tool to the formal educational process at our university. It involves 1 092 users, who have asked 379 questions and provided 517 answers so far. In addition, Askalot @mooc configuration is also already initially deployed in edX and it will be used in the selected courses during the spring 2016.

4   Designing Universal Experimental Infrastructure

We addressed the second open problem, namely how to effectively and flexible implement and evaluate methods for collaboration support, by designing a universal experimental infrastructure. It main benefits lie in (1) a modular approach, where all methods are loosely coupled from other methods or system itself, and in (2) a possibility to simply combine training/evaluation of methods on offline datasets (from Askalot or even from other datasets from standard CQA systems) with live experiments.

The proposed experimental infrastructure is fundamentally based on *publish-subscribe pattern*, which ensures its high modularity and loosely coupling. The experimental infrastructure can be divided into three main parts (see Fig. 2):

1. **Data conversion** – At first, it provides utilities to convert any datasets from CQA systems to a dedicated experimental database which has the same database schema as Askalot system. Currently, the convertor for Stack Exchange datasets (distributed under Creative Commons license in XML format) is implemented, however, it is easily possible to create converters for any additional CQA datasets.
2. **Event dispatching** – The second part of experimental infrastructure is responsible for *dispatching events* to subscribed listeners. Each event is represented by four attributes: (1) an initiator who created the event; (2) an action type (i.e. create, update, delete); (3) a resource which is related to the event (questions, answers, comments, views, votes, etc.); and (4) additional custom options. There are two possible sources of events – a *live system* in online experiments (Askalot is implemented to dispatch an event each time a relevant action in the system happens) and *datasets* (either from Askalot itself or from other CQA systems) in offline experiments.

   When using datasets, the experimental infrastructure performs an *event simulation job* which selects from the database all resources and each of these resources is converted to a list of events (e.g. a question which has been updated is converted to two events with actions types *create* and *update*). All generated events are consequently sorted by time when they originally happened (i.e. creation, update or deletion time). Finally, the event simulation job sets the current time in the experimental environment to this event time and dispatch the event. This solution allows us to reproduce events exactly in the same way as they would be created by the live system.

3. **Listeners and Profiles** – The third part is dedicated to implementations of research methods themselves by means of *listeners*. Listeners can select from all dispatched events only those they are interesting in and process them in any possible way. In general, there are two main types of listeners: *profilers*, which can model users and content (e.g. user expertise, question difficulty); and *method feeders*, which can trigger various research methods (e.g. a recommendation of new questions to potential answerers) and also directly evaluate their performance. The results of profilers

can be stored in *user/question/answer profiles* which can be easily used by the proposed research methods. These profiles are universal data structures based on four attributes: a value name (e.g. user expertise), a value (e.g. a numeral expression of expertise level), a probability (e.g. how sure we are about the calculated expertise), and a source (there can be even several profilers for expertise calculation).

The experimental infrastructure has been already successfully implemented and utilized in experimental verification of a question routing method based on non-QA data [13] and a reputation method [14], which we evaluated by means of three Stack Exchange datasets (with 10 to 20 thousands of questions in each of them) and consequently we took advantage of experimental infrastructure and we simply deployed its implementation in Askalot, where it is in production environment since May 2015.

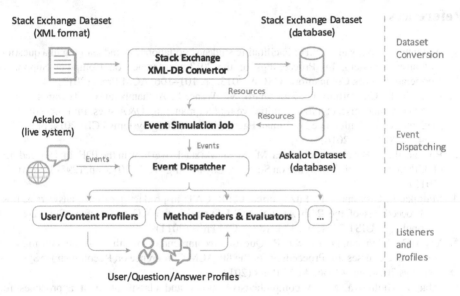

Fig. 2. Overview of experimental infrastructure.

5 Conclusion

Drawing upon the case study on CQA system Askalot, we showed several design recommendations how concepts of CQA systems can be adapted to an educational context and organizational environment with achieving high flexibility and scalability. It allowed us to deploy Askalot in three instances at two universities and in MOOC system edX. Askalot can be characterized also as an open platform based on the universal experimental infrastructure. It can be easily used to implement and evaluate various collaboration support methods (e.g. question recommendation) and even evaluate these methods with data from live system or offline datasets without any code modifications.

Our current primary goal is to deploy Askalot at several edX courses and collect feedback from students in order to make it even more suited for question answering in

MOOCs. In addition, we plan to study specifics of educational question answering process in more details and propose new adaptive support methods for (1) question routing and (2) question retrieval from archives of questions solved in the previous academic years or courses. Another possible direction for our future work is finding a solution how to tackle with performance decrease in experimental infrastructure which naturally appears at the cost of high flexibility.

Acknowledgement. This work was partially supported by grants No. VG1/0646/15 and KEGA 009STU-4/2014 and it is the partial result of collaboration within the SCOPES JRP/IP, No. 160480/2015. The authors wish to thank students participating in AskEd team, who contributed to design and implementation of Askalot and made its deploy in three different settings possible.

References

1. Aritajati, C., Narayanan, N.H.: Facilitating students' collaboration and learning in a question and answer system. In: Proceedings of the 2013 Conference on Computer Supported Cooperative Work Companion - CSCW 2013, pp. 101–106. ACM Press (2013)
2. Piccardi, T., Convertino, G., Zancanaro, M., Wang, J., Archambeau, C.: Towards crowd-based customer service: a mixed-initiative tool for managing Q&A sites. In: Proceedings of the 32nd ACM Conference on Human Factors in Computing Systems - CHI 2014, pp. 2725–2734. ACM Press (2014)
3. Ponzanelli, L., Bacchelli, A., Lanza, M.: Seahawk: stack overflow in the IDE. In: Proceedings of 35th International Conference on Software Engineering - ICSE 2013, pp. 1295–1298. IEEE (2013)
4. Matejka, J., Grossman, T., Fitzmaurice, G.: IP-QAT: in-product questions, answers & tips. In: Proceedings of the 24th Annual ACM Symposium on User Interface Software and Technology - UIST 2011, pp. 175–184. ACM Press (2011)
5. Yang, D., Adamson, D., Rosé, C.P.: Question recommendation with constraints for massive open online courses. In: Proceedings of the 8th ACM Conference on Recommender Systems - RecSys 2014, pp. 49–56. ACM Press (2014)
6. Srba, I., Bieliková, M.: A comprehensive survey and classification of approaches for community question answering. ACM Trans. Web (2016, submitted)
7. Gregg, D.G.: Designing for collective intelligence. Commun. ACM **53**, 134 (2010)
8. Reeves, S., Sherwood, S.: Five design challenges for human computation. In: Proceedings of the 6th Nordic Conference on Human-Computer Interaction - NordiCHI 2010m p. 383 (2010)
9. Mamykina, L., Manoim, B., Mittal, M., Hripcsak, G., Hartmann, B.: Design lessons from the fastest Q&A site in the west. In: Proceedings of the 2011 Annual Conference on Human Factors in Computing Systems - CHI 2011, pp. 2857–2866. ACM Press (2011)
10. Ortbach, K., Gaß, O., Köffer, S., Schacht, S., Walter, N., Maedche, A., Niehaves, B.: Design principles for a social question and answers site: enabling user-to-user support in organizations. In: Tremblay, M.C., VanderMeer, D., Rothenberger, M., Gupta, A., Yoon, V. (eds.) DESRIST 2014. LNCS, vol. 8463, pp. 54–68. Springer, Heidelberg (2014)
11. Srba, I., Bielikova, M.: Askalot: community question answering as a means for knowledge sharing in an educational organization. In: Proceedings of the 18th ACM Conference Companion on Computer Supported Cooperative Work and Social Computing – CSCW 2015, pp. 179–182. ACM Press (2015)

12. Williams, J.J., Heffernan, N.: A methodology for discovering how to adaptively personalize to users using experimental comparisons. In: Proceedings of the Late-Breaking Results at the 23rd Conference on User Modelling, Adaptation and Personalisation - UMAP 2015 (2015)
13. Srba, I., Grznar, M., Bielikova, M.: Utilizing non-QA data to improve questions routing for users with low QA activity in CQA. In: Proceedings of the 2015 IEEE/ACM International Conference on Advances in Social Networks Analysis and Mining 2015, pp. 129–136. ACM Press (2015)
14. Huna, A., Srba, I., Bielikova, M.: Exploiting content quality and question difficulty in CQA reputation systems. In: Wierzbicki, A., et al. (eds.) NetSci-X 2016. LNCS, vol. 9564, pp. 68–81. Springer, Heidelberg (2015). doi:10.1007/978-3-319-28361-6_6

A Matter of Words: NLP for Quality Evaluation of Wikipedia Medical Articles

Vittoria Cozza[1], Marinella Petrocchi[1(✉)], and Angelo Spognardi[2]

[1] IIT CNR, Pisa, Italy
{v.cozza,m.petrocchi}@iit.cnr.it
[2] DTU Compute, Kgs. Lyngby, Denmark
angsp@dtu.dk

Abstract. Automatic quality evaluation of Web information is a task with many fields of applications and of great relevance, especially in critical domains, like the medical one. We move from the intuition that the quality of content of medical Web documents is affected by features related with the specific domain. First, the usage of a specific vocabulary (Domain Informativeness); then, the adoption of specific codes (like those used in the infoboxes of Wikipedia articles) and the type of document (e.g., historical and technical ones). In this paper, we propose to leverage specific domain features to improve the results of the evaluation of Wikipedia medical articles, relying on Natural Language Processing (NLP) and dictionaries-based techniques. The results of our experiments confirm that, by considering domain-oriented features, it is possible to improve existing solutions, mainly with those articles that other approaches have less correctly classified.

1 Introduction

As observed by a recent article of Nature News [10], "Wikipedia is among the most frequently visited websites in the world and one of the most popular places to tap into the world's scientific and medical information". Despite the huge amount of consultations, open issues still threaten a fully confident fruition of the popular online open encyclopedia, like reliability and trustworthiness.

In this paper, we face the quest for automatic quality assessment of a Wikipedia article leveraging readability and reliability criteria, as well as additional parameters for completeness of information and coherence with the expected content. The notion of data quality we consider is strictly connected to the scope for which one needs such information, as suggested by recent contributions [12].

Our intuition is that groups of articles related to a specific topic and falling within specific scopes are intrinsically different from other groups on different topics within different scopes. We approach the article evaluation through machine learning techniques, that are not new to be employed for automatic

---

Work partly supported by the Registro.it project *My Information Bubble* MIB.

© Springer International Publishing Switzerland 2016
A. Bozzon et al. (Eds.): ICWE 2016, LNCS 9671, pp. 448–456, 2016.
DOI: 10.1007/978-3-319-38791-8_31

evaluation of articles quality. As an example, the work in [16] exploits classification techniques based on structural and linguistic features of an article. Here, we enrich that model with novel features that are domain-specific. As a running scenario, we focus on the Wikipedia medical portal. Indeed, facing the problems of information quality and ensuring high and correct levels of informativeness is even more demanding when health aspects are involved. Recent statistics report that Internet users are increasingly searching the Web for health information, by consulting search engines, social networks, and specialised health portals, like that of Wikipedia. As pointed out by the 2014 Eurobarometer survey on European citizens' digital health literacy[1], around six out of ten respondents have used the Internet to search for health-related information. We anticipate here that leveraging new domain-specific features is in line with this demand of articles quality. Moreover, as the outcomes of our experiments show, they effectively improve the classification results in the hard task of multi-class assessment, especially for those classes that other automatic approaches worst classify. Remarkably, our proposal is general enough to be easily extended to other domains, in addition to the medical one.

We present in the next section the dataset used in our experiments and in Sect. 3 our domain-specific, medical model. Section 4 presents experiments and results. Sections 5 and 6 conclude with related work and final remarks.

2   Dataset

We consider the dataset consisting of the entire collection of articles of the Wikipedia Medicine Portal, updated at the end of 2014. Wikipedia articles are written according to the Media Wiki markup language, a HTML-like language. Among the structural elements of one page, which differs from standard HTML pages, there are (i) the internal links, i.e., links to other Wikipedia pages, different from links to external resources; (ii) categories, which represent the Media Wiki categories a page belongs to: they are encoded in the part of text within the Media Wiki "categories" tag in the page source, and (iii) informative boxes, so called "infoboxes", which summarize in a structured manner some peculiar pieces of information related the topic of the article. The category values for the articles in the medical portal span over the ones listed at https://en.wikipedia.org/wiki/Portal:Medicine.

Infoboxes of the medical portal feature medical content and standard coding. An infobox may contain explanatory figures and text denoting peculiar characteristics of the topic, such as a disease, and the value for the standard code of a disease (for example, in case of the Alzheimer's disease, the standard code is ICD9, as for the international classification[2]).

Thanks to WikiProject Medicine[3], the dataset of articles we collected from the Wikipedia Medicine Portal has been manually labeled into seven quality

---

[1] http://ec.europa.eu/public_opinion/flash/fl_404_sum_en.pdf.

[2] http://www.who.int/classifications/icd/en/.

[3] https://en.wikipedia.org/wiki/Wikipedia:WikiProject_Medicine/Assessment.

classes. They are ordered as *Stub, Start, C, B, A, Good Article (GA), Featured Article (FA)*. The Featured and Good article classes are the highest ones: to have those labels, an article requires a community consensus and an official review by selected editors, while the other labels can be achieved with reviews from a larger, even controlled, set of editors. Actually, none of the articles in the dataset is labeled as *A*, thus, in the following, we do not consider that class, restricting the investigation to six classes.

At the date of our study, we were able to gather 24,362 rated documents. Remarkably, only a small percentage of them (1 %) is labeled as *GA* and *FA*. Indeed, the distribution of the articles among the classes is highly skewed. There are very few (201) articles for the highest quality classes (FA and GA), while the vast majority (19,108) belongs to the lowest quality ones (Stub and Start). This holds not only for the medical portal. Indeed, it is common in all Wikipedia, where, on average, only one article in every thousand is a Featured one.

Dealing with imbalanced classes is a common situation in many real applications of classification learning. Without any countermeasure, common classifiers tend to correctly identify only articles belonging to the majority classes, clearly leading to severe mis-classification of the minority classes, since typical learning algorithms strive to maximize the overall prediction accuracy. To reduce the disequilibrium among the size of the classes, we have first randomly sampled the articles belonging to the most populated classes. Then, we have oversampled the data from the minority classes, following the approach in [6], the Synthetic Sampling with Data Generation. After such processing, we have 1015 articles from Start, Stub, B and C and 214 and 162 ones for GA and FA, respectively.

3 The Medical Domain Model

We apply a multi-class classification approach to label the articles of the sampled dataset into the six WikiProject quality classes. In order to have a baseline, we have first applied the state of the art model proposed in [16] to the dataset. This model is known as the actionable model and is based on five linguistic and structural features. For page limit, we do not detail the features and how we have extracted them from the dataset. A detailed description is available in [8]. The classification results according to the baseline model are in Sect. 4.

Then, we have improved the baseline model with novel and specifically crafted features that rely on the **medical domain** and that capture details on the specific content of an article. As shown in Fig. 1, *medical model features* (the bio-medical entities) have been extracted from the free text only, exploiting advanced NLP techniques and using domain dictionaries. In details, we newly define and extract from the dataset the following novel features: *InfoBoxNormSize, Category* and *DomainInformativeness*. The first represents the normalised size of an infobox that contains standard medical coding. *Category* is the category a page belongs to. *DomainInformativeness* is the number of bio-medical entities, namely, the domain dependent terms in the article (such as the ones denoting symptoms, diseases, treatments, etc.).

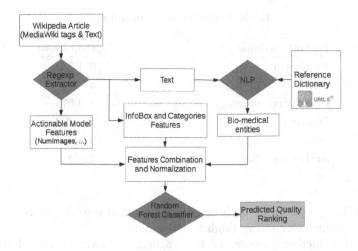

Fig. 1. Quality assessment process.

Infobox-Based Feature. We have calculated the *InfoboxBoxNormSize* as the $\log_{10}$ of the bytes of data contained within the MediaWiki tags that wrap an infobox, normalized it with respect to the article length feature, as in [16]. In this work, the authors noticed that the presence of an infobox is a characteristic featured by good articles. However, in the specific case of the Medicine Portal, the presence of an infobox does not seem strictly related to the quality class the article belongs to (according to the manual labeling). Indeed, it is recurrent that articles, spanning all classes, have an infobox with a schematic synthesis of the article topic. In particular, pages with descriptions of diseases usually have an infobox with the medical standard code of the disease (i.e., IDC-9 and IDC-10).

Category-Based Feature. For *Category*, we have leveraged the categories assigned to articles in Wikipedia, relating to the medicine topics available at https://en.wikipedia.org/wiki/Portal:Medicine. We have defined 5 upper level categories of interest: A, when an article is about *anatomy*; B, when an article is a *biography* or an event relevant for medicine; D, if it is about a *disorder*; F, when it is about *first aid* or emergency contacts; O otherwise. We have matched the article's text within the MediaWiki categories tag with an approximate list of keywords related to our category of interest.

Bio-medical Entities. For the extraction of the bio-medical entities, we consider the textual part of the article only, obtained after removing the MediaWiki tags, and we apply a NLP analysis. In particular, to obtain the *DomainInformativeness*, we have adopted a dictionary-based approach in order to extract the number of bio-medical entities from each Wikipedia article. The adopted approach (introduced for the Italian language in [1]) exploits lexical features and domain knowledge extracted from the Unified Medical Languages System (UMLS) Metathesaurus [4]. Since the approach combines the usage of linguistic analysis and domain resources, we were able to conveniently adapt it for

Table 1. Dictionary composition

Semantic groups	Definitions
Treatment	671,349
Sign or symptom	43,779
Body parts, organs, or organ components	234,075
Disorder	402,298
Drugs	5,109
Active ingredients	2,774

the English language, being both the linguistic pipeline and UMLS available for multiple languages (including English and Italian).

To build a medical dictionary for English, we have extracted definitions of medical entities from UMLS Metathesaurus [4] belonging to the following SNOMED-CT semantic groups: *Treatment, Sign or Symptom, Disease or Syndrome, Body Parts, Organs, or Organ Components, Pathologic Function*, and *Mental or Behavioral Dysfunction*, for a total of more than one million entries, as shown in Table 1 (where the two last semantic groups have been grouped together, under *Disorder*). Furthermore, we have extracted common Drugs and Active Ingredients definitions from RxNorm[4], accessed by RxTerm[5].

4   Experiments and Results

In this section, we describe our experiments and report the results for the classification of Wikipedia medical articles into the six classes of the Wikipedia Medicine Portal. We compare the results obtained adopting three different classifiers: the actionable model in [16] and two classifiers that leverage the ad-hoc features from the medical domain discussed in the previous sections. All the experiments were realized within the Weka framework [9] and validated through 10 fold cross-validation. For each experiment, we relied on the dataset presented in Sect. 2, and specifically, on that obtained after sampling the majority classes and oversampling the minority ones. The dataset serves both as training and test set for the classifiers. We have applied several classification algorithms (bagging, adaptive boosting and random forest). We report the results for the latter only.

4.1   Classifier Features

In Table 2, we report a summary of the features considered by the baseline model [16] and those introduced for the medical domain, that we adopted in two different models. In the *Medical Domain* model, we add to the baseline features the *Domain Informativeness*, as described in Sect. 3. The *Full Medical Domain*

---

[4] https://www.nlm.nih.gov/research/umls/rxnorm/.
[5] https://wwwcf.nlm.nih.gov/umlslicense/rxtermApp/rxTerm.cfm.

Table 2. Features and related information gain

	Actionable model features				
	ArticleLength	NumHeadings	Completeness	NumRefLength	Informativeness
InfoGain	0.939	0.732	0.724	0.621	0.377

	New features		
	DomainInformativ.	InfoBoxNormSize	Category
InfoGain	0.751	0.187	0.017

model also considers the features *InfoBoxNormSize* and *Category*. For each of the features, the table also reports the Information Gain, evaluated on the whole dataset (24,362 articles). Information Gain is a well-known metric to evaluate the dependency of one class from a single feature, see, e.g., [7].

We can observe how the Domain Informativeness feature has a considerably higher infogain value when compared with Informativeness [16]. We anticipate here that this will lead to a more accurate classification results for the highest classes, as reported in the next section. Leading to a greater accuracy is also true for the other two new features that, despite showing lower values of infogain, are able to further improve the classification results, mainly for the articles belonging to the lowest quality classes (Stub and Start).

4.2 Classification Results

Table 3 shows the results of our multi-class classification. For each of the classes, we have computed the *ROC Area* and *F-Measure* metrics [13].

Table 3. Classification results (In bold, the best results)

Metric	Baseline	Medical domain	Full medical domain
ROC Area Stub	0.981	0.982	**0.983**
ROC Area Start	0.852	0.853	**0.858**
ROC Area C	0.749	0.747	**0.76**
ROC Area B	0.825	0.832	**0.836**
ROC Area GA	0.825	0.908	**0.916**
ROC Area FA	0.977	0.976	**0.978**
F-Measure Stub	0.886	**0.891**	0.89
F-Measure Start	0.587	0.582	**0.598**
F-Measure C	0.376	0.367	**0.397**
F-Measure B	0.527	0.541	**0.542**
F-Measure GA	0.245	0.338	**0.398**
F-Measure FA	0.634	0.631	**0.641**

At a first glance, we observe that, across all the models, the articles with the lowest classification values, for both ROC and F-Measure, are those labeled C and GA. Adding the Domain Informativeness feature produces a slightly worse classification for C and FA articles, but better for the other four classes. This is particularly evident for the F-Measure of the articles of the GA class. A noticeable major improvement is obtained with the introduction of the features InfoBoxNormSize and Category in the *Medical Domain* model. The ROC Area increases for all the classes within the *Full Medical Domain*, while the F-Measure is always better than the *Baseline* and slightly better the *Medical Domain*.

The size of an article, expressed either as the word count, analyzed in [3], or as the article length, as done here, is able to discriminate the articles belonging to the highest and lowest quality classes. This is testified also by the results achieved exploiting the baseline model of [16], which poorly succeeds in discriminating the articles of the intermediate quality classes, while achieving good results for Stub and FA. Here, the newly introduced features have a predominant effect on the articles of the highest classes. This could be justified by the fact that those articles contain, on average, more text and, then, NLP-based features can exploit more words belonging to a specific domain.

Then, we observe that the ROC Area and the F-Measure are not tightly coupled (namely: high values for the first metric can correspond to low values for the second one, see for example C and GA): this is due to the nature of the ROC Area, that is affected by the different sizes of the considered classes. As an example, we can observe that the baseline model has the same ROC Area value for the articles of both class B and class GA, while the F-Measure of articles of class B is 0.282 higher than that of class GA.

Finally, the results confirm that the adoption of domain-based features and, in general, of features that leverage NLP, help to distinguish between articles in the lowest classes and articles in the highest classes, as highlighted in bold in Table 3. We notice also that exploiting the full medical domain leads us to the achievement of the best results.

5   Related Work

Automatic quality evaluation of Wikipedia articles has been addressed in previous works with both unsupervised and supervised learning approaches. The common idea of most of the existing work, like [3, 16–18], is to identify a feature set, having as a starting point the Wikipedia project guidelines, to be exploited with the objective in mind to automatically label the articles.

Recent studies specifically address the quality of medical information. In [2], the authors debate if Wikipedia is a reliable learning resource for medical students, evaluating articles on respiratory topics and cardiovascular diseases. In [11] the authors measure the quality of medical information in Wikipedia, by adopting an unsupervised approach based on the Analytic Hierarchy Process, a multi-criteria decision making technique [14]. The work in [5] aims to provide the web surfers a numerical indication of Quality of Medical Web Sites.

A similar measurement is considered in [15], where the authors present an empirical analysis that suggests the need to define genre-specific templates for quality evaluation and to develop models for an automatic genre-based classification of health information Web pages. In addition, the study shows that consumers may lack the motivation or literacy skills to evaluate the information quality of health Web pages. Clearly, this further highlights the importance to develop accessible automatic information quality evaluation tools and ontologies. Our work moves towards the goal, by specifically considering domain-relevant features and featuring an automatic classification task spanning over more than two classes.

6   Conclusions

In this work, we aimed to provide a fine grained classification mechanism for all the quality classes of the articles of the Wikipedia Medical Portal. An important and novel aspect of our classifier, with respect to previous works, is the leveraging of features extracted from the specific, medical domain, with the help of Natural Language Processing techniques. As the results of our experiments confirm, considering specific domain-based features, like Domain Informativeness and Category, can eventually help and improve the automatic classification results. We are planning to extend the work to include other domains, in order to further validate our approach.

References

1. Attardi, G., Cozza, V., Sartiano, D.: Adapting linguistic tools for the analysis of Italian medical records. In: Italian Conference Computational Linguistics, CLiC-it (2014)
2. Azer, S.A.: Is Wikipedia a reliable learning resource for medical students? Evaluating respiratory topics. Adv. Physiol. Educ. **39**(1), 5–14 (2015)
3. Blumenstock, J.E.: Size matters: word count as a measure of quality on Wikipedia. In: 17th World Wide Web, pp. 1095–1096. ACM (2008)
4. Bodenreider, O., McCray, A.T.: Exploring semantic groups through visual approaches. J. Biomedi. Inf. **36**(6), 414–432 (2003)
5. Cabitza, F.: An information reliability index as a simple consumer-oriented indication of quality of medical web sites. In: Pasi, G., Bordogna, G., Jain, L.C. (eds.) Quality Issues in the Management of Web Information. ISRL, vol. 50, pp. 159–177. Springer, Heidelberg (2013)
6. Chawla, N.V., et al.: SMOTE: synthetic minority over-sampling technique. J. Artif. Intell. Res. **16**, 321–357 (2002)
7. Cover, T.M., Thomas, J.A.: Elements of Information Theory (Wiley Series in Telecommunications and Signal Processing). Wiley, Hoboken (2006)
8. Cozza, V., Petrocchi, M., Spognardi, A.: A matter of words: NLP for quality evaluation of Wikipedia medical articles. CoRR abs/1603.01987 (2016)
9. Hall, M., et al.: The WEKA data mining software: an update. ACM SIGKDD Explor. Newsl. **11**(1), 10–18 (2009)

10. Hodson, R.: Wikipedians reach out to academics. Nature News, September 2015
11. Marzini, E., Spognardi, A., Matteucci, I., Mori, P., Petrocchi, M., Conti, R.: Improved automatic maturity assessment of Wikipedia medical articles. In: Meersman, R., Panetto, H., Dillon, T., Missikoff, M., Liu, L., Pastor, O., Cuzzocrea, A., Sellis, T. (eds.) OTM 2014. LNCS, vol. 8841, pp. 612–622. Springer, Heidelberg (2014)
12. Pasi, G., et al.: An introduction to quality issues in the management of web information. In: Pasi, G., Bordogna, G., Jain, L.C. (eds.) Quality Issues in the Management of Web Information. ISRL, vol. 50, pp. 1–3. Springer, Heidelberg (2013)
13. Powers, D.M.W.: Evaluation: from precision, recall and F-measure to ROC, informedness, markedness and correlation. Int. J. Mach. Learn. Technol. $2(1)$, 37–63 (2011)
14. Saaty, T.L.: How to make a decision: the analytic hierarchy process. Eur. J. Oper. Res. $48(1)$, 9–26 (1990)
15. Stvilia, B., et al.: A model for online consumer health information quality. Am. Soc. Inf. Sci. Technol. $60(9)$, 1781–1791 (2009)
16. Warncke-Wang, M., et al.: Tell me more: an actionable quality model for Wikipedia. In: 9th Symposium on Open Collaboration, pp. 8:1–8:10. ACM (2013)
17. Wecel, K., Lewoniewski, W.: Modelling the quality of attributes in Wikipedia infoboxes. In: Abramowicz, W., et al. (eds.) BIS 2015 Workshops. LNBIP, vol. 228, pp. 308–320. Springer, Heidelberg (2015). doi:10.1007/978-3-319-26762-3_27
18. Wu, K., et al.: Mining the factors affecting the quality of Wikipedia articles. Inf. Sci. Manag. Eng. 1, 343–346 (2010)

Middleware Mediated Semantic Sensor Networks

Cristian Lai[✉] and Antonio Pintus

CRS4 Center for Advanced Studies, Research and Development in Sardinia,
Ed. 1 Loc. Piscina Manna, 09010 Pula, CA, Italy
{cristian.lai,antonio.pintus}@crs4.it

Abstract. This paper investigates how the Internet of Things (IoT) can take advantage of Semantic Technologies when combined with a prototyping middleware. Although Sensor Networks within the IoT offer enormous potential, the surprising variability in terms of communication and interoperability among Things is a challenging problem. This paper proposes to move from the classic meaning of Sensor Networks to the concept of Semantic Sensor Networks. The proposed methodology uses Semantic Web technologies, based on machine-interpretable representation formalisms, for combining Sensor Networks and the Paraimpu middleware. We propose to prototype and deploy a Semantic Sensor Network, focusing on the semantic aspects, with the tangible advantage to delegate to Paraimpu the low-level network operations. As a result we obtain a shared RDF Knowledge Base useful for improving integration and communication between different networks.

Keywords: Internet of Things · Sensor network · Semantic Sensor Network · Ontology · RDF · Knowledge Base

1 Introduction

The Internet of Things (IoT) is the network of physical objects that contain embedded technology to communicate and sense or interact with their internal states or the external environment (Gartner Newsroom[1]). The IoT will grow to 26 billion units installed in 2020 representing an almost 30-fold increase from 0.9 billion in 2009. Nowadays it is possible to utilize wide networks with multiple elements (sensors, actuators) or in general *Things*. *Things* can be considered active participants in information processes and their heterogeneous nature makes interoperability among them a challenging issue. One specific issue is how to consider and manage networks' elements, namely devices and information obtained from raw data. This paper shows that semantic technologies, based on machine interpretable representation formalisms, appear as a promise for describing devices and data, sharing and integrating information together with other intelligent processing techniques. Data collected from sensors has to be exchanged among *Things* and other users on the Internet. Data originating from

---

[1] http://www.gartner.com/newsroom/id/2636073.

© Springer International Publishing Switzerland 2016
A. Bozzon et al. (Eds.): ICWE 2016, LNCS 9671, pp. 457–464, 2016.
DOI: 10.1007/978-3-319-38791-8_32

a device or a human being can be combined with other data to create different abstractions of the physical environment.

Semantics can support this integration and allows movement towards the concept of Semantic Sensor Networks (SSN). Our methodology proposes to encode sensor descriptions and observation data with Semantic Web technologies and to embed them directly within devices. Such descriptions compound a collection of semantic resources. Resources are linked to each other as well as to other types of virtual and/or real world objects through semantic links following the Linked Open Data principles[2]. Moreover, we propose to collect sensor data by using the cloud-based Paraimpu platform. The platform is used as a middleware and, thanks to its web API, freed us from handling all the low-level network operations, data collection and real-time data transformation/annotation.

This paper describes a dynamic and scalable SSN system supporting the following features:

– Geographically distributed sensors, grouped in stations, are able to form ad hoc networking topologies; not only sending measurements data but also announce themselves and their presence in the network;
– Raw data sent by sensors is semantically annotated and enriched on-the-fly by Paraimpu as it flows through the system, using Semantic Web formats;
– Resulting data and descriptions, semantically annotated, compose a shared RDF Knowledge Base useful to improve integration and communication processes between different networks.

The remainder of this paper is organized as follows: Sect. 2 briefly introduces related work; Sect. 3 introduces the proposed methodology; Sect. 4 illustrates the annotation and transformation processes; Sect. 5 introduces the Paraimpu middleware; Sect. 6 presents a case study; and Sect. 7 provides conclusions.

2   Related Work

In recent years, several middleware-like solutions for the IoT emerged to simplify the overall adoption of the IoT by companies and final users. This adoption process includes building new applications connecting and managing smart *Things*, sensors and devices and gathering data produced by them. Many existing platforms propose quite similar solutions and tools: API, web dashboards, data collection, while a large sub-set of them are simply cloud-based services. Available platforms such as Xively[3], Evrythng[4], Carriots[5], Paraimpu[6] and many others try to offer these services and tools to build and maintain new IoT applications. *Mineraud et al.* [6] report a gap analysis of today's IoT landscape and about available platforms, in particular aspects concerning a broad adoption of

---

[2] http://linkeddata.org.
[3] https://xively.com.
[4] https://www.evrythng.com.
[5] https://www.carriots.com.
[6] https://www.paraimpu.com.

the IoT. In that analysis, some of the emerged gaps concerning data are nonuniform data sharing formats and processing data streams efficiently and handling different formats and models. *Mineraud et al.* [6] recommend to address these gaps by aligning data models and semantic indexing to ease the uniform processing of data sharing and fusion. *Patni et al.* [7] proposed a framework for Linked Open Data (LOD) about sensor data collected from the physical environment, introducing a publishing method for LOD using RDF and SPARQL. An interesting part of this framework is the use of a sensor dataset description for LOD. Other interesting works include the knowledge representation for integrated IoT semantic services [12], but these works did not consider dynamic, semantic annotation and description of sensors and data in real time. As also remarked in an another relevant work [10], in IoT Sensor Networks, devices are dynamically added to sensor networks in real-time. To address this issue the authors [10] propose an integrated platform, which includes a web-based authoring tool and a service-based platform. This work tries to address the problems of a dynamic semantic expression of IoT resources/devices in real time and a semantic IoT data repository.

We did not focus on building a new semantic-enabled middleware platform from scratch. We decided to use an existing IoT platform in order to address our needs. After exploring many platforms, sorting by features, flexibility and data transformation tools, we decided to base our work on the Paraimpu platform. This middleware has been chosen mainly for its user-friendly workspace, for the simple but effective APIs and for its powerful embedded Javascript-based rule engine. This latter tool allows us to transform, in real-time, annotated data snippets coming from sensors in semantic descriptions.

3   Methodology

The open issues that our work tries to address can be summarized in two questions. How can sensors, stations and in general, smart, connected things, be instructed to provide semantic annotated data about their presence announcements in a SSN and related measurements? How can an existing IoT middleware platform be used to enrich data to transform it into Linked Open Data entities? Thus, our methodology addresses two objectives. The **first objective** focuses on sensors and observations data annotations, encoded through Semantic Web technologies. *Semantic annotations* are embedded within sensing stations based on Arduino microcontrollers. Sensing stations are basically devices that provide a small piece of information about their features; they are able to announce themselves in the network and declare what they observe. This information is minimized, in order to relieve sensors from details which keeps information representation very small. We consider some devices in order to easily lead the modeling and design of the basic set of sensing capabilities. We identify a set of basic components called *Things*, that can be shared within a sensor network and then used jointly (e.g., temperature and humidity sensor).

The **second objective** provides enriched *semantic descriptions* thanks to the idea of Linked Sensor Data [1–3,5,11], which facilitates in publishing and using enriched sensor data with the help of the Linked Open Data principles. Resources are enriched and associated with each other as well as with other types of virtual and/or real world objects through semantic links. The second step is based on the Paraimpu middleware and is automated starting from the annotations provided by devices. Devices are directly connected to Paraimpu through its web API. For this second objective, we divert our attention to the Paraimpu rule engine. We identify the rules necessary to transform semantic annotations to semantic descriptions. This approach allows us to create a distributed RDF Knowledge Base integrating the various annotations first embedded within sensors and then transformed into enriched descriptions through the Paraimpu middleware. We focus our attention on sensor network components such as *stations*, *sensors* and *observations*.

4   Semantic Sensor Networks

In our vision, a SSN is the set of devices, semantic meta-modeling formalisms and RDF Knowledge Bases. To address our purposes we use state-of-art ontologies while giving due consideration to the specific concepts and properties. As a result, we build the SSN Knowledge Base containing all the semantic descriptions. To implement our methodology, we apply the proposed technique to real-world devices. We generate semantic annotations, the so called *snippets*. Snippets are plain JSON objects and are embedded directly within devices. Snippets provide information concerning the sensing providers and the kind of sensing measures. We address two different cases: *(i) sensing features; (ii) sensing data*. In case of *sensing features*, a snippet is composed of an individual and an observed property. The individual identifies the specific sensor, while the observed property refers to the measure. Individuals become mainly from state-of-art ontologies, SSN [4] and CF[7]. In many cases we need to define our specific individuals. As a common convention we use specific namespaces inherited from state-of-art ontologies, whereas the base namespace is defined as ":".

5   The Paraimpu Middleware

In this work, a dynamic and scalable SSN system is based on the Paraimpu platform [8,9]. Platform main tool is the workspace. The workspace allows us to quickly prototype and deploy the whole system, focusing on the semantic aspects of research and delegating all the low-level, network operations to Paraimpu. The Paraimpu platform simplifies the connection, and the resulting collection of data, of an heterogeneous range of devices, applications and general data sources. By its API, almost any smart device able to communicate through the HTTP protocol can be connected in few simple steps, including Arduino boards sporting sensors and actuators to mobile applications, social networks and lighting systems. After the smart devices (from now we will refer to them as

---

[7] http://www.w3.org/2005/Incubator/ssn/ssnx/cf/cf-property.

Things) are connected to the platform they acquire a virtual peer on the visual Paraimpu workspace which allows them to be easily linked (inter-connected) with other Things. Adopting some abstraction paradigms, all things in Paraimpu can be considered as belonging to two main categories: *Sensors*, or any Thing capable of measuring and producing data, physical or not (e.g., temperature or humidity sensors, social networks or external API and web services); *Actuators*, or any Thing able to receive data and perform an action, such as a physical, connected device or another web service or API. On Paraimpu, a *connection* is a logic data flow between two things. When two things are interconnected, it is possible to write and set a variable number of rules for each separate connection. Rules can apply filters or transformations on data. The powerful, integrated, rule-based Javascript engine inside the platform allows the system to transform data coming from a heterogeneous range of Things in real-time such as raw measurements and packets, or structured Linked Data, in compliance with Semantic Web standards. Thanks to Paraimpu APIs it is then possible to retrieve transformed/semantic annotated data to be stored in a dedicated Knowledge Base.

6   Case Study

Raw data sources used in the experimentation includes several physical sensors deployed at CRS4 buildings along with others data sources, like weather streams and traffic information, queried in near real-time using the open-data provided by the Cagliari Municipality Government and released under the IODLv2.0 License. This section reports some details of the overall case study, including the deployment of the system.

Referring to Fig. 1, the Paraimpu platform acts as a middleware playing a very central role in the general architecture. Not only does it expose all the required API to let Things gather or push data, but also it provides the facilities to transform and annotate semantically data on-the-fly as it flows from them. Our SSN deployment using Paraimpu middleware is shown in Fig. 1. The numbered main modules/steps are as follows: (1) Physical things have been built using Arduino Yun programmable boards. The boards were equipped with temperature and luminosity sensors and connected to the Internet through WiFi. They were deployed inside the CRS4 HQ buildings and the software running on them allowed to announce their presence on the network sending data payloads to Paraimpu (i.e., temperature and luminosity values). The communication happens through the Paraimpu REST API which accepts sending data in JSON format. Other Things pushing heterogeneous data to the middleware included: city weather data, gathered through OpenWeatherMap[8] and traffic data measurements at several locations in the city of Cagliari, through their Open Data providers[9]. (2) All data sources are connected, managed and interconnected with ease by the facilities provided by the Paraimpu workspace. Incoming data, about network announcements and observations, are represented inside the Paraimpu

---

[8] http://openweathermap.org/.

[9] http://www.comune.cagliari.it/portale/it/openservice_info.page.

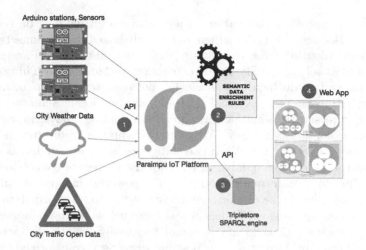

Fig. 1. The SSN deployment using the Paraimpu IoT platform

workspace as *Sensors* (see Sect. 5). Each of these sensors are connected to a corresponding *Actuator*. The *Registry* is a special *Actuator* that receives all the data concerning SSN network announcements. Thus, all Things are connected and all the connections are properly configured by *rules*. Rules are basically regular JavaScript expressions. They instruct the system about how to filter or transform data as it flows in near real-time from one Thing to another. We took advantage of this mechanism and wrote several semantic data enrichment rules to transform raw data, coming from direct measurements, to Linked Data formats to be sent to the actuators. (3) Every *Actuactor* registered in the Paraimpu platform can be reached by a REST API endpoint. Using APIs, we wrote an external service to gather semantic annotated data from the platform and to store it in a Triplestore. (4) As soon as data is stored in the Triplestore, a query-based event triggering is fired and a web-page automatically reflects the current status of the SSN, including sensor stations presence and related measurements. The web page shows an interactive bubble view of the SSN which updates in real-time through the websocket technology.

In this case study, the sensor sends an announcement annotated snippet to Paraimpu. The following example shows the snippet related to a temperature sensor:

{ "whois" : "sensor_Temperature_1",
"observes" : "cf-property:air_temperature" }

The snippet is composed of two key/value pairs. The *whois* key identifies the sensor, while the *observes* value addresses the observed property.

Paraimpu transforms the snippet into a semantic description and sends it (through the JSON-LD notation) to a connected Actuator representing our Registry. Data transformation/annotation is applied in real-time by a defined Paraimpu Rule (see Fig. 2). The semantic descriptions stored in the Triplestore

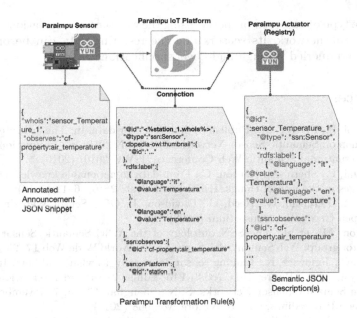

Fig. 2. Deployment of the SSN through Paraimpu sensor, actuator and connection abstractions, in case of a sensor announcement in the network.

compound a wide LOD knowledge base that allows to discover the interlinked information of the SSN.

Actually, a Rule can be seen as a generic data template, in which every snippet surrounded by the specific <%%> tag is dynamically executed as JavaScript code. Thus, the snippet can refer to data coming from a sensor to reduce the template to the sought real data.

7   Conclusion

In Sensor Networks, *Things* are active participants in information processes. In this paper we used semantic technologies for providing unambiguous data modelling, describing *Things*, sharing and integrating information. We discussed how to benefit from Semantic Web technologies in SSN. In our approach, devices are active parts of heterogeneous networks, able to announce themselves and to provide sensing data. Data originating from devices will be part of the world of Linked Sensor Data, through distributed RDF Knowledge Bases. To move from devices to Knowledge Bases we adopted the Paraimpu platform. The current Paraimpu connection model doesn't allow to group sensors together, thus the defined rules must be replicated in each new connection, event though they respond to similar aims. Future works will investigate how to avoid duplication of rules in connections sharing the same goal. In our vision, future networks will be able to exploit novel approaches of sensor analysis that infers semantic properties such as the type of observed property, using the raw sensor observations as input. In a SSN, the network, its sensors and the resulting data can be organized, managed and queried through high-level specifications.

References

1. Barnaghi, P., Presser, M.: Publishing linked sensor data. In: The 3rd International Workshop on Semantic Sensor Networks 2010 (SSN 2010) in Conjunction with the 9th International Semantic Web Conference (ISWC 2010) (2010)
2. Barnaghi, P., Sheth, A., Henson, C.: From data to actionable knowledge: big data challenges in the web of things. IEEE Intell. Syst. **28**(6), 6–11 (2013)
3. Botts, M., Percivall, G., Reed, C., Davidson, J.: OGC Sensor Web Enablement. The Open Geospatial Consortium (2008)
4. Compton, M., et al.: The SSN ontology of the W3C Semantic Sensor Network incubator group. Web Semant. Sci. Serv. Agents World Wide Web **17**, 25–32 (2012)
5. Kebler, C., Janowicz, K.: Linking sensor data - why, to what, and how? In: Taylor, K., Ayyagari, A., Roure, D.D. (eds.) Proceedings of the 3rd International Workshop on Semantic Sensor Networks, SSN , Shanghai, China, 7 November, CEUR Workshop Proceedings, CEUR-WS.org, vol. 668 (2010)
6. Mineraud, J., Mazhelis, O., Su, X., Tarkoma, S.: A gap analysis of Internet-of-Things platforms, Computer Communications, Special issue on the Internet of Things: Research challenges and Solutions, March 2016
7. Patni, H., Henson, C., Sheth, A.: Linked sensor data. In: Proceedings of the 2010 International Symposium on Collaborative Technologies and Systems (CTS), Chicago, IL, USA, pp. 362–370 (2010)
8. Paraimpu, a web platform for the Internet of Things. https://www.paraimpu.com
9. Pintus, A., Carboni, D., Piras, A.: Paraimpu: a platform for a social web of things. In: Proceedings of the 21st International Conference Companion on World Wide Web, pp. 401–404. ACM, Lyon (2012)
10. Ryu, M., Kim, J., Yun, J.: Integrated semantics service platform for the Internet of Things: a case study of a smart office. Sensors (Basel, Switzerland) **15**(1), 2137–2160 (2015)
11. Sheth, A., Henson, C., Sahoo, S.: Semantic sensor web. IEEE Inter. Comput. **12**(4), 78–83 (2008)
12. Wang, W., De, S., Cassar, G., Moessner, K.: Knowledge representation in the Internet of Things: semantic modelling and its applications. Automatika J. Control Meas. Electron. Comput. Commun. **54**, 388–400 (2013)

Vision Papers

I am a Machine, Let Me Understand Web Media!

Magnus Knuth$^{(\boxtimes)}$, Jörg Waitelonis, and Harald Sack

Hasso Plattner Institute, University of Potsdam, Potsdam, Germany
{magnus.knuth,joerg.waitelonis,harald.sack}@hpi.de

Abstract. The majority of web assets cannot be understood by machines, because of the lack of available explicit and machine readable semantics. By enabling machines to understand the meaning of web media, fully automated discovery, processing, and linking become feasible. Semantic Web technologies offer the possibility to enhance web resources with explicit semantics via linking to ontologies encoded in RDF. We demand to make the content of every web asset explicit for machines with the least possible effort for any content provider. Web servers should deliver RDF descriptions for any web document on request. To achieve this, we propose a framework that enables web content providers to connect to content-wise descriptions of their web assets via simple HTTP content negotiation in connection with on-the-fly automated multimedia analysis services. We demonstrate the feasibility of our approach with a prototype implementation.

Keywords: Machine understandability · Web media · Automated media analysis · Semantic web technologies · RDF · Content negotiation

1 Introduction

The Web is made for humans, not for machines. The majority of web assets cannot be understood by machines, because of the lack of available explicit and machine readable semantics. To fully automatically discover, process, and link web content, machines must be able to understand its meaning. Nowadays, multimedia documents such as images, video and audio files, but also other electronic documents such as PDFs, various formats for word processors, spreadsheets, slide show presentations, and file archives are indispensable constituents of the Web and use up the majority of the available bandwidth in the Internet. These documents largely contain unstructured data, partly in proprietary formats, which makes it intricate for machines to extract the actual content and meaning. Even though a web browser can display an image, it cannot understand the image content.

Consider the following scenario: someone uploads a holiday photograph to a web server so that it is publicly available to her friends. Those can download the image and admire her in front of that spectacular sight. But, if the image is downloaded by a computer it cannot see or recognize the content of the photograph like

© Springer International Publishing Switzerland 2016
A. Bozzon et al. (Eds.): ICWE 2016, LNCS 9671, pp. 467–475, 2016.
DOI: 10.1007/978-3-319-38791-8_33

a human. Given explicit metadata for that image the computer would know where the picture has been taken, which objects can be seen, etc. Using this knowledge, a machine could provide background information to the user, link it to the personal data of the user, make it retrievable by its content, and suggest to make use of the image for a particular purpose, e.g. as an illustration in a travel blog.

The Semantic Web [3] introduces languages such as the Resource Description Format (RDF) and the Web Ontology Language (OWL) to bring structure to the content of web pages with the goal to provide explicit and machine understandable semantics. One way to provide explicit semantics in HTML pages is the inclusion of microdata, such as RDFa [16] and schema.org[1], to annotate web documents with formal descriptions which are connected with the help of vocabularies to Linked Data resources.

Web documents are delivered via the Hypertext Transfer Protocol (HTTP). By using HTTP content negotiation different versions of the same web document can be identified and accessed via one unified URI [4]. To access information resources in the Web of Data, for Linked Data resources the same URI is used to access a human readable HTML document as well as a machine understandable RDF version of the same resource [7]. This mechanism should not be restricted to Linked Data resources only. Content providers should provide content-wise descriptions and metadata for every kind of asset on the Web including multimedia data. Moreover, this should be accomplished with minimal effort, i.e. without an overhead to laboriously create supplementary metadata in a manual way.

When requesting a web asset's URL via HTTP, the computer receives a copy of the original resource. In order to provide a machine understandable explicit semantic description of the web asset, HTTP content negotiation should be enabled and on request an RDF description of the content of the web asset can be delivered. This RDF description can be provided manually, from existing metadata, or with the help of automated analysis algorithms. Overall, the possibility to automatically receive machine readable metadata lowers the barrier for machines to understand and correctly interpret web assets.

In this paper we propose a framework based on standardized web protocols to enable the delivery of machine readable content related metadata for arbitrary documents on the web independent of the web document's type, modality, and encoding. To enable a smooth and least effort delivery of metadata we propose to utilize the content negotiation mechanism that enables to identify the original content as well as its metadata via the same URI. We demonstrate the feasibility of our approach with a prototype implementation that combines automated visual analysis as a web service with the content negotiation and metadata delivery mechanism with little effort for any content provider.

The paper is structured as follows: Sect. 2 describes technologies and description formats related to content representation, followed by potential use cases and service provisioning. Section 3 provides a detailed description of the prototypical implementation. Section 4 summarizes related approaches and Sect. 5 concludes the paper.

---

[1] https://schema.org/.

2   Content Representation and Content Negotiation

HTTP content negotiation is a well established mechanism that is used to deliver different representations of a document from a web server according to the demands and constraints of the user agent (client). By submitting a request to a web server, the client informs the web server what media types it understands including a ranking of preference. The client provides an HTTP accept header that lists acceptable media types, as e.g. `Accept: text/html`. In general, the accept header lists the MIME Types of the media that the client is willing to process [4]. The web server is then able to supply the version of the resource that best fits the user agent's needs.

In the Web of Data this mechanism is applied to identify resources, i.e. Linked Data resources, with the same URI providing a human readable HTML version as well as a machine readable (or even machine understandable) RDF version [7]. Thereby, various representations of the same information can be delivered using the same URI to identify this information.

2.1   Possible Contents of Descriptions

There exist different types of content descriptions. We classify these types into three different layers: *file metadata*, *provenance information*, and an actual *description of the content* (cf. Table 1). The most generic type of descriptions is *file metadata* which is often already available from the HTTP header. Depending on the file type there might also be *file type specific metadata*, in the case of an image that would be e.g. its pixel dimension and compression rate, for an audio or video file its duration, and for a PDF document the number of pages. A second type which is generically applicable and becomes increasingly relevant is *provenance information* such as the creator, creation and modification dates, and rights information. Images may contain Exif information with technical metadata such as the camera model, shutter speed, and geo-location.

The actual *description of the content* does strongly depend on the file type. For example, images could be described by color-space histograms, image type (e.g. photo, clip-art, line drawing, animated, etc.), or more sophisticated categorization methods, such as visual concept detection [9]. Audio transcriptions extracted from speech recognizers could be shipped along with any audible content. The textual content of such transcriptions as well as from rich text formats could be used to be categorized with extracted keywords or text summaries. Semantic named entity linking [19] could be used to identify meaningful elements in text and provide links to referenced resources.

2.2   Description Formats

For the content-wise description of multimedia documents various metadata schemata and vocabularies have been proposed for which also RDF based versions have been created. The following non-exhaustive list shows some prominent vocabularies within the context of the proposed system:

Table 1. Selection of Multimedia Content Descriptions

Generic	Image	Video	Audio	PDF (publication)
File metadata				
File size	Image width	Video width	Codec	Number of pages
File type	Image height	Video height	Duration	Page size
MIME type	Compression	Codec	Sample rate	
		Duration		
Provenance information				
Creator	Camera model	Camera model	Artist/speaker	Author
Rights	Exposure time		Recorder model	Publisher
Creation date	Aperture			DOI
Modification date	GPS position			
Content description				
	Image classification	Audio transcript	Audio transcript	Abstract
	Visual content detection	Shot boundaries	Genre	Keywords
	Face detection	Spatio-temporal	Title	Citations
	Object detection	Annotations	Album	Experimental data

- **DC Element Set/DC Terms:** The *Dublin Core vocabularies* provide a small set of elements for the description of web resources as well as of physical objects [15].
- **MIME Type:** the *Multipurpose Internet Mail Extensions* (MIME) clearly specify multimedia content types as well as content encodings [5].
- **Exif:** *Exchangeable image file format* (Exif) specifies a set of tags to describe image formats and technical metadata of camera and imaging devices. Kanzaki [12] provides an RDF vocabulary to encode Exif picture data [11].
- **COMM:** The *core ontology for multimedia* (COMM) [1] has been built re-engineering the multimedia annotation standard MPEG-7 [10].
- **Open Annotation Ontology:** the *Open Annotation Data Model* specifies an interoperable framework for creating associations between related resources and annotations [17].
- **NIF:** the *NLP Interchange Format* (NIF) is an RDF/OWL-based format that aims to achieve interoperability between natural language processing (NLP) tools, language resources and annotations on different levels [8].
- **Media Fragments:** the *W3C media fragments recommendation* specifies how to construct media fragment URIs and their utilization with the HTTP protocol [18].

2.3 Service Provisioning

Two options for deployment of such a feature are conceivable: *local* or *external* creation of RDF descriptions. If the content provider decides to host also the RDF descriptions, he has full control over the content and can integrate background knowledge, e.g. from media asset management tools. It would be reasonable to integrate this feature in content management systems. Otherwise, this task can also be transferred to a dedicated service provider, who analyses the file and generates the RDF description. Such a provider might be able to deploy more sophisticated content analysis tools to provide consistent descriptions. We demonstrate the latter approach in Sect. 3 since it allows a very simple setup for any content provider.

2.4 Potential Use Cases

There are plenty of application scenarios conceivable that would benefit from rich descriptions of web media.

- **Hypermedia and Accessibility.** Formal descriptions of web assets can support the accessibility for end users who are in any form impaired to perceive the original media format, e.g. a screen reader compiles and reads a natural language description of the visual content to a blind user. Such description does not need to be static as e. g. provided by the `alt` tag for images. Instead, intelligent tools could generate textual content-wise descriptions from sophisticated visual analysis results. Moreover, links to related resources can be attached to media files, e.g. sections in an e-learning video could be linked to forum discussions where learners discuss questions raised by the lecturer.
- **Multimodal Search, SEO, and Recommender Systems.** Search engine support within multimedia and other unstructured files is hard to achieve. A search engine needs to analyze the data first in order to index it properly. While big search providers can operate the needed infrastructure, i.e. computing power and algorithms, enterprise search engines are able to provide multimodal search based on the media's content descriptions. But also web scale search engines might provide better search results by using this explicit information and honor the provision of such.
- **Generic API.** Instead of developing and deploying new APIs for the distribution of metadata or content descriptions, content negotiation and RDF can be used to deliver such information in a generic way. E. g. video transcripts or subtitles are currently provided as an extra file, via dedicated APIs, or embedded in the video stream itself. Similar holds for chapter marks and shownotes[2] in podcasts. Whatever additional information shall be provided for web assets in future, the suggested mechanism can easily be applied to it.

3   Implementation and Demo

We have set up a prototype implementation that enables the creation and delivery of content-related RDF descriptions for images including basic technical metadata, Exif data, as well as descriptive metadata from automated visual concept detection. The overall architecture principle is depicted in Fig. 1. The demo consists of a standard web server and the content analysis server (COAL). The standard web server is considered to be an ordinary web server hosting some

---

[2] e.g. as provided at http://shownot.es/.

arbitrary website. The purpose of the COAL server is to provide RDF content descriptions for images as a service. The website publisher simply configures the web server to redirect specific content type requests to the COAL server. An exemplary rewrite rule, which redirects RDF data requests for image URLs to an external server and adds an alternate link header, is given in Listing 1.1.

In Fig. 1, the client, e.g. a web browser plugin or a search engine, requests a resource's machine readable RDF description from the web server by specifying the HTTP header field `Accept: application/rdf+xml` (1). The web server applies the rewrite rule and sends an HTTP 303 `redirect` back to the client including the new redirect location (URL) pointing to the COAL server (2). The client then requests the given URL from the COAL server (3), which subsequently retrieves the original file from the web server (4, 5) and ingests it to the analysis workflow. The analysis results are encoded as RDF and sent back to the client (7). A standard HTTP cache serves as temporary storage to ensure a resource is analyzed only once within a certain range of time.

```
<FilesMatch "\.(gif|jpg|jpeg|png|GIF|JPG|JPEG|PNG)">
  <IfModule mod_rewrite.c>
    RewriteEngine on
    RewriteRule ^ - [E=ORIGINAL_URI:http://%{HTTP_HOST}%{REQUEST_URI}]
    RewriteCond %{REQUEST_FILENAME} -f
    RewriteCond %{HTTP_ACCEPT} ^.*text/turtle.* [OR]
    RewriteCond %{HTTP_ACCEPT} ^.*application/n-triples.* [OR]
    RewriteCond %{HTTP_ACCEPT} ^.*application/rdf\+xml.* [OR]
    RewriteCond %{HTTP_ACCEPT} ^.*application/ld\+json.*
    RewriteRule . http://coal.s16a.org/resource?url=%{ENV:ORIGINAL_URI} [R
    =303,L]
    <IfModule mod_headers.c>
      Header append Link "<http://coal.s16a.org/resource?url=%{ORIGINAL_URI}e
    >; rel=\"alternate\"; type=\"application/rdf+xml\""
    </IfModule>
  </IfModule>
</FilesMatch>
```

Listing 1.1. Apache rewrite rule to redirect to the COAL server

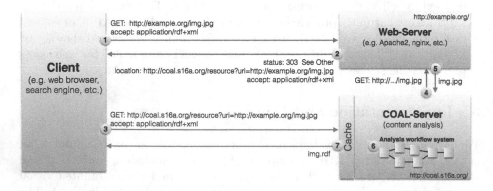

Fig. 1. Principle of content analysis with content negotiation for a given image

We have configured the rewrite rule on our Wordpress-based blog[3]. Image content descriptions can now easily be requested by specifying the desired content type:

```
curl -L "http://blog.yovisto.com/wp-content/uploads/2015/07/Bumper8.jpg" -H
"Accept:application/rdf+xml"
```

4 Related Approaches

The initial idea seemed so obvious that we did not expect not to find anyone who had at least tried it before, and indeed: already in 2002, Lafon and Bos released a W3C note [13] for describing photos with RDF and HTTP content negotiation. The approach of *Photo RDF* includes a manual annotation of digital images, supported by the *rdfpic* data entry program, and an extension for the Jigsaw server. A demonstration server for *Photo RDF* is also available[4]. *Photo RDF* already comes close to our vision, but it is limited to images and relies on manual annotation, which might be the main reason for its limited use.

The Adobe Extensible Metadata Platform (XMP)[5] allows to embed RDF descriptions in the file header of several file formats. Adobe recommends to use the Dublin Core vocabulary for provenance information and offers additional schemas. XMP is supported by a number of tools.

Semantic annotation of multimedia has been a field of research for over a decade. The goal is to provide rich machine processable descriptions of media contents using well defined properties. A number of models and tools have been created [14]. The most commonly used vocabularies are the W3C Media Ontology [2] and the Open Annotation Model [17]. Temporal and/or spatial regions in media assets are referenced via Media Fragment URIs [18]. These activities usually focus on individual collections and have not been applied at web scale. Furthermore, there is no common mode of publication for such media annotations, while content negotiation has been suggested [6], others such as SPARQL endpoints or individual APIs are also used.

DBpedia Commons[6] provides RDF descriptions for Wikimedia Commons including its multimedia resources [20]. The descriptions are extracted from the Wikimedia Commons wiki pages using the DBpedia extraction framework, i.e. they mainly include handcrafted annotations while low-level file information is not contained. Unfortunately, the data is not linked by its original source via standard HTTP protocols.

5 Conclusion and Outlook on Future Work

In this paper we have sketched our vision to realize a machine understandable web of media assets, which bases entirely on state-of-the-art web technologies

---

[3] http://blog.yovisto.com/.
[4] http://jigsaw.w3.org/Yves/Australia/1998/04/.
[5] http://www.adobe.com/products/xmp.html.
[6] http://commons.dbpedia.org/.

and to a great extent can be implemented in an automated way. We provided a number of use-cases that would benefit from explicit media content descriptions or are becoming possible by that. As always, it demands a significant amount of deployments to get real use of it. We have demonstrated that the actual deployment can be as easy as pie by using dedicated services.

Still, there are steps to take: a common set of ontologies to describe web assets and their content needs to be agreed. Furthermore, we plan to extend the COAL demo implementation in a modular way to support additional media and file types with more sophisticated analysis technologies.

References

1. Arndt, R., Troncy, R., Staab, S., Hardman, L., Vacura, M.: COMM: designing a well-founded multimedia ontology for the web. In: Aberer, K., et al. (eds.) ASWC 2007 and ISWC 2007. LNCS, vol. 4825, pp. 30–43. Springer, Heidelberg (2007)
2. Bailer, W., et al.: Ontology for media resources 1.0. W3C recommendation, (Feb 2012). https://www.w3.org/TR/mediaont-10/
3. Berners-Lee, T., Hendler, J., Lassila, O.: The semantic web. Sci. Am. **284**(5), 34–43 (2001)
4. Fielding, R.T., et al.: Hypertext transfer protocol - http/1.1. RFC 2616, RFC Editor (June 1999). http://www.rfc-editor.org/rfc/rfc2616.txt
5. Freed, N., Borenstein, D.N.S.: Multipurpose Internet Mail Extensions (MIME) Part One: Format of Internet Message Bodies. IETF RFC 2045 (Mar 2013). https://rfc-editor.org/rfc/rfc2045.txt
6. Hausenblas, M., et al.: Interlinking multimedia. In: CEUR-WS, Proceedings of the Linked Data on the Web Workshop. Madrid, Spain, vol. 538, April 2009
7. Heath, T., Bizer, C.: Linked Data: Evolving the Web into a Global Data Space, 1st edn. Morgan & Claypool, San Rafael (2011)
8. Hellmann, S., Lehmann, J., Auer, S., Brümmer, M.: Integrating NLP using linked data. In: Alani, H., et al. (eds.) ISWC 2013, Part II. LNCS, vol. 8219, pp. 98–113. Springer, Heidelberg (2013)
9. Hentschel, C., Sack, H.: What image classifiers really see – visualizing bag-of-visual words models. In: He, X., Luo, S., Tao, D., Xu, C., Yang, J., Hasan, M.A. (eds.) MMM 2015, Part I. LNCS, vol. 8935, pp. 95–104. Springer, Heidelberg (2015)
10. MPEG-7: Multimedia Content Description Interface (2001)
11. Exchangeable image file format for digital still cameras: Exif version 2.3 (2010). http://home.jeita.or.jp/tsc/std-pdf/CP3451C.pdf
12. Kanzaki, M.: Exif data description vocabulary (2003). http://www.kanzaki.com/ns/exif, last update in 2007
13. Lafon, Y., Bos, B.: Describing and retrieving photos using RDF and HTTP. W3c note, April 2002. https://www.w3.org/TR/photo-rdf/
14. Nixon, L., Troncy, R.: Survey of semantic media annotation tools for the web: towards new media applications with linked media. In: Presutti, V., Blomqvist, E., Troncy, R., Sack, H., Papadakis, I., Tordai, A. (eds.) ESWC Satellite Events 2014. LNCS, vol. 8798, pp. 100–114. Springer, Heidelberg (2014)
15. Powell, A., Nilsson, M., Naeve, A., Johnston, P.: Dublin core metadata initiative - abstract model (2005). http://dublincore.org/documents/abstract-model
16. RDFa 1.1 primer: rich structured data markup for web documents. W3C Working group note, March 2015. http://www.w3.org/TR/rdfa-primer/

17. Sanderson, R., Ciccarese, P., de Sompel, H.V.: Open annotation data model. W3C community draft, Febraury 2013. http://www.openannotation.org/spec/core/
18. Troncy, R., et al.: Media fragment URI 1.0. W3C recommendation, September 2012. https://www.w3.org/TR/media-frags/
19. Usbeck, R., et al.: GERBIL - general entity annotation benchmark framework. In: 24th WWW Conference (2015)
20. Vaidya, G., Kontokostas, D., Knuth, M., Lehmann, J., Hellmann, S.: DBpedia commons: structured multimedia metadata from the wikimedia commons. In: Arenas, M., et al. (eds.) ISWC 2015. LNCS, vol. 9367, pp. 281–289. Springer, Heidelberg (2015). doi:10.1007/978-3-319-25010-6_17

Situational-Context: A Unified View of Everything Involved at a Particular Situation

Javier Berrocal[1](✉), Jose Garcia-Alonso[1], Carlos Canal[2], and Juan M. Murillo[1]

[1] University of Extremadura, Cáceres, Spain
{jberolm,jgaralo,juanmamu}@unex.es
[2] University of Málaga, Málaga, Spain
canal@lcc.uma.es

Abstract. As the interest in the Web of Things increases, specially for the general population, the barriers to entry for the use of these technologies should decrease. Current applications can be developed to adapt their behaviour to predefined conditions and users preferences, facilitating their use. In the future, Web of Things software should be able to automatically adjust its behaviour to non-predefined preferences or context of its users. In this vision paper we define the Situational-Context as the combination of the virtual profiles of the entities (things or people) that concur at a particular place and time. The computation of the Situational-Context allow us to predict the expected system behaviour and the required interaction between devices to meet the entities' goals, achieving a better adjustment of the system to variable contexts.

Keywords: Internet of Things · Web of Things · Context-Aware

1 Introduction

The increased capabilities of embedded devices has enabled the development of smart things. These devices may be connected to the Internet, providing a virtual representation of themselves with which other devices can interact, enabling the development of the Internet of Things (IoT) [11]. The Web of Things (WoT) integrates the connected smart things in the web, facilitating their interactions with people [13]. One of the main goals of these paradigms is to simplify people life by making the technology work for them, either providing more information for decision-making or facilitating the accomplishment of some tasks.

It has been predicted that by 2020 there will be 50 to 100 billion of these devices connected to the Internet [23]. However, if we analyse the current state of how people interact with them, the benefits provided will not be as groundbreaking as expected. The reason is that, in order to increase usability, the behaviour of smart things and applications depends on the users preferences and their context, which can shift considerably overtime. However, how systems adapt to these context is still too manual. Manually configuring an increasing number of smart things connected to daily life activities will need too much attention. Moreover,

© Springer International Publishing Switzerland 2016
A. Bozzon et al. (Eds.): ICWE 2016, LNCS 9671, pp. 476–483, 2016.
DOI: 10.1007/978-3-319-38791-8_34

when there are changes in the context, these devices should be reconfigured. As an example we can consider a thermostat that allows its users to monitor and change their house temperature. To control this system the user establish a set of desired temperatures for specific times. This configuration can be manually overwritten when the user preferences or context change, for example if she is going to arrive home earlier she can put the heating on earlier. This manual control of WoT systems, that is acceptable when working with a small number of devices, will became a burden for users involved in dozens of systems.

Accordingly, solutions are needed to transparently and effortlessly integrate the people's needs, moods and preferences into the connected world of the WoT. There are researches working on gathering and processing the contextual information of users in order to create more comprehensive virtual profiles [1,10,15]. Even, the authors of this paper proposed to use the smartphone as a key element to create and maintain these profiles [12]. Nevertheless, an accurate and comprehensive virtual profile is not enough. Techniques to adapt the software behaviour to the context are also necessary. Currently, researchers are working on techniques such as Dynamic Composition [6] or Context Oriented Programming (COP) [14]. These techniques allow developers to predefine different behaviour of an applications depending on the identification of specific contextual information. They concur that the information and/or variables triggering the adaptations is detailed within the source code of the applications. Thus, the adaptation capabilities are limited to the set of predefined contexts. However, the variability of this information is very large and is difficult to identify and express every plausible situation in the development phase, especially for everyday environments in which interactions depend on each user and her context, i.e. her preferences, the people located around her, their history, etc. For example, when a person get into her home, the smartphone may automatically interact with the thermostat to establish the desired temperature, but this interaction can also depend on whether she is alone or accompanied, her mood, etc.

Here, we present a vision paper in which the authors outline a set of concepts for achieving adaptation in the defined context. Concretely, we propose the new concept of Situational-Context as a way to analyse the conditions that exist at a particular time and place; and how this analysis can be used to predict, at run-time, the expected behaviour of WoT systems. The Situational-Context is defined as the resulting context of composing the virtual profiles of the different entities (things and people) involved in a particular situation. In this composed context there will be entities providing goals that details specific conditions that are desirable to be achieved, and entities providing skills enabling the fulfilment of these goals. Thus, once the Situational-Context is composed, the ways in which the entities will better satisfy the goals should emerge from the Situational-Context itself. The Situational-Context will provide a higher level of automation of smart things with people. Currently, there is a large amount of works related with the Situational-Context in the Context-Aware [15], Ubicomp [5], User Modelling [16] and Ambient Intelligence [20] areas. Some of their results will be used to develop its technical aspects. The contribution of the Situational-Context to WoT will be not only the unified view of the virtual profiles and the emerging interactions from the situations, but also new programming models to develop applications aware of the situations will have to be defined.

To define the Situational-Context the rest of the paper is structured as follows. Section 2 presents the motivations and some related work. Section 3 details the Situational-Context concept, the technology required to support it and a proof of concept. And Sect. 4 presents some conclusions and future works.

2   Motivations and Related Works

In the WoT usually several devices are orchestrated to build complex systems [17]. However, as the WoT is more integrated into people daily activities this orchestration becomes more complex. The Ambient Intelligence (AmI) has emerge as a disciple for making the everyday environments sensitive and responsive to people [20]. AmI needs to be aware of the users preferences in order to know when a device should acts. This is even more challenging when the needs of a multiple entities should be analysed in order to predict the action to perform [7].

In this sense, there are different researchers focused on the identification of people's context. Concretely, the authors of this paper have been working on the People as a Service (PeaaS) and the Internet of People (IoP) approaches. PeaaS [12] is a mobile-centric computing model to infer the context of smartphones' owners and generate their sociological profile. IoP [21] propose an infrastructure and a manifesto for WoT systems that support this proactive adaptations. This manifesto indicates that the interactions between things and people must be *social*, must be *personalized* with the users profiles, must be *predictable*, and must be *proactive* and automatically triggered depending on the context.

The raw contextual information related to a person or a thing is very rich, however some times it can be too basic. Other research works focus on computing the raw information for making high level context deductions. In [22] the authors propose a system that can automatically recognize the high-level context of the users, i.e. activities, emotions, and relationships with other users. In [10], the authors indicate that the user context can be expressed as a combination of the user's activity, light conditions, social setting and geographical location. So, they propose a system to gather the user context and perform high level inferences.

One of the main goals of inferring high level information is to better adapt the applications behaviour to the users. The same authors of [10] reuse the deducted information to adapt the interface of an app to the user environment. The COP paradigm provides an additional dimension to standard programming techniques to dynamically switch among the behaviours associated with each context [24]. Most of the approaches defined in this paradigm group behaviour in layers related with a specific context. The activation of a layer is usually predetermined at the development stage. Even there are works decoupling the context from the layers, providing greater flexibility [19]. The Dynamic Composition paradigm is a step forward when the interactions between devices cannot be identified at the development stages. It allows developers to implement the application behaviour without defining the specific devices involved. Therefore, applications choose the devices involved in a specific interaction at run-time.

Therefore, there are a lot of proposals for building comprehensive virtual profiles. However, the techniques for developing systems adaptable to the users' profiles requires to predefine in the development phase when each behaviour is activated. This limits the customization of applications and makes it difficult to obtain WoT systems totally responsive to users. It would be desirable that the behaviours and interactions emerge from the concrete situations and that the system would be able to respond in an ad-hoc way to each situation.

The next section focuses on detailing how the context of the devices can be computed to identify situations of people and things, and how such situations can be used to predict at run-time the interactions to trigger.

3   Emerging Interactions from the Situational-Context

3.1   Situational-Context

The Situational-Context can be defined as the composition of the virtual profiles of all the entities involved in a situation. For a meaningful composition of these profiles, we consider that they contain, at least, the following information:

- A *Basic Profile* containing the dated raw information with the entity's status, the relationships with other devices and its history. This profile can be seen as a timeline with the changes and interactions that happened to the entity.
- *Social Profile.* This profile contains the results of high level inferences performed over the Basic Profile.
- The *Goals* detailing the status of the environment desired by the entity. These Goals can also be deducted from the Basic and Social Profiles.
- The Skills or capabilities that an entity has to make decisions and perform actions capable of modifying the environment and aimed at achieving Goals.

The result of composing the virtual profiles of the involved entities is not only the combined information of all entities. It contains the combined history of the entities ordered in a single timeline, the result of high level inferences performed over the combined virtual profiles, the set of Goals of the entities and their Skills. From the combined information of the Situational-Context, strategies to achieve Goals based on the present Skills should be identified. These strategies will guide the prediction of the interactions that must emerge from the context.

Furthermore, the Situational-Context is a dynamic abstraction of the combined profiles and therefore evolves through time. To analyse the instantaneity of this context, we use the concept of *Configuration*. A Configuration is the unified and stable view of the virtual profiles of the devices involved in the situation at a specific point in time. When changes in the environment happen, the Configuration is no longer stable and must be updated. Thus, a new Configuration must be defined from the updated/new virtual profiles of the devices. Thus, the Situational-Context can also be seen as a succession of Configurations.

Figure 1 shows the Situational-Context for controlling the temperature of a room. It contains a first configuration (C1) combining the virtual profiles of a thermostat and the smartphone of a person that is in the room. The smartphone defines the Goal to have a comfort temperature and the thermostat has a Skill to control the temperature of the room. When a new user with the same Goal in her profile enters the room, the situation change, a new configuration (C2) is computed and the strategies required to achieve the combined Goals are identified. Then, the interactions required for setting the adequate comfort temperature will emerge from this context.

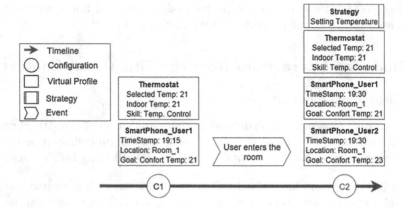

Fig. 1. Excerpt of a Situational-Context.

3.2 Technology for Supporting the Situational-Context

To support the Situational-Context, as described above, there are a number of technological issues that must be resolved.

First, which device or devices should compute the Situational-Context? This computation can be done in a Cloud environment. However, in order to reduce the network overhead and thanks to the increased capabilities of smart things, this computation can also be done either by a local device or distributively by a set of local devices [2]. Currently, Multi-Agent Systems [3] can be used to develop self-organised, reconfigurable and proactive systems. It should be evaluated what technique is the most appropriate for computing the Situational-Context or even if a combination of different techniques should be applied depending on the size and type of the virtual profiles to combine.

Second, how contextual information can be exchanged? There is a wide range of technologies for this purpose. There are middlewares homogenizing the communications in heterogeneous networks [8]. And there are works, like the SOFIA project [25], creating a semantic interoperability platform for making the information available for smart services. It is necessary to identify whether they can be used for identifying the devices involved in a configuration and to manage the interactions between them.

Third, how common Goals should be agreed for a specific configuration when the devices involved have different or, even, opposed Goals? Currently, there are algorithms for negotiating which device should perform a command [4] when in the surrounding there are several that have the capabilities to respond to it. In the Situational-Context, negotiation algorithms are needed to autonomously agree on a common Goal.

Fourth, how the strategies to achieve Goals should be identified? They can be predefined in order to be triggered depending on the Goals to achieve, but again this would compromise the applications flexibility. Should they also emerge from each specific configuration? The Spatial and Temporal reasoning areas [9] have been previously used to get a better understanding of the context in order to make sensible decisions. It should be evaluated whether is possible to infer the strategy to execute from the context using these techniques.

Finally, how the interactions can emerge from the Situational-Context and from each Configuration? The Self-Adaptive [18] software systems can modify themselves at run-time and, as detailed above, there are different proposals to develop applications that adapt their behaviour to the context. It should be assessed whether these approaches can be used to develop applications that autonomously compose the devices involved in a Configuration and trigger specific actions depending on the established Goals and Strategies.

3.3 Proof of Concept

Currently, we are working on a proof of concept for the computation of the Situational-Context. This proof of concept consist in an Android set-top box connected to a temperature sensor and an air conditioner, and a mobile app to control the temperature of a room that is installed on the users' phones.

The Android device has an application for controlling the air conditioner, for getting the room temperature from the sensor and for broadcasting information about the device. The mobile app sends commands for getting the temperature, stores the user contextual information and has rules for high level deductions and for its definition as Goals. Specifically, it has a rule to infer the user's comfort temperature from manual interactions.

In this case, the Situational-Context is locally computed by the smartphone. To that end, it constantly monitor the surrounding devices broadcasting information, identifies which ones have Skills for controlling the temperature, queries them to obtain the room temperature and, if it is different than the comfort temperature, the mobile app proactively trigger an strategy to set a new one.

Finally, this strategy has also defined a negotiation algorithm to agree a common temperature when there are several users. This algorithm, first, identifies all the devices involved in the conflict. For this, it broadcast a signal indicating that it wants to change the temperature, this signal is replied by the devices with a Goal defined involving the temperature. Subsequently, a communication is established between them to exchange the comfort temperature. The final temperature is the average of all temperatures and is notified to the Android device by the device that started the algorithm.

The tests conducted so far show us that the computation of the Situational-Context is feasible. However, more research work is still needed for the computation of complex situations.

4   Conclusions and Future Work

Current WoT applications can be implemented to have a specific behaviour depending on the preferences and the context of users. However, this adaptation is limited to the behaviours defined in the development phase. In the future these applications shall be fully self-adaptive and able to completely change their behaviour, at run-time, to cover the needs of any user or any group of users, and to use the capabilities of the new devices included in the system.

Here, we present a vision paper basing this adaptation in the Situational-Context. This facilitates the identification of the goals that should be pursued by the surrounding devices and the needed strategies and interactions to achieve them. We are currently working on formalizing the Situational-Context and its computation. For computing the Situational-Context, new programming models for the different development phases of WoT applications will be needed. These models will facilitate the development systems aware of the environment and able to react to its needs.

Acknowledgments. This work was supported by the Spanish Ministry of Science and Innovation (TIN2014-53986-REDT, TIN2015-67083-R and TIN2015-69957-R), by the Department of Economy and Infrastructure of the Government of Extremadura (GR15098), and by the European Regional Development Fund.

References

1. Abowd, G.D., Dey, A.K.: Towards a better understanding of context and context-awareness. In: Gellersen, H.-W. (ed.) HUC 1999. LNCS, vol. 1707, pp. 304–307. Springer, Heidelberg (1999)
2. Arslan, M., Singh, I., Singh, S., Madhyastha, H., Sundaresan, K., Krishnamurthy, S.: CWC: a distributed computing infrastructure using smartphones. IEEE Trans. Mob. Comput. **14**(8), 1587–1600 (2015)
3. Barbati, M., Bruno, G., Genovese, A.: Applications of agent-based models for optimization problems: a literature review. Expert Syst. Appl. **39**(5), 6020–6028 (2012)
4. Bauerle, F., Miller, G., Nassar, N., Nassar, T., Penney, I.: Context sensitive smart device command recognition and negotiation. In: Giaffreda, R., Vieriu, R.-L., Pasher, E., Bendersky, G., Jara, A.J., Rodrigues, J.J.P.C., Dekel, E., Mandler, B. (eds.) IoT360 2014. LNICST, vol. 150, pp. 314–330. Springer, Heidelberg (2015)
5. Caceres, R., Friday, A.: Ubicomp systems at 20: progress, opportunities, and challenges. IEEE Pervasive Comput. **1**, 14–21 (2011)
6. Chen, G., Li, M., Kotz, D.: Data-centric middleware for context-aware pervasive computing. Pervasive Mob. Comput. **4**(2), 216–253 (2008)
7. Cook, D.J., Augusto, J.C., Jakkula, V.R.: Ambient intelligence: technologies, applications, and opportunities. Pervasive Mob. Comput. **5**(4), 277–298 (2009)

8. Dubois, D., Bando, Y., Watanabe, K., Miyamoto, A., Sato, M., Papper, W., Bove, V.: Supporting heterogeneous networks and pervasive storage in mobile content-sharing middleware. In: Consumer Communications and Networking Conference, pp. 841–847 (2015)

9. Galton, A.: Qualitative Spatial Change. Oxford University Press, Oxford (2000)

10. Gronli, T.M., Ghinea, G., Younas, M.: Context-aware and automatic configuration of mobile devices in cloud-enabled ubiquitous computing. Personal Ubiquit. Comput. **18**(4), 883–894 (2014)

11. Gubbi, J., Buyya, R., Marusic, S., Palaniswami, M.: Internet of things (IoT): a vision, architectural elements, and future directions. Future Gener. Comput. Syst. **29**(7), 1645–1660 (2013)

12. Guillen, J., Miranda, J., Berrocal, J., Garcia-Alonso, J., Murillo, J.M., Canal, C.: People as a service: a mobile-centric model for providing collective sociological profiles. IEEE Softw. **31**(2), 48–53 (2014)

13. Guinard, D., Trifa, V., Mattern, F., Wilde, E.: From the internet of things to the web of things: resource-oriented architecture and best practices. In: Uckelmann, D., Harrison, M., Michahelles, F. (eds.) Architecting the Internet of Things, pp. 97–129. Springer, Heidelberg (2011)

14. Hirschfeld, R., Costanza, P., Nierstrasz, O.: Context-oriented programming. J. Object Technol. **7**(3), 125–151 (2008). ETH Zurich

15. Hong, J.Y., Suh, E.H., Kim, S.J.: Context-aware systems: a literature review and classification. Exp. Syst. Appl. **36**(4), 8509–8522 (2009)

16. Kobsa, A.: Generic user modeling systems. User Model. User-Adap. Interact. **11**(1–2), 49–63 (2001)

17. Kovatsch, M.: CoAP for the web of things: from tiny resource-constrained devices to the web browser. In: ACM Conference on Pervasive and Ubiquitous Computing Adjunct Publication, pp. 1495–1504. ACM, New York (2013)

18. Macías-Escrivá, F.D., Haber, R.E., Toro, R.M., Hernández, V.: Self-adaptive systems: a survey of current approaches, research challenges and applications. Expert Syst. Appl. **40**(18), 7267–7279 (2013)

19. Maingret, B., Mouël, F.L., Ponge, J., Stouls, N., Cao, J., Loiseau, Y.: Towards a decoupled context-oriented programming language for the internet of things. In: International Workshop on Context-Oriented Programming, pp. 1–6. ACM (2015)

20. Marzano, S.: The New Everyday: Views on Ambient Intelligence. 010 Publishers, Rotterdam (2003)

21. Miranda, J., Makitalo, N., Garcia-Alonso, J., Berrocal, J., Mikkonen, T., Canal, C., Murillo, J.: From the internet of things to the internet of people. IEEE Internet Comput. **19**(2), 40–47 (2015)

22. Park, H.S., Oh, K., Cho, S.B.: Bayesian network-based high-level context recognition for mobile context sharing in cyber-physical system. Int. J. Distrib. Sens. Netw. **2011**, 10 (2011)

23. Perera, C., Liu, C.H., Jayawardena, S., Chen, M.: Context-aware computing in the internet of things: a survey on internet of things from industrial market perspective. CoRR (2015)

24. Salvaneschi, G., Ghezzi, C., Pradella, M.: Context-oriented programming: a software engineering perspective. J. Syst. Softw. **85**(8), 1801–1817 (2012)

25. SOFIA Project: Smart Objects For Intelligent Applications (2009). http://www.sofia-project.eu/

The Direwolf Inside You: End User Development for Heterogeneous Web of Things Appliances

István Koren[✉] and Ralf Klamma

Advanced Community Information Systems (ACIS) Group,
RWTH Aachen University, Ahornstr. 55, 52056 Aachen, Germany
{koren,klamma}@dbis.rwth-aachen.de
http://dbis.rwth-aachen.de

Abstract. Mobile computing devices like smartphones have become a commodity. They are very convenient when connecting to ubiquitous Web of Things (WoT) appliances. However, WoT manufacturers are challenged to provide Web application interfaces for a multitude of mobile platforms in a short time. Moreover, end users are required to install dedicated Web apps for giving them access to these emerging technologies. To overcome this situational overburdening efforts, end user development in the form of component-based Web mashups has already been applied successfully in various domains. In this paper, we envision a framework for letting users create situational applications for opportunistic device usage. We explore the recent Web Component group of W3C recommendations as a foundation for peer-to-peer cross-platform, cross-application and cross-user Web applications. Our preliminary experiences may help the Web engineering community to build better Web infrastructures for a heterogeneous device landscape.

Keywords: Web of Things · End User Development · Web Components

1 Introduction

Over the last years, we have seen a massive growth in the number of smartphones used. They enable us to instantly access any kind of information while on the go; millions of platform-specific, native apps are serving individual needs like games, news, office and social networking applications. More recently, we encounter an exponentially growing number of everyday devices connected to the Internet: online TVs, intelligent power sockets, and many other ambient technologies form the basis of the *Internet of Things*, or *Web of Things (WoT)* in the context of the Web. Already, we are confronted with a multitude of WoT appliances, from interactive hotel rooms to conference venue systems that can be controlled from mobile devices. However, they often either require using provided hardware or installing a dedicated app on a personal mobile computer. Both options come with difficulties: We either have to learn how to use the provided input modalities, or we need to go to an app store to download an app. Thus, the time-consuming access methods of these WoT resources are not

© Springer International Publishing Switzerland 2016
A. Bozzon et al. (Eds.): ICWE 2016, LNCS 9671, pp. 484–491, 2016.
DOI: 10.1007/978-3-319-38791-8_35

adapted to the short-term situational context they are used in. Additionally, many companies producing these appliances are from industries not traditionally linked with the IT and software world; they are confronted with enormous economical challenges to provide user interfaces to a wide variety of end user smartphones and wearables. Yet, what unites both the WoT world and end user mobile tools is the universal access to the Internet, and in particular the standardized World Wide Web with browsers accessing HTML5 resources served over the HTTP protocol.

Software engineering traditionally strives to create development artifacts that are maintainable and reusable across projects. In the Web context, cleanly-cut responsibilities and functionalities are visible in the agile development of microservices and in the composition of Web 2.0 mashups [1]. These standards-based HTML5 mashups are ideal platforms for various situational use cases [2]. In this regard, *End User Development (EUD)* is commonly defined as a methodology to allow users of software systems to act as non-professional developers to create, modify or extend software artifacts [3].

In this article, we explore the research question, what infrastructure is needed for component-based Web engineering practices to unite the scattered world of mobile (smartphone and wearable) apps and everyday devices connected to the Web of Things. We embed our research in the field of End User Development in Sect. 2 and present related work. Section 3 discusses the extension of DireWolf, a platform for multi- and cross-device Web user interfaces. By including user interface elements referenced or served directly by WoT devices, our framework acknowledges the heterogeneity and fast evolution of device-specific proprietary APIs. Section 4 highlights implementational aspects building on the recent Web Components group of W3C recommendations[1]. Section 5 concludes the article by presenting a preliminary evaluation and giving an outlook on future work. We are confident, that using standardized HTML5 components will in the long run ease the development of user interfaces for various device types while at the same time liberating users from the tedious task of having to install separate apps for interacting with diverse everyday objects.

2   End User Development for the Web of Things

In traditional software engineering, usually developers are creating software to be used by users. The idea of End User Development is to break with this classical roles and give more power to the users to design their application. It is based on the idea, that end users know the best about their surroundings - the context, the tools and their constraints. Spreadsheets are generally considered as the first broad emergence of the EUD paradigm [4], in that users are creating formulas that resemble algorithms to calculate values based on fields. Since the early findings, a broad range of research has been carried out in the field, up to economical topics [5,6].

---

[1] https://www.w3.org/standards/techs/components.

Situational apps created for short-term needs in highly specialized environments are ideal candidates for End User Development [2,3]. In that sense, they resemble the characteristics of the *Long Tail* [7]. Originally conceived in the area of e-commerce, standing for the idea that the bulk of sales is not in the few top items but in the rest, the term is now also used for the large number of niche communities with specialized needs. Especially composite Web applications are now being associated with the Long Tail [8], as they allow context-dependent situational usage.

2.1   Related Work for the Web of Things

The world of everyday objects connected to the Internet is scattered with vendor- and device specific apps. On the protocol level, there exists a bewildering variety of standards such as XMPP, MQTT, CoAP and proprietary pseudo-standards like Z-Wave and EnOcean. The Web of Things by Guinard et al. [9] stands for the idea that every resource in the Internet of Things is accessible over the HTTP protocol, either directly or over gateways. In the WoT concept, the devices provide both, a JSON representation and a basic HTML interface [10], however advanced user interface concepts are not in the prime scope of the articles.

More recently, the Physical Web[2] approach by Google is based on the concept that devices broadcast a URL via Bluetooth that can be read out by users' mobile devices, pointing to a cloud-based application able to interact with the device through WebSockets. While this concept allows to access WoT devices through arbitrary Web-capable clients, it does not cater for building coherent applications out of composite parts; i.e. for controlling dozens of devices in a smart home, various bookmarks need to be kept around.

Snap-To-It is a platform for opportunistic discovery of devices based on photographs [11]. The authors performed user studies to find out the preferred way of consumers to interact with on- and offline devices in everyday situations. Neither QR codes nor list-based approaches were the preferred method of interaction; instead, photographs of hardware, software and physical artifacts like maps were favored and later implemented. To support the system, additional computing-intensive resources are needed in the network for the image discovery. While our work would benefit of the advanced object recognition capabilities to make connecting to objects easier, we take the coupling for granted and focus on the composability on the user interface level.

Multiple approaches for component-based Web applications have emerged over the last years in different domains, for instance the OMELETTE platform for telco mashups [12] and the ROLE SDK for personalized learning environments [13]. Special requirements arise as soon as mobile devices are included in these mashups. While advances have been made in the overlapping area of *Distributed User Interfaces*, another topic that profits by componentized interfaces, existing work has focused on native applications [14,15] and/or desktop-based

---

[2] https://google.github.io/physical-web/.

composition paradigms [15,16]. What is missing, is a framework that spans various types of Web-capable devices. In the next section, we discuss our vision towards device-agnostic componentized Web interfaces.

3 User Interfaces for the Web of Things

In our conceptual framework, we combine ideas of End User Development, the Web of Things and the Physical Web and allow devices to broadcast their own user interface and access logic. We are able to read in the user interfaces and display them in a common Web platform. To this end, we extend DireWolf, a framework for multi-device widget-based Web applications [17]. DireWolf already gives us the conceptual notion of sharing Web interfaces by synchronizing Web applications across multiple devices.

Figure 1 shows a system overview of the extended DireWolf framework in a smart ambient setting with intelligent lighting and a weather station connected to the Internet. The approach unites various flavors of end user devices with local and cloud-based solutions accessing the Web of Things. Smart things advertise an URL either by QR codes or Bluetooth Low Energy beacon signals. Either way, the URL points to a user interface element resource downloadable through HTTP. The actual interface to access device attributes and functionality, like temperature values and switching lights, is conceptually decoupled. It can either be served directly through the device or be hosted in the cloud, like in the case of the weather station that regularly pushes its data to a distant server. Beyond REST based interfaces on the device itself or through the cloud, in our approach, the devices can also be accessed over other communication channels available in Web browsers like Web Bluetooth and MQTT. Following the fundamental principles of XML and the Document Object Model in particular, imported elements are put in a tree, i.e. they may reference other components themselves to build up complex user interfaces. Beyond, the user interface elements are shared across instances. Due to Hypertext characteristics, particular elements can be

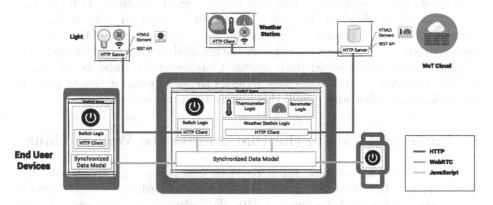

Fig. 1. Overview of the direwolf for the web of things system

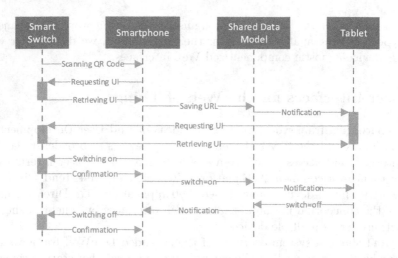

Fig. 2. Sequence diagram of the synchronization

bookmarked and linked either separately or as their combined representation, encapsulated within a structural or layout element.

Once coupled with the DireWolf platform, the user interface elements are aligned in flexible grids according to the concepts of *Responsive Web Design* [18]. All imported elements get access to a shared data model for cross-device synchronization of their state. An optional master flag on the device the element was imported on makes it the primary responsible entity to access the device and saving parameters in the shared model. This way, we avoid redundant requests to constrained devices. Rather, sensor and other values are only accessed once and distributed over the synchronization channel. In the case of the master disconnecting, the functionality is migrated to a new device. A master component could also be responsible for providing cached or interpolated data when certain WoT devices may be temporarily disconnected.

Figure 2 shows a sequence diagram of the overall communication. First, a *Smart Switch* is added to the system that could control an ambient light for instance. Then, the switch is turned on. As can be seen, only one of the DireWolf instances is directly communicating with the physical device, the rest is operating on the shared, synchronized data model. Changes in the data model trigger notifications that in turn may cause requests to the physical device to perform the action. The other way round, this applies to events as well.

4   Implementation of the Platform for the Web of Things

We implemented a prototype using the Web Components group of W3C recommendations that have brought much-needed standardization in the area of componentized frontends for the Web [19]. WoT components are imported using

Fig. 3. Screenshot of the scanning process

HTML Imports that define *Custom Elements*. These in turn define their UI elements in *HTML Templates* within their *Shadow DOM*. To provide backwards-compatibility with browsers not yet supporting the standards, a polyfill library is imported, that transparently handles all functionality that is not present on the current platform; if the methods are available natively, they are used instead. Parts of our implementation use the *Polymer*[3] library from Google that adds syntactic sugar on top of the Web Components JavaScript API calls. For example, a complete set of responsive, well-designed user elements are available through Polymer.

DireWolf provides application *spaces* for separating different applications. In our concept, all elements within the same space share a common data model. This is realized with a custom HTML5 element called `direwolf-space` that can be declaratively controlled with attributes. For instance, the `space` attribute defines the space's name. The `direwolf-space` element can be embedded in arbitrary HTML pages; we have already successfully deployed it in WordPress and ROLE SDK instances.

Elements wishing to use the shared data model need to implement the abstract class `DireWolf-Element-Behavior`. A `synced-properties` attribute can then be used to list all parameters of the element that should be synchronized across DireWolf instances. The synchronization layer is implemented using Yjs, our library for synchronizing data structures in a peer-to-peer way [20].

Figure 3 shows a screenshot of the Web application taken on a Laptop. It shows the space called "myspace". A toolbar button on the right opens a dialog that embeds a QR code scanner application. The scanner itself is developed natively with Web technologies. Upon scanning of a code, the interface of the WoT device is added to the space.

5   Conclusion and Future Work

In this article, we have introduced our conceptual extension of the DireWolf framework towards integrating heterogeneous Web of Things devices. The platform is based on state-of-the-art Web Components, thus the application spaces

---

[3] https://www.polymer-project.org/1.0/.

are embeddable in any kind of (responsive) HTML5 websites. User interface elements can be aligned in tree structures for delivering more complex applications.

To preliminarily validate the conceptual findings and use the results of the implementation in a real-world setting, we have set up a technical evaluation testbed using a variety of mobile devices and a number of commercially available and custom-made smart things connected to the Internet. Our scenario is based on Fig. 1 with a GSM-One WiFi smart socket and a Netatmo weather station. In both cases, designing the UI logic with Web Components could be performed in little time based on the broad documentation of Polymer UI components. The challenge was accounting for the vendor-specific API endpoints in the application logic: While for standards like XMPP and MQTT developers profit of a wide variety of Open Source libraries, both our test appliances required getting familiar with their proprietary REST APIs. Recent initiatives by global players such as Google and Mozilla are currently embedding further communication channels into the Web, including Web Bluetooth and mDNS; these technologies are a valuable add-on for DireWolf.

Because of the late-breaking style of this article, a thorough evaluation of our concept still has to be carried out. We are especially interested in the scalability of our concept, i.e. how many end users can use how many components for which number of WoT devices. Besides, we plan to analyze aspects of usability, accessibility and security. Technical challenges remain in JavaScript dependency management; in the current prototype, all imported elements need to reference the same version of 3rd party libraries to avoid undesired behavior. Module loaders that are currently being standardized in ECMAScript 6, the next generation of JavaScript, may solve this problem in the future. Finally, we envision headless DireWolf clients conceptually acting as microservices for performing the actual connection to WoT devices, while broadcasting results over the shared data model. They could as well serve as gate keepers for verifying access rights of users in collaboration with authentication and authorization providers. We are confident, that our framework can help build future Web infrastructures for a heterogeneous device landscape.

Acknowledgements. The work has received funding from the European Commission's FP7 IP Learning Layers under grant agreement no 318209.

References

1. Daniel, F., Matera, M.: Mashups: Concepts, Models and Architectures. Springer, Heidelberg (2014)
2. Balasubramaniam, S., Lewis, G.A., Simanta, S., Smith, D.B.: Situated software: concepts, motivation, technology, and the future. IEEE Softw. **25**(6), 50–55 (2008)
3. Lieberman, H., Paternò, F., Wulf, V.: End User Development. Human-Computer Interaction Series. Springer, Dordrecht (2006)
4. Burnett, M., Cook, C., Rothermel, G.: End-user software engineering. Commun. ACM **47**(9), 53 (2004)

5. Wulf, V., Jarke, M.: The economics of end-user development. Commun. ACM **47**(9), 41–42 (2004)
6. Sutcliffe, A.: Evaluating the costs and benefits of end-user development. ACM SIGSOFT Softw. Eng. notes **30**(4), 1 (2005)
7. Anderson, C.: The Long Tail: Why the Future of Business Is Selling Less of More. Hyperion, New York (2006)
8. Ogrinz, M.: Mashup Patterns: Designs and Examples for the Modern Enterprise. Addison-Wesley, Upper Saddle River (2009)
9. Guinard, D., Trifa, V.: Towards the Web of Things - Web mashups for embedded devices. In: Workshop on Mashups, Enterprise Mashups and Lightweight Composition on the Web (MEM 2009), in Proceedings of the 18th International Conference on World Wide Web. ACM, New York (2009)
10. Guinard, D., Trifa, V., Mattern, F., Wilde, E.: From the internet of things to the web of things: resource oriented architecture and best practices. In: Uckelmann, D., Harrison, M., Michahelles, F. (eds.) Architecting the Internet of Things, pp. 97–129. Springer, Heidelberg (2011)
11. de Freitas, A., Nebeling, M., Chen, X.A., Yang, J., Ranithangam, A.S.K.K., Dey, A.K.: Snap-to-it: a user-inspired platform for opportunistic device interactions. In: Proceedings of the 34th Annual ACM Conference on Human Factors in Computing Systems (CHI 2016) (to be published, 2016)
12. Chudnovskyy, O., Nestler, T., Gaedke, M., Daniel, F., Fernández-Villamor, J.I., Chepegin, V., Fornas, J.A., Wilson, S., Kögler, C., Chang, H.: End-user-oriented telco mashups: the OMELETTE approach. In: Proceedings of the 21st International Conference Companion on World Wide Web (WWW 2012 Companion), p. 235 (2012)
13. Govaerts, S., et al.: Towards responsive open learning environments: the ROLE interoperability framework. In: Kloos, C.D., Gillet, D., Crespo García, R.M., Wild, F., Wolpers, M. (eds.) EC-TEL 2011. LNCS, vol. 6964, pp. 125–138. Springer, Heidelberg (2011)
14. Häkkilä, J., Korpipää, P., Ronkainen, S., Tuomela, U.: Interaction and end-user programming with a context-aware mobile application. In: Costabile, M.F., Paternó, F. (eds.) INTERACT 2005. LNCS, vol. 3585, pp. 927–937. Springer, Heidelberg (2005)
15. Cappiello, C., Matera, M., Picozzi, M.: End-user development of mobile mashups. In: Marcus, A. (ed.) DUXU 2013, Part IV. LNCS, vol. 8015, pp. 641–650. Springer, Heidelberg (2013)
16. Chaisatien, P., Prutsachainimmit, K., Tokuda, T.: Mobile mashup generator system for cooperative applications of different mobile devices. In: Auer, S., Díaz, O., Papadopoulos, G.A. (eds.) ICWE 2011. LNCS, vol. 6757, pp. 182–197. Springer, Heidelberg (2011)
17. Kovachev, D., Renzel, D., Nicolaescu, P., Koren, I., Klamma, R.: DireWolf: a framework for widget-based distributed user interfaces. J. Web Eng. **13**(3&4), 203–222 (2014)
18. Marcotte, E.: Responsive Web Design. A Book Apart, New York (2011)
19. Krug, M., Gaedke, M.: SmartComposition: enhanced web components for a better future of web development. In: Proceedings of the 24th International Conference on World Wide Web, pp. 207–210
20. Nicolaescu, P., Jahns, K., Derntl, M., Klamma, R.: Yjs: a framework for near real-time P2P shared editing on arbitrary data types. In: Cimiano, P., Frasincar, F., Houben, G.-J., Schwabe, D. (eds.) ICWE 2015. LNCS, vol. 9114, pp. 675–678. Springer, Heidelberg (2015)

PhD Symposium Papers

A Semantic Model for Friend Segregation in Online Social Networks

Javed Ahmed[1,2(✉)]

[1] CIRSFID, University of Bologna, Bologna, Italy
[2] CSC, University of Luxembourg, Luxembourg City, Luxembourg
shahanijaved@gmail.com

Abstract. Online Social Networks exhibit many of the characteristics of human societies in terms of forming relationships and sharing personal information. However, the major online social networks lack an effective mechanism to represent diverse social relationships of the users. This leads to undesirable consequences of disclosing personal information of the users with unintended audiences. We propose a semantic model for friend segregation in online social networks. The relationship strength and social context of the users play vital role in friend segregation. The model infers relationship strength and social context from interaction pattern and profile similarity attributes of the users. We also conducted a research study with online social networks users. The study gives insight on user's information sharing behaviour and interaction pattern in online social networks. The findings reveal that personal information disclosure depends on relationship strength among the users.

Keywords: Online social networks · Privacy · Self presentation · Tie strength · Audience segregation

1 Introduction

Online social networks (OSNs) experienced exponential growth and attracted vast majority of the Internet users in recent years. OSNs offer the Internet users new and interesting means to communicate, interact and socialize with their family and friends. The users spend an unprecedented amount of time using online social networks and upload large quantities of personal information. In online social networks the uploader of the data must decide which of his friends should be able to access the data. This resulted in fundamental shift in status of an end user. An individual end-user becomes content manager instead of just being content consumer. The responsibility of managing appropriate privacy settings for every single piece of data shared on OSNs put a cognitive burden on the user and hence most of the users end up using default privacy settings. The

---

J. Ahmed—Author is doctoral candidate in Erasmus Mundus Joint International Doctoral (Ph.D.) program in Law, Science and Technology. Professor Leendert van der Torre, Guido Governatori, and Serena Villata supervise the author.

© Springer International Publishing Switzerland 2016
A. Bozzon et al. (Eds.): ICWE 2016, LNCS 9671, pp. 495–500, 2016.
DOI: 10.1007/978-3-319-38791-8_36

default privacy settings are very permissive in nature and lead to undesirable consequences of user's personal information disclosure with unintended audience and this poses serious privacy threat to the end-users. It is main reason privacy has received significant attention in the research community.

The current online social networks provide multitude of privacy settings to manage access to uploaded content. However, privacy-setting interface is too complicated to most of the normal users. The current interface has limited visual feedback, and promotes a poor mental model of how the settings affect the profile visibility [1]. Even after modifying settings, users can experience difficulty in ensuring that their settings match the actual desired outcome. Madejski [2] shows that privacy settings for uploaded content are often incorrect, failing to match user's expectations. Some of the online social networks provide features of lists and circles. These mechanisms help users in partitioning their contacts and then use these partitions to selectively share their content with an appropriate audience according to their preferences. The relationships in real life evolve with time and these features do not offer any mechanism to the user to deal with this evolution. The responsibility of maintaining the appropriateness of these lists lies solely on the user. As a result, it is unsurprising that many users do not use these features. We conclude that there is disparity between desired and actual privacy controls. The main reason for this disparity is social aspects of privacy that are ignored by existing technical solutions.

2   Problem Statement

Despite of the multitude of privacy controls, current online social networks fail to provide an effective mechanism to manage access to uploaded content of the users [2]. The main reason for this failure is shortcoming of the online social networks to represent diverse social relationships. Online social networks carry problematic assumptions in their implicit design of representing social relationships. All friends are created equal that means they have access to same identity, and same social context of the user. In real life people play diverse roles and disclose their personal information according to the role. Each individual has several role-based identities to preserve the contextual integrity of the information, which is being disclosed. The notion of privacy as contextual integrity is compromised by online social networks. For example, one may self-present in significantly different ways when in a business meeting versus when on a date. OSNs place employers and romantic partners on the same communication plane, make it more difficult for users to segment audiences and present varied versions of the self. Difficulty in disclosing information selectively to various life facets can lead to "context collapse" [3]. The collapsing of social contexts has emerged as an important problem with the rise of online social networks.

Most online social networks employ "friendship" as the only type of bidirectional relationship. The friendship is binary, static, and symmetric relationship of equal value between all the directly connected users, which provide only a coarse indication of the nature of the relationship. In reality social relationships are of varying tie strength (how close two individual are to one another), dynamic (change over time), and asymmetric in nature (one person pays attention to another, it does not mean the latter will reciprocate). It is challenging task to model dynamism, asymmetry, and relational strength in user relationships in contemporary online social networks. This is the motivation for our research work.

The main question for this research is how to represent diverse social relationships of the users in online social networks. More specifically, we want to explore whether a user's interaction pattern with his friends can be used as a basis for inferring relationship strength among users. We also examine link between profile similarity attributes and relationship context of the users. The strength and context of relationship are key factors to perform friend segregation. Friend segregation can play vital role to control personal information disclosure in online social networks. We break main research question into sub questions:

1. How interaction pattern and profile similarity attributes reveals strength and context of relationship among OSNs users?
2. How to develop a semantic model for friend segregation depending on strength and context of relationship among OSNs users?
3. How to evaluate the model for friend segregation in online social networks?

In human societies, the strength and context of relationship are crucial factors for individuals while deciding the boundaries of their privacy. We conducted a research study with OSNs users to examine their attitude towards online privacy and relationship forming. The main contributions of this research work are given below:

1. We conducted a user study to examine information sharing and relationship forming behaviour of OSNs users.
2. We developed a model for friend segregation in online social networks.
3. The evaluation of the model using set of predefined criteria and requirements.

3   Methodology

The methodology employed in this work is combination of mixed methods approach such as reviewing scientific literature to redefine privacy that suits needs of social web users, conducting a user study to establish link between interaction pattern and relationship strength among OSNs users, and iterative development of a semantic model for friend segregation in online social networks. The complicated nature of the problem is rationale for choosing such a methodology. In the first phase, we redefine privacy from social and technical perspective. This privacy definition is inspired from work of Pfitzmann et al. [4]. We customized this concept to suit needs of online social networks. This privacy definition includes three aspects that are contextual integrity, disclosure minimization and user control. The contextual integrity gives users ability to keep audiences separate and to compartmentalize their social life [5]. The notion of privacy as contextual integrity can be useful in addressing the problem of context collapse. The relationship strength plays vital role in disclosure minimization. Granovetter coined the term tie strength [6]. Tie strength is a quantifiable social network concept that measures the quality of relationships. Current online social networks provide simple access control mechanisms allowing users to govern access to information contained in their own spaces. Unfortunately, users have no control over data residing outside their spaces. Irwin Altman addresses this problem by enhancing user control to deal with both individual and collaborative boundary regulation [7]. We conducted a user study in the second phase to identify relationship between personal information disclosure and tie strength. The research survey was designed to examine interaction patterns of user with their diverse friend network in OSNs. The 323 participants took part in the study out of which 245 are males and 81 females, which leads to male bias. The results of survey are presented in following section. Finally, we developed a semantic model for friend segregation in online social networks. The model takes into consideration the three aspects of privacy described above.

4   Results

In this section, initially we present results of user study. According to the results 65 % of the participants added more than 200 people in their friend network, and 26 % of the participants reveal that they also added strangers to their friend network. Whereas, only 3 % of the participants are interested to share their personal information with strangers added in their friend network. The results show that vast majority of participants interact with friends and family on daily basis, and their interaction with colleagues and classmates is on weekly basis, whereas their interaction pattern with acquaintances and stranger is rarely or never. The preferred interaction type with strong ties is messaging, posting, commenting, and chatting. The participant's preferred interaction type with weak ties is either liking or not applicable. The most frequently used interaction types are messaging, liking, chatting, wishing, and posting, whereas, the least frequently used interaction types playing games and tagging. The results reveal that personal information disclosure depends on relationship strength among the users; the frequency of interaction is higher among the users with strong relational ties as compared to users with weak relational ties. The results also demonstrate that choice of interaction type for communication depends on relationship strength among the users.

An ontological model is developed using OWL as our modeling language. The ontology design methodology used is Methontology. The pool of competency questions is developed in the specification phase. In conceptualization phase, we identified entities and their relationships from competency questions. The model integrates some concepts from FOAF and PRO ontologies. The implementation of the model is done using Protege. Apart from checking consistency using various reasoners, the evaluation of the model is performed at assertional level by translating competency question into SPARQL queries and retrieving data. Figure 1 presents detail diagram of the model.

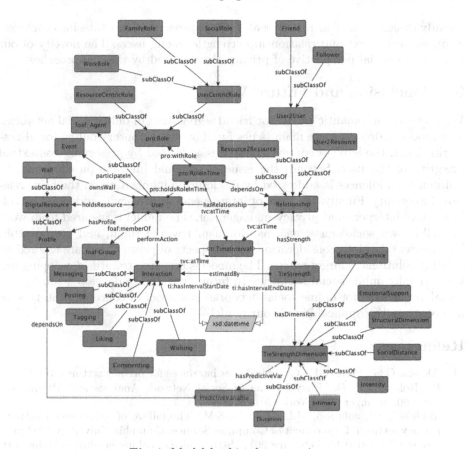

Fig. 1. Model for friend segregation

5   Related Work

The area of ontology based online social networks modeling is still in its early stages. One of the early solutions was proposed by Carminati et al. [8]. The authors propose online social network model based on semantic web technologies. The model considers the following five important elements of an online social network: (i) profiles, (ii) types of relationships among users (iii) resources, (iv) relationships between users and resources and (v) actions. The use of semantic web technologies allows the model to infer about the relationships among users and resources. Although the authors outline an access control framework, lack of formal descriptions and implementation leaves behind many ambiguities. A similar work is done by Masoumzadeh and Joshi [9,10], the authors propose ontology based access control model for online social networks. This model takes into account intricate semantic relationships among different users, data objects, and between users and data objects. The model enables expressing much more fine-grained access control policies on a social network knowledge base than already discussed by Carminati et al. Both approaches don't take into consideration social context and relationship strength among users. The novelty of our approach is social perspective of privacy that ignored by these approaches.

6   Conclusion and Future Work

We presented a semantic model for friend segregation in online social networks. The model addresses three main issues faced by contemporary online social networks. First, the issue of context collapse is addressed by preserving contextual integrity of the user. Second, the issue of personal information disclosure to unintended audiences is addressed by disclosure minimization on the basis relationship quality. Finally, the issue of interdependent privacy is addressed by collaborative interpersonal privacy management. The model is inspired from work of well-known sociologists such as Goffman, Irwin Altman, and Granovetter. The model takes into consideration social aspects of privacy that are ignored by existing solutions to larger extent. The model is first step towards developing privacy friendly online social networks. In future, we plan to develop a third party social application for online social networks as a proof of concepts prototype to demonstrate the applicability of our model.

References

1. Akcora, C.G., Ferrari, E.: Graphical user interfaces for privacy settings. In: Alhajj, R., Rokne, J. (eds.) Encyclopedia of Social Network Analysis and Mining, pp. 648–660. Springer, New York (2014)
2. Madejski, M., Johnson, M.L, Bellovin, S.M.: The failure of online social network privacy settings, Department of Computer Science, Columbia University, Technical report CUCS-010-11, February 2011. http://mice.cs.columbia.edu/getTechreport.php?techreportID=1459
3. Vitak, J.: The impact of context collapse and privacy on social network site disclosures. J. Broadcast. Electron. Media **56**(4), 451–470 (2012)
4. Borcea-Pfitzmann, K., Pfitzmann, A., Berg, M.: Privacy 3.0: = data minimization+ user control+ contextual integrity. IT-Information Technology Methoden und Innovative Anwendungen der Informatik und Informationstechnik **53**(1), 34–40 (2011)
5. Goffman, E.: The presentation of self in everyday life. In: Contemporary Sociological Theory, pp. 46–61 (2012)
6. Granovetter, M.S.: The strength of weak ties. Am. J. Sociol. **78**(6), 1360–1380 (1973)
7. Altman, I.: The Environment, Social Behavior: Privacy, Personal Space, Territory, and Crowding. Brooks/Cole, Monterey (1975)
8. Carminati, B., Ferrari, E., Heatherly, R., Kantarcioglu, M., Thuraisingham, B.: Semantic web-based social network access control. Comput. Secur. **30**(2), 108–115 (2011)
9. Masoumzadeh, A., Joshi, J.: OSNAC: an ontology-based access control model for social networking systems. In: IEEE Second International Conference on Social Computing (SocialCom), pp. 751–759. IEEE (2010)
10. Masoumzadeh, A., Joshi, J.: Ontology-based access control for social network systems. Int. J. Inf. Priv. Secur. Integrity **1**(1), 59–78 (2011)

Bootstrapping an Online News Knowledge Base

Klesti Hoxha$^{(\boxtimes)}$, Artur Baxhaku, and Ilia Ninka

Department of Computer Science, Faculty of Natural Sciences,
University of Tirana, Blv. Zogu I, Nr. 20/1, 1001 Tirana, Albania
{klesti.hoxha,artur.baxhaku,ilia.ninka}@fshn.edu.al

Abstract. News retrieval systems facilitate the process of quickly learning about events or stories reported in various online news providers. The traditional approach involves clustering articles that report about the same event using bag-of-words or concept based similarity measures, and offering personalized recommendations using various user modeling approaches. Knowledge bases have been extensively used in the recent years for powering search engines on entity based searches. The success of this approach, demonstrated by a now de-facto way of searching and browsing offered by commercial search engines and mobile applications, has created the need to incorporate semantic capabilities to news retrieval systems. In this paper we present a proposal for creating a knowledge base of entities, events and facts reported in Albanian online news providers. We aim to provide a news stream processing pipeline based in generally available open source toolkits and state-of-the-art research works about event and fact oriented knowledge bases.

Keywords: News retrieval · Fact extraction · Event mining · Semantic news

1 Introduction

Knowledge bases (KB) are nowadays powering most of the commercial search engines[1]. They are mostly used to provide quick facts about people, organizations, sport teams and other entities related to the provided search queries. It has been shown that entity enriched search results provide a better user experience on the related systems [2].

Very often news articles are centered around particular entities: a politician's visit to a particular place, the result of a football match, a public figure speech related to a certain question, a terrorist attack on a city, annual cultural events, etc. Even though most of the available news retrieval systems offer related stories discovery, content grouping and even story development timeline visualizations, they still lack of knowledge discovery features generally available in modern search engines.

---

[1] Two concrete examples: Google Knowlege Graph https://www.google.com/intl/es419/insidesearch/features/search/knowledge.html, and Microsoft Satori https://blogs.bing.com/search/2013/03/21/understand-your-world-with-bing/.

© Springer International Publishing Switzerland 2016
A. Bozzon et al. (Eds.): ICWE 2016, LNCS 9671, pp. 501–506, 2016.
DOI: 10.1007/978-3-319-38791-8_37

Let's consider a visit of Angela Merkel to Albania. A news retrieval system that makes use of a knowledge base, would detect that a certain news article about this event is related to Angela Merkel and Albania, furthermore it would store the fact that it is about a *politician's visit* to a certain country. An advanced use of the knowledge base in question can recommend news articles about Angela Merkel's visits to other Balkan countries, or any country in general. It can also suggest articles about previous visits of her to Albania, previous Chanchellors of Germany visits to Albania, and other similar related articles. This entity centered personalization approach has been reported in some previous works [3,4,10].

In this paper we describe the requirements and initial steps for creating a news-centered knowledge base for Albanian written news articles published online. It will store facts about certain events reported in the news using a custom knowledge representation model. We define a system architecture that allows for different implementations of it. This architecture can be also used by news retrieval systems that deal with articles written in any other language, however considering the fact that the natural language processing landscape for Albanian is lacking many enabler components, we aim to facilitate extensive experimentation.

2   Related Work

Works reported in literature regarding news knowledge base creation focus on three main aspects: entity linking and disambiguation, knowledge graph representations (ontologies) for news events, and news processing pipelines for knowledge base population.

Entity linking, the process of relating named entities found in the text of the processed documents with existing entries in a knowledge base, deals with the need of entity disambiguation. It is the process of finding the correct entry in a KB for orthographically different mentions of an entity, or identifying missing entries [7]. It has been shown in different works that entity disambiguation for news articles is done considering the textual context of a named entity appearance and concept similarity graphs [5,8]. Skenduli and Biba [9] have demonstrated that named entities in Albanian can be accurately recognized using trained classifiers provided by Apache OpenNLP[2].

Our intent is to create a news knowledge base that contains information and facts about events or stories related to people or places. We initially plan to link the identified entities with existing entries of people and places in some publicly available knowledge bases like DBpedia[3] and Yago[4].

News processing pipelines for KB population reported in literature use a combination of tools for achieving this. Some of them introduce a service oriented architecture. Regarding event or facts extraction there are two main approaches: machine learning NLP techniques or rule-based and topic clustering methods.

---

[2] https://opennlp.apache.org/.
[3] http://wiki.dbpedia.org/.
[4] https://www.mpi-inf.mpg.de/yago-naga/yago/.

An advanced multilingual news knowledge base is described by Rospocher et al. in [8]. They provide knowledge graphs of events reported in the news. It is created using a modular news processing pipeline with mostly custom build NLP tools for each involved language. Their approach processes a news collection all at once, not in an incremental manner.

XLike is another multilingual news processing pipeline [6]. It uses open source tools and generally available language corpora for implementing its NLP functionalities. News articles are clustered based on their topic, and a knowledge graph with facts and events is maintained. A similar architecture is described in [1], but lacking advanced NLP processing. It uses topic based clustering instead.

In [11] Zavarella et al. provide an example of a work that does not use a standard machine learning based NLP approach in its news processing pipeline. They describe a system that uses entity extraction grammars and semantic annotation through rule-based patterns. It is applied in crisis and security threat detection from news written in three Balkan languages.

3   Research Objectives

We aim to provide an initial setup of a news related knowledge base for news articles written in Albanian. Our main goal is to boost the user experience of news retrieval systems or news portals in general through advanced personalized news recommendation.

Due to the fact that the Albanian natural language processing landscape is still missing key components for creating advanced knowledge discovery systems, we can contribute in this regard as part of this work. This can be considered as another output of our research. In summary we have the following research objectives:

1. Propose a simple ontology for representing news events or facts.
2. Provide a software architecture for the news knowledge base that allows for extensive experimentation.
3. Contribute with corpora and tools for Albanian natural language processing.
4. Create an initial implementation of the proposed architecture using open source toolkits.

4   Methodology

We have started our work by developing a news aggregator for Albanian news using Scrapy[5]. In order to gain more context details (i.e. latest stories, important news) by the location of the page where the news is present, we do not use RSS feeds. News are stored in an intermediate representation using a NoSQL database (MongoDB[6]). For each article we also store extracted meta-data like publication

---

[5] http://scrapy.org/.
[6] https://www.mongodb.org/.

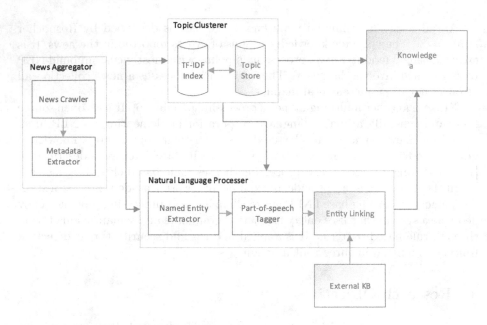

Fig. 1. Proposed architecture.

date, last update timestamp, author, extracted news category, number of comments, etc. We have also created a term-frequency index for the aggregated news using Apache Lucene[7]. This is used for clustering news articles about the same event using a term-frequency based similarity measure.

The proposed system architecture is shown in Fig. 1. We plan to use Apache OpenNLP for named entity recognition and part-of-speech tagging. Due to the lack of annotated corpora for this language, we are also creating them using the collected news as a corpus. Existing annotated corpora are also used for NLP processing in [6]. In order to allow experimentation with other NLP toolkits, we are using a custom annotation format that can be easily converted to the required format of the tool in question.

Because of the lack of quality annotated treebanks, we plan to skip machine learning techniques for semantic role labeling [6,8] and use a rule-based pattern matching approach similar to [11]. The set of events stored in the knowledge base will be limited in the initial stage. Table 1 shows a sample of the triples that will be created. For entity disambiguation [7] we plan to use the usage context with the help of the created term-frequency index. When linking to external knowledge bases we can also use location (for news about events happening in Albania) as a disambiguation feature. Entries in our knowledge base will also be linked to the source of the stored information, a single news or a topic cluster.

Considering that news article retrieval is a publication time sensitive task, the stream of news will be incrementally indexed and update the knowledge

---

[7] https://lucene.apache.org/.

Table 1. Sample triples included in the news KB.

Subject	Predicate	Object
Politician	spokeAbout	X
Politician	visited	Place
Parliament	approvedLaw	Law No.
Journalist	interviewed	Person
Artist	participatedIn	Concert
Concert	heldIn	Place
Accident	happenedIn	Place
Politician	met	Politician
SportMatch	endScore	X

base with new events or facts. The knowledge base will be accessible through a
RESTFul API. This allows an easier integration to third-party systems like news
search engines or news publication websites powering retrieval and personalized
content offering.

5 Conclusions

In this work we describe our approach and initial steps on creating a knowledge
base of events and stories reported in Albanian online news portals. We proposed
an architecture of a news stream processing pipeline based on the current state-
of-the-art solutions in this regard and implementable using various open source
toolkits.

The initial plan is to offer access to the created knowledge base through a
RESTFul API, however this can be extended also to the entity linking service of
our system. This would allow the incorporation of advanced knowledge discovery
features and facilitate personalized news recommendation to existing news search
engines and publishing portals.

To the best of our knowledge, this is the first reported attempt to create
a semantic knowledge base for documents written in Albanian. The datasets
and annotated corpora created in this work will also contribute to the Albanian
natural language processing landscape.

References

1. Amardeilh, F., Kraaij, W., Spitters, M., Versloot, C., Yurtsever, S.: Semi-automatic
   ontology maintenance in the virtuoso news monitoring system. In: 2013 European Intelligence and Security Informatics Conference (EISIC), pp. 135–138. IEEE
   (2013)

2. Arapakis, I., Leiva, L.A., Cambazoglu, B.B.: Know your onions: understanding the user experience with the knowledge module in web search. In: Proceedings of the 24th ACM International on Conference on Information and Knowledge Management, pp. 1695–1698. ACM (2015)
3. Cadilhac, A., Chisholm, A., Hachey, B., Kharazmi, S.: Hugo: entity-based news search and summarisation. In: Proceedings of the Eighth Workshop on Exploiting Semantic Annotations in Information Retrieval, pp. 51–54. ACM (2015)
4. Hare, J., Newman, D., Peters, W., Greenwood, M., Eggink, J.: Semanticnews: Enriching publishing of news stories (2014)
5. Kuzey, E., Vreeken, J., Weikum, G.: A fresh look on knowledge bases: distilling named events from news. In: Proceedings of the 23rd ACM International Conference on Information and Knowledge Management, pp. 1689–1698. ACM (2014)
6. Padró, L., Agić, Ž., Carreras, X., Fortuna, B., Garcia-Cuesta, E., Li, Z., Štajner, T., Tadić, M.: Language processing infrastructure in the xlike project. In: Ninth International Conference on Language Resources and Evaluation (LREC 2014) (2014)
7. Rao, D., McNamee, P., Dredze, M.: Entity linking: finding extracted entities in a knowledge base. In: Poibeau, T., Saggion, H., Piskorski, J., Yangarber, R. (eds.) Multi-source, Multilingual Information Extraction and Summarization 11. Theory and Applications of Natural Language Processing, pp. 93–115. Springer, Heidelberg (2013)
8. Rospocher, M., van Erp, M., Vossen, P., Fokkens, A., Aldabe, I., Rigau, G., Soroa, A., Ploeger, T., Bogaard, T.: Building event-centric knowledge graphs from news. Sci. Serv. Agents World Wide Web, Web Seman. (2016)
9. Skenduli, M.P., Biba, M.: A named entity recognition approach for albanian. In: 2013 International Conference on Advances in Computing, Communications and Informatics (ICACCI), pp. 1532–1537. IEEE (2013)
10. Tavakolifard, M., Gulla, J.A., Almeroth, K.C., Ingvaldesn, J.E., Nygreen, G., Berg, E.: Tailored news in the palm of your hand: a multi-perspective transparent approach to news recommendation. In: Proceedings of the 22nd International Conference on World Wide Web Companion, pp. 305–308. International World Wide Web Conferences Steering Committee (2013)
11. Zavarella, V., Kucuk, D., Tanev, H., Hürriyetoglu, A.: Event extraction for balkan languages. In: EACL 2014, p. 65 (2014)

Integrating Big Spatio-Temporal Data Using Collaborative Semantic Data Management

Matthias Frank[⊠]

Information Process Engineering, FZI Forschungszentrum Informatik,
Haid-und-Neu-Str. 10-14, 76131 Karlsruhe, Germany
frank@fzi.de

Abstract. Good decision support of geographical information systems depends on the accuracy, consistency and completeness of the provided data. This work introduces the hypothesis that the increasing amount of geographic data will significantly improve the decision support of geographical information systems, providing that a smart data integration approach considers provenance, schema and format of the gathered data accordingly. Sources for spatial data are distributed and quality of the data is varying, especially when considering uncertain data like volunteered geographic information and participatory sensing data. In our approach, we address the challenge of integrating Big Data in geographical information systems by describing sources and data transformation services for spatio-temporal data using a collaborative system for managing meta data based on Semantic MediaWiki. These machine interpretable descriptions are used to compose workflows of data sources and data transformation services adopted to the requirements of geographical information systems.

1 Introduction and Motivation

Geographical information systems (GISs) are important tools for decision support in various fields like civil planning, emergency management, agriculture or environment and nature protection. While the amount of data with a geographic context is increasing due to improved sensor technology and data created by mobile devices or users of social web applications, the reliability of these data may be uncertain and has to be evaluated when used in GIS. In addition, data values have different schemas to describe locations, like addresses, relative spatial relationships or different coordinates reference systems. Measured quantities and units that might be used for data values may also vary across data sources, leading to schema heterogeneity. In this approach, we use semantic Web technology to describe *(i) data sources and data transformation services* for GIS in a machine interpretable way. These semantic descriptions lay the foundation for *(ii) composing workflows* of data sources and data transformation services that fulfill different requirements of GISs on demand, even if these requirements

---

Ph.D. supervisor: Prof. Dr. York Sure-Vetter.

© Springer International Publishing Switzerland 2016
A. Bozzon et al. (Eds.): ICWE 2016, LNCS 9671, pp. 507–512, 2016.
DOI: 10.1007/978-3-319-38791-8_38

are not known at design time. In addition, provenance information and uncertainty of data are modeled using semantic Web technologies, which allows to *(iii) include volunteered geographic information (VGI)* and participatory sensing data. We hypothesise that the increasing amount of geographic data will significantly improve the decision support of GIS, providing that a smart data integration approach considers provenance, schema and format of the gathered data accordingly. This leads to the following research questions:

RQ1 How does the integration of uncertain data like VGI and participatory sensing data improve the decision support in GIS in terms of accuracy, consistency and completeness?

RQ2 Are domain experts provided with the necessary provenance information in order to compare the processed values of heterogeneous data sources within the result set?

In Sect. 2, we discuss related work and state our aims and objectives in Sect. 3. We introduce our research methodology in Sect. 4 and conclude in Sect. 5.

2   Related Work

In this section we discuss related work on the topics of *(i) data transformation and interoperability* of GIS, *(ii) semantic workflow composition* and *(iii) integration of VGI* and participatory sensing data.

2.1   Data Transformation and Interoperability of GIS

Transforming data from heterogeneous data sources into a unified schema and the interoperability of distributed systems is still an ongoing research topic where web services are commonly used for converting data. Kaempgen et al. [5] presented OLAP4LD, a framework for developers of applications over Linked Data sources reusing the Resource Description Framework (RDF) Data Cube Vocabulary. The Quantities, Units, Dimensions and Data Types Ontologies (QUDT)[1] can be used as a common standard for describing units and their conversation. In the context of GIS, transformation of spatial data across different coordinates reference systems was addressed by Atemezing et al. [1] which have published a dataset dedicated to the description of coordinates reference systems defined and maintained by the French national mapping agency. Similar requirements are also given for the Gauss-Krueger coordinates reference system used by national agencies in Germany. Li et al. [10] reported on their efforts to design and develop a geospatial cyberinfrastructure for urban economic analysis and simulation using a service-oriented architecture to allow widespread sharing and seamless integration of distributed geospatial data. For the interoperability of spatial data observed by sensors, the World Wide Web Consortium (W3C) Semantic Sensor Network Incubator Group introduced the Semantic Sensor Network (SSN) ontology[2] for describing sensors and observations.

---

[1] http://www.qudt.org/.
[2] http://purl.oclc.org/NET/ssnx/ssn.

2.2   Semantic Workflow Composition

Another challenge is to compose the workflow of data sources and transformation services that fulfills the requirements of any GIS. Gil et al. [4] have formalized an approach how the selection of application components and data sources can be automated in general using semantic Web technologies. Kopeck et al. [6] presented research in lightweight machine-readable service descriptions and semantic annotations for Web application programming interfaces (APIs), building on the Hypertext Markup Language (HTML) documentation that accompanies the APIs. Lanthaler [7] described an approach to build hypermediadriven Web APIs based on Linked Data technologies and developed Hydra [8], a small vocabulary to describe Web APIs. Lanthaler and Guetl [9] also introduced an approach to create machine-readable descriptions for RESTful services and show how these descriptions along with an algorithm to translate SPARQL Protocol and RDF Query Language (SPARQL) queries to Hypertext Transfer Protocol (HTTP) requests can be used to integrate RESTful services into a global read-write Web of Data. Calbimonte et al. [2] annotated sensor data and observations using an ontology network based on the SSN ontology and showed how to provide a highly flexible and scalable system for managing the life-cycle of sensor data in the context of the semantic Web of Things. Gemmeke et al. [3] have shown that semantic technologies can help to cope with data format heterogeneity, distribution of the data sets and interoperability issues in the medical domain, for example when processing medical images. Similar challenges have to be addressed in the domain of GISs when processing raster data created by satellites, drones or surveillance cameras.

2.3   Integration of Volunteered Geographic Information

In our approach, we also want to integrate uncertain data like VGI, Linked Open Data (LOD) and participatory sensing data to support decision with GISs. Lopez-Pellicer et al. [11] proposed a refinement of Linked Data practices, named Geo Linked Data, which defines a lightweight semantic infrastructure to relate URIs that identify real world entities with geospatial Web resources, such as maps. Stadtler et al. [12] elaborated on how the collaboratively collected Open-StreetMap[3] data can be interactively transformed and represented adhering to the RDF data model. They described how this data is interlinked with other spatial data sets, how it can be made accessible for machines according to the Linked Data paradigm and for humans by means of several applications, including a faceted geo-browser. The spatial data, vocabularies, interlinks and some of the applications are openly available in the LinkedGeoData[4] project.

3   Aims and Objectives

When integrating geographic data from different sources with different units of measurement, property definitions or coordinates reference systems, the data

---

[3] http://www.openstreetmap.org.
[4] http://linkedgeodata.org.

have to be transformed into a homogenous schema in order to receive a unified view of all sources. This requires not only a structure but also explicit and well defined semantics for meta data that represents the relations of the data that should be integrated as well as a mechanism for automated preprocessing and reliability quantification of uncertain data like VGI and participatory sensing data. By describing heterogeneous data sources for GIS and the input and output of available data transformation services semantically, we are able to implement services that dynamically compose workflows for processing these data and fulfill the requirements of different GISs. Data and index stuctures for the extraction and aggreation of relevant structures and the accessibility for analytics have to be covered by the composed workflows. For a complete representation of data, missing values have to be predicted by suitable algorithms. This approach enables domain experts to select any combination of data sources and receive a complete result set in different data schemas without the need of considering the format and completeness of the original sources. On the other hand, all provenance information has to be retained in order to make the values of different sources as well as predicted values comparable. Using semantic Web technology for managing geo temporal data does also enable semantic analytics for unstructured and remote sensing data. In our work we investigate a semantic workflow composition for integrating Big Data in GIS.

4   Research Methodology

In our approach, we design an infrastructure that gathers Big Data which may be needed to support decisions with GISs. The infrastructure itself has to be generic in order to fulfill the requirements of different GISs that may consume the gathered data for further processing. For the evaluation, this infrastructure is used for different use cases in order to prove the flexibility and answer the research questions stated in Sect. 1. To build up our infrastructure, we gather data from the regional environment authorities of Baden-Württemberg[5], the German weather service[6], mobile measurements on a urban railway[7] and remote sensing data from satellites operated by European Space Agency and National Aeronautics and Space Administration. More data sources should be integrated in a later stage of the project. Data of areas of interests which are not covered by the data gathered already will be collected by drones equipped with the necessary sensors where needed. The first step is to build a collaborative system based on Semantic MediaWiki (SMW) for managing meta data. This system does import and reuse commonly used vocabulary in the domain of GISs like SSN, QUDT and GeoVocab[8] and is used to describe data sources and transformation services. This information is used to dynamically build workflows consisting of the data sources and transformation services needed to fulfill the requirements defined

---

[5] https://www.lubw.baden-wuerttemberg.de/lubw.
[6] http://www.dwd.de.
[7] http://www.aero-tram.kit.edu/.
[8] http://geovocab.org/.

by the consuming GIS. We assume that these requirements are not know at design-time, therefore our infrastructure has to cover them on demand. For a first demonstration, we have used open refine[9] with the rdf plugin[10] in order to *(i) transform temperature data of weather stations* manually. We have used the SPARQL Inferencing Notation[11] to define unit conversation of thermodynamic temperatures using the information of QUDT. The prepared sources and services are then registered in SMW using suitable SMW-templates. The data of our SMW is stored in an Apache Jena[12] triple store which provides a Fuseki SPARQL endpoint. This endpoint provides the API for machine interpretable descriptions which we intent to use for *(ii) dynamically composed workflows of data sources and data transformation services* later in our work. The *(iii) integration of VGI and participatory sensing data* is not yet realized in this stage of our work.

5 Conclusions and Contribution to Web Engineering

In order to evaluate our contribution, we are going to investigate the output created by the dynamically created workflows of our infrastructure with regard to completeness, number and quality of integrated sources and the explanatory power of the provenance information within the result set. This will be made for a specific use case, which requires a set of records for thermodynamic temperature values from heterogeneous sources like weather stations, satellite data and thermal sensors of drones. With the gathered data as our training set, we plan to perform predictions for sub urban heat islands within the city of Karlsruhe, Germany, and evaluate the prediction with our test data set which is classified as measurements from sub urban heat islands in the same city. By varying the sources used as input for the predictions, we are going to evaluate the impact of these sources on the decision support in GISs. With our approach, we show how the decision support of a new generation of GISs can be improved by making big geo-temporal data including VGI and participatory sensing data available for analytics. We introduced the principles of this approach with the use case of thermal data gathered from various sources like weather stations, satellite observations and mobile sensors. By describing these data sources and appropriate data transformation services in a SMW we created machine interpretable descriptions. We intent to use this data for dynamically composed workflows of data sources and data transformation services later in our work.

Acknowledgements. This work was supported by the German Ministry of Education and Research (BMBF) within the BigGIS project (Ref. 01IS14012A). I thank Dr. Stefan Zander, Dr. Benedikt Kämpgen and Prof. Dr. Rudi Studer for guidance and insights.

---

[9] http://openrefine.org/.
[10] http://refine.deri.ie/rdfExport.
[11] http://spinrdf.org/.
[12] https://jena.apache.org/index.html.

References

1. Atemezing, G.A., Abadie, N., Troncy, R., Bucher, B.: Publishing reference geodata on the web: Opportunities and challenges for ign france. TC-SSN 2014 - Terra Cognita - Semantic Sensor Networks (2014)
2. Calbimonte, J.P., Sarni, S., Eberle, J., Aberer, K.: Xgsn: An open-source semantic sensing middleware for the web of things. In: Joint Proceedings of the 6th International Workshop on the Foundations, Technologies and Applications of the Geospatial Web, TC 2014, and 7th International Workshop on Semantic Sensor Networks, SSN 2014. CEUR Workshop Proceedings, vol. 1401, pp. 51–66. CEUR-WS.org (2015)
3. Gemmeke, P., Maleshkova, M., Philipp, P., Götz, M., Weber, C., Kämpgen, B., Nolden, M., Maier-Hein, K., Rettinger, A.: Using linked data and web apis for automating the pre-processing of medical images (2014)
4. Gil, Y., González-Calero, P.A., Kim, J., Moody, J., Ratnakar, V.: A semantic framework for automatic generation of computational workflows using distributed data and component catalogues. J. Exp. Theor. Artif. Intell. 23(4), 389–467 (2011)
5. Kämpgen, B., Harth, A.: OLAP4LD – a framework for building analysis applications over governmental statistics. In: Presutti, V., Blomqvist, E., Troncy, R., Sack, H., Papadakis, I., Tordai, A. (eds.) ESWC Satellite Events 2014. LNCS, vol. 8798, pp. 389–394. Springer, Heidelberg (2014)
6. Kopecký, J., Vitvar, T., Pedrinaci, C., Maleshkova, M.: Restful services with lightweight machine-readable descriptions and semantic annotations. In: Wilde, E., Pautasso, C. (eds.) REST: From Research to Practice, pp. 473–506. Springer, New York (2011)
7. Lanthaler, M.: Creating 3rd generation web apis with hydra. In: 22nd International World Wide Web Conference, WWW 2013, Rio de Janeiro, Brazil, May 13–17, 2013, Companion Volume, pp. 35–38. International World Wide Web Conferences Steering Committee/ACM (2013)
8. Lanthaler, M., Guetl, C.: Hydra: A vocabulary for hypermedia-driven web apis. In: Proceedings of the WWW2013 Workshop on Linked Data on the Web, Rio de Janeiro, Brazil, 14. CEUR Workshop Proceedings, vol. 996. CEUR-WS.org (2013), May 2013
9. Lanthaler, M., Gütl, C.: Seamless integration of restful services into the web of data. Adv. MM 2012, 586542: 1–586542: 14 (2012)
10. Li, W., Li, L., Goodchild, M.F., Anselin, L.: A geospatial cyberinfrastructure for urban economic analysis and spatial decision-making. ISPRS Int. J. Geo-Information 2(2), 413–431 (2013)
11. Lopez-Pellicer, F.J., Silva, M.J., Chaves, M., Javier Zarazaga-Soria, F., Muro-Medrano, P.R.: Geo linked data. In: Bringas, P.G., Hameurlain, A., Quirchmayr, G. (eds.) DEXA 2010, Part I. LNCS, vol. 6261, pp. 495–502. Springer, Heidelberg (2010)
12. Stadler, C., Lehmann, J., Höffner, K., Auer, S.: Linkedgeodata: A core for a web of spatial open data. Semant. Web 3(4), 333–354 (2012)

Extending Kansei Engineering for Requirements Consideration in Web Interaction Design

Maxim Bakaev[1](✉), Martin Gaedke[2], Vladimir Khvorostov[1], and Sebastian Heil[2]

[1] Novosibirsk State Technical University, Novosibirsk, Russia
{bakaev,xvorostov}@corp.nstu.ru
[2] Technische Universität Chemnitz, Chemnitz, Germany
{martin.gaedke,sebastian.heil}@informatik.tu-chemnitz.de

Abstract. In our paper we consider how the eminent Kansei Engineering (KE) method can be applied in computer-aided development of websites. Although principally used for exploring emotional dimension of users' experience with products, KE can be extended to incorporate other types of software requirements. In conjunction with AI Neural Networks (Kansei Type II), it then becomes possible to automate, up to a certain degree, evaluation of website quality in terms of functionality, usability, and appeal. We provide an overview of existing works related to KE application in web design, and note its certain gap with systematic Web Engineering. Then we summarize approaches for auto-validation of different types of requirements, with particular focus on computer-aided usability evaluation. Finally, we describe the ongoing experimental study we undertook with 82 participants, in which a Kansei-based survey with 21 university websites was performed, and outline preliminary results and prospects.

Keywords: Web interface design · Kansei Engineering · Non-functional requirements · Usability

1 Introduction

As the number of websites worldwide is approaching 10^9, systematic and efficient application of Web Engineering (WE) methodology continues to gain in importance – it is generally agreed that it could lead to more rapid, reliable, and economical web development. Web interaction design, which embraces HCI, information engineering, user interface design and testing, graphic design, etc., has long been affirmed as an integral part of WE, due to the crucial importance of positive user experience for website success. However, the application of formal and AI methods in this area remains quite limited, particularly in engineering usability and user satisfaction [1].

Kansei Engineering (KE) is a set of methods and techniques that originated in Japanese automotive industry in the 1980s and since then were successfully applied in

---

V. Khvorostov's Ph.D. Advisor is Assoc. Prof. Galina Kurcheeva.
S. Heil's Ph.D. Advisor is Prof. Martin Gaedke.

© Springer International Publishing Switzerland 2016
A. Bozzon et al. (Eds.): ICWE 2016, LNCS 9671, pp. 513–518, 2016.
DOI: 10.1007/978-3-319-38791-8_39

numerous other fields. KE's *analytical* method seeks to establish formal relations between target customers' feelings and impressions of existing or prospective products (expressed per measurement scales – *Kansei Words*) and particular attributes of the products. The *synthetic* method of KE aims to obtain the list of prospective product attributes from the desired Kansei (emotional feeling) of the target customer.

Probably the most recent and quite extensive review of KE applications for web design can be found in [2]; however the authors conclude that they are still relatively scarce. We discovered that a recurring theme in related research works (see e.g. [3, p. 2, 4]) was the contraposition of the emotional aspect vs. the other dimensions of website quality: this can best be summarized in a quote "… the new paradigm of producing desirable websites as opposed to current focus on website functional usability and performance" [4, p. 147]. Indeed, when applying KE, they virtually never consider unambiguous parameters related to users' interaction with a website beyond the emotional experience, and although proposals to construct KE/WE support knowledge bases were made repeatedly (e.g. [3, 5]), seemingly none of them were adopted by practicing web engineers. In one of our previous works [6], we proposed to employ an extended KE method as a core part in web interaction design on the basis of evolutionary algorithms (EAs). KE neural network (NN) could automatically evaluate candidate solutions per specified fitness function, so that (1) potentially deficient web interfaces are not presented to real users, and (2) the time gaps between generations of solutions are decreased, speeding up the algorithm's convergence. This approach in particular would allow adaptability to the ever-changing software requirements, owing to robust self-learning capabilities of KE NN [5].

Thus, our research work is dedicated to ensuring greater applicability of KE in web design, through enhancing it to consider all aspects of website interaction quality (or *fitness*, in terms of EA), not merely the generic emotional impression of the users. In Sect. 2 we explore how concordance of a website to various types of interaction-related requirements can be measured within the method's framework, at least in conventional projects with typical user tasks. In Sect. 3 we describe the ongoing experimental study seeking to illustrate the applicability of the proposed approach.

2   Kansei Engineering, Neural Networks, and Requirements

The synthetic KE method in essence attempts to automate the transition from requirements to design resolutions – long time a Holy Grail of software engineering – and implies a significant amount of pre-accumulated technological and usage knowledge in the industry. It would seem that WE is mature enough, with hundreds of millions of active websites, most of which are reasonably well accessible, since even the increasingly used AJAX technologies do not present an ultimate barrier for automated retrieval (NNs need lots of diverse data for self-learning). Still, our review of the field suggests that endeavors in improving KE application in the web design domain are mostly aimed towards the closer and more systematic involvement of users/customers [7, 8] – we were unable to find attempts to incorporate non-emotional requirements or established, even if not explicitly specified, interaction quality parameters.

Requirements engineering is widely recognized as the most crucial dimension of WE, essential for building and maintaining a web product within a reasonable timeframe and budget. There seems to be a multitude of requirement classifications, so the related common vocabulary even had to be organized as ontological concepts [9], while a very holistic work at cataloguing types of non-functional requirements (NFR) was carried out in [10]. The NFR types relevant for web systems are denoted as *Integrity, Interoperability, Performance, Privacy, Scalability, Security,* and, finally, *Usability*. In Table 1 we reason about the requirement types' applicability for interaction on the web and outline approaches for automating the evaluation of a website's compliance with them (validation), for the KE framework.

Table 1. Approaches for automated testing of compliance with requirements

Requirement type and relevance	Auto-validation approaches
Functional requirements in interaction are mainly represented as *Use Cases*	Test scripts, web interface test automation software: Selenium, HtmlUnit, etc.
Integrity and *Privacy* are in essence *Security* requirements. The main focus is on data entry, while channels and server security are not relevant	Web application security scanners, webform validators: SQLMap, W3AF, Metasploit Framework, etc.
Interoperability with applications and components is not relevant	For assessing quality of interaction with users see *Usability*
Performance for web interaction by and large means response/latency time per planned website capacity	Load testing/benchmarking, e.g. with tools like Apache JMeter that can use scripts to simulate user behavior
Scalability may refer to dealing with increasing complexity in user tasks (increasing number of users rather relates to *Performance*)	No known approaches for automation. Generally, creative interface re-designs are required when user tasks are complemented or modified
Usability is the major requirement type and may be sub-categorized into *do-goals* (in-use, achieving tasks) and *be-goals* (being satisfied, etc.)	*Usability in-use* evaluation can be interaction-based, metric-based, or model-based. *Satisfaction* is extensively measured with conventional KE

Understandably, *Usability* considerations, even if not explicitly specified in requirements, are the most important for web interaction design, but there are ongoing discussions about which measurement automation approach could accommodate the three peculiarities of usability, since it is by definition user-specific, task-specific, and context-specific. Probably the most widely applied one is *interaction-based* that infers usability evaluations (UE) from input in the course of real user interactions (like the promising WaPPU tool [1]), or from log data, which have to be previously accumulated. Another approach is *metric-based*, that attempts to identify a set of metrics that reflect a website's usability, from certain high-level design factors (e.g. the amount of text on a webpage), concordance to design guidelines [11], even users' opinions. A fundamental issue of determining the effect of different user tasks and contexts of use on the metrics' relative significance, however, seems to be unresolved.

The proposed KE NN evaluation method [6] belongs to *model-based* approaches, and conventionally the NN's input neurons are design factors, which we propose to supplement with requirements concordance metrics, and the output is user impressions or fitness evaluation for EA. Naturally, methods not involving real interactions can only provide approximate estimations of real usability, but this should be sufficient for application in EAs, for which fitness function approximations theory is reasonably well established. Also, since web interfaces are highly typical in terms of user tasks, technologies, standards, and platforms employed, compared to desktop or mobile software, the estimations should improve with NN training. So, in the next section we describe an ongoing experimental study undertaken to justify the proposed approach and illustrate how a factor of website cultural kinship affects user impressions.

3   The Experimental Study

To confirm the proposed idea that KE can be effectively enhanced to consider non-emotional requirements, we designed an experimental study, to be performed in two main stages. The setup of the first part is more or less typical for Kansei surveys, with target customers evaluating a number of websites varying in both visual design factors and unambiguous parameters stemming from NFRs. Then we are going to construct the extended KE NN, train it with data collected from the subjects, and use it to generate two "optimal" website designs, #1 considering purely emotional aspects, and #2 taking into account the extra parameters. In the second part of the experiment, in another survey with target customers we'll test the hypothesis that web design #2 rates significantly better than #1 and the control group of websites.

To date, we performed the first session of the first survey, collecting Kansei data from the two groups of subjects. First, there were 40 students (36 of whom were male) of a German university (14 of Bachelor and 26 of Master program), age ranging from 19 to 33 years, mean 24.5 (SD = 3.19). Second, there were 42 students (30 males) of a Russian university (23 of Bachelor and 19 of Master program), age ranging from 20 to 28 years, mean 21.7 (SD = 0.89).

All subjects were given a scenario to be performed with 21 real websites of several German and Russian universities (all websites were presented in their English versions), then rate them on 10 developed Kansei scales based on the ones used in similar research works [2–4, 12, 13]. The experimental scales and their evaluations (5-point Likert scale, with −2 meaning most prevalence of the first term, +2 most prevalence of the second term) are presented in Table 2. The websites' success in the suggested task (we call it *Overall* evaluation) was measured with the question *"Based on the website, would you recommend to your friend to go there for the Master's program?"*, answers were on the scale from 1 (*"definitely no"*) to 5 (*"definitely yes"*).

The correlation between the evaluations provided by German and Russian subjects was highly significant ($R^2 = .994$, $p < .001$). However, the results of the regression analysis for *Overall* evaluation have shown that significant factors (the single ones at $p \leq .01$) were different for the two groups of participants: *handcrafted – professional (HP)* for the German subjects ($R^2 = .718$) and *reasonable – premium (RP)* for the Russian

Table 2. The Kansei scales evaluations by German (DE) and Russian (RU) subjects

Scale	DE: mean (SD)	RU: mean (SD)
masculine – feminine	−0.15 (0.37)	−0.36 (0.38)
conventional – creative	−0.03 (0.68)	−0.16 (0.70)
homely – global	0.25 (0.30)	0.40 (0.39)
reasonable – premium	**0.02** (0.42)	**−0.18** (0.71)
academic – practical	**−0.12** (0.35)	**0.10** (0.30)
handcrafted – professional	0.13 (0.47)	0.43 (0.66)
natural – technical	0.19 (0.27)	0.64 (0.42)
stable – dynamic	−0.03 (0.61)	−0.08 (0.73)
exclusive – attainable	0.30 (0.21)	0.53 (0.34)
bright – temperate	**−0.21** (0.28)	**0.04** (0.71)
Overall	3.15 (0.39)	3.43 (0.58)

Table 3. Mean *Overall* evaluations per subject and website groups.

Subjects websites	German	Russian
German	3.22	3.20
Russian	3.07	3.69

ones ($R^2 = .805$). In Table 3 we illustrate how an objective factor of website's cultural kinship affects the resulting *Overall* evaluation for the two groups of subjects.

4   Conclusions

In our research work we seek to develop approaches for extension of Kansei Engineering beyond the conventional emotional aspect, so that the method could be used to consider other types of requirements and can be effectively applied in WE. The motivation for this stems from our existing work, in which we proposed to use extended KE NN to assess the fitness for solutions obtained in the course of evolutionary web interaction design [6]. The prototypical Web Design Support Intelligent System developed by our team (see description in [11]) takes requirements into account when generating a web interface wireframe, but in a quite rudimentary way that calls for further enhancement.

In this paper, we provided an overview of KE applications for web design and noted a certain contraposition between emotional aspect of user interaction and other types of software requirements. From research in requirements engineering, we extracted the most common types of NFRs and outlined the approaches towards an automated evaluation of website compatibility with the requirements. We gave particular focus to automated usability evaluation, noting pros and cons of interaction-based, metric-based, and model-based UE, as well as mentioning some existing testing automation tools.

To confirm that KE can be effectively enhanced to consider non-emotional requirements, we designed an experimental study and performed its first stage with 82 subjects evaluating 21 operating university websites per 10 specially developed Kansei scales. Our plan for future work involves the construction of the extended KE NN, training it with the experimental data, and justifying that web interface design created with extended KE is superior in comparison to the one generated with the conventional method that only considers the emotional aspect of web interaction.

Acknowledgement. The reported study was funded by RFBR according to the research project No. 16-37-60060 mol_a_dk. We'd like to thank Maximilian Speicher for his invaluable comments that helped improve this work.

References

1. Speicher, M., Both, A., Gaedke, M.: SOS: Does your search engine results page (SERP) need help? In: Proceedings of 33rd Annual ACM Conference on Human Factors in Computing Systems, pp. 1005–1014. ACM (2015)
2. Guo, F., et al.: Optimization design of a webpage based on Kansei engineering. Hum. Factors Ergon. Manuf. Serv. Ind. **26**(1), 110–126 (2016)
3. Lokman, A.M., Noor, N.M., Nagamachi M.: Kansei database system for emotional interface design of E-Commerce website. In: 4th International Cyberspace Conference on Ergonomics (2008)
4. Noor, N.M., Anitwati, M.L., Nagamachi, M.: Applying Kansei engineering to determine emotional signature of online clothing websites. In: 10th ICEIS, vol. 5. HCI (2008)
5. Lin, Y.C., Yeh, C.H., Wei, C.C.: How will the use of graphics affect visual aesthetics? A user-centered approach for web page design. Int. J. Hum.-Comput. Stud. **71**(3), 217–227 (2013)
6. Bakaev, M., Gaedke, M.: Application of evolutionary algorithms in interaction design: from requirements and ontology to optimized web interface. In: IEEE ElConRusNW, pp. 125–130. LETI, St Petersburg (2016)
7. Carreira, R., Patrício, L., Jorge, R.N., Magee, C.L.: Development of an extended Kansei engineering method to incorporate experience requirements in product–service system design. J. Eng. Des. **24**(10), 738–764 (2013)
8. Jiang, H., Kwong, C.K., Liu, Y., Ip, W.H.: A methodology of integrating affective design with defining engineering specifications for product design. Int. J. Prod. Res. **53**(8), 2472–2488 (2015)
9. Avdeenko, T., Pustovalova, N.: The ontology-based approach to support the completeness and consistency of the requirements specification. In: International Siberian Conference on Control and Communications (SIBCON). IEEE, Omsk (2015)
10. Mairiza, D., Zowghi, D.: Constructing a catalogue of conflicts among non-functional requirements. In: Maciaszek, L.A., Loucopoulos, P. (eds.) ENASE 2010. CCIS, vol. 230, pp. 31–44. Springer, Heidelberg (2011)
11. Bakaev, M., Avdeenko, T.: Indexing and comparison of multi-dimensional entities in a recommender system based on ontological approach. Computación y Sistemas **17**(1), 5–13 (2013)
12. Song, Z., Howard, T.J., Achiche, S., Özkil, A.G.: Kansei engineering and web site design. In: ASME 2012 International Design Engineering Technical Conferences and Computers and Information in Engineering Conference, pp. 591–601 (2012)
13. Qu, Q.X.: Kansei knowledge extraction based on evolutionary genetic algorithm: an application to e-commerce web appearance design. Theoret. Issues Ergon. Sci. **16**(3), 299–313 (2015)

Improving Automated Fact-Checking
Through the Semantic Web

Alex Carmine Olivieri[✉]

Data Semantics Lab - Institute of Information Systems,
Techno-Pole 3, 3960 Sierre, Switzerland
alex.olivieri@hevs.ch

Abstract. The Internet supplies information that can be used to automatically populate knowledge bases and to keep them updated, but the facts contained in these automatically managed knowledge bases must be validated before being trustfully used by applications. So far, this process, known as fact-checking, has been performed by humans curators with experience in the investigated domain, however, the big increase of the speed to which the internet provides information makes this way of doing inadequate. Nowadays techniques exist for automatic fact-checking, but they lack on modeling the domain of the information to be checked, thus losing the experience feature humans curators provide. This work designs a Semantic Web platform for automatic fact-checking, which uses OWL Ontology to create a specific knowledge base modeled on the domain concerning the facts to be checked, and it extends the knowledge available by linking this knowledge base to external repository of information and by reasoning about this extended knowledge. The fact-checking task is performed using a machine learning algorithm trained using the information of this extended knowledge base.

Keywords: Fact-checking · Linked open data · Semantic web · OWL ontology · Knowledge base · Accuracy

1 Introduction

The Internet supplies information that can be used to automatically populate knowledge bases and to keep them updated. The Semantic Web and the Linked Open Data provide the infrastructure to share and link structured data, allowing thus the reuse of such knowledge bases. Applications can then use these knowledge bases in order to drive their business logic. When applications integrate data from the open Web, they usually do not know the sources and do not have indicators about the quality of the data, thus providing data which contain trustworthy information becomes crucial [1]. Ensuring information trustworthiness implies that the facts containing such information must be checked.

The Oxford British Dictionary defines fact-check as the "act of verifying a fact, or checking or establishing the facts of a matter". In the knowledge base context fact-checking is the activity of evaluating the veracity of facts in order to

© Springer International Publishing Switzerland 2016
A. Bozzon et al. (Eds.): ICWE 2016, LNCS 9671, pp. 519–524, 2016.
DOI: 10.1007/978-3-319-38791-8_40

populate and update knowledge bases. Fact-checking was traditionally performed by humans. However, due to the enormous volume of information generated online nowadays, this activity has to be performed in an automated manner. Fact-checking is one of the main sub-tasks of an activity called Knowledge Base Population (KBP) [2]. KBP aims to automatically discover facts about entities and augments a knowledge base (KB) with these facts. The other main sub-task is Information Extraction (IE). Since IE provides facts automatically, these facts cannot be considered trustworthy a priori because they can come from misinformation [3], astroturf [4], malign behaviors [5] or they can be simply out of date [6]. Thus such facts cannot be used directly for KBP.

Previous research about KBP tried to evaluate inputs facts against general knowledge bases such as Wikipedia and his structured version DBpedia, Freebase and more recently Wikidata [7]. These works use approaches such as machine learning and/or graph theory [8, 10] in order to evaluate the veracity of input facts. Their contributions show interesting features, but, by using general knowledge bases, they lack in exploiting the concept of ontology itself, causing the accuracy to be good only under restricted conditions and thus making these approaches unreliable for real scenario usage. An ontology is a formal specification of a shared conceptualization [11], and without a clear formalization of the domain it is not possible to capture all its facets. Employing specific knowledge bases, modeled on appropriate ontologies and which contain only trustworthy information, can better the automatic fact-checking accuracy, and thus allow application which rely on external source of information, such as some web applications (e.g. Siri from Apple) to use KBP for managing their knowledge bases.

To fulfill my objective I propose to create a platform for fact-checking based on semantic web technologies. This platform uses domain specific knowledge bases that can be linked to external knowledge bases in order to increase the information available for the fact-checking task. When performing the fact-checking task, the platform uses a machine learning algorithm based on this extended knowledge base to rate the veracity of each input fact.

This research brings the following contributions: (1) it makes the fact-checking task able to deal with facts' updates; (2) it allows it to be easily adaptable to different scenario by changing the specific knowledge base; and (3) it makes it able to discover new information by linking the knowledge base dynamically to external knowledge bases and reasoning about this extended knowledge.

The rest of this paper is structured as follows: Section 2 summarizes the related work on the fact-checking field and points out its limitations; Sect. 3 describes the problem; Sect. 4 details the approach used to solve the problem; Sect. 5 describes the metrics used to evaluate the work; Sect. 6 concludes the paper.

2   Background

There is a growing number of research about fact-checking. Some contributions incorporate it in the full KBP process, while others treat it as an independent problem, abstracting from the Information Retrieval (IR) task. In this work I follow the second approach.

Dong et al. [8] use a knowledge base modeled on Freebase and estimate if new facts can be added to it. Machine learning methods in conjunction with graph theory are used for the estimation. This approach provides results having high accuracy, however it does not address possible hierarchical correlations between facts. Moreover, it lacks to address the temporal factor, which is essential when dealing with updates.

Lehmann et al. [9] calculate a confidence score for each input fact and then provide to users the confidence score and the evidences supporting it. To establish this confidence score they use a supervised machine learning algorithm trained with features deriving from the evidences found. Their approach provides promising results when dealing with facts referring to well-known pieces of information, but it shows limitations when they refer to pieces of information little known.

Ciampaglia et al. [10] use DBpedia as a prior knowledge base and they represent it as a knowledge graph. Nodes represent classes and edges represent relations between classes. To each node is associated a value, which expresses its generality. They define the *semantic proximity* concept, which derives from the transitive closure of knowledge graphs, and that consists on the path distance between two nodes. This distance is expressed as the sum of the generality of all nodes encountered in the path. They estimate the truth value of a new fact as: shorter the path, higher the truth value. As in [9] the results are promising with well-known pieces of information, but they worsen with peculiar ones. Moreover, weighting only the nodes and not the edges causes deficiency in dealing with relations' correlations.

Drummond et al. [12] represent a knowledge base as a 3-dimensional tensor and they predict new facts from existing ones by applying tensor factorization techniques. They demonstrate that the intrinsic open world semantics of RDF improves the possibility to predict missing facts based on similarity with facts already existing. However, they state that the possibility to access larger information sources can increment the set of predicted facts.

All contributions show some shortcomings. The use of general knowledge bases prevents fact-checking to capture details of a domain, which inevitably leads to a high rate of false positives. In contrast, omitting to capture the fundamental principles behind Semantic Web and Linked Data, such as Open World Assumption (OWA) [13] or reasoning over distributed knowledge bases, leads to a high rate of false negatives. I believe that addressing these deficiencies will improve the fact-checking accuracy and will make it suitable for real applications.

3   Problem Statement

Nowadays, through Linked Open Data, knowledge bases of structured data can be published online, and their content, once linked, can be used by applications in order to discover new knowledge through semantic queries. This work addresses the problem of increasing the accuracy of automatic fact-checking in order to populate knowledge bases automatically with correct information. By doing so, applications, such as web and mobile applications which may use external automatically created knowledge bases, can use them confidently.

4   Research Methodology

Automatically generated knowledge bases are still unsuitable for applications that demand trustworthy information because the methods for fact-checking lack to model the domain of the information and cannot adapt themselves to conditions' changes. The proposed approach evaluates the input facts against a knowledge base, modeled on an appropriate OWL ontology, that can be linked to external information repository in order to extend the available knowledge. The aim is to obtain a fact-checking methodology that provides high accuracy regardless the peculiarity of the different domains on which it is applied.

This work is based on Semantic Web, which represents data through the Resource Description Framework (RDF) [14], thus a fact is represented as an RDF statement, i.e. a triple *(s, p, o)* composed of a subject (s), an object (o) and a predicate (p) that connects the subject to the object. The evaluation of the veracity of a fact implies three steps that are described in detail below.

4.1   Step One: Investigating the Eligibility of a Fact

The Web Ontology Language and the RDF Schema define the structure of the knowledge base, and as a consequence the form that facts can have. For example, if I say that a predicate *eating* connects a subject of typology *Human* (the domain) with an object of typology *Food* (the range), a fact having a predicate *eating* can be considered eligible only if it connects an individual of the class *Human* to an individual of the class *Food*.

To investigate if a fact is eligible the method searches for synonyms of the predicate using WordNet [15] and creates an extended predicates' set. This step is fundamental because a predicate in the knowledge base could be expressed through a synonym of the input fact' predicate. The method then checks if it finds a match between the predicates' set and predicates contained in the knowledge base. If a match is found, it verifies if the subject belongs to the right domain and the object to the right range. Facts that do not have matches or that have subject and/or objects not belonging to the right domain/range get discarded. For the purpose of this work I consider that a fact contains also information about the classes for subjects and objects. Facts not discarded are considered eligible.

4.2   Step Two: Finding Evidences Supporting a Fact

For facts tagged as eligible the method has to find evidences that justify them. Since I do not consider input facts as the latest information, evidences supporting them may be somewhere. The internal knowledge base is considered reliable but it does not always contain the latest information. Thus external more dynamic repositories are needed for finding evidences. This work uses Linked Data to link the specific knowledge base with external knowledge bases and by doing so creating an extended knowledge base. In the specific I consider DBPedia as evidence provider. Nowadays DBPedia can be considered as reliable as more traditional encyclopedias [16], moreover it covers many topics, and because of its dynamism it can be used as a source for evidences. The input of this step is all the subject-predicate eligible couples. The platform uses OWL inferences to reason over the extended knowledge base and then creates a list of objects retrieved for each couple. This list also contains metadata for each item (when available) such as its timestamp and provenience information. These metadata joined with other characteristics of this list of objects are used as features for training the machine learning algorithm introduced in Sect. 4.3.

4.3 Step Three: Evaluating the Veracity of a Fact

The evaluation phase involves two cases: update and addition. Update concerns relations having a functional property as restriction, while all other relations are considered addition. The difference lies behind the fact that an update involves the elimination of prior knowledge, thus it requires stronger evidences.

For evaluating the veracity the method uses a machine learning regression algorithm based on the logistic function (sigmoid function). The algorithm has two versions: a *weak* version used to evaluate addition, which uses as input for the algorithm only the list of objects provided as output in Sect. 4.2 and a *strong* version used to evaluate updates, which considers also the object already in the knowledge base to be part of the algorithm. The full list of features for training the algorithm has not been decided yet.

5 Evaluation Plan

For the evaluation I calculate the provided accuracy (F-measure) using the following performance metrics.

$$Precision = \frac{TFsKB \cap TFs}{TFs} \qquad Recall = \frac{TFsKB \cap TFs}{TFsKB} \qquad (1)$$

where, TFs is the average number of facts (a random subset of the test set) evaluated as trustworthy by experts and TFsKB is the number of facts of the test set considered trustworthy by my approach. For obtaining TFs I plan to use the crowdsourcing platform Amazon Mechanical Turk[1].

The purpose is to improve the current best accuracy - 0.88 - provided by [9], in every situation and not only when dealing with not well-known information as it does. For this purpose the dataset will be an RDF triple stores about tourism in Switzerland, which can be considered little-known information.

6 Conclusions

This work proposes a Semantic Web oriented platform which uses a novel approach for automatic fact-checking. It produces the following contributions:

---

[1] https://www.mturk.com/mturk/welcome.

(1) by using a specific knowledge base the fact-checking can capture the peculiarity of the specific domain and thus efficiently deal with updates; (2) it allows to expand the explicit knowledge by linking the specific internal knowledge base to needed external ones; (3) by dynamically changing the specific knowledge base it can be easily adapted to various domain. I believe that such approach has the potential of greatly increasing the accuracy of automatic fact-checking and bringing the KBP to be more employed by applications.

Acknowledgements. I would like to thank my supervisors, Prof. Philippe Cudre-Mauroux and Prof. Maria Sokhn, for their support.

References

1. Heath, T., Bizer, C.: Linked Data: Evolving the Web into a Global Data Space. Synthesis Lectures on the Semantic Web. Morgan & Claypool Publishers, Seattle (2011)
2. Ji, H., Grishman, R.: Knowledge base population: successful approaches and challenges (2011)
3. Castillo, C., Mendoza, M., Poblete, B.: Predicting information credibility in time-sensitive social media. Internet Research **23**(5), 560–588 (2013)
4. Ratkiewicz, J., et al.: Detecting and tracking political abuse in social media. In: ICWSM 2011 (2011)
5. Maddock, J., et al.: Characterizing online rumoring behavior using multi-dimensional signatures. In: CSCW, pp. 228–241 (2015)
6. Berti-Equille, L., et al.: Sailing the information ocean with awareness of currents: discovery and application of source dependence (2009)
7. Michael, F., et al.: A Comparative Survey of DBpedia, Freebase, OpenCyc, Wikidata, and YAGO (2015)
8. Don, X., et al.: Knowledge vault: a web-scale approach to probabilistic knowledge fusion. In: KDD 2014, pp. 601–610 (2014)
9. Lehmann, J., Gerber, D., Morsey, M., Ngonga Ngomo, A.-C.: DeFacto - deep fact validation. In: Cudré-Mauroux, P. (ed.) ISWC 2012, Part I. LNCS, vol. 7649, pp. 312–327. Springer, Heidelberg (2012)
10. Ciampaglia, G.L., et al.: Computational fact checking from knowledge networks. CoRR abs/1501.03471 (2015)
11. Gruber, T.R.: Toward principles for the design of ontologies used for knowledge sharing? Int. J. Hum. Comput. Stud. **43**, 907–928 (1995)
12. Drumond, L., Rendle, S., Schmidt-Thieme, L.: Predicting RDF triples in incomplete knowledge bases with tensor factorization. In: SAC 2012, pp. 326–331 (2012)
13. Baader, F., et al.: The Description Logic Handbook: Theory, Implementation, and Applications. Cambridge University Press, Cambridge (2003). ISBN: 0-521-78176-0
14. Bechhofer, S.: OWL: Web ontology language. In: Liu, L., Özsu, M.T. (eds.) Encyclopedia of Database Systems, pp. 2008–2009. Springer, Heidelberg (2009)
15. Princeton University About WordNet. WordNet. Princeton University (2010). http://wordnet.princeton.edu
16. Giles, J.: Internet encyclopaedias go head to head. Nature **438**(7070), 900–901 (2005)

Using Spatiotemporal Information to Integrate Heterogeneous Biodiversity Semantic Data

Flor Amanqui[1,2(✉)], Ruben Verborgh[1], Erik Mannens[1], Rik Van de Walle[1], and Dilvan Moreira[2]

[1] Data Science Lab, Ghent University - IMinds, Ghent, Belgium
{ruben.verborgh,erik.mannens,rik.vandewalle}@ugent.be
[2] SCC-ICMC, University of Sao Paulo, Sao Paulo, Brazil
{flork,dilvan}@icmc.usp.br

Abstract. Biodiversity is essential to life on Earth and motivates many efforts to collect data about species. These data are collected in different places and published in different formats. Researchers use it to extract new knowledge about living things, but it is difficult to retrieve, combine and integrate data sources from different places. This work will investigate how to integrate biodiversity information from heterogeneous sources using Semantic Web technologies. Its main objective is to propose an architecture to link biodiversity data using mainly their spatiotemporal dimension, effectively search these linked data sets and test them using real use cases, defined with the help of biodiversity experts. It is also an important objective to propose a suitable provenance model that captures not only data origin but also temporal information. This architecture will be tested on a set of representative data from important Brazilian institutions that are involved in studies of biodiversity.

Keywords: Semantic web · Linked data · Biodiversity

1 Problem Statement

Biological diversity is essential to life sustainability on Earth [1]. The large amount of data generated by researchers in biodiversity has led to discussions about how to find the best ways to organize this data and provide tools and environments that stimulate and facilitate the search for information. Currently, when using search tools for biodiversity data, experts specify their queries using one or more terms of interest. However, these terms may not match those that are part of the documents and, therefore, some relevant documents are not recovered [2].

In Brazil, there is a network of Amazonian and extra-Amazonian institutions that are involved in studies of biodiversity. This network is integrated by important institutions, such as the National Research Institute for the Amazon (INPA)[1], the National Institute for Space Research (INPE)[2], the Global Biodiversity Information Facility (GBIF)[3], the Emilio Gueldi Museum in Par?

---

[1] http://portal.inpa.gov.br/.
[2] http://www.inpe.br/ingles/.
[3] http://www.gbif.org/.

© Springer International Publishing Switzerland 2016
A. Bozzon et al. (Eds.): ICWE 2016, LNCS 9671, pp. 525–530, 2016.
DOI: 10.1007/978-3-319-38791-8_41

(MPEG)[4], and Brazilian Agricultural Research Corporation (EMBRAPA)[5]. These organizations collect and contribute large amounts of data about biodiversity. One of the most frequent problems, reported by biodiversity researches, is how to retrieve and integrate information simultaneously from the big number of data sources found on the various biodiversity databases. Typically, these users utilize the biodiversity data to visualize integrated information about the collected specimens [1].

The problem is that a specialist may specify one or more terms (strings) for a search and, due to the large amount of available data, get responses with too many results (not all relevant) [1]. He then has a lot of work sifting through the results for the desired information, because the results provided are very broad and may not even contain the targeted data. This activity is not particularly well supported by biodiversity software tools based on keyword searching (the kind usually found in the Web) [2].

Even if a search is successful, it is the biodiversity specialist who must browse the selected documents to extract the information he/she is looking for. There is not much support for retrieving the actual information from the documents, a very time-consuming activity, and put it in a suitable format [1]. Of course, there are tools that can retrieve texts, split them into parts, check the spelling, and count their words. But, when it comes to interpret sentences and extract useful information for biodiversity specialists, the capabilities of current software are still very limited. It is simply very difficult to distinguish the meaning of the following query:

Return all occurrences of records of insects that belong to the ant family (Formicidae) and have been found in an aquatic habitat in the Brazilian Amazon forest

For instance, an SQL query, in a traditional database, would only succeed if records have the exact information (strings) asked in the query. In this case, a record of a *Paraponera clavata* specimen (bullet-ant) that was found in a swamp would not be returned. The strings *Paraponera clavata* and *swamp* are not in the query.

Biodiversity specialists also need more complex queries, e.g., requiring spatiotemporal query processing, such as deriving co-occurrence of species in a given spacetime frame. Such processing is seldom supported. Other queries involve biodiversity relations among species, e.g., farms within a protected area. Such relationships are not stored, and must be deduced by the scientist after performing a sequence of queries and simulations.

2   Research Questions

The main question research is:

- How can we integrate biodiversity information from heterogeneous sources using their spatial location and temporal data?

---

[4] http://www.museu-goeldi.br/portal/.
[5] https://www.embrapa.br/en.

To answer this question, we also need to find an answer to the following questions:

- How can we improve the interoperability of the biodiversity data?
- How can we improve the location accuracy of biodiversity data?
- How to improve the trust in biodiversity data?

3 Hypotheses

The main hypotheses related to this research are:

- Representing biodiversity data as Linked Data will improve the integration it with data from different and independent data sources (if they share common ontology terms).
- Using biodiversity data as Linked Data will resolve advanced and complex querying that was not possible before.
- Capturing the spatiotemporal characteristic from biodiversity data will perform more accurate locations.
- Reusing the provenance model will improve the trust of the biodiversity datasets and scientists could trust the data links provided by the network of Amazonian and extra-Amazonian institutions.

4 Research Approach

Initially, we will analyze and extract spatiotemporal data of biodiversity and geographic databases (such as soil, rivers, deforestation) from different data sources (INPE, INPA, MPEG, EMBRAPA). Once the spatiotemporal data is extracted, the next step is to find the links between different sources. For this reason, we will identify the vocabularies and ontologies with specific relationships to biodiversity and geospatial information. Following this, we will map biodiversity data and the ontologies describing them, considering data provenance. We will convert biodiversity data in the Semantic Web format (mapping). In order to provide a better feedback on the quality of the data. The mapping will be implemented using state of the art Semantic Web tools and tested on a set of representative data about biodiversity.

We will then develop a new Linked Data architecture to integrate biodiversity information from heterogeneous sources using their spatial location and temporal data. A first prototype, based on this architecture, will be implemented. This prototype will permit data integration from different triple stores, checks for inconsistencies and new knowledge extraction. The generated linked information will be retrievable in a friendly way. After that, an experimentation phase, based on controlled experiments, will be carried out. To conclude, we will test various use cases.

5   Evaluation Plan

There are different aspects of the proposed architecture which need to be assessed:

- The interlinking between biodiversity vocabularies and ontologies with other domains. Interlinking is provided by RDF triples that establish a link between the entity identified by the subject with the entity identified by the object.
- The performance in process complexity SPARQL and GeoSparql queries.
- The accuracy, precision and recall of the retrieved links in conjunction with other domains.

6   Related Work

In this Section, we will review the related work on the use of Linked Data and Provenance in biodiversity domain.

Linked Data is gaining traction in the scientific community. One of the earliest investigation relates with Amazon Rainforest was conducted by Cardoso et al. [3]. They describe a geographical gazetteer that associates place names to geographic coordinate data from two large biodiversity repositories: GBIF and the SpeciesLink[6]. However, there is still a fundamental lack to answer complex queries with spatiotemporal characteristics (e.g., farms within a protected area between 2005 and 2011).

Kauppinen et al. [4] describe the Linked Brazilian Amazon Rainforest Dataset (LBARD) using ontologies and vocabularies. However, the authors only show the Amazon Rainforest data using the R program. Users have to invest a considerable amount of time in programming in R, and perform many manual tasks, to obtain the needed datasets.

Garcia et al. [5] propose a data mining framework for primary biodiversity data analysis. This approach uses relational database to store the biodiversity data. Rocca-Serra et al. [6] describe how resources of the Open Biological and Biomedical Ontologies (OBO)[7] have been used to provide a semantic framework enabling the presentation of biodiversity information as Linked Data. Wieczorek et al. [7] describe the Darwin Core data standard for publishing and integrating biodiversity information. We plan to use the Darwin Core standard to capture complex aspects of the biodiversity domain.

A critical look at the available literature indicates that most of existing approaches suffer of the following limitations: (i) A number of techniques have been developed for using ontologies to retrieve relevant documents in response to a query. However, none of the works focused on the problem of storage, retrieval and link RDF triples using their spatiotemporal information. (ii) The approaches do not provide an explicit visualization of the geospatial and biodiversity dataset. There is still a fundamental lack of approaches to visualizing linked biodiversity data that use spatial and temporal relations.

---

[6] http://splink.cria.org.br/.
[7] http://www.obofoundry.org/.

Provenance describes how a data object came to be in its present state, and thus, it describes the evolution of the object over time [8]. There are a number of studies, which have used provenance in the biodiveristy domain [9–11]. For example, Beserra et al. [11] propose a provenance-based approach to manage long term preservation of scientific data. Their approach is based on the Open Provenance Model (OPM) [12]. However, this approach does not provide support to connect curated metadata with LOD, which would allow breaking down disciplinary boundaries among repositories and enhance reuse.

The PROV specification[8] defines a core data model for provenance for building representations of the entities, people and processes involved in producing a piece of data or thing in the world. However, there is a lack of expressiveness using this generic W3C recommendation to model the different types of organisms that co-occur in time and space (geospatial relations).

A critical look at the available literature indicates that a number of techniques have been developed for using provenance models, such as OPM and DCMI, in the different scientific domains. Despite the variety of models, there is currently no unified, conceptual model for biodiversity information and provenance that can be applied to different datasets and setups, while remaining both expressive and generic enough to cover many use cases.

7   Reflections

The main difference of this thesis proposal compared to existing works on linked biodiversity data is that we (i) introduce the idea of use the spatiotemporal information from biodiversity heterogeneous sources data to interlinking with other domains; and (ii) another important facet, when dealing with scientific data, is provenance. We plan to specialize the PROV provenance model for biodiversity data.

Acknowledgments. The research activities described in this paper were funded by Ghent University, iMinds, the IWT-Flanders, the FWO-Flanders, and the European Union, and the FINCyT Science and Technology Program from Peru.

References

1. Magnusson, W., Braga-Neto, R., Pezzini, F., Baccaro, F., Bergallo, H., Penha, J., de Jesus Rodrigues, D., Verdade, L.M., Lima, A., Albernaz, A.L., Hero, J.M., Lawson, B., Castilho, C., Drucker, D., Franklin, E., Medonca, F., Costa, F., Galdino, G., Castley, G., Zuanon, J., do Vale, J., dos Santos, J.L.C., Luizao, R., Cintra, R., Barbosa, R.I., Lisboa, A., Koblitz, R., da Cunha, C.N., Pontes, A.R.M.: Biodiversity and Integrated Environmental Monitoring. Program for Planned Biodiversity and Ecosystem Research (PPBio) (2013)

---

[8] https://www.w3.org/TR/prov-overview/.

2. Amanqui, F.K., Serique, K.J., Cardoso, S.D., Santos, J.L., Albuquerque, A., Moreira, D.A.: Improving biodiversity data retrieval through semantic search and ontologies. In: 2014 IEEE/WIC/ACM International Joint Conferences on Web Intelligence (WI) and Intelligent Agent Technologies (IAT), vol. 1, pp. 274–281, August 2014
3. Cardoso, S.D., Amanqui, F.K., Serique, K.J., dos Santos, J.L., Moreira, D.A.: SWI: a semantic web interactive gazetteer to support linked open data. Future Gener. Comput. Syst. **54**, 389–398 (2015)
4. Kauppinen, T., de Espindola, G.M., Jones, J., Sanchez, A., Gräler, B., Bartoschek, T.: Linked brazilian amazon rainforest data. Semant. Web J. **5**(2), 151–155 (2014)
5. Fontes, S.G., Stanzani, S.L., Correa, P.L.P.: A data mining framework for primary biodiversity data analysis. In: Rocha, A., Correia, A.M., Costanzo, S., Reis, L.P. (eds.) New Contributions in Information Systems and Technologies: Volume 1. AISC, vol. 353, pp. 813–821. Springer, Heidelberg (2015)
6. Rocca-Serra, P., Walls, R., Parnell, J., Gallery, R., Zheng, J., Sansone, S.A., Gonzalez-Beltran, A.: Modeling a microbial community and biodiversity assay with OBO foundry ontologies: the interoperability gains of a modular approach. Database 2015 (2015)
7. Wieczorek, J., Bloom, D., Guralnick, R., Blum, S., Döring, M., Giovanni, R., Robertson, T., Vieglais, D.: Darwin core: an evolving community-developed biodiversity data standard. PLoS ONE **7**(1), 1–8 (2012)
8. Omitola, T., Gibbins, N., Shadbolt, N.: Provenance in linked data integration (2010)
9. Zhao, J., Klyne, G., Shotton, D.: Provenance and linked data in biological data webs. In: Bizer, C., Heath, T., Idehen, K., Berners-Lee, T. (eds.) Proceedings of the WWW 2008 Workshop on Linked Data on the Web (LDOW 2008) (2008)
10. Wang, S., Padmanabhan, A., Myers, J.D., Tang, W., Liu, Y.: Towards provenance aware geographic information systems. In: Proceedings of the 16th ACM SIGSPATIAL International Conference on Advances in Geographic Information Systems, GIS 2008, p. 70:170:4. ACM, New York (2008)
11. Beserra Sousa, R., Cintra Cugler, D., Gonzales Malaverri, J., Bauzer Medeiros, C.: A provenance-based approach to manage long term preservation of scientic data. In: 2014 IEEE 30th International Conference on Data Engineering Workshops (ICDEW), pp. 162–133, March 2014
12. Moreau, L., Freire, J., Futrelle, J., McGrath, R.E., Myers, J., Paulson, P.: The open provenance model: an overview. In: Freire, J., Koop, D., Moreau, L. (eds.) IPAW 2008. LNCS, vol. 5272, pp. 323–326. Springer, Heidelberg (2008)

Demonstration Papers

Automatic Page Object Generation with APOGEN

Andrea Stocco[1(✉)], Maurizio Leotta[1], Filippo Ricca[1], and Paolo Tonella[2]

[1] DIBRIS – Università di Genova, Genova, Italy
andrea.stocco@dibris.unige.it, {maurizio.leotta,filippo.ricca}@unige.it
[2] Fondazione Bruno Kessler, Trento, Italy
tonella@fbk.eu

Abstract. Page objects are used in web test automation to decouple the test cases logic from their concrete implementation. Despite the undeniable advantages they bring, as decreasing the maintenance effort of a test suite, yet the burden of their manual development limits their wide adoption. In this demo paper, we give an overview of APOGEN, a tool that leverages reverse engineering, clustering and static analysis, to automatically generate Java page objects for web applications.

1 Introduction and Motivation

Automated web test code created for tools such as Selenium[1] is renowned for being difficult to maintain as the application under test evolves [1]. When the same functionality must be necessarily invoked within multiple test cases (e.g., user login), a major drawback is the duplication of code within the test suite.

Page objects can effectively improve the maintainability and longevity of a web test suite [1], because they hide the technical details about how the test code interacts with the web page behind a more readable and business-focused facade. Indeed, they can be considered as an API toward the web application: the web pages are represented as object-oriented classes, encapsulating the functionalities offered by each page as methods. In this way, the tests specification is well separated from their concrete implementation.

There are clear advantages stemming from the adoption of page objects within the test code [1]. However, their manual development is expensive and existing tools offer poor assistance in the creation of the source code [5]. In short, most of the page objects development effort is still on the shoulders of the tester.

Our tool APOGEN [5,6] is the first solution providing a considerable degree of automation, offering a more complete page objects generation tool, that can be used as a baseline to create well-architected, and thus more maintainable, web test suites.

The demo paper is organised as follows: Sect. 2 describes the high level architecture of APOGEN. Section 3 illustrates the tool functioning from the user's perspective, by means of a running example. Conclusions are drawn in Sect. 4.

---

[1] http://www.seleniumhq.org/projects/webdriver/.

© Springer International Publishing Switzerland 2016
A. Bozzon et al. (Eds.): ICWE 2016, LNCS 9671, pp. 533–537, 2016.
DOI: 10.1007/978-3-319-38791-8_42

2   Tool Architecture

We now explain the tool architecture, how a web tester can automatically generate page objects using APOGEN, and how such page objects are used for the construction of a web test case. APOGEN has been developed in Java and makes use of several external libraries and tools. Figure 1 shows the high level architecture of APOGEN [6].

The Crawler (1) is built on top of Crawljax [4], a state of the art tool for fully customisable exploration of highly-dynamic web applications. Since the model retrieved by the Crawler can be huge, the Clusterer (2) groups conceptually correlated web pages within the same cluster [6], using clustering algorithms available from the popular machine learning library Weka.

The Cluster Visual Editor (CVE) (3) is a web-based tool developed using the D3 library[2]. It supports the tester with an interactive cluster visualisation and editor facility, allowing her to inspect and modify the clustering results. Indeed, CVE allows the tester to interactively move nodes to the cluster they should belong to, in order to manually refine the output of the Clusterer (see the stickman in Fig. 1).

The Static Analyser (4) uses JavaParser[3] and XMLUnit[4]. The former is used to gather information from the web pages Document Object Model (DOM) and build an abstract representation for each cluster of web pages. The latter, instead, is used to collect the dynamic portions of the web pages within the same cluster (performing *intra-cluster DOM differencing*), on top of which the tester might create test case assertions.

In the last step, the Code Generator (5) transforms each cluster into a Java page object, tailored for the Selenium WebDriver framework. The Code Generator uses JavaParser to iteratively create from scratch the abstract syntax trees (AST) of the Java page objects. The class constructor contains a Selenium WebDriver variable to control the browser and resorts to the *PageFactory* pattern to

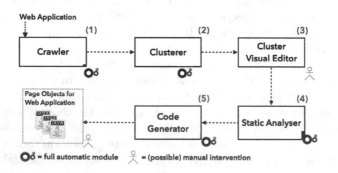

Fig. 1. High level architecture of APOGEN

---

[2] http://d3js.org/.
[3] http://javaparser.github.io/javaparser/.
[4] http://www.xmlunit.org/.

initialise the web elements at once. The methods that APOGEN generates are of three types: *navigations* between page objects, representing the links and the graph transitions (e.g., login page → home page), *actions* wrapping every data-submitting form and exposing the associated functionality (e.g., the login form), and *getters* – methods which retrieve textual portions of a web page that can be used to verify the behaviour of the web application through test case assertions (e.g., the total of a shopping cart).

The output of APOGEN is a set of Java page objects that reflect the pages of the web application, organised using the Page Factory design pattern, as supported by the Selenium WebDriver framework. A more detailed description and evaluation of the tool can be found in our recent papers [5,6], while a web page containing the source code and demo videos is available at: http://sepl. dibris.unige.it/APOGEN.php.

3   Running Apogen on PetClinic

Let us consider PetClinic[5], a veterinary clinic web application allowing veterinarians to manage data about pets and their owners. PetClinic makes use of technologies as Java Spring Framework, JavaBeans, MVC presentation layer and Hibernate. It consists of 94 files of various type (Java, XML, JSP, XSD, HTML, CSS, SQL, etc.), for a total of about 12 kLOC, of which 6.1 kLOC accounting for Java source files (63 Java classes). Hence, it is a medium size web system, with features and technologies that are quite typical of many similar systems available on the web.

We provided APOGEN with the URL of PetClinic, together with the data necessary for the login and form navigation. This task can be performed either via the tool's GUI, or by setting a configuration file. In the next step, the Crawler (1) reverse-engineered a graph-based representation of the web application, coming up with 26 nodes, i.e., 26 dynamic states of the web pages, and 105 event-based transitions between such nodes.

However, the manual inspection of such graph was challenging. Indeed, the high number of dynamic states (26) and transitions (105) made the visualisation of the graph quite tangled, definitely undermining its understandability and reducing the effectiveness of the automated page object creation. For this reason, the Clusterer (2) executed a clustering algorithm over the graph, with the aim of grouping within the same cluster web pages conceptually correlated among each other. Clusterer's default setting is [clustering algorithm= *"Hierarchical Agglomerative"*, feature vector= *"DOM tree-edit distance"*], because this was empirically found to be effective in producing clusters of web pages close to those manually defined by a human tester [6]. In the case of PetClinic, 10 clusters were found and displayed by CVE (3). We manually inspected such clusters. The Clusterer was able to find the best page-to-cluster assignment automatically, thus no manual adjustments were necessary. It is worth to mention that, by disabling clustering, APOGEN would have been generated 26 page objects for PetClinic (a 160 %

---

[5] https://github.com/spring-projects/spring-petclinic.

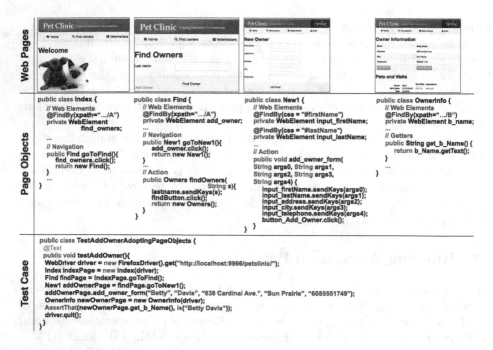

Fig. 2. Page objects generated by APOGEN to support a web test case development

increment in the amount of generated page objects, and therefore of duplicated and useless code). In the next steps of the approach, the Static Analyser **(4)**, and the Code Generator **(5)** ran to completion and automatically generated 10 Java page objects for PetClinic.

Figure 2 shows a Selenium WebDriver test case for the "Add Owner" functionality of PetClinic, developed using the methods of the page objects generated by APOGEN. For space constraints, we limit the code only to the methods that are used by the test, in the considered test scenario. We can see how the page objects effectively realise the use case scenario steps as methods, and thus, are an effective aid for the tester during the creation of a real web test case for PetClinic.

4   Conclusions and Future Work

We presented APOGEN, a prototype research tool for the automatic generation of page objects to be used for web applications testing. APOGEN leverages a combination of non-trivial techniques, such as reverse-engineering, machine learning, web-visualisation, HTML static analysis and differencing, and AST creation. APOGEN represents the most advanced state of the art tool for the automatic generation of page objects for web applications, because it is the first solution providing a high degree of automation. As future work, we plan to experiment with case studies involving human subjects to measure the efficacy in supporting the development of web test suites. The maintainability of the generated page objects can also benefit from robust web element localisation techniques [2,3]. At last, we plan to enhance the level of automation, by employing MDE techniques as, for instance, templates.

References

1. Leotta, M., Clerissi, D., Ricca, F., Tonella, P.: Approaches and tools for automated end-to-end web testing. Adv. Comput. **101**, 193–237 (2016)
2. Leotta, M., Stocco, A., Ricca, F., Tonella, P.: Using multi-locators to increase the robustness of web test cases. In: Proceedings of 8th International Conference on Software Testing, Verification and Validation, ICST, pp. 1–10. IEEE (2015)
3. Leotta, M., Stocco, A., Ricca, F., Tonella, P.: ROBULA+: an algorithm for generating robust XPath locators for web testing. J. Softw. Evol. Process **28**(3), 177–204 (2016)
4. Mesbah, A., van Deursen, A., Lenselink, S.: Crawling Ajax-based web applications through dynamic analysis of user interface state changes. TWEB **6**(1), 1–30 (2012)
5. Stocco, A., Leotta, M., Ricca, F., Tonella, P.: Why creating web page objects manually if it can be done automatically? In: Proceedings of 10th International Workshop on Automation of Software Test, AST, pp. 70–74. IEEE (2015)
6. Stocco, A., Leotta, M., Ricca, F., Tonella, P.: Clustering-aided web page object generation. In: Bozzon, A., Cudré-Mauroux, P., Pautasso, C. (eds.) ICWE 2016. LNCS, vol. 9671, pp. 132–151. Springer, Heidelberg (2016)

SnowWatch: A Multi-modal Citizen Science Application

Roman Fedorov[✉], Piero Fraternali, and Chiara Pasini

Dipartimento di Elettronica, Infomazione e Bioingegneria, Politecnico di Milano,
Piazza Leonardo da Vinci, 32, Milan, Italy
{roman.fedorov,piero.fraternali,chiara.pasini}@polimi.it

Abstract. The demo presents SnowWatch, a citizen science system that supports the acquisition and processing of mountain images for the purpose of extracting snow information, predicting the amount of water available in the dry season, and supporting a multi-objective lake regulation problem. We discuss how the proposed architecture has been rapidly prototyped using a general-purpose architecture to collect sensor and user-generated Web content from heterogeneous sources, process it for knowledge extraction, relying on the contribution of voluntary crowds, engaged and retained with gamification techniques.

Keywords: Rapid prototyping · Citizen science · Crowdsourcing

1 Introduction

The diffusion of mobile devices, social networks and online games has spawned a novel generation of hybrid applications, associated under the generic label of "citizen science", which harness the online, voluntary contribution and cooperation of common people for the resolution of complex tasks in a variety of domains, including computer vision, transport, environment monitoring, biomedical research, and more [4]. The common traits of these applications include: (i) the use of people as soft sensors to acquire data about the physical environment to be monitored or analysed (ii) the fusion of heterogeneous data, coming not only from people, but also from conventional sensors (iii) the need of validating data, for improving input accuracy and training/tuning data processing algorithms (iv) the provision of mechanisms for recruiting, engaging, and retaining people, who contribute voluntarily and should be acknowledged for their participation.

This demo presents SnowWatch, a citizen science application for the acquisition and processing of mountain images for the purpose of extracting snow information, predicting the amount of water available in the dry season, and supporting a multi-objective lake regulation problem.

The work has been partially funded by the EC and Regione Lombardia, under the FP7 SmartH2O and FESR PROACTIVE projects.

A. Bozzon et al. (Eds.): ICWE 2016, LNCS 9671, pp. 538–541, 2016.
DOI: 10.1007/978-3-319-38791-8_43

SnowWatch has been realized on top of a Web/mobile software architecture for the rapid development of citizen science applications, based on three main tiers: (i) a back-end that supports the composition of data processing workflows, by the collation of independent, loosely-coupled data acquisition and analysis modules (ii) a client tier, which can hosts multiple applications, fixed Web and mobile, that implement common interfaces for publishing tasks to workers and collecting their contributions (iii) a middle tier independent of both the data processing back-end and of the client crowdsourcing applications, which factors out the engagement policies and achievement rewarding rules enacted to secure people participation and durable commitment.

2   The SnowWatch Application and Rapid Prototyping Architecture

The SnowWatch project [1], in which the architecture and application have been developed, supports the low cost analysis of environmental mountain phenomena. Several state-of-the-art methods try to virtualize permanent measurement stations, e.g., for snow and other mountain environment parameters, through aerial and terrestrial image analysis [3], but require high quality images, which are scarce and costly, and are insufficient to build and calibrate a really usable mountain environmental model. On the other hand, the visual UGC publicly available on the Web is almost unlimited and a significant portion of it consists of outdoor photos. Based on such content, SnowWatch tackles the problem of mountain environment monitoring with a Citizen Science application for the collection of public mountain images and the extraction of snow indexes usable in water prediction models. The system crawls a large number of images from content sharing sites and touristic webcams, classifies those images that portrait mountain peaks and contain the location of shooting, identifies visible peaks by automatically aligning each image to a synthetic rendition computed from a public digital terrain model, finds the pixels of each peak that represent snow and calculates useful snow indexes (e.g., minimum snow altitude). These indexes are then used to feed existing water prediction models and compared with other official sources of information. Crowdsourcing is also employed, for three tasks: validating the classification of images that contain visible mountain profiles; validating the peak identification computed automatically; collecting images on demand, e.g., portraying mountain for which there is not enough UGC and no webcams are available.

SnowWatch is implemented by instantiating the general architecture of Fig. 1, reusing standard components and adding domain-specific services. The image processing and computer vision algorithms used in the project are explained in detail in [1,2].

Two *Image source connectors* and one *Data Aggregator* have been configured, for acquiring images from sharing sites, webcams, and users. A *Flickr Crawler* specializes the generic, keyword-search, image source connector with three filtering criteria: the photo must be geo-tagged and located within a rectangular

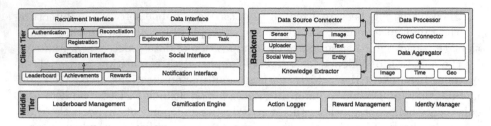

Fig. 1. Citizen science development architecture used in SnowWatch

region provided in input, and the altitude of the shooting location must be higher than a minimum threshold. The *Mountain webcam crawler* specializes the generic webcam source connector with a filtering step. Since cloudy meteorological conditions are very common at high altitudes, the connector discards images with bad weather conditions. The *Image aggregator* specializes the Data Aggregator interface to collapse a set of input mountain images, taken in good weather conditions, into one daily median image. This steps removes even small transient clouds and boosts the precision of the subsequent image processing steps that must identify accurately the edges of a mountain range.

The *Data Processor* interface is the one most heavily specialized, to incorporate the domain-specific algorithms for mountain image analysis. The realized specializations include: (1) *Mountain photo classifier*, used in the *Mountain relevance classification* automatic task, applies to each candidate photo a supervised learning Support Vector Machine (SVM) binary classification step, discarding the photos that do not contain a clearly visible mountain profile. (2) *Photo orientation estimator*, used in the *Mountain peak identification* automatic task, given as input a geo-tagged photo, estimates the direction of the camera using a matching algorithm on the photo edge maps and a rendered view of the mountain silhouettes that should be seen from the photographers point of view [1]. (3) *Snow pixel detector*, used in the *Snow mask computation* and automatic task, receives as input an image for which the direction of shooting is known and computes for each pixel representing the terrain a Boolean label (snow, no-snow). It outputs a binary snow mask representing for each pixel the presence or absence of snow. The *Crowd Connector* has been instantiated as follows: a task GUI has been added in the client tier, enabling the execution of the task. And a crowd connector has been allocated in the back-end, to support the recruitment of the contributors.

Finally, the *Knowledge Extractor* has been instantiated with a *Snow Index Computation* service. This service transforms the snow masks into real-valued indexes that represent virtual snow measurements (e.g. area covered by snow in km^2 or minimum altitude of snow in m). The time series of these indexes produced for the mountains of interest are the final output of SnowWatch and can be fed to environmental machine learning models that exploit this information for predicting water availability and taking decisions in water allocation problems.

The Middle Tier (Gamification Engine) has been used to configure the Gamification Data Model, by creating: *(i)* actions that can be performed by a user (e.g. upload a photo, share a photo with friends, comment a photo, validate a photo, manually align a photo, etc.); *(ii)* achievements and actions required to obtain them; *(iii)* rewards that can be provided to users for their achievements.

The Client Tier of the application has been customized by adding the GUIs needed for supporting the execution of human tasks and an exploratory Web portal interface for the general public:

- *Exploratory Web portal*[1]: it customizes the Exploration Data Interface to support browsing the geo-located image collection, in two ways: with a map view, placing the images on a map in the positions they were shot; and with a gallery view that publishes all images into a scrollable grid.
- *Mountain photo classification validation*: the user can label as negative (does not contain mountains) a photo that was erroneously classified as positive.
- *Manual photo-to-terrain-model alignment*: the user can adjust the automatically computed alignment of the photo to the rendered terrain view.
- *Mountain photo shooter*: it is a mobile application supporting the human task whereby the user can take photos of mountains with the peak names automatically overlaid onto the image.

At the moment, SnowWatch has collected more than 174 k user-generated photos and 30 M webcam images. Over 3500 webcams in the Alpine region have been identified and ~2000 of them have been registered to the application as they point to mountains of interest. The utility of the SnowWatch virtual snow indexes has been validated in a simulation exercise about the regulator of the water level of the Como lake, optimizing a two-objectives problem: flood risk vs water availability. The simulation shows that using the information of the virtual snow indexes helps the regulation of the lake to make more informed decisions on water release and thus attain a policy closer to the optimum Pareto frontier.

References

1. Fedorov, R., Camerada, A., Fraternali, P., Tagliasacchi, M.: Estimating snow cover from publicly available images. IEEE Trans. Multimedia PP(99) (2016)
2. Fedorov, R., Fraternali, P., Tagliasacchi, M.: Snow phenomena modeling through online public media. In: 2014 IEEE International Conference on Image Processing (ICIP), pp. 2174–2176. IEEE (2014)
3. Garvelmann, J., Pohl, S., Weiler, M.: From observation to the quantification of snow processes with a time-lapse camera network. Hydrol. Earth Syst. Sci. **17**(4), 1415–1429 (2013)
4. Memarsadeghi, N.: Citizen science [guest editors' introduction]. Comput. Sci. Eng. **17**(4), 8–10 (2015)

---

[1] The portal is reachable at the address: http://snowwatch.polimi.it.

CroKnow: Structured Crowd Knowledge Creation

Jasper Oosterman$^{(\boxtimes)}$, Alessandro Bozzon, and Geert-Jan Houben

Delft University of Technology, P.O. Box 5031, 2600 GA Delft, Netherlands
{j.e.g.oosterman,a.bozzon,g.j.p.m.houben}@tudelft.nl

Abstract. This demo presents the *Crowd Knowledge Curator* (`CroKnow`), a novel web-based platform that streamlines the processes required to enrich existing knowledge bases (e.g. Wikis) by tapping on the latent knowledge of expert contributors in online platforms. The platform integrates a number of tools aimed at supporting the identification of missing data from existing structured resources, the specification of strategies to identify and invite candidate experts from open communities, and the visualisation of the knowledge creation process status. `CroKnow` will be demonstrated through a case study focusing on the enrichment of the Rijksmuseum Amsterdams digital collection.

Keywords: Crowd identification · Semantic representation · Knowledge creation

1 Introduction

Fuelled by the ever-growing need for open and semantically rich data sources, Knowledge Crowdsourcing (KC) is rapidly becoming a common tools for organisations to outsource knowledge creation to (possibly anonymous) individuals and communities willing to contribute with their domain-specific expertise. We refer to these contributors as *expert contributors* (or *experts*), so to stress their experience of, or their insight into, a targeted domain of knowledge. Artwork annotation is a known example of a KC task. There, successful contributors must be able to understand the abstract, symbolic, or allegorical interpretation of the reality depicted in the artwork, as well as to identify and recognise the occurrences of visual classes (e.g. plants, animals, objects) in the artwork [7,8]. Knowledge crowdsourcing is also fundamental to train expert systems (e.g. IBM Watson), or, in general, artificial intelligence methods focused on knowledge-related reasoning and prediction.

Previous work focusing on the identification of expert contributors for KC tasks, demonstrated how expert contributors could be approached and engaged to capitalise their familiarity with a domain of knowledge in order to execute activities such as content production, image annotation, etc. Candidate experts can be identified exploiting user modelling techniques relying on topic-based profiling [3], contextual properties (e.g. geographical location) [2], or Web content consumption [4]. In a recent work, we have shown how online social platforms

© Springer International Publishing Switzerland 2016
A. Bozzon et al. (Eds.): ICWE 2016, LNCS 9671, pp. 542–546, 2016.
DOI: 10.1007/978-3-319-38791-8_44

such as `reddit` are a viable source of contributors [5], and that carefully crafted expertise identification and invitation strategies can enable the interaction with large amount of expert contributors.

This paper presents the *Crowd Knowledge Curator* (`CroKnow`), a novel web-based platform that streamlines the processes required to enrich data sources by tapping on the latent knowledge of expert contributors in online platform[1]. The ultimate goal of `CroKnow` is to provide organisations with a tool that simplifies the crowdsourced creation and evolution of structured data sources (e.g. Wikis, or generic knowledge bases) by: (1) identifying missing data and specifying the knowledge to be created both at schema and instance level; (2) defining strategies for the identification and invitation of candidate experts from open communities; (3) supporting such experts in the knowledge creation task; and (4) keeping track of the knowledge creation process status.

The platform integrates and implements state-of-the-art methods and tools for each of these steps. Section 2 introduces the reader with the architecture of `CroKnow`, highlighting the components devoted to the identification and invitation of candidate experts, and to the extraction and quality assessment of knowledge from them. The demo will showcase the application of `CroKnow` to an artwork annotation problem, with a case study developed with the Rijksmuseum Amsterdam and their collection of 1M prints.

2   CroKnow Architecture

`CroKnow` has been developed with a modularity and customisation as main design goals. Figure 1 depicts its building blocks, each interacting with a centralised `Orchestrator`. Each component maps onto a process step in the crowd knowledge creation process, indicated with the numbers in the red circles.

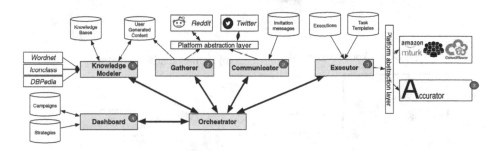

Fig. 1. `CroKnow` architecture (Color figure online)

- The `Knowledge Modeler` ❶ handles the interaction with external knowledge bases to be enriched, and includes algorithms designed to assess the suitability of user generated content w.r.t. to a targeted knowledge model;

---

[1] A demonstration video is available at http://www.wis.ewi.tudelft.nl/ICWE2016_CroKnow.

- The `Gatherer` ➋ and `Communicator` ➋ respectively cater for the gathering of user generated content from online social platforms like `reddit` or `Twitter`, and the communication with users of such platforms;
- The `Executor` ➌ handles the creation and deployment of knowledge creation tasks by instantiating pre-defined templates. Tasks can be deployed on existing crowdsourcing platforms (e.g. Amazon Mechanical Turk), or on our own execution platform `Accurator`. The `Executor` is also responsible for the collection of runtime statistics about task executions.
- Finally, the `Dashboard` ➍ provides an easy-to-use interface where crowd knowledge campaigns can be specified and monitored by users. A campaign specification implies the specification, for each component, of suitable strategies.

Individual components of `CroKnow` have previously been instrumented, tested and used; `Knowledge Modeler` in [6], `Gatherer` and `Communicator` in [1,5], `Executor` and `Accurator` in [8]. The `Dashboard` component is a new addition resulting from the need to visualize the orchestration of the other components.

`CroKnow` had been implemented in Java and uses the web framework ERRAI for the front-ends of the dashboard and for the `Accurator` execution platform. Figure 2 depicts several instances of the user interfaces provided by the `CroKnow` `Dashboard` and by `Accurator` task execution interface.

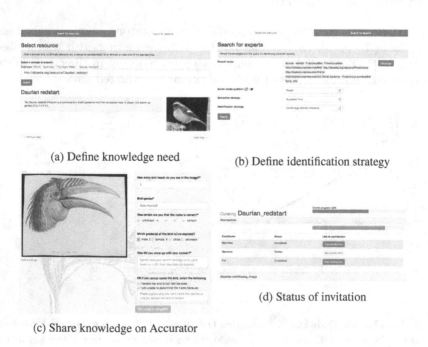

(a) Define knowledge need

(b) Define identification strategy

(c) Share knowledge on Accurator

(d) Status of invitation

Fig. 2. Screenshots of `CroKnow` components

Figure 2a shows the selection of a resource in a semantic repository, e.g. a resource from DBPedia. The resource selection is the minimal knowledge need specification for the process, but it can also be extended by including an (automated) identification of missing properties w.r.t. to similar resources of the same type.

Figure 2b shows the definition of a search strategy (targeted online platform, queries for expert identification etc.) based on a knowledge need specified in the previous step. The knowledge need can require different levels of expertise. For example, the creation or retrieval of a descriptive image arguably requires a lower level of expertise, compared to the task of determining the name of a bird species. CroKnow supports the formulation of queries using (a combination of) keywords, properties from the structured resource and structured knowledge bases such as ontology's, taxonomies and vocabularies. The specificity of the query and the search strategy influences the amount of identified candidate contributors. CroKnow allows assessment and refinement of the chosen query and search strategy by providing feedback on the volume and relatedness of the identified candidates. The search strategy defines the target platform (reddit, Twitter etc.) and the method to extract user generated content from the target platform.

Figure 2c shows a task we have deployed for extracting domain specific knowledge (names of depicted bird species on artworks).

Lastly Fig. 2d shows the status of a campaign by visualising the status of the invitation and the executions. This feedback can serve as input to invite more candidates or to change the search strategy.

3   Demonstration Scenario - Artwork Annotation

We demonstrate CroKnow on the use case of artwork annotation, an actual use case developed together with Rijksmuseum Amsterdam. We will show how semantic resources can be used to define the knowledge need, and how the reddit and Twitter platform could be exploited to identify users with knowledge related the ornithology domain. The dashboard component (see Fig. 1) will provide users with an overview of the status of the crowd knowledge generation process.

References

1. Balduini, M., Bocconi, S., Bozzon, A., Valle, E.D., Huang, Y., Oosterman, J., Palpanas, T., Tsytsarau, M.: A case study of active, continuous and predictive social media analytics for smart city. In: Proceedings of the 5th SSC Workshop, Riva del Garda, Italy, 19 October 2014, pp. 31–46 (2014)
2. Cheng, Z., Caverlee, J., Barthwal, H., Bachani, V.: Who is the barbecue king of texas?: a geo-spatial approach to finding local experts on twitter. In: Proceedings of SIGIR2014, SIGIR 2014, pp. 335–344. ACM, New York (2014)
3. Difallah, D.E., Demartini, G., Cudré-Mauroux, P., Pick-a-crowd: tell me what you like, and i'll tell you what to do. In: Proceedings of the WWW 2013, pp. 367–374 (2013)

4. Ipeirotis, P.G., Gabrilovich, E.: Quizz: targeted crowdsourcing with a billion (potential) users. In: Proceedings of the WWW 2014, WWW 2014, pp. 143–154. ACM, New York (2014)
5. Kassing, S., Oosterman, J., Bozzon, A., Houben, G.: Locating domain-specific contents and experts on social bookmarking communities. In: Proceedings of the SAC 2015, Salamanca, Spain, 13–17 April 2015, pp. 747–752 (2015)
6. Nottamkandath, A., Oosterman, J., Ceolin, D., Fokkink, W.: Automated evaluation of crowdsourced annotations in the cultural heritage domain. In: Proceedings of the 10th URSW Workshop, Riva del Garda, Italy, 19 October 2014, pp. 25–36 (2014)
7. Oosterman, J., Nottamkandath, A., Dijkshoorn, C., Bozzon, A., Houben, G., Aroyo, L.: Crowdsourcing knowledge-intensive tasks in cultural heritage. In: ACM Web Science Conference, pp. 267–268 (2014)
8. Oosterman, J., Yang, J., Bozzon, A., Aroyo, L., Houben, G.-J.: On the impact of knowledge extraction and aggregation on crowdsourced annotation of visual artworks. Computer Networks 90, 133–149 (2015)

ELES: Combining Entity Linking and Entity Summarization

Andreas Thalhammer[✉] and Achim Rettinger

AIFB, Karlsruhe Institute of Technology, Karlsruhe, Germany
{andreas.thalhammer,achim.rettinger}@kit.edu

Abstract. The automatic annotation of textual content with entities from a knowledge base is a well established field. Applications, such as DBpedia Spotlight and GATE enable to identify and disambiguate entities of text at high levels of accuracy. The output of such systems can be used in many different ways. One way is to show knowledge panels which provide a fact-based summary of an entity and provides further information as well as browsing options. Such fact-based summaries are produced by entity summarization systems.

This paper presents ELES, a lightweight combination of DBpedia Spotlight and the SUMMA entity summarization interface. DBpedia Spotlight analyzes text and links fragments to entities of the DBpedia knowledge base. The LinkSUM summarizer (interfaced via the SUMMA API definition) produces fact-based summaries of DBpedia entities. The two applications are combined on the client side through the "Internationalization Tag Set 2.0" W3C recommendation and lightweight jQuery-based interfaces.

1   Introduction

The field of linking fragments from text to entities of a knowledge base is currently at an advanced stage: words and compounds can be identified and disambiguated at high levels of accuracy [1,2,8]. Entity linking usually enables to provide further information on the entities, browsing, or recommendation. In this work, we consider the use case of providing a knowledge panel that pops up on mouse over entities that were identified through annotation. The knowledge panel is used to explain the entities identified by the annotator with concise fact-based information units and also enables further browsing (i.e. navigating through related entities). Entity summarization enables to filter all information that is available about an entity (often more than 1000 facts) and to select a small fraction that will be presented to the user.

With this demo, we propose loose coupling between automatic entity linking and entity summarization systems with the "Internationalization Tag Set 2.0" (ITS 2.0) W3C recommendation [3]. We exemplify the feasibility of the lightweight integration with the applications DBpedia Spotlight [1] (as a entity linking tool) and LinkSUM [4] (as an entity summarization tool interfaced via the SUMMA API [5]). Both applications use DBpedia[1] as a knowledge base.

---

[1] DBpedia – http://dbpedia.org.

© Springer International Publishing Switzerland 2016
A. Bozzon et al. (Eds.): ICWE 2016, LNCS 9671, pp. 547–550, 2016.
DOI: 10.1007/978-3-319-38791-8_45

2   Implementation

We make use of ITS 2.0 by using the `its-ta-ident-ref` attribute as the combining element between entity linking and entity summaries. This attribute can be used with HTML elements such as `<span>` tags (for an example see Listing 1). The system is implemented in accordance to the following workflow:

1. Automatically identify and annotate entities of a text.
2. Register a knowledge panel for each identified entity (on mouseover).

Listing 1. Example use of `its-ta-ident-ref` in a `<span>` tag.

```
She spent her summers in
<span its-ta-ident-ref="http://dbpedia.org/resource/Dublin,_Ohio">Dublin</span>.
```

We had to extend the DBpedia Spotlight jQuery plugin in order to enable ITS 2.0 output.[2] The system uses a Web service in order to anntoate one or more text paragraphs with entities from the DBpedia knowledge base. The entity summaries are produced by LinkSUM [4]. The produced summaries are displayed as knowledge panels via the summaClient[3] implementation [5]. The original implementation has been extended by the qSUM method. It registers mouseover events

Fig. 1. Automatically annotated excerpt of a Wikipedia article (https://en.wikipedia.org/w/index.php?title=Angela_Merkel\&oldid=709980123.) and the summaClient knowledge panel with a summary by LinkSUM.

---

[2] ITS 2.0 for DBpedia Spotlight – https://github.com/dbpedia-spotlight/demo/pull/5.
[3] summaClient – http://athalhammer.github.io/summaClient/.

for all elements with an `its-ta-ident-ref` attribute. The respective knowledge panel is then shown at the position of the respective annotation. The LinkSUM entity summarization system can be easily exchanged by another entity summarization system that implements the SUMMA API.

A screenshot of an automatically annotated text is provided in Fig. 1 and a do-it-yourself example is provided in Listing 2.

Listing 2. Full HTML example with the jQuery (UI), DBpedia Spotlight, and the SUMMA client libraries included.

```
<!DOCTYPE html><html><head><title>Example</title>
<style>span {background-color:#AAAAAA}</style>
<link rel="stylesheet" type="text/css"
href="http://athalhammer.github.io/summaClient/css/summaClient.css" />
<script src="http://code.jquery.com/jquery-2.2.1.min.js"></script>
<script src="http://code.jquery.com/ui/1.11.4/jquery-ui.js"></script>
<script src="http://dbpedia-spotlight.github.io/demo/dbpedia-spotlight-0.3.js"></script>
<script src="http://athalhammer.github.io/summaClient/js/summaClient.js"></script>
<script>
$(document).ready(function() {
  // selector on HTML element(s)
  var select = ".annotate";

  // as soon as the annotations are ready, start registering mouseover events
  // parameters: topK, language, fixed properties, service
  $(select).bind("DOMSubtreeModified", function() {
    qSUM(5, "en", null, "http://km.aifb.kit.edu/services/link/sum");
  });

  // DBpedia Spotlight configuration and annotation
  var settings = { "endpoint" : "http://spotlight.sztaki.hu:2222/rest", "its" : "yes",
    "spotter" : "Default" };
  $(select).annotate(settings); $(select).annotate("best");
});
</script></head><body><div class="annotate">Angela Merkel is TIME Person of the Year 2015.
</div></body></html>
```

3   Related Work

Our work on ELES was inspired by Denny Vrandečić's qLabel[4] project. qLabel is a jQuery-based application that uses text fragments, annotated with `its-ta-ident-ref` references to Wikidata [7], for translation between different languages. For this, qLabel leverages the wealth of multi-lingual labels available in Wikidata. A Wikidata-based summarization system that uses the SUMMA API can be easily combined with qLabel via qSUM.

There are also a number of proprietary solutions that combine annotation and knowledge panels. The refer[5] application, partly described in [6], supports automatic annotation in combination with knowledge panels. The application is well integrated with additional browsing features and a complete graph panel that can be enabled at the top of each page. Other proprietary solutions include the Bing Knowledge Widget[6] and Ontotext's Now[7]. Most of the proprietary

---

[4] qLabel – http://googleknowledge.github.io/qlabel/.
[5] refer – http://refer.cx/.
[6] Bing Knowledge Widget – https://www.bing.com/widget/knowledge.
[7] Ontotext Now – http://now.ontotext.com/.

solutions are highly customized and the annotation and knowledge panel parts are often strongly connected.

4   Summary

With ELES, we propose loose coupling between automatic entity linking and entity summarization systems via ITS 2.0. We exemplify the lightweight integration approach with the applications DBpedia Spotlight and the qSUM method of the SUMMA entity summarization interface.

Acknowledgements. The research leading to these results has received funding from the European Union Seventh Framework Programme (FP7/2007–2013) under grant agreement no. 611346 and by the German Federal Ministry of Education and Research (BMBF) within the Software Campus project "SumOn" (grant no. 01IS12051).

References

1. Daiber, J., Jakob, M., Hokamp, C., Mendes, P.N.: Improving efficiency and accuracy in multilingual entity extraction. In: Proceedings of the 9th International Conference on Semantic Systems (I-Semantics) (2013)
2. Damljanovic, D., Bontcheva, K.: Named entity disambiguation using linked data. In: Proceedings of the 9th Extended Semantic Web Conference (2012)
3. Filip, D., McCance, S., Lewis, D., Lieske, C., Lommel, A., Kosek, J., Sasaki, F., Savourel, Y.: Internationalization Tag Set (ITS) Version 2.0. W3C recommendation. W3C, October 2013. http://www.w3.org/TR/2013/REC-its20-20131029/
4. Thalhammer, A., Lasierra, N., Rettinger, A.: LinkSUM: using link analysis to summarize entity data. In: Proceedings of the 16th International Conference on Web Engineering (ICWE 2016) (2016, to appear)
5. Thalhammer, A., Stadtmüller, S.: SUMMA: a common API for linked data entity summaries. In: Cimiano, P., Frasincar, F., Houben, G.-J., Schwabe, D. (eds.) ICWE 2015. LNCS, vol. 9114, pp. 430–446. Springer, Heidelberg (2015)
6. Tietz, T., Waitelonis, J., Jäger, J., Sack, H., Navigator, S.M.: Visualizing recommendations based on linked data. In: Industry Track at the International Semantic Web Conference (ISWC 2014), vol. 1383. CEUR-WS (2015)
7. Vrandečić, D., Krötzsch, M.: Wikidata: a free collaborative knowledgebase. Commun. ACM **57**, 78–85 (2014)
8. Zhang, L., Rettinger, A.: X-LiSA: cross-lingual semantic annotation. In: Proceedings of the VLDB Endowment (PVLDB), the 40th International Conference on Very Large Data Bases (VLDB), vol. 7, no. 13, pp. 1693–1696, September 2014

Liquid, Autonomous and Decentralized Stream Processing for the Web of Things

Masiar Babazadeh[✉]

Faculty of Informatics, University of Lugano (USI), Lugano, Switzerland
masiar.babazadeh@usi.ch

Abstract. In recent years we have witnessed the rise in number of smart devices and sensors connected through the Web. This led researchers to explore the World Wide Web as a platform to orchestrate such devices. In this demo we show how we are able to harmonize heterogeneous hardware for home automation systems with the Web Liquid Streams (WLS) framework. The WLS framework lets developers implement topologies of data streams across a heterogeneous pool of devices thanks to Node.JS and the Web browser. By using JavaScript, the lingua franca of the Web, we are able to write the stream operators once and run them anywhere a Web browser or Node.JS can run. The demo shows a home automation system application that can seamlessly run on different kind of devices.

Keywords: Web of things · Streaming applications · Liquid software · Home automation systems

1 Introduction

The increase in the number of smart devices and sensors has led developers to explore the Web as a platform to organize and make these devices interoperate. The accessibility of such hardware has also led the rise of the Maker culture [1], a subculture that extends in a technological way the Do It Yourself (DIY) movement. Makers often have a basic understanding of electrical engineering concepts and programming paradigms, and are able to program their microcontrollers to automatise (part of) their houses. Given the lack of programming experience, integrating different kinds of microcontrollers through the Web may appear a rather difficult task for Makers, which either fragment their home automation in small set-ups, or have to deal with data streams and data synchronization in a heterogeneous environment.

In this demo paper we demonstrate the use of the Web Liquid Streams framework [2,3] to help Makers build topologies of distributed data stream operators that are able to run on different kind of hardware: from a small microcontroller, passing to laptops and big Web servers.

WLS follows the Liquid software paradigm [4], by which applications can exploit computational resources from all the devices owned by the user, and dynamically migrate from one device to the other, for example in faulty scenarios. This turns out to be very useful when applied to a distributed streaming

© Springer International Publishing Switzerland 2016
A. Bozzon et al. (Eds.): ICWE 2016, LNCS 9671, pp. 551–554, 2016.
DOI: 10.1007/978-3-319-38791-8_46

application scenario, where the data stream is expected to be up and flowing for a very long time.

2   Framework

While building Web applications across Web enabled devices may nowadays appear a relatively simple task thanks to Node.JS, WebRTC and WebSockets, it is much more difficult to setup an infrastructure that is able to arbitrarily exploit the JavaScript Event Loop on the available hosting machines.

With the Web Liquid Streams framework, developers can create topologies of distributed streaming operators and run them across a pool of heterogeneous hardware resources. Thanks to JavaScript, topologies may be implemented using a single programming language and the WLS' primitives. The WLS runtime is then in charge to deploy the implemented operators on the available devices, connect them through sockets and start the data stream.

WLS is able to tolerate faults and changes in the computing environment at runtime, by migrating the execution of the operators on other available devices, and re-routing the topology accordingly. This is done by a control infrastructure which is also in charge of solving bottlenecks in the computation, by increasing or decreasing the allocated resources on the host.

WLS can be used by Makers that can program in JavaScript and want to automate their homes with Web-enabled sensors and microcontrollers. After developing the operators scripts, Makers have only to define a topology description file that tells the WLS runtime how the operators have to be wired. Makers do not have to worry about the actual communication channels, it is the runtime's task to create the right sockets to make two arbitrary machines communicate.

3   Demo

The demo focuses on integrating a streaming topology across a pool of heterogeneous devices, simulating a home environment. We make use of temperature, pressure, and humidity sensors as well as a microphone to monitor the environment in different rooms. The available hardware, that in WLS we call "peers", are two Raspberry Pis (first model), two Tessels (first model), one laptop and one smartphone with the Google Chrome Web browser installed, and two Web servers running Node.JS. We show how these peers can interoperate seamlessly thanks to our framework by just installing it, and writing both the script operators and the topology description file.

Figure 1 illustrates the demonstrated topology. We setup three producers, two running on Tessels (peer 0 and peer 1) and one on a Raspberry Pi (peer 2). The data gathered is sent both to a consumer (peer 3), running on a smart phone with the Chrome Web browser installed, and to a filter (peer 4) running on a Web server. The Web browser consumer receives the data from the sensors and displays the status of the microcontrollers. If one producer dies, the Web browser

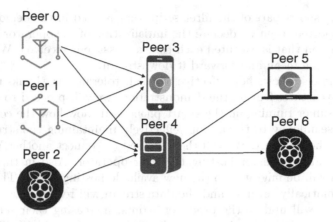

Fig. 1. The demonstrated topology.

will show it on the page. The Web server instead gathers the data, stores it into a database and computes a mean of the last received values. These measures will then be forwarded to both the consumers at the end of the topology. The Web browser consumer (peer 5) graphically shows the obtained measurements by the means of interactive graphs, while the Raspberry Pi consumer (peer 6) works as an actuator, turning a fan on if the temperature is too high, and lighting red alert lights if the noise level is too high.

Listing 1.1. Example filter script

```
 1  var k = require('WLS.js');
 2
 3  //initialize operator state
 4  k.createOperator(function(measurements) {
 5      //store the measurements
 6      k.db_store("temperatures",
 7      {
 8        "room_id" : measurements.id,
 9        "temp" : measurements.temperatureData
10      });
11      //[...] store all the other measurements
12
13      //compute means of that room
14      var toBeSent = {};
15      toBeSent.tempMean = avg( k.db_get("temperatures",
            measurements.id, 1000) );
16      //[...] compute all the other averages
17
18      //send data downstream
19      k.send(toBeSent);
20  });
```

Listing 1.1 shows part of the filter script that is used in the demo. First our library is imported, then we declare the initialization of the operator and pass a callback function that is executed each time a message is received. We store the data, retrieve the mean and forward it downstream.

This demo also shows how effective our fault tolerance is, thanks to our controller infrastructure. During the demonstration, we will proceed to disconnect the first consumer running on the smart phone and show how the computation is migrated seamlessly to the laptop, effectively maintaining the structure and semantics of the topology. We will then proceed to connect another Web server and cause a fault in server hosting the filter operator. Also in this case, the computation will be migrated to the new available hosting server. The topology will be automatically rewired, and the data stream will restart.

Finally, we will update the producer scripts, increasing their sending rate. This will create a small bottleneck on the filter operator, which will be solved autonomously by the controller infrastructure by allocating more resources on the hosting peer, effectively parallelising the execution of the operator.

4   Conclusions

In this demo we have shown how the Web Liquid Streams framework can be used by Makers to develop their personal streaming topologies, passing through their microcontrollers, personal computers or home Web servers. Thanks to JavaScript, Makers only have to know JavaScript and install WLS across their devices. The WLS runtime will then take care of deploying the implemented operators on the available devices and start the data stream. Thanks to our controller interface, the topology becomes fault tolerant, being able to autonomously migrate the faulty operators on other available machines and rewiring the topology, maintaining its structure and semantics intact.

Acknowledgments. The work is supported by the Hasler Foundation with the Liquid Software Architecture (LiSA) project of the SMARTWORLD initiative.

References

1. Anderson, C.: Makers : The New Industrial Revolution. Random House Business Books, London (2012)
2. Babazadeh, M., Gallidabino, A., Pautasso, C.: Decentralized stream processing over web-enabled devices. In: Dustdar, S., Leymann, F., Villari, M. (eds.) ESOCC 2015. LNCS, vol. 9306, pp. 3–18. Springer, Heidelberg (2015). doi:10.1007/978-3-319-24072-5_1
3. Babazadeh, M., Gallidabino, A., Pautasso, C.: Liquid stream processing across web browsers and web servers. In: Cimiano, P., Frasincar, F., Houben, G.-J., Schwabe, D. (eds.) ICWE 2015. LNCS, vol. 9114, pp. 24–33. Springer, Heidelberg (2015)
4. Mikkonen, T., Systä, K., Pautasso, C.: Towards liquid web applications. In: Cimiano, P., Frasincar, F., Houben, G.-J., Schwabe, D. (eds.) ICWE 2015. LNCS, vol. 9114, pp. 134–143. Springer, Heidelberg (2015)

Migrating and Pairing Recursive Stateful Components Between Multiple Devices with Liquid.js for Polymer

Andrea Gallidabino[✉]

Faculty of Informatics, University of Lugano (USI), Lugano, Switzerland
andrea.gallidabino@usi.ch

Abstract. With the continuous development of new Web-enabled devices, we are heading toward an era in which users connect to the Web with multiple devices at the same time. Users expect Web applications to be able to flow between all the devices they own, however the majority of the current Web applications was not designed considering this use case scenario. As the number of devices owned by a user increases, we have to find new ways to give Web developers the tools to easily implement the expected liquid behaviour into their software. We present a new contribution provided by the Liquid.js for Polymer framework, allowing the migration of recursive component-based Web applications from a device to another. In this demo paper we will show how to create recursive components, how to migrate them among devices, and how their state can be paired among the various components.

Keywords: Web components · Liquid software · Liquid web applications · Stateful web components

1 Introduction

The Liquid.js for Polymer framework is based on the *Liquid software* paradigm [1,2]. As a poured liquid adapts to the shape of the containers holding it, a software adapts to the resources of the devices running it [3]. Liquid applications are specifically designed to run on multiple devices following the users focus whenever the application flows among them [4]. From the user point of view these applications run either: (1) **sequentially**: at any given moment in time an application runs only on a single device, however the users may decide to move the application to a different one. The state of the application in a sequential scenario is never accessible from two devices simultaneously; (2) **simultaneously**: the application has to be shared among multiple devices, while its state has to be kept in sync.

Liquid.js for Polymer [5] is a novel framework for easily create liquid Web applications. In a previous demo publication we showed how to create liquid Web applications by using our framework API, in this demo we focus on a new feature: while in the past the migration was only possible on *flat* components,

© Springer International Publishing Switzerland 2016
A. Bozzon et al. (Eds.): ICWE 2016, LNCS 9671, pp. 555–558, 2016.
DOI: 10.1007/978-3-319-38791-8_47

today we make a distinction between *container* and *leaf* components. Finally we show how these complex structures can be paired with each other by invoking methods provided by our API.

2 Liquid Framework

Liquid.js for Polymer extensively exploits the most recent HTML5 standards. This approach allows to target as many devices as possible, achieving an increased compatibility with any system or hardware able to run a Web browsers complying with HTML5, like Google Chrome or Mozzilla Firefox.

The goal of Liquid is to automatise how an application is *shared* between multiple devices, the framework transparently decides where data has to be stored in such a way it is always available and as close as possible to the source using it [5]. The environment created by Liquid is highly decentralised, the decentralisation is achieved by delegating clients of storing data in a peer-to-peer mesh instead of storing it in a central server and, whenever possible, clients also distribute the application assets whenever they are requested. The server in a Liquid application is used as a fallback whenever P2P technologies are not available, and as the initial orchestrator of the P2P mesh by exchanging signalling messages between the clients.

Liquid expects the developer to be able to build component-based application by using the WebComponents standard, specifically by using the Polymer library[1]. A developer has to decompose an application into smaller components and he has to *explicitly* define which parts of the application are expected to be shared between devices. In order to do so Liquid provides an API and gives default tools to the Web developers for easily *migrate*, *fork* and *clone* stateful liquid Polymer components between multiple devices: – **migrate**: the migrate primitive moves a component from a device to another, the state of the component is migrate as the component does. No trace of the component and the state is kept on the initial device; – **fork**: Liquid makes a copy of a component and its current state on another device. The state of the initial component and the newly created one is not synchronised, meaning that upon state change they don't affect each other; – **clone**: Liquid makes a copy of a component and its current state on another device, while keeping the state of the two components automatically synchronised. These three behaviours can be imported into any Polymer component by adding our liquid behaviour to it, in the case a Polymer components import the liquid behaviour we call it a liquid component.

3 Demo

The demo will focus on a new feature of Liquid.js: *liquid container components*. While the liquid components, discussed in the previous session, only import the three liquid primitives into a solid component, they do not allow the composition

---

[1] https://www.polymer-project.org/1.0/.

of multiple liquid components into one, which is an expected use case scenario whenever developers decide to use the WebComponents standard and the component-base architectural style. For this reason we introduce the concept of *container* and *leaf* components in Liquid.js: – **container components**: like a normal liquid component, a container component imports the liquid behaviour. Additionally it is possible to add into the containers any number of liquid components, they can be either other containers or leaves. Whenever a liquid primitive is invoked, the containers automatically broadcast the primitive invocation to all subordinated components. – **leaf components**: leaf components do not accept any subordinated liquid component. Whenever the application tries to create a liquid component inside of a leaf component, it automatically rejects the operation.

In the demo we will present how to create container components by importing the new *liquid container behaviour* into the Polymer behaviour list (Listing 1.1), moreover we will show what is the expected behaviour of the component in a live demonstration.

Listing 1.1. Liquid Container Paper-Input Component

```
1   <dom—module id="liquid-component-test">
2     <template>
3       ...
4     </template>
5     <script>
6       Polymer({
7         is: 'liquid-component-test',
8         behaviors: [LiquidBehavior, LiquidContainerBehavior],
9         properties: {
10          ...
11        },
12      });
13    </script>
14  </dom—module>
```

In this demo we will also present how it is possible to pair variables in Liquid.js. The pairing happens by invoking the *pairVariables* method passing two URLs into the method (*pairVariables(variableURL_1, variableURL_2)*). In fact all liquid variables in our framework are accessible by a unique URL (routing 1) which defines: – **device**: the device identifier which contains the component with the registered liquid variable; – **component**: the component identifier that registered the liquid variable; – **variable**: the name of the desired liquid variable.

$$/ : device/ : component/ : variable \tag{1}$$

Developers are allowed to use **wildcards** (*) whenever they write a variable URL. Routing 2 shows the routing that resolves as *all registered variables named text registered in all components contained in any devices.*

$$/ * / * /text \tag{2}$$

Moreover developers are allowed to write [**componentNames**] (surrounded by brackets) whenever they write a variable URL. Routing 3 shows the routing that resolves as *all registered variables named image inside the 'liquidImage' components in any device.*

$$/*/[liquidImage]/image \tag{3}$$

With this approach it is possible to pair liquid variables among any registered variable in the distributed application. Example 4 show a possible pair case in which the variable *image* registered by component *c1* contained in device *d1*, is paired with all other registered *image* variables in the system.

$$pairVariable('/d1/c1/image', '/*/*/image') \tag{4}$$

4   Conclusion and Future Work

Liquid.js provides the default mechanisms to migrate flat and recursive applications between devices. In the future we will add a new level of abstraction to the variables URL routing, namely *:users*. In fact users own a set of devices, and by adding the users resource in our routing, it is possible to reference all devices owned by a single user. Moreover by introducing the concept of user in the system, we are also looking forward to implement *black* and *white* lists, which will increase the sharing security whenever users work with sensitive data.

Acknowledgments. This work is partially supported by the SNF and the Hasler Foundation with the Fundamentals of Parallel Programming for Platform-as-a-Service Clouds (SNF-200021_153560) and the Liquid Software Architecture (LiSA) grants.

References

1. Taivalsaari, A., Mikkonen, T., Systa, K.: Liquid software manifesto: the era of multiple device ownership and its implications for software architecture. In: 2014 IEEE 38th Annual Computer Software and Applications Conference (COMPSAC), pp. 338–343. IEEE (2014)
2. Gallidabino, A., Pautasso, C., Ilvonen, V., Mikkonen, T., Systä, K., Voutilainen, J.P., Taivalsaari, A.: On the architecture of liquid software: technology alternatives and design space. In: Accepted at WICSA 2016 (2016)
3. Mikkonen, T., Systä, K., Pautasso, C.: Towards liquid web applications. In: Cimiano, P., Frasincar, F., Houben, G.-J., Schwabe, D. (eds.) ICWE 2015. LNCS, vol. 9114, pp. 134–143. Springer, Heidelberg (2015)
4. Levin, M.: Designing Multi-device Experiences: An Ecosystem Approach to User Experiences Across Devices. O'Reilly, Sebastopol (2014)
5. Gallidabino, A., Pautasso, C.: Deploying stateful web components on multiple devices with liquid.js for Polymer. In: Accepted at CBSE 2016 (2016)

A Universal Socio-Technical Computing Machine

Markus Luczak-Roesch[1][✉], Ramine Tinati[1],
Saud Aljaloud[1], Wendy Hall[1], and Nigel Shadbolt[2]

[1] Electronics and Computer Science, University of Southampton, Southampton, UK
mail@markus-luczak.de
[2] Department of Computer Science, University of Oxford, Oxford, UK
http://social-computer.org

Abstract. This is an attempt to develop a universal socio-technical computing machine that captures and coordinates human input to let collective problem solving activities emerge on the Web without the need for an a priori composition of a dedicated task or human collective.

1 Introduction and Background

Since the advent of the *Social Machines* paradigm as abstractly described by Tim Berners-Lee [1], scholars have witnessed various attempts to underpin it with a formal theory and practice. The current range of theories includes a scheme to classify Web applications along a dedicated set of socio-technical properties [9,10] as well as an archetypal framework to reflect upon sociality in collective action on the Web [11]. These two qualitative and small scale approaches are complemented by a quantitative information-centric view to Social Machines [4–6]. It turns out that, while these approaches provide novel means to retrospectively look at the interplay of the technical and the social on the Web, their constructive dimension – the practice – is somewhat limited.

Here we describe a novel architecture of a universal socio-technical computing machine – or short, a *Social Computer*. In contrast to the classification work, but in-line with ideas of archetypal narratives, our approach assumes Social Machines being the emergent output of human activity rather than any fixed engineered input. We ultimately seek to develop an engine that allows for actively shaping the morphology of the archetype of a collective action as it emerges in near real-time. Our approach differs from the typically coordinated approach in human computation and crowdsourcing [3,7], where research commonly calls for methods to pre-engineer the way a human collective is going to perform a task [8]. Based on the principle that *the accumulated information sharing activities of individuals on the Web can compose purposeful collective action* [4], we designed a system that lets the human participants determine the computational program by their real-time inputs, while the technical components simply facilitate information flow to other technical systems to reach further human participants. Or to put it differently, we developed a system that reacts upon bursts of information occurring on the Web and engages with human participants on various platforms to let a coordinated problem solving activity emerge.

© Springer International Publishing Switzerland 2016
A. Bozzon et al. (Eds.): ICWE 2016, LNCS 9671, pp. 559–562, 2016.
DOI: 10.1007/978-3-319-38791-8_48

2   System Architecture

For the principled design of our system we rely on the representational state transfer (REST) principles of the Web architecture [2] and take a data-centric approach. That means that the central interface between system components is a data repository that is read from and written to by the individual components via RESTful request. The data in the repository is semi-structured so that the system allows for flexible expansion. Figure 1 depicts how the individual components of the system interact.

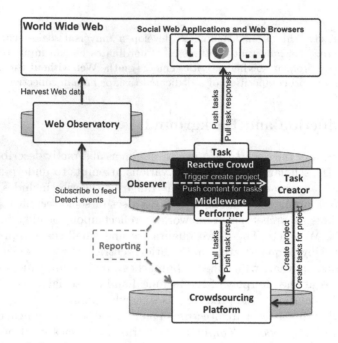

Fig. 1. Principled architecture of our universal socio-technical computing machine.

The source of data to be observed is any system on the World Wide Web. In order to decrease the necessary effort to implement individual data harvesters per system that can be accessed it is recommended to instantiate or link with a real-time Web Observatory [12], which is a decentralised approach to enable access to historic and real-time data from and about systems on the Web. The observer component subscribes to a unified activity feed on a Web Observatory and implements (a) an information extraction mechanism to look for patterns in the content elements of the feed that are regarded relevant; and (b) a threshold heuristic to indicate a relevant burst of activity around a particular pattern. When the heuristic indicates a burst, a project to manage crowdsourcing tasks on all incoming content containing the respective pattern is kicked off. The task creator manages that, from now on, any content element with that pattern is persisted in a crowdsourcing platform, which maintains a specific part of the overall data repository focused on crowdsourcing analytics for making decisions about the completion of particular tasks and projects. The task performer component revisits the projects and tasks maintained in the data repository regularly and pushes them back to the Web to call for contributions from the crowd. This component also pulls responses to those published tasks back from the Web and persists them as task runs in the crowdsourcing database. This setup allows contributions to the crowdsourcing tasks in various ways: (1) participants of systems to which tasks are pushed (e.g. Twitter or facebook, see Fig. 2) can simply reply to the shared content that contains the tasks (these are registered or unregistered participants, depending on the remote system's policies); (2) participants can subscribe to the RESTful interface of the task performer and pick up pushed tasks and post task runs; (3) participants can log into the crowdsourcing platform that is part of this architecture and contribute to the tasks through the system's Web interface. Our system is ultimately designed to allow for orchestrating arbitrary task workflows solely by the input from human users. In its current development state fixed workflow templates for translate, question answering and annotation tasks are provided.

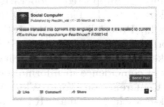

Fig. 2. Two ways to contribute human input to our Social Computer: Twitter and facebook.

3   Summary and Outlook

In this paper we presented a system design of a middleware to enable the autonomous creation and management of crowdsourcing tasks workflows. The approach automatically spins up crowdsourcing tasks for topics that feature temporally high activity on the Web in near real-time. We called this autonomous reactive crowdsourcing approach a *universal socio-technical computing machine* (or a Social Computer) because in its ultimate vision it shall allow for the composition of arbitrary workflows solely by the input of human participants through a set of primitive built-in tasks, which would form the basic instruction set of the Social Computer to form complex algorithms. This requires future work on the definition of this fundamental and generic instruction set and to implement it in a way that it can be used by the crowd in their responses to pushed out tasks rigorously but still intuitively. Comprehensive experimentation is needed to understand the properties and impact of varying activity and consensus thresholds, and a completely new set of analytics to observe the system needs to be devised. Our Social Computer is configured by the content stream that is taken in and by the patterns to react upon within that stream, which allows for realizing either completely open or context specific work to be carried out. We see great potential for the approach to be used in scenarios that are inherently broadcasting orientated and do not feature a pre-defined online community to engage with. We find those in real-time event response such as disaster management using social media as well as in citizen science. The system also shows great potential to be used in organisations to let coordinated collaboration emerge when related activity around a topic is detected in independent organisational units.

References

1. Berners-Lee, T., Fischetti, M., Foreword By-Dertouzos, M.L.: Weaving the Web: the Original Design and Ultimate Destiny of the World Wide Web By Its Inventor. HarperInformation, New York (2000)
2. Fielding, R.T.: Architectural styles and the design of network-based software architectures. Ph.D. thesis, University of California, Irvine (2000)
3. Kittur, A., et al.: The future of crowd work. In: Proceedings of the 2013 Conference on Computer Supported Cooperative Work, pp. 1301–1318. ACM (2013)
4. Luczak-Roesch, M., Tinati, R., O'Hara, K., Shadbolt, N.: Socio-technical computation. In: Proceedings of the 18th ACM Conference Companion on Computer Supported Cooperative Work & Social Computing, pp. 139–142 (2015)
5. Luczak-Roesch, M., Tinati, R., Shadbolt, N.: When resources collide: towards a theory of coincidence in information spaces. In: Proceedings of the 24th International Conference on World Wide Web Companion, pp. 1137–1142 (2015)
6. Luczak-Roesch, M., Tinati, R., Van Kleek, M., Shadbolt, N.: From coincidence to purposeful flow? properties of transcendental information cascades. In: Proceedings of the 2015 IEEE/ACM International Conference on Advances in Social Networks Analysis and Mining 2015, pp. 633–638. ACM (2015)
7. Malone, T.W., Laubacher, R., Dellarocas, C.: Harnessing crowds: Mapping the genome of collective intelligence (2009)
8. Minder, P., Bernstein, A.: *CrowdLang*: a programming language for the systematic exploration of human computation systems. In: Aberer, K., Flache, A., Jager, W., Liu, L., Tang, J., Guéret, C. (eds.) SocInfo 2012. LNCS, vol. 7710, pp. 124–137. Springer, Heidelberg (2012)
9. Shadbolt, N.R., et al.: Towards a classification framework for social machines. In: Proceedings of the 22nd International Conference on World Wide Web Companion, pp. 905–912. International World Wide Web Conferences Steering Committee (2013)
10. Smart, P., Simperl, E., Shadbolt, N.: A taxonomic framework for social machines. In: Miorandi, D., Maltese, V., Rovatsos, M., Nijholt, A., Stewart, J. (eds.) Social Collective Intelligence. Computational Social Sciences, pp. 51–85. Springer, Switzerland (2014)
11. Tarte, S., et al.: Archetypal narratives in social machines: approaching sociality through prosopography (2015)
12. Tinati, R., Wang, X., Tiropanis, T., Hall, W.: Building a real-time web observatory. IEEE Internet Comput. **19**(6), 36–45 (2015)

Web Objects Ambient: An Integrated Platform Supporting New Kinds of Personal Web Experiences

Gabriela Bosetti[1], Sergio Firmenich[1(✉)], Gustavo Rossi[1], Marco Winckler[2], and Tomas Barbieri[1]

[1] LIFIA, Facultad de Informática, Universidad Nacional de La Plata, La Plata, Argentina
{gbosetti,sfirmenich,gustavo}@lifia.info.unlp.edu.ar
[2] ICS-IRIT, University of Toulouse 3, Toulouse, France
winckler@irit.fr

Abstract. The Personal Web arose to empower end users with the ability to drive and integrate the Web by themselves, according to their own interests. This is usually achieved through Web Augmentation, Mashups or Personal Information Managers (PIM), but despite the diversity of approaches, there are still scenarios that require to be solved through the combination of their features, which implies the end user knowing diverse tools and being able to coordinate them. This paper presents WOA, a platform conceived under the foundations of the Personal Web for supporting the harvesting and materialization of information objects from existing Web content, and their enhancement through the addition of specialized behaviour. This makes it possible to conceive multiple Web information objects coexisting in a same space of information and offering the end user with different modes of interaction, therefore, with multiple kinds of personal Web experiences.

Keywords: Personal web · Web augmentation · Mashups

1 Introduction

Web contents are daily growing in size and diversity, and it is increasingly likely that much of the information we need for achieving any of our daily activities is already available somewhere on the Web, although not always part of the same information source. Several approaches have addressed the need of consuming and offering the user with content or services from different sources in order to achieve their personal goals; Mashups [2] can integrate both of them in a new application that reuses existing information for accomplishing a new purpose that the original context did not contemplate; Personal Information Management (PIM) systems [3] allow the user to collect information objects for further making them available in a personal information space for performing specific operations; Web Augmentation [1] enhances existing Web pages according to the user's requirements, by adding or adapting specialized behaviour, styles or content. Each of the mentioned applications and techniques empower users with the capability of interacting with existing content, but they work isolated, thus making it difficult to have a complete Personal Web experience. Even worst, a concrete application might lack some desirable feature that makes it possible the integration with another

© Springer International Publishing Switzerland 2016
A. Bozzon et al. (Eds.): ICWE 2016, LNCS 9671, pp. 563–566, 2016.
DOI: 10.1007/978-3-319-38791-8_49

application. E.g. it could be designed to consume just static or dynamic, structured or unstructured data; to empower the end users or just to support developers; to provide sharing mechanisms for individual information objects or the whole information space; to conceive the stored data as application independent, or making it hard to externally consume it in a straightforward way (often inconceivable for end users); to consider Reactive Web [5] capabilities; to consume content from multiple sources; to augment a Web page with such information.

The Personal Web, as explained in [4], is intended to "empower ME, as a common internet user of generally limited technical skills, the autonomy and ease of control in assembling and aggregating integrate-able web elements across the web for a particular sphere of context of my concern". This promises to completely change the user experience in the WWW, because it claims him as the axis of such extensive space.

In this light, we present Web Objects Ambient (WOA), a platform for achieving full interactive Personal Web experiences by reusing existing Web content and improving them with specialized behaviour artefacts, enabling diverse modes and contexts of interaction with such information objects under a common environment.

2   The Web Objects Ambient

In order to guarantee complete Personal Web experiences, it is not only desirable that the multiple features of the aforementioned applications to be provided by a single integrated platform, but also that the created information objects could be reusable in diverse contexts and consumed from an application-independent storage. We implemented our platform by extending the Firefox browser capabilities, which provided us high-level permissions to access the file system, to create custom browser user interfaces, to clone objects into diverse contexts and to manipulate the Web with almost no restrictions (e.g. no same-origin policy). But despite technical issues, it is mainly required that the experience could be produced by the same person who knows, in detail, the business logic and data needs to meet; the end user himself. To do so, we empowered him with the capability of composing his own information space, a common environment where personal information objects "live" and can be enhanced with specialized behaviour. We refer such objects as *Concepts*, and they are instantiated from *Concept Templates* (CT). To define a CT, the user should navigate to the Web page containing the content of his interest and enable the WOA *Collectors* by clicking a toolbar button. When this option is enabled, all the behaviour of the opened documents in the browser are prevented, the DOM elements matching the mouse pointer position are highlighted, and a special context menu is added to the UI description of the browser, where diverse mechanisms for content extraction will be displayed. Then, as shown in step (1) of Fig. 1, he can collect Web content into the WOA by right clicking the highlighted DOM element. This event makes WOA to ask a set of specialized data *Collectors* to analyse the DOM element, to look for properties of their interest and to render an item in the context menu, if applicable. Such properties depends on the type of data such extractor supports; the aim is to provide the user with some auto-completed data in the materialization process. E.g. processing the itemtype attribute of a microformatted element, to suggest the user certain tag for his template; this facilitates him the cognitive process of abstracting the representations and choosing a proper tag matching a semantic class of our ontology. Once the user clicks on a context menu item, a form opens in the sidebar for defining the values for the template, as shown in step (2). Some of them are transparent to the user (as the URL or the XPath), other are automatically filled by the *Collector* in charge (as the tag), and the remaining ones should be filled by the user himself. Once the template is saved, the user can see its thumbnail in the sidebar and, by right clicking on its configuration icon (the gear at top-right), he can access a contextual menu with some options for accessing the template edition, the concept instances view, some general purpose template (class) messages, and the template removal, as seen in step (3).

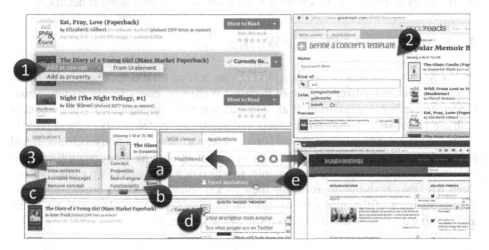

Fig. 1. Materializing and interacting with WOA information objects

Once a concept template has been created, it could happen that the retrieved instances are not presented in a single DOM, because there is a navigation bar or a search engine in the original site. As shown in marker (a) of Fig. 1, the end user can configure a WOA search engine, so he can browse and interact with all the instances provided by the site. Back to structuration, the user should also collect and materialize Properties in the same way he did with Concepts; the only difference is he should click the second menu item in step (1) of Fig. 1, and he will see an extra combo in step (2) for associating the *Property Template* to any existing CT. When the user define all the templates he requires, their instances are available in the ambient but he might not be able to interact with them yet. When a CT is created, it is automatically associated with a *Decorator* [6], which will wrap and provide every one of its concept instances with specialized behaviour for meeting a concrete purpose. *Decorators* have defined a set of keywords and a set of semantic classes, and their values are used for matching a *Concept* with the most specific available *Decorator*. If there is no specific decorator for a certain tag, it applies the one devoted to general purposes. Every *Decorator* has a set of selectable and configurable messages, and such configuration consists in a series of parameters matching a property.

If their names do not match, it is necessary that the user links them from the *Decorator* configuration. Decorators can be changed, and so their messages and parameters. This could be accessed by the CT's context menu, by choosing "Functionality" as shown in marker (b) of the figure. Finally, when templates are created and decorators are configured for properly working with such templates, it is possible to interact with the concept instance's messages through the WOA Viewer (c), in-situ augmentations (d) (provided by specialized decorators), or domain-specific WOA applications; by importing a regular Web application that uses the WOA API for accessing the collected concepts and decorators (e).

WOA also considers a second user role; a *developer*, in charge of extending and providing end users with new Collectors, Decorators and Applications. But for the sake of simplicity and space, in this work we just addressed end-user support details.

3   Conclusion and Further Work

In this paper we introduced WOA, a platform supporting a novel approach for enabling end users to create a diverse range of Personal Web experiences, by abstracting, structuring and enhancing existing Web content. We fully implemented such common ambient and a set of specialized artefacts to demonstrate the feasibility of the approach. Now, we are extending the platform in order to support new extraction mechanisms and to provide the end users with a broader spectrum of specific functionality for their objects. We are also working on the implementation of an end user tool for empowering them with the capability of producing their own applications, and we are designing the first experiment of the approach, focused on end users. For more details about WOA and demo videos, please visit the Web site of our project.

References

1. Díaz, O., Arellano, C.: The augmented web: rationales, opportunities, and challenges on browser-side transcoding. ACM Trans. Web 9(2), 8 (2015)
2. Ennals, R., Garofalakis, M.: Mashmaker: Mashups for the masses (demo paper). In: Proceedings of the 2007 ACM SIGMOD International Conference on Management of Data (2007)
3. Karger, D.R., Bakshi, K., Huynh, D., Quan, D., Sinha, V.: Haystack: a customizable general-purpose information management tool for end users of semistructured data. In: Proceedings of the CIDR Conference, January 2005
4. Ng, J.: The personal web: smart internet for me. In: Proceedings of the 2010 Conference of the Center for Advanced Studies on Collaborative Research, pp. 330–344, November 2010
5. Van Kleek, M., Moore, B., Karger, D.R., André, P.: Atomate it! End-user context-sensitive automation using heterogeneous information sources on the web. In: Proceedings of the 19th International Conference on World Wide Web, pp. 951–960. ACM, April 2010
6. Gamma, E., Helm, R., Johnson, R., Vlissides, J.: Design Patterns: Elements of Reusable Object-Oriented Software. Pearson Education, India (1994)

WeatherUSI: User-Based Weather Crowdsourcing on Public Displays

Evangelos Niforatos[✉], Ivan Elhart, and Marc Langheinrich

Università della Svizzera italiana, Via Giuseppe Buffi 13, 6900 Lugano, Switzerland
{evangelos.niforatos,ivan.elhart,marc.langheinrich}@usi.ch

Abstract. Contemporary public display systems hold a significant potential to contribute to in situ crowdsourcing. Recently, public display systems have surpassed their traditional role as static content projection hotspots by supporting interactivity and hosting applications that increase overall perceived user utility. As such, we developed WeatherUSI, a web-based interactive public display application that enables passers-by to input subjective information about current and future weather conditions. In this demo paper, we present the functionality of the app, describe the underlying system infrastructure and present how we combine input streams originating from WeatherUSI app on a public display together with its mobile app counterparts for facilitating user based weather crowdsourcing.

1 Introduction

Public display systems are increasingly becoming part of the urban landscape. Most public displays today are simple slide-show systems that broadcast content in the form of static images. However, public displays envisioned in the near future will not only integrate content from a number of different sources, but also serve as data collection stations. Indeed, research has shown that public displays may hold a significant potential in "crowdsourcing", when motivational design and feedback validation mechanisms are employed [2]. Crowdsourcing is a process where a large number of volunteer users contribute information through an online platform. A well-known example of crowd sourcing is Wikipedia.

Crowdsourcing has recently been gaining ground in mobile devices leveraging both their abundance and their increasingly available on-board sensors. Within this context we previously developed Atmos [5], a mobile app that collects both human and sensory weather related input, for providing highly localized weather information via a network of mobile devices. Collected input is clustered by location, processed and instilled back into the network of mobile devices. In order to increase the system's user base, along with the android and iOS counterparts, we recently designed a public display version of Atmos, called WeatherUSI and deployed it at University of Lugano (USI) [3]. With WeatherUSI we plan to explore how the act of weather crowdsourcing on public displays differs from the existing use of Atmos on mobile devices. In fact, we have found that humans can be somewhat accurate when they estimate current weather conditions and even when they perform short-term weather predictions, on a mobile

© Springer International Publishing Switzerland 2016
A. Bozzon et al. (Eds.): ICWE 2016, LNCS 9671, pp. 567–570, 2016.
DOI: 10.1007/978-3-319-38791-8_50

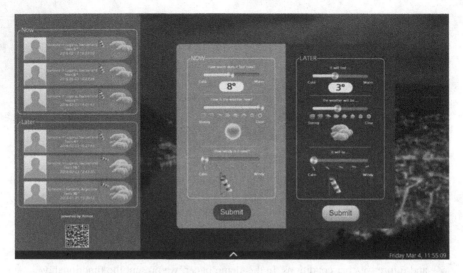

Fig. 1. The WeatherUSI app interface comprised of "NOW" panel for obtaining user input on current weather conditions (i.e. report) and "LATER" for future weather conditions (i.e. prediction), respectively. On the left part, global crowd updates are displayed, as they get collected.

device [4]. Apart from the data collected through the weather reporting interface, we also hope that the public nature of display systems will open up novel ways of studying crowdsourcing activities in situ through direct observations, an opportunity that is much more difficult in a mobile setting. Next, we present the app deployed on the University's public displays and showcase the underlying infrastructure.

2   The WeatherUSI Application

WeatherUSI app (see Fig. 1) encompasses a modern interface for obtaining user input about weather conditions. Passers-by can input how they are currently experiencing the weather and/or how they think it will develop in the short future, using a three bar layout. Similar to Atmos android and iOS mobile apps, the public display interface collects user generated information about current and future temperature (in °C), weather phenomena (e.g. sunny, stormy or cloudy) and wind intensity in a qualitative scale. After the user presses the submit button, all input is collected, processed and merged with data collected via the mobile app counterparts (i.e. Atmos android and iOS apps) and presented both in the WeatherUSI interface as well as, Atmos apps. Moreover, upon submitting a user weather report or prediction, the respective panel flips, displaying weather information downloaded from the Weather Underground API, allowing one to compare one's input with the measurement of a nearby weather station. This feature aims at increasing user participation through gamification, enabling to compare their accuracy in estimating current and future weather conditions with that of a ground meteorological station.

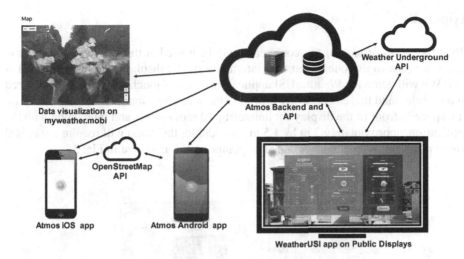

Fig. 2. Atmos Ecosystem comprised of Atmos android and iOS mobile apps and WeatherUSI public display app for aggregating user input. OpenStreetMap API is used for reverse geocoding, whereas Weather Underground API is used for obtaining ground truth for performing comparisons. Data visualization is available at myweather.mobi.

2.1 System Architecture

The WeatherUSI app is part of the broader "Atmos ecosystem" (see Fig. 2) for collecting both human (i.e. manual) and sensor (i.e. automated) generated weather information. Apart from user input, collected across all three versions of the apps, sensor input is also aggregated by the mobile apps, via polling any weather-related sensor (e.g. environmental pressure sensor) found on a mobile device. Ultimately, we envision Atmos ecosystem will offer a particular advantage for weather forecasting in places with microclimates, where current weather models prove insufficient. Atmos is entirely web-based architecture that combines Restful and WebSocket services.

Currently, we are deploying WeatherUSI on a interactive and multi-application public display at our university [1] and employing machine-learning algorithms for efficiently combining both human input and sensor data and generating our own hybrid weather models. WeatherUSI application uses WebSocket technology to communicate with the backend in order to increase the responsiveness of the data exchange to and from the display. Responsiveness of WeatherUSI application is very important as its interface immediately visualizes the reported weather data through the touch interface. Our approach utilizes the power of crowds, individually (mobile devices) and collectively (public displays), combining both explicit (human input) and implicit (automated sensor readings) sampling to significantly improve the accuracy of weather forecasting in areas with challenging climatic conditions.

Acknowledgments. The authors acknowledge the financial support of the Future and Emerging Technologies (FET) programme within the 7th Framework Programme for Research of the European Commission, under FET Grant Number: 612933.

Appendix

Since the demo session of the conference will be hosted at the University of Lugano (USI), we plan to use one of our four interactive public displays currently installed at USI. We will demo the WeatherUSI application on a 46" touch-enabled display placed on a mobile stand that can be easily moved to the demo location. The demo will require free space in front of the display for uninterrupted movements and interaction with the application, approximately 2 m by 1.5 m. In addition, the demo will require a standard power plug and Internet connection. The planned setup is shown in Fig. 3.

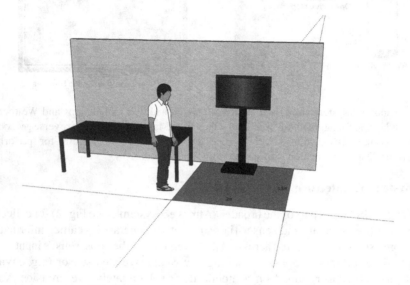

Fig. 3. Demo setup for WeatherUSI application.

References

1. Elhart, I., Langheinrich, M., Memarovic, N., Heikkinen, T.: Scheduling interactive and concurrently running applications in pervasive display networks. In: The International Symposium on Pervasive Displays. ACM (2014)
2. Goncalves, J., Ferreira, D., Hosio, S., et al.: Crowdsourcing on the spot: altruistic use of public displays, feasibility, performance, and behaviours, p. 753. ACM Press (2013). doi: 10.1145/2493432.2493481
3. Niforatos, E., Fouad, A., Ivan, E., Langheinrich, M.: WeatherUSI: crowdsourcing weather experience on public displays. In: The 4th ACM International Symposium on Pervasive Displays. ACM (2015)
4. Niforatos, E., Vourvopoulos, A., Langheinrich, M.: Weather with you: evaluating report reliability in weather crowdsourcing. In: The 14th International Conference on Mobile and Ubiquitous Multimedia (MUM 2015), pp. 152–162. ACM Press (2015). doi:10.1145/2836041.2836056
5. Niforatos, E., Vourvopoulos, A., Langheinrich, M., Campos, P., Doria, A.: Atmos: a hybrid crowdsourcing approach to weather estimation (poster abstract). In: Proceedings of the 2014 ACM International Joint Conference on Pervasive and Ubiquitous Computing: Adjunct Publication, pp. 135–138. ACM (2014). doi:10.1145/2638728.2638780

Discovering and Analyzing Alternative Treatments Hypothesis via Social Health Data

Paolo Cappellari[(✉)], Soon Ae Chun, and Dennis Shpits

City University of New York, New York, NY, USA
{paolo.cappellari,soon.chun,dennis.shpits}@csi.cuny.edu

Abstract. User-generated social health data can provide valuable information to extend the status of the medical knowledge. We present a tool geared towards social health data exploration and reasoning. Starting from a repository of semantically linked social health data, we enable researchers to discover alternative treatments as well as similar conditions by exploring the semantic repository via potentially compatible concepts. Researchers are prompted with the features of the concepts under investigation to analyze similarities and contradictions, when present. Concepts are enriched with confidence values that help researchers in assessing the reliability of the information they are analyzing.

Keywords: Social health data · Linked data · Data exploration

1   Introduction

With the growth of the web resources and social networks dedicated to health subjects, the web is becoming a huge repository of medical knowledge. While official medical records are the primary source of information, health data volunteered by patients provide a truthful description of how medical knowledge is applied in practice. For instance, the (controversial) practice of off-label drug use is all but uncommon: practitioners treat a condition using drugs not meant for such condition (thus off-label). The American Cancer Society acknowledges that cancer treatment often involves using certain chemotherapy drugs off-label[1].

One of the biggest challenges is to make sense of such a dispersed knowledge to help improve the general health of a population. With this work we want to facilitate the investigations of medical hypothesis against a knowledge base of semantically linked user generated health data. Specifically, we want to help practitioners discovering alternative, not yet known, treatments to a condition. Consider the following scenario: a medical researcher hypothesize that two conditions $C1$ and $C2$, unrelated in the current medical knowledge, have similar traits and, as a consequence, a treatment for condition $C1$ could be used to

---

[1] http://www.webmd.com/a-to-z-guides/features/off-label-drug-use-what-you-need-to-know.

© Springer International Publishing Switzerland 2016
A. Bozzon et al. (Eds.): ICWE 2016, LNCS 9671, pp. 571–575, 2016.
DOI: 10.1007/978-3-319-38791-8_51

treat condition $C2$. In other words, she wants to verify her hypothesis: whether a treatment $T1$ used to treat condition $C1$ can be used to treat condition $C2$, and whether or not the side-effects are compatible for a patient. She also wonders if there is any replacement (off-label) treatment $T2$ for the current treatment $T1$ for a condition $C1$, to alleviate a side-effect of $T1$.

Approach. The core idea in our approach is to enable users to reason on a medical hypothesis by comparing features of related concepts from the Linked Data of Social Health knowledge base. To illustrate our approach, let us consider the small excerpt from our RDF knowledge base in Fig. 1. The excerpt shows a few conditions (in rectangles) linked to a known set of treatments (rounded rectangles) that, in turn, are linked to a side-effects (ovals). Assuming a researcher wants to explore an alternative, not known, treatment to the *"Addison's disease,"* it make sense to start by analyzing treatments that have some commonality with it. In figure, condition *"Rheumatoid Arthritis"* share a treatment with *Addison's disease*, that is *"Predinisone."* One can speculate that *Rheumatoid Arthritis* and *Addison's disease* are somehow related. If so, one may wonder whether a treatment for the former, e.g. *"Leflunomide,"* could be used for the latter.

A researcher can start reasoning on such a hypothesis by comparing the features of the treatments in question, i.e. side-effects and purposes. The goal is to find evidence that denies or reinforces such notion of common traits by discovering contradictions or further commonalities. It is not our intention to provide medical recommendations: we want to enable medical researchers to discover alternative treatments by reasoning and analyzing case based evidence health practice from social data. Many works tackle the problem of assisting health practitioners for identifying off-label drug uses, ranging from machine learning [1] to artificial intelligence [2], to classification rules [3], and more.

2   Demonstration

Our inference tool relies on a RDF repository of semantically linked health data extracted from public sources, where equivalent entities have been identified and linked [4]. The core medical concepts in the knowledge base are: condition, treatment, purpose, symptom, and side-effect. We also have aggregate data on treatment usages as reported by patients, which we use to provide users with a confidence value for the visualized information.

The demonstration shows the scenario of a researcher exploring alternative treatments for condition the *MODY* (Maturity onset diabetes of the young). The following functionality (in bold) are demonstrated.

Search Treatments. In Fig. 2, the user searchers for *MODY* by using the search box in the top left-most panels. All known treatments for *MODY*, that is *"Glipizide"* and *"Glyburide,"* are shown in the panel below the search box.

Related Conditions and Treatments. The user selects *Glipzide* in the bottom left-most panel, see Fig. 2, to obtain the list of conditions and treatments related to it. She founds one related condition, *"Diabetes Type 2,"* and multiple treatments, *"Glimepiride"* etc. These can be regarded as conditions and treatments potentially compatible to *MODY* and *Glipizide*.

Ranked List of Treatments. Above lists can be ranked by number of patients' report or by the number of purposes in common, so to show most reliable/promising information at the top.

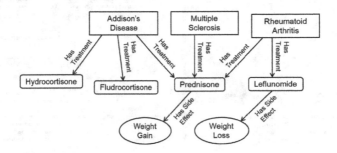

Fig. 1. Excerpt of the semantic health knowledge base.

Comparison of Treatments. The user wants to investigate *Glimepiride* as an alternative treatment to *Glipizide*. Upon selecting the two treatments on the GUI, the user is prompted with all information about these treatments and can start a comparison analysis, see four right-most panes in Fig. 2. The top two panels show the list of side-effects; the bottom two display the list of purposes. The user can reason on what information could be in support of or against

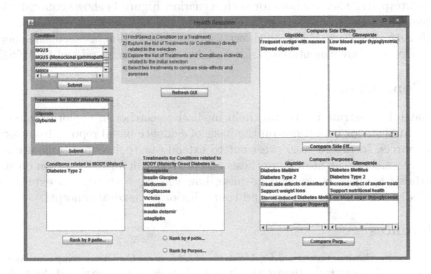

Fig. 2. Related treatments with contradiction in purposes.

the compatibility of the two treatments. In this case, there are two purposes in opposition: "*Elevated blood sugar*" for *Glipizide*, and "*Low blood sugar*" for *Glimepiride*. This can be regarded as a contradicting information, in the sense that the objectives of the two treatments were conceived with different traits. The researcher may want to backtrack her exploration to pursue other paths.

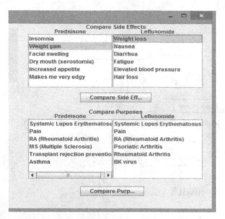 

(a) Contradiction between side-effects.   (b) Cross-contradiction between side-effects and purposes.

Fig. 3. Examples of contradictions between side-effects and purposes.

We plan to show further scenarios where conflicts are raised between side-effects or between the purposes of one and the side-effects of the other. Figure 3 show two (partial) screenshots for such scenarios. Figure 3a shows contradiction between side-effects for treatments *Prednisone* and *Leflunomide*, related to condition *Addison's disease*; Fig. 3b shows a cross-contradiction between side-effects and purposes of treatments *Glipizide* and *Insuline Glargine*, related to *MODY*.

3   Conclusion

We have demonstrated a tool to help medical researcher in exploring alternative treatments for conditions on the basis of evidence based reports from social data sources. In future work we want to extend our tool with a semantic reasoner: researchers can state hypothesis and the tool can formally reason on such hypothesis against the knowledge base; however, we first need to extend the knowledge base with coherency and contradiction of medical concepts.

References

1. Alonso, F., Caraça-Valente, J.P., Martínez, L., Montes, C.: Discovering similar patterns for characterizing time series in a medical domain. Knowl. Inf. Syst. 5(2), 183–200 (2003). http://dx.doi.org/10.1007/10.1007/s10115-003-0098-5

2. Becerra-Fernandez, I.: The role of artificial intelligence technologies in the implementation of people-finder knowledge management systems (2000)
3. Freitas, A.A.: A survey of evolutionary algorithms for data mining and knowledge discovery. Advances in Evolutionary Computing, pp. 819–845. Springer-Verlag New York Inc, New York (2003)
4. Ji, X., Cappellari, P., Chun, S.A., Geller, J.: Linking and using social media data for enhancing public health analytics. J. Inf. Sci. $\mathbf{I}(25)$ (2016)

Towards Handling Constraint Network Conditions Between WoT Entities Using Conflict-Free Anti-Entropy Communication

Markus Ast[✉] and Martin Gaedke

Technische Universität Chemnitz, Chemnitz, Germany
{markus.ast,martin.gaedke}@informatik.tu-chemnitz.de

Abstract. Deploying and composing Web of Things entities in scenarios where connections are subject to network constraints, like disconnected operations, intermittent connections or limited bandwidth, requires handling changing network conditions properly. Therefore, this work proposes to utilize both eventual consistent data structures and corresponding eventual consistent communication for such scenarios. This enables composition and collaboration of WoT entities in network constraint scenarios.

Keywords: Web of Things · Distributed systems · Network constraints

1 Introduction

The emerging field and availability of Web of Things (WoT), results in the need for making such things, e.g. devices, sensors, etc., available for all kinds of scenarios. When composing WoT entities together, one challenge that arises, are network constraints that disrupt communication with or between them. Such network constraints can be (1) disconnected operations so that there is no connection at all for a long period of time, (2) intermittent connections where recurring loses of connection happen at irregular intervals, and (3) limited bandwidth in terms of having a slow connection.

Taking these network constraints into account, connections between WoT entities could be considered irregular and loosely. To still allow for composition and therefore for collaboration of WoT entities, this work provides an experimental approach that ensures eventual communication of WoT entities using conflict-free replicated data types that are distributed using anti-entropy communication.

This work is thereby about all scenarios of WoT entities collaborating together under changing network conditions. When being connected wirelessly, network constraints can be due to natural reasons, e.g. mountainous regions where changes in weather conditions easily affect network quality, or due to catastrophic events. Furthermore, entities like sensors can also be deployed out of reach and therefore rely on being connected manually, e.g. research sensors inside caves.

© Springer International Publishing Switzerland 2016
A. Bozzon et al. (Eds.): ICWE 2016, LNCS 9671, pp. 576–580, 2016.
DOI: 10.1007/978-3-319-38791-8_52

The rest of this paper is organized as follows: at first, in Sect. 2, an analysis is conducted and used technologies is introduced accordingly. Afterwards, an overview of the approach is given in Sect. 3. Finally, related work is summarized in Sect. 4, and a conclusion is given in Sect. 5.

2 Analysis

Let $V = \{e_0, e_1, ...\}$ be a set of composed WoT entities. Each entity has a set of peers P, where $P \subseteq V$. Consider these entities as a graph $G = (V, E)$, where E is the set of edges that indicate an available connection for communication between two entities. The resulting graph is neither guaranteed to be connected completely nor guaranteed to be connected at all. However, the graph is being considered to be connected eventually, since it is only disconnected because one or more of its connections are not available for a finite amount of time. Consequentially, the graph is only disconnected for a finite amount of time, too.

According to the CAP theorem [1], a distributed system can only have two of the following three properties at the same time: consistency, availability and partition-tolerance. In the described scenario, WoT entities have to work well, despite possible partitions of the network. Since partitions are not guaranteed to be resolved within a reasonable short amount of time and since achieving consistency requires communication, pursuing the property of consistency would lead to unresponsive WoT entities. This would in return lead to bad user experience or even stagnate important functionalities. That is, according to the CAP theorem, trade-offs will be made in consistency instead of in availability.

With achieving both availability and partition-tolerance the systems ends up being *eventual consistent*. *Eventual consistency* is "simply an acknowledgement that there is an unbounded delay in propagating a change made on one machine to all the other copies" [4]. That is, each operation will be eventually be applied to all entities. This requires a total global order using something like vector clocks [3]. However, changes between entities are potentially communicated in different order—compared to their initial occurrence. Therefore, the property of *eventual consistency* can be extended with the even stronger condition of *strong convergence*: "correct replicas that have delivered the same updates have equivalent state" [7]. With this so called strong *eventual consistency*, there are no roll backs necessary to resolve conflicts with updates in different orders.

Strong eventual consistency is provided by using *Conflict-free Replicated Data Types* (CRDT). CRDTs are data types "for which some simple mathematical properties ensure eventual consistency" [7]. A simple example for such a CRDT would be a replicated counter, "which converges because the increment and decrement operations commute (assuming no overflow)" [6]. With CRDT, updates do not require synchronization, they can rather be executed immediately when being received. They are both scalable and fault-tolerant and most data structures are reasonable easy to implement.

A way of replicating state with weak consistency requirements, are anti-entropy protocols - or also called gossip protocols. Anti-entropy protocols work, simply put, as follows. An entity $p \in V$ periodically selects a peer $q \in P_p$. Then, p either pushes its state to q or sends a digest (only keys and version numbers of its data) to q to retrieve only the necessary updates from q afterwards. To not create a huge backlog of unsynchronized pending state updates and to keep the network usage minimal to tackle the constraint of limited bandwidth, the *Scuttlebutt Reconciliation* [5] is used.

For providing each entity with information about the current network state, a failure detector is required. Treating failure information as a state that is synchronized with all other entities allows for providing each entity with information of the overall network. This allows entities to know about the state of other entities even though they may not have a direct connection to them on their own.

Traditionally, failure detection is boolean only: a node is either available or not. However, this does not work well with changing network conditions. That is, an adaptive failure detector that allows for adapting its predictions according to changing network conditions is necessary. This allows each entity to make its own predictions about the network, taking its entity-specific requirements and constraints into account. To provide such an adaptive failure detector, that provides a scale of confidence rather than a boolean value, the Φ *Accrual Failure Detector* [2] is used. This failure detector is easily integrated into the gossip communication. Each state replication reports its timestamp to the *Accrual Failure Detector*, which keeps a sampling window of previous reports to adapt its estimation for the next report accordingly.

3   Approach

Resulting from the analysis, our approach for tackling network constraint WoT entities combines conflict-free replicated data types with gossip protocol communication and integrates the *Accrual Failure Detector* for failure detection. This yields an eventual consistent system and therefore allows for being very tolerant to changing network conditions. This enables deployment of WoT entities in network constraint scenarios.

The interaction between these introduced components works as follows. Each entity acts as a replicated state machine. States are based on CRDT data structures. Periodically, each node selects another peer in the network randomly. This selection, however, favors peers that appear to be accessible above peers that appear to be inaccessible. The entity's knowledge about the accessibility is provided by employing the *Accrual Failure Detector*. Each incoming request or response from a peer is reported to the failure detector to maintain its sampling window and make predictions about its accessibility accordingly. Additionally, reports from other entities and the accessibility to other network participants from their point of view are integrated as well.

Upon peer selection, state between both connected entities is synchronized using *Scuttlebutt Reconciliation*. Doing so, and employing proper flow control, allows for efficient usage of network bandwidth. That is, the communication scales for both high and low bandwidth availability. The usage of the *Accrual Failure Detector* thereby adds the possibility to give each entity its own local view of the overall network. Having a probability scale of each entities connectivity state, allows each entity to adapt its own response or functionality accordingly, e.g., notify on the entity working users immediately about connection changes, or reduce gossip rate according to the received prediction.

4   Related Work

Replicating state in distributed systems is often done using consensus algorithms. That is, data types like CRDTs are not required. However, on each node disconnect, the selection of a new master may be required and synchronization during network partitions can lead to conflicts.

With Riak 2.0, CRDT found their way into distributed databases recently[1]. Riak also uses a gossip protocol to communicate ring state and bucket properties across its cluster. However, these are only parts of Riak and Riak itself is not targeted towards the described scenarios.

That is, the application of CRDTs and gossip protocol communication for WoT entities is not widely experimented with, yet. Since it should apply to minimal hardware, like sensors, too, it also yields new challenges for CRDT and gossip protocol approaches, like partial state synchronization.

5   Conclusion

This paper introduced an experimental approach for handling constraint network conditions between WoT entities by employing CRDT data types that are replicated using gossip protocol communication. With this approach, connected WoT entities are less prone to network failures or constraint network conditions.

While first experiments yielded promising results, there is still a huge potential for succeeding experiments and other future work, like allowing for partial state replication. Partial state replication will be a crucial part, because simple sensors to not need to have the whole state of other entities locally. For them, it is probably enough to replicate their own state and state related to remote configurations.

Acknowledgement. The authors gratefully acknowledge funding by the DFG (GRK 1780/1).

---

[1] https://docs.basho.com/riak/2.0.1/dev/using/data-types/.

References

1. Gilbert, S., Lynch, N.A.: Brewer's conjecture and the feasibility of consistent, available, partition-tolerant web services. SIGACT News **33**(2), 51–59 (2002)
2. Hayashibara, N., Défago, X., Yared, R., Katayama, T.: The Φ accrual failure detector. In: Proceedings of the 23rd IEEE International Symposium on Reliable Distributed Systems, pp. 66–78. IEEE (2004)
3. Lamport, L.: Time, clocks, and the ordering of events in a distributed system. Commun. ACM **21**(7), 558–565 (1978)
4. Oracle: De-mystifying "eventual consistency" in distributed systems, June 2012
5. van Renesse, R., Dumitriu, D., Gough, V., Thomas, C.: Efficient Reconciliation and Flow Control for Anti-Entropy Protocols (2008)
6. Shapiro, M., Preguiça, N., Baquero, C., Zawirski, M.: A comprehensive study of Convergent and Commutative Replicated Data Types, p. 50, January 2011
7. Shapiro, M., Preguiça, N., Baquero, C., Zawirski, M.: Conflict-free Replicated Data Types, July 2011

Poster Papers

RESTful Conversation with RESTalk

The Use Case of Doodle

Ana Ivanchikj[(✉)]

Faculty of Informatics, University of Lugano (USI), Lugano, Switzerland
ana.ivanchikj@usi.ch

Abstract. With the availability of multiple Web services, offering identical or similar utilities, their ease of use has become a valuable success factor, highly influenced by API's documentation quality. Tools are available for documenting the various technical details pertaining to the static structure of RESTful services. Additionally, we have identified interest in and usefulness of also depicting API's behaviour, i.e., the viable RESTful conversations defined as multiple client-server interactions necessary to utilize certain service functionality. RESTalk, the REST domain specific language we have designed for modeling RESTful conversations, facilitates the conceptual modeling and visualisation of API's behaviour. In this poster paper, we extend RESTalk with new language constructs and apply it on a real RESTful API, the Doodle API, which refers to RESTful conversations between multiple clients and one server.

Keywords: RESTful web services · Multiparty conversations · Domain Specific Language · Real API · Use case · Doodle

1 Introduction

The idea behind the Representational State Transfer (REST) architectural style is to introduce simplicity through constraints and standardization. This has inevitably brought about its popularity, with an ever-growing number of Web Application Program Interfaces (APIs) declaring REST compliance. While the awareness for the need of documenting the low-level HTTP details of REST API's static structure has resulted with several tools, such as RAML or Swagger[1], there is still a lack of support for conceptual modeling and visualisation of REST API's dynamics. Reaching a certain resource state, frequently requires undertaking a predefined sequence of interactions or choosing among different alternative paths, thus shifting from the concept of a single RESTful interaction to the concept of a RESTful conversation [1]. As conversations become more complex, visualising them can help decrease the cognitive load of API designers, who need to communicate their design to the developers, or of API clients, who need to use the API. Currently, mainly UML Sequence Diagrams or UML State Machines are used to model API's behaviour. However, they lack the ability

---

[1] http://raml.org; http://swagger.io.

© Springer International Publishing Switzerland 2016
A. Bozzon et al. (Eds.): ICWE 2016, LNCS 9671, pp. 583–587, 2016.
DOI: 10.1007/978-3-319-38791-8_53

of concisely presenting important REST tenets, such as HTTP methods, URIs, headers, hypermedia flow, status codes, etc.

Therefore, in [2] we have proposed the first version of RESTalk, a Domain Specific Language (DSL) for modeling RESTful conversations. In [3] we have conducted an exploratory survey, among practitioners and researchers, to obtain initial feedback on its cognitive characteristics, and its perceived usefulness. In this poster paper, based on the survey feedback, we extend RESTalk with additional language constructs to support modelling of multiple participants in the conversation and their roles, as well as to present resource state transitions, and asynchronous email communication. We use this extended version of RESTalk to model the behaviour of Doodle, a well known scheduling Web service[2] which depicts RESTful conversations between multiple clients and one server.

2   RESTalk

To model RESTful interactions, Nikaj and Weske [4] add REST-specific annotations to the Choreography diagram of the Business Process Model and Notation (BPMN) 2.0 standard. With RESTalk we go further and modify the standard notation in order to visually draw the attention to what is essential in RESTful interactions, i.e., the content of the exchanged messages.

The results from the above mentioned exploratory survey [3], have revealed missing constructs in RESTalk for depicting: 1) roles of the conversation participants, when viable interactions depend on such roles; 2) multiparty conversations where multiple clients interact with the server; 3) client-server interactions which lead to changes in the related resource's state; and 4) asynchronous interaction through email notifications sent to participants. Thus, in this poster paper, we propose a way to extend RESTalk to represent such important details. Figure 1 shows a summary of all the language constructs relevant to the Doodle use case which we will describe in Sect. 3. The semantics of the existing RESTalk constructs, i.e., the ones not added to the language with this poster paper, are explained in detail in [2].

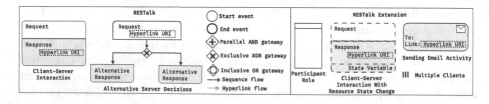

Fig. 1. RESTalk Constructs

---

[2] http://doodle.com.

3   The Doodle Use Case

To show-case the appropriateness of RESTalk for documenting real RESTful APIs, we have decided to use it to model Doodle's API. Doodle's basic free offering is a Web service which facilitates event scheduling between multiple participants. We have opted for modeling this basic service, where no log-in is required. Due to the lack of detailed API documentation[3], we have used a prescriptive instead of descriptive approach in modeling its dynamics.

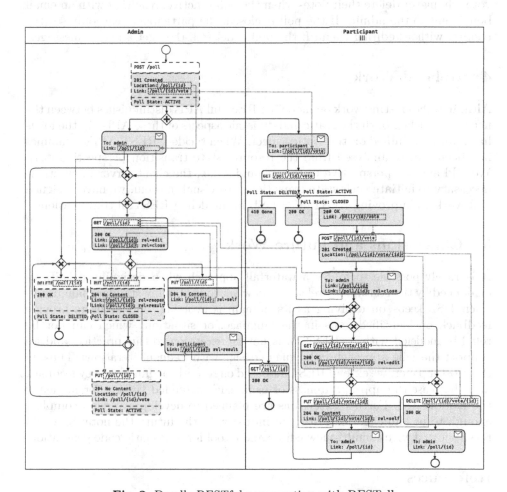

Fig. 2. Doodle RESTful conversation with RESTalk

Following is the natural language description of the conversation modelled in Fig. 2. The client can take two distinct roles leading to different privileges. The admin role, assigned to the client who has created the poll, and the participant

---

[3] http://support.doodle.com/customer/en/portal/articles/664212.

role, assigned to the clients who are invited to participate in the poll. After the admin creates the poll, emails are sent to the admin, with a link to the poll resource, and to all participants, with a link to the poll voting resource. The poll can have three states: active, closed, or deleted. The interaction which results with entering in a certain state is marked with a dashed line and the state variable is noted under the response box. The admin can edit, close or delete the poll at any time, as well as reactivate it if closed. When the poll is closed, an email notification may be sent to the participants. The participants can only vote, change or delete their votes when the poll is active, resulting with an email being sent to the admin. If the poll is closed, the participants can only see the results, without editing them. If the poll is deleted, they get an error message.

4   Related Work

Although the existing work on modeling RESTful APIs distinguishes between the need of modeling both the static and dynamic aspects of these APIs [5], the focus has mainly remained on the static aspect. When tackled, REST API's dynamics has been mostly analysed from the resource state transition perspective [6,7]. We add another perspective to the dynamics, i.e., the client-server interactions necessary to initiate such state transitions. To visualise them, we have designed and work on improving RESTalk, a DSL for modeling RESTful conversations.

5   Conclusions and Future Work

It is rarely possible to follow a waterfall approach when designing a DSL, as evidenced by the continuous release of new versions of many standard languages. Each DSL keeps on evolving as its domain is evolving, and as users provide feedback on identified gaps in the language, or situations which can not be reliably modeled with it. RESTalk is not an exception to this practice, and we support the agile approach in language design with frequent iterations. Thus, in this poster paper, we extend RESTalk based on recently acquired survey feedback and showcase the appropriateness of using such extended version for modeling the Doodle API. Further extensions are planned to develop a version complete enough to be launched for testing in industry. In the future the notation could be supported with a multi-view editor and a tool for automatic code generation.

References

1. Haupt, F., Leymann, F., Pautasso, C.: A conversation based approach for modeling REST APIs. In: Proceedings of the 12th WICSA 2015, Montreal, Canada, pp. 165–174 (2015)
2. Pautasso, C., Ivanchikj, A., Schreier, S.: Modeling RESTful conversations with extended BPMN choreography diagrams. In: Weyns, D., et al. (eds.) ECSA 2015. LNCS, vol. 9278, pp. 87–94. Springer, Heidelberg (2015). doi:10.1007/978-3-319-23727-5_7

3. Ivanchikj, A., Pautasso, C., Schreier, S.: Visual modeling of RESTful conversations with RESTalk: an exploratory survey. J. Softw. Syst. Model. (2016, Under review)
4. Nikaj, A., Weske, M.: Formal specification of RESTful choreography properties. In: Proceedings of the ICWE 2016, Springer (2016) (to Appear)
5. Schreier, S.: Modeling RESTful applications. In: Proceedings of the Second International Workshop on RESTful Design, pp. 15–21. ACM (2011)
6. Rauf, I.: Design and validation of stateful composite RESTful web services. Ph.D.thesis, Turku Centre for Computer Science (2014)
7. Mitra, R.: Rapido: A sketching tool for web API designers. In: Proceedings of the 24th WWW 2015, Florence, Italy, pp. 1509–1514 (2015)

Supporting Personalization in Legacy Web Sites Through Client-Side Adaptation

Jesús López Miján[1], Irene Garrigós[1(✉)], and Sergio Firmenich[2,3,4]

[1] WaKe Research, I.U. Investigación Informática, University of Alicante, Alicante, Spain
jlm76@alu.ua.es, igarrigos@dlsi.ua.es
[2] LINVI, Universidad Nacional de la Patagonia San Juan Bosco, Puerto Madryn, Argentina
sergio.firmenich@lifia.info.unlp.edu.ar
[3] LIFIA, Universidad Nacional de La Plata, La Plata, Argentina
[4] CONICET Argentina, Buenos Aires, Argentina

Abstract. Immersed in social and mobile Web, users are expecting personalized browsing experiences, based on their needs, goals, and preferences. However, adding personalization to an existing Web site is not a simple task for Web owners who are not personalization experts. Most of the existing personalization approaches imply extending the backend application or paying for a *personalization as a service* solution, which are more focused on improving conversion rates than on improving the user browsing experience. In this work we present a methodology to add client-based personalization to an existing Web site oriented to non-developer designers or Web sites owners. This approach allows them to define a set of personalization rules to be applied in the client-side with minimum alterations on the backend application.

1 Introduction

Nowadays, immersed in the social and mobile Web, users are expecting a personalized browsing experience, which adapts to their needs, goals, and preferences. This is especially important in those sites where personalization is a crucial factor and the fidelity of the user should be maintained and improved. However, adding personalization to an existing Web site is not a simple task, in fact, the cost associated to provide personalization (either by designing and implementing one or paying for PaaS - Personalization as a Service - products) could be one of the reasons behind the fact that vast Web sites do not offer any form of personalization.

From the academy, personalization was tackled from several points of views. The design of user profiles and recommendation systems were strong contributions to the field, but they require developing complex software components on the backend. In the context of model driven, there are several approaches for creating a personalized Web site from scratch [1, 3, 4]. Reverse engineering techniques [5] also allow us extracting the models from an existing Web (originally created with no models) and then applying one of these model-driven approaches to add personalization support. However, the owner of the Web site is most of the times a non-expert user, who is not knowledgeable about models and depend on others to implement this kind of solution. In this work, we present an approach for allowing Web site owners to

© Springer International Publishing Switzerland 2016
A. Bozzon et al. (Eds.): ICWE 2016, LNCS 9671, pp. 588–592, 2016.
DOI: 10.1007/978-3-319-38791-8_54

include personalization artefacts defined without requiring either advanced programming skills or advanced configuration. For this purpose, our contribution is a personalization framework, which provides them with a way of defining a personalization component to be injected in the final Web site. This component is formed by a set of ECA (event-condition-action) personalization rules that will act over certain parts of the DOM of the site. For building these rules we have considered the PRML (Personalization Rules Modelling Language) [3] set of events and actions. However, the approach proposes a rule-based generic engine that let us adding new kind of personalization effects.

The outline of the paper is as follows. Section 2 introduces our approach from a conceptual point of view illustrated by a simple case study. Section 3 shows the implementation details, and finally, in Sect. 4 we discuss about the strength of the approach and present future work.

2 Personalization Support in Legacy Web Systems

In this section we present our personalization framework with the aim of giving support to non-expert users (our target are owners/designers of Web sites) in defining personalization strategies in a legacy Web system.

In Fig. 1 we can see the overall process and architecture of the framework. For demonstration purposes we have used the framework to add personalization to an existing Web site: "*La Guia X*" (http://www.laguiax.com.ar/), which is a shop guide of La Plata city. We describe the process next.

In order to define the elements of the Web site over which we are going to define a personalization strategy, the first step needed is the annotation of the Web site (i.e. we define the parts of the DOM where a personalization action can be defined). This step is driven by the designer/owner (using a visual tool). The framework's extension implemented for the case study (which is shown in the following section) includes personalization strategies that act over the navigation. However, other kind of personalization strategies may be added. In the case study we considered two elements to annotate *La Guia X*: links and menus (e.g. set of links), as Fig. 2 shows. The different Web pages are also annotated with an *id* in order to refer to them in the personalization rules.

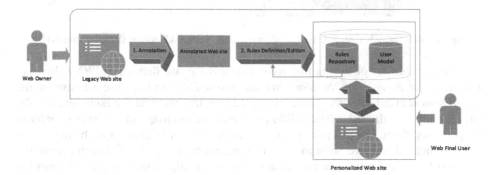

Fig. 1. Personalization framework overview

Fig. 2. Case study - http://www.laguiax.com.ar/: annotation

Once the Web site has been annotated, the next step is defining the personalization strategies to be applied. The strategies are defined as ECA (event-condition-action) rules considering the PRML language set of events and actions [3], as Fig. 3 shows. In this example, we want to sort the set of links with *id* = *"Rubros"*, the personalization strategy we want to define is: "sort the set of links by use, where the most used links are on the top of the list". For this purpose, we select the action "SortLink". Once selected, we have to define the event and condition for applying this action.

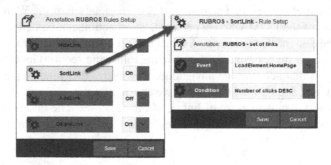

Fig. 3. Rules attached to annotation "Rubros" and "SortLink" personalization rule details

The possible set of events that we consider is the one defined in PRML lite (i.e. *LoadElement, Navigation, SessionStart and SessionEnd*). In this case we have set the *LoadElement* event over the home page, so every time we load the home page of the site the rule is evaluated. The condition will evaluate the usage of the links in order to properly sort them. For this purpose, we check the number of clicks done by the user of every annotated link we want to sort. This information is stored for each user in the client-side (i.e. in the local storage of the browser). An algorithm compares the number of clicks sorting them in descending way.

As we explain in the following section, the defined rules are stored in a script, which is integrated in the Web site. Although in this paper we have implemented the PRML set of events and actions, new rules can be easily added. In spite of the concrete rules, the main contribution is a little architecture for adding personalization in legacy Web sites, which are not maintained by developer teams, but still could improve the user experience with adaptation mechanisms.

3 Implementation

The implementation of our approach is composed by two components. The first one is an authoring tool (based on visual programming) that allows Web site owners to annotate and define the rules, and a rules engine that must be embedded in the Web site in order to execute the rules when a Web page is loaded on the client-side.

The authoring tool is implemented using a client-side plugin that allow Web owners/ designers to create and edit the rules. It is implemented with common client-side Web technologies such as JavaScript, HTML5 and CSS. At the end of the definition process, this tool produces a minimized JavaScript artefact with the specification of the personalization strategy. These specifications should be added to the Web site (just by adding the JavaScript file in those Web pages where the personalization will work). Once added these specifications together with the rule engine JavaScript library, the personalization effects can be performed on the client-side. In this way, any end-user who visits the Web site has the new mechanism available.

4 Conclusions and Future Work

Personalization is a powerful mechanism to improve the user experience, but it is not broadly implemented in other domains than e-commerce. However, users are really interested on making adaptive the Web sites they use as shown by some trends such as Web Augmentation, even more, they can do it with end-user programming tools [2]. However, this kind of tools do not reach the whole amount of Web site visitors and do not allow Web owners taking advantage of tracking the user behavior. In this work, we use client-side adaptation to provide Web site owners with a framework for adding personalization rules to their Web site with minimum efforts and little technical knowledge. Then the rules are added to the Web site and consequently available for every visitor. As future work, we will work on an assisted annotation tool for abstracting DOM elements into business domain objects, which will allow to define more complex personalization effects such as item recommendations, etc. We are currently developing a server-side component for sharing data among devices, which also will allow deploying our approach as a third-party application included on the Web sites, in the same way than common social widgets or analytics. Moreover, we plan to do usability tests in order to improve the Web owners experience.

References

1. De Troyer, O., Casteleyn, S., Plessers, P.: WSDM: web semantics design method. In: Rossi, G., Pastor, O., Schwabe, D., Olsina, L. (eds.) Web Engineering, pp. 303–351. Springer, London (2008)
2. Díaz, O., Arellano, C., Aldalur, I., Medina, H., Firmenich, S.: End-user browser-side modification of web pages. In: Benatallah, B., Bestavros, A., Manolopoulos, Y., Vakali, A., Zhang, Y. (eds.) WISE 2014, Part I. LNCS, vol. 8786, pp. 293–307. Springer, Heidelberg (2014)
3. Garrigós, I., Gómez, J., Houben, G.-J.: Specification of personalization in web application design. Inf. Softw. Technol. **52**(9), 991–1010 (2010)
4. Koch, N., Kraus, A., Zhang, G., Baumeister, H.: UML-based web engineering - an approach based on standards. In: Rossi, G., Pastor, O., Schwabe, D., Olsina, L. (eds.) Web Engineering, pp. 157–191. Springer, London (2008)
5. Martin, A., Cechich, A.: A model-driven reengineering approach to web site personalization. In: Proceedings of the Third Latin American Web Congress, LAWEB, p. 14. IEEE Computer Society, Washington, DC (2005)

A Lightweight Semi-automated Acceptance Test-Driven Development Approach for Web Applications

Diego Clerissi, Maurizio Leotta[✉], Gianna Reggio, and Filippo Ricca

DIBRIS, Università di Genova, Genova, Italy
diego.clerissi@dibris.unige.it,
{maurizio.leotta,gianna.reggio,filippo.ricca}@unige.it

Abstract. Applying Acceptance Test Driven Development (ATDD) in the context of web applications is a difficult task due to the intricateness of existing tools/frameworks and, more in general, of the proposed approaches. In this work, we present a simple approach for developing web applications in ATDD mode, based on the usage of Screen Mockups and Selenium IDE.

1 Introduction

The emerging relevance of web-based software in everyday human activities arises the need for effective development approaches helping developers in the realization of high quality products. It is well-known that web applications are prone to frequent changes due to customers' requests and requirements evolution. In this context, agile approaches are considered appropriate for web application development.

Acceptance Test Driven Development [2] (from now, ATDD) is a cornerstone practice that puts acceptance testing on top of the software development process and focuses on the communication among customers and software professionals, such as business analysts and software testers.

Even if ATDD is often tool assisted [1], its usage in the context of web applications is still a problematic task, since the available web testing tools often require the presence of the application itself and the knowledge of technical details related to the used programming languages and frameworks. As a result, a non-trivial manual intervention to convert acceptance test cases into executable test scripts is required (i.e. it is very difficult to define web test scripts before implementing the web application).

In this work, we propose a lightweight semi-automatic approach that, starting from textual requirements and screen mockups, is able to generate executable Selenium IDE[1] functional test scripts (i.e. black box tests able to validate a web application by testing its functionalities), which in turn drive the development of web applications.

---

[1] http://www.seleniumhq.org/projects/ide/.

© Springer International Publishing Switzerland 2016
A. Bozzon et al. (Eds.): ICWE 2016, LNCS 9671, pp. 593–597, 2016.
DOI: 10.1007/978-3-319-38791-8_55

2   ATDD in the Context of Web Applications

ATDD is an agile development practice adopting the strategy of TDD, where test scripts are defined before software implementation and used as acceptance criteria for validating it through business objectives. However, ATDD is not limited to agile contexts where requirements can be expressed with user stories (i.e. descriptions consisting of one or more short sentences). Indeed, even more formal requirements specifications based on well-structured use cases [8,9] can be used with the ATDD practice. Usually, in these cases, acceptance tests are defined by following the scenarios composing the use cases.

A large number of ATDD tools usable in the web applications context emerged in the last years. For instance, Fitnium[2], an integration of FitNesse[3] (where test cases can be represented in a tabular form by using the natural language), and Selenium IDE (a Firefox plug-in that allows to record, edit, and execute web test scripts). Some other tools require a different template for acceptance test cases (like, e.g., the "given-when-then" template of Cucumber[4]) or a freely HTML format which is later enriched by tags to interpret the text and execute it (as for Concordion[5]). Unfortunately, in all these tools, the connections between test cases and web application under development (i.e. the so-called fixtures) have to be written by the developer. Besson et al. [1] are among the first researchers to describe an ATDD approach for web applications trying to overcome this burdensome activity. In that work, a web application is modelled with a graph of pages and the paths of the given graph are the test cases, which must be validated by the customer and subsequently transformed into test scripts. Conversely to Besson et al., our approach does not require the web application modelling phase, which is substituted by a simpler recording phase of user actions by means of Selenium IDE executed upon the previously produced screen mockups.

3   The Approach

The approach we propose in this work is based on the following tasks (see Fig. 1):

Requirements Analysis aims at producing the requirements specification for the web application under development. It includes the following subtasks: (1) gathering the requirements from future users, customers and other stakeholders, (2) determining whether the requirements are complete, consistent, and unambiguous, (3) writing the requirements specification as use cases or user stories depending on whether, respectively, a more prescriptive or more agile development approach is adopted.

---

[2] https://fitnium.wordpress.com/.
[3] http://www.fitnesse.org/.
[4] http://cucumber.io/.
[5] http://concordion.org/.

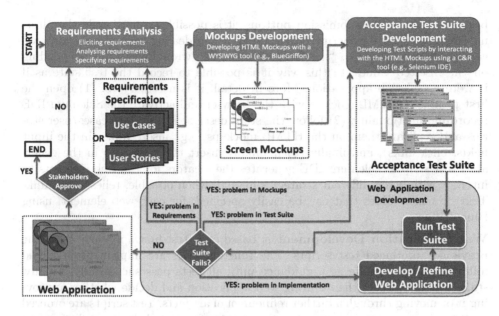

Fig. 1. From the requirements analysis to the web application development

Mockups Development aims at creating a set of screen mockups used for prototyping the user interface of the web application to develop [3,7]. In order to reduce as much as possible the need of manual intervention required to run the automated acceptance test scripts on the web application under development, the mockups have to represent quite accurately - from a functional point of view - the interfaces of the web application (e.g., all the web elements of the web pages to interact with must be shown in the mockups while the layout or the styles can be just sketched). To produce the mockups, it is possible to follow the method described by Reggio et al. [8] helping in capturing and writing requirements specifications enriched with screen mockups. Since we chose to adopt the state of the practice web testing tool Selenium IDE, mockups can be quickly developed in HTML using a WYSIWYG content editor for web pages such as BlueGriffon[6]. Adopting a capture-replay DOM-based [5] tool like Selenium IDE allows to pay little attention to the mockups graphical aspect and focus on the user interaction, with clear advantages in terms of effort required for creating the test scripts [4]; for this reason we avoid to adopt both visual or programmable [5] web testing tools, such as Sikuli[7] or Selenium WebDriver[8] respectively.

Acceptance Test Suite Development. Once the mockups are available it is possible to record the test suite by interacting with them. To make this task easier we suggest to implement the links among the web pages and the submission

---

[6] http://www.bluegriffon.org/.

[7] http://www.sikuli.org/.

[8] http://www.seleniumhq.org/projects/webdriver/.

buttons. Concerning submission buttons, it is possible to hard-code the alternative links using JavaScript; for instance, when dealing with a login form we can reach two mockups, "homePage.html" and "wrongPage.html", depending on the inserted values. In this way it is possible to record the test suite as if it were a real web application. More in detail, it is necessary to: (1) open the first produced HTML mockup with the browser and activate the Selenium IDE recording functionality, (2) follow the steps described in the use cases/user stories and replicate them on the HTML mockups (e.g., insert values in the input fields, click links), and finally (3) manually insert the assertions in the generated test scripts. Selenium IDE generates the locators for the web elements to interact with using different strategies [6] and, when possible, relies on id, link-Text or name values that can be easily specified, for each web element, using BlueGriffon.

Web Application Development is based on a test-first approach using the previously produced test scripts. The functionalities are implemented/refined following the test suite as a guidance until all tests pass successfully. Finally, stakeholders evaluate the resulting web application and decide whether approving it or moving through a further refinement of artifacts. Test scripts are ordered starting from the ones concerning the simpler functionalities (e.g., login) and grouped by use case/user story. It is important to notice that the web application development can be conducted with any technology – e.g., Ajax, Flash, etc. – and any development process – e.g., traditional, model-driven (e.g., using WebRatio) or by means of mashups. The only constraint is to use the same text (e.g., for linkText locators) or id/name attribute values used in the produced mockups. Moreover, developing the mockups and defining the links among them allows also to produce a preliminary but "working" prototype of the web application that can be shown to the stakeholders. This is very useful for detecting, as soon as possible, problems and misunderstandings in the requirements [10].

4   Conclusion and Future Work

In this work, we have proposed a novel approach for developing web applications adopting the ATDD practice. The novelty regards the usage of screen mockups for generating, with a limited effort, acceptance test scripts able to drive the development of the target web application. The approach has been successfully applied on a sample case study (weBlog application) to show its feasibility. As future work, we intend to validate and refine our approach by means of experiments and with real industrial case studies. In this way, we will be able to measure the additional costs required for generating the mockups and gather feedbacks on the effectiveness and usefulness of our approach.

References

1. Besson, F.M., Beder, D.M., Chaim, M.L.: An automated approach for acceptance web test case modeling and executing. In: Sillitti, A., Martin, A., Wang, X., Whitworth, E. (eds.) XP 2010. LNBIP, vol. 48, pp. 160–165. Springer, Heidelberg (2010)

2. Downs, G.: Lean-agile acceptance test-driven development: better software through collaboration by Ken Pugh. ACM SIGSOFT Softw. Eng. Notes **36**(4), 34–34 (2011)
3. Hartson, H.R., Smith, E.C.: Rapid prototyping in human-computer interface development. Interact. Comput. **3**(1), 51–91 (1991)
4. Leotta, M., Clerissi, D., Ricca, F., Tonella, P.: Capture-replay vs. programmable web testing: an empirical assessment during test case evolution. In: Proceedings of 20th Working Conference on Reverse Engineering (WCRE 2013), pp. 272–281. IEEE (2013)
5. Leotta, M., Clerissi, D., Ricca, F., Tonella, P.: Approaches and tools for automated end-to-end web testing. Adv. Comput. **101**, 193–237 (2016)
6. Leotta, M., Stocco, A., Ricca, F., Tonella, P.: ROBULA+: an algorithm for generating robust XPath locators for web testing. J. Softw. Evol. Process **28**(3), 177–204 (2016)
7. O'Docherty, M.: Object-Oriented Analysis and Design: Understanding System Development with UML 2.0, 1st edn. Wiley, New York (2005)
8. Reggio, G., Leotta, M., Ricca, F.: A method for requirements capture and specification based on disciplined use cases and screen mockups. In: Abrahamsson, P., et al. (eds.) PROFES 2015. LNCS, vol. 9459, pp. 105–113. Springer, Heidelberg (2015). doi:10.1007/978-3-319-26844-6_8
9. Reggio, G., Ricca, F., Leotta, M.: Improving the quality and the comprehension of requirements: disciplined use cases and mockups. In: Proceedings of 40th Euromicro Conference on Software Engineering and Advanced Applications (SEAA 2014), pp. 262–266. IEEE (2014)
10. Ricca, F., Scanniello, G., Torchiano, M., Reggio, G., Astesiano, E.: Assessing the effect of screen mockups on the comprehension of functional requirements. ACM Trans. Softw. Eng. Methodol. **24**(1), 1–38 (2014)

The WoT as an Awareness Booster in Agile Development Workspaces

Olivier Liechti[1]([⊠]), Jacques Pasquier[2], Laurent Prévost[1], and Pascal Gremaud[2]

[1] Institute for Information and Communication Technologies,
University of Applied Sciences Western Switzerland,
1400 Yverdon-les-bains, Switzerland
`olivier.liechti@heig-vd.ch`
[2] Department of Computer Science,
University of Fribourg, 1700 Fribourg, Switzerland

Abstract. Continuous feedback is one of the most important concepts in agile development. We argue for the need to increase the awareness that the team maintains of various facets of the development activity. We then introduce iFLUX, an event-driven middleware designed for the Web of Things. We explain how it provides a platform that facilitates the creation of augmented workplaces that connect various information sources with physical displays, also known as *information radiators*.

Keywords: Agile development · Awareness · Feedback · Web of things · Middleware · Team work

1 Introduction

Agile methodologies make the development of web applications more efficient. On the flip side, web applications also make agile methodologies more efficient. Just think about issue tracking, source code management and communication. All of these software engineering tasks are now commonly handled via the web, especially in remote teams. Looking at this dual relationship, we see the Web of Things as a particularly interesting web engineering domain. In our research, we are interested by two questions. Firstly, we want to understand how agile practices can be applied to the development of WoT systems. For instance, what does it mean to build continuous delivery pipelines and to implement an automated testing strategy in a WoT environment? Secondly, we want to explore how WoT applications can make agile development teams more productive.

This paper focuses on the second question. We demonstrate how the WoT is a powerful mediation platform for continuous feedback in agile workspaces. We first look at the importance of feedback and awareness in agile methodologies. We then explain how an event-driven middleware provides a foundation for designing workspaces augmented with WoT components. Finally, we illustrate this concept with a usage scenario and a demonstration setup. While space prevents us to give a lot of implementation details, we explain how the APIs defined by the iFLUX

© Springer International Publishing Switzerland 2016
A. Bozzon et al. (Eds.): ICWE 2016, LNCS 9671, pp. 598–602, 2016.
DOI: 10.1007/978-3-319-38791-8_56

event-driven middleware [1] can easily be implemented to connect information sources (e.g. code repositories, quality management platforms, etc.) to physical displays (e.g. Arduino-based devices).

2   The Importance of Feedback in Agile Development

Feedback is one of the most important principles in agile practices, at all levels. Software is developed in short iterations, so that customers can give frequent feedback about the software functionality and user experience. Developers write automated tests, so that they can get frequent feedback about the software quality. Teams do regular retrospective meetings, to capture feedback about their work practices and fuel a continuous improvement process.

The notion of feedback is closely related to the concept of *awareness*, which as been extensively studied in the Computer Supported Cooperative Work literature. Dourish and Belotti [2] have defined awareness as *an understanding of the activities of others, which provides a context for your own activity*. In our context, this raises two questions. Firstly, how can we capture the activity of a software development team (what are tasks to be considered? where are these tasks performed? how can we monitor and record them?). Secondly, how can we make this activity visible to the whole team (what are the appropriate presentation modalities? how do we deal with information overhead?).

Agile practitioners have looked at these questions for a long time. The reason for sticking post-it notes and charts on walls is to make information publicly available, thereby giving a shared context to the team. Cockburn [3] has coined the term of *information radiators*, which should make information easy to read and frequently updated. Information radiators [4,5] are often low-tech: when status changes, someone needs to update the status with pen and paper. We have often observed a tension between physical and digital boards. Physical displays tend to be more impactful. Digital boards, on the other hand, enable archiving, searching and remote collaboration. This is precisely where we see a huge potential for applying the WoT to agile development workspaces. With the adequate technical infrastructure, it is now easy to create digital widgets that augment physical boards, thereby combining the benefits of both approaches.

3   Rapid Prototyping with an Event-Driven Middleware

The idea of using "smart objects" to display notifications is not new. Many agile developers have hacked lava lamps and sirens to notify breaking builds. Our contribution is to make this process easier. We aim to offer an open and lightweight integration platform for wiring activity sources and information radiators. We want to empower agile teams, who should be able to experiment with new ideas and to integrate custom components. Working with many agile teams, we have seen the value of "making", "hacking" or simply put "cool" activities. Beyond the immediate outcome of these activities, it is the impact on the team culture and the sense of belonging that is extremely valuable.

The core of our *agile awareness platform* is the open source iFLUX event-driven middleware. We have initially created iFLUX in the context of a research program on smart cities. However, the middleware is generic and is well-suited for any kind of WoT system. Its programming model was inspired by popular lightweight service integration services, such as IFTTT and Zapier. It follows the Event Condition Action (ECA) paradigm [6] and is based on three core abstractions: (i) *event sources*, (ii) *action targets* and (iii) *rules*. *Event sources* and *action targets* are meant to be developed by third-party developers, independently from any specific application (to encourage reuse). Application developers implement workflows on top of available *event sources* and *action targets*, by defining stateless rules. Essentially, they express rules such as "*if* an event with properties that match these conditions is notified, *then* trigger an action on this target, with the following properties".

4   Usage Scenario and Illustrative Setup

For illustration purposes, let us consider two important facets of the software development activity and that the team should maintain awareness of:

– *awareness of team activities.* When people share a physical space, they unconsciously process audio-visual cues (e.g. body language, side conversations) and have a general sense of what others are doing. The situation is different when people do most of their tasks in digital systems (e.g. in a code repository), or when they work remotely.
– *awareness of software quality.* The goal of an agile team is to deliver *working* software. It is therefore critical for the team to keep track of what measures software quality: passing and failing tests, feedback from users, number of issues, etc. This information must be extracted from different systems.

4.1   Capture Information with iFLUX Event Sources

Creating a source of information with iFLUX is easy. The middleware exposes a REST endpoint (/`events`). Event sources `POST` simple payloads, with an event type, a timestamp and a list of custom properties. Consider two examples:

– an agent, which uses the GitHub API to monitor events occurring in the code repository such as commits, pull requests, comments, etc. The agent issues `POST` requests to forward GitHub events to iFLUX.
– an agent, which fetches information in the Probe Dock agile testing platform. The agent emits iFLUX events whenever a suite of automated tests is run (indicating the number of failing tests). The agent also emits events when new tests are added to the test suite.

4.2   Represent Information with iFLUX Action Targets

Creating *information radiators* with iFLUX is also easy. When a rule is triggered, the middleware issues a POST request to the URL declared in the rule. Creating an information radiator means implementing a /actions REST endpoint. The endpoint has to process JSON payloads, which also have a simple structure: an action type and a list of custom properties. Consider two examples:

- a custom device, built by integrating an Arduino board with a color LED ring. The embedded HTTP server accepts JSON payloads. The payloads have an action type property with the value setColorPattern and a custom property pattern with one of the defined values (e.g. solid-green-bright).
- an analytics dashboard, built as a web app displayed on a large public display. The web application maintains the state of various metrics and exposes the /actions endpoint. It accepts payloads where the action type property has a value of updateMetric and where the id and the value of the metric are specified in custom properties.

4.3   Connect Sources and Targets with iFLUX Rules

The iFLUX components are loosely coupled. The LED display can be used to represent activity happening in any of the connected event sources. Similarly, activity detected in the GitHub space can be represented in any of the connected action targets. Once the sources and targets have been implemented and deployed, it is up to the development team to define event-condition-actions rules. They do that by posting payloads on the /rules endpoint exposed by the iFLUX middleware. A first rule could specify that" if the event type is probedock.testRun and the custom property numberOfFailures is greater than 0, then send an action target to the LED display with the action type set to setColorPattern and the pattern custom property pattern set to pulse-red-fast. Another rule could specify that if a new commit is detected in GitHub, the LED light should blink twice and the metric numberOfDaily-Commits should be increased in the analytics dashboard.

5   Conclusion

We have shown how the iFLUX middleware facilitates the integration of various event sources and information displays, and thus the creation of informative workspaces. We have used such WoT installations in different agile environments. We have witnessed the value of making team activities and software quality continuously and physically perceptible. Something as simple as knowing that new code has just been committed may not seem very helpful. But we have observed that it positively impacts the team dynamics. More information about iFLUX is available on http://www.iflux.io.

References

1. Liechti, O., Prévost, L., Delaye, V., Hennebert, J., Grivel, V., Rey, J.P., Depraz, J., Sommer, M.: Enabling reactive cities with the iflux middleware. In: Proceedings of the 6th International Workshop on the Web of Things, p. 1. ACM (2015)
2. Dourish, P., Bellotti, V.: Awareness and coordination in shared workspaces. In: Proceedings of the 1992 ACM Conference on Computer-Supported Cooperative Work, pp. 107–114. ACM (1992)
3. Cockburn, A.: Agile Software Development Agile Software Development. Addison-Wesley Professional, Boston (2001)
4. Paredes, J., Anslow, C., Maurer, F.: Information visualization for agile software development. In: 2014 Second IEEE Working Conference on Software Visualization (VISSOFT), pp. 157–166. IEEE (2014)
5. Mateescu, M., Kropp, M., Burkhard, R., Zahn, C., Vischi, D.: aWall: a socio-cognitive tool for agile team collaboration using large multi-touch wall systems. In: Proceedings of the 2015 International Conference on Interactive Tabletops & Surfaces, pp. 361–366. ACM (2015)
6. Qiao, Y., Zhong, K., Wang, H., Li, X.: Developing event-condition-action rules in real-time active database. In: Proceedings of the 2007 ACM Symposium on Applied Computing, pp. 511–516. ACM (2007)

A Model-Driven Process to Migrate Web Content Management System Extensions

Dennis Priefer[1,2]([✉]), Peter Kneisel[2], and Gabriele Taentzer[1]

[1] Philipps-Universität Marburg, Marburg, Germany
taentzer@mathematik.uni-marburg.de
[2] KITE - Kompetenzzentrum für Informationstechnologie,
Technische Hochschule Mittelhessen, Gießen, Germany
{dennis.priefer,peter.kneisel}@mni.thm.de

Abstract. Developing and maintaining software extensions for Web Content Management Systems (WCMSs) like Joomla, WordPress, or Drupal can be a difficult and time consuming process. This poster presents a model-driven process which addresses typical challenges during the migration of software extensions for WCMSs. We introduce JooMDD as a prototypical environment for the development and maintenance of Joomla extensions. JooMDD consists of a domain-specific modelling language for WCMS extensions, a reverse engineering tool to create models based on existing WCMS extensions, and a code generator for software extensions, which can be used to enrich Joomla-based applications. The use of JooMDD within our research demonstrates the application of a model-driven migration process for WCMS extensions.

Keywords: Model-driven development · Web Content Management Systems · Joomla · Software extensions · Software migration

1 Introduction

Today's web mainly consists of dynamic web applications, often instances of web content management systems like Joomla, WordPress, and Drupal. These systems provide the necessary functionality for administrators to create these instances independent of their experience in web development.

One of the biggest advantages of using a WCMS as platform for dynamic websites is the functional extensibility through standardised extension types. Through the use of APIs, extensions can be implemented without changing the platform itself. The dependency on these APIs has a large impact on the maintenance of developed extensions. If the API of the underlying WCMS platform changes, e.g. through a new major release, extensions must be changed as well. Normally, developers have to change their extension's code by hand. This can lead to inconsistencies within the extension, if the responsible developers do not meticulously update all altered dependencies. Consequently, if developers have to migrate multiple extension, the overall effort can increase exponentially. The same applies to both platform internal and platform external extension migration.

© Springer International Publishing Switzerland 2016
A. Bozzon et al. (Eds.): ICWE 2016, LNCS 9671, pp. 603–606, 2016.
DOI: 10.1007/978-3-319-38791-8_57

Due to the amount of schematically recurring code in standard WCMS extensions, independent of their underlying platform, we propose a *model-driven* approach to migrate WCMS extensions faster and more easily in comparison to manual migration. In addition, we obtain the typical benefits of model-driven approaches, such as reusability and enhanced code quality.

Using a model-driven approach for software migration on a higher abstraction level is seen as a promising approach in today's research. In [4] the authors introduce a meta-model for the definition of migration processes. These processes are based on model-driven sub-processes as are ours. The reengineering method and reverse engineering tool as presented in [5] deal with the migration of complete CMSs. As our work progresses, we plan to incorporate these approaches into our research and check their suitability for the migration of WCMS extensions. In [3] we consider similar model-driven approaches such as presented in [1], whereby existing work deals with complete systems, web applications in general, or the data of concrete WCMS instances and not the migration of their extensions' code.

Our main contribution is a **concept for a model-driven migration process explicitly for WCMS extensions** and prototypical tools to migrate Joomla extensions. Our set of tools encompasses:

- a domain-specific modelling language for the abstract description of WCMS extensions,
- a transformation tool for creating models from existing Joomla extensions (supporting usual extension types like components, modules, plugins, and libraries),
- a code generator for installable Joomla extensions based on an extension model

2   Model-Driven Migration Process

As an alternative to manually performed migration of the source code, a model-driven migration process of WCMS extensions is done at a higher abstraction level. This allows the use of common model-driven engineering practices, like model refactoring for improving the software quality.

Figure 1 illustrates the migration process of installable WCMS extensions which is divided into three main steps (cf. [2,5]):

Reverse Engineering: Existing extension packages (code) are used as input for an automated text-to-model (*T2M*) transformation. This transformation should be as complete as possible. To consider individual code fragments, we suggest to create code models, which contain platform-specific code fragments and can be bound to abstract extension models.

Model Migration: Models can be refactored, extended, or migrated to models based on differing modelling languages through model-to-model (*M2M*) transformations. These transformations can be performed semi-automatically (e.g. model refactoring), or manual (e.g. model extension).

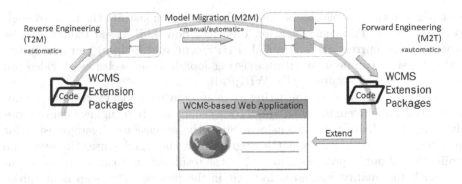

Fig. 1. Model-driven migration process

Forward Engineering: Through an automated model-to-text ($M2T$) transformation, models can be transformed to software code, in our case to installable WCMS extensions.

3 Prototypical Realisation

To test our approach, we have developed an environment (**JooMDD**) for the model-driven migration of Joomla[1] 3.x extensions. We provide the *domain-specific language (DSL)* **eJSL**, which divides a Joomla extension into **entities** (data model), **pages** (views), and **extensions** (extension structure and meta data). For the creation and maintenance (or reengineering) of eJSL models, we provide plugins for the current development environments (IDEs) Eclipse, IntelliJ IDEA, and PHPStorm. These plugins consist of textual editors which support the modellers with features such as auto completion and model validation.

In addition, we developed the prototype **jext2eJSL** to support reverse engineering by a model extractor. The tool uses existing Joomla 3.x extensions (PHP, HTML, JavaScript, and SQL files) as input and creates a domain model based on the eJSL language. It supports the common Joomla extension types (*components, modules, plugins, libraries*, and *templates*), on the conditions that they follow the Joomla coding standards and use the typical design pattern for the particular extension type (e.g. *Model-View-Controller* within components or *Observer* within plugins), meaning that jext2eJSL searches for prescribed file and code schemes expected by the Joomla platform. In order to support WordPress and Drupal extensions, we plan to incorporate the tools presented in [5]. Even though these tools were developed to migrate web-based to WCMS-based applications, we believe the parsers could be further developed to handle the code of WCMS extension as well.

For the forward engineering step we created a **code generator** for installable extension packages for Joomla 3.x. If the Joomla platform is changed, the generator has to be updated, but because of the nature of model-driven approaches,

---

[1] We selected Joomla as the target platform, because it is one of the most widely used WCMSs (according to http://w3techs.com/technologies/overview/contentmanagement/all).

most parts of the models can be reused. In [3] we demonstrate the forward engineering process. The demonstration describes how eJSL-based models can be created within current IDEs (IntelliJ, PHPStorm, and Eclipse) and how generated extensions can be used within existing Joomla-based websites. A video can be found at https://youtu.be/Uy_WBIjPldI.

We applied our process, consisting of an automated model extraction, a semi-automated model reengineering, and a code generation, to reengineer conventionally developed Joomla 3.x extensions. Since the extensions already existed for the current platform, this is not a migration in the usual sense. However, the application of our approach ensures that the resulting extensions are in compliance with the quality standards implicit in the process. This step is an initial investment for further migrations.

4 Perspective

We plan to abstract the modelling language and simplify the migration process as much as possible to support further WCMSs and provide a simpler integration of our approach into existing development processes.

To ensure the correctness and usefulness of our approach we will test it extensively by migrating actual WCMS extensions. We expect the next major release of Joomla (version 4.x) within the next two years. Since we are developing and maintaining different types of Joomla extension for the academic sector, we have an adequate set of reference extensions for testing our proposed migration process. Our intention is to reduce the effort involved in the migration of the reference extensions to the new Joomla version as much as possible. In addition we plan an empirical evaluation of our approach to assess the model-driven migration speed and the quality of the migrated extensions.

References

1. Brambilla, M.: Interaction Flow Modeling Language: Model-Driven UI Engineering of Web and Mobile Apps with IFML. Morgan Kaufmann, Waltham (2015)
2. Demeyer, S., Ducasse, S., Nierstrasz, O.M.: Object-Oriented Reengineering Patterns. The Morgan Kaufmann Series in Software Engineering and Programming. Morgan Kaufman Publishers, San Francisco (2003)
3. Priefer, D., Kneisel, P., Taentzer, G.: JooMDD: A model-driven development environment for web content management system extensions. In: ICSE Companion 2016: Companion Proceedings of the 38th International Conference on Software Engineering. ACM, New York (in press, 2016)
4. Ruiz, F.J.B., Ramón, Ó.S., Molina, J.G.: Definition of processes for MDE-based migrations. In: Proceedings of the Third Workshop on Process-Based Approaches for Model-Driven Engineering, PMDE 2013, pp. 1–9. ACM, New York (2013)
5. Trias, F., de Castro, V., López-Sanz, M., Marcos, E.: RE-CMS: a reverse engineering toolkit for the migration to CMS-based web applications. In: Proceedings of the 30th Annual ACM Symposium on Applied Computing, SAC 2015, pp. 810–812. ACM, New York (2015)

Tutorials

Using Docker Containers to Improve Reproducibility in Software and Web Engineering Research

Jürgen Cito[1]([✉]), Vincenzo Ferme[2], and Harald C. Gall[1]

[1] University of Zurich, Zurich, Switzerland
{cito,gall}@ifi.uzh.ch
[2] University of Lugano (USI), Lugano, Switzerland
vincenzo.ferme@usi.ch

Abstract. The ability to replicate and reproduce scientific results has become an increasingly important topic for many academic disciplines. In computer science and, more specifically, software and web engineering, contributions of scientific work rely on developed algorithms, tools and prototypes, quantitative evaluations, and other computational analyses. Published code and data come with many undocumented assumptions, dependencies, and configurations that are internal knowledge and make reproducibility hard to achieve. This tutorial presents how Docker containers can overcome these issues and aid the reproducibility of research artifacts in software and web engineering and discusses their applications in the field.

Keywords: Reproducibility · Containers · Cloud

1 Motivation

Reproducibility can be described as the repeatability of a certain process in order to establish a fact or the conditions under which we are able to observe the same fact [1]. The ability to replicate and reproduce scientific results has become an increasingly important topic for many academic disciplines. In computer science and, more specifically, software and web engineering (SE/WE), contributions of scientific work rely on developed algorithms, tools and prototypes, quantitative evaluations, and other computational analyses.

However, even if code and data are published alongside the paper as open source artifacts, they come with many undocumented assumptions, dependencies, and configurations that make reproducibility hard to achieve [2]. Reproduction of results often requires internal knowledge that is missing from the published manuscript.

Docker container [3] is an open source technology that can address the issues of reproducibility in SE/WE research. Containers can be seen as lightweight virtual machines that allow to set up a computational environment, including all necessary dependencies (e.g., libraries), configuration, code and data needed,

© Springer International Publishing Switzerland 2016
A. Bozzon et al. (Eds.): ICWE 2016, LNCS 9671, pp. 609–612, 2016.
DOI: 10.1007/978-3-319-38791-8_58

within a single unit (called *image*). The steps necessary to achieve the state in such an image are documented within a *Dockerfile*, a script that holds all infrastructure configuration and commands. Images can be distributed publicly and seamlessly run on Linux, and also have support for major operating systems through Docker machine. The major difference to virtual machines is that Docker images share the kernel with the underlying host machine, which enables much smaller image sizes and higher performance. This has made Docker particularly attractive to industry and has thus seen a steep rise in adoption of the technology [4,5].

Containers address the shortcomings of previous approaches (e.g., open sourcing) and make artifacts in SE/WE research immediately usable to reviewers, interested readers, and future researchers and improves dissemination of scientific results.

This tutorial aims on giving a hands-on introduction to Docker, and show how researchers can package an existing research project in the SE/WE community within a Docker container.

2   Importance to the Web Engineering Community

In recent years, software and web engineering conferences have started to encourage the submission of artifacts that support replication (e.g., replication packages at FSE[1], data showcase at MSR[2]), signaling the importance of reproducibility in the field.

Reproducibility can be further improved if all artifacts belonging to a paper are packaged and documented in Docker containers. This allows others to immediately make use of the package without the need of internal knowledge and without dependency issues.

This tutorial will offer an opportunity to familiarize the audience with how Docker containers work and how SE/WE researchers can leverage this technology to provide a reproducible package to their own research. More specifically, it will give a hands-on tutorial on how existing prototypes can be packaged to form a reproducible entity.

3   Outline

The tutorial is supposed to take half a day (3 h). It will first introduce the basics of container technology, how it differs to virtual machines, and why it has gained widespread attraction in industry. It will then convey the basic building blocks of how an image can be constructed. In addition, it will give guidance on how to best produce a Dockerfile out of working containers. It will then continue to apply these basic techniques to a specific use case in the Web Engineering domain. The tutorial will conclude with a discussion on the advantages, challenges, and

---

[1] http://esec-fse15.dei.polimi.it/replicationPack.html.
[2] http://2016.msrconf.org/#/data.

limitations of the use of containers to enable reproducibility in SE/WE research. The detailed outline of the tutorial is described in the following.

1. Introduction to Containers and Reproducibility of SE/WE Research.
The tutorial will start by introducing the term reproducibility in relation to SE/WE research. It will continue to introduce container technologies and how they can help with reproducibility.

2. Docker Container Basics.
The tutorial will cover a short overview of the Docker ecosystem and will introduce the basic building blocks and its tooling. This block in the tutorial will also walk through the process and concrete instructions necessary to build an initial container.

3. Web Engineering Use Case.
This part of the tutorial will walk through a concrete use case that could be found in web engineering. The use case is based on a distributed, real-time node.js application, realized by multiple services. The concrete instructions to construct the Docker image will be elaborated along the way.

4. Open Challenges and Limitations.
We conclude the tutorial with a discussion on the open challenges that still remain in the area of reproducibility, what kind of limitations exist.

All materials covered in this tutorial, including all scripts and resulting artifacts, will be made available online at:
http://www.ifi.uzh.ch/seal/people/cito.html.

4   Target Audience

This tutorial is suitable for both academic researchers and industry professionals that want to learn more about Docker containers and reproducibility in general. No prior knowledge of Docker or any other container technology is necessary. To follow along with the instructions, we assume basic skills in working with the Linux console (e.g., `bash`). The audience will be pointed to further material, for those who want to learn more about container technologies.

5   About the Organizers

The material to be included in the tutorial is authored by Jürgen Cito, Vincenzo Ferme, and Harald C. Gall.

Jürgen Cito is a Ph.D. candidate at the University of Zurich, Switzerland. In his research, he investigates the intersection between software engineering and cloud computing. In the summer of 2015, he was a research intern at the IBM T.J. Watson Research Center in New York, where he worked on cloud analytics based on Docker containers. That year he also won the local Docker Hackathon in New York City with the project `docker-record`[3].

More information is available at: http://www.ifi.uzh.ch/seal/people/cito. html.

Vincenzo Ferme is a Ph.D. candidate at the University of Lugano (USI), Switzerland. In his research, he is involved in the BenchFlow Project. The goal of the project is to design the first benchmark for assessing and comparing the performance of workflow management systems. In the context of the project, he is developing a framework for automated software performance benchmarking that largely relies on Docker[4].

More information is available at: http://www.vincenzoferme.it.

Harald C. Gall is a professor of software engineering in the Department of Informatics at the University of Zurich, Switzerland. His research interests include software engineering, focusing on software evolution, software quality analysis, software architecture, reengineering, collaborative software engineering, and service centric software systems. He was the program chair of the European Software Engineering Conference and the ACM SIGSOFT ESEC-FSE in 2005 and the program co-chair of ICSE 2011.

More information is available at: http://www.ifi.uzh.ch/seal/people/gall. html.

References

1. Mockus, A., Anda, B., Sjøberg, D.I.: Experiences from replicating a case study to investigate reproducibility of software development
2. Boettiger, C.: An introduction to docker for reproducible research. ACM SIGOPS Oper. Syst. Rev. **49**(1), 71–79 (2015)
3. Merkel, D.: Docker: lightweight linux containers for consistent development and deployment. Linux J. **2014**(239), 2 (2014)
4. Gerber, A.: The state of containers and the docker ecosystem: 2015. Technical report, White paper
5. Cito, J., Leitner, P., Fritz, T., Gall, H.C.: The making of cloud applications: an empirical study on software development for the cloud. In: Proceedings of the 10th Joint Meeting on Foundations of Software Engineering, ESEC/FSE 2015, pp. 393–403. ACM, New York (2015)

---

[3] https://github.com/citostyle/docker-record.
[4] https://github.com/benchflow.

A Declarative Approach to Information Extraction Using Web Service API

John Samuel[1(✉)] and Christophe Rey[2]

[1] Université de Lyon, LIRIS, CNRS, UMR-CNRS 5205, Lyon, France
`john.samuel@liris.cnrs.fr`
[2] Université Blaise Pascal, LIMOS, UMR-CNRS 6158, Aubière, France
`christophe.rey@univ-bpclermont.fr`

Abstract. The number of diverse web services that we use regularly is significantly increasing. Most of these services are managed by autonomous service providers. However it has become very difficult to get a unified view of this widespread data, which in all likelihood is substantially important to enterprises. A classical approach followed by the enterprises is to write applications using imperative languages making use of the web service API. Such an approach is not scalable and is difficult to maintain considering the ever-evolving web services landscape. This tutorial explores a semi-automated declarative approach to information extraction from the web services using a classical virtual data integration approach, namely mediation, that relies on a well-known query rewriting algorithm, namely the inverse-rules algorithm. It is targeted to audience from both industry as well as academia and requires a basic understanding of database principles and web technologies.

Keywords: Data integration · Web services · Application programming interface · Declarative programming

1 Introduction

Internet has become an inherent part of our lives. Web services emerge in the market offering services in different niches. It has made our lives significantly easier without requiring us to understand the various intricacies of the underlying complex systems. But it is now significantly harder to get a unified view of the data spread across diverse, autonomous web services, sometimes even spanning across different continents. Service providers often provide API so as to facilitate the integration of their services and the internal applications of clients.

The enterprises make use of the imperative programming languages to integrate with each of the dependent services. Such an approach is not scalable requiring to write applications using imperative programming languages. Several machine readable languages are being proposed by the research community that can be used to automatically generate code for integrating with these web services. But as we analyse various web services in the market, we find their

© Springer International Publishing Switzerland 2016
A. Bozzon et al. (Eds.): ICWE 2016, LNCS 9671, pp. 613–615, 2016.
DOI: 10.1007/978-3-319-38791-8_59

widespread adoption missing. Developers are still dependent on the (human-readable) API documentation to code the applications and periodically check associated sites to receive updates on any API changes.

In this tutorial, we explore a declarative approach to integrate with numerous web services based on authors' recent research work [3,4]. Its aim is to transform the coding effort needed to use web services APIs into an easier and hopefully faster administration task. To reach this objective, the keypoints are (i) to replace imperative programming languages by declarative one, and (ii) to use a query rewriting algorithm to automate the process as much as possible. This approach has been implemented as the ETL technique of DaWeS [4], which is a data warehouse fed only with data coming from web services APIs.

2   Tutorial Objectives

The tutorial is intended to audience from both industry and academia and requires a basic knowledge of database principles and web technologies like HTTP, XML or JSON. Its main objectives are given below:

- to get an insight into the *current-generation web services* available in the market, their heterogeneity and evolving nature, their API, various technologies used by them and their documentation.
- to comprehend the various ways by which enterprises currently *integrate with the web services* and how the web service providers also offer services to achieve faster integration time.
- to get an understanding of various *declarative languages* used in databases and web domain, their purpose and how they are being currently used.
- to get an *overall view of data integration* [2] field, especially the mediation approach and query rewriting technique [1] and related declarative languages.
- to get an overall idea of building a platform to *extract data from web services using the mediation approach* both from a research and development perspective.
- and finally to discuss *various open problems* studied and researched by the scientific community, especially related to user-friendly query languages.

Taking an example of a social networking web service domain, this tutorial will present an end-to-end example for extracting information using its API and associated (human-readable) documentation.

3   Tutorial Content

This half-day tutorial will require a PC-projector and (optional) wifi/wireless connection. Given below is the list of issues that will be discussed throughout the tutorial:

1. Introduction to Data formats and Declarative Languages
   - Data formats (XML, JSON)

- Data validation (XSD, JSON-Schema)
- Data transformation (XSLT, JSONT)
- Conjunctive query, datalog query, SQL
- Imperative programming versus declarative approach
2. Web Services
   - Application Programming Interface (API)
   - API libraries
   - Machine-readable and human-readable documentation
   - Heterogeneity and evolving nature
   - Authentication Mechanism (Basic HTTP Authentication and OAuth)
3. Mediation for data integration
   - Virtual data integration
   - Rewriting algorithms
   - Access patterns
4. Web service Information Extraction Platform
   - Query rewriter
   - Query evaluation engine
   - Web service wrapper
5. Open problems:
   - Manual and automated efforts
   - Query Languages

References

1. Duschka, O.M., Genesereth, M.R., Levy, A.Y.: Recursive query plans for data integration. J. Log. Program. **43**(1), 49–73 (2000)
2. Halevy, A.Y.: Theory of answering queries using views. SIGMOD Rec. **29**(4), 40–47 (2000)
3. Samuel, J.: Towards a data warehouse fed with web services. In: Presutti, V., d'Amato, C., Gandon, F., d'Aquin, M., Staab, S., Tordai, A. (eds.) ESWC 2014. LNCS, vol. 8465, pp. 874–884. Springer, Heidelberg (2014). http://dx.doi.org/10.1007/978-3-319-07443-6_61
4. Samuel, J., Rey, C.: Dawes: datawarehouse fed with web services. In: Actes du XXXIIème Congrès INFORSID, Lyon, France, 20–23 Mai 2014, pp. 329–344 (2014). http://inforsid.fr/actes/2014/20_paper_20.pdf

Distributed Web Applications with IPFS, Tutorial

David Dias$^{(\boxtimes)}$ and Juan Benet

Protocol Labs, Lisbon, Portugal
mail@daviddias.me, juan@benet.ai

Abstract. The contents of this document describe the tutorial session delivered at ICWE 2016, focused on Building Distributed Web Applications with IPFS. IPFS, the InterPlanetary File System, is the distributed and permanent Web, a protocol to make the Web faster, more secure and open. The tutorial format focuses in key elements of IPFS and how to use it to build applications with

Keywords: IPFS · Web · Distributed · P2P · Cryptography · Merkle-Tree · MerkleDAG · IPLD · Go · JavaScript · Application · Apps · Blockchain · Hash · Secure · Data · File system · Files · Graphs · Database

1 Introduction

IPFS [1], the InterPlanetary File System, is the distributed and permanent Web, a protocol to make the Web faster, more secure, open and available. IPFS can be described "as Git meets a BitTorrent swarm", exchanging objects within one Git repository. In other words, IPFS provides a high throughput content-addressed block storage model, with content-addressed hyperlinks. This forms a generalised MerkleDAG, a data structure that can be used to build versioned file systems, blockchains, unix like file systems, amongst other options. IPFS combines a Distributed Hash Table, an incentivised block exchange and a self-certifying namespace. IPFS has no single point of failure, and nodes do not need to trust each other.

The tutorial will focus on the IPFS Application Stack, including: libp2p, the networking layer; bitswap for data exchange;IPLD and the MerkleDAG, the thin waist data structure of IPFS and how to use IPFS interface to build distributed applications. The full length of the tutorial is 6 h.

2 Motivations and Goals

Distributed Applications are naturally complex, it is known that a ton of work and energy has been put by professionals from the Academia and the Industry to solve some of the toughest problems to deliver guarantees and semantics that applications can use and trust.

All links were last followed on March 10, 2016.

© Springer International Publishing Switzerland 2016
A. Bozzon et al. (Eds.): ICWE 2016, LNCS 9671, pp. 616–619, 2016.
DOI: 10.1007/978-3-319-38791-8_60

IPFS builds on top of the knowledge gathered along the last decades, offering semantics that are similar to those of a file system, but built with the Web in mind. This tutorial covers the core challenges of building a distributed application and offers a structure to solve those problems through IPFS.

3   IPFS, The InterPlanetary FileSystem

A complete IPFS description can be found on the IPFS paper [1] and the specifications repository[1] inside the IPFS organization on Github. Here we present a distilled version on each layer of IPFS.

3.1   libp2p

libp2p[2] is the networking layer library built for IPFS, which exists as a standalone project. libp2p is a modularized and extensible approach to the network stack, that reuses existing transports and system capabilities to offer NAT Traversal, Peer Discovery, Routing, Stream Multiplexing, Protocol Multiplexing, Encryption, Authentication and more.

3.2   Data Exchange

The IPFS Data Exchange takes care of negotiating bulk data transfers, exchanging blocks that are wanted by a given peer in a market like approach.

3.3   MerkleDAG

The ipfs merkledag is a directed acyclic graph whose edges are merkle-links. This means that links to objects can authenticate the objects themselves, and that every object contains a secure representation of its children.

This is a powerful primitive for distributed systems computations. The merkledag simplifies distributed protocols by providing an append-only authenticated datastructure. Parties can communicate and exchange secure references (merkle-links) to objects. The references are enough to verify the correctness of the object at a later time, which allows the objects themselves to be served over untrusted channels. Merkledags also allow the branching of a datastructure and subsequent merging, as in the version control system git. More generally, merkledags simplify the construction of Secure CRDTs, which enable distributed, convergent, commutative computation in an authenticated, secure way.

3.4   Data Structures

Any kind of Data Structure that can be described in a graph format can be mounted on top of the IPFS MerkleDAG. A practical example is the included UnixFS, a Data Structure that is built into IPFS offering a native way to handle files in familiar way to filesystems in Unix environments.

---

[1] https://github.com/ipfs/specs.

[2] https://github.com/ipfs/specs/tree/master/libp2p.

3.5   Naming

Naming inside IPFS is governed by IPNS, the InterPlanetary Naming System. IPNS takes ideas from SFS [2] to enable the creation of cryptographically signed mutable pointers, which can be used to the creation of name records inside the network.

4   Tutorial

The format of the tutorial is a sum of a lecture and a laboratory class. Participants will get a common base of understanding of what is IPFS through a lecture, followed by an hands on laboratory class, where each individual will work in parallel and build a Distributed Web Application with IPFS. This tasks will be divided in a series of steps, starting from the network, followed by the data model, design decisions on desired guarantees and so on.

During these practical steps, participants will interact with the several layers of IPFS and their respective APIs.

4.1   Learning Outcomes

During this session, it is expected that attendees learn how to:

- Install IPFS
- Use IPFS through the CLI, HTTP-API and available client libraries
- Load an application to and from IPFS
- Dial between peers, using IPFS (libp2p)
- Learn how to build data structures on top of the Object (DAG) API
- Learn how to use UnixFS

4.2   Target Audience

General interest in cryptography, distributed systems, data structures and P2P protocols is recommended. Familiarity with JavaScript or the Go programming languages are a bonus, however any knowledge of CS programming will suffice.

4.3   Curriculum

This tutorial covers the IPFS stack and topics to have into account when building distributed applications, including:

- Merkle'lized Data Structures, such as: Merkle Trees, MerkleDAG, IPLD
- Hashing functions
- Distributed Hash Tables, P2P Routing strategies and Protocols
- Transport protocols
- IPFS Core API, HTTP API and CLI
- Data Exchange, namely bitswap
- Self Describable Data Formats

The tutorial is custom build for ICWE2016 audience, taking into consideration participants experience with the subject and interest.

5   Presenter

David Dias is a P2P Software Engineer and Researcher at Protocol Labs (http://ipn.io), the company behind IPFS. Before, David worked on the security and web development industry at Lift Security.

David holds a P2P Masters in Science, having built the first P2P DHT using WebRTC specifically for the Web Platform for job execution distribution.

David's speaking history with regards to P2P, security and distributed systems has been the following:

- Dec 2015 | Linux Foundation Node.js Interactive Conference. Stellar Module Management, using IPFS for code package distribution.
- May 2015 | Data Terra Nemo, the P2P Conf. "webrtc-explorer", distributed browser computing platform using volunteered shared resources.
- Feb 2015 | OpoJS. Resource Discovery for the Web Platform on top of a P2P Overlay Network powered by WebRTC.
- Apr 2014 | JSConf Brazil. Securing Node.js Applications by the community and for the community.

Currently I'm also an invited Professor at the University of Lisbon, having developed a new post graduation course on modern web development.

Other relevant previous work:

- Developed a 2 day WebRTC Training for O'Reilly Fluent Conf 2015
- Node Security researcher
- Part of the European research project SynergyVM while a researcher on the distributed systems group at INESC-ID

6   Conclusion

With this tutorial, participants will become knowledgeable of the components that compose IPFS, its architecture design decisions and be comfortable to build Web Applications with IPFS.

The materials built for this tutorial will be made available under MIT License, under the IPFS organization on GitHub[3]. Participants are encouraged to consult them at any time or distribute amongst their colleagues in their organization. We will continue to improve the content as IPFS evolves.

We would like to acknowledge and send our appreciation to the organizing committee behind ICWE 2016 for having invited us to make this Tutorial happen.

References

1. Benet, J.: IPFS - Content Addressed, Versioned, P2P File System (2014)
2. Mazieres, D., Kaashoek, F.: Self-certifying file system (2000)

---

[3] https://github.com/ipfs.

Recommender Systems Meet Linked Open Data

Tommaso Di Noia[✉]

SisInf Lab, Polytechnic University of Bari, Via Orabona 4, 70125 Bari, Italy
tommaso.dinoia@poliba.it

Abstract. Information overload is a problem we daily experience when accessing information channels such as a Web site, a mobile application or even our set-top box. There is a clear need for applications able to guide users through an apparently chaotic information space thus filtering, in a personalized way, only those elements that may result of interest to them. Together with the transformation of the Web from a distributed and hyperlinked repository of documents to a distributed repository of structured knowledge, in the last years, a new generation of recommendation engines has emerged. As of today, we have a huge amount of RDF data published as Linked Open Data (LOD) and available via a SPARQL endpoint and the number of applications able to exploit the knowledge they encoe is growing consistently. Among these new applications and services, recommender systems are gaining positions in the LOD arena.

1 Recommender Systems

Recommender Systems (RSs) are software tools and techniques providing suggestions for items to be of use to a user [9]. The main aim of RSs is to help users in satisfying their information needs when dealing with huge information spaces. To achieve this, RSs try to select the subset of items which best match the users' preferences and tastes. Among the several definitions given in the literature, we report the one proposed by [2] which says: *the recommender system term indicates any system that produces individualized recommendations as output or has the effect of guiding the user in a personalized way to interesting or useful objects in a large space of possible options.* A formal formulation of the recommendation problem has been given in [1] and it is defined as follows. Let U represent the set of users and I the set of items in the system. Potentially, both sets can be very large. Let $f : U \times I \to R$, where R is a totally ordered set, be a utility function measuring the usefulness of item $i \in I$ for user $u \in U$. Then, the recommendation problem consists in finding for each user u such item $i^{max,u} \in I$ maximizing the utility function f. More formally, this corresponds to

$$\forall u \in U, \ i^{max,u} = \arg \max_{i \in I} f(u, i)$$

Typically, the utility of an item is represented by a rating, which indicates how a particular user liked a particular item. The central problem of recommender systems is that the utility is not defined on the whole $U \times I$ space, but only a subset of it is actually available. For each user only a portion of her ratings is known.

A. Bozzon et al. (Eds.): ICWE 2016, LNCS 9671, pp. 620–623, 2016.
DOI: 10.1007/978-3-319-38791-8_61

Hence, the main task of the system concerns the estimation of the utility function from the available data. Once the utility function is obtained it can be used to predict unknown values and recommendations are eventually generated by selecting for each user the best N items with highest utility (recommendation list).

Recommendation Techniques. In the literature, there are different types of recommendation techniques. The main two are: collaborative filtering and content-based. Besides these two, an important class of recommender systems which are often used in real systems are the hybrid recommenders [2] which combine different strategies to improve their separate performance and obtain higher recommendation quality. Collaborative Filtering is the process of filtering or evaluating items using the opinions of other people. In this approach personalized recommendations for a target user are generated using opinions of users having similar tastes to those of the target user [8]. Content-based RSs recommend an item to a user based upon a description of the item and a profile of the user's interests [7]. Differently from collaborative filtering, such recommendation approach relies on the availability of content features describing the items. The main idea behind hybrid recommender systems is to combine two or more classes of algorithms in order to mitigate the weaknesses of the individual approaches and obtain better recommendation quality. In [2] a taxonomy of several hybridization schemes is given. One of the main limitation of traditional content-based approaches is that they completely ignore the semantics associated to the item attributes because they rely on keyword-based representations. Such textual approaches are incapable of capturing more complex relationships among objects at a deeper semantic level based on the inherent properties associated with these objects [3]. For example let us consider two generic movies $m1$ and $m2$, which have $a1$ and $a2$ as directors, respectively. Let make the case that even if the two movies have different directors $a1$ and $a2$, those directors have however many things in common such as they both were born in the same country and they both won a particular award. It is reasonable to assume that if a user likes $m1$ because of $a1$ then she might like with a certain degree $m2$ because $a2$ is similar to $a1$. In this case, an approach based on keyword matching would fail because the two values for the attribute director are different. The system needs a better representation of the items content. As described in [6] **semantic analysis** and its integration in personalization models is one of the most innovative and interesting approaches proposed in literature to solve those problems. The key idea is the adoption of knowledge bases for annotating items and representing profiles in order to obtain a *"semantic"* interpretation of the user information needs. The availability of additional semantic knowledge can allow the system to go beyond the simple keyword matching. Common-sense and domain-specific knowledge may be useful to give some meaning to the content of items, thus helping to generate more informative features than "plain" attributes [10].

2   What Linked Open Data Can Do for Recommender Systems

Several works on ontological or semantics-aware recommender systems have been proposed in the past before the Linked Open Data initiative was officially launched [5]. Most of them exploit ontological knowledge of items to boost collaborative filtering systems or to build better content-based ones. However, we argue that those approaches are not particularly suited for working with LOD datasets and new techniques are required for properly incorporating Linked Open Data into RSs and effectively exploiting their semantics. We recognize two main reasons why new approaches are needed. The first reason is that those ontological recommendation algorithms developed before the LOD initiative referred principally to the usage of specific domain ontologies and taxonomies. Linked Open Data datasets have the peculiarity of being published according to the Semantic Web technologies and of using a graph-based data model. Such aspects require specific models and paradigms for their effective usage and incorporation into recommender systems. Past works on ontology-based RSs base on the usage of taxonomies, controlled vocabulary and limited domain ontologies. With the advent of LOD new interesting possibilities appear for realizing better recommendation applications. The main advantages of using Linked Open Data for content-based and hybrid recommender systems can be summarized as: (i) availability of a great amount of multi-domain and ontological knowledge freely available for feeding the system; (ii) Semantic Web standards and technologies to retrieve the required data and hence no need for content analysis tasks for obtaining a structured representation of the items content; (iii) the ontological and relational nature of the data allows the system to analyze item descriptions at a semantic level.

Semantic Analysis. The main advantage of using LOD is the availability of well structured graph-based item descriptions. In fact, items are connected to entities by means of semantic relations. Such entities are classified in more or less complex classes. The semantics of those classes and relations is described by means of ontologies. For example if we consider the resource `dbpedia:Bruce_Willis` in DBpedia, it is instance of the class `dbpedia-owl:Person` which in turn is subclass of `dbpedia-owl:Agent`. In such ontology it is also defined the semantics of properties. For example the property `dbpedia-owl:starring` which connects `dbpedia:Pulp_Fiction` to `dbpedia:Bruce_Willis` has domain `dbpedia-owl:Work` and range `dbpedia-owl:Actor` which is sub-class of `dbpedia-owl:Person`. Thanks to the semantic relations among entities [4] the system can perform a deeper semantic analysis of the item content. In a keyword-based representation the system is limited to compute the syntactic match between keywords. Instead, thanks to the availability of semantic entities the system can potentially detect complex associations between the user profile and the items.

3   Tutorial Description

The main goals of this tutorial are: (i) Provide an introduction to recommender systems by describing the main approaches available to design and feed a recommendation engine; (ii) Show how to exploit the information available in the Linked Open Data cloud to develop a new generation of recommender systems. The tutorial starts with a brief introduction to the problem of information overload with examples taken from everyday life. Then we move to the definition of the recommendation problem and introduce all the elements needed to define, design and evaluate a recommender system. Starting from the user-item matrix, some collaborative approaches are described showing their strong and weak points. The same is done with content-based approaches. The second part of the tutorial is devoted to the presentation of how to exploit the knowledge encoded in LD datasets while computing a recommendation list. We see how to leverage both the structure and the semantics of a knowledge graph for feature selection by using a single attribute or a chaining (paths) of attributes and resources. Hybrid approaches together with their evaluation close the tutorial.

References

1. Adomavicius, G., Tuzhilin, A.: Toward the next generation of recommender systems: a survey of the state-of-the-art and possible extensions. ieee trans. knowl. data eng. **17**(6), 734–749 (2005)
2. Burke, R.D.: Hybrid recommender systems: survey and experiments. User Model. User-Adapt. Interact. **12**(4), 331–370 (2002)
3. Dai, H., Mobasher, B.: A road map to more effective web personalization: integrating domain knowledge with web usage mining. In: Proceedings of the International Conference on Internet Computing, IC 2003, Las Vegas, Nevada, USA, 23–26 June 2003, vol. 1, pp. 58–64 (2003)
4. Di Noia, T., Ostuni, V.C., Rosati, J., Tomeo, P., Di Sciascio, E., Mirizzi, R., Bartolini, C.: Building a relatedness graph from linked open data: a case study in the IT domain. Expert Syst. Appl. **44**, 354–366 (2016)
5. Di Noia, T., Ostuni, V.C., Tomeo, P., Di Sciascio, E.: Sprank: semantic path-based ranking for top-n recommendations using linked open data. ACM Trans. Intell. Syst. Technol. (TIST) (2016)
6. Lops, P., Gemmis, M., Semeraro, G.: Content-based recommender systems: state of the art and trends. In: Ricci, F., Rokach, L., Shapira, B., Kantor, P.B. (eds.) Recommender Systems Handbook, pp. 73–105. Springer, New York (2011)
7. Pazzani, M.J., Billsus, D.: Content-based recommendation systems. In: Brusilovsky, P., Kobsa, A., Nejdl, W. (eds.) Adaptive Web 2007. LNCS, vol. 4321, pp. 325–341. Springer, Heidelberg (2007)
8. Resnick, P., Iacovou, N., Suchak, M., Bergstrom, P., Riedl, J.: Grouplens: an open architecture for collaborative filtering of netnews. In: Proceedings of the Conference on Computer Supported Cooperative Work, CSCW 1994, Chapel Hill, NC, USA, 22–26 October 1994, pp. 175–186 (1994)
9. Ricci, F., Rokach, L., Shapira, B., Kantor, P.B. (eds.): Recommender Systems Handbook. Springer, New York (2011)
10. Semeraro, G., Lops, P., Basile, P., de Gemmis, M.: Knowledge infusion into content-based recommender systems. In: Proceedings of the Third ACM Conference on Recommender Systems, RecSys 2009, pp. 301–304. ACM, New York (2009)

Author Index

Printed in the United States
By Bookmasters